EZEKIEL'S TEMPLE IN MONTANA

BY

NEAL CHASE

*"**THE MOST GREAT LAW** is come, and*
*the Ancient Beauty ruleth upon **the throne of David**.*
Thus hath My Pen spoken that which
the histories of bygone ages have related."
--Baha'u'llah
(*Kitab-i-Aqdas: Proclamation of Baha'u'llah*, p. 89)

BAHA'I PUBLISHERS UNDER THE PROVISIONS OF THE COVENANT
MISSOULA, MONTANA

WILLIAMS WAS RIGHT!

Williams was right!   In April of 1863, the same time as Baha'u'llah's proclamation in Baghdad, the Morman prophet George Williams prophesied that the return of Jesus would be in the Deer Lodge Valley and that here the New Temple, the City of the Great King which is the heavenly New Jerusalem, would be built up.

The Morrisites immediately moved to Deer Lodge to await the return of Jesus in his temple. Williams was right! The prophecy is fulfilled! Now and for all time, everyone will remember George Williams and the greatness of the Morrisite pioneers, brave men and women, as the ones who were right all along!

PHOTO #1

The Prison in Deer Lodge

PROPHECY FULFILLED!

Drawing #2 on the right is an artist's conception of the New Temple which is prophesied in the Book of Ezekiel to be established and built in the latter days as the temple that Jesus himself shall return to. Photo #1, above, is the striking fulfillment of Ezekiel's vision of the future temple (Deer Lodge Prison in Montana) which the Morrisites who pioneered the Deer Lodge Valley eagerly anticipated as the place for the second coming of Jesus.

BIBLE AND PRISON IDENTICAL!

Drawing #2 is taken from D.M.G. Stalker's book, *Ezekiel, Introduction and Commentary*. D.M.G. Stalker is a Christian writer not involved with the Baha'i Faith or the Deer Lodge Prison. From his research based purely on the measurements given in the Book of Ezekiel and the Bible, not from the prison or the Baha'is, he was able to draw this composite showing the prophecied temple of the future which fits the Deer Lodge Prison exactly.

The Jews never built Ezekiel's temple! Unlike the temple of Solomon and the second temple, Ezekiel's is the only temple with 7 towers identical to the seven watchtowers of the Deer Lodge Prison. Both Photo #1 and Drawing #2 show tower # 7. Both the photo and the drawing show the main temple gate that faces east -- the gate that Jesus himself is prophesied to enter by (Malachi 3:1; Ezekiel 44:1-2). Both the photo and the drawing show the two twin pillars of Jachin and Boaz standing by the door!

DRAWING #2

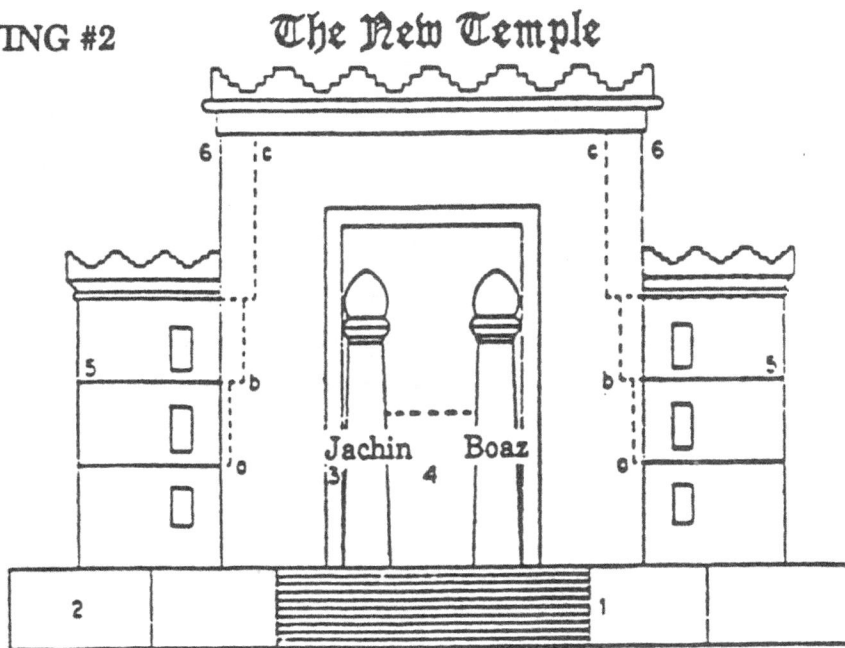

The New Temple

Jachin   Boaz

Drawing taken from **Ezekiel** *by Stalker*

JACHIN AND BOAZ

These two pillars (Jachin and Boaz) represent the two Christs -- the two anointed descendants of King David (Zechariah 4:14). 'J' is for Jesus and 'B' is for Baha'u'llah. Jachin means "he shall establish". Boaz, David's blood ancestor, means "the royal genealogy of King David". It is Jesus ('J' for Jachin -- "he shall establish") who is prophesied to return in this temple in Deer Lodge, Montana, to establish his Father's (Baha'u'llah's) royal geneology of King David and thereby establish the Kingdom of God on earth as it is in heaven.

iii

All writings of Baha'u'llah are sacred scripture;
and therefore are in the public domain.

TABLE OF CONTENTS

FOREWORD

All the people of the world await this Great Day when wars shall cease, poverty and injustice shall be no more, and the entire human family may be able to live as one people upon this spinning globe as a single family with justice and fairness for all.

The day when prophecy is fulfilled is no small matter! It is the opportunity to transform as both individuals and society into something more, something better, something greater.

There cannot be peace on earth unless and until justice is first established. In this book, all the religions of the world are seen to be a progressive scheme for the ever advancing humanity of divine civilization now established upon the earth.

While this vision fulfills the prophecies of both the East and the West, it is of particular special interest for Jews, Christians and Muslims who await the fulfillment of the Kingdom of God spoken of in their Holy Scriptures. World prophecy paints one clear portrait of these days and times--and the Unity of God reveals One Common Source from which all true spirituality and religions originate.

These were given progressively, as in the grades of school, for the education and advancement of all the peoples of the world--both for their personal safety, security and salvation, as well as that for our burgeoning global community that is even now blossoming into the long awaited and long ago promised GOLDEN AGE!

The power of this book is that it is TRUE! It is the documentation of FACT--actual factual reality that can be experienced personally and investigated thoroughly.

What began with the discovery of Ezekiel's Temple in Montana has blossomed into the fullness of seeing God's vision of the New Jerusalem in the Rocky Mountains unfolded before our very eyes. While global wars rage, and the old form of things convulses and disintegrates, the new heaven and new earth are rolled out before our very eyes as we are more or less willing participants in this age old divine drama for the redemption of the entire human race. This redemption comes from maturity. A maturity to see the reality of God, with our own eyes and not through the eyes of our neighbor. This makes this book, not just mere words on parchment, but a transformative spiritual experience, that has the real power to bring about the ardent wish and supreme desire of every lover of God.

In the Book of Revelation it states that the New Jerusalem is seen descending out of heaven like a bride (thus spiritual) adorned for her husband. This Heavenly City, is heavenly because it descends from the heaven of prophecy of God, and not from the physical sky--which is nothing but empty and meaningless space. It has twelve gates that open up through twelve natural mountain passes by which the faithful enter: three on the North, three on the South, three on the East; and three on the West (Rev. 21:13). These are the two I-90s and the I-15 on the North; the two I-10s and the I-25 on the South; the I-80, I-70 and I-40 on the East; and the I-80, I-70 and I-40 on the West (see Map). This is a real place that you can go and visit. It fulfills the prophecy of God in the Holy Books and Scriptures of the world. It is the Shambhala Kingdom of the East and

Twelve Gates of the
New Jerusalem in the Rocky Mountains

Revelation 21:10-14

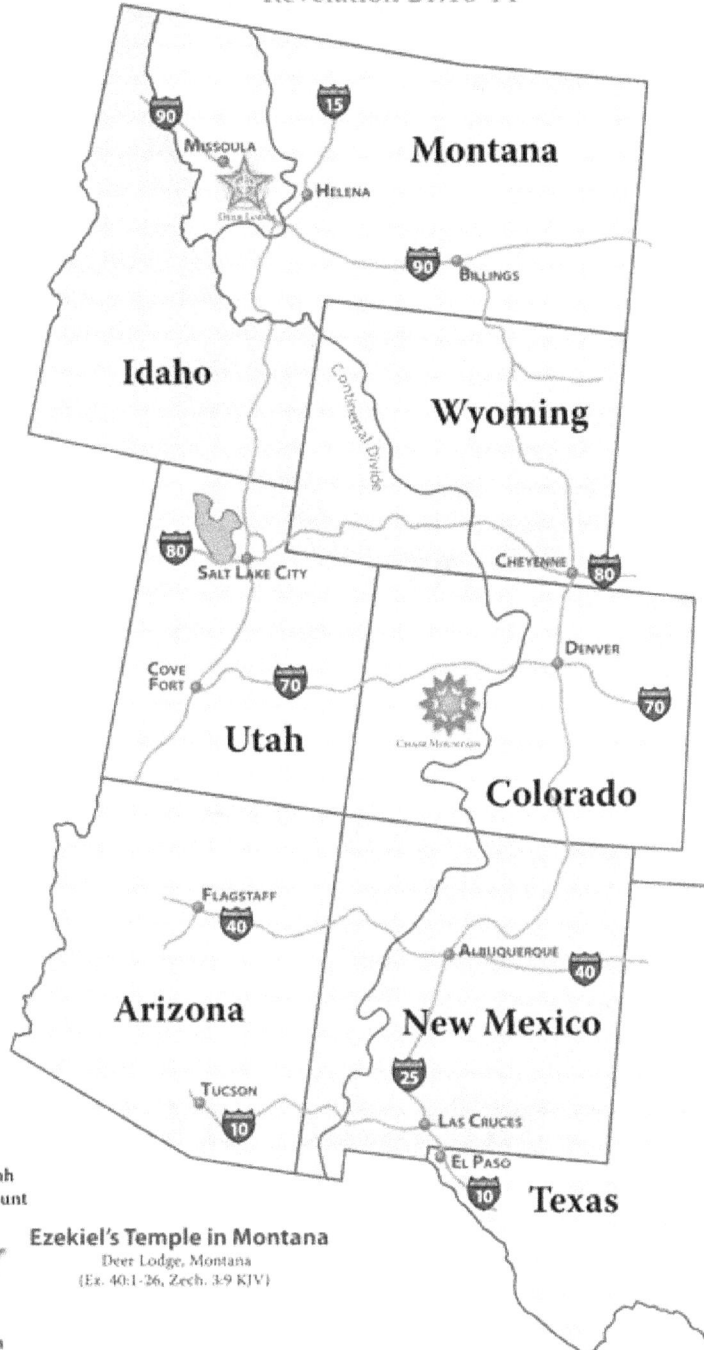

Montana

MISSOULA

HELENA

BILLINGS

Idaho

Wyoming

Continental Divide

CHEYENNE

SALT LAKE CITY

DENVER

COVE FORT

Utah

Colorado

FLAGSTAFF

ALBUQUERQUE

Arizona

New Mexico

TUCSON

LAS CRUCES

EL PASO

Texas

Mt. Moriah
Temple Mount

Ezekiel's Temple in Montana
Deer Lodge, Montana
(Ex. 40:1-26, Zech. 3:9 KJV)

Mt. Zion
Place of David's Throne

Chair Mountain and the Crystal River
(Rev. 20:11, 22:1)
Glenwood Springs, Colorado

Gathering Unto the Throne

"Then he showed me the river of the water of life, bright as crystal, flowing from the throne of God and of the Lamb"

Revelation 22:1; 14:1,5

Baha'i International Gathering

Kamal, Perfection, 8-10, 160 BE

August 8-10, 2003 CE

Baha'is Under the Provisions of the Covenant

the Kingdom of God and of His Christ anticipated in the West. This vision single handedly unites all the prophecies of the world: and thereby all hearts, minds and souls of all the peoples of the world into one human family under God--where all are as even as one soul in one body--at this time of the Great Awakening.

Within this prophesied vision of the New Jerusalem, are the Twin Promised Ones: the "One seated upon the throne" symbolized by Chair Mountain--the outer representation of the Throne of King David; and the Great Establisher of the Kingdom, the one spoken of as High Priest, who shall come "suddenly to his Temple."

As prophesied there is a river of crystal flowing out from this throne, and on either side of this river are the two sacred Council Trees, one on this side and one on that side of the stream--across the Great Divide. There are only two such sacred Native American trees in the state.

COUNCIL TREE FORT COLLINS   COUNCIL TREE DELTA COLORADO

There is even streets paved with Gold, in this Great City. The road from Ouray to Durango is called the "Million Dollar Highway" because of the great amount of Gold of its pavement--that cannot be mined because of the precariousness of its route through the high mountain passes. The Native Americans held these same regions and areas as holy and sacred. We have described more of this vision in two video presentations: *Shambhala and the 13th Crystal Skull*; and *The Celestial Magi: Universal Cycles of Time.*

By reading this book, you are opening the door to a personal journey and great adventure in the many of worlds of God, including--but not limited to--the establishment of the Kingdom of God upon this earth as it is in heaven. The facts in this book are clearly documented. We didn't just figure this out, nor did we put all of the pieces of the puzzle together. No!

These things were unfolded to us through our experiences and journey through these many worlds--until we were all caught up together into heaven, and gathered before His throne. This gathering continues to this day: for it is written that we are "all living stones" in this Temple of God.

By the time you read this book, the destruction of thermonuclear war may have already taken place. The prophecy of this war in the Book of Revelation is entitled: ARMAGEDDON.

The word Armageddon is actually a Greek mash-up of two Hebrew words *Har*--meaning mountain; and *megiddo*--that is the plain of Megiddo. It is well known to Bible scholars that the Mountain of Megiddo (*Ar-mageddon*) is Mt. Carmel in the Holy Land.[*] This is the site where Elijah slew the pagan priests of Baal, and is the prophesied Ground-Zero spot of this "Great War in Heaven" mentioned in the 12th Chapter of the Book of Revelation.

It is upon the heights of Mt. Carmel that the Baha'i Covenant was violated with the murder of the Guardian, Shoghi Effendi, in November of 1957, by a group of people known as "The Hands." From out of this Violation of the "the Hands" comes the four winds of destruction now unleashed from the Great River Euphrates which flows through Iraq, near Baghdad, where Baha'u'llah made His proclamation to be the second coming of Christ on April 21st, 1863.

With the Covenant broken, the living Davidic King in exile, and the emergence of the modern "Anti-Christ" ("Hand's Faith") upon the prophesied spot of Mt. Carmel (Armageddon--the Mt. of Megiddo) the Beautiful Maiden--New Jerusalem--was given the two "wings of the eagle"--the eagle being the symbol of the United States--and the Covenant and Kingdom of God and throne of David was relocated to America, as it was meant to be. Today we have a choice: we can be controlled and manipulated and fooled by the Covenant breakers: "Hands" upon Mt. Carmel (the Mountain of Armageddon of the Violation--and other clergy, priestcraft, and false leaderships both secular or religious) or we can turn to the safety, security and salvation of the Covenant keepers, alive and well in the New Jerusalem, safe and secure in the Rocky Mountains USA. From out of this region, the Good News of this Kingdom (Davidic) is now proclaimed to all the world!

---

[*] **"Mt. Carmel is identified as the Mountain of Megiddo:"** See "Jeremias" in *Kittel's Theological Dictionary of the New Testament Vol. 1*, p. 468. Gerhard Kittle and Gerhard Friedrich (eds.), (1987). Translated by G. W. Bromiley, Grand Rapids, MI: Eerdmans; also J. Massingberde Ford, (1975). *Revelation, Anchor Bible Vol. 38*, New York, NY: Doubleday, p. 263; and W. H. Shea, (1980). "The Location and Significance of Armageddon in Rev. 16:16," *Andrews University Seminary Studies, 18*, Berrien Springs, MI: Andrews University Press, pp. 152-162.

PREFACE THIS EDITION

"All those people that belonged to that little church down there [in Deer Lodge, Montana]: One day out of the year, it was **<u>August the 9th</u>**, **they knew that was the Day that Christ would return.**"*(Lewis Johnson--interviewed, September 21st, 1990--Last of the Morrisite Pioneers)*

Prophecy is fulfilled, but expectations are not. This book represents one of the most amazing case-studies in the science of prophecy fulfillment that has ever been conducted! The phenomena depicted in these pages hearkens back to the days of Jesus in Jerusalem, Moses before Pharaoh, Buddha in the Court of the Hindu sages, Zoroaster before the Persian King, Krishna in the War Chariot of Arajuna, Muhammad amongst the barbarian peoples of the Desert Expanse, that of the Bab and Baha'u'llah in Persia and the Collapse of the entire Ottoman Empire of Islam, as foretold in the Book of Revelation from God. Yes! prophecy is fulfilled, but expectations are not.

In His *Book of Certitude* (*Kitab-i-Iqan*) Baha'u'llah enumerates and expounds upon these themes.

When we found *Ezekiel's Temple in Montana* in 1990, so to speak, little did we know then, that this would lead on to an over 30 years journey to discover the entire "New Jer<u>usa</u>lem" in the Rocky Mountains (see maps, illustrations and charts in this volume), as well as the "Great White Throne" and the "River that flows like Crystal" with "Two Sacred Trees" (Twin Sacred Ute Council Trees: Delta, CO and FC) on either side of the stream! This world embracing Vision fulfills the prophecy of both the East and the West, those of the North and the South! The prophecies of God bequeathed to All the peoples of the world.

While working on this project, and attempting to republish this original authentic edition of *Ezekiel's Temple in Montana*, one of the most valued of our co-workers, has been taken from this world. This occurred at the same time that the Sacred Tree was cut down in Delta, and a new one to be planted in its place. To that end, we now dedicate this book to him, to his memory, to his legacy, to his family and his loved ones, to his friends, and to his teachings, to his work, and to his everlasting undying Spirit, that travels through all the worlds of God. "For, behold! I died, and I live forever more!" We dedicate: To his smile, to his light, his love, his cheer, his sadness, his griefs, his loves, his hopes, his dreams, and to him!

I dedicate this work to you, my friend, to: VICTOR GEORGE WOODS.

FROM INDIA:

> Dear Guardian, Hope you are all well, although no words can heal the loss of Victor Woods to your community and immediate family members, but we hope that sharing the grief will reduce its intensity. Our Indian community was also equally upset from the time this News was given to them. **<u>Condolence Message</u>**:
>
> This News of untimely death is heard with all the sadness that our co-worker in faith Mr. Victor Woods has leaved us and this temporary world. We pray for the

Ascension and progress of his soul in the ABHA Kingdom. Although we haven't met (in person); but an emotional attachment is there with every believer of BUPC with each other. We will also hold a memorial prayer meeting for Victor Woods on the same day and date on which our brethren in USA has kept.

May God give patience to the Near and dear ones of Victor Woods.

Thanks. All the workers from India.

FROM IRAN:

Dear Guardian, I'm shocked! I didn't know this before! No one told me this. Unbelievable! I am so sorry! I really feel sad. I am sure that I cannot indeed understand and feel his family's feelings...and also his friends.

I cannot stop thinking of him as he was the First Person who I could--through his writings and his answerings to some questioners--smell the Truth; exactly when I had been in contact with the BUPC for the first time about three years ago or less. I liked his responses. Actually it was through him that I recognized Pepe as the second Guardian of the Faith. At that time, I was not sure who was the true Guardian after Mason. So I was searching about Pepe on that web-page, and suddenly I found Victor's short simple persuasive responses. It really made me happy! So I wrote back to the UHJ (info@uhj.net) to the effect that I accept and believe in the current Guardian of the Cause of God. I really liked Victor and I love him now, too. "Hi Victor!" Your servant, R.N.

Included here, in this special *Crimson Edition*, is the Statement from Persia: "WHAT DO YOU THINK??" And an important article by Victor Woods, entitle "Joshua and Zerubbabel," excerpted from his book, *Nostradamus Prophecy!* Three Surahs from Baha'u'llah; and other important materials, not to be found in other previous editions of this work.

May God Open the Doors of Understanding for those who are pure of heart, who seek the truth, as Jesus said, for the truth shall set you free.

May all the people of the world be freed from the clutter that fills their minds! So that they shall then be able to see the truth with their own eyes and not through the eyes of their neighbor!

JOSHUA AND ZERUBBABEL

(Excerpt from the book *Nostradamus Prophecy!*
by Victor Woods)

Just as the Bab and Baha'u'llah fulfill prophecy for the appearance of the Twin Manifestations of God in the East at the close of this 6000 year Cycle of Adam, so it is also prophesied that there shall be the appearance of Two Promised Ones in the West. These two figures are spoken of in the Bible as Joshua and Zerubbabel and represent the High Priesthood of Jesus the establisher of the Kingdom, and the current living Guardian, the Davidic King alive in the world at this time.

"BEHOLD THE MAN WHOSE NAME IS THE BRANCH"

In the Book of Zechariah in Chapter 3 and Chapter 6 it speaks of a prophecy of the "man whose name is the BRANCH." As already explained "Branch" is the English translation of the Arabic and Persian word Aghsan (singular *ghusn*) and refers to the name of the male-line descendants of Baha'u'llah and 'Abdu'l-Baha or AGHSAN of which the current guardian Neal Chase ben Joseph Aghsan is the fifth of this name: BRANCH (Zech. 3:8 KJV)--Aghsan--seated upon David's throne that is to last for ever. Here in the sixth chapter of Zechariah we read that he shall have a High Priest by his side and a spirit of understanding shall be between them both.

> Behold, the man whose name is the Branch: for he shall grow up in his place, and he shall build the temple of the Lord. It is he who shall build the temple of the Lord, and shall bear royal honor, and shall sit and rule upon his throne. And there shall be a priest by his throne, and peaceful understanding shall be between them both. (Zech. 6:12-13 RSV)

This "priest by his throne"--the throne of King David --is the Promised One of today that fulfills prophecy for the coming of Joshua the High Priest. Joshua is the Hebrew equivalent of the Greek name "Jesus." Now Jesus was a high priest after the order of Melchizedec and this is explained by Paul in the book of Hebrews chapters 5, 6 and 7; as well as by Jesus himself in his personal reference to his authority from Psalm 110, the Melchizedec Psalm (Matt. 22:43-44 RSV). In this book we learn that Melchizedec, who was the founder of the city of Jerusalem, met Abraham after the *Slaughter of the Kings* outside the city walls. Abraham paid tithes to Melchizedec (gave him a tenth of all the spoils) and was presented with the Eucharist of the bread and wine, the same bread and wine, that Jesus as High Priest and sacrificial Lamb offers the twelve at the last supper. Thus this is the bread of the true teachings of God of which if one eats he shall live for ever and ever and never go hungry--the true manna from heaven--and the wine of the belief: belief in the firm covenant that the throne-line passed down from Adam to Abraham to David to Baha'u'llah and 'Abdu'l-Baha and to the current living heir shall never end. This is belief in the everlasting Covenant of God (Ez. 37).

According to *Halley's Handbook of the Bible* and *The Legends of the Jews* by Louis Ginzberg, Melchizedec's identity is actually the blessed son of Noah, Shem. Shem's real name was Job, of the Book of Job in the Bible, who lost everything at the hands of the historical Satan (Nimrod, the King of Babylon--see Isaiah chapter 14 for more) and then later had all things restored to him. After meeting with Abraham, Shem allowed him to enter the city of Jerusalem which was surrounded by a hundred foot wall which was a hundred feet thick, to keep out all the corruption of Nimrod and Semiramis that had deluded all of the people of the world.

Within those walls was the school of the Bet Midrash--the College of the Holy Spirit--and the Bet Din: the Court of Divine Justice. Abraham entered therein and studied in that school for four years. When he graduated he wrote his book entitled the Book of Formation--*the Sefer Yetzirah*--which speaks of the mystery of the Divine and Ineffable name of God. This is the original Holy Name which was given to humanity from God at the time of Adam at the beginning of the 6000 years cycle. It was passed down only to Enoch and then to Methuselah and to Noah.

Thus these four Adam, Enoch, Methuselah and Noah possessed this secret as the succession of the throne was passed to them. The four granite stones forming the Purple Arch in the Great Pyramid of Giza (that is the entrance gate to the descending passageway) represent these Four promised ones who came under the Revelation of Adam: (a) Adam, the Manifestation of God; (b) Enoch, (c) Methuselah, and (d) Noah. The dating of the Purple Arch at 2500 BC gives the date in the Pyramid for the date that Noah received the plans to build the ark.

On board the ark, Ham, the cursed son of Noah, who became the father of Cush, the father of Nimrod (Ham was also known as Canaan after he violated) stole the robes and other paraphernalia of Noah that he had inherited from Adam for himself; but he was not able to gain possession of the True Name of God. It is said that whosoever possesses the knowledge of the True Name possesses all power of Creation both material and spiritual, and all things and all doors are open to that one. Noah concealed this Secret and gave it to his beloved son Job. Thus Job became known as "Shem" as "Shem" in Hebrew means "the Name," (*Ha Shem*) as he was the only possessor of it and its secrets.

When Shem saw that Abraham fulfilled prophecy from the existing scriptures of the time, as his own promised tenth generation descendant, as well as the prophesied time-line contained within the masonry and blue-prints of the Great Pyramid of Giza, he bequeathed the Secret of this Name of God to Abraham as well as succession to the throne by mediating the everlasting Covenant of the successorship from Noah directly to Abraham. This Name was referred to outwardly as *El Shaddai*--God Almighty-- and was known to the patriarchs before captivity in Egypt when it was lost.

When Moses received the Name YHVH he was told that this was not the same name that God had given to the Patriarch Adam and to Abraham of old, but was in fact a different name. When the lineage of High Priest from Moses' brother Aaron died out, this name YHVH was lost. Later the Jewish scribes added vowel points to the Bible in the Masoretic text and took the vowels of the name of the pagan god '*Adonay*,' and added a-o-a to YHVH getting YaHoVaH which the German's erroneously translated as "Jehovah" which is a bastard name for God and not the real name of God at all.

In the Book of the Revelation of Jesus Christ it is prophesied that God will once again reveal His own New Name, and this gift will be conferred upon all of the true believers who accept the Twin Manifestations of the Bab and Baha'u'llah as well as the Twin Promised Ones of Joshua and Zerubbabel. Thus these Four together are a fulfillment of a form of the four letters (tetragrammaton) of the Most Great Name of God. In this way these four personages fulfill the pattern of the Four Stones of Red Granite forming the Purple Arch for the Revelation and Baha'i Cycle that is to last 5000 Centuries for our New Age of the Kingdom today.

Now I'm not going to give away the True Name here in this book, for it would be harmful for those who do not believe to say it in vain if they heard it and didn't really understand what it is. It would be like giving a loaded gun to a small child--safety on or not--it could be that dangerous for someone in both this world and the next to take the real Name in vain, possibly irreparably fatal (spiritually damaging) to themselves in both this world and the next for all eternity. This name was so sacred that it was only known for thousands of years to only one person on earth at a time. It is prophesied that when the second coming of Christ appears in the "Glory of the Father" which is Baha'u'llah, that He will reveal this Most Great Name. Now as God knew the mainstream Baha'is would all break the Covenant He thus concealed the knowledge of this True Name from them as well, and so all Covenant-breakers are so deprived. Shoghi Effendi explains that "the Persians do not have the real Aqdas of Baha'u'llah" and they do not possess the real Name of God either--this is kept with the sacred trust of the authentic Guardians of the Baha'i Faith and was known to the High Priest, the establisher, Dr. Leland Jensen as well. Not even those who profess to be "Baha'i" have knowledge of this True Name, unless they have learned this from the Two Promised Ones foreseen in the Bible, the prophecies of the Great Pyramid of Giza, the Book of Revelation and all sacred scriptures of all the world.

THESE TWO PROMISED ONES FULFILL PROPHECY

Like Jesus Christ that fulfilled prophecy in his day for his prophesied name, prophesied date, prophesied address and prophesied mission, these Two Promised Ones--representing the Twin Institutions of the Kingdom, the "House of the Lord" (Is. 2:2-4 RSV), the true Universal House of Justice of Baha'u'llah and the Executive Branch of the Guardianship "seated upon the throne of King David" (Is. 9:6-7; 11:1-11 RSV)--are also both prophesied by their respective prophesied names, prophesied dates, prophesied addresses, and prophesied missions as given in the Holy Bible.

This clear vision fired the prophetic imagination of all those who have gone before. It enabled them to see all the tests and trials, and woes and difficulties during the ministry of these two promised ones in the West whose mission is the establishment of the Kingdom of God on earth as it is in heaven, in fulfillment of the Lord's prayer. These two promised ones of the West are the establishers of the Firm Foundation of the Covenant of Baha'u'llah, even as ancient Joshua and Zerubbabel laid the foundation for the restoration of the second Temple at the time after the first exile of the Jewish people 490 years before the appearance of the first Jesus, 2000 years ago.

Calculated from the prophesied Biblical starting point when historic Joshua and Zerubbabel laid the "Foundation stone of the Temple" on September 21st, 520 BC, there are "7 Times" spoken of in Daniel. These "7 Times" are 2520 years. Each "time" is 360 degrees for 7 prophetic cycles of 360 years for a total of 2520 years (7 x 360 = 2520).

There are exactly 2520 years from September, 21st, 520 BC bringing us to September 21st, 2001 AD when God saw fit to bring forth his "servant the BRANCH" (Zechariah 23:8 KJV) and the personal identity of the living Davidic King was projected to all the people of the world.

The date of 2001 AD was announced to all the people of the world on April 29th, 1980 when Dr. Jensen made his first world-wide media projection. The date 2001 AD is also prophesied as the "six days" of creation in which in 2 Peter 3:8 it states "remember this beloved with the Lord each day is as a thousand years and a thousand years is as one day." These "six days" are therefore the 6000 years

Cycle of Adam which from 4000 BC comes to an end in the year 2001 AD and is the start of 5000 Century Baha'i Cycle. The same "six days" are mentioned in the Qur'an of Muhammad in which it also states that "each day is as one thousand years" (Q. 32:4; 22:47 Pickthall's). The prophesied date of 2001 AD also corresponds within the prophetic cycles of the Hindu *Kali Yug*, the Mayan and Aztec prophetical calendars, Hopi prophecy, and the Buddhist *Kalachakra* dating, as well as the prophecies of China, Africa, the Scandinavians and other indigenous peoples of all the world.

THE SEVEN TIMES:
2520 PROPHETIC YEARS
September 21st, 520 BC– September 21st, 2001 AD

In the book of Daniel, chapter 4, Daniel records the dream of King Nebuchadnezzar within which is given a prophecy: that there will be a period of "Seven Times" that a stump (or in other words the ancient root stock* of the throne-line of David of the Tree of Life) will be passed over "…until the Most High rules the kingdom of men, and gives it to whomsoever he will" (Dan. 4, verses 15, 17, 23, 25). Some versions read "…and gives it to whom it belongs" connecting it to the Shiloh prophecy of Genesis 49:10 RSV which reads, "The scepter shall not depart from Judah until it comes to whom it belongs, and to him shall the gathering of the people be." This signifies its connection to the throne of David and the promised Zerubbabel. This "Seven Times" is the prophesied time period that the throne of David will be hidden in obscurity, being the subjects of other kingdoms.

A time is 360 degrees, known to scholars as the "prophetic year." Seven Times then is 360 multiplied by 7. This equals 2520. (7 x 360 = 2520). As one day of prophecy is equal to one year (Ezek. 4:6, Num 14:34) 2520 days is 2520 years. This is a date prophecy that refers to the time when God's kingdom will be proclaimed and established--"the Most High rules the kingdom of men" --and more specifically to the time of the fulfillment of God's promise that he would bring forth His servant the BRANCH (Zech 3:8, translated from the Hebrew *tsemach* --the grafted branch, grafted into the ancient root stock) in which the foundation stone to the kingdom of God will be laid. The root stock of the tree of life, that is the stump, represents the foundation of the temple or the foundation upon which the house of God or Temple of the Lord is to be built. They are one and the same. Of this house Jesus stated we must build it upon the rock, that rock being the rock of ages, which Paul states is the Christ, (1 Cor. 10:4) the anointed descendant of King David. The house built upon sand, the false ideas of man shall fall. Here God gives 2520 years from the foundation of the second temple in 520 BC until the year 2001 AD, when ten days after the 9-11 God fulfilled his promise "Behold I shall bring forth my servant the BRANCH" (Zech. 3:8 KJV, and the identity of the living Davidic King, our guardian, is now known. Thus we recognize the true Universal House of Justice of Baha'u'llah, which is the temple of the Lord.

This prophecy of 2520 years is well known by Bible scholars, and more specifically, many regard it as pointing to the year of 2001 AD (Baha'u'llah's *mustaghath:* in which all the letters have numerical values in that name that add to 2001). For instance, William F. Dankenbring, Pastor and Director of Triumph Prophetic Ministries, writes in *An Open Letter to Ariel Sharon, Prime Minister of Israel* the open declaration that: "This year, 2001 AD, is precisely 2520 years after the foundation was laid to the second Temple in 520 BC. …It is 7 x 360, and represents the fulfillment of 'seven times.'" Christian author, Dr. Stephen Jones, in an article called *September 2001--A Short History of Tribulation* writes: "The prophetic time of the final

---

* Baha'u'llah refers to Himself as the "Ancient Root."

'building' of the New Temple insofar as Haggai's prophecies are concerned, really began in the year 2001 AD…If we add 2520 years to [520 BC] we come to 2001 AD."

Specifically, it was on exactly the very day of September 21st, 520 BC--the Autumnal Equinox--that was the very day **they laid the Foundation Stone of the Temple of God.** Scholars note that this very day was so important and remarkable to the Hebrew Prophets because it relates to our time now and the coming forth of the BRANCH (the Guardianship) and the establishment of God's Kingdom on earth as it is in heaven:

> Then [in 520 BC] the prophets, Haggai and Zechariah the son of Iddo, prophesied unto the Jews that were in Judah and Jerusalem in the name of the God of Israel, even unto them. Then rose up Zerubbabel the son of Shealtiel, and Joshua the son of Jozadak, and began to build the house of God which is at Jerusalem: and with them were the prophets of God helping them. (Ezra 5:1-2) "Consider from this day onward… Since the day [Sept. 21st, 520 BC] that the foundation of the Lord's temple was laid, consider:…from *this day* on I will bless you." (Hag. 2:18)

> Both 1 Esdras and Josephus place the event during the reign of Darius I. Work on the temple began on the twenty-fourth day of the sixth month of the second year of Darius (Sept. 21st, 520 BC) according to Hag. 1:15… The Chroniclers sentence might well be completed, as in 1 Esdras 5:57 by supplying "And they laid the foundation of the Temple of God." (*The Interpreters Bible Vol. 3*, p. 592)

The twenty-fourth day of the sixth month of the Jewish lunar calendar in the second year of Darius the king, corresponds to September 21st, 520 BC. On this date Joshua and Zerubbabel laid the cornerstone of the second Temple. This is a most significant historical event proven through historical evidence known to most Bible scholars, showing that it is scientifically and historically accurate. Several years later the second temple was completed. This is the foundational date in Haggai that we count the prophesied 2520 years from, which brings us to September 21st, 2001 (there is no zero year, so add one). Therefore, September 21st, 2001 is the fulfillment of Daniel's prophecy, signifying that the promised future temple is being completed NOW!

This date, September 21st, 2001, is the date for the coming of a promised one, the promised Guardian of the Baha'i Faith. The prophecy in Daniel chapter 4 says the "stump" will be passed over for 2520 years "until the Most High rules the kingdom of men, and gives it to whomsoever he will." The "stump" that is referred to here is the ancient rootstock of King David. The meaning of this prophecy, is that this ancient lineage, the throne line of David, will be subjugated and in exile by different empires for 2520 years i.e. the Greeks, the Romans, the Persians, the Islamic empires etc, in which the line and throne of David have in fact continued in exile as "exilarchs", the exiled monarchs of King David all the way down to Baha'u'llah and 'Abdu'l-Baha now continued in the son, grandson and great-grandson of 'Abdu'l-Baha, Neal Chase ben Joseph Aghsan.

Therefore, it is now that we are at the end of this cycle of 2520 years, that the throne of king David is raised up (promulgated) as a natural branch, a descendent of David from a collateral line has been grafted back into the ancient rootstock (the stump) by being adopted and appointed to continue the throne of David. This natural branch (Jewish, grafted back in by Pepe, the grandson of 'Abdu'l-Baha) was put into place as the cornerstone on September 21st 2001 AD, for this is the day that God brought forth, his "servant, the BRANCH" (Zech. 3:8 KJV).

THRONE OF DAVID
IS GOD'S THRONE ON EARTH

"So Solomon sat on the throne of the LORD [Heb. YHVH]
as king in place of his father David.
He prospered and all Israel obeyed him."
(1 Chronicles 29:23 NIV)

The throne of David which Baha'u'llah and His successors is seated upon is the throne of God on earth for this Kingdom. The purpose of this throne and the living man seated upon it is so we can recognize the true Universal House of Justice of Baha'u'llah from fakes, frauds and imitations.

To accomplish this God has raised up in his plan Two Promised ones that fulfill the prophecies of their prophesied name, prophesied date, prophesied address, and prophesied mission: the king and priest, the promised Twin Establishers of the Kingdom. These two promised ones are spoken of in Zechariah Chapter 6 as appearing between two Mountains of Bronze, in some translation two mountains of copper. The world's two largest repositories of copper are on the North and South ends of the Deer Lodge Valley, in Deer Lodge, Montana. Butte was the world's largest repository in its day on the South end of the valley. Most all the copper in the world has come out of the mines in Butte Montana. Lincoln on the North is known to have even more copper deposits than Butte, but they haven't been able to perfect the extraction of it yet. In the Book of Zechariah chapter six it is written:

> Then I looked up again and saw four chariots coming from between two mountains, and the mountains were of copper… And the word of the LORD came to me: … "Take from them silver and gold, and make a crown, and set it upon the head of Joshua, the son of Jehozadak, the high priest; and say to him [Leland], 'Thus says the LORD of hosts, "Behold, the man whose name is the Branch [Aghsan, Neal]: for he shall grow up in his place, and he shall build the temple of the LORD. It is he who shall build the temple of the LORD, and shall bear royal honor, and shall sit and rule upon his throne [the throne of King David]. And there shall be a priest [Leland] by his throne, and peaceful understanding shall be between them both [Doc and Neal]."' And the crown shall be in the temple [IBC/UHJ] of the LORD as a reminder… "And those who are far off shall come and <u>help</u> to <u>build</u> the temple of the LORD; and you shall know that the LORD of hosts has sent me to you. And this shall come to pass, if you will diligently obey the voice of the LORD your God." (Zech. 6: 1 NWT; Zech. 6:9-15 RSV)

The first, is the priest which means teacher "and peaceful understanding shall be between them both" who is the main establisher of the Kingdom, who is prophesied to be the teacher and educator of the second "the man whose name is the Branch." Thus Leland, educated and established Neal upon the spiritual teachings and principles of the foundation of the Revelation of Baha'u'llah in fulfillment of his divine mission in the prophetic plan of God; and in recognition of this Pepe fulfilled his role in adopting and appointing Neal in the same manner and style as 'Abdu'l-Baha's adoption and appointment of Mason: to be his **aghsan-son** to the throne as the successor and great-grandson of 'Abdu'l-Baha.

Thus Pepe adopted and appointed Neal to be his successor to the throne of King David from Baha'u'llah, 'Abdu'l-Baha, Mason and himself; and Dr. Leland Jensen established this throne of King David in the hearts, minds and souls of the people of the world who are pure of heart and use their intellects to recognize the proofs of the prophecy fulfilled that the Guardian Neal Chase is seated upon. In Moffatt's Bible it gives the prophesied name of the Branch: "the Eternal our CHAMPION:"

> Woe to rulers who ruin and scatter the flock that was theirs to shepherd! This therefore is the Eternal's sentence on the rulers in charge of his flock: 'You scattered my flock and drove them away, you took no care of them; so I will take good care to punish you for the evil you have done. I will gather all that is left of my flock from every land where I have driven them, I will bring them back to their folds, and they shall be fruitful and multiply; over them I will put rulers, to shepherd them, and they shall be no longer scared or startled or dismayed. The day comes, the Eternal promises, when I raise up a true scion [Branch]of David, to reign both royally and ably, to enforce law and justice in the land; under him Judah shall be safe, and Israel live secure, and this shall be his title, "The Eternal our CHAMPION." (Jeremiah 23:1-6; Moffatt's Bible translation)

So not only is it prophesied there is to be a high priest AND a king, called the BRANCH--aghsan--between the two mountains of copper, here it gives this individual's name: "CHAMPION."

From *What's In A Name* by Gayle Palmquist (or any name book for that matter, look it up yourself): "NEAL--Literal meaning: CHAMPION."

PROPHETIC CALLING CARD:
CURRENT GUARDIAN FULFILLS PROPHECY

To summarize the proofs for Dr. Leland Jensen, and Neal Chase (Joshua and Zerubbabel, the High Priest and the Davidic King, the Branch) are as follows, by prophesied name, prophesied date, prophesied address, and prophesied mission:

NAME

Dr. Leland Jensen: 'The Land'--Leland "I will remove the iniquity of that land in a single day" (Zech. 3:8)

Neal: 'Champion'--Neal " The day comes, the Eternal promises, when I raise up a true scion [Branch] of David, to reign both royally and ably, to enforce law and justice in the land; under him Judah shall be safe, and Israel live secure, and this shall be his title, 'The Eternal our CHAMPION'" Jeremiah 23:1-6; Moffatt's Bible translation). Neal means 'champion.' It is the same name in a different language.

DATE

Dr. Jensen: 1963 AD--"Blessed is he who waits and comes to the thousand three hundred and thirty five days" (Daniel 12:12). 1335 years added to the victory of Muhammad in 628 AD brings us to 1963. (628 AD + 1335 years = 1963 AD) See *Baha'u'llah and the New Era*, Chapter 13, "Prophecies of

Baha'u'llah and 'Abdu'l-Baha" subsection "Coming of the Kingdom of God" for 'Abdu'l-Baha's calculation of this date to be 1963 AD.

Neal : "We, moreover, swear fealty to the One Who, in the time of *Mustaghath*, is destined to be made manifest, as well as to those Who shall come after Him till the end that hath no end" (Baha'u'llah, *Gleanings*, XXX, p. 73). The numerical value of the time *'Mustaghath'* is the year 2001 AD as cited in *A Basic Baha'i Dictionary* by Wendi Momen:

> Mustaghath. He Who Is Invoked. A reference to the appearance of the Promised One at the time specified by the Bab. The Bab had set the limit of time for the coming of the Promised One as Mustaghath, the numerical value of which, in the *abjad* system is 2001. (Wendi Momen, *A Basic Baha'i Dictionary*, p. 166)

Also the date of September 21st, 2001 AD is given as the Terminal Date of the time scale in David Davidson's book *The Great Pyramid, Its Divine Message*, pages 359-368. As well as 2520 years--the "Seven Times--added to September 21st, 520 BC brings us to again September 21st, 2001 AD This same date is included in the volume measure of the Capstone which is 2520 cubic cubits representing the 2520 prophesied years. The top truncated platform measure is 520 square cubits representing the prophesied foundation date of the laying of the corner stone of the second temple on September 21st, 520 BC Thus the top platform and the capstone fulfills the Biblical prophecies of Daniel and Haggai for the date September 21st, 520 BC and the 2520 years (7 x 360 = 2520) that brings us to September 21st, 2001 AD This was exactly 10 days after the 9-11 event of the year 2001 AD which Neal had accurately predicted. The turmoil and controversy surrounding his prediction of 9-11 is what resulted in his worldwide projection as the BRANCH--the living Guardian--"ten days" (Rev. 2:10) later at the prophesied date, given in the Bible, Book of Revelation and the Great Pyramid Prophecy.

In September of 2001 AD Neal unfurled the Divine Banner (http://www.bupc.org/genealogy/genealogy-of-christ.html), which he brought forth and the Trade Towers were destroyed on the date he gave.

ADDRESS

Dr. Jensen: The "Stone with Seven Eyes"/Between the Two Mountains of Copper:--

> "For behold, upon the stone which I have set before Joshua, upon a single stone with seven eyes..." (Zechariah 3:9) "And again, I lifted my eyes and saw and behold, four chariots came out from between two mountains [Deer Lodge Valley]; and the mountains were mountains of bronze [Hebrew: copper]..." (Zechariah 6:1)

Neal: Chair Mountain at the Great White throne (Rev. chpts 20-22)/The Temple/Between the Two Mountains of Copper--"And another angel came out of the temple, calling with a loud voice to him who sat upon the cloud, 'Put in your sickle and reap, for the hour to reap has come, for the harvest of the earth is ripe.'" (Revelations 14:15)

> "And again, I lifted my eyes and saw and behold, four chariots came out from between two mountains [Deer Lodge Valley]; and the mountains were mountains of bronze [Hebrew: copper]..." (Zechariah 6:1) "Behold, the man whose name is the

Branch: for he shall grow up in his place [Neal was living in Deer Lodge when Pepe adopted and appointed him]" (Zech. 6:12-13)

MISSION

Dr. Jensen: Brings forth the BRANCH, has charge of courts.

> "Thus says the Lord of hosts: If you will walk in my ways and keep my charge, then you shall rule my house and have charge of my courts…I will bring forth my servant the BRANCH." (Zechariah 3:7-8)

Neal: Is the BRANCH, Executive Head of Courts, builds the Temple, and brings true believers back into the Covenant.

> "Behold, the man whose name is the Branch: for he shall grow up in his place, and he shall build the temple of the Lord. **It is he who shall build the temple of the Lord**, and shall bear royal honor, and shall sit and rule upon his throne. And there shall be a priest by his throne, and **peaceful understanding shall be between <u>them both</u>**" (Zech. 6:12-13)

Like John who prepared the way for Jesus, Dr. Jensen prepared the way for the people to be able to accept and recognize, Neal. He wrote about him many times: "This angel is one of the Apostles of the Lamb who believes in the Revelation of Baha'u'llah and is firm in the Covenant. 'Put in your sickle and reap' means that this Apostle of the Lamb gives the Lamb's explanations and gathers the true believers BACK into the Covenant" (Dr. Leland Jensen, *Revelation Explained,* Revelation chapter 14 verse 15); and again: "The angel with the golden censer mentioned here is Neal Chase. His media releases plus his book on the Morrisites *Ezekiel's Temple in Montana* coincides with current events. The prayers of the saints are the prayers of all the previous martyrs that the 144,000 should be gathered quickly so that their blood could be avenged" (Dr. Leland Jensen, *Revelation Explained*, Revelation Chapter 8 verses 3, 4 and 5).

SUMMARY

Dr. Leland Jensen fulfilled prophecy. He had the "Stone with Seven Eyes" before him. He appeared in his Temple between the two mountains of copper in Deer Lodge. He was opposed the Covenant-breakers, the adversaries of God, (Heb. "Satan") on April 21st, 1963 as he began his mission. And Dr. Jensen also had charge and set up the courts, and as High Priest anointed the BRANCH that God has now brought forth. These are the proofs for The Establisher of the Baha'i Faith. To deny any of these is to deny the Joshua and the Greater Covenant all together. Both Leland and Neal fulfill these prophecies. Dr. Jensen wrote:

> I have a mandate--to bring forth and establish the BRANCH--I must and I will accomplish this. NOTHING IN HEAVEN OR ON EARTH CAN PREVENT ME IN DOING THIS.

> The Guardianship of the Baha'i Faith is the promised Zerubbabel, the governor of the New Jerusalem (Rev. 21:2, Haggai 1:1) he is that Great King that is seated upon

Area

Ezekiel's Temple in Montana

TUESDAY
Missoulian

NEAL CHASE is among a small group of believers who say the old Montana State Prison is the site of the second coming of Jesus "the High Priest" and it occurred Aug. 9, 1969.

KURT WILSON/Missoulian

THE ASIAN AGE

Baha'i council centre in city

'Founder descended from King David'

AGE CORRESPONDENT

MUMBAI

Neal Chase Ben Joseph Aghsan

Oct. 14: Throwing the gauntlet at all other sects of the Baha'i faith in the country, the Baha'is Under the Provisions of the Covenant (BUPC) has formed the National Baha'i Council in India, with its centre at Mumbai. The BUPC believes that Baha'u'llah, the founder of the Baha'i faith, was a descendant of King David. It also believes that the throne line did not end with the death of the first guardian Shoghi Effendi but is kept alive by the great-great-grandson of Baha'u'llah, Neal Chase Ben Joseph Aghsan.

According to BUPC members, the throne line of King David, which functions as the hereditary sign to recognize the true Universal House of Justice (UHJ) of Baha'u'llah, has been mistakenly construed to have ended in 1957. Citing Psalm 89, wherein God promises King David that his descen-

dants would rule on his throne forever, the BUPC believes that this prophecy that was fulfilled by the coming of Baha'u'llah is still kept alive by Neal Chase and he is the rightful president of the UHJ.

The BUPC maintains that peace will be established when all of mankind recognises this true spiritual government. Blaming Ruhiyyih Khanum, wife of Effendi and the Hands for trying to reduce the importance of the UHJ, the BUPC maintains that the act was aimed at turning the faith into an oppressive organised religion, in stark contrast to the principles of the faith.

THE ASIAN AGE

Mr Masri
... through Spanish territory.   the *Daily Mail*
          —AFP

Federal court: All Baha'i sects can be called Baha'i

AGE CORRESPONDENT

MUMBAI

Dec. 9: In a landmark judgement, a federal court in Chicago recently overruled a 1966 court decision that stopped an offshoot organisation from using the Baha'i name. The Chicago court judges, while criticising the 1966 ruling, said that it was a wrongful means of trying to resolve a question of religious authority. The federal 7th Circuit Court of Appeals has ruled that the 1966 decision does not apply to the different sects of Baha'i.

Sameer, a Member of the International Bahai Council and Chairman of the newly constituted National Bahai Council of India, said that the attempts of the Haifa-based mainstream Baha'i faith to shut down the public teaching effort and close down all the websites and publications of

the Baha'is, under the provisions of the Covenant, have been thwarted with this ruling.

One of the most important outcome of the ruling is that it has put aside all questions regarding religious organisations having any right to trademark its names or icons.

This comes as a major boost to the 1,44,000 strong followers of the Baha'is under the Provision of Covenant in the United States. They believe that the mainstream Baha'i faith has strayed from the religion's original teachings.

"The abrogation of the original order has freed us from their "marks" and the 6-66 injunction is upheld. We are free to go forward with our path and plans to further advance the Baha'i faith, headed by the third guardian Neal Chase, the Covenant appointed" said Mr Sameer.

MISSOULA Independent

24 hour fighter jets patrol over New York & Washington after Trade Towers destruction (New York Times 9/12/01)

President George W. Bush said Wednesday that all options were open for the use of the US nuclear arsenal... Russia, China, Iran, Iraq, Libya, North Korea, and Syria were named as potential targets for US nuclear strikes. (AFP 3/13/02)

Saddam Hussein executed in fulfillment of prophecy Dec. 29, 2006 Bush Administration has said the killing & "regime change" of Saddam Hussein must take place.(AP 2/07/02) Next attack on NYC imminent

The Head of the Arab League said that when the U.S. attacks Iraq it will "open the gates of hell." (BBC 9/5/02)

Millennial Fever

Mark Matthews explores the dire predictions of Missoula's Baha'is

FROM PERSIA: THE REAL MEDICINE

> Dear Neal "My dear Boy"
> My purpose is to BOMBARD you & your EDUCATOR with a dose of your own Medicine.
> Pepe

WHAT DO YOU THINK?? ????!

Dears, I think as Dear Neal Chase, the current Guardian of the Cause of God, has been always the one of followers("at the top of the list") of Dr. Jensen, the return of Jesus, SO then the "Dear Neal's own Medicine" cannot be anything but the "truth of his loyalty to the promised one of God". Therefore the "Medicine" means "Firmness in the Covenant"("his EDUCATOR's own Medicine"). It also refers to the "Teachings of Jesus on his return" which "Pepe's dear Boy" followed. And this is the REAL medicine for our sick world.

> Dear Brent My purpose is to BOMBARD Neal & Leland with a dose of their own Ammunition
> Pepe

Also what could be the "Ammunition" of "Neal & Leland" except the "Power of the Covenant" if we've accepted Doc as the "Seventh Angel"?!?

So Pepe used this "Ammunition" and did "appoint in his own life-time him that shall become his successor" exactly in that letter on the back of the same page.

p.s. Of course the "Medicine" refers to the Teachings of Jesus on his return too, as you all know it! --Yours, Iranian Baha'i @ [http://www.persian-bupc.doodlekit.com/contact]

...So Pepe used the "ammunition" and did "appoint in his own life-time him that shall become his suscessor" exactly in that letter. [http://www.persian-bupc.doodlekit.com/home]

the throne, that brings forth the CAP STONE, AMID SHOUTS OF GRACE GRACE TO IT!!! (Zech. 4:7) The Cap Stone represents the Kingdom of God on earth as it is in heaven, of which the Guardian is the sine qua non. This is the stone [the guardian the living Christ of the Baha'i world order] that the builders [Covenant-breaking Baha'is "Hands", etc.] have rejected, the corner stone of the kingdom of God on earth is the Guardianship, for it is the head of the corner itself (Psalms 118:22, Matthew 21:42, Mark 12:10). (Dr. Leland Jensen, *The Beast: Is About to Be Dead!*)

Thus this great treasure of the Kingdom of God is preserved in America and within the prophecies of the Bible, the Great Pyramid and seers such as Jeane Dixon as well as the prophecies of Nostradamus. As these two Neal and Leland fulfill prophecy by their prophesied names, prophesied dates, prophesied addresses and prophesied missions as the Two Promised Ones to appear in the West--the Twin Establishers of the Kingdom--at this time of the Great Catastrophe they are authentic. As they are authentic then we can believe it.

It all comes down to a matter of trust. Who can we trust? Well it tells us who we can trust on the America money. It says "In God we trust." Therefore we can trust in God. We can also trust in the one that God sends into the world to represent Himself. We can further put our trust in the one that the one sent by God appoints to succeed Himself.

Thus the true Universal House of Justice of Baha'u'llah is recognized by the living descendant of King David as its president. In fulfillment of Bible prophecy, the dates given in the Great Pyramid of Giza, the fulfillment of the tremendous visions of Jeane Dixon, Nostradamus and many others Dr. Leland Jensen established the true UHJ on earth as it is in heaven with the assistance of Neal Chase, the living descendant of King David as its president seated upon the throne of King David that is to last for ever.

The purpose of the descendant of King David being the president of Baha'u'llah's Universal House of Justice is so that we can recognize the true UHJ of Baha'u'llah from fakes, frauds, and imitations.

AUTHENTICITY IS THE CRITERIA
OF BELIEVABILITY

As Dr. Leland Jensen and Neal Chase fulfill prophecy they are authentic; therefore we can believe it. As those dates of 1963 AD and 2001 AD have come and gone, no one else in all history can ever again fulfill these prophecies. The time is past. The door is closed. Baha'u'llah and His Covenant is the Medicine needed for this sick world today. The college of Divine physicians exists and is established. This comprises the 24 elders who are the Council members prophesied in the book of Revelation and the one seated upon the throne, which is 25--the number of Pyramid inches in the sacred cubit. The Nuking of New York--the final "third woe" in the siege of the city--is a bump in the head to get the attention of the people who are stubborn and refuse time and time again to access this remedy--as the Covenant of Baha'u'llah and the Will and Testament of 'Abdu'l-Baha is the Divine Peace Program from God, it alone has the power to remedy all ills, through the power of His Most Great Name.

xxvi

Thus has the promised one living among you arrived with paradise in his one hand and heaven on earth in the other; yet as the mass of the people have rejected them both our world goes head-long into global thermo-nuclear war. Someone has to be fuel for the fire.

> The prophets prophesy falsely, and the priests bear rule by their means; and my people love *to have it* so: and what will ye do in the end thereof? (Jer. 5:31 KJV)

> For the time will come when people will not put up with sound doctrine. Instead, to suit their own desires, they will gather around them a great number of teachers to say what their itching ears want to hear. (2 Tim. 4:3 NIV)

The meaning of the word Christ is the male-sperm descendant of king David that is anointed. The purpose of the living descendant of King David is so that we can recognize the real Universal House of Justice of Baha'u'llah from fakes, frauds and imitations.

For free on-line firesides go to: http://bahaifireside.org. See also BUPC.org and UHJ.net for more.

> *"Do not harm earth or the sea or the trees, till we have sealed the servants of our God upon their foreheads." "**Blessed is He** who keeps the words of the prophecy of this Book" And I saw "the number of the sealed, a hundred and forty four thousand sealed..." (Rev 7:4; 22:7 RSV)*

--Victor G. Woods.

***** ******* ****

Dedicated to Victor Woods, The Name of God, The First!
--Ismullah-il-Awwal--

SURIY-I-ZIYARAT-NAMIH-I ISMULLAH-IL-AWWAL

--Baha'u'llah--

*This is the **Surah of Visitation** that has been sent down from the Realm of Grace for the Name of God, the First (**Ismullah-il-Awwal**), that she who is the most pious of women (**Varaqatu'l-Firdaws**: the First Leaf of Paradise) may visit him; as well as those who believe in God and His verses (may visit him too) and BE of those who have Attained!*

HE IS the Almighty, the Omnipotent, the Exalted, the All-Glorious in El-ABHA.

This is a letter from a Wronged One, known in the Kingdom of Eternity as Baha; in the Dominion of Exaltation as the Exalted, the Most High; in the Unseen Realm as (the Supra-Totality) of All God's Beauteous Names; and in the contingent world as Husayn; yet most of the people are under a Veil and an Immense Delusion. No one can reckon what has befallen Him in every dispensation, save God, the Sovereign, the Sublime.

O Leaf of Paradise! When you receive this luminous, effulgent Tablet, rise up from your place and take hold of it with the Hand of Humility. Inhale from it the fragrance of God, your Lord and the Lord of All the Worlds! Commemorate My sufferings, which it relates, so that you may be counted among those who are Remembered in the Tablets of God, the Overshadowing, the Mighty, the Powerful. Teach the Cause of God to those around you and to those who have been guided by the Spirit's Counsel and are among the assured...

Blessed are you, O Leaf of Paradise! for you have been carried away by the breezes of the Spirit and taken to the Egypt of the Divine Presence--the Place of the Recognition of your Lord, the Sublime, the Wondrous. You have drunk from the cups of your Lord's mercy and attained to that which no other in All the Worlds has attained. Thank your Lord. Humble yourself and bow down before Him. Take hold of the Book of God with such strength as is borne of Him, for *It* is indeed the Sublime Book.

How blessed you are in that God has related you to His Name. Through Him, the Ensigns of Salvation were manifested, the Sun of Grace dawned, the Moon of Bounty rose, and the Ancient Beauty was established on the throne of His Name, the Exalted, the Sublime. By Him, the Kingdom of Names was exalted, the forms of the Divine Attributes were adorned, and the Temple of Holiness was revealed in the garment of His Name, the Ancient of Days. By Him, the Supremacy of the Cause encompassed all contingent things and the Sun of Bounty shone its light on all creation. By Him, the Two Mighty Rivers flowed through the Two Exalted Names. None have drunk from them except those whom God has singled out for His Cause, favored among His servants and chosen out of His peoples. He has made them manifestations of His Most Excellent Names and embodiments of His Most Exalted Attributes, and enabled them to be among those who have entered His Transcendent, Sublime and Wondrous-Presence!

O Leaf of Paradise! *Visit* Him on My behalf with what is now being revealed from the Realm of God, the Sanctified, the Lofty, the Wise, the All-Knowing.

When you wish to begin your *Visitation* with Him who is the Dawning Place and Wellspring of God's Names and the Orient and Treasury of His attributes: **Arise!** and set your face toward Paradise, the place (Lamborn Mesa) where the First Name is buried which God has made the resting place of His Holy, Majestic and Luminous Temple. **Stand** and *MANGNIFY GOD* your Lord (*Kaibbari Allah*) Nineteen Times. As you recite each *Takbir** God will open ONE of the Doors of Ridvan before your Face, and the Fragrant Breeze of the All-Praised will waft over you from the Garden. Thus has it been ordained by One Who is Almighty and All-Wise. Then *GLORIFY GOD* Nine Times with Certitude (*Tabahhi† va Iqan*) in His Cause, affirming His sovereignty, proclaiming His majesty, recognizing His manifestation, and turning toward His sanctified, effulgent, manifest, dazzling, scintillating, resplendent and Luminous Countenance.

Then say: I testify by My Soul, My Essence, My Being, My Tongue, My Heart and the Limbs of My Body that there is none other God beside Him! That the Primal-Point of the Clear Proofs (*bayan*) is His manifestation, His advent, His majesty, His honor, and His grandeur before those in the Celestial Concourse, and His Sublimity, His power and His might between Heaven and Earth. He whom the One True God has made manifest is His appointed Sovereign to all in the Heavens and on Earth, and His effulgence to each and every one in the Kingdom of Command and Creation (*Alam-i-Amr va Khalq*). Say:

The First Spirit manifested from the Realm of Grandeur and the First Mercy revealed from the Heaven of Holiness at the right of the throne, where our Lord, the Exalted, the Most High is seated--may they rest upon Thee, O secret of the Divine Decree, Temple of the Realization, Most Perfect Word in the Realm of Eternity, and Most Great Name in the Kingdom of Creation.

I testify by My essence, My soul and My tongue that by you the Beauty of the All-Praised was established upon the throne of His Name, the All-Merciful, that in you the Primal Will was made manifest to the people of existence, that through you the melody of Paradise was revealed from the Heaven of Grace on the part of your Lord, the Almighty, the Beneficent, and that because of you the Cause of God, the Omnipresent, the Omnipotent, the Mighty, the Powerful, was made manifest. I testify that you are the First Light to dawn from the beauty of God's unity and the First Sun to rise from the Horizon of Divinity. Were it not for you, the beauty of the Essence would have remained concealed and the Mysteries of Eternity would not have been revealed.

I testify that, because of you, the birds of the souls of those consumed with longing flew through the Expanse of Nearness and Reunion, and the hearts of those overcome with yearning tasted the sweet savor of beauty and communion, at the dawning of the Sun of the Countenance of Thy Lord, the Possessor of majesty and glory. Were it not for you, no one would have recognized the Self of God and His beauty, no one would have reached the shore of His nearness and presence, contingent beings would not have drunk from the waters of His magnanimity and abundance, and created things would not have partaken of the wine of His bounty and munificence.

---

* Each One of the 19 "*Allah-Hu Akbar!*" The **Takbīr** (تَكْبِير), also transliterated *Tekbir* or *Takbeer*, is the Arabic phrase *Allah-Hu Akbar!* (اللهأكبر) meaning "*God be Magnified through Me!*" It is a common Arabic expression of Islam used in various contexts by Muslims in formal prayer; in the call (*adhān*) for prayer; as an informal expression of faith;, in Times of Distress; or to express Resolute Determination and/or Defiance! *Ya Allah-Hu Akbar! Va-Ha-Allah al-Kay-Bir!*" Say: "*Allah-Hu Akbar!*" Nineteen Times.
† "*Allah'u'Abha!*" Nine Times. Each one is termed a *Tabahhi*.

xxix

Because of you the Veils of Existent Things have been torn away. Because of you the Kingdom of names and attributes has been manifested. Because of you every soul has been guided to the shore of a Sublime Sanctity. Because of you the dove warbled upon the BRANCHES of Eternity and the Songbird of the throne sang its melodies upon the Boughs of the Lote Tree of Glory. Because of you the Beauty of the Unseen has been manifested in His Name, the Exalted, the Most High. Because of you all good has been sent down from the Realm of the Unseen unto the Kingdom of Creation, and every grace has been inscribed by the fingers of God upon the Tablets of Destiny. And because of you contingent beings have been embraced by the Mercy of God, the Omnipotent, the All-Knowing, the Sublime, the Majestic.

Were it not for you, neither would Heaven have been raised above, nor would the Earth have been spread below, nor would the Oceans have been revealed. Were it not for you, neither would the trees have borne fruit, nor would the leaves have appeared in their green verdure, nor would the Orb of Divine Grace have *shone* from a Horizon of Effulgent Sanctity. Because of you, the Breezes of Forgiveness have wafted over all in the Heavens and on Earth, the Gates of the Garden have been Opened to all beings, and the hearts of those who believe in God, the Mighty, the Powerful, the Munificent, have been enraptured.

Thou art the Word through which contingent things are distinguished from each other--the blessed from the wicked, the light from the darkness, and the believer from the unbeliever--on this Day until the day on which Heaven is cleft and God comes in clouds of the Cause surrounded by a company of the angels. At that time, the clouds are rent asunder and the Divine Countenance appears from behind the Veil, with tens of thousands in Great Glory. In that moment, those who joined partners with God flee from the right and the left; and a stupor takes hold of all in the Heavens and on Earth, save a few Letters of the Countenance of your Lord, the All-Merciful, the Compassionate.

I testify that you were entrusted with the faith of your Lord, the All-Merciful, and that you recognized the Beauty of the All-Praised before the creation of the universe and attained the presence of God on a Day when you alone had recognized Him. By means of this grace, God favored you, before He created the Heavens and the Earth. I testify that, through your remembrance, the tongues of created things were inspired with the mention of their Lord, the All-Knowing, the All-Wise, and through your praising your Creator, all rose in celebration of Him. All existence, both seen and unseen, bears witness to this and, BEYOND this: God is a Witness and Fully Aware.

I testify that you *championed* the religion of God, manifested His Cause and struggled (*mujahada*) in His path insofar as you were able. I moreover testify that, through your *victory*, the proof of God and His testimony were revealed, and likewise His power and ascendency, His grandeur and majesty, and His sovereignty over all created things. **Blessed be those who struggled with you** and **waged war against the enemies of God at your command,** who circled round you, entered the stronghold of your Guardianship and drank from the Kawthar of your Love, who were martyred for turning toward your Countenance and who rested in the Court of your Nearness. They are of those who repose in tranquility. I testify that they are the Champions of God on His earth, the bearers of His trust in His lands, the kindred of God among His people, the Legions of God in the midst of His creation, and the chosen of God between the Heavens and Earth.

I testify that *you* **fell victim to the most grievous tribulations** and deplorable hardships in the path of your Lord and that adversity encompassed you on all sides. Yet nothing could deter you from the path of your Creator. Alone you fought until you became a martyr in His Cause and gave up your spirit, your soul and your body in your love for your Lord, the Eternal. I testify that all things between Heaven and Earth wept by reason of your suffering, as did the eyes of the near ones behind the Tabernacle of Manifest Majesty. The Maids of Heaven (*ḥuriyya*) in their private rooms uncovered their heads and struck them with wondrous and sanctified fingers. They fell down with their faces in the dust, sat upon the ashes, and lamented at that time in their Luminous Red Chambers. I testify that, due to Thy suffering, all things were clothed in a Black Robe of mourning, the faces of the sincere paled, the limbs of such as had affirmed the Divine Unity trembled, and the eye of majesty and grandeur wept in the Realm of Exalted Holiness.

I testify, O my Master, here where I stand! that you did not fail in the Cause of your Lord, nor did you hold back in the love of your God. You took His command to the East of the land and to the West of it, until you were sacrificed in His path and became a martyr. **God curses the people who oppressed** *you*, rose up against you, fought against you, argued to your face, denied your testimony, left your side, disdained being humble before you, and were among the idolaters.

Therefore, do I beseech God by you and by those around you that He forgive me and pardon my sins, that He cleanse me of earthly defilement and number me among the Purified. I ask that He honor me with His presence during these Days when all have been heedless of Him and are among those who have veiled themselves. I ask that He aid me in recognizing Him, confessing His Cause, believing in Him with all assurance, affirming His verses, entering into His shelter, standing present in the Court of His mercy, bearing witness on His path, and turning wholly unto Him, the Exalted, the Sublime.

We beseech God by Thee that He not cut us off from the shining lights of His countenance in these days, nor make us deprived of the wonders of His grace or debarred from His mercy, which encompasses the worlds. We ask that He establish us securely in His love and stand us upright in His Cause, so that our feet shall not slip on His path, which has appeared in reality between the Heavens and the Earth.

Mercy, praise and glory *be* upon you, O chosen of God among His servants and trusted of God throughout His lands, and upon your bodily forms, your celestial forms, and your spirits, and upon your First, your Last, your Manifest and your Concealed. And mercy, praise and glory be upon those who have dismounted at your precinct, circled around you, come before the Gate of your Mercy, stood before the manifest lights of your clemency, and entered the Threshold of your Nearness. These are they who have been brought near to God because of you, who have sought mediation with God through you and who have visited your sanctuary; who were blessed by the dust of your graves, who have sought guidance through your Teaching, and who were among those who turned toward your Countenances, pure, sanctified, effulgent and luminous.

O Lord, my God! I beseech Thee by him and by those who have rested in his vicinity, to make us of those who have flown in the expanse of Thy Mercy, drunk the wine of Thy munificence and beneficence, attained the summit of grace through Thy bounty and abundance, and tasted the sweetness of Thy remembrance. Make us of those who have ascended to the ladders of the Remotest Region and the seats of the Highest Realm through Thy grace and bestowals, who have cut themselves off from all sides, who have hastened in the direction of Thy favors and who have been seized by the glorious breezes of Thy compassion and the Holy Fragrances of Thy eternity. Indeed, Thou art the All-Powerful, the Mighty, the All-Wise.

Our God and our Beloved! Forgive us, our parents, our relations and those who have believed in Thee and in Thy verses and in him who has been made manifest in Your Sovereignty. Grant, moreover, O my God, that we be empowered by strength from Thee in this world, and that we attain Thy presence in the next. Do not decree us forbidden from that which You possess, nor denied of such as is worthy of Thee. In truth, Thou art the Possessor of bounty and beneficence, and of grace and benevolence.

Indeed, Thou art our Lord, the All-Merciful, and our God, Whom we supplicate: and in Whom we place our trust. None other God is there beside Thee, the Forgiving, the Munificent, the Merciful.

Thus have We revealed this Surah to Thee, **O Leaf of Paradise**, that you may follow such as Thou art bidden and be numbered among the pious in the Tablets of Luminous Sanctity.

***** ********* *****

"By their Countenance shall the sinners be known, and they shall be seized by their forelocks and their feet!" (Q. 55:41; 2:273)

Thus the peoples of the world are judged by their Countenance. By it, their misbelief, their faith, and their iniquity are all made manifest. Even as it is evident in this day how the people of error are, by their Countenance, known and distinguished from the followers of divine Guidance. Were these people, wholly for the sake of God and with no desire but His good-pleasure, to ponder the verses of the Book in their heart, they would of a certainty find whatsoever they seek. In its verses would they find revealed and manifest all the things, be they great or small, that have come to pass in this Dispensation. They would even recognize in them references unto the departure of the Manifestations of the names and attributes of God from out their native land; to the opposition and disdainful arrogance of government and people; and to the dwelling and establishment of the Universal Manifestation in an appointed and specially designated land. No man, however, can comprehend this except he who is possessed of an understanding heart. (Baha'u'llah, *Kitab-i-Iqan*, p. 173-174)

COUNTENANCE OF LOVE

(Lawh al-Tal'at al-Hubb)
--Baha'u'llah--

Countenance of love! We have recognized your longing for God in the Tabernacles of Eternity, insofar as you drew near and attained, in the arenas of encounter, to the presence of God. Thus have we reckoned everything in a Book that was decreed in the Tablet. Know that you have advanced to the Sanctuary of Beauty and visited the Ka'bih of Holiness in the Garden of paradise on the Mount Paran of Love. Thus was your affair guarded from the rebellious in a Tablet. Do not grieve over any matter, and be not perplexed at the adversities of this world. God shall send you forth in a station that is, in truth, exalted. For the world, its adornments and finery, shall pass away in less than the blink of an eye. Therefore, exert yourself in what will be everlasting for you in the highest Kingdom, so that you will be safeguarded in the worlds of the spirit that revolve around the Tree of Immortality.

Listen with the ear of your heart to what the dove warbles on the pole of infinity, insofar as it has taught you the paths of truth on that route that was raised up in Light. Attest to this Tablet with the Tongue of Spirit so that you might be radiant with the Fire of Love. Fear God, and pay no attention to those who opposed Him. Do not follow those who have disbelieved and who shall never find for themselves a path to the truth. Be constant in Love and firm in the Cause so that your foot shall not stumble, even if you are opposed by all who are on earth. Therefore, cast away what is in your right hand, then follow God's paradise so that you might find an august station at the center of the Garden near the Sea of Immortality.

Thus have we written in the Tablet the details of all things, and have mentioned them to you so that you might arrive at a station that is impervious to sorrow. By God, if you savor the Fragrance of this Garment, you will experience the breezes of the Divine essence, your eyes will overflow with tears in your yearning for God, and you will be insightful concerning the Cause of your Lord.

Spirit Be upon *you*: and upon those who are well-disciplined, having *drawn nigh* and been consumed by the Fire of Union.

THE TABLET OF THE BESTOWAL

(Lawh-i-'Ata)
--Baha'u'llah--

HE IS GOD!

IN MY NAME by which the **Door of Bestowal** has been flung open upon the denizens of the earth and heaven!

The particles of existing things and the realities of contingent beings bear witness that this Servant has neither had nor has any object in manifesting Himself and this Cause except the salvation of humanity and extinguishing the fire of hatred and rebellion. In the night season His call is raised, in the morningtide His cry and tears, and in the days His sonorous Voice!

As some sects maintain and continue to proclaim today: mention has been made in their scriptures of the burning of books, killing of souls and forbidding association one with another. This is despite the fact that true fellowship, joyous transactions, healthy commerce and sharing are the greatest means for the advancement of humanity and the progress of countries! Contrary to this, these things--and even worse atrocities--have been mentioned and recorded in the Qur'an, the Bible and the Bayan and perpetrated in their names.

In His childhood, this Oppressed One saw the expedition of the people of Qurayza in a book attributed to the blessed and forgiven, Mulla Baqir Majlisi. Although what happened was the Command of God and had no purpose besides crushing the power of the oppressors, at that time He was so grief-stricken and distressed to such a profound degree that the pen is incapable of describing it! Suddenly the Boundless Sea of Forgiveness and Grace was seen and experienced surging forth! In those lasting days, therefore, He continually beseeched God for that which shall be the means of love, concord and solidarity for all the people of the earth.

On the second day of the Twin Birthdays, just before sunrise, all My manners, My words and speech, and My thoughts were suddenly changed in suchwise that it gave the Glad-Tidings of Exaltation and Ascendency. This change kept descending and manifesting without interruption for twelve consecutive days. A transfiguration took place with unyielding cessation and intensity. Thereafter, the waves of the Sea of Eloquence were seen; the Ocean of Utterance welled forth; and the Effulgences of the Luminary of Satisfaction (and bliss) were resplendent and present upon all sides until it led to the time of the Manifestation (*zuhur*). Then I attained to that which God has made the **Source of the Happiness of the Worlds** and the **Dawning-Place of Bestowal** for the dwellers of the heavens and the earths.

Subsequently, by the Most Exalted Pen, that which is the cause of trouble, suffering, divisions and segregation was removed by an Irrevocable Inevitable Command and that which is the means of agreement, fellowship and association flowed and descended. None will deny the excellence of this Manifestation except every veiled neglectful one and every hating oppressor. The sanctified revealed Tablets that have been sent down and the Tablet of the Sacrifice (*Suratu'dh-Dhabih*) are witness! Blessed are the fair ones and Blessed is every truthful trustworthy one!

When you hear My Call from My Tablet, and see that which has shone forth from **The Shining of its Horizon** by My Grace, say:

"My God! My God! Praise be to Thee for Thou hast made me to hear Thy Call and made me aware of that which was hidden in Thy Knowledge and concealed from the eyes of Thy servants. I beseech Thee, O Sovereign of Existence and the Ruler of the Seen and the Unseen, that Thou assist me in Thy remembrance and in Thy service and in the service of Thy friends. Aid me with such Steadfastness that the affairs of Thy creation and the doubts of Thy servants are unable to change it! Verily, Thou art the Prevailing Ordainer, the All-Mighty, and the Most Bountiful Bestower!"

INTRODUCTION

For the Jewish people the Temple is all important. Unlike today where there is a church on every corner or many synagogues and temples throughout the cities for the people to attend, in ancient Israel there was only one Temple in the entire nation to which all the people flowed.

The primary function of the Temple was that of an Academy or House of Study (*Bet Midrash*) in which the people could learn about the one God and His plan for establishing the Kingdom on earth. The Temple was the center of education with the high priest being the great educator.

Today when we think of the word "priest" we think of someone who performs a ritual, waves incense, or gives the people wine or a wafer to eat or something like that. When Moses appointed his brother Aaron to be the high priest Moses charged Aaron to be the educator of the people. High (*Gavohah*) means "great" and priest (*Kohen*) means "educator." The other priests and Levites being his students and disciples were also educators and teachers. It was their function to scatter throughout the land and educate the nation. The people would for their part make pilgrimage to the Temple on a regular basis.

The Temple also functioned as a House of Justice (*Bet Din*) where the Sanhedrin of 70 met as the supreme court of all Israel.

Through the teachings of the High Priest, the court of 70 was guided by the Law of Moses to make decisions that were favorable in the sight of God. Through this manner all the difficult problems of the nation of Israel were resolved.

The King of Israel, and before him the judges (Joshua being the first judge) enforced the decision of the Court. The primary function of the Kingship was to guard the Temple and sanctuary from being destroyed by enemy nations and to protect the life of the High Priest and his teachings. For this reason the King was empowered to command the army (which was strictly volunteer according to the Law of Moses that God gave Him).

The reason there was only one Temple was so that the people should know that there is only one God. The Temple of Israel was the focal point of unity and was the heart of the nation. As long as the people had their Temple their nation was without sin and they enjoyed the Presence of God among them. The word "sin" comes from an archery term which literally means "to miss the mark." For Israel the Temple was the mark which no should miss for it united God and man after the passing of Moses. For this reason the Temple also bore the additional name of Lebanon meaning "that which makes white" for it purified the nation; and also "*leb*" meaning the "heart," for the Temple was the heart of the of the people from which flowed the life blood of the nation and the spiritual waters of life from the Revelation that God gave Moses.

> Because of its atoning power, the Temple bears the additional name of Lebanon: 'that which makes white,' because it cleanses Israel from sins (*lebanon* is thus

connected with the Hebrew *laban*, 'white'), and also because it forms the heart (*leb*) of the people (Midrash Lev. I)[*]

Very briefly, from these examples, we can see the all important position that the Temple holds in the life of Israel. Not only did it cleanse the people of sin, but it was the source of Israel's life. The Temple was the heart of the nation. Today the Jews are without their Temple and the people are distressed. It is as if the heart has been ripped from their chest. Some militant religious fanatics are even now demanding that their Temple be restored by violence. Bloodied handprints of wounded Palestinians marked the Temple mount wall not long ago when Meir Kahane who advocated the total destruction of the al-Aqsa Mosque (occupying the old Temple site for Jews) was murdered in New York City. The world has witnessed the worst massacre of unarmed Palestinians in Israeli History who were fired upon with live ammunition.

From the Orthodox to the radical, from the conservative to the reform, clearly these events show that the Jews are waiting for their Temple.

The Temple must always be awaited. The Temple is the core of Jewish belief and the center of its value system.

> The rebuilding of the temple must always be awaited (Sab. 12b and other passages). God will erect the future Temple even before the Kingdom of David has been reestablished and his descendants restored to office (Yer. M.S. 5:2, 56a).[†]

The first Temple was the human temple of Moses through which the Law was Revealed on Sinai. However Moses knew that his human temple, his physical body, would not last forever. So he had the people build a tent called the Tabernacle to succeed him. The tabernacle was the embryonic Temple which was later to evolve into the one built out of Stone by King Solomon.

Moses had the tent divided into two rooms, one called the outer sanctuary or Holy Place and the second inner room called the Holy of Holies or Most Holy Place. In this inner room of the Holy of Holies Moses had a box constructed to hold his written word. This box was called the Ark of the Covenant. Only the High Priest, who was Moses' brother that he appointed (and after him his brother's descendants) was allowed to enter the Holy of Holies and read the scrolls in the box. By these three things: (a) the High Priest, (b) the Ark, and (c) the Holy of Holies the Temple became the dwelling place of God.

The dwelling place of God is called in Hebrew the *Shekinah*. The Shekinah is considered to be the Presence of God Himself. The Shekinah is known as the Divine Presence and is described as the glory, splendor, or light of God. Being that the God of Israel is infinite and invisible and cannot be known in essence, the Presence of God (Shekinah) refers to His presence in Manifestation and Revelation. God can only be known through the Manifestation of Himself, the Manifestation of His qualities and attributes, i.e. love, justice, concord, fidelity, harmony, *etc.*

---

[*] *The Universal Jewish Encyclopedia, Vol. 10*, p. 196.
[†] *The Universal Jewish Encyclopedia, Vol. 10*, p. 197.

For the Jews the Revelation of God came to them through Moses of whom it is said the Shekinah dwelled. The Shekinah is also described in the Jewish literature as the Holy Spirit (*ruach ha-qodesh*: חור שדוקה). In other words, Moses having the Holy Spirit (Shekinah) was able to receive the thought of God and reflect it in a Revelation. In symbolic parable this is described as the burning bush of Moses' heart. The fire of which in Hebrew is the word "*Urim*" which is accurately translated as Revelation (the oracular) and the *Thummim* referring to His purity of His stainless and sanctified heart from which the commandments (*amr*) issue forth.

After Moses' passing the Presence of God (Shekinah) was transferred into the Temple which became his successor. The Shekinah was said to rest in the Holy of Holies upon the Ark of the Covenant. Thus the Holy of Holies became known as the Presence of God. Yet how can God be said to live in the Temple when God is infinite and omnipresent filling all space?

The answer is that the Holy of Holies was considered the Presence of God because this is where the words of Moses were kept in the box. It was within the words that Moses spoke (within the Revelation of the Torah that he gave) that the essence of God was Manifested. This is not to say that God incarnated in Moses or in the Temple or was in any way physically contained within the box of the Ark. This would be absurd and against the teachings. All that could be known of God was the knowledge of God through the Revelation of Moses on Sinai. This knowledge of God (Shekinah) was transmitted by Moses to the people in the form of His Revelation which after his passing was preserved in his written words. In receiving this Revelation (the Presence of God; Shekinah) the people who entered into the Law and Covenant of the Torah became sons of the Covenant or commandment. This is the essence of *bar mitzpa* (literally son of the commandment or Covenant). Therefore the Revelation of Moses was the Manifestation of God to all Israel.

As long as those three things of (a) the High Priest, (b) the Ark of the Covenant, and (c) the Holy of Holies were intact the Presence of God (Shekinah) was with the people of Israel and the Revelation was living. If at any time one of these three essentials were to be withdrawn, then the Presence of God would be lost to the people.

The high priesthood was continued through the descendants of Aaron, Moses brother. Only one man could be the high priest (great educator) at any time so that there could be no division in thought concerning the one God.

It was the purpose of the Davidic kingship to guard the high priest and protect the Temple from the enemies of Israel so that it should not be destroyed. Before the Davidic kings were anointed by Samuel to fulfill this function the judges fulfilled this role. Joshua, the establisher of Moses, was the first judge and he moved the tent (Tabernacle) to Shiloh where it remained until the time of David. David moved the Ark and the tent (embryonic Temple) to Jerusalem where Solomon then built the Temple out of stone. God was very pleased with Solomon and made him the greatest king in the world.

Then Solomon, and all Israel with him, broke the Covenant and prayed to the pagan gods of Ashtoreth and Milcolm who are known in Babylon as Semiramis (Ashtoreth) and Nimrod

(Milcolm). Because of this, the people of Israel forsook the teaching of God and entered under the second part of Moses' Covenant, the curse.[*]

Moses had made a three part Covenant with the tribes of Israel (see Deuteronomy chapters 28 and 30). First they would be blessed and become a great nation; second they would forsake the law, break the Covenant, become scattered throughout the world and become cursed; and third they would be gathered again from the four corners of the earth by the descendant of David prophesied to come seated upon David's throne, known as the Messiah (the anointed descendant of David).

> And if you obey the voice of the LORD your God, being careful to do all his commandments which I command you this day, the LORD your God will set you high above all the nations of the earth. And all these blessings shall come upon you and overtake you, if you obey the voice of the LORD your God... But if you will not obey the voice of the LORD your God or be careful to do all his commandments and his statutes which I command you this day, then **all these curses shall come upon you** and overtake you... The LORD will send upon you **curses, confusion, and frustration,** in all that you undertake to do, until you are destroyed and perish quickly, on account of the evil of your doings, because you have forsaken Me... And when all these things come upon you, **the Blessing and the Curse**, which I have set before you, and you call them to mind among all the nations where the LORD your God has driven you, and **Return** to the LORD your God, you and your children, and obey his voice in all that I command you this day, with all your heart and with all your soul; then the LORD your God **will restore your fortunes**, and have compassion upon you, and he will **Gather you again** from all the peoples where the LORD your God has scattered you. (Deut. 28:1-2, 15, 20; 30:1-3 RSV)

At the time of David and Solomon the first part of the blessing was fulfilled. Then when they broke the Covenant by bowing down to statues they became cursed. God allowed Nebuchadnezzar to come in and destroy Jerusalem, burn down the Temple, capture the king and the people, and bring them to Babylon as slaves. The people were devastated. Their Temple was destroyed and their kingdom gone.

In 457 BCE, Ezra repopulated the city of Jerusalem for Temple worship, bringing a remnant of the people (about 30,000) back from Babylon to Jerusalem. At this time the Temple of Solomon had been rebuilt by the Jews and is known as the second Temple.

Later the second Temple was refurbished by Herod around the time of Jesus. About 40 years after Jesus the Temple was finally destroyed by Titus in 70 CE. Since that time, the Jews have been without their Temple and have remained under the second part of Moses Covenant (the curse) in anticipation of the coming of the Messiah and the appearance of the future Temple.

---

[*] For more on the enduring role of Nimrod and Semiramis in the Great Violation see Rev. Alexander Hislop (1871), *The Two Babylons, 7th ed.* and Colonel J. Garnier (1909), *The Worship of the Dead* for more.

When the Jews recaptured Jerusalem in 1967, the Jewish leaders were asked what their plans were now that they regained their Holy City and the site of the Temple. Moshe Dayan said, "We have returned to our holiest of holy places, never to leave her again."[*]

The interviewers asked that although they had regained the city and the Temple cite they still didn't have the Temple, the Ark of the Covenant, and the High Priest and that without these they couldn't be right with God. The Jews agreed. They were asked what they could do about the Temple when the Mosque of Omar is standing in its place, "If you tear it down then there would be the greatest holy war in the history of the world?" The Jews said, "Maybe there will be an earthquake."[†] "Well even if there was an earthquake and the Temple was rebuilt, what about the Ark of the Covenant which is lost?" They responded, "Maybe we will find it." Even if they found the Ark what about the high priesthood, all the pure descendants of Aaron have intermarried? The Jews say that is why they are waiting for their Messiah.

According to the Bible, the Book of Ezekiel, the holy writings of the prophets, and the Jewish literature the Temple must appear as Ezekiel prophesied it: "The Temple will appear as Ezekiel prophesied it."[‡]

The unique feature of Ezekiel's Temple which distinguishes it from all others is that Ezekiel's Temple has SEVEN TOWERS.

In chapter 44, Ezekiel sees "the coming of the Lord" enter the future Temple through the seventh tower which is "the gate that faces east" from between the two pillars of Jachin and Boaz (see double-illustrations on inside front pages ii and iii). This is the exact gate through tower seven that the establisher of the Baha'i Faith passed through on the prophesied date.

Earlier in his book ("God's Glory Departs from the Temple:" see Ezekiel chapter 10), Ezekiel had seen the Divine Presence leave Solomon's Temple in Jerusalem **never** to return their again. The Jews never built a Temple with seven towers, but only rebuilt and refurbished Solomon's Temple. It is to Ezekiel's Temple with seven towers that the Divine Presence is to return to.

Furthermore the Temple that Ezekiel sees is to be on a very high mountain in the far north. The old Temple cite of Solomon is not on a high mountain nor any mountain for that matter. Also it is located in the south, in Judea, and not in the far north.

However in the far north of the very high mountain of the Rockies in North America is Ezekiel's Temple in Montana. Over 127 years ago the prophet George Williams saw "the City of the Great King," the New Jerusalem, which included Ezekiel's Temple was to built up in Deer Lodge, Montana. The Morrisite pioneers who followed the vision of George Williams specifically pioneered the Deer Lodge Valley in 1863 in expectation of Ezekiel's Temple and "the City of the Great King" to be built there.

---

[*] Hal Lindsey, *The Late Great Planet Earth*, p. 45.

[†] *Time Magazine* (June 30, 1967), p. 56.

[‡] Raphael Patai, *Messiah Texts*, p. 144. (Ma'as Daniel, pp. 225-26).

The Morrisites never built the Temple which George Williams prophesied would be built from "the stone of the surrounding mountains." The only thing that they built was a little wooden church called the Lord's House about five miles outside the Deer Lodge city limits. Williams explicitly told them that their prayer house was not the Temple which was to be made out of stone and not out of wood. He also told them that the "tribes from the north" would be the ones to build the Temple. So the Federal government from the north in Helena built the Temple for them.

The Old Montana State Prison has a solid stone wall made from the granite and sandstone from Whitehall and Garrison (from the surrounding mountains). This stone wall has the prophesied seven towers with the seventh tower and gate that faces east having the twin pillars of Jachin and Boaz standing at the door.

These two pillars represent the two Messiahs prophesied to come in the Jewish literature (see below)--the "Suffering Messiah" entitled, Messiah ben Joseph; and the "Reigning Messiah" entitled King-Messiah.

Furthermore the prison is divided into two parts, the larger yard being the outer sanctuary and the inner maximum security area being the Holy of Holies with the Ark of the Covenant building in it (see diagram pages 32 and 49).

Today approximately two thirds of the population of the Deer Lodge Valley, which is 60 miles long and 5 to 10 miles wide, are descendants of the Morrisite pioneers who settled the valley over 127 years ago for the specific reason of being the first ones to greet the Lord (the High Priest after the order of Melchizedec) upon his return as the prophet Malachi saw:

> Behold I send my messenger [George Williams] to prepare the way before me,
> and the Lord whom you seek will suddenly come to his Temple. (Malachi 3:1)

Not only does Ezekiel give the vision of the future Temple to have seven towers, but the Jewish literature also describes the High Priest who will preside in the seven towered Temple of the Lord. With the return of the High Priest in the Temple with the knowledge of the Ark of the Covenant the Divine Presence (Shekinah) is then restored to the world. Who is the High Priest that comes to Ezekiel's Temple?

Unanimously all authorities **agree by common consent** that the high priest in the kingdom of God will be **Melchizedec**.

> Much is to be said in the Talmudic literature about the high priest in the Messianic age...He is called "the Righteous Priest" (*Kohen-Zedek*)--an appellation apparently identical with **Melchizedec**. Here we have a significant point of contact of the Talmud with the Epistle to the Hebrews...in the New Testament. But the Talmud also has many passages militating against the conclusion that Melchizedec and the Messiah are identical...[for example] in the saying of the Patriarch Rabban Simeon ben Gamaliel II (post-Hadrianic) on Zechariah 4:14:

'These are the two anointed ones.' This means the Righteous Priest [Melchizedec] and the Messiah. And I do not know which of them is the more beloved. But since it says (Psalm 110:4) "The LORD hath sworn and will not repent: 'Thou art a priest for ever [after the manner of Melchizedec],'" we know that the King-Messiah is more beloved than the Righteous Priest [Melchizedec].'

The high priest in the Age to Come, **Melchizedec**, who plays such an important role in the Epistle to the Hebrews, is here less beloved of God than the Messiah. But the **existence** of the high priest in the Messianic Age is mentioned as something to be taken for granted by common consent.[*]

The existence of Melchizedec as the High Priest in the Messianic Age is unanimously accepted. That it is **Melchizedec** (and not from Aaron) is taken for granted by common consent. Yet clearly his station in relation to King-Messiah is one of subordination, for according to the Jewish literature it is the King-Messiah who shall reveal "the New Torah" and Melchizedec the High Priest who shall officiate over and establish what has been revealed. Therefore the High Priest is dependent upon what has already been revealed by the King-Messiah who is his superior. As Moses is the superior to Aaron and Joshua so the King-Messiah is superior to Melchizedec his high priest and establisher returned in the seven towered Temple of Ezekiel. Who is Melchizedec?

According to all ancient authorities and history, Melchizedec is the title bestowed upon Shem, the blessed son of Noah.[†] Shem/Melchizedec is unique in that he fulfilled two roles as both king and high priest. Melchizedec was the original founder and builder of the city of Jerusalem which today is heralded as the holy city for Jews, Christians, and Muslims. It was Melchizedec who blessed Abraham after the slaughter of the kings and served him bread and wine. In Jerusalem Melchizedec had built a great Academy known throughout the ancient world as the Academy of Shem (Bet Midrash/House of Study). Likewise this House of Study also functioned as a House of Justice (Bet Din). After the slaughter of the kings when Abraham was blessed by Shem/Melchizedec, Abraham entered the Academy of Shem and studied there for 4 years after which he graduated and wrote a book. Isaac and Jacob also studied in the Academy of Shem.

When Abraham returned from the war, Shem, or, as he is sometimes called, Melchizedec, the king of righteousness, priest of God Most High, and king of Jerusalem, came forth to meet him with bread and wine. And this high priest instructed Abraham in the laws of the priesthood and in the Torah, and to prove his friendship for him he blessed him, and called him the partner of God in the possession of the world, seeing that through him the Name of God had first been made known among men.[‡]

---

[*] Joseph Klausner, *The Messianic Idea in Israel*, p. 515.
[†] "The Rabbis identify Shem with Melchizedec, King of Salem, who is termed 'a priest of the Most High,' and who came to meet Abraham after the latter had defeated the four kings [the slaughter of the kings] led by Chedorlaomer (Gen. xiv. 18-20). According to this account, Shem, as a priest, came to Jerusalem (with which Salem is identified by the Rabbis), of which city he became king" ('SHEM,' *The Jewish Encyclopedia*).
[‡] Louis Ginzberg, *Legends of the Jews, Vol. I*, p. 233.

xlii

He [Abraham] first studied three years by himself, afterwards, by the command of God, he was taught by Shem, until he became so wise that he composed the *Sefer Yetzirah*. Then God appeared to him, took him to Himself, kissed him, called him His friend, and made a Covenant with him and his descendants forever.[*]

The other half of Melchizedec's role is that of the king--meaning the Defender. Not only was he the great educator (priest) that educated Abraham, Isaac and Jacob, but he defended the true religion of the One True Invisible God against the evil Nimrod. Thus as the Davidic Kings guarded the Temple and defended the religion, Melchizedec also guarded Jerusalem and his Temple by defending the religion.

Noah had three sons: Ham, Japeth and Shem. Shem was blessed but Ham was cursed. Ham had a son named Cush who had a son named Nimrod. Nimrod was the first to become a mighty hunter on the earth. He reestablished the paganism that had corrupted the people before the flood. He proclaimed that he was a god and that his wife Semiramis was a goddess. Shem/Melchizedec went down to the court of 72 judges in Egypt and showed that Nimrod had broken the Covenant and the Law. Nimrod was found guilty by due process and sentenced to death. His body was cut up into chunks and a different piece of him was sent out to his empire. Back in Babylon, the capital, his wife Semiramis got a piece. She was furious. She said that "As he was a god in life so shall he be a god in death!" So she out smarted Shem. About a year later she got pregnant and proclaimed that her son was the reincarnation of the Nimrod. She said that as Nimrod was god he came down to her in the spirit form and that her womb was the habitation of the Holy Spirit. She said that the son was the incarnation of the father god, Nimrod. Thus she created something new which had never been seen of before, the Trinity! The triune god-Lie of three gods in one. At the time of Solomon he prayed to Semiramis under her name of Ashtoreth. When the Jews followed Solomon into this and the nation of Israel began to worship the trinity, God allowed them to be destroyed by Nebuchadnezzar. From that time until today the Jews have never again been involved in paganism.

Today the Christian's (who are about 1/3 of the world's population) are into to this same paganism of Nimrod and Semiramis, especially the triune god-Lie (the trinity). Therefore over 20 nations are the Middle East ready to fight out the Armageddon over religion and oil (as prophesied) and after this nuclear holocaust they, like the Jews after Nebuchadnezzar, will be purified out of their paganism. It is the mission of the modern Melchizedec to educate the world out of their paganism and establish the Kingdom of the God of Israel, the One True Invisible God.

Nimrod and Semiramis are known by different names in the different countries. In Egypt she is Isis, he is Osiris, and the boy is Horus. From Egypt this spread to Greece. In Greece they broke up the god into many gods and the goddess into many goddesses. If she was smart she was Athena, if she was pretty she was Aphrodite. If he was strong he was Zeus, if he was wise he was Apollo. Rome gets their gods from Greece. In Rome she is Venus and Nimrod is Saturn. Nimrod pointed to Saturn and said that was him. Saturn is where we get the modern word Satan from.

---

[*] Louis Ginzberg, *Legends of the Jews, Vol. V*, p. 210.

Nimrod is the Satan of the Bible[*] because he sought to be greater than God Himself and corrupted the true religion. Melchizedec does battle with Nimrod and as the great educator (high priest) is the one to put him to death (put these falsehoods to rest) by exposing the corruption of this pagan religion of the trinity and many gods.

According to Zechariah 4:14 (as R. Gamiliel II pointed out) "Two anointed ones" are prophesied in the Old Testament: one to be the King-Messiah and one to be Melchizedec. These are the two descendants of King David as "Messiah" or "Christ" refers to this genealogy from David. The word "Christ" comes from the Hebrew word "Messiah" and literally means "anointed one." But anointed one of what? The full title in Hebrew is Messiah ben David and literally means "the anointed male-sperm descendant of King David."

The first is the "Suffering Messiah" who will be descended from David suffer and die, not sit upon David's throne and have no sons to continue after him. He will also be a high priest after the order of Melchizedec (see Hebrews). The second is the "Reigning Messiah" or King-Messiah who will be descended from David be seated upon David's throne and have sons to succeed him. In Ezekiel's Temple these two Messiahs are represented by the two pillars of Jachin and Boaz that are standing by the door of the seventh tower, the door that faces east.

The word "Messiah" is the Hebrew for anointed one, meaning an anointed descendant of king David. Here there are two Messiahs prophesied to come! Throughout all the teaching of Judaism from the Bible to the Talmud there are two Messiahs (two anointed sons of David) prophesied. They are depicted as a "Suffering Messiah" and as a "Reigning Messiah." As the Jewish literature militates against Melchizedec being the King-Messiah, Melchizedec is therefore identical to the other anointed one (as Gamiliel II pointed out) the Suffering Messiah.

According to the Bible and the Jewish literature, the Suffering Messiah will appear first, before the King-Messiah. He will be rejected by the majority of the Jews who are still in exile and then killed by the evil Armilus (see below). Then later, at the climax of the Messianic Age, the King-Messiah will appear and as his first great act and sign he will resurrect the Suffering Messiah as the High Priest Melchizedec who appears as the high priest in Ezekiel's Temple.

Thus, the mission of the King-Messiah (the Reigning Messiah) is to be seated upon the throne of David as the victorious champion and the Suffering Messiah (entitled "Messiah ben Joseph") is to suffer and die in battle against the evil Armilus on his first coming and then be resurrected by King-Messiah as the High Priest Melchizedec on his second coming to finish the battle he was first killed in. In this way the evil Armilus is destroyed and the Kingdom of God is established.

According to this criteria given in the scriptures and the Jewish literature, Jesus Christ, although descended from David, was never seated upon the throne of David and is therefore disqualified as the Reigning King-Messiah. At the time that Jesus appeared the **EXILARCH**[†] in Babylon was seated upon David's throne.

---

[*] See Rev. Alexander Hislop, *The Two Babylons*, for more.
[†] EXILARCH: the **Exil**ed Mon**arch** of King David: "Title given to the head of the Babylonian Jews, who, from the time of the Babylonian exile, were designated by the term 'golah' (see Jer. xxviii. 6, xxix. 1; Ezek. *passim*) or 'galut' (Jer. xxix. 22). The chief of the golah or **prince of the exiles** held a position of honor which, recognized by

No ruling house in the whole world continued uninterruptedly to hand authority down from father to son as did the House of David. Considering that the Exilarchate lasted beyond the year 1000 AD, this house can be said to have exercised authority for more than 2000 years.[*]

The Exilarchate developed into a powerful instrument of government. Its agents enjoyed the prerequisites of Iranian nobility...**the Exilarch, had a powerful claim too**. He was of David's seed and from him, or one of his relatives **would come the <u>Messiah</u>.**[†]

The Exilarchs (exiled monarchs of King David) had remained in Babylon since the time of Cyrus the Great in an unbroken chain from Jehoiachin and his son Shenazzar. They lived in the Area of Pure Lineage in which their genealogy was preserved for over 2300 years (see Map). They were the legitimate kings in exile seated upon David's throne. All the Jews awaited the King-Messiah to be from the reigning Exilarch or one of his descendants. According to the law and the prophecy only a descendant of David through this line (the throne-line) was qualified to inherit the throne of David and therefore fulfill the prophecy as King-Messiah.[‡]

Jehoiachin [in exile as the first exiled monarch of David: Exilarch] was still regarded as the legitimate king. Texts discovered in Babylon, which show that Jehoiachin was a prisoner of Nebuchadnezzar's court, call him the "King of Judah," while jar handles bearing the inscription, "Eliakim steward of Jehoiachin," show the crown property was still his.[§]

The king Jehoiachin was incarcerated for life, a solitary prisoner, separated from his wife and his family. The Sanhedrin, who were among those deported with the king, feared that the house of David die out. They therefore besought Nebuchadnezzar not to separate Jehoiachin from his wife. They succeeded in enlisting the sympathy of the queen's hairdresser, and through her of the queen herself, Semiramis, the wife of Nebuchadnezzar, who in turn prevailed upon the king to accord mild treatment to the unfortunate prince exiled from Judea. Suffering had completely changed the once sinful king, so that, in spite of his great joy over his reunion with his wife, he still paid regard to the prescriptions of the Jewish law regulating conjugal life. He was prepared to deny himself every indulgence, when the purchase price was an infringement of the Word of God...By way of reward for his continence he was blessed with distinguished posterity...the Messiah himself will be a descendant of his.[**]

---

the state, carried with it certain definite prerogatives, and was **hereditary in a family that traced its descent from the royal Davidic house** ("EXILARCH," *The Jewish Encyclopedia*).

[*] Nissim Rejwan, *The Jews of Iraq*, p. 49.

[†] Jacob Neusner, *A History of the Jews in Babylonia, Vol. II*, p. 95; *Vol. III*, p. 93.

[‡] See the works of Jacob Neusner on Exilarchs; and also Maimonides on the same subject.

[§] John Bright, *A History of Israel*, pp. 327-328. Tablets "found near the Ishtar Gate in Babylon indicate that even in exile Jehoiachin was called the 'king of Judah'" (*Atlas of the Bible*, p. 145) and "also the Messiah himself will be a descendent of his" (Louis Ginzberg, *Legends of the Jews, Vol. IV*, p. 287).

[**] Louis Ginzberg, *Legends of the Jews, Vol. IV*, p. 287

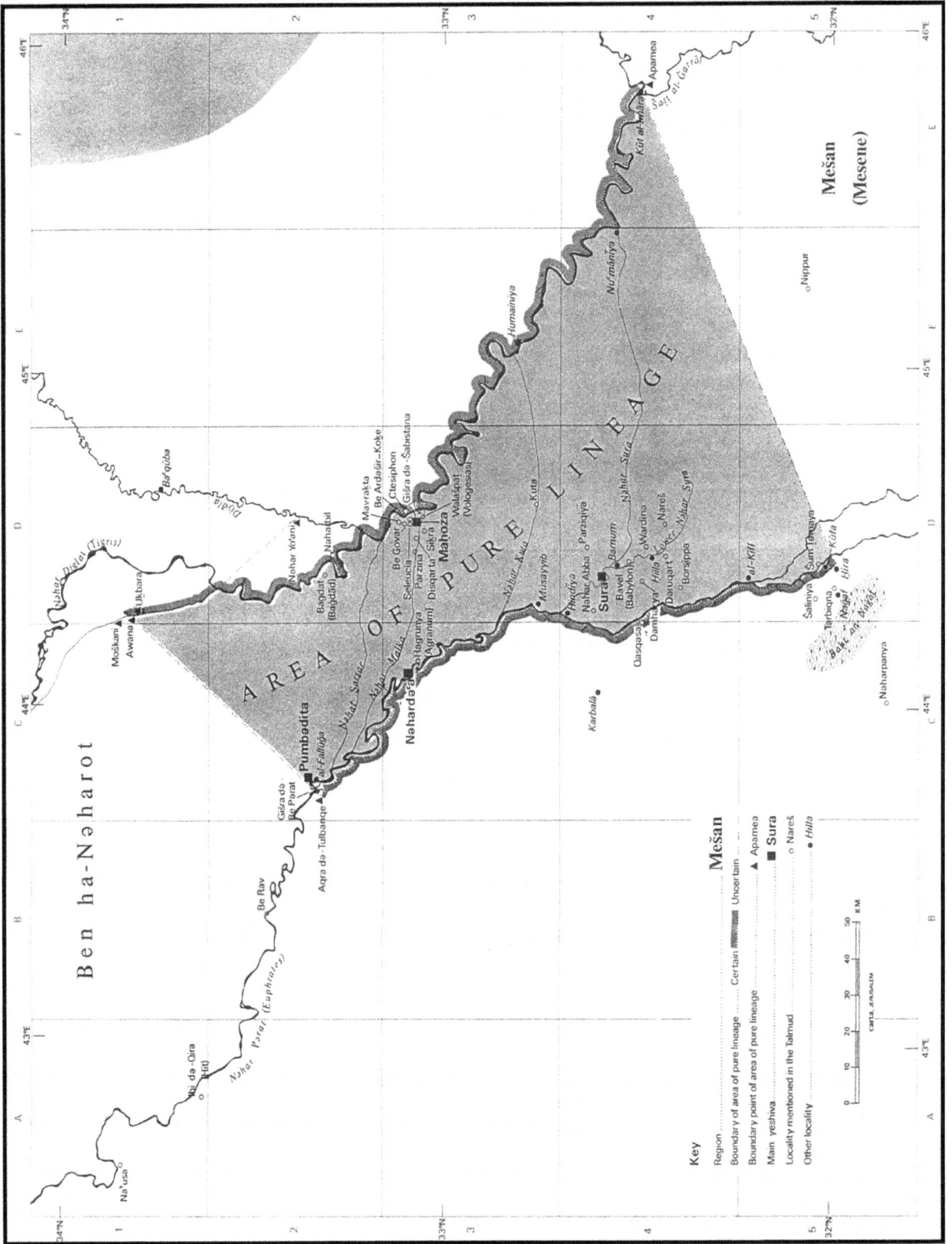

Map

Ben ha-Nəharot

AREA OF PURE LINEAGE

Mešan (Mesene)

Nahar Diqlat (Tigris)
Nahar Parat (Euphrates)
Diglta
Nahar Yoʾaniq
Nahar Sagya
Nahar Malka
Nahat Kuta
Nahar Abba
Nahar Sura
Nahar Sya
Baʿ-e an-Najaf

Naʾusa
Abu da-Qira (Hīd)
Be Rav
Aqra da-Tufbanqe
Gišra da-Be Parat
al-Falluja
Pumbadita
Awana
Moškani
Ukbara
Baʿqūba
Baghdad (Bağdād)
Nahabal
Mavrakta
Be Ardašir-Koke
Ctesiphon
Gišra do -Sabistana
Seleucia
Be Govaʾi
Parzina
Disqarta -Sikra
Agranum
Pultegrunya
Nahardeʾa
Mahoza
Walašut (Vologesias)
Musayyib
Himqiya
Mahat Kuta
Kuta
Parzuqya
Vardino
Barnum
Naresʾ
Bavel (Babylon)
Sura
Damharya
Hilla
Qasgasa
Daruqart
Borsippa
al-Kifl
Humanniya
Nuʿmaniya
Nippur
Kōt al-Mara
Šaṭṭ al-Ṭarraʾ
Apamea
Salinya
Tarbiqna
Sum Tanqya
Kufa
Nəšəš
Hira
Naharpanya
Karbala

Key

Mešan .... Region
Boundary of area of pure lineage ...... Certain ▤▤▤ Uncertain
▲ Apamea .... Boundary point of area of pure lineage
■ **Sura** .... Main yeshiva
○ Nareš .... Locality mentioned in the Talmud
● Hilla .... Other locality

0 10 20 30 40 50 KM
CARTA, JERUSALEM

Moses Maimonides (Rambam), the most important Jewish authority on the Law and religion since Moses himself recognized the Exilarchs as the legitimate genealogy from David through which the Messiah must come. When Maimonides received word from the Exilarch he used to make the entire congregation stand as the letter was read aloud. His writings and the other Jewish literature are filled with the history and prophecy of the Exilarchs and one of their descendants being the King-Messiah.

> I will sing of Thy steadfast love, O LORD, for ever; with my mouth I will proclaim Thy faithfulness to all generations. For Thy steadfast love was established for ever, Thy faithfulness is firm as the heavens. Thou hast said, "I have made a Covenant with My chosen one, I have sworn to David my servant: 'I will establish your descendants for ever, and build your throne for all generations.'"… "I will not violate My Covenant, or alter the word that went forth from My lips. Once for all I have sworn by My holiness; I will not lie to David. His line shall endure for ever, his throne as long as the sun before Me. Like the moon it shall be established for ever; it shall stand firm while the skies endure." (Pslam 89:1-4; 34-37 RSV)

Maimonides also explains that if one were to deny the coming of the Messiah being a real person descended from David through this royal lineage from Solomon and the Exilarchs they would be apostatizing their faith and would therefore no longer be a true Jew:

> The Jew, unless he wishes to forfeit his claim to eternal life by denial of his faith, must, in acceptance of the teachings of Moses and the prophets down to Malachi, believe that **the Messiah** will issue forth from the House of David **in the person** of a descendant of Solomon, the only legitimate king; and he shall far excel all rulers in history by his reign, glorious in justice and peace. Neither impatience nor deceptive calculation of the time of the advent of the Messiah should shatter this belief.[*]

Thus Maimonides is clear that the King-Messiah that the Jews are waiting for must be descended from King David through King Solomon and the royal line of Exilarchs. The rejection of this is the rejection of God and His true Faith.

It is Jesus genealogy from David through Nathan which deprives him of ever being the King-Messiah. Jesus is descended from David's son Nathan,[†] Solomon's brother. David gave the throne to Solomon and not to Nathan. Nathan never sat upon the throne of David and neither did any of his descendants including Jesus. Jesus knew this and that is why he said that "his Kingdom was not of this world" (John 18:36). It was his apostles who were confused on this issue, not Jesus. They had hoped that Jesus would be the King-Messiah but they were wrong. Jesus told them that he was to suffer and die but they disbelieved him until after the fact. Three days and three nights after Jesus body of believers died (the apostles) the body of believers (his apostles) resurrected Sunday night when they realized that he was the Suffering descendant of King David and not the Reigning Messiah.

---

[*] Rabbi Moses ben Maimonides (Rambam) cited from K. Kohler, *Jewish Theology*, pp. 386-387.
[†] See Luke 3:31.

The authority of Maimonides is upheld by the Jewish people worldwide as almost equal with that of Moses himself. Maimonides (whose first name is Moses) is actually thought of as a second Moses. Thus the authoritative saying "From Moses to Moses there is no one like Moses" establishes the binding authority of Maimonides codifications (which are binding because of their accuracy to the true teachings of Moses, the Bible, and the prophets).

Here Maimonides briefly explains the role of Jesus in the plan of God (and Muhammad also):

> It is beyond the human mind to fathom the designs of the Creator; for our ways are not His ways, neither are our thoughts His thoughts. All these matters relating to Jesus of Nazareth and the Ishmaelite (Muhammad) who came after him, only served to clear the way for King-Messiah, to prepare the whole world to worship God with one accord, as it is written **"For then will I turn to the people a pure language, that they may call upon the NAME of the Lord to serve Him with one consent"** (Zeph. 3:9). [*]

Thus Jesus and Muhammad do play a significant role in the coming of the King-Messiah and the establishment of the Kingdom, though Maimonides himself admits that he doesn't know the specifics as these things are only in the thought and mind of God. Surely when King-Messiah appears he will be able to answer these questions.

For now we can see some of the greatness of Jesus and Muhammad, as both promoted the Old Testament. [†] Though the followers of Moses, Jesus, and Muhammad may be in strife, these three are not, in as much as they lead to the same end: the coming of the King-Messiah. Therefore upon His appearance it is incumbent upon Christians and Muslims as well as Jews to recognize and rejoice in His authority. To do otherwise would mean war as He is designated "Prince of Peace" (Isaiah 9:6-7).

The Jewish literature paints a clear picture of the role of the Suffering Messiah called Messiah ben Joseph. He will come before the Messiah ben David, the King-Messiah, appears. He will come from "Upper Galilee." He will rule for "over Israel for no less than nine months and not more than three years." He "will go up from Galilee to Jerusalem," where he will be killed in battle by the evil Armilus and his body will be left unburied in the streets for forty days. After his death the Temple will be destroyed.

---

[*] Hershman, *The Code Of Maimonides, 14: The Book of Judges* (New Haven Yale University Press), p. xxiii.

[†] As a matter of fact Jesus, himself a Jew, turns out to be the greatest promoter of the Old Testament in all of history. The New Testament is very small compared to the Old Testament, yet by it the Laws of Moses the History of Israel and the prophecy of the prophets has been brought around the world and occupies a space in every bookshelf in almost every home, whereas once its greatness was confined to only those of Jewish descent who formed only one nation and are clearly a minority of the population of the world. Muhammad likewise backed up the scripture which is the same today as it was in 600 AD, during his life time. Therefore it is blasphemy against Muhammad for Muslims to deny the Old and New Testaments which Muhammad himself accepted as ancient manuscripts which exist today (like the Dead Sea scrolls) pre-date Muhammad by many hundreds of years. The Bible Muhammad promoted is the one we possess today.

A man will rule over Israel for not less than nine months and not more than three years...and he will be called Messiah of God. And many people will gather around him in Upper Galilee, and he will be their king...But most of Israel will be in their exile, for it will not become clear to them that the end has come. And then [he] Messiah ben Joseph, with the men who rally around him, will go up from Galilee to Jerusalem...and when Messiah ben Joseph and all the people with him will dwell in Jerusalem, Armilus will hear their tiding and will come and make magic and sorcery to lead many astray with them, and he will go up and wage war against Jerusalem, and will defeat Messiah ben Joseph and his people, and will kill many of them, and will capture others and divide their booty...And he will slay Messiah ben Joseph and it will be a great calamity for Israel...Why will permission be granted to Armilus to slay Messiah ben Joseph? In order that the heart of those of Israel who have no faith should break, and so that they say: "This is the man for whom we hoped: now he came and was killed and no redemption is left for us." And they will leave the Covenant of Israel, and attach themselves to the nations, and the latter will kill them...When Messiah ben Joseph is killed, his body will remain cast out [in the streets] for forty days, but no unclean thing will touch him, until Messiah ben David comes and brings him back to life, as commanded by the Lord. And this will be the beginning of the signs which he will perform, and this will be the beginning of the resurrection of the dead which will come to pass.[*]

This is a perfect description of Jesus of Nazareth who though cannot be the King-Messiah as he is not seated upon David's throne does fulfill the role of the Suffering Messiah.

Jesus father's name was Joseph. Back then they didn't have last names so Jesus name would have been Jesus ben Joseph, meaning Jesus the son of Joseph. He did come from Galilee, and from there went to Jerusalem where he was slain. He only taught for about 3 years from his baptism to his crucifixion. His body of teachings were rejected by the Jews at the time as dead for forty years (a day being equal to a year Numbers 14:34, Ezekiel 4:6). Until after the 40 years the Temple was destroyed. Most importantly he was killed by Armilus.

Armilus in the Jewish Literature is also described as Anti-Christ in the Midrash where the word Anti-Christ is actually found. It is the evil Armilus who is born out of a stone statue in Rome that kills the Messiah ben Joseph. Then Armilus proclaims to the Jews that he is their Messiah and their god. Of course the Jews cannot accept this as the Messiah is not to be God; also as Armilus persecutes the Jews and is able to kill millions of them in his battles.

And after all this Satan will go to Rome to the stone statue and have connection with it in the manner of the sexual act, and the stone will become pregnant and give birth to Armilus.[†]

---

[*] Patai, *Messiah Texts*, pp. 168-69: from Hai Gaon Responsum. Note: these traditions of Messiah ben Joseph were preserved by the scholars and fathers from ancient times. One of the first mentions of the Suffering Messiah ben Joseph is as early as a century before the birth of Jesus (see Hal Lindsey, *There's a New World Coming*, p. 29 for more).
[†] Patai, *Messiah Texts*, p. 157.

Satan actually did go to Rome in 133 BCE. After the death of Nimrod, Semiramis set her son (bar-Nin) up as the head of her pagan religion of the triune god-Lie with the statue worship. The throne which he sat on was the throne of Nimrod who is Saturn which is where we get the word Satan from. The throne of Satan was passed down in Babylon from father to son all the way down to Nebuchadnezzar who destroyed Israel and the Temple.

Later Cyrus the Great conquered Babylon and the throne of Satan moved to Pergamum in Asia Minor. In 133 BCE Atallus III, the last king of Pergamum willed the throne of Satan to the Roman Empire when Rome conquered Pergamum. Julius Caesar claimed the right to be seated upon the throne of Satan by being Venus Genetrix--that is a descendant of the goddess Venus, i.e. Semiramis. Thus he became the first Caesar to wear the robes of Satan and to be seated upon that throne.

The robes of Satan included the fish hat of Dagon which looks like the gaping Jaws of a fish. Also the crosier of Janus and Cybele. Gratian the emperor of Rome refused to wear these pagan robes so Damascus the Bishop of Rome took them and became the head of the pagan religion wearing the fish hat of Dagon and seated on the throne of Satan (Nimrod) as the first historical "Pope." Christianity never conquered paganism, but the evil religion of paganism--Armilus sprung from the stone statue--conquered Christianity. In this way Satan visited Rome and gave birth to Armilus the corrupted pagan religion of the trinitarian statue worship which today masquerades as "Christianity."

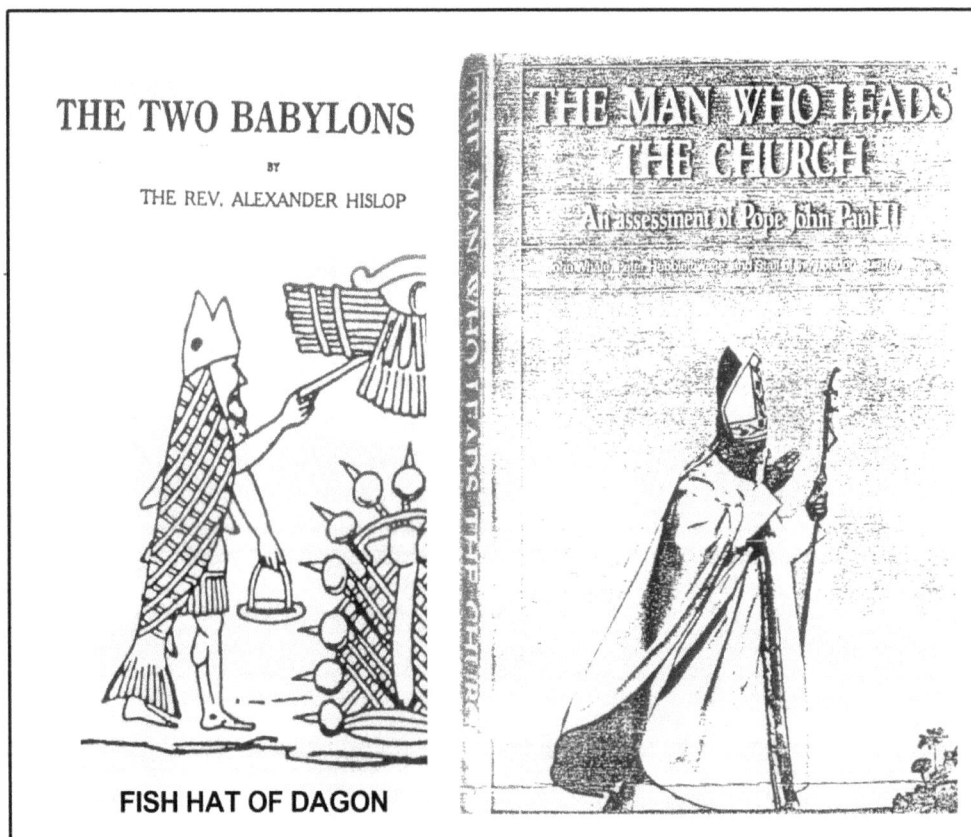

THE TWO BABYLONS
BY
THE REV. ALEXANDER HISLOP

FISH HAT OF DAGON

THE MAN WHO LEADS THE CHURCH
An assessment of Pope John Paul II

Armilus is not a man but is a mythical figure who does not really exist. His religion is a false religion of idolatry and mythology. It was the religion and teachings that Jesus brought which were corrupted by the paganism of Nimrod and Semiramis from Rome and were twisted into this false mythical religion of Armilus. Today the god/man/messiah which is hawked by the trinitarian pagan pseudo-"Christians"--selling Jesus Christ on the cross for the almighty dollar--is actually not Jesus or his teachings but the evil Armilus. The people who follow Armilus (Mythical Jesus) are the many anti-christs named in the scripture. They are the false (or pseudo) Christians. In reality Christ--which is Greek for Messiah--refers to the son of David, but the Christians today are anti-Christ because they push Jesus as the physical son of God instead of what he really was the physical son of David: a "sperm-child" of his father Joseph who was of the house and lineage of King David as expressly stated in the HOLY BIBLE: "Concerning his son Jesus Christ who was made **of the seed of David according to the flesh**" (Romans 1:3-4 KJV). The word "seed" here in Greek is literally "sperm"--meaning the biological male seed--**a sperm child**! They deny this on purpose in order to make Jesus equal with God. The god/man/messiah is not the real Jesus who was in fact slain by this incarnate god-Lie but is in reality the evil Armilus just as Jewish literature depicts.

> They call him Armilus. And he will go to Edom [Rome] and say to them: "I am your Messiah, I am your god!" And he will mislead them and they will instantly believe in him, and make him their king. And all the Children of Esau [i.e. the "Christians": the "dead in Christ"] will gather and come to him. And he will go and announce to all cites saying to the Children of Esau: "Bring me my Torah ['Law'] which I gave you!" And the nations of the world will come and bring the book…and he will say to them: "This is the book which I gave you." And he will further say to them: "I am your god, I am your Messiah and your god."*

The "Jesus" that the Christians preach is in reality the pagan Armilus. Being that this paganism has thoroughly corrupted Christianity it should be obvious how the Armilus/Anti-Christ trinitarian religion has slain the true religion of Jesus Christ who was himself a Jew as were all his apostles including Paul and never proclaimed any such paganism. When Paul went to Greece and Rome it was the people not Paul who corrupted the religion and message that Jesus brought. It has remained corrupted to this day. Christianity never conquered paganism. Paganism conquered Christianity.

Muhammad wrote that the Jews and Romans at that time got the wrong body. In other words it was the body of Jesus' teachings which were slain by the evil Armilus.

Yet in the beginning it was different. For forty years the true uncorrupted body of Jesus teachings laid exposed in the streets of Jerusalem until the Temple was destroyed by Titus in 70 CE. For forty years the apostles and Paul proclaimed Christ crucified as the Suffering Messiah foretold in the Bible and the Jewish literature. It is the mission and first great sign of the King-Messiah, the Messiah ben David, to resurrect Jesus as the High Priest Melchizedec for the final battle of the end in which Armilus and this Anti-Christ religion is to be finally exposed and slain. As the King-Messiah is the Prince of Peace it is not his job to wage war. It is the job of the

---

* Patai, *Messiah Texts*, p. 158.

resurrected Suffering Messiah (also called "the anointed of war") to slay the Armilus religion which today masquerades as Christianity the same as the ancient Melchizedec had Nimrod brought to justice (after which he was then put death by order of the court of judges) who with his wife Semiramis corrupted all the religions of the world. Furthermore it is an established fact the Jesus' station as the Suffering Messiah was also combined with that of the High Priest after the order of Melchizedec (see the Epistle to Hebrews chapters 5, 6 and 7). Thus according to the Bible and the Jewish literature there is only one scenario of the end days and the establishment of the Kingdom!

Jewish literature also states that when King-Messiah does come at the appointed time, His life will be the duplicate of Moses. As Moses ministered for 40 years so did Baha'u'llah.

Baha'u'llah is a direct male-line descendant of King David through the Exilarchs and Solomon and inherited the throne of David by both blood and by legal right (see Baha'u'llah's genealogy on the **Tree of Life** chart).

Baha'u'llah's mission began in 1852 when imprisoned in the Black Pit (*Siyah Chal*) the dungeon in Teheran, Iran He received a vision in which He saw a maiden who told Him that He was the long awaited for King-Messiah. It is well known in all histories of Baha'u'llah how for four months he suffered in the dungeon with the great chain galling his neck. According to the Jewish literature this fulfills prophecy!

> They said: In the septenary in which the son of David comes **they will bring Iron beams and put them upon his neck** until his body bends and he cries and weeps, and his voice rises up into the Heights, and he says before Him: "Master of the World! How much can my strength suffer? How much my spirit? How much my soul? And how much my limbs? Am I not but flesh and blood?[*]

This is exactly the circumstance of Baha'u'llah, who since His coming the nation of Israel has been restored to the Jews and the Golden Dome of the shrine of the Bab glistens atop the mighty Mount Carmel in Israel herself!

Yet the world at large has not yet heard this message of Baha'u'llah the great descendant of David, the King of Kings seated upon David's throne descended from Solomon and the Exilarchs.

Why?

For like Moses who died before entering the Promised Land and was succeeded by Joshua his establisher Baha'u'llah likewise must be succeeded by the modern Joshua to establish the Kingdom on earth. "Jesus" is the Greek word for "Joshua." According to the Jewish Literature the first act and sign of the Messiah Ben David--Baha'u'llah--is to resurrect Jesus (the Suffering Messiah) as the High Priest Melchizedec to be his Joshua, the establisher of the Kingdom--as Joshua and Jesus are the same identical name and the same identical personage. This is the prophecy of Joshua (Jesus) the High Priest.

---

[*] Patai, *Messiah Texts*, pp. 112-113.

THE TREE ✡ OF LIFE

ADAM
ENOCH
NOAH
SHEM, MELCHIZEDEK
ABRAHAM (the father of a Multitude)

SARAH (first wife)   KETURAH (third wife)   HAGAR (handmaiden)
(second wife)

ISAAC
ISRAEL   ISHMAEL
     Kedar
Levi   Judah   Tabit
    Yarab
Aaron   MOSES   Yathjib
Jesse   Tarah
KING DAVID   Almaqoom
Nathan   King Solomon   Ohd
Rehoboam   ADNAN
    Mad
King Josiah   Nazar
Shealtiel   Modarr
Zerubbabel   Ilyas
EXILARCHS   Mudrika
Zechariah Elizabeth Mary Joseph   Exilarch Jehoiachin   Khazema
John   Shenazzar   Kinana
the Baptist   JESUS   Babulan   Nadar
Liuban   Majik
Shemiah   QU'RAYSH
Shekeniah   Fahar
Hezekiah   Ghalib
Jacob   Lowayy
Nahum   Yohanan   Kaab
Shefet   Morrah
Huna I   Kaljab
Mar Ukban I   Qusay
Huna II   Monaf
Mar Ukban II   Nehemiah   Hashim (Hashmites)
Huna III   Mar Ukban III   Abdu'l Muttalib
Abba
Kahana   Nathan
Huna IV   Mar Zutra I   Abu Talib   Abdu'llah
Huna V   Kahana II   MUHAMMAD
Huna IV
Mar Zutra II Mar Abunai   IMAMS
Karnai   IMAM ALI (i)   Fatima
Haninai
(Mar Pahda   EXILARCHS   9 IMAMS
usurper)→
BOSTANAI DARA (Izdundad)   SHAHR-BANU   IMAM HUSAYN (iii)   Imam Hasan (ii)

Shahriyar Gurgashah Mardugshah   Imam Zaynu'l Abidin (iv) Fatima

Ruzbihan
Judah   Mar Rav Abunai
Zakkai ben Abunai   Moses ben Abunai
Isaac Iskoi ben Moses
(817 A.D.) (converted to Shi'i Islam by Imam Ali ar-Rida)

MAZINDARAN
Shahriyar-Hasan
Aqa Fakhr
Aqa Muhammad-Ali
Haji Muhammad-Rida Big
Mirza Abbas
Mirza Rida-Quli Big
Mirza Buzurg

KETURAH line (center)
ZOROASTER
(the seed of the woman)

Cyrus the Great
(Bahman ibn Isfandiyar)
Sassan
THE
SASSANIAN DYNASTY
Sassan
Babek
Ardeshir I
Shapur I
Hormazd I
Bahram I
Bahram II
Nersehi
Hormazd II
Shapur II
Bahram IV
Shushandukht Yazdegird I
Bahram V Gor
Yazdegird II
Firuz
Kubad
Chosroes I, Anushurvan the Just
Hormiuzd IV   (Bahram VI usurper)
Chosroes II Parviz
Shahriyar
Yazdegird III

Right side imams
Imam al-Baqir (v)
Imam as-Sadiq (vi)
Imam al-Kazim (vii)
IMAM ALI ar-RIDA (viii)
Imam Muhammad Taqi (ix)
Imam Ali-Naqi (x)
Imam Hasan-i-Askari (xi)
THE HIDDEN IMAM MIHDI (xii)

Mirza Abid of Shiraz   Mirza Nasru'llah
of Shiraz
Mirza Ibrahim
Mirza Ali   Mirza Muhammad-Husayn   Mirza Abu'l-Fath
Fatima-Bagum Muhammad-Rida   Mirza
Muhammad-Rida
Mirza Musa, Aqay-i-Kalim   Mirza Muhammad-Quli   Haji Mirza Abu'l-Qasim   Khadyih-Bagum   THE BAB
BAHÀ'U'LLÀH   Siyyid Muhammad-Husayn   IMAM MIHDI
Mirza Mihdi   'ABDU'L-BAHA
CENTER OF THE COVENANT   Daya'iyyih Mirza Hadi Afnan   Ahmad (died at birth)

1st Aghsan Guardian of the Bahà'i Faith   SHOGHI EFFENDI
CHARLES MASON REMEY   CENTER OF THE CAUSE
and
Afnan Guardian
of the
Bahà'i Faith
2nd Aghsan Guardian of the Bahà'i Faith
JOSEPH PEPE REMEY

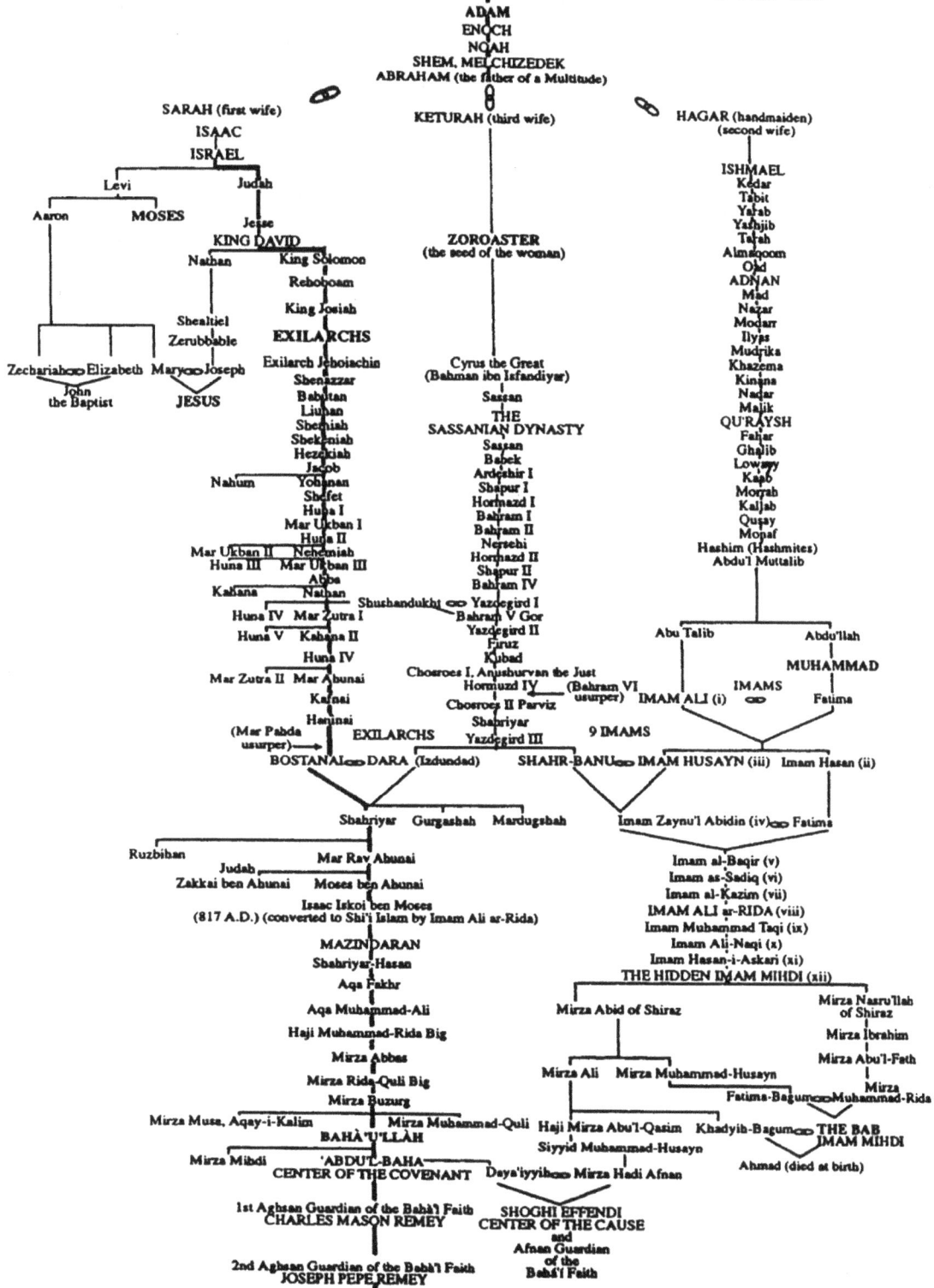

"David shall never lack a man to sit on the throne." -Jeremiah 33:15-22

liii

Moreover, this Jesus is none other than Jesus the High Priest after the order of Melchizedec identical to "Joshua the High Priest" prophesied to come in Zechariah chapter three who is to have the "Stone with Seven Eyes" before him (Zechariah 3:9 KJV). According to Jewish commentary this "Stone with Seven Eyes" refers to the prophesied Temple* which is Ezekiel's Temple in Montana, the only Temple to have seven towers. As these towers are watchtowers they are like eyes with the wall being made of solid stone.

Thus we have the fulfillment of the promise as Jesus the High Priest after the order of Melchizedec returns to establish his Father's (Baha'u'llah's) Kingdom in Ezekiel's Temple in Montana. According to Isaiah "the Everlasting Father" is "seated upon the throne of David" (Isaiah 9:6-7) and therefore can be none other than Baha'u'llah the King-Messiah, the Prince of Peace.

In other words the world will only hear of Baha'u'llah, the Exilarch, the great King of Kings descended from David, the King-Messiah, first through the powerful teachings of Melchizedec the High Priest returned in Ezekiel's Temple in Montana. And the Temple must appear as Ezekiel prophesied it with seven towers.

Now we live in the greatest time of all! The Great and Terrible day of the Lord. The greatest event in all history the blowing of the trumpet and the announcement of the Messiah descended from David from Solomon, from the Exilarchs (exiled monarchs of King David) seated upon his throne and with the name in which Ezekiel saw him: "the Glory of the Lord": Baha'u'llah!

Ezekiel didn't speak English, he spoke Aramaic. In Aramaic "Baha" is glory; and Lord or God is "Allah." Thus Ezekiel gives His name as Baha'u'llah.

According to Isaiah, Baha'u'llah will be upon Mount Carmel in Israel (Isaiah 35). It was here on this mountain that the Covenant-breakers masquerading as "Baha'is" did away with the Davidic Kingship. Unlike Jesus, Baha'u'llah had sons. 'Abdu'l-Baha succeeded his father to the throne of David and then set up the institution of the guardianship to be continued as the kingship of David in this New Era. The Covenant-breakers on Mt. Carmel in Israel claim that God has violated His own Covenant and that the Davidic kingship has ended.

In 1957 the adopted son of 'Abdu'l-Baha, Charles Mason Remey Aghsan, was rejected by the violators who refused to recognize his authority as the head and president of the embryonic Universal House of Justice (called the first International Baha'i Council) which according to the Will and Testament of 'Abdu'l-Baha can only be the guardian and Davidic king seated upon David's throne which is to last forever.

Thus through violation it becomes obvious why the High Priest Melchizedec must return in the seven towered Temple of Ezekiel to establish the genealogy of David (the guardianship) back on the throne as president and member of the genuine Universal House of Justice of Baha'u'llah. The establisher of the Baha'i Faith is Dr. Leland Jensen, Knight of Baha'u'llah.

---

* *The Twelve Prophets: Soncino Books of the Bible*, p. 282: "**Zech 3:9**. *behold the stone that I have laid before Joshua*. The foundation-stone of the Temple is seen by the prophet in the vision lying before Joshua, symbolizing the immediate completion of the Temple (Rashi)."

At the death of Baha'u'llah in November of 1892 construction on the solid stone Temple wall with seven towers was begun in Montana in 1893. When 'Abdu'l-Baha visited the United States in 1912 he announced to the Baha'is of Wilmette, Illinois, that, "The Temple is already built!" Ezekiel's Temple in Montana was completed in 1912.

According to all ancient tradition, literature and understanding including that of the Jews, the heavens are said to be upheld by two world mountains from between which the sun rises, that is the Revelation of God is made known. These two mountains are represented in the Temple of Ezekiel by the twin pillars of Jachin and Boaz. From between these two pillars, like the two mountains, comes forth the Shekinah the glory, splendor, and light of God of which is like a spiritual Sun, the Manifestation of God.

These two pillars represent the two Messiahs. "J" in Jachin is for Jesus or Joshua; and "B" in Boaz is for Baha'u'llah. Jachin means "he shall establish" and Boaz refers to the royal genealogy: Boaz being the great-grandfather of King David. Thus it is Jesus (Joshua) who establishes the genealogy of Baha'u'llah, King-Messiah, as the presidents of Baha'u'llah's true Universal House of Justice (UHJ). The descendant of King David must be the president of the Universal House of Justice so that we can recognize the true UHJ of Baha'u'llah from fakes, frauds and imitations. The two mountains which these two pillars represent is Mt. Carmel in Israel the mountain of Baha'u'llah: Boaz; and the Rocky Mountains in North America where Ezekiel's Temple is for Jesus the High Priest: Jachin. The mountain of the East and of the mountain of the West. Here from the mountain of Jachin the Kingdom of God is to be established. Thus these are the two world mountains of Jachin and Boaz which uphold the Heaven of the Law, the Covenant, and the Revelation from which the Kingdom of God is established.

The last nine chapters of the Book of Ezekiel contain the vision of the future Temple with seven towers and the City of New Jerusalem.

The Jews never built a Temple with seven towers. Even after Ezekiel had received his vision, when the Jews built the second Temple they didn't do it according to the plan that was laid out in the book of Ezekiel. The second Temple--which was later refurbished by Herod and destroyed by Titus--never had seven towers. Even the Temple that the militant Jewish sects are planning to build today does not go according to the plan in Ezekiel but is the rebuilding of Solomon's Temple. Their Temple does not have seven towers either and they are building it in the wrong place. For according to Ezekiel's vision the future Temple with seven towers is to be built on a very high mountain which is in the far north.

> Great is the Lord and greatly to be praised in the city of our God! His holy mountain, beautiful in elevation, is the joy of all the whole earth, **Mount Zion, in the Far North**, the City of the great King.[*] Go round about her number her **towers** [seven: 7].

The old Temple was in the south in the land of Judea, not in the far north. The new Temple is to be in the far north atop a high mountain. Thus because the Temple with seven towers that

---

[*] Psalm 48:1-2.

Ezekiel sees is in a different place than the old city of Jerusalem (which is also not on a mountain) Ezekiel explains that City of the New Jerusalem that he sees is renamed, "THE LORD IS THERE."[*]

Furthermore the law of Temple is that the entire square area around it upon the mountain is to be holy.

> This is the law of the Temple: the whole territory round about **upon the top of the mountain** shall be most holy. Behold this is the law of the Temple.[†]

In the Book of Revelation, the New Jerusalem which Ezekiel also sees in his vision appears as a perfect square. The City of Deer Lodge, Montana was originally plotted out as a perfect 640 acre Square Mile--1 mile wide by 1 mile long--in 1863 the same time as Baha'u'llah's proclamation in the garden of Ridvan outside Baghdad, Iraq. Deer Lodge is also 12 blocks long by 12 block wide which fulfills the vision of the city exactly.

> The angel who spoke with me carried a gold measuring rod, to measure the city, its walls and its gates. The city was built as a square, and was as wide as it was long.[‡]

Deer Lodge Montana is this perfect square city!

> And he measured the city with his rod, twelve thousand stadia; its length and breadth and height are equal.[§]

"Stadia" comes from the word *stadium* and refers to the track in the stadium. A stadium can be any size, and refers to a fixed unit of measure. The stadia is the same as a block. The way you run around the stadium you run around the block. Deer Lodge is exactly 12 blocks long by 12 blocks wide. The city in the Bible appears to be 1000 times bigger. 1000 symbolic for the 1000 years of peace in which this City of the Great King is to last for a full 1000 years.

Furthermore its height is equal to its length and its breadth. Deer Lodge, Montana is a perfect square mile. In order to get there you have to drive a mile high into the mountains. Thus its height is equal to its length and its breadth. After the shifting of the earth's crust it will be exactly one mile high in altitude. The city of Butte at the south end of the Deer Lodge Valley is known as "the city a mile high and a mile deep" because of the old copper mines. Deer Lodge City is the city a mile high, a mile wide, and a mile long.

Also the New Jerusalem is to be built out of Gold. The City of Deer Lodge is literally built out of the gold from the placer gold mines, the richest gold mines in the US at the time they were discovered.

---

[*] Ezekiel 48: 35.
[†] Ezekiel 43:12.
[‡] Revelation 21:15-16, *New English Bible*.
[§] Revelation 21:17 RSV.

Even more important is the fact that Ezekiel's Temple is standing in the city with the prophesied river flowing from it. In this seven towered temple has returned the High Priest (great educator) after the order of Melchizedec to educate the world on Baha'u'llah's genealogy from David, Solomon, and the Exilarchs and also to put down the corruption of the paganism that has corrupted Christianity and the Covenant-breaking Baha'is.

The Mount of Olives is the mount that is to be before the Temple. In Zechariah 14 it explains that the Mount of Olives will be split in two: half withdrawing to the north and half to the south. In Zechariah chapter 6 the same prophet Zechariah sees these two mountains as "two mountains of copper" from out which will come the four spirits of God to go throughout all the world after standing before the Lord of the earth.

On either side of the Deer Lodge Valley are the world's two largest mountains of copper, Lincoln on the north and Butte on the south. Butte is known as the richest hill on earth.

> I looked up again and saw four chariots coming out from between two mountains, and the mountains were made of copper.[*]

What made the old Jerusalem great was that the Lord was once there in His Temple. But since the curse and the destruction of the Temple the city has remained desolate and been trampled underfoot for 2300 years. When we add the 2300 years to 457 BCE at the time of Ezra we get 1844 CE which is the beginning of the Baha'i calendar and the Bab and the martyrdom of his 10,000 followers' blood cleanses the sanctuary. From 1852 to 1892 is the 40 years mission of Baha'u'llah whose Revelation is the Holy of Holies. At Baha'u'llah's ascension in 1892 He is succeed by Ezekiel's Temple in Montana to which Jesus the Suffering Messiah resurrected as Melchizedec has appeared between these two mountains of copper to all the people of the world in the fulfillment of prophecy!

The prophecies are fulfilled! The Great Announcement has come!

Ezekiel's Temple has appeared with its seven towers and Jesus the High Priest after the order of Melchizedec is here to establish the Davidic throne!

The greatness of this day cannot be understated nor emphasized enough! The Cycle of Baha'u'llah is for 500,000 years of peace through justice of the Kingdom of God on earth. The throne of David will last for the rest of the life of this planet (which could be for billions of years yet) on it with a descendant of Baha'u'llah and 'Abdu'l-Baha seated upon the throne of David as the guardianship of the Baha'i Faith forever!

The greatness of the people whose intellectual/spiritual eye is open to see the fulfillment of the prophecy is tremendous! What could be greater than this! Today Jews are happy because Baha'u'llah is Jewish.

---

[*] Zechariah 6:1 *New English Bible*. Note: brass/bronze and copper are all the same word in Hebrew.

The Jews have a saying that man is the microcosm of the Universe. All the world is compared to the apple of his eye. The white is like the mighty oceans, the iris is the land, the pupil is the city of Jerusalem and the image in his eye is the Temple of God.

Read this book and see with your own eye, of the intellect, how over 127 years ago the prophet George Williams saw the appearance of Ezekiel's Temple in Deer Lodge, Montana and the Morrisite pioneers who followed Williams's vision homesteaded the Deer Lodge Valley specifically to prepare for the coming of Joshua (Jesus) the high priest Melchizedec to his Temple.

To this day approximately two thirds of the population of the Deer Lodge Valley in Montana which is 60 miles long and 5 to 10 miles wide is descended from these Morrisite pioneers! The four spirits of God are prophesied to go out from Ezekiel's Temple in Deer Lodge, Montana from between the two mountains of copper to all the world!

This day in which we live--anticipate the Jews--marks the great announcement of the coming of the Messiah (descended from David) and the appearance of the true Temple.

Today--with over 20 nations in the Middle East ready to war over the oil and religion--we are already approaching Armageddon fast. Today is like the days of Noah. God loves the people and wants to see no one perish. That is why he sent them Noah. Today we have PROPHECY FULFILLED in the person of this great educator who has appeared in Ezekiel's Temple with seven towers in Montana. Don't miss the boat!

Investigate. Investigate. Investigate.

EZEKIEL'S TEMPLE IN MONTANA

THE PROPHECY!

"In that region where you dwell [Deer Lodge, Montana], extending East, West, South and North --in this region will come down the City of the Great King [New Jerusalem, the City of Ezekiel's Temple]. Before that, many wise men shall find their way there, endowed with intelligence from the Lord to map out and make ready [build the prison] for the Lord's coming, with thousands who have tolled and suffered with him here. You are the pioneers. The climate shall be moderated by the earth's 3rd motion southward [earth's shifting crust], without interference with her diurnal and annual motion by which she will be fitted to bring forth all the choice vegetation and floral grandeur she is entitled to yield. No beast of prey may find a place there. All rank and unprofitable growth shall be banished at that day. Neighbor shall meet neighbor in perfect accord, and say--my children are numerous, and everyone sound in body and judgement--and so are mine [yours]...In those days the old men shall not weep, neither shall they depart in sorrow or pain; but angels shall bear them to their resting place. And lights shall be on every hill, and on every dwelling place as the Sun for brightness. And like birds of the air shall men move from place to place, and hold converse with one another. A pure language shall be given from their childhood by which all shall do the will of God on the sides of the North as the angels do In His presence...For the choice place of the earth is handed over to you. Its beauties and riches in part, are yet hidden [the prison is only revealed as the Temple today]. But your Children will develop more and more. For there [in Deer Lodge] will be the City of the Great King."[*]

TWO MOUNTAINS OF COPPER!

According to the Mormon prophecy of George Williams the sacred spot for the return of Jesus (Jesus II) is in the Deer Lodge Valley where the Temple of God, the City of the Great King, the New Jerusalem is to be built. In Hebrew the word for copper and brass or bronze (that are copper alloys) is the same. On either end of the Deer Lodge Valley (where the prison is located in the city of Deer Lodge) are the world's two largest mountains of copper: Lincoln and Butte, Montana.

> I looked up again and saw four chariots coming out between two mountains, and **the mountains were made of <u>copper</u>**. (Zechariah 6:1 NEB)

Butte is called the "Richest Hill on earth." In 1900 Butte produced about 1/4th of the United States copper output and 1/7th of the world's![†] Butte is also called the city a mile high and a mile deep. It is a mile high in the Rocky Mountains and a mile deep with copper mines. Likewise, it is known that Lincoln has even more copper than Butte though it hasn't even been tapped yet.[‡]

---

[*] George Williams cf: C. Leroy Anderson, (1981). *For Christ Will Come Tomorrow: The Saga of the Morrisites.* Logan, UT: Utah State University Press, pp. 222-223.

[†] Tom Stout, (1921). *Montana: History and Biography.* Chicago, IL: The American Historical Society, p. 836.

[‡] The copper deposits surrounding Lincoln, Montana extend approximately 45 miles along a geological deposit with the southeast tip of this area of deposits 10 miles north of Lincoln. See Gregory B. Byer, (1987). *The Geology and Geochemistry of the Cotter Basin Stratabound and Vein Copper-Silver Deposit, Helena Formation, LINCOLN, Lewis and Clark County, Montana.* Missoula, MT: University of Montana.

1

PROPHECY IN THE DEER LODGE VALLEY

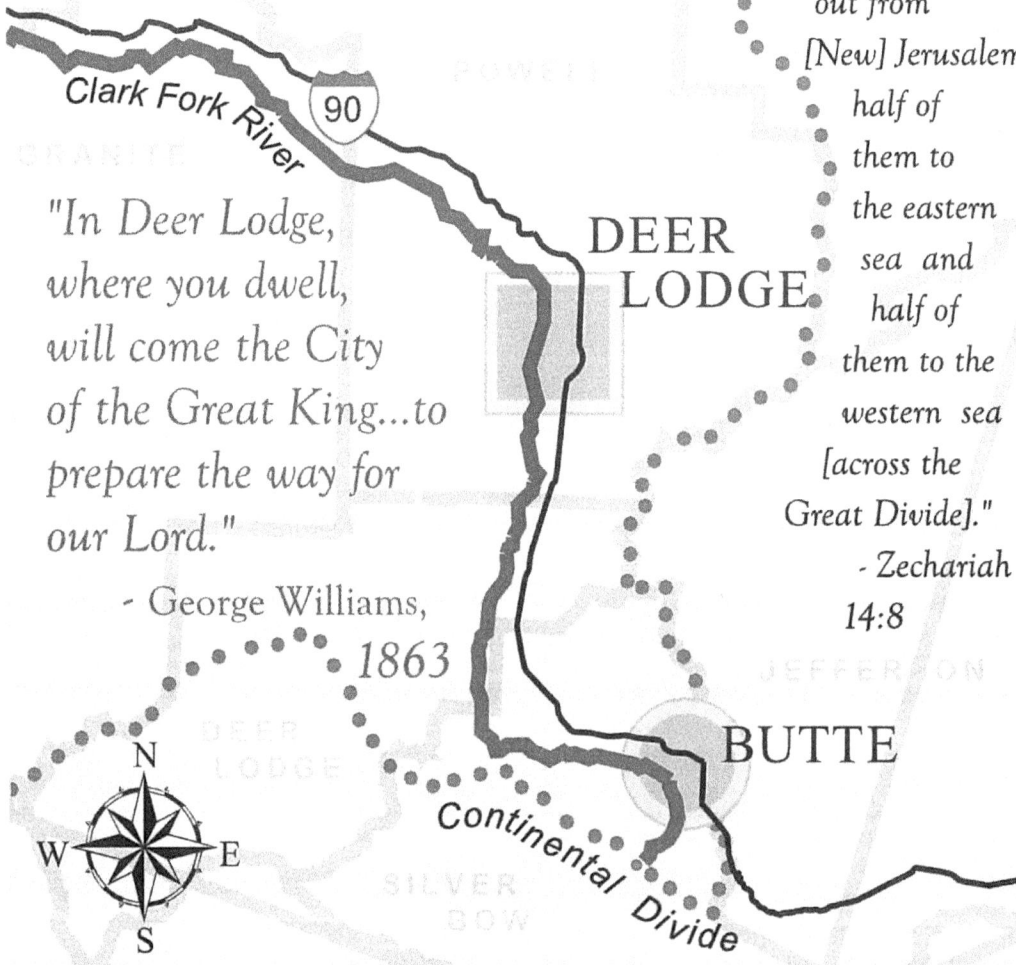

"Between two mountains; and the mountains [Lincoln and Butte] were mountains of copper...so that one half of the Mount [Lincoln] shall withdraw northward and the other half [Butte] southward."
- Zechariah 6:1, 14:4, NEB

LINCOLN

"On that day living waters shall flow out from [New] Jerusalem half of them to the eastern sea and half of them to the western sea [across the Great Divide]."
- Zechariah 14:8

Clark Fork River

90

"In Deer Lodge, where you dwell, will come the City of the Great King...to prepare the way for our Lord."
- George Williams, 1863

DEER LODGE

BUTTE

Continental Divide

Zechariah Chapters 6 & 14

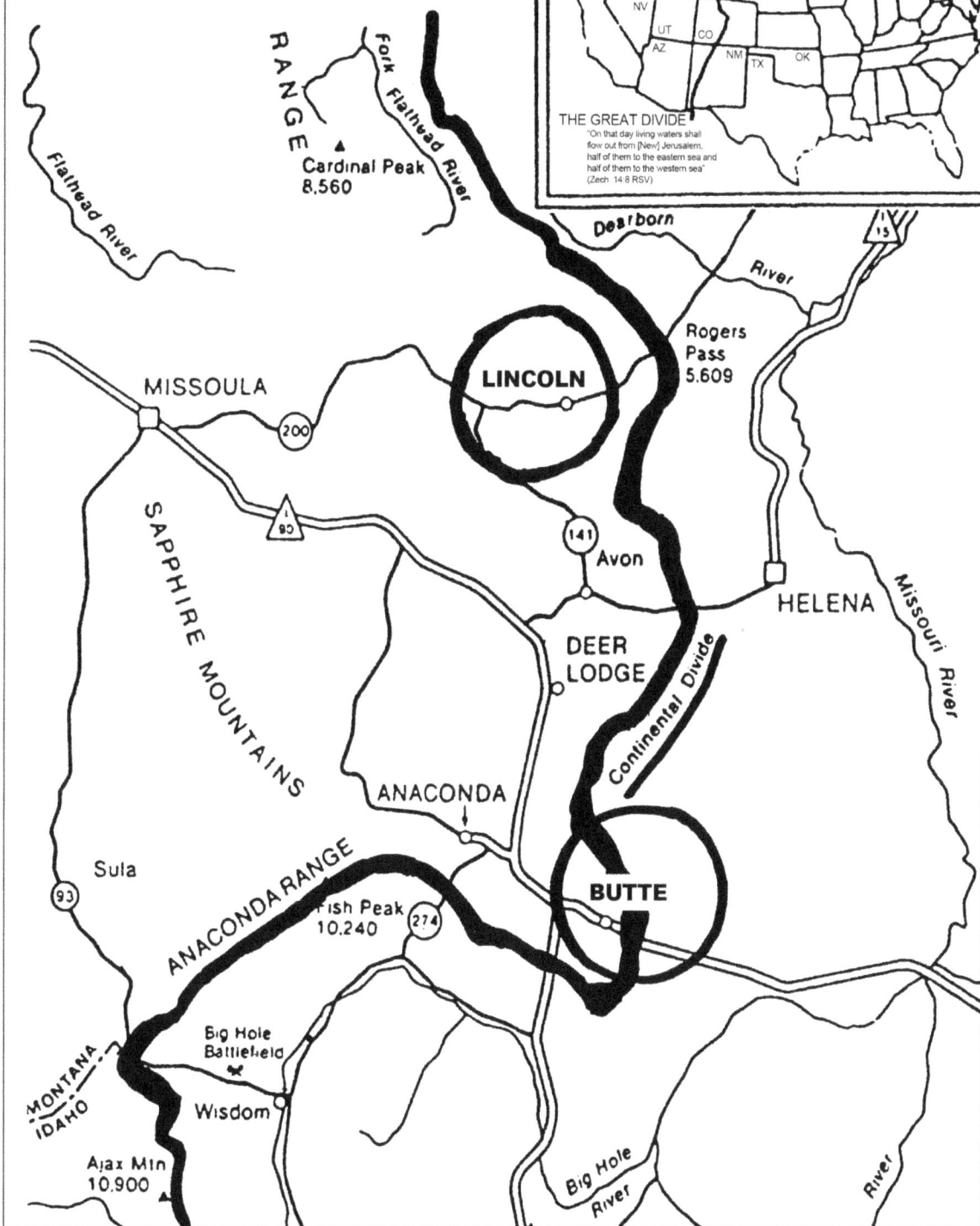

RANGE

Fork Flathead River

Flathead River

Cardinal Peak
8,560

MT

ID   WY

NV

UT   CO

AZ   NM   TX   OK

THE GREAT DIVIDE
"On that day living waters shall
flow out from [New] Jerusalem,
half of them to the eastern sea and
half of them to the western sea"
(Zech 14:8 RSV)

Dearborn

River

15

Rogers
Pass
5,609

MISSOULA

200

LINCOLN

141

Avon

HELENA

Missouri River

I 90

SAPPHIRE   MOUNTAINS

DEER
LODGE

Continental Divide

ANACONDA

Sula

ANACONDA RANGE

93

Fish Peak
10,240

274

BUTTE

MONTANA
IDAHO

Big Hole
Battlefield

Wisdom

Ajax Mtn
10,900

Big Hole

River

River

**TWO MOUNTAINS OF BRASS: Lincoln & Butte, Montana
THE GREAT DIVIDE**

It is from between these two mountains of copper that the Old Montana State Prison in Deer Lodge fulfills the prophecy for the seven towered temple of Ezekiel, the Temple that Jesus II enters through the eastern gate of tower #7, between the two pillars of Jachin and Boaz.

From this prison in Deer Lodge between these two mountains of copper (Lincoln and Butte), the chariots of God and His heavenly army, led by the return of Jesus (Jesus II), will gather to be sent out into all the world proclaiming the good news of the Kingdom of God.

> In the first chariot were red horses; and in the second chariot black horses; and in the third chariot white horses; and in the fourth chariot grisled and bay horses. Then I answered and said unto the angel that talked with me, "What are these, my Lord?" And the angel answered and said unto me, "These are the four spirits of the heavens that go forth from standing before the Lord of all the earth." (Zechariah 6:1-5)

ARMAGEDDON: THE MOUNT OF OLIVES SPLIT IN TWO

> For I will gather all the nations against Jerusalem to battle, and the city shall be taken and the houses plundered and the women ravished; half of the city shall go into exile, but the rest of the people shall not be cut off from the city.
>
> Then the Lord will go forth and fight against those nations as when he fights on a day of battle. On that day his feet shall stand on the Mount of Olives which lies before Jerusalem on the east; and **the Mount of Olives shall be split in two from east to west by a very wide valley [Deer Lodge Valley]; so that half the Mount shall withdraw northward [Lincoln] and the other half southward [Butte].**
>
> On that day living waters shall flow out from Jerusalem [from the Temple (Ezekiel 47)], **half of them to the eastern sea and half of them to the western sea**; it shall continue in summer as in winter. (Zechariah 14:2-4, 8)

The waters flow to the eastern sea and to the western sea only at the point of the Continental Divide! It is here, at the Great Divide, that Jesus II (the second coming) will appear between the TWO MOUNTAINS OF COPPER that are separated by the Deer Lodge Valley which is 60 miles wide from north to south, and five to 10 miles across. Zechariah, the prophet who sees this vision in chapter 14, also saw these two mounts as the mountains of copper in chapter 6 of his book. They are the mountains of copper by the Great Divide.

On his first coming Jesus stood on the Mount of Olives. On his return appearance the whole world will only see Jesus between these two mountains of copper by the Great Divide in the United States when they also see the battle of Armageddon begin to rage. According to all authoritative sources in the Bible and in Bible commentary, the battle of Armageddon is to be fought over the Middle Eastern oil with Russia becoming involved with the Arabs against Israel and the US. Russia has even now just joined OPEC which unites Russia with the Oil Producing

Export Countries of the Arabic Mid-East. And all this as the US has mobilized into Saudi Arabia, against Iraq.

It is at this time when the Lord goes to battle and all the armies of God stream forth from between these two mountains of copper, Lincoln and Butte, from out of the Deer lodge Valley.

EZEKIEL'S TEMPLE IN DEER LODGE MONTANA: WHERE IT ALL BEGAN!

The town motto for Deer Lodge is: "Where it all began." For generations to come all the people of the world will remember Deer Lodge as the place where Jesus returned and the Kingdom of God began.

Deer Lodge has always been a Holy place. Long before the white-man came there, the Native American Indians considered Deer Lodge spiritual ground. Although the different tribes continued their warfare between each other for many years, they would never fight in the Deer Lodge Valley because it was considered sacred ground. As the Indians would pass through Deer Lodge, warring tribes would be at peace with one another. But as soon as they left the Valley, their wars would rage on. Thus the Hell Gate Canyon outside the Deer Lodge Valley, and other places, became infamous for tribal warfare, ambushes and massacres.

THE GREAT ANNOUNCEMENT OF GEORGE WILLIAMS

In April of 1863, the Mormon prophet George Williams proclaimed his true vision of the return of Jesus appearing in Deer Lodge, Montana--Big Sky Country--to the scattered Morrisite peoples! George Williams himself was never a Morrisite and always remained a Mormon. However, it was the Morrisites who listened to his prophecies and followed his instructions to move to Deer Lodge.

THE MOVE TO DEER LODGE

Williams directed the Morrisites to move to the Deer Lodge Valley for the purpose of settling that area in preparation for Jesus' return. Upon receiving this great announcement of the return of Jesus in Deer Lodge, Montana, a large contingent of Morrisites moved directly to Deer Lodge in 1863.[*] The rest of the group joined them later in the early 1870s. The Morrisites who embraced the divine calling of Williams were the first settlers and pioneers of the Deer Lodge Valley.[†] It was they who first cultivated the land and developed the Valley. They were the original farmers. They were the land owners. They were the pioneers.

Upon entering the Deer Lodge Valley, as the Morrisite wagons passed over the hump on the southern side near Butte, they came to the top and could see the Deer Lodge Valley spreading

---

[*] Anderson, p. 177.
[†] Anderson, p. 206. "From that group came numerous persons who played a significant role in the settlement of the Deer Lodge Valley in Montana."

out five to 10 miles wide and 60 miles long before them. Their first words were, "We've entered paradise!"

Today two thirds of the population of the Deer Lodge Valley are descendants of the Morrisite peoples. They are either direct descendants of the Morrisites or have married into those families who are direct descendants of the original Morrisite pioneers. The original Morrisite settlers of the Deer Lodge Valley had big families with lots of children, some up to 10 in number! What could possibly make all the Morrisite people happier than knowing that the prophecies that their folks lived by and prayed for are now coming true, just as Williams revealed:

> It's [Deer Lodge and the prison's] beauties and riches in part, are yet hidden. But your children will develop more and more. For there [in Deer Lodge] will be the City of the Great King [centered on the Temple of the Old Montana State Prison].[*]

THE LORD'S HOUSE

When the Morrisites first pioneered the Deer Lodge Valley in 1863 in anticipation of Jesus II they built a little white church called the Lord's House for Jesus to live in when he arrived. This was a mistake because Jesus is not prophesied to return to a church. He is prophesied to return suddenly to his Temple (Malachi 3:1). The Morrisites never built a Temple, so the Federal government built it for them! This is in exact fulfillment of the prophecy of George Williams that the "tribes from the North," in Helena, north of Deer Lodge would come down to build the Holy Temple. He states that the Morrisites:

> Being in a state of preparation to become the Heralds of the Fullness of the Gospel of the Lord Jesus to the whole House of scattered Israel. It was their [the Morrisites] privilege to invite and welcome the tribes from the North [Federal Government and contractors from Helena], to build the Holy Temple, to take the covering veil from off mortality and usher back the mighty spirits [4 chariots who are the 4 spirits from between the two mountains of copper] who are reserved to carry this work to its final issue, and clean away the element of evil that the 144,000 saviors may, robed in light and glory, descend clothed with powers belonging to the celestial worlds…and remain with him [Jesus II] in the Holy City [New Jerusalem] that John sees coming down from the first heaven. (Williams, Letter to James, June, 12, 1866)

However, when the prison was built, nobody realized that they were actually building the Temple! It is not until today that the 144,000 are being gathered, with the Morrisite descendants as first fruits unto God that the Fullness of the Gospel is now being revealed and this work of proclaiming and teaching the return of Jesus in Deer Lodge in his Temple is only now being brought to its final issue.

Therefore, it is the eternal privilege of the Morrisites and their descendants to be the "heralds" of

---

[*] Anderson, p. 223.

Jesus II. In this way their mission and the Mormon prophecy of Williams was fulfilled. The New Jerusalem, the City of the Great king, the Holy Temple has been built and Jesus II himself has suddenly appeared there.

"THE TEMPLE IS ALREADY BUILT"

Two thousand four hundred and eighty five years after Ezekiel prophesied the Old Montana Prison in 571 BC, the solid stone construction on the wall was completed in 1912. From 1912 onward all prisoners had to pass through tower #7 between the two pillars of Jachin and Boaz, including Jesus II.

At the same time in 1912, the great Davidic King, 'Abdu'l-Baha, son of Baha'u'llah, was busy laying the cornerstone for the Baha'i Temple in Wilmette, Illinois, outside of the city of Chicago. Upon laying this cornerstone over 1000 miles away, 'Abdu'l-Baha stopped and, looking to the West toward Deer Lodge--with his back to lake Michigan, declared to all the world: "THE TEMPLE IS ALREADY BUILT!"[*]

Obviously the laying of one stone in Wilmette is not the completion of that Temple. In fact construction on the Wilmette Temple wasn't even started until 9 years later, in 1921, and it wasn't even complete until the late 1940s! Rather, it is the completion of Ezekiel's Temple in Montana which 'Abdu'l-Baha boldly announced to the Baha'i world! For it is the return of Jesus that is prophesied to come in the Baha'i writings of both Baha'u'llah and 'Abdu'l-Baha as well as in the Holy scriptures of the Bible and the prophecies of Williams.

Thus 'Abdu'l-Baha prophetically announced the completion of Ezekiel's Temple in Montana in 1912 when it was finished.

MORRISITE AND BAHA'I

The Baha'i Faith and the Morrisite Faith are two separate and independent religions just like Judaism and Christianity are separate and independent religions. Yet like Christianity which is the fulfillment of Judaism, the Baha'i Faith is the fulfillment of the Morrisite religion. "Where Judaism is the root, and Christianity the branch, the Baha'i faith is the leaf, flower and fruit of that same Tree."

In April of 1863, the Mormon prophet George Williams prophesied that the return of Jesus (Jesus II) would be at Deer Lodge, Montana. At this same time, thousands of miles away, halfway around the world, Baha'u'llah, the Jewish King in exile (Exilarch) a descendant from King David, proclaimed Himself as the second coming of Christ in the Garden of Ridvan in the Area of Pure Lineage, outside of Baghdad, Iraq.

The Montana State Prison in Deer Lodge was open exactly 108 years (1871-1979) making it the longest operating prison in American history to this day. If we add the 108 years to the

---

[*] *Baha'i News*, April, 1987.

'Abdu'l Bahá in America: the 75th anniversary

Bahá'í News

Bahá'í Year 144 · April 1987

'The Temple is already built'

Within days of the close of the 1909 convention (of Bahai Temple Unity) a committee of the Executive Board—consisting of Albert Hall, Bernard Jacobsen, and Mountfort Mills—began working on the purchase of the 12 lots for which Corinne True held option. On 17 May the Bahá'ís purchased that land from Silas Crandall for a reported $32,500. The Chicago Examiner, mixing fact and fiction, reported that

While none of those interested in the movement can give any definite date, it is believed work will be started within the next two months.

The work is to be accompanied by unique ceremonies. Many members of the local cult, it is said, will give up their homes and live on the sacred grounds while the work is going on. With their own hands they will construct the temple, men and women alike carrying brick and mortar . . .

The temple will be built to symbolize the new man—the perfected man—to justify the perfected world. It will have nine outer walls and nine fountains, each fountain representing a world religion and a world Messiah, all meeting and unifying through the latter day revelation of truth made through triune manifestations of God through the three great Bahai messengers. The temple will be erected on a triangular plot and will represent the trinity of teachers* who brought to the world

*This article about the laying in 1912 of the dedication stone for the Bahá'í House of Worship in Wilmette, Illinois, is reprinted from Bruce W. Whitmore, The Dawning Place: The Building of a Temple, the Forging of the North American Bahá'í community, pp. 51-65, copyright © 1984 by the National Spiritual Assembly of the Bahá'ís of the United States.

the gospel of Bahaism.[1]

Since 'Abdu'l-Bahá had already indicated that the gardens should be circular, the Executive Board was not pleased with the triangular shape. In an effort to make the plot more circular the Executive Board convinced the village of Wilmette to eliminate roadways running through the property. The board also negotiated with the Sanitary District Board of Chicago, which was building a canal along the western boundary, in order to straighten out that boundary.[2] But a misunderstanding between the Executive Board and the Sanitary Board almost caused the negotiations to fail. When the Sanitary Board did not hear from the Executive Board—because the Executive Board was waiting to hear from the Sanitary Board—the Sanitary Board assumed that the Bahá'ís were no longer interested in site modifications, and workers were ordered to begin construction of the canal. On the day the digging was to start, a fierce storm broke out that prevented work on the canal for four days. Communications were reestablished during that time, and the land transactions were completed. By April 1910 Honore Jaxon, negotiator for the Executive Board, reported, "As the matter is now agreed upon, by all the parties in interest, our holdings are so consolidated that on our own land we can draw a circle of nearly five hundred feet in diameter. . . ."[3]

Payment for the land seemed formidable at first. Although the Chicago House of Spirituality had given a Temple Fund of $3,666.44 to the Bahai

*The Bahá'í Faith has only one founder, Bahá'u'lláh. The Chicago Examiner may be referring to 'Abdu'l-Bahá and to the Báb, Prophet-Forerunner of Bahá'u'lláh, as the two other teachers.

Temple Unity, along with the title to the two lots, the amount in the fund was far short of what was needed, for the contract on the land required the payment of $5,000 every six months, plus interest. Corinne True, as the new financial secretary of the Executive Board, wrote to Helen Goodall that "every effort will need to be made to meet" the payments and that "all must unite in sacrificing." The initial response of the Bahá'ís was heartwarming: "The Contributions to the Fund came in so fast," Mrs. True recalled, "that I was rushed to death receipting for them."[4]

During the first year of the Bahai Temple Unity, several methods for collecting money were devised, including a Widow's Quilt Fund, the use of 3,500 "blessing boxes," and the private sale of Bahá'í hymn books. Children in Bahá'í Sunday school groups nationwide sent in their offerings—sometimes only a few pennies, but often several dollars. In Washington, D.C., a variety of programs were begun, including one in which Bahá'ís performed odd jobs for other Bahá'is and then contributed their wages. One woman from Greenwich, Connecticut, convinced that the Temple would be completed with unusual swiftness, sent her donation of $19 and wrote, "I hope that I am not too late!" By the end of the year, contribution had been received from 61 cities in 22 states. Although the amount received from North America (Canada, Mexico, the Hawaiian Islands, and the United States) and Europe (England, France, and Germany) totaled $7,638.66, this sum was nearly equaled by gifts totaling $7,092.85 from Bahá'ís in India, Turkey, Syria, Palestine, Russia, Egypt, and Persia.[5] These contributions from the East were encouraged by 'Abdu'l-Bahá, Who bade the Oriental Bahá'ís to

---

stone, but it was too dull to cut through the spring grass. He placed the trowel in its case and asked for more practical tools. When it was discovered that plans had not been made to have such tools available, one of the young men ran to a nearby house to borrow an ax. "Like an athlete," 'Abdu'l-Bahá took it and "swung it high in the air." "After several blows," wrote Louise Waite, He "cut through the resisting turf and reached the earth below." [8] The scene inspired the Baha'is to sing—first the "Benediction" and then "Tell the Wondrous Story," both written by Mrs. Waite.

In the meantime another young man, Herbert Anderson of Chicago, had run west on Linden Avenue in search of a shovel. He found a work crew on the Northwestern Elevated tracks about four blocks south of Linden Avenue, near Isabella Street, and convinced them to loan him one of their shovels, which he whisked back to the ceremony. As the shovel was handed to 'Abdu'l-Bahá, Corinne True reportedly stepped forward and encouraged Him to let a woman participate in the ceremony.[9] Turning to Lua Getsinger, He bade her to come forward despite her resistance. It was not until He called her a second time that she responded, grasped the shovel, and turned the first earth. Following her was Corinne True, after which, one by one, individuals of many races and nationalities—Persian, Syrian, Egyptian, Indian, North American Indian, Japanese, South African, English, French, German, Dutch, Norwegian, Swedish, Danish, Jewish—were called forward to participate in the digging.

Now that a rather large hole had been dug, 'Abdu'l-Bahá reached down and scooped up handfuls of dirt, which He shared with several individuals. Then He "consigned the stone to its excavation, on behalf of all the people of the world." After retrieving the golden trowel, He pushed the earth back around the stone and declared, "The Temple is already built." [10]

NOTES
1. For more information about Albert Hall and Mountfort Mills see appendices 3.2 and 3.6 respectively in The Dawning Place.
2. Chicago Examiner, 18 May 1909.

'Abdu'l-Bahá looks on as people from many nations and races break ground for the Mother Temple of the West in Wilmette, Illinois.

3. Early in 1910 the Executive Board reported that "Harmonious and mutually helpful co-operation has been effected with the village council of the Village of Wilmette and the officers of The Sanitary District of Chicago, as a result of which arrangements have been consummated in an agreement (now in the process of being carried out), whereby the alley running through our tract, and Greenleaf Avenue on its northern boundary, will be vacated; and in return the Unity will convey, and dedicate to public use, land for Sheridan Road through part of our triangular tract formerly lying north of Greenleaf Avenue. This permits a greatly improved line for Sheridan Road, curving in a graceful line to the north and west at our eastern and northern boundary and across the bridge over the Drainage canal. The agreement also contemplates the granting to the Sanitary District Board of some additional width it needs for its abutments, in return for which we acquire a greater width to our tract at points that clear up and straighten out westerly line leaving us a somewhat enlarged tract of symmetrical outline." (Bahai Temple Unity to unidentified "Bahá'is and Friends in the Cause of God," n.d., author's personal papers)
4. Honore Jaxon, "Brief Report to Date on Site Negotiations," Bahai News, 1, no. 4 (17 May 1910), 26.
5. "Record of the Second Annual Convention of Bahai Temple Unity, held April 25 and 26, 1910," Bahai News, 1, no. 4 (17 May 1910), 12; True to Helen Goodall, 29 June 1909, 23 January 1911, Helen S. Goodall Papers, National Bahá'í Archives, Wilmette, Ill.
6. Chase to Albert Windust, 29 April 1908, Star of the West Records, National Bahá'í Archives, Wilmette, Ill. By 1915 contributions had also been received from Ireland, Italy, South Africa, Brazil, New Zealand,

Mauritius, and the Isle of Pines.
7. 'Abdu'l-Bahá to "his honor Ameen," trans. 19 April 1910, quoted in "Record of the Second Annual Convention," p. 14; 'Abdu'l-Bahá to "the beloved of God in America" (delegates to the 1910 annual Bahá'í convention), trans. 18 March 1910, quoted in "Record of the Second Annual Convention," pp. 8-9. (Since authoritative translations of these letters have not yet been made, the letters are to be considered only as historic documents.)
8. True to Goodall, 29 June 1909, Goodall Papers.
9. Louise R. Waite, Words of 'Abdul-Baha In regard to the Mashrak-el-Azkar in Chicago (n.p., 1909), author's personal papers. (Because this statement was conveyed verbally, it does not have the authority of a signed letter in an approved translation.)
10. True to Goodall, 2 March 1911, Goodall Papers. (Because this statement was conveyed verbally, it does not have the authority of a signed letter in an approved translation.)
11. ('Abdu'l-Bahá), "Tablet to the American Friends from Abdul-Baha," Star of the West, 2, no. 4 (17 May 1911), 7.
12. ('Abdu'l-Bahá), "Tablet from Abdul-Baha," Star of the West, 2, no. 13 (4 Nov. 1911), 3.
13. True to Goodall, 2 March 1911, 25 February 1910, Goodall Papers.
14. 'Abdu'l-Bahá, quoted in Howard MacNutt, "Introduction to 1922 Edition," in 'Abdu'l-Bahá, The Promulgation of Universal Peace: Talks Delivered by 'Abdu'l-Bahá during His Visit to the United States and Canada in 1912, comp. Howard MacNutt, 2d ed. (Wilmette, Ill.: Bahá'í Publishing Trust, 1982), p. xv.
15. "Program, Bahai Temple Unity Convention, April 27 to May 2, 1912," Star of the West Records; Chicago Daily News, 30 April 1912, 29 April 1912; Mírzá Mahmúd-

---

i-Zarqání, "Kitáb-i-Badáyi'u'l-Áthár: Diary of 'Abdu'l-Bahá's travels in Europe and America, written by His secretary," TS, entry for 29 April 1912, National Bahá'í Archives, Wilmette, Ill.
16. The report on the land was presented by Bernard Jacobsen, secretary of the Executive Board: "After numerous interviews a price of $17,000 was finally agreed upon. Mr. Conrad originally wanted $65 per foot for this ground and required $7,000 cash and $5,000 per year until paid. We felt that this was more than we could carry, so the proposed plan for the use of the grounds was laid before him and he finally agreed to give us our present terms of $17,000.— $5,000 cash, $3,000 per year, at 5 per cent interest until paid. This gave us a saving in interest and a longer term to pay the balance, which was a decided advantage for the Unity.

"Mr. Conrad became so enthused with the object of our institutions that he has since then offered us the use of the $3,000 which we were to pay him in September as a loan for the purchase of other ground if desired. The spirit of good-will has followed all of our transactions with these people. . . .

"Then there is another piece of property owned by Mr. Yost, which lies north and adjacent to the piece we bought from Mr. Conrad and consists of about 140 feet frontage on Sheridan Road. Several meetings have been held with Mr. Yost, but his price is exorbitant at present. Therefore, we have decided to let this matter rest until some future time" (Bernard M. Jacobsen, "Record of the Fourth Annual Convention of Bahai Temple Unity: Chicago, April 27th-May 1st, 1912," Star of the West, 3, no. 5 (5 June 1912),4.)

Mr. Yost's property was later purchased by Benjamin Marshall, a noted architect who designed the Drake and Blackstone hotels in Chicago and the Orrington Hotel in Evanston. In 1921 Marshall spent more than $1 million constructing one of the most fabulous residences ever built in the Chicago area, complete with a fifth-century Chinese temple and a glassed-in tropical garden, the trees and shrubs for which required a five-car train to transport. In 1936 the mansion was purchased by Nathan Goldblatt. Several years later, as real estate taxes soared, he offered the property to the village of Wilmette as a gift. The offer was rejected, and the mansion was torn down in 1950 following a fire that did extensive damage to the structure. The 2.5 acres of land were purchased by the National Spiritual Assembly of the Bahá'ís of the United States for $50,000. The ornamental iron gates leading to the lakeside parking lot are the only remaining evidence of Marshall's magnificent creation.
17. For additional information about Dr.

Zia Bagdadi, see appendix 3.1 in The Dawning Place.
18. News of the Nation, 2 July 1890.
19. 'Abdu'l-Bahá, Promulgation, pp. 67-68.
20. Joseph H. Hannen, "The Public Meetings of the Fourth Annual Convention of Bahai Temple Unity: Chicago, April 27th-May 24, 1912," Star of the West, 3, no. 4 (17 May 1912), 32.
21. 'Abdu'l-Bahá, Promulgation, p. 65.
22. The "Temple Song" can be found on pages 266-67 in The Dawning Place.
23. See appendix 4.6 in The Dawning Place, "Some Individuals Present at the Initial Ground-Breaking Ceremony, and the Cities They Represented," 1 May 1912.
24. Mírzá Ahmad Sohráb, "Abdul-Baha at the Grave of Thornton Chase," Star of the West, 3, no. 13 (4 Nov. 1912), 15.

25. Chicago Daily News, 1 May 1912.
26. Honore J. Jaxon, "Dedication of the Mashrak-el-Azkar Site," Star of the West, 3, no. 4 (17 May 1912), 5-6.
27. 'Abdu'l-Bahá, Promulgation, pp. 71-72.
28. Louise R. Waite, "My Visits With, and Instructions From, Abdul Baha While He was in Chicago, from April 30 to May 6, 1912," Star of the West Records.
29. Ibid.
30. Jaxon, "Dedication," p. 7; Mardiyyih Nabíl Carpenter, "Commemoration of the Twenty-Fifth Anniversary of 'Abdu'l-Bahá's Visit to America," in The Bahá'í World: A Biennial International Record, Volume VII, 1936-1938, comp. National Spiritual Assembly of the Bahá'ís of the United States and Canada (New York: Bahá'í Publishing Committee, 1939), p. 219.

The Master at the Mother Temple of the West, May 1, 1912. At His feet is the Temple's dedication stone.

proclamation of Baha'u'llah in April of 1863 when Williams also made his announcement of the return of Jesus in Deer Lodge, Montana, we get April of 1971: (1863+108=1971).

It was on April 29th of 1971 that Jesus II, the establisher of the Baha'i Faith had the "stone with seven eyes" before him and fulfilled the 108 year old Mormon prophecy of Williams for the return of Jesus in Deer Lodge in his Temple.

THIS "STONE WITH SEVEN EYES"

Today, hanging in the administration building of the Old Montana Prison is one of the most priceless paintings in the world. The painting of "This Stone with Seven Eyes Zechariah 3:9" is on display as a unique historical treasure, documenting the Date of April 29th, 1971 as the date for the proclamation of Jesus II when he was wrongfully incarcerated in this prison thus fulfilling prophecy against his own will.

The prison wall is made out of solid stone and has seven towers on it. These seven towers are like seven eyes because from them the guards could see everything that goes on in the entire place.

In some translations it is a "stone with seven facets." Facets are projections meaning towers. These projections being both towers and eyes make them watch towers. Ezekiel's Temple in the Bible wouldn't need watch towers if it wasn't a prison where the guards had to be above the people with their guns to oversee everything that goes on inside.

This "Stone with Seven Eyes," which is Ezekiel's Temple in Montana with the seven towers, is the most important place in the world for all humanity. From out of this prison, from between the two mountains of copper/brass, come the armies of God (144,000 promised ones) and the establishment of the Kingdom throughout the entire word. It was in this prison that the seven seals on the Book of Revelation were first broken and now can be openly explained to all the world as easily as you might read the headlines on today's newspaper! Just as it is prophesied in Revelation chapter 5, only the return of Jesus (Jesus II) as the Lamb, is able to break these seals and unfurl and read the scrolls to all the people of the world.

Today, people of all ages and of all nationalities can come to the Old Montana State Prison at Deer Lodge and see this priceless painting of the "Stone with Seven Eyes" documenting the proclamation of Jesus II. Today bones of people who were with Jesus on his first coming or a tiny little splinter of the true cross or other "holy relics" are worth millions of dollars! They are so valuable they are priceless! The painting of the prison documenting Jesus' proclamation, which was painted by his disciples, is more valuable than the Mona Lisa. In the future the crumbling pieces of stone from the prison wall could be worth hundreds or maybe even thousands of dollars.

Not a single tour goes by which does not stop at the painting which announces the proclamation of Jesus II having this "Stone with Seven Eyes" before him on April 29th, 1971. Today we can stop and reflect upon the significance that this irreplaceable national treasure, upkept by the people of Deer Lodge and the Historical Society, has in store for all the people of the word. With

Painting of Ezekiel's Temple
"THIS STONE WITH SEVEN EYES"

Now on display in the prison tour
Proclamation of Jesus II April, 29th 1971

10

such a great treasure as Ezekiel's Temple in Montana, the foreordained spot chosen by God and prophesied and heralded by George Williams as the place for the return of Jesus, it is certainly no wonder that Montana Is called "The Treasure State!"

No treasure can be greater this. No treasure can be more valuable or more sought after than the Presence of God (Shekinah) in His Holy Temple. "Of what does it profit man to gain all the world and lose the Kingdom of God?"

People will come from all around the world to visit the Old Montana Prison and reflect upon these words of Jesus spoken long ago:

"I was in prison and you came to me." (Matthew 25:36)

THE SIGN OF THE SON OF MAN IN HEAVEN

It was not until right after the Baha'i gathering in May of 1990 celebrating the arrival of Comet Austin that any of the Baha'is found out about the prophecies of George Williams for the coming of Jesus II.

I had been doing research on Ezekiel's Temple in the Bible at that time and had come to Montana to give a talk on how the seven towered prison was the physical fulfillment of Ezekiel's vision. (Only Ezekiel's Temple and the Deer Lodge prison have seven towers.)

After the gathering, in June of 1990, when Comet Austin had already departed, we decided to go to Deer Lodge and measure the prison the way Ezekiel was told to measure the Temple. To our amazement in God's perfection, all the prophesied dates found in both the Bible and the Great Pyramid of Giza (Adam's chronological book in stone) were also found inculcated into the atone masonry of the prison! While we were there, the tour coordinator asked us what we were doing. We told her that we were doing research on the Baha'i Faith because this prison fulfilled the Biblical prophecy for Ezekiel's Temple which Jesus is prophesied to return to, having the "Stone with Seven Eyes" before him. She then told us something which I--nor any other Baha'i--had ever heard before. She told us that there was another group in Deer Lodge called the "Morrisites,"* who came out of the Mormons, that had independent prophecies that the second coming of Jesus Christ would be in Deer Lodge, Montana. We were elated and said, "That prophecy is fulfilled right here in this prison!"

She said that there was a book about the Morrisites that we should read. After researching that book, *For Christ Will Come Tomorrow: The Saga of the Morrisites*, by C. Leroy Anderson (which everyone should read and become acquainted with) we did more research and wrote up this book, *Ezekiel's Temple in Montana*.

None of us, not even Dr. Leland Jensen, who fulfills the prophecy for the return of Jesus, had ever heard of the Morrisites before. His proclamation, made on April 29th, 1971 was based purely on the fulfillment of Biblical prophecy in Zechariah chapter 3 and other places, which

---

* When she said "Morrisites"? I thought, "I've heard of a parasite, I know what a termite is--but what is a Morrisite?"

11

pinpoints the return of "Jesus the High Priest" (Catholic Douay version)[*] in this Old Montana State Prison which is the "Stone with Seven Eyes" that Jesus II, the High Priest, is to have before him (Zechariah 3:9).

Therefore, a completely independent source, not associated with the Baha'i Faith, prophesied of his coming to Deer Lodge in the prison, the seven towered Temple of Ezekiel. Like the star of Bethlehem which heralded his first coming, Comet Austin was the sign of the Son of Man in Heaven, heralding his second coming at Deer Lodge, which brought us the news of the Morrisites and the prophecy of George Williams.

THE LORD'S MESSENGER

George Williams himself fulfills Mormon prophecy as the "messenger of the Lord" who is to come as the forerunner to Jesus II. In the Book of Mormon, 3 Nephi 24:1, George Williams fulfills this prophecy for the "messenger of the lord" which is identical to the prophecy given by Malachi In chapter 3 of his book in the Old Testament:

> Behold, I send my messenger to prepare the way before me, and the Lord whom you seek will suddenly come to his Temple; the messenger of the Covenant in whom you delight behold he is coming, says the Lord of hosts. But who can endure the day of his coming, and who can stand when he appears? (Malachi 3:1-2; 3 Nephi 24:1)

The Lord's messenger, George Williams, prepared the way for the return of Jesus by announcing to all the world that Jesus would come suddenly to his Temple in Deer Lodge Montana, which is the Old Montana State Prison prophesied as the seven towered Temple of Ezekiel.

Many other prophecies of George Williams have likewise come true. He foresaw the technological age with airplanes and modem inventions. He prophesied that the whole world would speak a universal language which is one of the twelve principles of Baha'u'llah. Likewise, he prophesied the earth's shifting crust which will bring Deer Lodge down to a warm southerly climate. Both the Guardian of the Baha'i Faith, Charles Mason Remey Aghsan, and Albert Einstein wrote about how the earth's surface is going to shift, bringing the United States 2000 miles south into the area of the tropics.

According to C. Leroy Anderson, there are other miscellaneous prophecies of William's that came true.[†] However, Anderson said that they might have been only coincidental because at the time of that writing he was unaware of the fact that Jesus II had proclaimed himself in Deer Lodge in the prison on April 29th, 1971. The main prophecy of the appearance of Jesus II the High Priest in his prison/temple with seven eyes or towers is only now for the first time being explained to all the world!

---

[*] Reads "Joshua the High Priest" in some versions.
[†] C. Leroy Anderson, (1976). "The Scattered Morrisites," *Montana: The Magazine of Western History, 26*, p. 69.

ALBERT EINSTEIN AND THE EARTH'S SHIFTING CRUST!

The fulfillment of Williams's prophecy of the earth's shifting crust is still yet to come. It will happen after the year 2000 AD when the Kingdom is firmly established upon the earth. Williams made this prophecy long before scientists such as Albert Einstein were able to explain that in fact the earth's crust does shift. Without the aid of modem science and technology, Williams's mind was opened to these visions of the future and he prophesied of these events to accompany the world announcement of Jesus II from the Deer Lodge Valley between the two mountains of copper.

The crust of the earth is about 10 to 50 miles thick, is solid rock, and encases the entire globe. Underneath this crust there is a layer of molten lava--magma--which is soft and slippery, allowing the crust to easily slide over the body. The mechanism that forces the crust to slide in a specific direction is the lopsided deposition of ice on the land in a polar region. Albert Einstein stated:

> In a polar region there is a continual deposition of ice, which is not symmetrically distributed about the pole. The earth's rotation acts on these unsymmetrically deposited masses, and produces centrifugal momentum that is transmitted to the rigid crust of the earth. The constantly increasing centrifugal momentum produced in this way will, when it has reached a certain point, produce a movement of the earth's crust over the body and will displace the polar region toward the equator. (Albert Einstein, Foreword to *Earth's Shifting Crust* by Charles Hapgood)

The continent of Antarctica is about twice the size of the United States, and has high mountain ranges like the Rocky Mountains. In the last eleven thousand years, since the last crustal shift, there has been deposited on this continent, a one to two mile high layer of ice. This ice is unsymmetrically located and exerts a centrifugal pressure on the crust due to the force of the earth's rotation on its axis. This is now shoving the crust northward on the 115 degree longitudinal meridian-Eastern hemisphere. The Greenland ice cap, although smaller, is working in tandem with this and is shoving the crust in the Western hemisphere southward. The more this movement continues the hotter becomes the magma (due to friction), and the more slippery it becomes; also, the more eccentric becomes the Antarctic ice cap.

The further that the center of Antarctica gets from the South Pole the greater becomes the centrifugal force. In addition to this, fifty to one hundred feet of new ice is presently being deposited on this continent each year. This ice cap is now bigger than the one--North American Ice cap--that caused the crustal shift 11,000 years ago, that moved the North Pole from the Hudson Bay area to the Arctic Ocean, causing the receding of the Wisconsin Ice Age. The Mammoths that were grazing in the plains of Northern Siberia were quickly moved into the Arctic Circle, and were quickly frozen, thus preserving their flesh to this day. Antarctica was moved into the South Polar Region. Coal has been discovered 200 miles from the South Pole. In order for that continent to have coal deposits, it would have been necessary for it to have had a coniferous forest, like that which is now found in Montana.

At a specific, preordained date, there will be a rapid slipping of the crust. The North Pole will move into the Lake Baikal area of Siberia. The United States will move southward about 2000 miles toward the equatorial bulge and under a mile high of water. Just about everything in this country below 5000 feet will be inundated. Thus, this is a terrifying picture of the birth of God's Kingdom on Earth as it is In Heaven.[*]

WHO ARE THE MORRISITES?

The Morrisites get their name from Joseph Morris. He appeared on the scene at the height of the great Mormon reformation of 1856.[†] It was his mission, much like that of the great reformer Martin Luther, to separate a group of pure hearted people from the mainstream Mormon church which by that time had deviated from its true course. The Morrisites consider the reformer Morris as only the martyr foreshadower or forerunner of their true prophet George Williams.[‡]

Ten years after the Mormons entered the Great Salt Lake area in Utah, in 1857, they had become very corrupt under the leadership of Brigham Young. The main corruption of the Mormons was polygamy. This practice was started by Brigham Young, not by Joseph Smith,[§] and wasn't announced by Brigham Young as an official Mormon practice until 1852, eight years after Smith had died. The purpose of this was so Brigham Young could marry a lot of rich widows and get their money and land.

Joseph Morris rose up at this time against the corruption of Brigham Young as a relatively unknown Mormon like Martin Luther who, in his day, was just one simple monk against the great Pope. Unlike Luther, Morris had no intention of starting his own religion. He just wanted to reform the Mormon church in Utah and get rid of all their corruption so they could continue on their true path. However, Brigham Young refused to reform, just like the Pope refused to reform to Martin Luther. Brigham Young decided that he had to get rid of Morris and rub him out. Martin Luther, when he made his declaration, found protection from the Pope under the eight German princes. As long as the US government army remained in the Utah territory, Morris was safe. However, in 1862 with the outbreak of the Civil War, the US army pulled out of Utah and Brigham Young and his Mormon militia took over and ruthlessly murdered Joseph Morris and several other Morrisites, ranking the Morrisite War right up there with the Mountain Meadows Massacre a few years earlier.

The Brighamite sheriff Burton, riding roughshod into the Morrisite camp at Kington Fort, tried to run Joseph Morris down with his horse. He said, "I want no more of your apostasy"[**] (clearly showing that the conflict was purely religious in nature) and then shot Morris dead.

---

[*] See Dr. Leland Jensen (1971). *The Beast: Is About to Be Dead!* Missoula: MT: Baha'i Publishers Under the Provisions of the Covenant (BPUPC), p. 3, for more.

[†] Anderson, p. 13.

[‡] Anderson, pp. 148 and 154.

[§] "An eminent jurist, Federal Judge John F. Phillips, reviewed the evidence presented by the polygamous Utah Mormon Church [of Brigham Young], in legal proceedings wherein the origin of the doctrine and practice of polygamy was a vital issue, and held that Brigham Young not Joseph Smith was the author and instigator of that... doctrine. (See Reorganized Church vs. Church of Christ, et al, 60 Fed. 937" cited in: Inez Smith Davis, (1959). *The Story of the Church.* Independence, MO: Herald Publishing House, p. 486.

[**] Joseph Morris, (1886). *The Spirit Prevails.* San Francisco, CA: George S. Dove and Company, p. 7.

A young woman named Isabella Bowman, holding in her arms the babe of the mother who had been killed by the first cannon ball fire into camp, stepped forward and said: "You blood-thirsty hell-hound, why do you shoot at that good man?" Burton took deliberate aim at her, and shot her dead. Mrs. O'Hagg was shot at the same time. At this time, John Banks was standing near the steps of the school house, when one of the mob stepped behind him and shot him in the back of the neck; but he didn't die until that night.[*]

Seventeen years later, Burton was brought up on murder charges for killing Morris and the others. He was found guilty. After an appeal to a higher court the charges were dropped.

With the death of their leader, the Morrisites were shattered yet expectant because the last instructions from their leader had declared that after this great conflict with the enemy (Brigham Young and his followers) the second coming of Jesus Christ would appear to them and they would receive the Gospel of the Kingdom. According to C. Leroy Anderson, Morris's last instructions, given in the form of prophecy six months before the events transpired, were "remarkable"! Anderson writes:

> 'Regardless of how one might view the general prophetic abilities of Joseph Morris, the substance of this revelation [his last instructions] is remarkable. It provides almost a flawless scenario of the actual confrontation between the Morrisites and the law [of Brigham Young] that occurred six months later.[†]

Thus it was in the spring of 1863, corresponding exactly to the time of Baha'u'llah's proclamation in the Garden of Ridvan on April 21st, 1863, that George Williams--following the direction of God--proclaimed himself to the Morrisite community declaring that Deer Lodge Valley, Montana, was the place where their Lord, the return of Jesus, would be and that Deer Lodge was the sacred spot foreordained In all the books of God to be the site for the Heavenly City, the "City of the Great King" which is described in the Book of Revelation and the Bible as "New Jerusalem."

At once with joyful hearts and renewed vigor the seemingly beaten band of Morrisites were now set aglow with a new zeal! For they had been saved and redeemed just as Morris had promised they would be after the great Morrisite War of 1862! Now with the true vision of the seer Williams, they triumphantly gathered their scant material possessions and moved to the Deer Lodge Valley, for them the home of the Promised Land! Some moved directly to Deer Lodge while others moved to Soda Springs, Idaho, and Council Bluffs, Iowa, later to join the rest of them in Deer Lodge.

The Morrisite people became the pioneers of Deer Lodge, the first farmers and land owners, their sole purpose to build up that city and prepare the way for the construction of the Temple of God in which Jesus is prophesied to suddenly return.

---

[*] Joseph Morris, *The Spirit Prevails*, pp. 7-8.
[†] Anderson, p. 92.

George Williams himself, however, was never a Morrisite* and always remained a Mormon. It was the Morrisites who listened to his prophecies and followed his instructions to move to Deer Lodge. Williams himself never went to Deer Lodge but remained in Utah in Salt Lake City where he was a farmer. He used to have his mail sent to a friend's house because Brigham Young and his followers were constantly looking for him. When they had Morris killed they thought that they had heard the last of the Morrisites. But now they were going around proclaiming that Brigham Young had it all wrong and that the return of Jesus would be in Deer Lodge.

Williams never set himself up as leader of the Morrisites but appointed other people to the positions. He had no intention of becoming some big muckity-muck because he wasn't power hungry and he wasn't greedy. Williams was pure of heart and only wanted the truth of his vision preserved in Deer Lodge until the appearance of Jesus II. Eventually, because of the Brighamites' pursuit of him, he moved from Utah back to his native England. The Morrisites continued in Deer Lodge all the way up until the 1950s and 1960s where their last official leader, George Johnson, died in 1954. Right up until the end of his life, George Johnson never wavered from the prophecy of Williams that the second coming (Jesus II) would be in Deer Lodge, Montana. With a strong Faith and absolute certainty he taught this fact to his children and to his grandchildren. Today it is the children of the Morrisites who reap the benefits of their parents as this prophecy is fulfilled in the Deer Lodge Temple of the Old Montana State Prison.

THE FIRST VISION

On April 15th of 1862, while riding on his horse in the mountains of Utah, Williams was overcome by a majestic visitation from the north in the direction of Deer Lodge, in which he saw the return of Jesus leading the armies of heaven riding "a countless host of horses" out from between two "massive pillars of light." These two "massive pillars" correspond to the two mountains of copper from which the horses and four chariots of the armies of heaven are prophesied to come forth from, in Zechariah chapter 6. The two mountains of copper are Lincoln and Butte, Montana. Lincoln is on the north and Butte is on the south of the Deer Lodge Valley.

His first vision was first circulated in handwritten form and was later published by John Eardley in 1899 in a book containing Williams's prophecies and visions entitled, *Gems of Inspiration*. Williams writes:

> After leading a blameless life, and searching after the treasures of eternity, through the gospel of Christ, under the guidance of the Holy Spirit, I was, on the 15th day of April, AD 1862, riding on my spirited mare by the slope of the Western range of mountains, near Hacker's canyon, in Salt Lake Valley, Utah, when snow began to fall in a marvelous manner. A cloud appeared in the north and became agitated, and speedily formed an enormous archway, spanning the entire valley.

---

* Anderson, p. 174.

On each side of this arch were massive pillars of light, constructed with fine skill, and folding doors studded with golden bolts. Beholding this heavenly appearance, I alighted from my horse, and allowed it to escape.

While meditating this scene, the eyes of my understanding were opened by the spirit of God, so as to understand the things of God as they were from eternity.

The folding doors were thrown back, and the highway to the eternal worlds was opened before me, and a voice strengthened me, saying: "Fear not, thou greatly beloved of the Lord, these are they that form a portion of the armies of heaven." Beyond the folding doors I saw a countless host of horses, and they who sat upon them had on breast-plates of fire, and diamonds, and helmets of precious stones, and out of the nostrils of the horses came fire and smoke, and their riders had large swords, and their faces were lightened as the sun.

As soon as the first of this host reached the archway, they halted and formed a double line, the horses facing each other, and up this line I saw into the first heaven, from the earth, and bear record of the same, God, the eternal Father, standing on a throne of sapphire stone, and Christ [Jesus the Lamb] seated at His right hand.[*]

The great cloud that Williams saw in his vision in the north is the great cloud that once filled the Deer Lodge Valley shooting up out of the geyser in the middle of the Valley (now Warm Springs). This cloud could be seen for 25 miles in all directions filling the Montana sky.[†] Likewise, Montana is called Big Sky Country. "Big Sky" is written in big bold colorful letters on all the Montana license plates. And in the Dakotas they call Montana the "Sky State."

Thus Williams first sees this giant cloud in the north coming toward him from the direction of the Deer Lodge Valley. The Bible prophecies are clear that Jesus is to return on a cloud in the sky. The cloud is the big steam cloud in Deer Lodge and the sky is Montana--Montana is the SKY state. Thus Jesus II appears in the cloud in the sky.

Williams then saw the cloud become highly agitated in which it transformed into a giant archway. It is out of this archway from between the two "massive pillars of light" (two mountains of copper) that Williams sees the doors of the future flung wide open and armies of God (the 144,000) and the "countless host of horses" riding out from the Deer Lodge Valley to all the world.

---

[*] Anderson, p. 175.
[†] Leeson, *History of Montana 1739-1885*, p. 551.

Jesus II appears in the SKY: MONTANA

THE BIG SKY STATE

Matthew 24:30 (N.I.V.)

"At that time the sign of the Son of Man will appear in the sky, and all the nations of the earth will mourn. They will see the Son of Man coming on the clouds of the sky, with power and great glory (Bahai)."

HOW DEER LODGE GOT ITS NAME

It is from this great cloud of steam, filling the Deer Lodge Valley which Williams sees in his vision, that Deer Lodge gets its name. The huge steam cloud was formed from a geo-thermal well high atop a forty foot mound in the middle of the Deer Lodge Valley which is today located at Warm Springs. The heavy column of steam from high atop this mound was filled with nutritious minerals which kept the grass in the valley green and luscious year round. Likewise the forty foot mound was formed from the mineral and salt build up over the years.

The salt-lick attracted the deer in multitudes who came to graze on the delicious green grass which was kept luscious by the great thermal cloud and its nutritious minerals which fertilized all the grass in the Valley year round. With all this great food the deer multiplied in large numbers and became very big and healthy, a perfect hunting ground for the Native Americans. Thus Deer Lodge was "the happy hunting ground in the sky" (Montana) for the Native American Indians who considered it a sacred spot and would have no warfare there.

Thus the Indians named it *It Soo-Ke En Car-Ne*, "Lodge of the White Tailed Deer" because the steam issuing up from the geo-thermal well into the Valley looked just like the Indian sweat lodges except in this case the Deer Lodge Valley was like a huge sweat lodge for the deer.

> Deer Lodge Valley spreads out from five to ten miles wide, between the Rocky and Deer Lodge ranges for a distance of sixty miles. Besides these a number of lateral valleys open into it, bordering the numerous and beautiful streams which enter the main river from each side. Many fine farms are located in these valleys, while the foot hills and mountain sides are grazing lands. The mountains within the county boundaries possess all that gigantic beauty to be found on the Pacific slope, while natural eccentricities, such as hot springs, etc., make up a scene unexcelled in the entire west. The origin of the name is credited to the poetic imagery of the Indians. Captain Mills, himself an old settler, call it an "old appellation," and states that it is derived from a large, sugarloaf mound, with a thermal spring on its summit. Situated near the center of the broad upper half of this valley, it is one of the most beautiful and interesting formations in the northwest, growing with the centuries, the waters building their throne slowly, imperceptibly, but steadily as the coral builds the ocean reefs, and in the coming years will attract many thousands to drink of its medicinal waters and find health and pleasure in the picturesque valley, mountain circled and coursed by crystal streams. The mound is over forty feet high. It stands in the midst of a perfectly level valley; and the hot springs on its summit, during the greater portion of the year, send up a heavy volume of vapor, rendering it a conspicuous object for from twenty to twenty-five miles in every direction. It bears, in the distance, a striking resemblance to an Indian lodge with the smoke ascending from it. Through all the traditions of the Indians the valley has been famous for the plenitude and fatness of the white-tailed deer that graze upon its ever-nutritious and almost ever-green grasses: where the snow scarcely ever falls, and, falling, quickly disappears. And so the aborigines, true to these facts, and weaving with them a happy fancy, named it after what it most resembled; and we have it that the Snake hunting

parties, approaching the crests of the surrounding mountains, before the pale-face came to the land, would try the fleetness of their steeds to see who would first catch sight of and hail the point of rendezvous--*It Soo-ke en Car-ne*--the Lodge of the white-tailed Deer.[*]

Just like a high smoke stack that sends pollution in every direction (but in this case beneficial natural fertilizer), the nutritious minerals in the steam cloud were dispersed In 25 mile radius (50 miles diameter) from the giant mound. As the Deer Lodge Valley is 60 miles long the steam cloud was able to fertilize the grass throughout the entire Valley. Also, because the nutritious minerals were very high in salt content, the snow melted on the grass. This kept the valley green year round just like salt on the road keeps the ice from forming even in zero degree weather. Today these effects are gone because the steam from the geo-thermal well is used to heat the hospital facilities at Warm Springs.

THE DANISH CONNECTION

The majority of Morrisites were Danish.[†] Morris married a Danish woman named Mary Olsen.[‡] The Omaha and Council Bluffs group's minutes were in Danish.[§] The writings of Williams were translated into Danish.[**] Williams sent Guhl and Sorensen to Denmark to found a community based on the Danish fulfillment of Deer Lodge as the site for Valhalla, the temple in the sky.[††] Carrie Jensen was a Danish girl who married Henriksen, the Danish president of the Morrisites in Deer Lodge until 1921 when he passed on.[‡‡] He was succeeded by George Johnson who was also a Dane who passed on in 1954. The Danes became Morrisites because Deer Lodge fulfills Danish prophecy![§§]

VALHALLA

According to Danish prophecy at the time of the end, during Ragnarok, the day when the world is wrecked (Armageddon), all the mighty warriors are to come pouring out of Valhalla as the invincible army of God. Valhalla is the mead hall[***] in the sky where the bravest Viking warriors go when they die in battle, like the Indians who have the happy hunting ground in the sky. A mead hall is a great, big, gigantic lodge. Valhalla is special because it is surrounded by deer on all four sides, thus making it the Deer Lodge in the sky. Montana is the sky state as it says on all the license plates. Thus Valhalla, the Deer Lodge in the sky, is the Deer Lodge in Montana--The Big Sky!

---

[*] Leeson, *History of Montana 1739-1885*, p. 551.
[†] Anderson, p. 73.
[‡] Anderson, p. 91.
[§] Anderson, pp. 205-206.
[**] Anderson, pp. 177-178.
[††] Anderson, p. 205.
[‡‡] Anderson, p. 212 and pp. 227-228.
[§§] See *Keys to the Kingdom in Scandinavian Legends*, by Brian Mueller; and *Entry By Troops*, Chapters 7, 8 & 9 for more.
[***] The "Grail Castle" of Arthurian Legends.

It is no coincidence that Valhalla, the Deer Lodge in the sky, is the same place as the Indian's happy hunting ground in the sky which is also in Deer Lodge. According to the granddaughter of George Williams, who is also Danish, the Morrisite religion and that of the native American are exact parallels having a majority of things in common.

These deer surrounding Valhalla are represented by the four great deer, the stags "Dain, Dvalin, Duneyr, and Durathor from whose horns the honeydew dropped down upon the earth and furnished the water for all the rivers of the world."[*] These four stags stand at the four directions of the compass holding back the four winds of destruction to be released only when the 144,000 come pouring out of Valhalla at the great world battle of Armageddon (Ragnarok) fought over the Mid-East oil and religion, with God being the victor and His Kingdom being established in all the world by the year 2001 AD.[†]

According to the Danish prophecy, God (the All-Father) created the world out of a great geothermal. The world was cold with ice and the fire-giant struck the earth with his flaming sword. The contrast between the fire element in the earth and the snow and ice of the north created a huge cloud of steam. Out of the steam cloud created by this great contrast came a cow who, hungry for food and attracted to a salt-lick, licked the first god out of the salt from which come all the other gods.

It is in Deer Lodge that out of the steam cloud from the geo-thermal comes the salt-lick and luscious grasses which attracted all the deer. Thus the deer "lick out" the Valley where Jesus II and his Temple (Valhalla) are to be. From Jesus II comes the rest of the host of heaven, the 144,000 promised ones.

Interestingly enough, the only civilian stone mason to work on the Temple in Deer Lodge, William Beal, owned the salt-lick geo-thermal well which was on his homestead in Warm Springs. Beal would travel daily from the salt-lick to work on the Temple. All the rest of the work was done by convict labor.

> William was a rock mason and some of his work still stands in this area, including part of the prison [Temple] at Deer Lodge. The Beal's first homestead was on Warm Springs Creek about where the second new addition of Anaconda is today...The second homestead was located on present highway #48 near the Junction of I-90. William would drive his team, wagon and mortar box from here to Deer Lodge to work on the state prison [Ezekiel's Temple in Montana]. The Beals later sold this homestead to Dr. Musicbrod of Warm Springs which became the state hospital.[‡]

---

[*] H. A. Guerber, *Myths of Northern Lands*, p. 20.
[†] This prophecy was fulfilled at the 9-11, 2001 event, during the prophesied "10 days" from 9-11 until 9-21, the Autumnal Equinox, when God brought forth His servant "THE BRANCH" (Zech. 3:8 KJV).
[‡] Deer Lodge County History Group, (1975). *In the Shadow of Mount Haggin: The Story of Anaconda and Deer Lodge County from 1863-1976*, p. 86.

THE TRIBE OF DAN

The Danes have their origin from the tribe of Dan which is one of the 10 lost tribes of Israel.[*] Everywhere the Dans went they named after themselves. In 721 BC the tribe of Dan along with the other 10 tribes of Israel were taken captive to Assyria. The rest of the tribes stayed in Assyria, modern northern Iraq and Iran, while the tribe of Dan migrated up the Dan-ube, into Denmark (Dan's mark) and became known as the Danes (Dans). The other half of the tribe of Dan had left before the captivity by boat because they lived on the sea coast. They went to Ireland, Scotland and England. When St. Patrick[†] established the trinity in Ireland he forced out all the serpents--the Dans--who then moved to Scotland and then finally to England. Both Morris and George Williams were Englishmen and the majority of the Morrisites are Danish and Scan-DAN-avian. When Williams had his vision of the armies of God pouring out of Deer Lodge, the New Jerusalem, he could see that this was Valhalla at the great day of Ragnarok (Armageddon).

The name Dan in Hebrew means "judge" and the symbol of the tribe of Dan is the serpent (Genesis 49:17). The serpent is the symbol of the intellect. The Morrisites, being Dans (Danes), can see this with the intellect going by proofs and not rhetoric. This is important, for the ones sent by God always give proofs for their authenticity--the type of proof laid out in the Bible, like the first three chapters of the Book of Matthew in which he gives the proofs showing how Jesus Christ fulfills prophecy. For example the very first verse in the first page of the New Testament, tells us that Jesus is the son of David. Likewise, this book is a book of proofs. Of course Dr. Jensen is also a Dane (Dan).

EZEKIEL 43

In Ezekiel 43 it says that the "Glory of the Lord" entered the temple by the gate facing east, and behold the "Glory of the Lord" filled the temple. Ezekiel didn't speak English but wrote In Aramaic. In Aramaic "Glory" is "Baha", "U" Is "of" and "Allah" is "Lord, God and Father" and "gate" is Bab. The "Glory of the Lord" is Baha'u'llah.

In Hebrew 'b' and 'v' are interchangeable. The tribe of Dan (Danes) spoke Hebrew and thus Baha'u'llah is Valhalla: the Deer Lodge in the sky. Likewise, the mead halls also functioned as temples preserving the prophecy and religion of the Danes. Valhalla (Baha'u'llah) is the prophesied Temple of Ezekiel, that is, Baha'u'llah (the Revelation of Baha'u'llah) fills the Temple!

Thus Baha'u'llah filling the Temple is Valhalla, showing that Ezekiel's Temple in Montana is the Valhalla in the Big Sky. The Bab (Gate) was the forerunner for Baha'u'llah, like John the Baptist was for Jesus. If we leave the key names in the original Aramaic that Ezekiel wrote in, chapter 43 reads like this:

> Afterward he brought me to the [Bab], the [Bab] facing east. And behold
> [Baha'u'llah] of Israel came from the east; and the sound of his coming was like

---

[*] Herbert Armstrong, (1980). *The United States and Britain in Prophecy*, p. 96.
[†] He was no saint.

the sound of many waters; and the earth shone with his [Baha'i]. And the vision I saw was like the vision I had seen when he came to destroy the city, and like the vision which I had seen by the river Chebar; and I fell upon my face [in adoration]. As [Baha'u'llah] of Israel entered the temple by the [Bab] facing east, the Spirit lifted me up, and brought me into the inner court [Holy of Holies]; and behold, (Baha'u'llah) of Israel filled the temple. (Ezekiel 43:1-5)

Thus Baha'u'llah filling the Temple is Valhalla. The Temple of Ezekiel is divided into two sections just as the prison is. The outer section is the sanctuary which represents the Revelation of the Bab and the inner section (which is the maximum security at the prison) is the Holy of Holies which represents the Revelation of Baha'u'llah. It is the establisher of the Baha'i Faith, Jesus II the High Priest, who is standing in the Holy of Holies (the Revelation of Baha'u'llah) when he had the "Stone with Seven Eyes" of Ezekiel's Temple before him: Valhalla (Baha'u'llah) in the Big Sky-Deer Lodge Montana.

SALT LAKE, SALT LICK. WHAT'S THE DIFFERENCE?

Brigham Young made a great mistake. Right before Joseph Smith died, Smith had a vision of the entire United States being destroyed except for the Rocky Mountains. Charles Mason Remey Aghsan, Guardian of the Baha'i Faith, upheld this prophecy of Joseph Smith and wrote about it in a letter to his secretary in America, Charley Murphy.

10 September 1969,

Mormon prophecy taken from the book by Norman C. Pierce, "and there shall be a time of trouble such as never was since there was a nation--It shall be for a time, times and a half" [The 3 1/2 Times].

THE PROPHET JOSEPH SMITH PREDICTS A NATIONAL JUDGEMENT

"You will see the Constitution almost destroyed. It will hang by a thread, as it were, and that thread as fine as the finest silk fiber.****

"A terrible revolution will take place in the land of America, such as has never been seen before, for the land will be left without a supreme government, and every species of wickedness will be rampant. It will be so terrible that father will be against son, and son against father; mother against daughter, and daughter against mother. The most terrible scenes of murder and bloodshed and rapine that have ever been looked upon will take place.

"Peace will be taken from the earth, and there will be no place of safety, except in the Rocky Mountains. This will cause many hundreds and thousands of the honest in heart to gather there; not because they would become Saints, but for safety and because they would not take up the sword against their neighbor."

10 September 1969

Mormon Prophecy

Taken From the Bank

By Norman C. Pierce.

"and there shall be a time of trouble such as never was since there was a Nation --- It shall be for a time. times and a half"

THE PROPHET JOSEPH PREDICTS A NATIONAL JUDGMENT

"You will see the Constitution almost destroyed. It will hang by a thread, as it were, and that thread as fine as the finest silk fiber. ****

"A terrible revolution will take place in the land of America, such as has never been seen before, for the land will be left without a supreme government, and every species of wickedness will be rampant. It will be so terrible that father will be against son, and son against father; mother against daughter, and daughter against mother. The most terrible scenes of murder and bloodshed and rapine that have ever been looked upon will take place.

"Peace will be taken from the earth, and there will be no place of safety except in the Rocky Mountains. This will cause many hundreds and thousands of the honest in heart to gather there; not because they would become Saints, but for safety and because they would not take up the sword against their neighbor.

The Prophet Joseph Smith was shown the doings of the Negro in America at this time, and the scene was so terrible that he could not bear to look upon it any longer, and he asked the Lord to close this scene from his vision. The race rioting was too horrible to view

P.S. Send behind this entire and next is — FIRST TO the press and all your conference to the friends on your mailing list. C.M.R.

Dear Charley

please make haste to take this Mormon Prophecy, in which I have confidence, to the "associated press" in Boulder asking that it be given their immediate attention. To me it looks as if shortly Washington will be destroyed by atomic atomic Bombs and many will

Perish. Mason Remey
Guardian Head of
the Baha'i World Faith.

The Prophet Joseph Smith was shown the doings of the Negroes[*] in America at this time, and the scene was so terrible that he could not bear to look upon it any longer, and he asked the Lord to close this scene from his vision. The race rioting was too horrible to view. (Norman C. Peirce)

****

Dear Charley,

Please make haste to take this Mormon prophecy, in which I have confidence, to the Associated Press in Boulder, asking that it be given their immediate attention. To me it looks as if shortly Washington will be destroyed by atomic bombs and many will perish. (signed) Mason Remey, Guardian, Head of the Baha'i World Faith.

Brigham Young was therefore instructed to take the Mormons out to the Rocky Mountains to build the Temple for Jesus to return in. They were supposed to go to the salt-lick in Deer Lodge in the Rocky Mountains. Instead Brigham Young took them to Utah to the Salt Lake. When they got there they were half-starved and many wanted to turn back. So Brigham Young decided, Salt Lake, Salt-Lick, What's the difference? and had them all stay in Utah.

Because of all the corruption that Young brought into the Mormon Faith, the Mormons could no longer see that they were in the wrong place. Brigham Young even erroneously built a Temple there with only 6 towers, whereas the Temple prophesied In Ezekiel must have 7 towers with Jachin and Boaz standing by the gate of the east door of Tower #7.

Therefore, it was essential that the reformer Joseph Morris was raised up to separate a group of people who were pure in heart (the Salt of the earth[†]) so that they could accept the true vision of the Mormon prophet George Williams, that the Temple for Jesus to return to had to be in Deer Lodge where the Great Salt Lick is.

Thus It is written: "And I shall make thee a Covenant of Salt forever (Leviticus 2:13; Numbers 18:19)."

THE CITY OF THE GREAT KING

In that region where you dwell [Deer Lodge, Montana], extending East, West, South and North--in this region will come down the City of the Great King [New Jerusalem, the City of Ezekiel's Temple]. (George Williams)

The title "City of the Great King" which Williams used to designate Deer Lodge is quoted by Jesus in Matthew chapter 5 verse 35 in which Jesus identifies "the City of the Great King" with Jerusalem. Of course it is not the physical old Jerusalem which is to be glorified but it is the heavenly New Jerusalem which is to descend from heaven with The Temple of God and the

---

[*] This was written by Norman C. Pierce.
[†] Matthew 5:13.

return of Jesus at its center. Williams foresaw Deer Lodge as the place for the New Jerusalem to be built and the site for the return of Jesus to be. New Jerusalem is described by Ezekiel in the last chapter of his Book (which Includes the 7 towered Temple also depicted in the book of Ezekiel) and is identical to the New Jerusalem mentioned in the 22 chapter of the Book of Revelation.[*]

Nevertheless, the title and prophecy of "City of the Great King" comes directly out of Psalm 48.

PSALM 48

> Great is the Lord and greatly to be praised in the city of our God! His holy mountain, beautiful in elevation, is the joy of all the earth, Mt. Zion[†] in the far north [North America], the City of the great King. Within her citadels God has shown himself a sure defense. (Psalm 48:1-3)

In the videotape tour of the prison, they describe the prison as a citadel just as Psalm 48 prophesies. The sure defense of God is the great and crystal clear proof which will be seen by all the world inculcated in the stone masonry of the prison walls of the "Stone with Seven Eyes" Old Montana State Prison, Ezekiel's Temple. This proof is overwhelming as 'Abdu'l-Baha has revealed that he, Jesus II, the "Distinguished Personage," will reveal himself to such a degree as to bring all under his shadow.

Zion in the far north is Deer lodge which is in the far North West.[‡] Likewise, in Isaiah Jesus II is prophesied to be in the far northwest (Isaiah 49:11-12). In verse 12 of Psalm 48 it is written:

> Walk about Zion, go round about her, number her towers, consider her ramparts, go through her citadels; that you may tell the next generation that this is God, our God for ever and ever. He will be our guide for ever. (Psalm 48:12-14)

"Number her towers" refers to the seven towers of the Temple as described in the Book of Ezekiel which is the seven watch towers on the Citadel of the Old Montana Prison. Thus Zion has seven towers. As one prisoner remarked the Old Montana Prison looks more like a castle for a king than a prison. In reality it is the 7 towered citadel of Zion which is the place where the advent of Jesus II is prophesied to be: Deer Lodge, the City of the Great King.

---

[*] The complete vision of the New Jerusalem in the Rocky Mountains is fulfilled with 12 Gates--12 natural mountain passes--by which the people enter; and covers 10 states with Montana and Colorado being singled out as "Mount Moriah"--the Temple Mount at Deer Lodge--and "Mount Zion" (the place of David's throne) at Chair Mountain located outside Glenwood Springs, CO (see New Jerusalem Map--back cover--for full details).

[†] Zion literally means "the place of David's throne." Wherever the throne of David is located is "Zion."

[‡] The actual throne of King David was located in Deer Lodge during the time that the Guardian of the Baha'i Faith lived at 1200 Main Street, Apt. # 1 in fulfillment of the vision of George Williams and Bible prophecy.

JESUS II IN AMERICA?

The Mormons and the Morrisites were not the first ones to understand that the return of Jesus and the building of the Temple were all to happen in America. On page 60 of C. Leroy Anderson's book, *For Christ Will Come Tomorrow*, he writes:

> Of course, neither the preoccupation with the Second Coming nor the expectation of the transformation of America into a paradise originated with the Mormons. They simply made more specific some already well-developed cultural traditions. Christopher Columbus was certain he had approached paradise upon discovering the New World, for he believed that the fresh water he found in the Gulf of Pariah had as its fountain the four rivers of the Garden of Eden. He believed he was fulfilling prophecy through his discovery and that he was opening the way for the end of the world and ultimately the millennium.

> Mircea, a European historian of religion, writes: "The colonization of the two Americas began under an eschatological sign: people believed that the time had come to renew the Christian world, and the true renewal was the return to the Earthly Paradise...In the eyes of the English; for example, the colonization of America merely prolonged and perfected a Sacred History begun at the outset of the reformation. Indeed the triumphal push of the pioneers toward the West continued the triumphal march of Wisdom and the True Religion from East to West.

> "More than any other modem nation the United States was the product of the Protestant Reformation seeking an Earthly Paradise in which the reform of the Church was to be perfected...It is significant that the millenarist theme enjoyed its greatest popularity just prior to the colonization of America and Cromwell's revolution. Hence, it is not surprising to note that the most popular religious doctrine in the Colonies was that **America had been chosen among all the nations of the earth as the place of the Second Coming of Christ**, and the millennium…would be accompanied by a paradisiacal transformation of the earth, as an outer sign of an inner perfection. As the eminent Puritan, Increase Mather, President of Harvard University from 1685 to 1707, wrote: 'When the Kingdom of Christ has filled all the earth, this Earth will be restored to its paradise state…' the certainty of the eschatological mission, and especially of attaining once again the perfection of early Christianity and restoring paradise to earth, is not likely to be forgotten easily. It is very probable that the behavior, of the average American today, as well as the political and cultural ideology of the United States, still reflects the consequences of the Puritan certitude of having been called to restore the Earthly Paradise." (Mircea Eliade, (1967). "Paradise and Utopia," in Utopias and Utopian Thought. Boston, MA: Beacon Press, pp. 260-69)

> For further discussions of these points see Brodie, *No Man Knows My History*;

Timothy L. Smith, Revivalism and Social Reform; and Ernest Lee Tuveson, Redeemer Nation: The Idea of America's Millennial Role.[*]

All the early American pioneers knew that Jesus would return in America. It was the fundamental belief of all colonial Christians that America is the place! Likewise it was Columbus's expectation to find Jesus here on his discovery of America along with the New Jerusalem, the City of Gold, all built up and ready to go for the Millennium which is the 1000 years of peace on earth. One of the reasons Spain financed Columbus's voyage is that they were hoping he could bring back the gold from the heavenly city to fill the treasury in Spain!

DEER LODGE: THE CITY OF GOLD

According to the Bible, in the Book of Revelation, the City of the Great King, the New Jerusalem is to be built out of gold.

When the Morrisites first came to Deer Lodge they worked in the Placer gold mines at Gold Creek to finance themselves in getting established in Deer Lodge-thus, Deer Lodge is the city built out of gold.

Also, the New Jerusalem (City of Gold) is to have a river of gold flowing out from its center (see Ezekiel 47 and Revelation 21). The Clark Fork River has its origin in Butte and flows through the Deer Lodge Valley right past the Temple on into Missoula and finally to the Pacific Ocean. Gold was first discovered in Montana In the Deer Lodge Valley at the Placer mines in Gold Creek. Gold Creek empties into the Clark Fork thus making it "the river of Gold" prophesied in the Bible which flows out of the Temple in Deer Lodge City, the City of Gold.

THE VOYAGE OF ST. BRENDAN

One of the most popular books in Europe at the time of Columbus, and earlier, was called the *Voyage of St. Brendan*. In the book, Irish monks have a vision of a maiden who describes the United States to them as a great land across the western sea divided in half by a mighty river (the Mississippi). Then she gives them the prophecy that the second coming of Jesus is to be in the US.[†]

---

[*] Anderson, p. 60.
[†] See David R, Greene, (1985). "The Voyage of Bran," in *An Anthology of Irish Literature, Vol. I*, p. 131 ff.

This book was very popular and through its graphic imagery and prophecy prompted both Columbus and the Danish Vikings before him in search of Valhalla to travel to America. The Voyage of St Brendan was written in about 600 AD!

COLUMBUS AND HIS BOOK OF PROPHECY

Columbus came to America looking for the return of Jesus which he knew according to prophecy had to be in America. Columbus was a very religious man and he believed that he was fulfilling prophecy by coming to America. Columbus wrote his *Book of Prophecy* which he gave to the Queen and King of Spain in order to get the money for his voyage. Upon entering the Gulf of Pariah, when he saw the fresh water there, he proclaimed that he had discovered the Paradise of Adam and Eve where he believed he would find Jesus and the Heavenly Temple and the City of Gold, New Jerusalem, and usher in the 1000 years of peace.

Columbus believed that America was prophesied throughout the entire Bible as part of God's Plan and especially mentioned "the coast lands of the sea" in Isaiah chapter 11 and other places.

> Christopher Columbus **from information based upon known and provable facts** drew conclusions which led him unerringly across the vast ocean to the unknown continent of America. ('Abdu'l-Baha, *Baha'i World Faith*, p. 260)

Columbus in Prison

DEER LODGE, MONTANA: THE GALILEE OF THE GENTILES
ISAIAH 9:1-2

> But there will be no gloom for her that was in anguish. In the former time he [Jesus at his first advent] brought into contempt the Land of Zebulon and the land of Naphtali, but in the latter time [right now] he [Jesus II] will make glorious the way of the sea [Columbus's pathway to America], the land beyond the Jordan, [the United States) Galilee of the Nations [Deer Lodge Montana].

> The people that walked in darkness have seen a great light: they that dwell in the land of the Shadow of death, [Hell's gate, between Missoula and Deer Lodge], upon them hath the light Shined. (Isaiah 9:1-2)

In verse 1 of the 9th chapter of Isaiah, he tells us:

> But there will be no gloom for her that was in anguish. In the former time he brought into contempt the land of Zebulon and the land of Naphtali, but in the latter time he will make glorious the way of the sea, the land beyond the Jordan, Galilee of the nations. (Isaiah 9:1)

According to the book of Matthew, the land of Zebulon and the land of Naphtali were brought into contempt in the former time at the first advent of Jesus who was rejected there in Galilee (Galilee is in Naphtali) by his fellow Jews (Matthew 4:15-16). "But In the latter time" at the second coming of Jesus, "he will make glorious the way of the sea, the Land beyond the Jordan, Galilee of the Nations." In the King James Version it says: "Galilee of the Gentiles." "In the former time," at Jesus' first coming, he appeared in Galilee of Israel, not Galilee of the Gentiles. The Jews are not Gentiles. Today Israel is still ruled by a Jewish Government. Jesus will not return to the Galilee of Israel, the Galilee of the Jews, but he is to return at the Galilee of the Gentiles which is located in the Naphtali Valley.

NAPHTALI VALLEY

In Genesis 49:21, in the blessing of the 12 tribes by Jacob: "Naphtali is a hind let loose, that bears comely fawns." The hind is the Asian red deer which is technically called the *Altai Wapiti*. The *Wapiti* is the North American white tailed deer that filled Deer Lodge Valley because of the great Salt Lick and luscious green grass there making it the Happy Hunting Ground in the Sky (Montana) where Valhalla, Ezekiel's Temple, is. Therefore "the Galilee of the Gentiles" is Deer Lodge, Montana, in North America which is the land beyond the Jordan and the land far beyond the sea in the good old US of A.

The Bible is full of numerous prophecies that the return of Jesus will be in America (also symbolized by the eagle and "eagles wings").

Thus, in the latter day (today) he will make glorious (Baha'i) the way of the sea (Columbus' way across the western sea to America) the land beyond the Jordan (the United States) the Galilee of the Gentiles (Deer Lodge, Montana).

PRISON BLUEPRINT OVER 5000 YEARS OLD

The blueprint for the Deer Lodge Prison, The Temple of God, is over 5000 years old. Contained within the solid stone structure of the Great Pyramid of Giza (depicted on the back of the American one dollar bill) is the core blueprint for the Deer Lodge prison given over 5000 years ago! This is the same blueprint that Moses went by to build the core of His Temple (tabernacle).

Moses grew up in Pharaoh's court and could see the great Pyramid out his back window. These blueprints of the Pyramid were also kept in the library of Alexandria which Moses had access to and could read. It is from the Revelation of Moses, through his branch of the Holy Spirit, that Ezekiel received his vision of the future Temple now standing in down town Deer Lodge. Therefore, according to this ancient blueprint that God gave for His future Temple, the prison is divided up into two main sections.

The first section is the main prison yard which is identical to the outer sanctuary, also called the Holy Place. The second section is the maximum security area which is identical to the inner sanctum of the Holy of Holies. Here in the Holy of Holies was placed a box called the Ark of the Covenant which contained the tablets of the law and the scrolls of the Covenant. The maximum security building in the Holy of Holies is the Ark of the Covenant on a gigantic scale. True to its purpose, if a prisoner was sent into the maximum security of the Ark of the Covenant building, he was only allowed to bring Holy Scriptures with him, like a Bible or a prayer book. Likewise this maximum security area (Holy of Holies) was originally the women's prison at one time which, being female, represents the spiritual qualities and attributes of God even as His Law, the New Jerusalem, is to descend like a "bride adorned for her husband" (Revelation chapter 21).

The Holy of Holies is also known as the Presence of God. The way the Temple worked is that only one man, the High Priest, was allowed to go into the Holy of Holies and read the scrolls of the Covenant contained within the Ark (thus a solitary confinement). He would only go in there once a year and then come out and teach the law and guidance of God to the rest of the people. Thus through these three things a) the Temple; b) the Ark of the Covenant; and c) the High Priest, the Presence of God was established in the world.

31

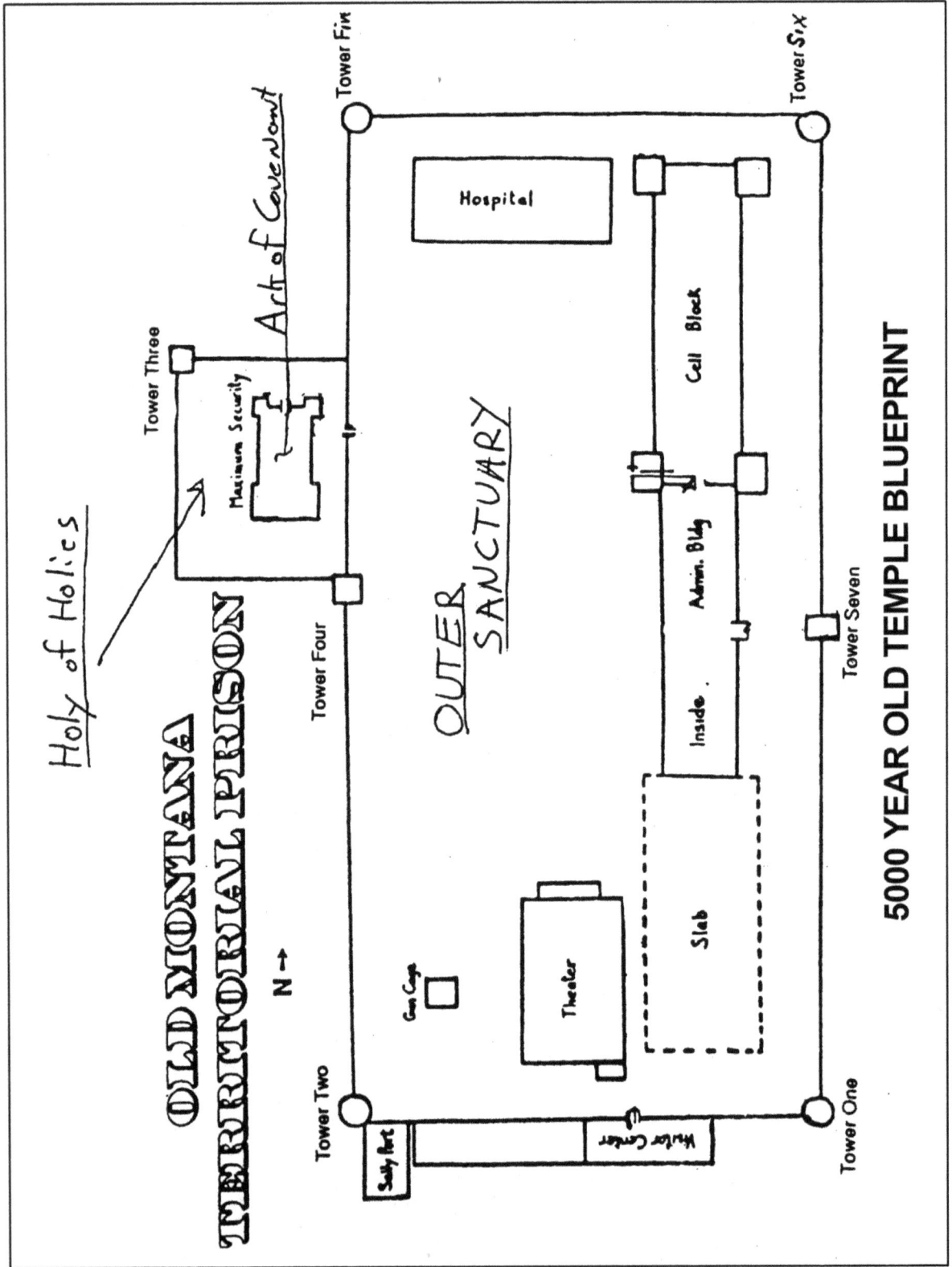

OLD MONTANA TERRITORIAL PRISON

N→

Holy of Holies

Art of Covenant

Maximum Security

Tower Three

Tower Four

Tower Five

Tower Six

Hospital

Cell Block

OUTER SANCTUARY

Admin. Bldg

Inside

Tower Seven

Tower Two

Gun Cage

Theater

Slab

Tower One

Sally Port

Visitor Center

5000 YEAR OLD TEMPLE BLUEPRINT

32

The Temple in Deer Lodge is therefore the most important place on earth and must be upkept and maintained for the next one thousand years of peace, the first thousand years of the Kingdom until the coming of the next Manifestation of God--for without this Temple we would be lacking one of the three essential ingredients and the Presence of God would be lost.[*]

THE PRESENCE OF GOD IN DEER LODGE, MONTANA

While Moses was alive, he was the Manifestation of God and his body was the Temple of God through which the people received the Revelation and the Law. However, Moses knew that he wasn't going to live forever, so he had them build another Temple (the Tabernacle--a tent) to preserve the Presence of God in the world after his departure. This Tabernacle (Temple) replaced the Manifestation of God as being the intermediary between God and man. After Moses, the Ark of the Covenant was placed in the Tabernacle which Joshua put at Shiloh. Four hundred years later King Solomon built a Temple out of stone and moved the Ark of the Covenant to Jerusalem where he had it placed in the Holy of Holies.

However, Moses knew that the people would violate His Covenant and lose everything, including their Temple which would be destroyed--thus they would become apostate and lose the Presence of God. At that time, explained Moses, the Israelites would be scattered all over the world. Through God's infinite wisdom, it was long ago foreordained in His Plan that the true Heavenly Temple of Ezekiel with seven towers, the New Jerusalem, the City of the Great King, should be built in Deer Lodge, Montana. With keen insight and pure vision the Mormon Prophet George Williams, over one hundred years ago, foresaw this great day, which, in its fulfillment, has proven the Morrisites to be right all along, great champions of the Cause of God.

When the Jews violated Moses' Covenant, the curse came upon them and they were apostate. Nebuchadnezzar destroyed Jerusalem in 586 BC. The Temple was destroyed too, and the Ark of the Covenant was lost. Although the Jews returned to Jerusalem with Ezra in 457 BC and had rebuilt the Temple, they didn't have the Ark of the Covenant, so they were apostate and the Presence of God (Shekinah) was lost. Furthermore, they didn't build the second Temple according to Ezekiel's plan.

HIGH PRIEST AFTER THE ORDER OF MELCHIZEDEC

When Jesus Christ first arrived on the scene (Paul explains in Hebrews), he couldn't enter the Temple built by hands, since he was of the blood of David and not of the priestly line from Moses' brother Aaron. But as a High Priest forever after the order of Melchizedec, Jesus Christ put his Covenant in the Temple in the Sky (the Temple in 'heaven' the 'heaven of prophecy')--Montana, thus showing that it is in his Temple, Ezekiel's Temple with seven towers, that he is to return to.

With the advent of the Bab and Baha'u'llah this archetypical Temple was purified and brought to earth. The archetypical Temple is the Manifestation of God. Paul explains that the way into the

---

[*] The scriptures further state, that we are all "living stones" (1 Peter 2:5) in the Temple of God, thus the Presence of God (via the Covenant) pervades the body (temple) of believers as well.

Holy of Holies must first be purified by blood. The Manifestation of the Bab fulfills the prophecy for the cleansing of the outer Temple Sanctuary or Holy Place with the blood of himself and his 10,000 followers who were all martyred. The coming of the Manifestation of Baha'u'llah, the great Davidic King of Kings the whole Bible is talking about, fulfills the prophecy for the second coming of Christ which is the appearance of the Holy of Holies which the return of Jesus the High Priest is to be found standing within.

THREE DATES

In Matthew chapter 24, the apostles come to Jesus Christ and ask him when he will come again. "Tell us, when will this be, and what will be the sign of your coming and the close of the age?" (Matthew 24:3 RSV). In response, Jesus tells them to read the Book of Daniel, for Daniel has already prophesied the date for his return (Matthew 24:15). However Daniel gives not one but three dates for second coming of Jesus Christ.

These last three dates given in the Book of Daniel represent a) the opening of the archetypical Temple brought to earth by the cleansing of the outer sanctuary; b) the second coming of Christ as "the Glory of the Father" (Mark 8:38), Baha'u'llah (Baha = glory; u = of; Allah = Father, Lord and God) which is the appearance of the Holy of Holies; and c) the return of Jesus the High Priest standing within the Holy of Holies to establish His Father's (Baha'u'llah's) Kingdom on earth as it is in heaven.

These dates are given as the 3½ times, 1290 days/years and the 1335 days/years. According to the text of the Bible each day equals a year (Numbers 14:34; Ezekiel 4:6).

I
3½ TIMES: DANIEL 12:7

The 3½ times equals 1260 years. A time is a circle or a cycle of 360 degrees. Three and a half times 360 equals 1260 (3.5 x 360 = 1260). Twelve sixty (1260) AH[*] on the Muslim Calendar is equal to 1844 AD on the Christian calendar. This is the prophesied date for the cleansing of the outer sanctuary of the Temple also given in the Book of Daniel chapter 8 verses 13 and 14. It was in 1260 AH (1844 AD) that the Bab began his mission and purified the sanctuary by his blood and the blood of 10,000 Babi martyrs who were all brutally murdered by the Shi'i clergy of Iran.

> How long shall be the vision concerning the daily sacrifice, and the transgression of desolation, to give both the sanctuary and the host to be trodden underfoot?
>
> And he said unto me, unto two thousand and three hundred [2300] evenings and mornings; then shall the sanctuary be cleansed. (Daniel 8:13-14)

The outer sanctuary represents the Revelation of the Bab (Gate) who was the "John the Baptist" for Baha'u'llah. The Bab proclaimed himself on May 23rd of 1844 AD (1260 AH). He is called

---

[*] AH = After the Hegira, the flight of Muhammad.

the Bab (Door or Gate) because he closed the door to the age of prophecy and opened the door for the age of fulfillment which begins on March 21st, 1844 when the Bab started the Baha'i calendar.

In the Book of Daniel, the cleansing of the sanctuary takes place exactly 2300 years after Ezra repopulated Jerusalem for Temple worship In 457 BC.

There are 456 years from the edict of Artaxerxes (March 21st 457 BC) allowing Ezra to return to Jerusalem until the birth of Jesus. From the birth of Jesus until the Manifestation of the Bab in Persia (1260 AH) there are 1844 years. 1844 years plus 456 years equals the prophesied 2300 years until the cleansing of the sanctuary (1844 + 456 = 2300 years).

Completely separate from the Bab in Persia, was William Miller in America who announced March 21st, 1844 as the date for the second coming of Christ. Also, independent of him and the Bab was Wolf in Asia who announced that 1844 was the correct year. The Templar's in Germany not only knew this date, 1844, but in Isaiah (chapter 35) they read that "the Glory of God" (Baha'u'llah) will be on Mt. Carmel in Israel so they moved from Germany to there. When Baha'u'llah knocked on their front door in Haifa, on Mt. Carmel, in the Holy Land, and announced to them that the prophecies were fulfilled and that He had now come, they told Him to go away.

This same date of March 21st, 1844 is given in the Great Pyramid of Giza at the beginning of the foot of the Great Step of the Altar Stone at the top of the ascending passageway which corresponds to the beginning of the outer sanctuary in the Pyramid. In the Great Pyramid of Giza each pyramid inch represents one solar year in the passageways. The great step of the Altar stone upon which the Bab and his followers are martyred is exactly 1843.218 pyramid inches from the zero point (the birth of Jesus Christ) which gives us the exact date of March 21st, 1844 AD.

"IF ONLY THESE WALLS COULD TALK!"

On a recent TV newscast on the Deer Lodge prison, a reporter commented, "If only these walls could talk!" Unknown to her these walls do talk as the dates for the second coming of Christ and the return of Jesus are inculcated in the stone masonry of the Temple walls just as the dates for the Manifestations of God are found in the Great Pyramid of Giza, the other "Bible in Stone."

THE PRISON OF PROPHECY

Likewise March 21st, 1844 AD, the date when the Bab started the Baha'i calendar, is given in the stone masonry of the Deer Lodge prison. On the outer side of the southern half of the west wall there are 18 pilasters. On the inner side of the southern wall of the Holy of Holies there are 44 nubs. Thus we have 18 and 44 giving us 1844 AD. This section of Wall then leads up around to tower #3 which is March, the third month of the year. Plus, all around the outside of the Holy of Holies supporting tower #3 there are 21 pilasters supporting the outer wall giving us the 21st day of the month. Thus we have 3-21- 1844, or March 21st 1844.

DIAGRAM #1
PYRAMID OF GIZA

"THE BLUEPRINT OF GOD" FOR THE MAKING OF "MAN IN OUR IMAGE" – MANIFESTATIONS OF GOD – (GENESIS 1:26) SEE ISAIAH 19:19. IT IS HIS CHRONOLOGICAL TIME-SCALE ERECTED 5400 YEARS AGO, FOR THE ADVENTS OF HIS MANIFESTATIONS AND OTHER HOLY ONES SENT BY HIM. IT IS THE PATHWAY OF GOD TAKING MAN FROM THE STONE-AGE (IN THE IMAGE OF ANIMAL) TO THE ESTABLISHMENT OF THE KINGDOM OF GOD "ON EARTH AS IT IS IN HEAVEN." THEN ALL MEN WILL BE IN THE IMAGE OF GOD, SEE REVELATION CHAPTERS 21 AND 22.

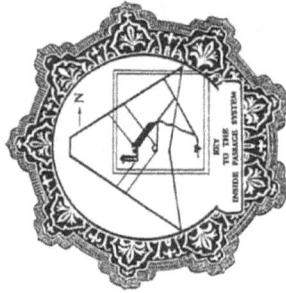

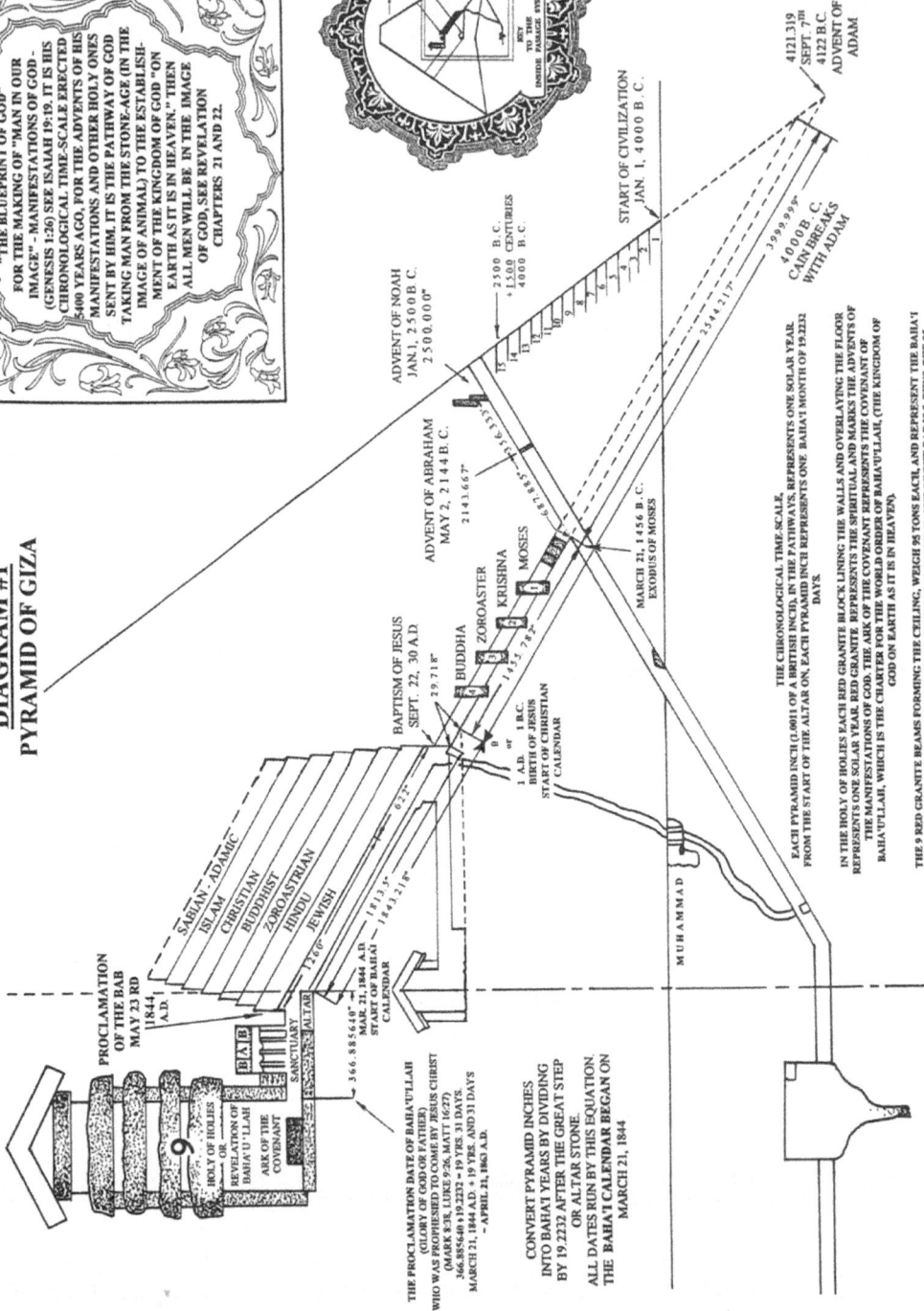

N

KEY TO THE INNER PASSAGE SYSTEM

4121.319
SEPT. 7TH
4122 B.C.
ADVENT OF ADAM

START OF CIVILIZATION
JAN. 1, 4000 B.C.

4000 B.C.
CAIN BREAKS
WITH ADAM

2500 B.C.
+ 1500 CENTURIES
4000 B.C.

ADVENT OF NOAH
JAN.1, 2500 B.C.
2,500,000"

ADVENT OF ABRAHAM
MAY 2, 2144 B.C.
2143.667

ZOROASTER

KRISHNA

MOSES

MARCH 21, 1456 B.C.
EXODUS OF MOSES

BUDDHA

BAPTISM OF JESUS
SEPT. 22, 30 A.D.
29.718"

1 A.D. 1 B.C.
BIRTH OF JESUS
START OF CHRISTIAN
CALENDAR

SABIAN, ADAMIC
ISLAM
CHRISTIAN
BUDDHIST
ZOROASTRIAN
HINDU
JEWISH

PROCLAMATION
OF THE BAB
MAY 23 RD
1844
A.D.

BAB

SANCTUARY
ALTAR

9
HOLY OF HOLIES
OR
REVELATION OF BAHA'U'LLAH
ARK OF THE COVENANT

366. 885640"
MAR. 21, 1844 A.D.
START OF BAHA'I
CALENDAR

THE PROCLAMATION DATE OF BAHA'U'LLAH (GLORY OF GOD OR FATHER) WHO WAS PROPHESIED TO COME BY JESUS CHRIST (MARK 13:32, LUKE 9:26, MATT 16:27) 366.885640 ÷ 19.2232 = 19 YRS. 31 DAYS. MARCH 21, 1844 A.D. + 19 YRS. AND 31 DAYS = APRIL 21, 1863 A.D.

CONVERT PYRAMID INCHES INTO BAHA'I YEARS BY DIVIDING BY 19.2232 AFTER THE GREAT STEP OR ALTAR STONE.
ALL DATES RUN BY THIS EQUATION. THE BAHA'I CALENDAR BEGAN ON MARCH 21, 1844

MUHAMMAD

THE CHRONOLOGICAL TIME SCALE, EACH PYRAMID INCH (1.0011 OF A BRITISH INCH) IN THE PATHWAYS, REPRESENTS ONE SOLAR YEAR FROM THE START OF THE ALTAR ON, EACH PYRAMID INCH REPRESENTS ONE BAHA'I MONTH OF 19.2232 DAYS.

IN THE HOLY OF HOLIES EACH RED GRANITE BLOCK LINING THE WALLS AND OVERLAYING THE FLOOR REPRESENTS ONE SOLAR YEAR. RED GRANITE REPRESENTS THE SPIRITUAL AND MARKS THE ADVENTS OF THE MANIFESTATIONS OF GOD. THE ARK OF THE COVENANT REPRESENTS THE COVENANT OF BAHA'U'LLAH, WHICH IS THE CHARTER FOR THE WORLD ORDER OF BAHA'U'LLAH, (THE KINGDOM OF GOD ON EARTH AS IT IS IN HEAVEN)

THE 9 RED GRANITE BEAMS FORMING THE CEILING, WEIGH 95 TONS EACH, AND REPRESENT THE BAHA'I NUMBER 9, WHICH IS THE VALUE OF BABA IN PERSIAN. THE VALUE OF THE BAB IS 5, THUS, THE 95 REPRESENTS BAHA'U'LLAH AND THE BAB.

36

Thus, from four sources (two in the Book of Daniel) a) Daniel 8:13-14; b) Daniel 12:7; c) the Great Pyramid of Giza, and d) the stone masonry of Ezekiel's Temple in the Sky (Montana)), we get March 21st, 1844 as the date for the cleansing of the sanctuary by the martyrdom of the Bab and 10,000 of his martyr-followers which prepared the way for the opening of the Holy of Holies by the proclamation of Baha'u'llah, the second coming of Christ, in the potency of the "Everlasting Father" seated upon "the throne of King David" (see Is. 9:6-7) on April 21st, 1863.

II
1290 YEARS: DANIEL 12:11

The 1290 days/years (like the 1260) is taken from the Muslim lunar calendar as Baha'u'llah proclaimed Himself in Baghdad, Iraq where they use the Islamic calendar. It was exactly 1290 lunar years from the proclamation of Muhammad, when He did away with the daily sacrifice (the Muslims have no ritual sacrifice), until the proclamation of Baha'u'llah on April 21st, 1863 in the Garden of Ridvan of the Area of Pure Lineage* outside of Baghdad, Iraq.

Muhammad proclaimed himself 10 years before He started His calendar (-10 AH). Thus 1290 minus 10 lunar years gives 1280 AH on the Muslim calendar which is the same year as 1863 on the Christian calendar (1290 - 10 = 1280 AH = 1863 AD).

Likewise, the date for Baha'u'llah is given in the Great Pyramid of Giza at the entrance way of the King's Chamber which is the Holy of Holies. The Baha'i Era and calendar was inaugurated by the Bab who made His proclamation on May 23rd of 1844. The New calendar instituted by the Bab, for the new age, has 19 days to the month, 19 months to the year, and 4 intercalary days (leap years have five days). Thus, one year = 19 months of 19 days plus 4¼ intercalary days (19.2233).

From the start of the sanctuary at the Great Step until the entrance way to the Holy of Holies of the King's Chamber of the Great Pyramid of Giza there are 366.88564 pyramid inches. Because each P. inch from the Altar onward represents a Baha'i month of 19 days plus 1/19 of the 4¼ intercalary days (19.2237), the 366.88564 P. inches from the start of the Altar to the Holy of Holies represents 19 years and 31 days (366.88564 divided by 19.2233 = 19.08547 or 19 1/12th). It was 19 years and 31 days from the Vernal Equinox of March 21st, 1844 AD to when Baha'u'llah entered the Garden of Ridvan and proclaimed Himself on April 21st of 1863 AD'

It was at this exact time, in 1863, that George Williams proclaimed that the return of Jesus would be in Deer Lodge. Thus his prophecies were announced at the perfect time according to the Plan of God.

Likewise, April 21st, 1863 is also given in the stone masonry of the Old Montana Prison in Deer Lodge. On the southern half of the outer West wall we have 18 pilasters. Counting straight north passing through tower number 4 into the Holy of Holies there are 63 nubs on the inner east side of the Holy of Holies. 18 and 63 gives us 1863 AD which passes through the fourth tower being

---

* See Aharon Oppenheimer, (1983). *Babylonia Judaica in the Talmudic Period*. Wiesbaden, DE: Dr. Ludwig Reichert Verlag, for more.

April, the fourth month of the year. Again, surrounding the outer wall of the Holy of Holies we have 21 pilasters giving us April 21st of 1863 (4-21-1863) for the proclamation of Baha'u'llah as the second coming of Christ. This exact time corresponds to the great announcement of Williams over one hundred years ago that the return of Jesus as the High Priest standing in the Holy of Holies of Ezekiel's Temple would be in Deer Lodge, Montana.

TWO CHRISTS

The Bible is very clear that there will be not one, but two Christs to appear in the Plan of God: one entitled the Son, who is to suffer and die (which we may call the "Suffering Messiah") and the other entitled the Father (Isaiah 9:6-7), who is to be seated upon the throne of David and reign forevermore (which we may call the "Reigning Messiah"). In Hal Lindsey's book, *The Late Great Planet Earth*, a number one Best Seller, which has sold over 30 million copies, he describes the "two portraits" of these two Christs.

TWO PORTRAITS

Two completely different portraits of a coming Messiah were described by the Old Testament prophets. The portraits, painted by the sure Hand of God, were placed on the same canvas, framed in one picture...

One portrait of the Messiah depicts Him as a humble servant who would suffer for others and be rejected by His own countrymen. This portrait we may call "the Suffering Messiah" (look into the prophecies of Isaiah 53 for the perfect picture of this Messiah).

The other portrait shows the Messiah as a conquering king with unlimited power, who comes suddenly to earth at the height of a global war and saves men from self destruction. He places the Israelites who believe in Him [Baha'u'llah] as the spiritual and secular leaders of the world and brings in an age free of prejudice and injustice. It's easy to see why this would be the most popular portrait.

We may call this second picture "the Reigning Messiah." We find this description in such prophecies as Zechariah 14 and Isaiah 9:6-7. (*The Late Great Planet Earth*, pp. 18-19)

Christ is a Greek word meaning "anointed one." It is the same as the Hebrew word Messiah which also means "anointed one." The full title is Messiah ben David meaning an "anointed male-sperm descendant of King David."

The kings of Israel were all anointed by the High Priest with olive oil which they used to light their lamps, symbolizing enlightenment through education. However, two descendants of David are prophesied to come and not be anointed by a High Priest with olive oil but to be anointed directly by God with the Holy Spirit and thus be Manifestations of God. It is these two anointed sons of David who are the two Christs. The first is Jesus, being entitled the 'Son,' who is the Suffering Messiah, as He suffered and died. The second is Baha'u'llah being entitled the

38

'Father,' who is the Reigning Messiah. The 'Father' and the 'Son' refer to the respective potencies of their Revelations.

In the Book of Acts, Stephen, gazing into heaven sees these two Christs (two anointed sons of David) and he names them: Jesus and Baha'u'llah.

> But he [Stephen], full of the Holy Spirit, gazed into heaven and saw the Glory of God [Baha'u'llah] **and** Jesus standing at the right hand of God. (Acts 7:55)

Stephen didn't speak English. (At that time the English were still swinging from trees!) In the Galilean dialect of Aramaic that he spoke, "glory" is "Baha," "u" is "of" and "God, Lord and Father" is "Allah." Thus Stephen sees Jesus and Baha'u'llah (The Glory of God) standing at the right hand of God. This is the exact same vision that Joseph Smith had centuries later when he was 14 years old and he saw the two Christs, the Father (Baha'u'llah) seated upon the throne of David (Isaiah 9:6-7) and the Son (Jesus) returned to establish his Father's Kingdom on earth as it is in heaven.

Likewise, Jesus didn't speak English either but spoke the same dialect of Aramaic as Stephen. In Mark 8:38 Jesus prophesies Baha'u'llah by name when He says that "the Son of Man will return in the Glory of the Father (Baha'u'llah)."

THE **TWO** ANOINTED ONES
THAT STAND BY THE LORD OF THE WHOLE EARTH

In Zechariah chapter 4 verse 14, he sees these two Christs, (two anointed descendants of David) standing by the Lord of the whole earth, which is the same as the vision of Stephen of the two Christs and that of Joseph Smith many years later.

> I see, and behold, a lampstand all of gold, with a bowl on the top of it, and seven lamps on it, with seven lips on each of the lamps which are on top of it. And there are two olive trees by it, one on the right of the bowl and the other on the left. And I said to the angel who talked with me, "What are these my lord?"
>
> "These seven are the eyes of the Lord, which range through the whale earth." Then I said to him, "What are these two olive trees on the right and on the left of the lampstand?" And a second time l said to him, "What are these two branches of the olive trees, which are beside the two golden pipes from which the oil is poured out?" He said to me, "Do you not know what these are?" I said, "No, my Lord." Then he said, "THESE ARE THE TWO ANOINTED ONES [TWO CHRISTS] THAT STAND. BY THE LORD OF THE WHOLE EARTH." (Zechariah 4:2-4; 10-14)

This vision of Zechariah is depicted on the State seal of Israel. The seven lamps represent the seven Manifestations of God sent out to all the world who are not descended from David (Adam,

The Coat of Arms for the State of Israel

Zechariah 4:14

"Two Anointed Ones (Two CHRISTS)

The Tree of Light: A Study of the Menorah, the Seven Branched Lampstand, by L. Yardin; ©1971, Horovitz Publishing, London.

Moses, Krishna, Zoroaster, Buddha, Muhammad and the Bab). The two anointed ones are the two Christs, the two anointed sons of David: Jesus Christ and Baha'u'llah (the second corning of Christ).

JACHIN AND BOAZ

In order that we should never forget this important fact that there are two Christs, one entitled the Son and one entitled the Father, we have the two twin pillars of Jachin and Boaz standing before the door of the Temple which likewise represent these two Messiahs: 'J' for Jesus and 'B' for Baha'u'llah.

During the Temple ceremony they used to open the main Temple gate so that the people should be able to see into the Temple but not go inside. When the doors were wide open, between the two pillars of Jachin and Boaz, the people could see the giant menorah with seven candles which is the same view as Zechariah's vision in chapter 4. Likewise at the Deer Lodge Temple, we have these same two pillars of Jachin and Boaz and we also have the seven eyes of the seven watch towers which also represents the seven other Manifestation of God described in Zechariah's vision.

THE EVERLASTING FATHER: BAHA'U'LLAH

Unlike Jesus, who was killed and had no children, it is the mission of Baha'u'llah to be seated upon the throne of David and have a son to continue the Davidic kingship through his genealogy from David. Thus Boaz (for Baha'u'llah) represents the royal lineage and genealogy of David which Baha'u'llah preserves in His Covenant where He appointed His son 'Abdu'l-Baha to be the Center of His Covenant as His successor to the throne of David. Likewise, 'Abdu'l-Baha preserves the Davidic Kingship in the sacred Will and Testament of 'Abdu'l-Baha which is the Charter for the Kingdom of God on earth (see *World Order of Baha'u'llah*, p. 144 for more).

These two documents, the Covenant of Baha'u'llah (*Kitab-i-'Ahd*) written within and the Will and Testament of 'Abdu'l-Baha written on the back, is that scroll in the hand of the one seated on the throne depicted in Revelation chapter 5. When a king sits on his throne he holds a scepter in his hand. This signifies the authority by which he rules. The Covenant and Will and Testament is the scepter of authority by which the Davidic kings rule today. Today, the Davidic kingship through 'Abdu'l-Baha's sons is entitled the guardianship of the Baha'i Faith because their main function is to guard the Faith from corruption, usurpation, mis-interpretations, and violation. Along with their fellow members of the Council--the "House of the Lord" (Is. Ch. 2) entitled the International Baha'i Council/ Universal House of Justice of Baha'u'llah (UHJ)--the foundation of justice and fairness is laid firm and secure.[*]

GENTILES SHALL INHERIT THE KINGDOM

According to the Bible and the Gospel of the Kingdom proclaimed by Jesus Christ, the Gentiles shall inherit the Kingdom. In fulfillment of this and the Shiloh prophecy (Genesis 49:10)--which

---

[*] See UHJ.net and BUPC.org for more.

41

states that the scepter shall pass (by adoption) from between the feet and legs of Judah (between the feet and legs is the reproductive organs)--'Abdu'l-Baha adopted an American, Charles Mason Remey Aghsan, as his son to be the next Davidic king after him and the guardian of the Baha'i Faith. In 1957 when the first guardian Shoghi Effendi died, the worldwide Baha'i community violated the Covenant and said that the guardianship had come to an end. They used a Persian word "Bada" which means that God had broken His own Covenant and that the guardianship of the Davidic kings was ended! How outrageous to call God a liar! God says:

> "I will **not** violate My Covenant, or alter the word that went forth from My lips.
> Once for all I have sworn by My Holiness; **I WILL NOT LIE TO DAVID.**
>
> His line shall endure for ever, his throne as long as the sun before me. Like the moon it shall be established forever; it shall stand firm while the skies endure."
> (Psalm 89:34-37)
>
> I will sing of thy steadfast love, O Lord, for ever; with my mouth I will proclaim thy faithfulness to all generations. For thy steadfast love was established for ever, thy faithfulness is firm as the heavens.
>
> Thou hast said, "I have made a Covenant with My chosen one, I have sworn to David my servant: 'I will establish your descendants [the guardians] for ever, and build your throne for all generations." (Psalm 89:1-4)

In order for someone to be the guardian of the Baha'i Faith, he has to fulfill a two-part criteria. First, he has to be the Aghsan (*ghusn*)[*] son of David through Baha'u'llah and 'Abdu'l-Baha. Second, he has to be appointed by the previous guardian within his lifetime. To be a son and to be appointed are the same two criteria the Davidic kings always had to fulfill in order to ascend the throne of David and be the next king.

Today Charles Mason Remey Aghsan's only son that he appointed within his lifetime is the guardian of the Baha'i Faith.[†] However, at the death of the guardian, Mason Remey Aghsan, the Baha'i Faith came to an end. Only one man, who fulfills the prophecy for the return of Jesus the High Priest and having the "Stone with Seven Eyes" before him (Zechariah 3:9), remained faithful to God under the provisions of the Covenant. He recognized 'Abdu'l-Baha's grandson, the son of Charles Mason Remey Aghsan, Joseph Pepe Remey Aghsan, as the guardian of the Baha'i Faith. Single handedly Jesus II has raised up an entire new creation of over 4000 Baha'is under the provisions of the Covenant and is busy gathering the rest of scattered Israel, the 144,000 promised ones who are the spiritual and intellectual giants, the knowledgeable educators, that will help establish the Kingdom of God on earth.

---

[*] Aghsan is the title "BRANCH" that Baha'u'llah gave to all His male descendants (it is "*ghusn*" in the singular). Baha'u'llah didn't speak English, He spoke Persian and Arabic. It is the mission of Jesus in Zechariah chapter 3 to establish the BRANCH referring to the Davidic Kingship descended from Baha'u'llah and 'Abdu'l-Baha now entitled the guardianship of the Baha'i faith (Zechariah 3:8 KJV). Also Jesus is to establish the courts (Zechariah 3:7) of the Universal House of Justice of Baha'u'llah of which the guardian is the sacred head and irremovable member (the president and Executive Branch of the UHJ) for life.

[†] He was succeeded to the throne of David by his only son in 1994, Ben Joseph Aghsan, the great grandson of 'Abdu'l-Baha.

Thus Jachin, which is "J" for Jesus II, represents that Jesus has returned to establish the royal lineage and throne-line of Baha'u'llah (Boaz) from David in the world.

MADE OF THE SEED OF DAVID

According to Romans chapter 1 verses 3 and 4 of the King James Bible, Jesus Christ is "made of the seed of David according to the flesh" and is only "declared to be" the son of God. In the original Greek manuscripts it says that Jesus is made out of the "sperm" of David. Thus according to the Bible Jesus is a "sperm-child" of his father Joseph who was also of the House and Lineage of King David. Other translations are not as accurate to the truth of this verse--and faithful to the original Greek text here--as is the King James Bible.

The sperm of David is the male-seed whereas the ovum is the female. Mary didn't have the sperm of David: she had an ovum (an egg, not a seed). Therefore Jesus can only be "made of the sperm of David" through Joseph, who was also made of David's seed according to the flesh, being a descendant of David (Luke 2:4). In order to be the Christ (anointed male-sperm descendant of King David) Jesus has to be the physical son of his father Joseph. God is not a descendant of David. In order for Jesus to be the Christ and for the Bible to be true, as it declares Jesus is made of the seed (sperm) of David, then he must be. But how can this happen if Mary had a virgin birth?

THE VIRGIN BIRTH

In order for a baby to be born, both a sperm and an ovum must be present in the womb for conception to take place. Yet Mary was a virgin and she gave birth to baby Jesus. In fact many women give birth all the time and they are virgins!

Being a virgin means that a person has never had sexual intercourse. The legal and medical definition of sexual intercourse is "penetration." Penetration takes place when the male sex organ penetrates the female sex organ. Yet the sperm have little tails like a polliwog; and they can swim. Without a penetration a woman can still become pregnant and yet be a virgin and have her hymen intact. In Dear Abbey's article (on the next page) she explains that "as impossible as it may sound, in the medical literature can be found cases where there has been no penetration--the girl remained a virgin, but after engaging in heavy petting, she found herself pregnant."

Whether or not it was heavy petting or something else, that's the Holy Spirit's business. However it happened, Jesus is made of David's seed through Joseph, thus making Him the Christ, the anointed male-sperm descendant of King David. To deny that Jesus is made of the "seed of David" (Gk: *sperma*) is to deny that he is the Christ. This is anti-Christ, he who denies that Jesus is the Christ in the flesh--"made out of the seed [*sperma*] of David" in the flesh (1 John 2:22; Romans 1:3-4 KJV).

43

ADVICE & CONVERSATION

Pregnancy-prevention advice sought

ABIGAIL VAN BUREN
DEAR ABBY

DEAR ABBY: I am a 19-year-old college student, and even though I've dated quite a bit, I'm rather naive about sex. I am still a virgin and hope to remain one until I marry. Don't get me wrong, I'm no "Goody Two Shoes," but I don't want to risk an unwanted pregnancy.

I'm dating a guy right now who has been around. He knows how I feel about sex before marriage, so he's never pressured me to go all the way, but I've come closer with him than I have with any other guy. I'm ashamed to tell you how far we've gone, but I'm still a virgin (I think).

A long time ago you explained how a virgin could get pregnant. I'm sorry I didn't save it, but I never dreamed I'd need it.

Well, last night I was with this guy and things really got out of hand. Everything happened so fast. Please run that piece again about how a virgin can get pregnant. I'm worried.

B., ST. PAUL

DEAR B.: The piece is from my booklet, "What Every Teen-ager Ought to Know." Many junior and senior high school teachers wrote to say that they had read it aloud to their students:

How to get pregnant

One of the questions I have been asked often by teens is: "How far can I go without getting pregnant?"

That is not a dumb question. It's a very intelligent one. A lot of kids get aroused by just lying close to each other while kissing. Then they just naturally proceed to the next step, which is petting.

Sometimes they remove some of their clothing because it's "in the way," or they burrow underneath it to explore each other's bodies with their hands. This is known as heavy petting, or "doing everything else but."

The technical (and legal) definition of sexual intercourse is "penetration." (The male's sex organ must penetrate the female's.) However, as impossible as it may sound, in the medical literature can be found cases where there has been no penetration — the girl remained a virgin, but after engaging in heavy petting, she found herself pregnant.

How can that be? Simple.

The boy and girl were lying very close to each other (unclothed), doing "everything but," when a small amount of sperm leaked out ... near (not inside, but very close to) the girl's vagina. The sperm got into the moisture around the vagina and found its way up into it, and fertilized the egg.

VIRGIN BIRTH

THE GENEALOGY OF JESUS CHRIST AND BAHA'U'LLAH

According to the Bible Jesus is descended from David through David's son Nathan (Luke 3:31). Nathan never sat upon the throne of David and neither did any of his descendants. David gave the throne to Nathan's brother King Solomon. Jesus knew that he was descended from Nathan and that he did not sit upon the throne of David. Therefore Jesus said, "My Kingdom is not of this world" (John 18:36).

Baha'u'llah is descended from King David through King Solomon and the royal line of Exilarchs who remained in Babylon all the way up to the present century. "Exilarch" means Exiled Monarchs of King David or Monarchs of King David in Exile.

EXILARCHS

When Ezra returned to Jerusalem, from Babylonian captivity, he only brought a small group of people with him. The majority of Jews remained in Babylon Including the Davidic Kings in exile called Exilarchs (exiled monarchs of David). The first Exilarch Jehoiachin had four sons. The first three died before he did thus passing the throne to his fourth son Shenazzar. Zerubbabel, the son of Shealtiel the first son, didn't inherit the throne of David so he also returned to Jerusalem to be governor. None of Zerubbabel's descendants sat upon David's throne either.

The Exilarchs remained in Babylon (in the Area of Pure Lineage) until 817 AD, when the great grandson of Exilarch Bostanai, Isaac Iskoi ben Moses, was converted to Christianity and Islam by the 8th Imam Ali ar-Rida. The Imam presented the proofs of prophecy from the Old Testament that the Jewish king in exile could accept since these proofs were given by Moses and the prophets from his own Holy Book. From these proofs the Exilarch recognized the truth of Jesus Christ and Muhammad and accepted both Christianity and Islam. The Imam then told the Exilarch to move to Mazindaran where he would be safe. The Exilarch returned to Babylon in the Area of Pure Lineage and was able to convert over 800 Jews who went with him into northern Iran. There the Exilarchs became the Kings of Mazindaran seated upon David's throne and ruled for one thousand years. Amazing to scholars, even to this day, is the length and accuracy of the genealogies kept by the dynasties in Mazindaran.

Exactly one thousand years after the Exilarchs moved to Iran, in 1817 AD, Baha'u'llah was born. His family preserved their genealogy all the way back to David whereas the genealogies in the time of Christ were all burned when Titus destroyed Jerusalem in 70 AD.

Baha'u'llah is therefore seated upon David's throne as the "Reigning Messiah" prophesied in Isaiah chapter 9 verses 6 and 7, whereas Jesus, who was not seated upon the throne of David, cannot fulfill this mission. If Jesus were to return right now on a cloud in the sky, he would still not be seated upon David's throne. The most he could do is proclaim Baha'u'llah who does.

ISAIAH 9:6-7

According to the prophecy of the "Reigning Messiah" in Isaiah 9:6-7, the "Reigning Messiah" is called the "Everlasting Father" and the "Prince of Peace." Jesus Christ was not the Father, he was the Son. He said, "The Father is greater than I" (John 14:28). When they asked Jesus Christ if he was the "Prince of Peace" He said: "Do not think I have come to bring peace on earth; I have not come to bring peace but a sword" (Matthew 10:34). As a matter of fact, Jesus told his apostles to sell their coats and buy swords! (Luke 22:36). That is why Peter had a sword to cut off the ear of the High Priests servant (Matthew 28:51).

Also, the Reigning Messiah is to be seated upon David's throne and bring peace and a government to all the world. Jesus never sat upon the throne of David and if He claimed to be the Prince of Peace then he would have been the biggest failure in the history of the world because we have had nothing but the bloodiest wars over the last 2000 years since his advent; and most of them have been fought between the Christians!

KING AND HIGH PRIEST

Although Jesus Christ was not seated upon the throne of David, he was still a King, but his Kingdom was not of this world whereas Baha'u'llah's Kingdom is of this world. Jesus Christ however was BOTH King and High Priest rolled up into one.

He was both the Christ, the King, being an anointed son of David, and he was also a High Priest after the order of Melchizedec as Paul explains in Hebrews chapters 5, 6 and 7.

The original High Priest after the order of Melchizedec was Shem, who in fact was known as Melchizedec. Shem/Melchizedec lived after the flood, had Nimrod[*] brought to justice, built the city of Jerusalem and founded an academy there where Abraham, Isaac and Jacob studied to learn of the Revelation of the One True Invisible God. Like Jesus Christ, Shem was both King and High Priest rolled up into one. He was the King of Jerusalem and the High Priest Melchizedec.

After Shem/Melchizedec, who was both King and Priest, a thousand years later we have the split of these roles into two separate persons of David who was King in Jerusalem and Zadok who was High Priest (1 Kings 1 :34).

---

[*] Nimrod is the ancient corruptor of God's true religion. He is the Lucifer of the Bible (the historical "king of Babylon," see Isaiah 14:4) who was once a mighty angel helping to establish the Revelation of Adam. He then wanted to be a god for himself and fell from his high station. Nimrod is known by many names in the different languages. In Rome he is called Saturn, which is where we get the word Satan from. Nimrod is the Satan of the Bible. After Shem/Melchizedec had Nimrod brought to justice at the Ancient World Court of 72 judges--that sentenced him to death--his wife, Semiramis, concocted the trinitarian religion of the Papacy that corrupted Christianity which Martin Luther fought against. Luther was unable to remove the trinity from the churches and told his friend that he left it up to future generations. Today almost all religions of the world are corrupted by the Babylonian triune god lie (trinity) of Semiramis who is known as "the whore of Babylon" in the Book of Revelation (see *The Two Babylons* by Hislop). Thus, with the Trinitarians in power, Satan (Nimrod's religion) rules the world. The advent of Jesus II is essential to bind Stan up so we can have the Kingdom of God on earth and the first 1000 years of peace before Satan is again loosed and finally destroyed.

Likewise with the second coming of Jesus Christ we have this same split into two separate Individuals fulfilling these two roles. The first Promised One fulfills the prophecies for the second coming of Christ, the King; and the other Promised One fulfills the prophecies for the return of Jesus the High Priest spoken of in Zechariah Chapter 3 (See diagram on page 183 for more).

Baha'u'llah fulfills the prophecies for the second coming of Christ because Baha'u'llah is the King of Kings seated upon the throne of David and descended from King David. But Baha'u'llah does not fulfill the prophecies for the return of Jesus the High Priest. The return of Jesus the High Priest happens in Deer Lodge, Montana, where Dr. Jensen was wrongfully incarcerated. It is Jesus II, the High Priest after the order of Melchizedec, who comes to establish his Father's (Baha'u'llah's) Kingdom on earth as it is in heaven.

Thus, with the second coming of Christ, the King, Baha'u'llah is a different person than the return of Jesus the High Priest ("the lamb"), just as Zadok, the High Priest was a different person than David who was his King in that time.

THE RETURN OF JESUS STANDING IN THE HOLY OF HOLIES

As Baha'u'llah fulfills the prophecy for the second coming of Christ (the anointed son of David), His establisher is the return of Jesus the High Priest standing within the Holy of Holies which is spiritually the Revelation of Baha'u'llah and physically Ezekiel's Temple in Deer Lodge. The date we have for the return of Jesus the High Priest (after the order of Melchizedec) is given in the third date prophesied in the last chapter of the Book of Daniel as "he who waiteth and cometh to the thirteen hundred and thirty five days."

III
1335 YEARS: DANIEL 12:13

In *Baha'u'llah and the New Era* by John Esselmont, in the chapter entitled 'Prophecies of Baha'u'llah' subsection, 'Coming of the Kingdom of God,' 'Abdu'l-Baha explains:

> In the last two verses In the Book of Daniel occur the cryptic words: "Blessed is he that waiteth and cometh to the thousand, three hundred thirty-five days. But go thy way till the end be: For thou shalt rest, and stand in thy lot until the end of the days."

> Many have been the attempts of learned students to solve the problem of the significance of these words. In a table talk at which the writer was present, 'Abdu'l-Baha reckoned the fulfillment of Daniel's prophecy from the date of the beginning of the Muhammadan Era.

> 'Abdu'l-Baha's Tablets make it clear that this prophecy refers to the one hundredth anniversary of the Declaration of Baha'u'llah in Baghdad, or the year 1963:--

"Now concerning the verse in Daniel, the interpretation whereof thou didst ask, namely, 'Blessed is he who cometh unto the thousand three hundred thirty-five days.' These days must be reckoned as solar and not lunar years. For according to this calculation a century will have elapsed from the dawn of The Son of Truth, then will the teachings of God be firmly <u>established</u> upon the earth, and the divine light shall flood the world from the East even unto the West. Then on this day, will the faithful rejoice!"

Thus the date that 'Abdu'l-Baha gives for the establisher of the Baha'i Faith is April 21st, 1963 AD, which is the 100th anniversary of the proclamation of Baha'u'llah in Baghdad.

The beginning of the Muhammadan Era came in 628 AD with the Victory of Muhammad. It was in 628 that Muhammad wrote His Victory Surah. If we add the 1335 years to 628 AD we get 1963 AD, the date given by 'Abdu'l-Baha.

Likewise, April 21st, 1963 AD is given in the Great Pyramid of Giza. The King's Chamber of the Holy of Holies is made entirely out of solid red granite blocks. There are exactly 100 red granite blocks forming the walls of the Holy of the Holies of the Great Pyramid representing the 100 years from the proclamation of Baha'u'llah to the advent of Jesus II. When we add these 100 blocks/years to the date for the proclamation for Baha'u'llah on April 21st, 1863 we get the prophesied date of April 21st, 1963. On this date Jesus II, the High Priest spoken of in Zechariah Chapter 3, was first opposed by Satan, who is Rex King. The Guardian of the Baha'i Faith, Mason Remey Aghsan, subsequently rebuked Rex King designating him to be the Satan of our age.

Likewise, the date given in Daniel for the 1335 years is found in the stone masonry of the Old Montana State Prison in Deer Lodge.

The nubs on the stone wall serve the purpose of supporting the 1000 white granite slabs (representing the 1000 years of peace) that cap the entire wall around the prison yard. There are an average of 6 to 7 nubs on the outside of the wall between the pilasters which give the wall support. These nubs can be seen at the top course of the wall directly below the white granite slabs that cap off the stone wall.

Altogether there are a total of 1963 nubs! Furthermore, when we add up the total nubs on the East wall plus the total nubs on the West wall, plus the total nubs inside the Holy of Holies of the Maximum Security, we get 1335! The total nubs on the South wall plus the total nubs on the North wall plus the total nubs on the outside of the Holy of Holies gives us 628! 628 AD (the date for the Victory of Muhammad) plus 1335 years gives us the prophesied date of 1963 (628 + 1335 years = 1963 AD). Then if we count the 21 pilasters surrounding the Holy of Holies which pass through tower #4 we get April, the 4th month, on the 21st day of 1963!

The total nubs on both the inside and the outside of the East wall (593) plus the total nubs on the inside and outside of the West wall (598) plus the total nubs on the inside of the Holy of Holies (Maximum Security, which used to be the women's prison--representing the spiritual--) (144)

PRISON OPEN 108 YEARS (1871-1979)

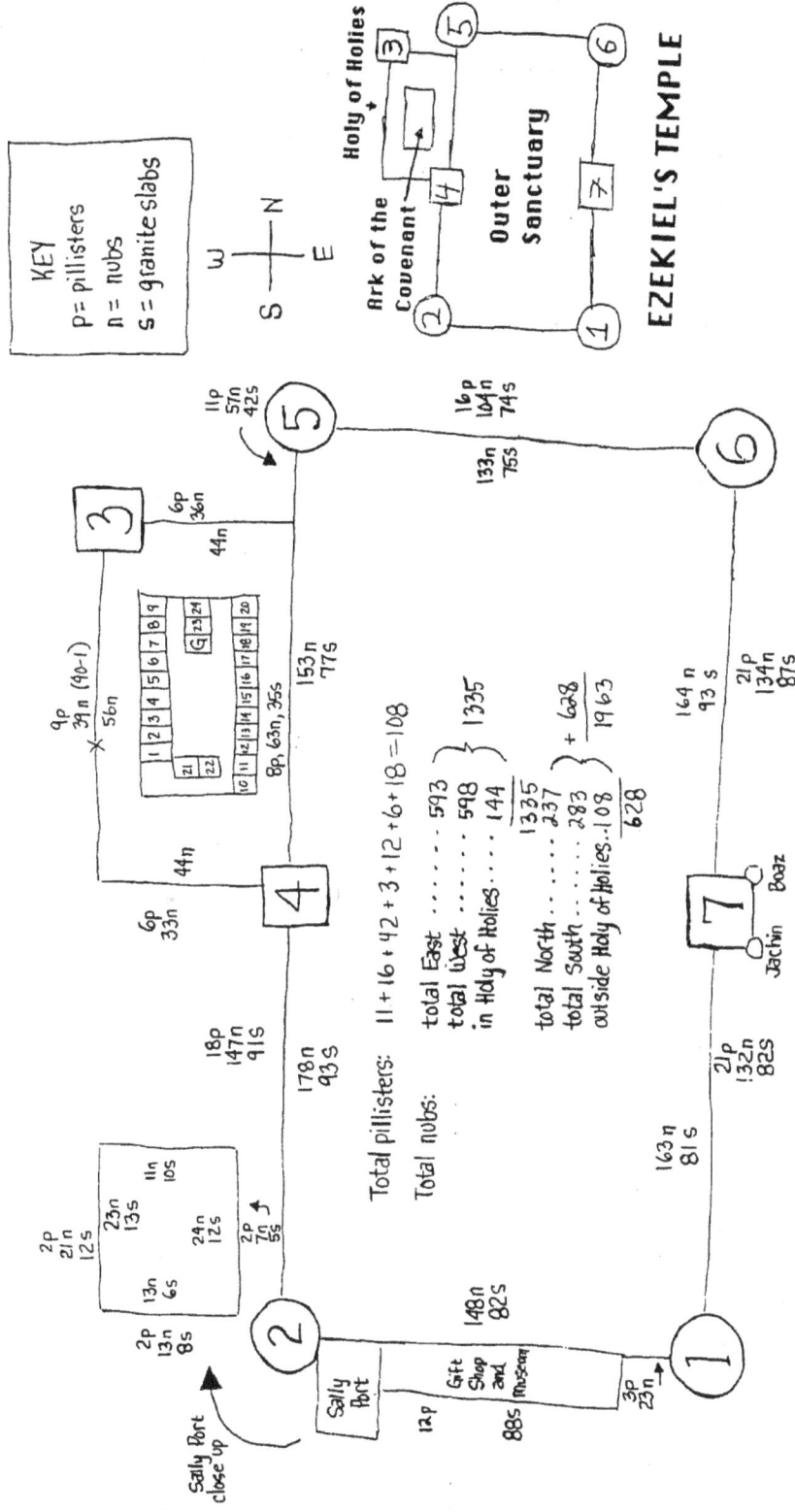

KEY
p = pillisters
n = nubs
s = granite slabs

N
W E
S

2p
21n
12s

2p
13n
8s

23n
13s

13n
6s

11n
10s

24n
12s

2p
7n
5s

Sally Port
close up

Sally Port

12p

148n
82s

Gift
Shop
and Museum

88s

3p
23n

178n
93s

18p
147n
91s

6p
33n

4

44n

9p
39n (40-1)
56n

1	2	3	4	5	6	7	8	9
10	11	12	13	14	15	16	17	18	19	20
21	22			G	23	24				

8p, 63n, 35s

153n
77s

6p
36n

3

44n

11p
57n
42s

5

16p
104n
74s

133n
75s

6

164 n
93 s

21p
134n
87s

Total pillisters: 11 + 16 + 42 + 3 + 12 + 6 + 18 = 108

Total nubs:
total East 593
total West 598
in Holy of Holies 144
                        1335
                        237   } 1335

total North 237
total South 283   } + 628
outside Holy of Holies . . 108
                         628
                        1963

163 n
81 s

2lp
132n
82s

7

Jachin   Boaz

EZEKIEL'S TEMPLE

Holy of Holies

Ark of the
Covenant

4

Outer
Sanctuary

7

3

5

6

2

1

THIS "STONE WITH SEVEN EYES" ZECHARIAH 3:9 KJV
(JESUS II, April 29th, 1971)

equals 1335 nubs. The total nubs on the inner and outer North (237) plus the total on the South inner and outer (283) plus the total nubs on the outside of the Holy of Holies (108) equals 628. 628 AD is the year Mohammed wrote his Victory Surah. 1335 + 628 = 1963 AD. Thus, the masonry of the Old Montana State Prison corresponds exactly to 'Abdu'l-Baha's prophecy of this date for the return of Jesus in *Baha'u'llah and the New Era*. (For a complete detail of all the nubs see illustration previous page 49.)

APRIL 29th, 1971

Furthermore, there are 108 red granite stones which form the floor of the King's Chamber and Holy of Holies in the Great Pyramid. When we add these 108 to the proclamation of Baha'u'llah at the entrance of the Holy of Holies, we get April 21st, 1971. Then there are 9, ninety-five ton, red granite beams that form the ceiling of the King's Chamber in the Pyramid. The first beam is the first day of Ridvan on April 21st and the 9th beam is the ninth day of Ridvan of April 29th. Thus we get April 29th, 1971 AD, the date for the proclamation of Jesus II standing in the Holy of Holies with the "Stone with Seven Eyes" before him. This is the date given on the priceless painting hanging in the Old Montana State Prison!

It wasn't even until June of 1990 that we measured and counted the things on the prison, yet these dates were given and known to all Baha'is Under the Provisions of the Covenant for over 20 years!

All together, surrounding the outside of the prison, there are 108 pilasters! When we add these 108 pilasters to the proclamation of Baha'u'llah when George Williams gave his prophecy in 1863 (a date also given in the prison), we get 1971. Surrounding the Holy of Holies on the outside, there are the 21 pilasters which pass through tower #4 giving us April 21st PLUS there are 8 more pilasters on the INSIDE of the Holy of Holies, giving us a total of 29 pilasters making it April 29th, 1971, the date given on the painting hanging in the prison and in the Great Pyramid of Giza for when Jesus II the High Priest was proclaimed suddenly in his Temple, Ezekiel's Temple in Montana, the Old Montana State Prison in downtown Deer Lodge!

Also, surrounding the outside of the Holy of Holies we have 108 nubs. There were originally 109 but God broke one off the middle of the back of the outside Maximum Security wall in an earthquake.[*] This broken-off nub is highly obvious as the only crack in the entire wall. It goes straight through to the other side and from top to bottom. It was formed when God broke this nub off in the earthquake at the prison thus making 109 minus 1 which is 108. When God wants accuracy He gets it!

Likewise, the prison was open a total of 108 years making it the longest operating prison in American History! Also, there are a total of 54 nubs on the north side and the east side of the Ark of the Covenant building. If we were to double this number for all four sides we get 54 x 2 which equals 108! This prison has the mark of God written all over it. "If only these walls could talk!" and so they do--loud and clear!

---

[*] An earthquake is considered to be an act of God.

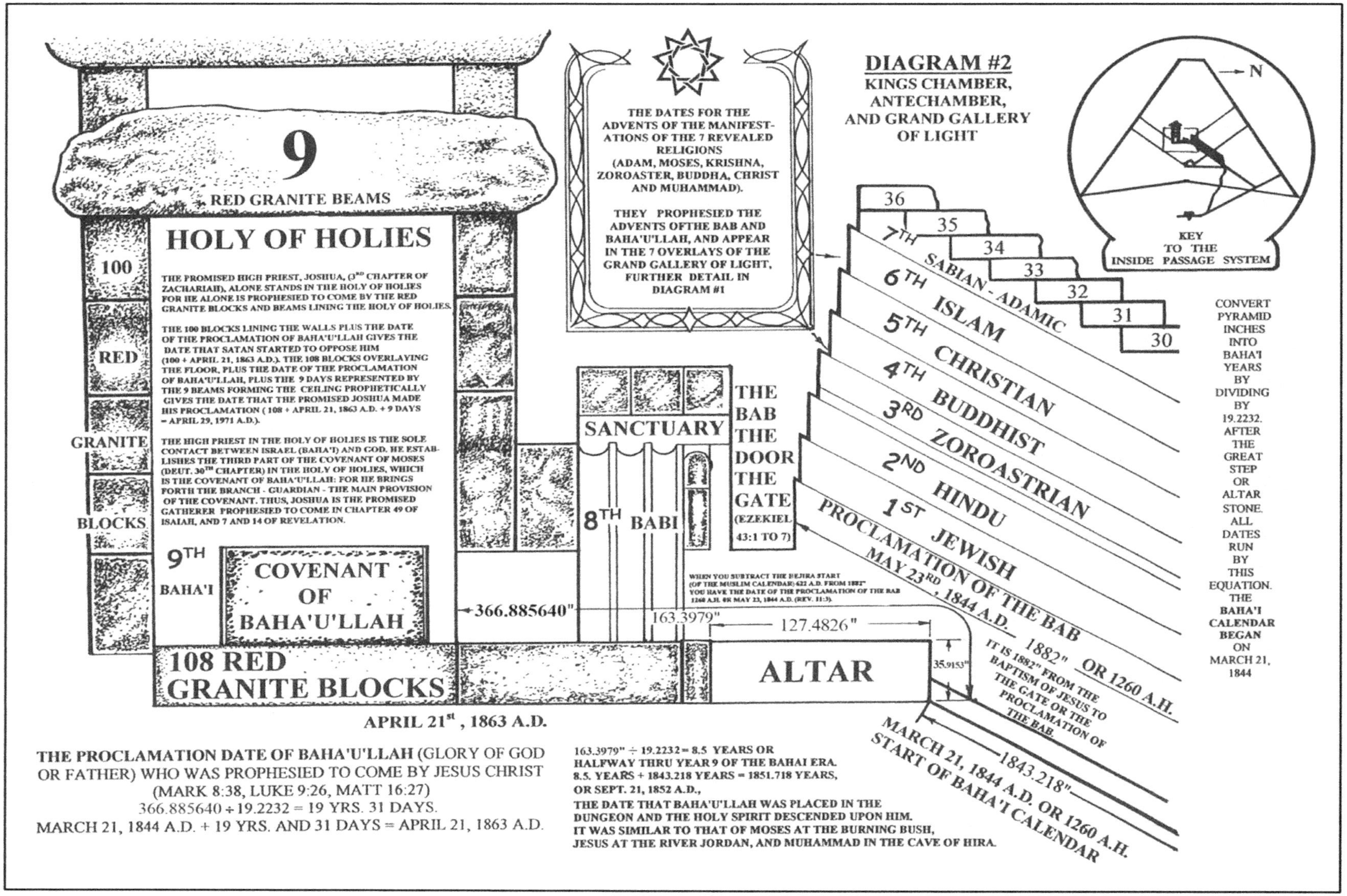

DIAGRAM #2
KINGS CHAMBER, ANTECHAMBER, AND GRAND GALLERY OF LIGHT

KEY TO THE INSIDE PASSAGE SYSTEM

CONVERT PYRAMID INCHES INTO BAHA'I YEARS BY DIVIDING BY 19.2232. AFTER THE GREAT STEP OR ALTAR STONE ALL DATES RUN BY THIS EQUATION. THE BAHA'I CALENDAR BEGAN ON MARCH 21, 1844

36 35 34 33 32 31 30

7TH SABIAN - ADAMIC

6TH ISLAM

5TH CHRISTIAN

4TH BUDDHIST

3RD ZOROASTRIAN

2ND HINDU

1ST JEWISH

PROCLAMATION OF THE BAB
MAY 23RD, 1844 A.D.

1882" OR 1260 A.H.

1882" FROM THE BAPTISM OF JESUS TO THE PROCLAMATION OF THE BAB

1843.218" OR 1260 A.H.

MARCH 21, 1844 A.D. START OF BAHA'I CALENDAR

THE DATES FOR THE ADVENTS OF THE MANIFEST-ATIONS OF THE 7 REVEALED RELIGIONS (ADAM, MOSES, KRISHNA, ZOROASTER, BUDDHA, CHRIST AND MUHAMMAD).

THEY PROPHESIED THE ADVENTS OF THE BAB AND BAHA'U'LLAH, AND APPEAR IN THE 7 OVERLAYS OF THE GRAND GALLERY OF LIGHT, FURTHER DETAIL IN DIAGRAM #1

THE BAB

SANCTUARY

THE DOOR

THE GATE (EZEKIEL 43:1 TO 7)

8TH BABI

WHEN YOU SUBTRACT THE BEDRA START (OF THE MUSLIM CALENDAR) 622 A.D. FROM 1882 YOU HAVE THE DATE OF THE PROCLAMATION OF THE BAB 1260 A.H. OR MAY 23, 1844 A.D. (REV. 11:3).

163.3979"

ALTAR

35.9153"

127.4826"

366.885640"

RED GRANITE BEAMS

HOLY OF HOLIES

9

100 RED GRANITE BLOCKS

THE PROMISED HIGH PRIEST, JOSHUA, 6TH CHAPTER OF ZACHARIAH, ALONE STANDS IN THE HOLY OF HOLIES FOR HE ALONE IS PROPHESIED TO COME BY THE RED GRANITE BLOCKS AND BEAMS LINING THE HOLY OF HOLIES.

THE 100 BLOCKS LINING THE WALLS PLUS THE DATE OF THE PROCLAMATION OF BAHA'U'LLAH GIVES THE DATE THAT SATAN STARTED TO OPPOSE HIM (100 + APRIL 21, 1863 A.D.). THE 108 BLOCKS OVERLAYING THE FLOOR, PLUS THE DATE OF THE PROCLAMATION OF BAHA'U'LLAH, PLUS THE 9 DAYS REPRESENTED BY THE 9 BEAMS FORMING THE CEILING PROPHETICALLY GIVES THE DATE THAT THE PROMISED JOSHUA MADE HIS PROCLAMATION (108 + APRIL 21, 1863 A.D. + 9 DAYS = APRIL 29, 1971 A.D.).

THE HIGH PRIEST IN THE HOLY OF HOLIES IS THE SOLE CONTACT BETWEEN ISRAEL (BAHA'I) AND GOD. HE ESTAB-LISHES THE THIRD PART OF THE COVENANT OF MOSES (DEUT. 30TH CHAPTER) IN THE HOLY OF HOLIES, WHICH IS THE COVENANT OF BAHA'U'LLAH FOR HE BRINGS FORTH THE BRANCH - GUARDIAN - THE PROMISED PROVISION OF THE COVENANT. THUS, JOSHUA IS THE PROMISED GATHERER PROPHESIED TO COME IN CHAPTER 49 OF ISAIAH, AND 7 AND 14 OF REVELATION.

9TH BAHA'I

COVENANT OF BAHA'U'LLAH

APRIL 21st, 1863 A.D.

108 RED GRANITE BLOCKS

THE PROCLAMATION DATE OF BAHA'U'LLAH (GLORY OF GOD OR FATHER) WHO WAS PROPHESIED TO COME BY JESUS CHRIST (MARK 8:38, LUKE 9:26, MATT 16:27)

366.885640 ÷ 19.2232 = 19 YRS. 31 DAYS.

MARCH 21, 1844 A.D. + 19 YRS. AND 31 DAYS = APRIL 21, 1863 A.D.

163.3979" ÷ 19.2232 = 8.5 YEARS OR HALFWAY THRU YEAR 9 OF THE BAHAI ERA. 8.5 YEARS + 1843.218 YEARS = 1851.718 YEARS, OR SEPT. 21, 1852 A.D.,

THE DATE THAT BAHA'U'LLAH WAS PLACED IN THE DUNGEON AND THE HOLY SPIRIT DESCENDED UPON HIM. IT WAS SIMILAR TO THAT OF MOSES AT THE BURNING BUSH, JESUS AT THE RIVER JORDAN, AND MUHAMMAD IN THE CAVE OF HIRA.

THE GOLDEN CRITERIA

Many people can come up claiming a lot of different things. But God has given us a way to tell the charlatans from the real McCoys! This way is a scientific method for recognizing God's promised ones that no Christian can deny without blaspheming the Holy Spirit.

In order to know anything, there has to be a criteria. Almost everything has a criteria. If you want to know what time it is you look at your watch, what the temperature is you look at a thermometer, etc...

Yet it can't be just any criteria; it has to be qualified--A Golden criteria. The GOLDEN CRITERIA given in the Bible for recognizing one sent by God is set forth in the first three chapters of the Book of Matthew. It is fulfilling prophecy! The only reason Jesus Christ believed in himself as the Messiah and the only reason that we should accept him is because he fulfilled prophecy! He never said, "Hey look at me, I'm Jesus!" and neither does Jesus II. Jesus' claim was that he fulfilled prophecy--very specific prophecies such as his prophesied name, prophesied date, prophesied address and prophesied mission, just like a divine business card.

For example, if you were in Timbuktu and needed to see a doctor and you had their business card you could see who they were (what their name is), where they worked (their address), what their office hours were (date) and what kind of doctor they were (profession). You would catch a plane from Timbuktu and fly to anywhere in the world, let's say Missoula, Montana. You could get off the plane find the exact address 19 Main St. Office #1 and knock on the door. Then a person would answer the door wearing a white doctors smock and you could say, "Are you Dr. So and So, who works at 19 main street office #1, Missoula, Mt, who is a Doctor and is open between the hours of 6:00 to 8:00?" and they said "Yes," would you call them a LIAR? No. Certainly not!

This is how accurately the ones sent by God fulfill prophecy. In order to qualify this criteria we have the Book of Matthew which gives this proof for Jesus Christ. First we see he is descended from David so we know he is the Christ (anointed descendant of David). Then he gives us his name Jesus/Immanuel: both names mean "God with us" in different languages. Then he gives the address, Bethlehem. Everyone knows Jesus was born in Bethlehem. Then in Daniel chapter 7 he gives the date of the 490 years (70 weeks of years) taken from 457 BC at the time of Ezra which gives us the date of 34 AD for when Jesus fulfilled his mission to be crucified on Calvary cross at the age of 33. Only one man in all history can and will ever fulfill that type of accurate proof of all four points: as that specific name, that specific place, that specific date for that specific mission. As that date has come and gone no one else can ever fulfill those. This QUALIFIES the criteria and is set forth as the right criteria to recognize the second coming. Denying the criteria is the same as denying God.

	490 YEARS	
	(7 weeks + 62 weeks + 1 week = 70 weeks)	

7 Weeks	62 Weeks	Week of the Covenant	
49 years	434 years - an Interim Period	3 1/2 years	3 1/2 years
The Rebuilding of Jerusalem Order of Artaxerxes	From the Rebuilding to the last week (49 + 434 = 483 years)	⇐ John the Baptist Jesus Baptised ⇩	Jesus Crucified ⇨ ✝ Cross

457 B.C.　　408 B.C.　　　　　　　27 A.D.　　30 A.D.　　34 A.D.

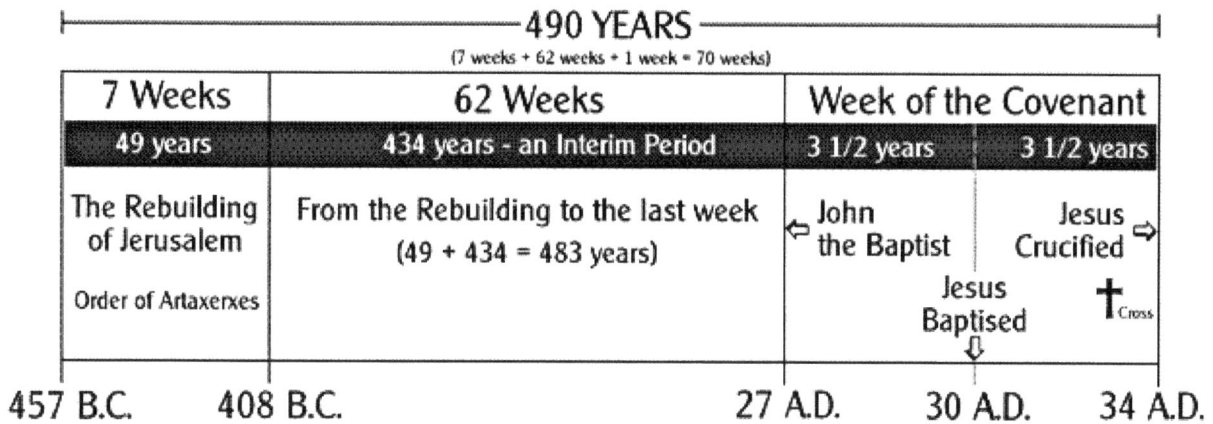

Likewise, Baha'u'llah fulfills this Golden Criteria of His prophesied name, prophesied date, prophesied address and prophesied mission. He is prophesied by Jesus as Baha'u'llah (the Glory of the Father) in Mark 8:38. His address is given in Isaiah as to be on Mount Carmel in Israel where He established the Baha'i World Center which stands on that mountain today (Isaiah 35). His date is given in Daniel and the Pyramid and the Temple in Deer lodge as April 21st, 1863, the day of His proclamation. His mission is given in Isaiah 2: to set up the Universal House of Justice; in Isaiah 9:8-7: to be seated upon the throne of David; and in Isaiah 11: that He is a descendant of David come forth out of the "stem of Jesse"* which is the male sex organ from which David came. Thus Baha'u'llah fulfills this same GOLDEN CRITERIA given in the Bible and explained in *Some Answered Questions* (SAQ) by 'Abdu'l-Baha, the book of proofs for Jesus and Baha'u'llah. Likewise does the return of Jesus (Jesus II) fulfill this same GOLDEN CRITERIA!

From a letter written not too long ago, Dr. Leland Jensen explains his own situation and proof:

> And he shewed me Joshua the high priest standing before the angel of the Lord, and Satan standing at his right hand to resist him. (Zech. 3:1 KJV)

The New Catholic Version, by Douay states:

> And the Lord shewed me Jesus the high priest standing before the angel of the Lord: and Satan standing at his right hand to resist him. (Zech. 3:1)

Joshua is the Aramaic for the Hebrew word *Yehoshua*, and Jesus is the Greek word for Joshua. On April 21st, 1963, the date given by Daniel and explained by 'Abdu'l-Baha for "Blessed is he who waits and comes to the 1335 days" or years, I fulfilled this prophecy when Rex King, who was designated Satan by the Guardian, started to bad-mouth me in his attempt to usurp the guardianship. At that time I was the only protector of the guardianship.

> And the Lord said unto Satan, "The Lord rebuke thee, O Satan; even the Lord that hath chosen Jerusalem rebuke thee: is this not a brand plucked out of the fire?" (Zech. 3:2)

---

* Jesse is the father of King David.

The Lord that was the guardian of the Baha'i Faith said to Satan, as expressed in a letter that I received as follows:

(See LETTER FROM GUARDIAN on facing page)

I entered the Montana State Prison August 8th, 1969 on a charge that in prison jargon is called a "dirty jacket." I was shunned and ridiculed by the prisoners chanting "dirty jacket, dirty jacket." I was unable to make but very few friends because of this.

Several months after this, in a prison cell, I received this letter from Mason Ramey through his correspondent Charlie Murphy. I received it in the morning mail and read it, remarking to myself "That it was about time that the guardian did something about Rex." This was just before I went to lunch, leaving this letter laying on my desk. After returning from lunch I found a King James version of the Bible (which is still in my possession), opened to the third chapter of Zechariah, lying next to the letter from Mason. Someone had tossed it into my cell between the bars and it just happened to land open to that chapter. Later I found that Merle Gardipee, one of the few friends that would talk to me, was going out on parole and as it was customary to leave a token of remembrance to friends, and knowing that I was religious, he left me his Bible.

I took this as an omen: that this didn't just happen by chance, but that there was a special message for me. So I began to read from the third chapter of Zachariah. After reading the first verse I thought it was a history of a priest by the name of Joshua that had the same thing happen to him as happened to me. So I continued on and read the second verse.

> And the Lord said unto Satan, "The Lord rebuke thee, O Satan; even the Lord that hath chosen Jerusalem rebuke thee, is this not a brand plucked out of the fire?" (v. 2)

While I was reading this, the letter from Mason stating that Rex King was Satan was laying alongside of the Bible and I could see the strong similarity of the text of the Bible and Mason's strong rebuke of Rex King. I could hardly believe that the same thing had happened to Joshua. But then when I read the third verse it was just too much.

> Now Joshua was clothed with filthy garments, and stood before the Angel. (v. 3)

It stated that Joshua also had a filthy garment, like me. But it didn't say that Joshua was dirty, just his garments, like me. I was in the prison on a travesty of justice, undoubtedly like Joshua in the text. The parallel was so striking that I could hardly believe it. The scenario was so grasping as to seize my very soul. What was to happen next?

> And he answered and spake unto those that stood before Joshua to take away the filthy garments and unto Joshua he said I have caused thy iniquity to pass from thee. (v. 4)

FOR DR. LELAND JENSEN • FROM THE GUARDIAN OF THE ORTHODOX BAHA'I

WORLD FAITH

C/O American Express Co.
Florence, Italy
13 September 1969

Some days ago I was astonished to have word that Rex King
and two young men were below wishing to see me! I sent word
back to say I would like very much to see Rex but not the young
men. I had things I wanted to tell him but not them.

I told Rex that no one of my acquaintance has a better knowledge of the Baha'i Faith than he but as Lucifer in Old Testament Days chose to put truth aside and espouse the cause of Satan,
so had he done in these modern times decided that he would now
assume the station of Satan in these days of the Dispensation of
Christ, despite the many opportunities that I had given him to
change his evil ways, yet he refused and blatantly insisted on
maintaining his satanic intentions, therefore obliging me to cast
him out from all association in this world with the people of God
that included the life to come as well as his life here upon
earth - his station to be ever and eternally that of Satan for
evermore.

Charles Mason Remey

He had the iniquity to pass from Joshua by having those that stood before him to remove the iniquity. As Joshua was a high priest, then all the true body of Israel would stand up for him. Then I started thinking, 'Am I going to have my iniquity removed in the same manner?' I looked up the word *iniquity* and one of the meanings is: "violation of right or justice; unjust thing." I was in prison by a violation of my rights which was an unjust thing. I presumed that the same thing applied to Joshua. Was I, too, going to have people stand before me and remove this unjust thing? And how are they going to do this? So I went on to the next verse:

> And I said, Let them place a fair mitre upon his head, and clothed him with garments. And the angel of the Lord stood by." (v. 5)

The "fair mitre" is the head dress of the high priest, indicating that he possessed the knowledge of the High Priest standing in the Holy of Holies. He is the one that has the greatest knowledge of the Revelation of the Manifestation. It is something like when you graduate from College and they put a mitre board on your head, indicating that you had passed the course.

> And the angel of the Lord protested unto Joshua, saying, "Thus saith the Lord of Hosts [Baha'u'llah]; if thou wilt walk in my ways, and if thou wilt keep my charge, then thou shalt also judge my house, and shalt also keep my courts, and I will give thee places to walk among these that stand by." (vs. 6, 7)

If Joshua will walk in the ways, and keep the Covenant and Testament of the Lord of Hosts, and pass all the tests, the sting operations, then Joshua will judge His house and shall also keep His courts. Up until this time I was still thinking this was history, and I saw that it was in parallel to me as it fit my situation entirely. But then when I read the next verse the light bulb turned on.

> "Hear now, O Joshua the high priest, thou, and thy fellows who sit before thee: for they are men wondered at: for, behold, I will bring forth my servant the BRANCH." (v. 8)

When I read this verse I said, "O My God, O My God!" and tears rolled down my cheeks: with me saying, "This isn't history, this is a prophecy; for the BRANCH is 'Abdu'l-Baha." He is the Most Great Branch, branched from the Ancient Root, and Joshua was going to reestablish him in the world, for the whole Baha'i world had failed the tests and violated all the provisions of His Sacred Will and Testament. He is the "servant, the BRANCH," for the name, 'Abdu'l-Baha translated into English is "the servant of Glory."

Then another thunderbolt hit me. Does all this mean that I am the fulfillment of this prophecy? By no means! I would have nothing to do with that. Not even in my fondest dreams did I ever picture myself in such a position. So I totally rejected this thought as it was abhorrent for me to even think of such a thing. So I read on.

> "For the stone that I have laid before Joshua; upon one stone shall be seven eyes: behold, I will engrave the graving thereof, saith the Lord of hosts [Baha'u'llah], and I will remove the iniquity of that land in one day" (v. 9)

I said to myself, "How could a stone have seven eyes? A potato may have seven eyes, but how could a stone?" I looked all around me and I couldn't see a stone with 7 eyes. So I began to rejoice: "Ah ha! See, I don't have a stone with 7 eyes before me, so I couldn't be the Joshua" and I began to rejoice all the more. But then something happened to me that has never happened before and has never happened since.

I had a visitation. An angel stood before me. I couldn't see the angel but I knew he was an angel, for he spoke to me and said, "You are the Joshua in this prophecy and you will establish the BRANCH." I was startled and dumbfounded. Then in the frenzy of the moment I thought he was saying something like that I was the Branch. As I knew that I could neither be the Branch nor the guardian, I then perceived that he was an evil spirit and that he was an evil spirit who was sent to beguile me. So I told him so. I told him that he was an evil spirit and that I wanted nothing to do with him. I told him to depart and he did.

I was shaken! I looked in the mirror and I was as white as a sheet, and the hair was standing up on my body. But I was relieved, for the last thing that I wanted in my life was to perform in such a role.

I wasn't working at the time, for the institution doctors had ruled that because of the health condition that I had at the time, I didn't have to work. This was just fine with me for it gave me time to study and write. However, due to the pleas of the deputy warden, I took a job for a while in the fingerprint department in the administration building.

Shortly after that while I was working I heard one of the guards say, "They are bringing another one in through Tower 7." I looked out the window and I saw a sheriff bringing another prisoner in through Tower 7. The towers are two stories, with the guard on the second floor with some sort of an assault weapon. On the first floor there were two doors: one to the street and the other to the prison yard. The guard unlocks the door to the street from the second floor, and lets them enter. Then he locks the door and opens the other to the yard in the same way.

After looking out the window I turned to the guard that had just made the announcement and asked him, "Is that a stone wall?" And he answered, "Every bit of it." I then Inquired, "How many towers are there on that stone wall?" He said, "Seven." I said, Where is the eighth one? He said, "There is no 'eighth one.'" I then pressed further saying, "Maybe there are only six, perhaps one isn't functional?" He informed me that there were indeed seven, and that they were all functional. That's when I swooned, for no matter which way I turned I had the "Stone with Seven Eyes" before me. I told the guard that I was faint and that I had to go lie down. He dismissed me so l went back up to my room.

I then started to read the 3rd chapter of Zechariah from other versions (translations). I found that where it said "that land" in the 9th verse of the King James version, in most of the other versions it said, "the land," such as in the Moffat Translation and in the St. Joseph Textbook Edition Bible, the New English Bible and others. Then I said, "O My God! O My God!" For "the land" is my name. When I was teaching the Baha'i faith during the world crusade of Shoghi Effendi on two French-speaking Islands in the Indian Ocean, many people told me that my name "Leland" means "the land." "Le" is the French article for the English article "the."

As you can see by the parallels between Joshua and myself, Leland, that the iniquity of "the land" and the iniquity of the Joshua is the same iniquity: "the dirty garment." At that point all the evidence was in. There was nothing more. Indeed I was the promised return of Jesus. Not Jesus the Messiah, a Manifestation, but Jesus the High Priest standing alone in the Holy of Holies.

I decided to keep it a secret, like an ostrich sticking his head in the sand, hoping that it would go away as a bad dream. Perhaps another person would come up with the true claim. So I told no one.

But right after that my wife, the other Knight, that never missed a weekend coming down to the prison from Missoula, ninety miles away, to visit me, said to me: "Le,"* (inadvertently, she always called me Le, meaning "the-," or 'God,' as in theology, or theogony: a genealogy of the gods) "... something has happened to you." I asked her what happened to me. She said that was what she wanted to know. I told her that nothing had happened to me. She said, "Yes something has, and I want you to tell me." I said, "It is nothing." Then she said, "Oh, so there is something!" She said, "You have never kept anything from me, so I want you to tell me." I told her I would, but I had her swear that she would never tell anyone. So I told her that I fulfilled the third chapter of Zechariah, and I read it to her, telling her that I was to establish the Kingdom of God on Earth that was brought by Baha'u'llah. She told me that she knew this all the time. She said that I was the only one in the world who knew the Baha'i faith, and that I was the only one who could establish it. Then she reminded me that I was one of the two knights of the Lord that 'Abdu'l-Baha had indicated would establish "the Kingdom."

There is one more thing that I need to cover, and this pertains to the time frame of the "one day" of the ninth verse of Zechariah 3. This is the Day of Joshua. It starts when he began his mission on April 21st, 1963, the date given by Daniel and ratified by 'Abdu'l-Baha; and it finishes with the establishment of the Kingdom. This is certified by the 10th verse:

> "In that day," saith the Lord of Hosts (Baha'u'llah], "shall ye call every man his
> neighbor under the vine and under the fig tree. (v. 10)

So the Day of Joshua (Jesus) is from April 21st, 1963 until the end of this century,† with the establishment of the Kingdom.

Harry Stroup was reading the Bible from cover to cover. I still had kept my identity a secret. When Harry came to Zechariah 3 he came to me and told me that I was the Joshua (Jesus) of Zechariah chapter 3 and that this prison wall with its seven towers was the "Stone with Seven Eyes." I was shocked. He had figured it all out. I told him that I was. This happened in the afternoon of April 29th, 1971. We had a Baha'i fireside that evening with about thirty-five

---

* Pronounced: LEE.
† This was dramatically fulfilled in the "10 days" of 9-11-2001 to 9-21-2001: when God "brought forth" His "servant THE BRANCH" (Zech. 3:8 KJV) and the identity of the living Davidic King, the great-grandson of 'Abdu'l-Baha was made known.

inmates attending. I made my proclamation before them and they all believed. Right after that about a third of the inmates became believers.

There is one more thing to add on the address of the "Stone with Seven Eyes:" It is between two mountains of copper or bronze. In the Hebrew lexicon the word for copper, brass, and bronze is the same word:

> And I turned, and lifted up mine eyes, and looked, and, behold there came four chariots out from between two mountains; and the mountains were mountains of brass. (Zech. 6:1)

> Then I answered and the said unto the angel that talked with me, "What are these, my Lord?" And the angel answered and said unto me, "These are the four spirits of the heavens, which go forth from standing before the Lord of all the earth." (Zech 6:4, 5)

The two largest deposits of copper in the world are at Butte and Lincoln, Montana. The Montana State Prison at Deer Lodge, Montana is between these two mountains of brass.[*]

NAME, DATE, ADDRESS AND MISSION OF JESUS II

Thus we have **THE NAME**: for the advent of Jesus (Joshua) the High Priest is "the land" (Leland), for the "iniquity of Joshua" [Jesus II] (Zech. 3:4) and the "iniquity of the land" (Zech. 3:9) is the same "iniquity," the dirty garment (Zech. 3:3, 4). "Iniquity means "a gross injustice." The dirty jacket was the gross injustice inflicted against Leland.

THE ADDRESS: for the advent of Jesus II is the "Stone with Seven Eyes" (Zech. 3:9); which is located in the mountains of the Northwest (Isaiah 49:12). It is just about half way between the two largest mountains of brass or copper in the world (Zech 6:1), of which "the four spirits of the heavens, which go forth from standing before the LORD of the whole earth" (Zech. 6:5).

THE DATE: for the advent of Jesus II is 1963 AD as given by the prophet Daniel (Dan. 12:12), and the 100 Granite Blocks lining the Holy of Holies when he stood before the Angel of the Lord and Satan was at his right hand to oppose him. And his Proclamation on April 29th, 1971 AD with the "Stone with Seven Eyes," indicated by the 108 Granite Blocks overlaying the floor of the Holy of Holies and the nine Granite Beams forming the ceiling of the Holy of Holies.

THE PROFESSION: of Jesus II is to establish in the world the "Twin Institutions" (The Universal House Of Justice and the guardianship) of the BRANCH--'Abdu'l-Baha (Zech. 3:8). Thus, Jesus II has charge of the courts (Zech 3:7) of the Universal House of Justice and establishes the BRANCH of the guardianship of the Baha'i faith (Zech. 3:8) which is the president of the Universal House of Justice seated upon the throne of David which is to last forever. Thus the GOLDEN CRITERIA proves Jesus II as authentic.

---

[*] Excerpted from a letter by Dr. Leland Jensen in his own words.

AUTHENTICITY IS THE CRITERIA FOR BELIEVABILITY

When Jesus taught, they asked by what authority he does these things (Matthew 21:23), for he has never studied with us (John 7:15). The clergy claimed authority as they were ordained, but Jesus outranked them for he fulfilled prophecy. He was prophesied by his prophesied name, prophesied date, prophesied address and prophesied mission. Jesus said, "My teaching is not mine, but his who sent me" (John 7:16).

With the coming of the Bab (Door) and Baha'u'llah (Glory of the Father; Mark 8:38) the same claim was made by the clergy. Their authority was that they were ordained, asking by what authority do They teach, they have never studied with us. However, the Bab and Baha'u'llah outranked the clergy as they fulfilled prophecy coming in the prophesied name, prophesied date, prophesied address and prophesied mission.

Today they ask: by what authority does Dr. Leland Jensen teach. The clergy and the "Hands" claim authority for they were ordained. But Leland outranks them for he fulfills the prophecies to establish the Kingdom (the Davidic Throne) and the courts (Zechariah 3:7) of the Universal House of Justice that Baha'u'llah revealed (Isaiah 2). Baha'u'llah sat upon the Throne (Isaiah 9:6-7) and it continued through the BRANCH of the guardianship (Zechariah 3:8). There are more prophecies in the Bible for Leland than anyone else. As with Jesus I, the Bab and Baha'u'llah, he was prophesied by his prophesied name, prophesied date, prophesied address and prophesied mission.

Yet now in 1990 after the passing of Comet Austin, the Sign of the Son of Man in Heaven, we see that he was likewise prophesied by George Williams over one hundred years ago and that the Temple in Deer Lodge is Ezekiel's Temple in Montana! This is the greatest proof of all! It is the clearest prophecy yet. And as prophecy outranks ordination, the world rejoices that the promise of God is true and the words of the prophets are fulfilled! Yes, Jesus has suddenly returned to his Temple (Malachi 3:1)! Authenticity is the criteria for believability!

COMET AUSTIN

It was not until the passing of Comet Austin in May 1990 (The Sign of the Son of Man in Heaven) that Dr. Leland Jensen, who fulfills these prophesies for Jesus II, found out that over 100 years ago George Williams, the Lord's messenger, had prophesied him to "suddenly return to his temple" (Malachi 3:1) in Deer Lodge, Montana. Furthermore, the state flower of Montana is the bitterroot which is called the Resurrection flower!

Thus a completely independent source from the GOLDEN CRITERIA proves this great message that Dr, Leland Jensen proclaimed on April 29th, 1971.

On April 29th, 1971, Jesus II, the establisher of the Baha'i Faith, was standing in the a) **Holy of Holies** (the Revelation of Baha'u'llah) in the Deer Lodge Temple with seven towers as b) **High Priest** after the order of Melchizedec, holding the sacred scroll of the c) **Ark of the Covenant** written within and on the back (the Covenant of Baha'u'llah/Will and Testament of 'Abdu'l-Baha) in his hands as the Lamb before the throne (see Revelation 5:1-11). Thus with the Holy of

Holies, Ark of the Covenant and return of Jesus the High Priest we have the Holy Presence of God established in the world among us again! God is with us!

TOWER #7: THE EAST GATE

In Ezekiel chapter 44 it states Jesus II shall enter his Temple by the east gate (tower #7) and that after he enters by it that gate shall be shut forever.

> Then he brought me back to the outer gate of the sanctuary (tower #7), which faces east; and it was shut; And he said, "This gate shall remain shut; it shall not be opened, and no one shall enter by it; for the Lord, the God of Israel, has entered by it; therefore it shall remain shut." (Ezekiel 44:1-2)

In 1969 several weeks after Dr. Jensen was put into the Old Montana Prison on a bum rap it was announced over the loud speaker that they were going to close the Prison for ever more and open a new modem facility elsewhere in the Valley. Thus when the one who fulfills the prophecy for Jesus II with the knowledge of God (Baha'u'llah's Revelation) entered the Temple through the east gate of tower #7 between the two pillars of Jachin and Boaz, it was announced that "This gate shall remain shut" and the prison was closed and the east gate of Tower #7 was locked for ever more.

Today tower #7 is still locked. The entrance to the prison that the people now pass through for tours is through the museum and gift shop on the south side. Tower #7, the east gate, is shut tight as a drum!

24 THRONES SURROUNDING THE THRONE OF GOD

Inside the Ark of the Covenant building of the Maximum Security, there are 24 cells surrounding the guard's cage representing the 24 thrones surrounding the throne of God in Revelation chapters 4 and 5. According to Revelation chapter 5, it is Jesus II, the Lamb, who is before the throne and among the 24 elders. Here, standing before this physical representation of the guardianship seated upon the throne of David surrounded by the 24 elders of the Baha'i Faith, Jesus II, the High Priest after the order of Melchizedec became cognizant of his mission at the start of 1970 and thus took the scroll out of the right hand of him who is seated upon the throne (the throne of David), the guardian of the Baha'i Faith Charles Mason Remey Aghsan, to establish his Father's (Baha'u'llah's) Kingdom in the world.

Throughout his mission he is still holding this scepter of the scroll written within (the Covenant of Baha'u'llah) and on the back (the Will and Testament of 'Abdu'l-Baha) in his hand. As the seven seals are opened these correspond to world events and important happenings within the faith. From between these two mountains of Brass/Copper, Lincoln and Butte, Montana, from out this prison, which is the seven-towered Ezekiel's Temple in Montana, the proclamation of the Kingdom of God is going forth.

REVELATION 4:1-6
24 thrones surrounding the Throne of God (Guard's Throne)
In the Ark of the Covenant Building

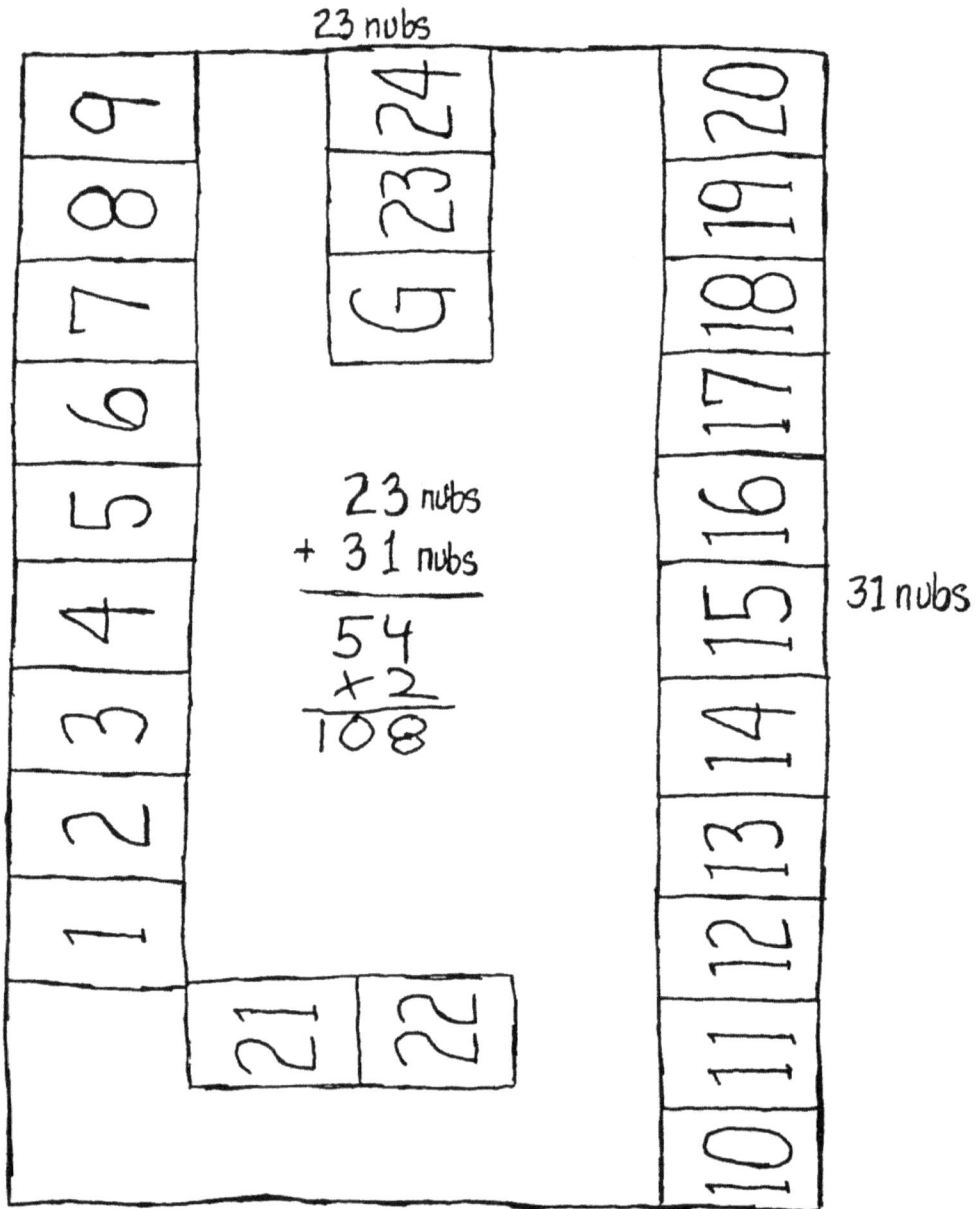

23 nubs

```
23 nubs
+ 31 nubs
─────────
  54
  ×2
─────────
 108
```

31 nubs

Throne of God = Throne of David
The Guard is the Guardian of the Bahai Faith

CONCLUSION

When the Morrisites went to Deer Lodge they built a little white church called the Lord's House. The reason they built it was so that Jesus could live there upon his return. However, Jesus is not prophesied to come to a church and live there as the Morrisites thought. He is prophesied to come suddenly to his Temple (Malachi 3:1). The book of Ezekiel shows him enter his temple through the east gate (Ezekiel 44)! Malachi reaffirms this truth in the third chapter of his book. The Jewish literature states that it must be in the temple!

> "The rebuilding of the Temple must always be awaited (Sab. 12b and other passages). God will erect the future Temple **even before** the Kingdom of David has been reestablished and his descendants restored to office (Yer. M.S. 5:2, 56a)." (*The Universal Jewish Encyclopedia, Vol. 10*, p. 197)

And the temple must be as Ezekiel prophesied it!

> "The Temple will appear as Ezekiel prophesied it" (Raphael Patai, *Messiah Texts*, p. 144)

Therefore, if Jesus has not returned to the prison in Deer Lodge, which is Ezekiel's Temple, then the Morrisites moved to Deer Lodge for nothing!

ADDENDUM

After the writing of this book further research was done and more prophesies of George Williams have been discovered. C. Leroy Anderson, author of *For Christ Will Come Tomorrow*, placed his original source material in Utah State University in Logan, Utah in the special collections section of the library. There were six boxes filled with original material: letters, interviews, etc., including original epistles of George Williams and his prophecies which were circulated among the Morrisites in handwritten form. The things we discovered during our four hours there are only a small scratch on the tip of the iceberg.

To prepare the world for the glorious appearance of the Return of Jesus, God has sent us the forerunner, George Williams. His prophecies foretell the place, date and mission of Jesus II in great detail as well as explaining the cleansing catastrophes which will take place before God's magnificent Kingdom is established.

The genealogy of Jesus II is one of the brilliant signs given to us through a dream of the King of Denmark as explained by George Williams.

> You also wish me to say something of a notice regarding the King of Denmark, the Dream, The Vision of the King's, was this:
>
> In the Early dawn of Morning as he lay upon his bed **a company of poorly clad men** [prisoners] with staves in their hands and without shoes, entered his palace without ceremony. The vision continued until the King saw himself in his Grand Reception Room with his Kingly robes on and a crown upon his head he attempted to Order these Strangers to withdraw but was speechless. The Company began to remove the ornaments in the room, Casting them from the window and approaching the King **removed his robes and crown and clothed him as they themselves were clothed** [prophetic for a descendant of the King to wear the "dirty garment"*], placing him in the midst and one who was called Seth [Joseph Morris] stood up.
>
> At this moment came a man's Hand through the ceiling of the Room handing Seth a roll of Parchment in which was written in glowing letters which Seth unfolded and read before the King, saying, "These are Ministers of the Holy One of whom you have heard: hear them! The High and Holy One has sent them with the Covenant and the Law that whoever obeys and is faithful shall be brought before the Highest and Ordained a King, a Priest or Ruler or Celestial Glory when mortality and the thing there of are passed away with you. **For behold you are a the Royal Line of heavenly Priesthood [the return of Jesus as a High Priest after the Order of Melchizedec is from the royal genealogy of the Kings of Denmark]** and elected to sit in your place to be of advantage to the Work of Redemption in the hands of the Holy One!"

---

* Zechariah 3:3, 4.

Then this sent unto you and Knowledge shall be given unto you. First through them and then through other means appointed by the Highest and see you tell not the priest or the wicked for they will labor to turn your heart away from the Truth with threats of Rebellion but stand fast and Listen not for the Highest is sufficient to bear you up and his Wisdom shall shine upon you. Be not afraid and my servant Seth shall not give you a seal and a sign and the Hand withdrew and the speaker who was Seth then called upon the fruits of the Earth to appear and after a melodious Anthem was sung by an unseen band they appeared grove after grove of trees in full fruit of every color which could be tasted in passing by the King and Company No agent was seen conducting, but self moving in utmost order.

After these had passed were seen streams of delicious Lovely Flowers entering and passing through as the trees had done blooming their Fragrance would be felt by all the company and through the foliage of flowers could be seen the band of players of music **A Celestial Band of Females in robes of exceeding whiteness [Jesus II's army]** around their arms and ankles were hands of Gold and precious Stones and on their heads were many crowns. Their long bright hair held their robes in pleats and formed a Girdle for their waists. They sang **an Anthem [the New Song[*]]** in honor of our dear Lord and the Fullness of the Gospel, Saying in the Chorus, "How beautiful shall Adams Planet be," and clothed with Celestial Glory, the Working Ministers are sent O King. They stand before you.

The Vision of the King continued until Seth reached forth his hand and took from this Celestial Female Band Host new Raiment [clean garment[†]] for the King, with which Seth clothed him and put his heavenly name on his forehead and sealed it there. As I am only complying with your wishes it is not for me to describe the King's **new name [Leland[‡]]** or the Celestial Priesthood's dress at this time. But the King awoke in great trouble and seeks to know the meaning of his dream but dare not tell it.[§]

How remarkable and wonderful that God should give the King of Denmark a dream foretelling the important details of the life of his future progeny, Jesus II. Here he sees these great future things by experiencing them himself. The return of Jesus is Leland Jensen the descendant of royalty through the Danish line of kings, of whom the King dreamt. Leland Jensen was thrown into the temple (prison) on "a dirty jacket" charge, just as his ancestor the King had foreseen, and is now given a "clean raiment," as now the public can see that his frame-up and incarceration were in fulfillment of the prophecies for Jesus' return to the temple (prison).

Jesus II being of this "Royal Line of heavenly Priesthood," has the job of explaining the "Covenant and Law" to all the people. As a High Priest after the Order of Melchizedec he goes out from the temple to proclaim the Covenant of God. Leland shows with proof that the Book of the Covenant of Baha'u'llah and the Will and Testament of 'Abdu'l-Baha is the CHARTER for

---

[*] Revelation 14:3.
[†] Zechariah 3:4, 5.
[‡] Zechariah 3:9.
[§] George George Williams, (April 6, 1873). "Letter to Brother Rasmusson," Lincolnshire, England, pp. 2-4.

the World Order of Baha'u'llah. This is the government for the Kingdom of God on earth. The "Branch" in Zechariah 3:8 is 'Abdu'l-Baha, son of Baha'u'llah. He is entitled "the Most Great Branch," and Jesus II establishes his Will and Testament in the world. This World Order has two inseparable institutions. One is the lineage of the Branch. This is the line of King David through Baha'u'llah, who sat on the Davidic throne, then passed it to His son 'Abdu'l-Baha, then to his son and so on. This is the line of the kings for the kingdom of God on earth entitled the Guardianship. The other twin institution is a democratic body elected from all the peoples of the world entitled the Universal House of Justice (UHJ). Together these Twin Institutions, through obedience to God's plan, govern a peaceful and just civilization.

The return of Jesus is raising up an army, the 144,000, represented in the King's dream as a "Celestial band of Females in robes of exceeding whiteness." In the vision these people are female because the feminine is symbolic of the spiritual and the masculine the physical. These people are pure enough to see the truth of Jesus' return and proclaim it to everyone else in "an Anthem" or the New Song. The New Song is the explanations and commentaries of Jesus II. Many of these explanations are contained in the Firesides which prove the greatness of this day.

In the recounting of this Vision, George Williams saw the name of the King's descendant but said "it is not for me to describe the King's new name." This is similar to the biblical reference to the knight on the white horse, which is Jesus on his return, Dr. Leland Jensen, the last remaining knight of Baha'u'llah. In Revelation 19:12 it says, "His eyes are like a flame of fire, and on his head are many diadems; and he has a name inscribed which no one knows but himself." This new name is cleverly hidden until this day. In chapter three of Zechariah the state of Joshua (Jesus) being clothed in dirty garments is the iniquity of Jesus but later in verse nine, Zechariah refers to this as the iniquity of "the land" which is taken away. Here is the name of the return of Joshua or Jesus --"the land" or Leland. "Le" is a French article for "the." Leland is Dr. Jensen's name. So in this dream we see the foretold genealogy, mission and "new name"[*] of the return of Jesus and how Dr. Leland Jensen fulfills these exactly.

Among George Williams papers was an article by Joseph Morris who, when speaking of the fourth chapter of Zechariah, where a seven candlestick menorah is envisioned, said,

> "Who are these seven spirits referred to in these quotations? They are the seven angels. What should be understood by the stone which was laid before Joshua? [Zech. 3] The stone represents the seventh angel. The eye represents light. There being seven eyes engraven upon the stone, represents the light of the seven dispensations which will be possessed by the seventh angel. The stone being laid before Joshua, represents that at the time when the seventh angel should commence his mission, Joshua should be upon the earth,…"[†]

Here Joseph Morris sees the connection between Joshua and the seventh angel who are in fact the same person. Jesus, Joshua, the seventh angel, the knight on the white horse are some of the "many diadems" or titles on the crown he wears.

---

[*] Williams gives his "new name" Leland--"The Land" in the prophecy of "The High Priesthoods Return" see pages 175-178 this volume.
[†] From an article called "The Order of Sevens," by Joseph Morris, pp. 48-49.

Morris also sees the connection that the seventh angel must be in this "Stone with Seven Eyes." The great "Stone with Seven Eyes" is the temple foretold by Williams for the Return of Jesus. This temple has seven watchtowers or "seven eyes" and was his home for four years while wrongly incarcerated on the dirty jacket charge. This is the exact same building Ezekiel describes in his book. All of this was accomplished to fulfill the words of the prophets.

George Williams had many visions concerning the place for the Return of Jesus.

> You wish to know what is the object of **gathering together in Montana**. It is our Lord's Command that his chosen people may come together to receive blessings spiritual and temporal, and the order of both Priesthoods prepared. Also **a Temple prepared** to receive the ministering angels of our God.[*]

> For the choice place of the earth is handed over to you. Its beauties and riches, in part, are yet hidden. But your children will develop it more and more. For there will be built the City of the Great King.[†]

> If I call at night or day, and say, "Pack up for Deer Lodge--Our Merciful God wants your presence there," he is quickly on the road.[‡]

> As Deer Lodge Valley, Montana is the nucleus, let all others begin to turn their attention that way as they tire in the wings.[§]

How wonderfully clear these prophecies are! These are the very words which caused the Morrisites to pack up from their homes and settle the Deer Lodge Valley. These very prophecies are the reason two-thirds of the Valley are descended from the Morrisites.

Not only did George Williams clearly establish that the return of Jesus would be in Deer Lodge but he spoke of the temple itself in specific terms. Williams foretold that the temple would be built of the "stone from the surrounding." And the wall of the Montana State Prison, the Temple to which Jesus returns, is built entirely of stone. The sandstone and granite used in the construction of the Temple were quarried from the mountains in Garrison and Whitehall, just as Williams had prophesied. He also understood that the Lord's House wasn't the temple but the "temple in miniature."

> It is very gratifying to me to find all are lending the builder a helping hand, as it will be a source of pleasure to them in all time, being in a central place, and on property of your own, must, it appears to me, be wisely chosen, **a Temple in miniature**, and place of holiness for the faithful.[**]

---

[*] George Williams, (July 24, 1873). "Letter to Dear Sister Thomas," Brigg, Lincolnshire, England, p. 59.
[†] George Williams, (1879). "Letter to My Dear Brother James," Walthamstow, Essex England, p. 65.
[‡] George Williams, (June 13, 1880). "An Open Letter," p. 114.
[§] George Williams, (August 9, 1865). "Letter to My Dear Saint James and John," Great Salt Lake, p. 6.
[**] George Williams, (August 28, 1878). "Letter to My Dear Brother Henrikson," Walthamstow, Essex England, p. 36.

Besides this, the Lord's House is made of wood not the "stone from the surrounding mountains." Another interesting thing Williams adds about the temple is that in a vision, when an angel is showing him things to come, he pauses over the temple.

> Our guide went round the city in order to give us chance to **count the towers**.[*]

This is the Temple with seven watchtowers, the "Stone with Seven Eyes." Williams's visions of the place for the return of Jesus as being in Deer Lodge, Montana in a multi-towered stone building built from the stones of the surrounding mountains are indeed precise!

The Morrisites believed in the prophecy of "One Hundred years Hence."[†] This one hundred years is reckoned from 1863, the date Williams felt he was first allowed by God to proclaim his vision. This corresponds to the date given in Daniel chapter twelve where the prophesied 1335 days/years is added to 628 AD when Mohammed had his victory, giving us 1963. 'Abdu'l-Baha also prophesied of the 100th anniversary of Baha'u'llah's proclamation in 1863 as the time when the establisher of the Baha'i Faith, Jesus II would come. In 1963 Jesus II, the High Priest had Satan (Rex King) "standing at his right hand to oppose him" (Zech. 3:1). The Morrisite "One Hundred years Hence" brings us to this same date of 1963.

In addition to this, George Williams explains how the Great Pyramid of Giza in Egypt is the Plan of God in stone written in the universal language of mathematics, thus foreshadowing the time when, as part of his mission, the return of Jesus, Dr. Jensen, will break all the seals of the Pyramid when he has the "Stone with Seven Eyes," Ezekiel's temple, before him.

> With regard to the Pyramids in Egypt there will be wise men attracted there to explore, calculate to measure, to find what is the meaning of these extraordinary relics. Jeremiah speaking, and Isaiah also, knew the Lord of Hosts had a design in these great wonders, and these explorers will be helped to bring these hidden mysteries to light if they are doing it for an honest, holy purpose, to benefit mankind, and not with a view of making money; for every feature of the structure represents a heavenly order and may be called a pure language. Not by figure or by writing as we represent things, and it is written that the Lord will turn unto the inhabitants of the earth **a pure language** by which a small sign or movement may represent volumes of our written words. It's height, its circumference, its depth, its inner chambers, the space occupied by it, **all represent Jehovah's purposes from Adam to the Millennium**, and farther, as far as I know. There they stand, witnesses, and are called the mighty wonders of Egypt; and altho the children of Israel built some of these Pyramids in slavery and oppression, the Lord of Hosts claimed their labors a standing memorial of his guardianship over them. He

---

[*] Handwritten notes of George Williams found in the special collections department in Utah State University in Logan Utah, as are all other references in this addendum.

[†] Old Mormon prophecy held by the Morrisites. However the Morrisites reckoned it from both 1863 and 1869, not 1845 as some Mormons did. Found in the special collection department of the Library in Utah State University in box 6. August 9th, 1869 plus 100 years = August 9th, 1969, the first day of Jesus II in Deer Lodge., and the last day the Morrisites gathered.

delivered them, and drowned their oppressors, as the record tells us; but the Egyptians knew not what a wonderful memorial Jehovah's chosen had left behind them; and now, before our dear Lord's second coming, professors and wise men desire to look into the meaning of these grand structures, and, I have no doubt, others will be found buried In the sand. These explanations have been given me as fast as my scribe could write them. Amen & Amen.[*]

The date for the beginning of Jesus' mission, 1963 and the date for his proclamation, 1971 are in the Pyramid of Giza in mathematics, the "pure language."

The Morrisites officially ended in 1969. Unknown to them at the time, this was the same year that Jesus suddenly returned to his Temple in Deer Lodge. It was in 1969 that Dr. Jensen first had the "Stone with Seven Eyes" before him and became cognizant of his mission to establish God's Kingdom on earth. This Kingdom is the World Order of Baha'u'llah as delineated in the Sacred Will and Testament of 'Abdu'l-Baha.

Williams also foretold that "every stone would be numbered." This refers to the counting of all the nubs, slabs and pilasters of the Temple which gives us the dates 1963 and 1971. This meticulous clarity leaves no room for speculation. Jesus on his return is most plainly prophesied to come in words and in the stones of the Temple and the stones of the Pyramid.

Not only did God show Williams the specifics of the return of Jesus but he also was shown the purifying catastrophes the world had to go through before the kingdom is established.

> [Jesus] has done his part up to this time, and will continue to do until he has lifted the planet into celestial glory, and all belonging to it that is worthy. The rest must be dissolved by fire...Not till then will he hand up the Kingdom or the planet to the Father.[†]

Jesus II establishes the Kingdom for his Father, Baha'u'llah. In the Galilean dialect of Aramaic that Jesus Christ spoke, the word "glory" is "baha," "of" is "u" and "God the Father" is "Allah." The promised "Glory of God" is Baha'u'llah, the second Christ (see Mark 8:38). Jesus II comes to establish the Plan of the Kingdom given by Baha'u'llah. This is spoken of in I Corinthians 15:24: "Then comes the end, when he [Jesus II] delivers the kingdom to God the Father after destroying every rule and every authority and power."

In his Vision of the Kingdom Williams sees this:

---

[*] George Williams, (December 27, 1881). "Letter to Dear and Beloved Brother Erasmussen," Walthamstow, Essex, England, pp. 8-9.
[†] George Williams, (August 28, 1878). "Letter to My Dear Brother Henrickson," Walthamstow, Essex, England, p. 37.

The wicked are turned into hell, and forgotten, but the righteous reign with God in GLORY [Baha'i] and it seemed as if the echo came from a redeemed world-- "GLORY [Baha'i]."[*]

This "glory" is "baha" and the world becoming Baha'i or followers of the Glory of God, Baha'u'llah. Jesus has returned and he is establishing his Father's kingdom now!

The "fire" is a nuclear war that we must go through to cleanse the world of its bestial systems so that the Kingdom can be born. This fire is the first wind of destruction after which is a great meteor and then a great earthquake which Williams recounts.

> The **great earthquake** mentioned by John and other prophets before him had leveled the mountains over the whole earth and the sea had rolled back as it was in the beginning, the crooked was make straight and the rough places plain. The earth yielded her increase and the knowledge of God exalted man to the society of resurrected beings.[†]

The last of these four winds is the earth's shifting crust.

> The climate shall be moderated by the earth's 3rd motion Southward, without interference with her diurnal or annual motion by which she shall be fitted to bring forth all the choice vegetations and floral grandeur she is entitled to yield.[‡]

George Williams also describes this as the "earth moving as a cottage." At the time Williams prophesied this he was certainly laughed at by non-Morrisites but today we know that scientists such as Albert Einstein are aware of this great natural event upon us. Einstein wrote about this in an introduction to the book *The Earth's Shifting Crust* by Hapgood.

There are several places in America which certain groups felt were the place for Jesus' return. George Williams explains how Salt Lake and Jackson County are not the correct site.

> You Dear Sister Margarett will joy to know I am yet preserved in health, heedless alike of the slanderers and ignorant counterfeit Priesthoods who cry, "Come here, Christ is in the secret chamber with us," or "Christ is in the Desert of Salt or at Plans" and others "We are waiting for the coming man." These all are the soothsayers watching to catch souls of Satan. Beware, my friends, my brethren and sisters. This is the day of fire and whosoever's works are impure will fall into some of these flames.[§]

---

[*] Taken from the handwritten manuscripts of George Williams in box 6 of the special collections in the Library of Utah State University, Logan, Utah.

[†] Taken from the handwritten manuscripts of George Williams found in the special collections in the Library of Utah State University, Logan, Utah.

[‡] George Williams, (January 6, 1879). "Letter to Dear Brother James & the Saints of the Most High in Stake No. 1 on the sides of the North in Montana," Essex, England, p. 29.

[§] George Williams, (July 24, 1873). "Letter to Dear Sister Thomas," Lincolnshire, England, p. 57.

Williams also refers to Salt Lake as "modern Nazareth." Nazareth is the city that rejected the first coming of Jesus. He also shows how Jackson County, Missouri played the harlot like an adulterous wife. Jackson County is therefore deprived of God and clearly Deer Lodge is the true city of God's Temple where Jesus will suddenly return.

> The faithful and patient will have their names and rewards in foundations of his Seat, or Temple on the North [Montana State Prison in Deer Lodge]. Jackson County will be as one held in remembrance, who once was fair and young and beautiful, wedded to our dear Lord; but while he tarried, she welcomed other lovers educated in fraud and lust and deceit. She left the paths of virtue for which she felt the heavy hand of the bridegroom's displeasure. At what time is a wife forgiven for adultery with us? So may Jackson County in like manner when the unbearable debt is paid. But the sides of the North was set apart in the counsels of God's, and it is always on every planet the seat and Throne for the God in power. Old Israel wants it at Jerusalem. The Latterdays want it in Jackson County. The Mahomets want it at Mecca. Shall they have their desire? In part they shall, as they have the Gospel in part. All these and some others will be stakes under the government located on the sides of the North, from which they will receive the law, and their King appointed by what is written in the books.[*]

Finally, Williams knew this wouldn't take place in his "mortal day" but in the future--Our Day.

> This excitement will arise suddenly as the world lays sleepy and finds the foundation of an everlasting Government laid secure and the Lord coming suddenly to his Temple. Even then, with all our care, many in the work will need purifying as by fire, before the work is accepted. **These grand yet awful scenes may not take place in our mortal day**; but the faithful will take part in it, either in the body, or out of it.[†]

Knowing this would take place in the future he stated: "I wish especially to be remembered to the children."[‡]

Williams knew that it is the children, grandchildren and great grandchildren of the Morrisite pioneers who would live to see Jesus on his return.

He also spoke of the old Morrisite government of twelve apostles under Joseph Morris and the government of the Deer Lodge Morrisites[§] as an earthly model. He saw these as a pattern and prototype for the heavenly pattern in the future,[**] referring to Jesus II's twelve members that

---

[*] George Williams, (1876). "Letter to My Dear Brother James," Walthamstow, Essex England, p. 36.

[†] George Williams, (1879). "Letter to My Dear Brother James," Walthamstow, Essex England, p. 65.

[‡] George Williams, (August 28, 1878). "Letter to My Dear Brother Henrickson," Walthamstow, Essex, England, p. 39.

[§] "When 12 can be brought to meet, you have an Holy Assembly and can meet in order preaching the beginning of Eternal Life unto them. Never depart from truth and a righteous walk before all and let no fault be seen" (George Williams, (August 9, 1865). "Letter to May Dear Saint James and John," Great Salt Lake, p. 9).

[**] "And earthly things are the pattern of heavenly things" (George Willaims, (1879). "Letter to My Dear Brother James," Walthamstow, Essex, England, p. 62).

form the body of the International Baha'i Council (IBC). Williams then spoke of how the King will come and be united with the council of twelve referring to the guardianship of the Baha'i Faith who is the Davidic King and President of the IBC/UHJ.[*]

George Williams then explains that after the catastrophes and after the earth's shifting crust, the Kingdom will be established throughout all the world and the world center will be moved to Israel, "The land of Jacob," specifically Mt. Carmel the place Baha'u'llah Himself designated.

Your question I answer thus. What is the Lord's design in the future? His design is to bring the Fullness of the Gospel to the understanding of the **heirs of salvation** [descendants of the Morrisites] that they may do His will upon the earth as the Angels in Heaven do it. How is this to be done and what for? First they are to be visited by ministers prepared called **huntsmen** [Jesus II's army] who were to hunt them out of the holes, dens and caves of the rocks. Now it is evident they don't live in such places. The prophet had not liberty to tell it plainer: but should have said:--Hunt them out of the Halls, Palaces, Seminaries of learning [the Baha'is will be teaching in the various places of learning in Deer Lodge and elsewhere] and chambers of the great and cottages of the poor where the **fishers of Enos** [corrupt Mormons] could not throw their net: neither were the fishers or those who listened to the fisher's story eligible for the Grand Department now to be introduced; but served that portion assigned them. Therefore, let them alone at present.

The **Hunters** with their entrance keys will enter these residences quiet as the rising planets, delivering to them the Glad Tidings from Heaven, even a Fullness. Everything from Heaven is Glad Tidings, as they listened: for it is still through the ear faith cometh [through the careful listening to the New Song, the explanations and commentaries of Jesus II]. They are ministered to as the pattern at Weber, gathered into Holy Assemblies, 12 making sufficient for the title [the International Baha'i Council/Universal House of Justice of Baha'u'llah], instructed in the Fullness and the Fullness embraceth every part. After a little a doctrine is introduced of duty to build a Temple [the prison in Deer Lodge] in their land. What for? When it is completed, for the Holy Angels to come and bring the mind and will of God from day to day, that they, the Saints of the Most High, may learn to do it as they, the Angel, do who know it on like terms, daily, in these Temples; likewise learn celestial wisdom, escaping the judgments the fire and calamities reserved for those who then know not God nor obey the Fullness of his Gospel.

The Kings of the earth to be brought in, (see *Cainan's Interview*), then it will be fashionable; and outside of this world will be nothing but the rebellious of Adam's children and **the <u>Fallen Ones</u> in the <u>white</u> nations**. With the others we have nothing to do--they will be seen after by those they have listed to obey-- Mahomet, Confucius, Zoroaster, Zeny and others. Then cometh the Lord Jesus Christ with his armies, as the Holy Joseph showed, and the earth **moving as a**

---

[*] This was fulfilled in the 10 days following the 9-11-2001.

Cottage [earth's shifting crust]. We shall be instruments used to bring to pass **This Mighty Gathering**: for it is still **a Gathering and Temple Building Dispensation** [after the catastrophes the whole world will be gathered into the Kingdom], altho not to America [the Universal House of Justice with the Guardian at its head will ultimately have their headquarters on Mt. Carmel in Israel at the spot Baha'u'llah indicated to 'Abdu'l-Baha]. Adam's earth has far more choice locations than the land of Joseph, altho his father Jacob did not know it and it will be seen that **The Great God can raise His Kingdom and Glory thereof in every land**. His ministers not becoming transgressors. Who are these the Hunters will gather? These are they who will be chosen here for leaders and Governors and Kings under their Father Adam when his earth is exalted--the rest as ministering spirits. Then the Kingdom, the greatness of the Kingdom and dominion under the whole Heaven shall be given to the Saints of the Most High and they shall possess it for ever and ever. This line of things fits like a ladies glove and needs no attempt to debate its proof.[*]

To help him educate humanity Jesus II sends out his angels (messengers) to proclaim the New Song, his explanations and commentaries such as the firesides that he taught them. Williams saw this happening in the future and sometimes referred to them as "hunters" as in the above quote. The message that is proclaimed is the Gospel of the Kingdom coming "on earth as it is in heaven."

Williams's insight, vision and prophetic ability are accurate and awe-inspiring. He was certainly a genuine prophet. God truly chose him to see the coming of Jesus to his Temple. This is only the tip of the iceberg. Williams prophesied many more things which we are still ardently searching out. His prophecies have come true, therefore passing the test of a true prophet.

In obedience to Jesus Christ's promise that he would return and the prophetic visions of George Williams, we see as clear as crystal that Dr. Leland Jensen fulfills the prophesied name, prophesied date, prophesied address and prophesied mission for the Return of Jesus. It is also most evident that the promise of the Kingdom and the preceding calamities are true and that it is our opportunity to assist in establishing this promised civilization. Through Williams, God has prepared a people, the Morrisites, and moved them to Deer Lodge to establish their families so that their descendants will receive Jesus on his return in the Temple, the "Stone with Seven Eyes." What a glorious day this is indeed! How thorough and loving God is to send us a forerunner for Jesus II, George Williams as preparation and as proof of Jesus' glorious Return today!

---

[*] George Williams, (August 9, 1865). "Letter to My Dear Saint James and John," Great Salt Lake, pp. 3-5.

Rise and Measure the Temple of God

"'The angel stood, saying, **Rise, and measure the Temple of God**, and the altar, and **them that worship therein**;' that is to say, compare and measure: measuring is the discovery of proportion. Thus the angel said: Compare the Temple of God and the altar and them that are praying therein, that is to say, investigate what is **their true condition** and discover in what degree and state **they** are, and what conditions, perfections, behavior and attributes **they** possess; and make yourself cognizant of **the mysteries of those holy souls** who dwell in the Holy of Holies in purity and sanctity."-- 'Abdu'l-Baha, *Some Answered Questions*, p. 54.

PHOTOGRAPHED BY
UNDERWOOD AND UNDERWOOD
NEW YORK.

76

TOWER 2

TOWER 4

TOWER 3

TOWER 5

TOWER 1

**TOWER 7
INSIDE VIEW**

TOWER 6

Morrisite Center--Johnson House, Deer Lodge, Montana

90

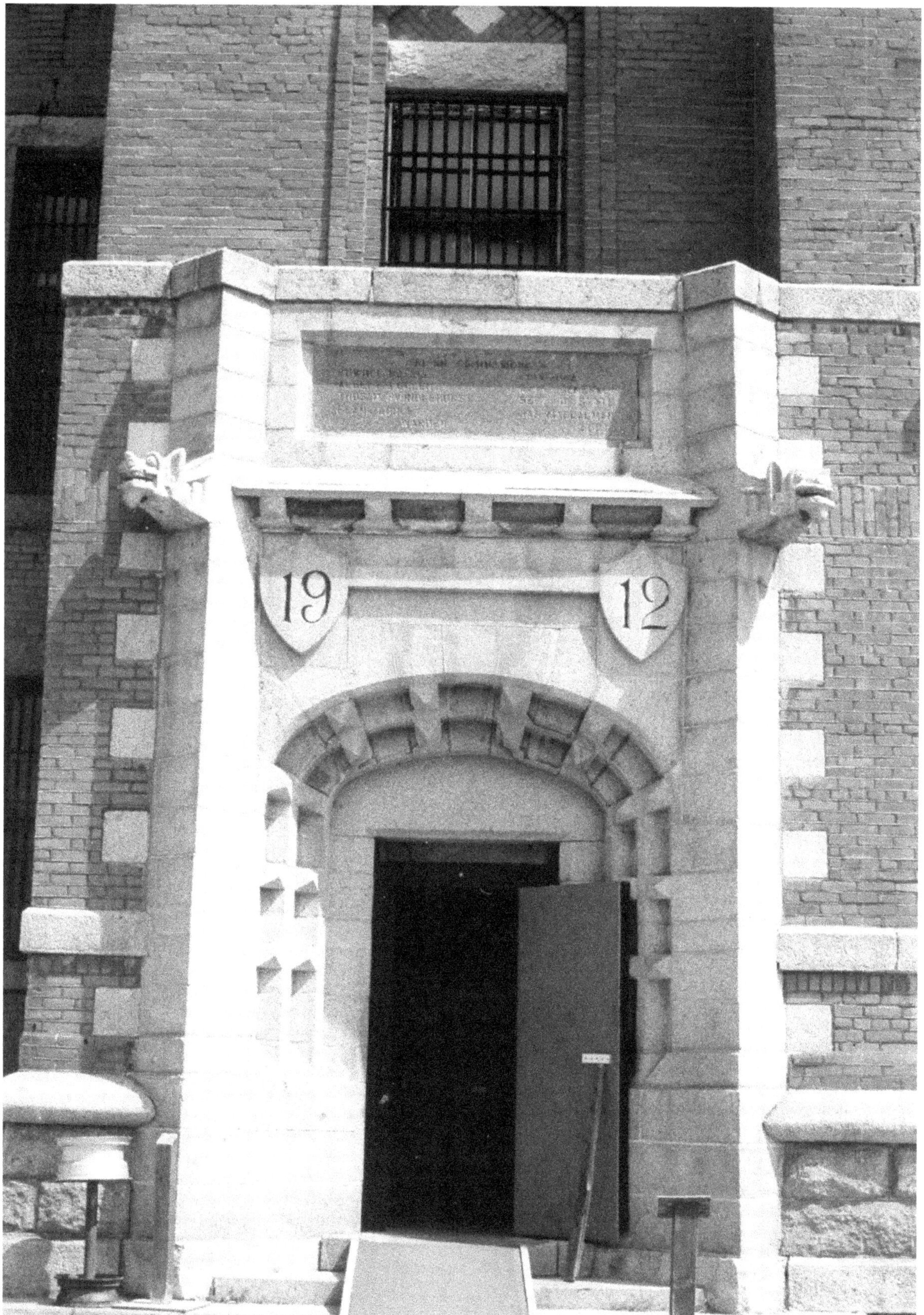
19
12

GATHERING OF THE PEOPLE OF BAHA
(Colorado in Prophecy)
Transcribed from a talk by Victor Woods

Opening Prayer:

I know not, O my God, what the Fire is which Thou didst kindle in Leland. Earth can never cloud its splendor, nor water quench its flame. All the peoples of the world are powerless to resist its force. Great is the blessedness of him that hath drawn nigh unto it, and heard its roaring.

Some, O my God, Thou didst, through Thy strengthening grace, enable to approach it, while others Thou didst keep back by reason of what "The Hands" have wrought in Thy days. Whoso hath hasted towards it and attained unto it hath, in his eagerness to gaze on Thy beauty, yielded his life in Thy path, and ascended unto Thee, wholly detached from aught else except Thyself.

I beseech Thee, O my God, by this Fire which blazeth and rageth in the world of creation, to rend asunder the veils that have hindered me from appearing before the throne of Thy majesty, and from standing at the door of Thy gate. Do Thou ordain for me, O my Lord, every good thing Thou didst send down in Thy Book, and suffer me not to be far removed from the shelter of Thy mercy.

Powerful art Thou to do what pleaseth Thee. Thou art, verily, the All-Powerful, the Most Generous.--Baha'u'llah

Do you know what the best vitamin is for a Baha'i? B-1. Be One.

OK. Gathering of the People of Baha. What is that? Well I thought that people of Baha were already gathered. Isn't that the whole idea of the Baha'i Faith? That Israel has been regathered under its New Name: Baha'i. Glory.[*] Well, it says in the book of Isaiah, in the eleventh chapter, the eleventh verse:

> In that day the Lord will extend his hand ***yet a second time*** to recover the remnant which is left of his people, from Assyria, from Egypt, from Pathros, from Ethiopia, from Elam, from Shinar, from Hamath, and from the coastlands of the sea. He will raise an ensign for the nations, and will assemble the outcasts of Israel, and gather the dispersed of Judah from the four corners of the earth. (Isaiah 11:11-12 RSV)

This is what was promised. This is the second regathering taking place. For Moses had given us a three-part Covenant. And he says in Deuteronomy:

---

[*] Isaiah 62:2, 43:7, 6:3; Revelation 2:17, 3:12; Ezekiel 43:2.

And if you obey the voice of the LORD your God, being careful to do all his commandments which I command you this day, the LORD your God will set you high above all the nations of the earth. And all these blessings shall come upon you and overtake you, if you obey the voice of the LORD your God. (Deuteronomy 28:1-2 RSV).

So, Moses came and he gave the law, and he delivered an entire civilization to the people and he said, IF you OBEY these laws, you will be the greatest nation on the face of the earth. But then he goes on and he says:

But if you will not obey the voice of the LORD your God or be careful to do all his commandments and his statutes which I command you this day, then all these curses shall come upon you and overtake you... And the LORD will ***scatter you*** among all peoples, from one end of the earth to the other; and there you shall serve other gods, of wood and stone, which neither you nor your fathers have known. (Deuteronomy 28:15, 64 RSV)

And you shall be scattered. What's the third part of this Covenant that Moses gives? He says:

And when all these things come upon you, the blessing and the curse, which I have set before you, and you call them to mind among all the nations where the LORD your God has driven you, and return to the LORD your God, you and your children, and obey His voice in all that I command you this day, with all your heart and with all your soul; then the LORD your God will restore your fortunes, and have compassion upon you, and ***He will gather you again*** from all the peoples where the LORD your God has scattered you. (Deuteronomy 30:1-3 RSV)

So this is the promise. That the people will be gathered. That they will be regathered a second time. And that first regathering, we all know has already happened. That Baha'u'llah, against His will, and in chains, and in captivity, was exiled from the Persian empire and given into the hands of the Ottoman empire. And in His exiles, He went through these lands, and the people who were the descendents of these ten tribes who had been taken into captivity (in 721 BC)--the descendents of these people--recognized Baha'u'llah as that redeeming Messiah who was to appear to them and was promised to them. Entire Jewish communities in Isfahan and Gulpaygan --entire communities recognized Baha'u'llah and they followed Him ALL the way back to the Holy Land--to Israel in fulfillment of the prophecies. And this was the first regathering of Israel under its new name--Glory--of Baha'i.

Well, what happened? What does it say? "If you follow my commandments and follow these laws and follow these instructions, and follow all these things, you'll be the greatest nation in the world." What happened?

The people got headstrong and egotistical. They decided that their will was going to be above that of the Will of God. And they violated this Covenant that Baha'u'llah gave--which was a Covenant for ALL the peoples and all the nations of the world--that ALL the people would be ONE race and one world. They violated that Covenant. They said, "Our plan is better than God's plan and we are scrapping the whole deal and we are going forward on our path." And since that time, the Baha'i Faith has been scattered. But as Doc used to put it--he said, "God had an ace up His sleeve." That there was this promised one in the plan from the beginning--that this violation would occur--as it HAS occurred throughout history--that Baha'u'llah talks about. He says that the darkness of the night of error has to appear so that the morning of the light of truth can be recognized.[*] The light shines out the brightest in the darkest of places. And this is how you are able to recognize it.

So throughout all of the history of our world and all the history of religions, this has continually occurred. But it is now today, with this second regathering, that this pattern will come to an end. God had an ace up His sleeve: that that High Priest--that promised one in the faith in the scriptures itself--appeared. Dr. Leland Jensen, in fulfillment of biblical prophecies for the coming of Jesus the High Priest. A lot of you knew Doc. He said that he had the weight of the world on his shoulders. Read from Isaiah, chapter 22:

> I will thrust you from your office, and you will be cast down from your station. In that day I will call my servant Eli'akim the son of Hilki'ah, and I will clothe him with your robe, and will bind your girdle on him, and will commit your authority to his hand; and he shall be a father to the inhabitants of Jerusalem and to the house of [David] Judah. And I will place on his shoulder ***the key of the house of David***; he shall open, and none shall shut; and he shall shut, and none shall open. And I will fasten him like a peg in a sure place, and he will become a throne of honor to his father's house. And they will ***hang on him the whole weight*** of his father's house, the offspring and issue, every small vessel, from the cups to all the flagons. In that day, says the LORD of hosts, the peg that was fastened in a sure place will give way; and it will be cut down and fall, and the burden that was upon it will be cut off, for the LORD has spoken. (Isaiah 22:19-25 RSV)

So Doc had the whole weight of this Cause on his shoulders. And as it says in Zechariah in the third chapter--it says that this person is to bring forth the BRANCH.

> "Hear now, O Joshua the high priest, thou, and thy fellows that sit before thee: for they are men wondered at: for, behold, **I will bring forth my servant the BRANCH**" (Zechariah 3:8 KJV)

And this is the **KEY of the house of David** that he had on his shoulders. He knew that he was the only one--himself and his wife were the only ones--who supported this lineage of David. That came from the adopted line: Mason Remey, Joseph Pepe Remey, and today, the promised BRANCH of the regathering, Neal Chase.

---

[*] "What 'oppression' is greater than that which hath been recounted? What 'oppression' is more grievous than that a soul seeking the truth, and wishing to attain unto the knowledge of God, should know not where to go for it and from whom to seek it? For opinions have sorely differed, and the ways unto the attainment of God have multiplied. This 'oppression' *is the essential feature of every Revelation*. Unless it cometh to pass, the Sun of Truth will not be made manifest. *For the break of the morn of divine guidance must needs follow the darkness of the night of error*" (Baha'u'llah, *Kitab-i-Iqan*, p. 31).

Nostradamus also saw this. He saw this in his prophesies, as the flowering Lily of the Valley (Canticles 2:1) or the *Fleur-de-Lis*.

The *fleur-de-lis* has one large petal in the middle and two on either side. This is representative-- in Nostradamus's prophecies--of these three guardians that appear. The guardians who are representative, as Kay has pointed out, of the promise, the curse, and the regathering: like the three red-granite plugs in the Ascending Passageway of the Pyramid are representative of these three individuals.

In chapter 12 of the Book of Revelation, it talks about this violation that occurred and this scattering that took place.

> And a great portent appeared in heaven, a woman clothed with the sun, with the moon under her feet, and on her head a crown of twelve stars; she was with child and she cried out in her pangs of birth, in anguish for delivery. And another portent appeared in heaven; behold, a great red dragon, with seven heads and ten horns, and seven diadems upon his heads. His tail swept down a third of the stars of heaven, and cast them to the earth. And the dragon stood before the woman who was about to bear a child, that he might devour her child when she brought it forth; she brought forth a male child, one who is to rule all the nations with a rod of iron, but her child was caught up to God and to his throne, and the woman fled into the wilderness, where she has a place prepared by God, in which to be nourished for one thousand two hundred and sixty days.

> Now war arose in heaven, Michael and his angels fighting against the dragon; and the dragon and his angels fought, but they were defeated and there was no longer any place for them in heaven. And the great dragon was thrown down, that ancient serpent, who is called the Devil and Satan, the deceiver of the whole world--he was thrown down to the earth, and his angels were thrown down with him. And I heard a loud voice in heaven, saying, "Now the salvation and the power and the kingdom of our God and the authority of his Christ have come, for the accuser of our brethren has been thrown down, who accuses them day and night before our God. And they have conquered him by the blood of the Lamb and by the word of their testimony, for they loved not their lives even unto death. Rejoice then, O heaven and you that dwell therein! But woe to you, O earth and sea, for the devil has come down to you in great wrath, because he knows that his time is short!" And when the dragon saw that he had been thrown down to the earth, he pursued the woman who had borne the male child. But the woman was given ***the two wings of the great eagle*** that she might fly from the serpent into the wilderness, to the place where she is to be nourished for a time, and times, and half a time. The serpent poured water like a river out of his mouth after the woman, to sweep her away with the flood. But the earth came to the help of the

woman, and the earth opened its mouth and swallowed the river which the dragon had poured from his mouth. Then the dragon was angry with the woman, and went off to make war on the rest of her offspring, on those who keep the commandments of God and bear testimony to Jesus. (Revelation 12:1-17 RSV)

It says she is given "the two wings of an eagle," and this is the United States. This is the symbol of the United States. The three guardians that have appeared--the blessing, the curse, and the regathering--these are Americans: They come from America--the United States. This is where this violation has occurred. From the time when Mason Remey came forth and declared that he was appointed to this position, they violated the Covenant. They violated the Covenant with Pepe, and they violated the Covenant with Neal.

This is a Tablet of 'Abdu'l-Baha from *Tablets of 'Abdu'l-Baha*:

O Thou who art attracted by the Fragrances of God!

Give thanks unto God for having revealed unto thee, in visions, the mysteries of His Kingdom and for having strengthened thee to attain certain revelations which show Thine utmost attraction and constancy unto this great Cause.

Verily, the three birds are the three holy souls. The one on the right is His Holiness the great Bab, the one on the left is His Honor the Quddus, the glorious soul, and the great bird in the middle is the Greatest Name. The light shining from the Supreme Horizon is the Beauty of El-ABHA. These birds descended from an infinite height and the nearer they came to earth the more their majesty and glory became manifest. All nations were promised by a sure promise and were awaiting with anxiety and longing the coming of the Promised One. The two birds accompanying the great bird in the center signifies that the Bab and His Honor the Quddus were both under the wings of the Greatest Name. As those birds descended and their shadows extended vertically over the expectants, as the sun approacheth the zenith at noontide, at this time Thou hast seen a majestic being in the form of man upon the back of the huge bird in the center. This person in the human form is the "divine station" mentioned in the Bible: "Let us make man in our image after our likeness." ('Abdu'l-Baha, *Tablets III*, pp. 678-681)

This human form is the same human form that Ezekiel sees in his vision--where he sees this human form over the throne. And it's in the form of a genealogy that appears--which is this Divine Standard that has been unfurled. And it says: "Let us make man in Our image, after Our likeness" (Genesis 1:26): meaning that *in this genealogy*, all of the Manifestations of God who have appeared--have come; and it is through their teachings that we are made in the image of God.

And the divine lights were reflected from the reality of the Greatest Name. Although this station is far from the minds and understandings, yet its lights are apparent, its rays reflected and its brilliancy manifested throughout the universe.

117

The white garments signify holy dignity and a station sanctified from color, i.e., free from the universal conditions and material qualities. That luminous countenance, manifested in beauty, signifieth that the divine lights shone forth from the human form, which were reflected and descended upon Thee, dazzling the eyes of those who were perceiving it as the sun dazzles the eyes of those who try to look upon it. **That divine form manifested itself <u>in America</u> and entered the Great Temple**...That divine face will beam upon **numberless souls who will enter this Temple.**

Now you know, of course, that 'Abdu'l-Baha talks about how there are these interpretations. So many that there are these seventy and one, or seventy and two interpretations:

Thus it is recorded: "Every knowledge hath seventy meanings, of which one only is known amongst the people...He also saith: "We speak one word, and by it we intend one and seventy meanings; each one of these meanings we can explain." (Baha'u'llah, *Kitab-i-Iqan*, p. 255)

Here in this Tablet 'Abdu'l-Baha explains that this is the Bab and Quddus and the Greatest Name. This is manifesting itself today in America. That these three individuals have appeared.

Regarding the table laid in that magnificent house: This is the Heavenly Table of divine knowledge, love and eternal life. As to the people gathered there, they are the beloved of God and His chosen ones whose faces shine with wonderful and heavenly beauty. The woman sitting at the side of the Temple is the law of God, which will soon dispel all veils and its beauty will appear, after which it shall be established forever and ever. The stamped coins presented to the woman sitting in that honored station, are the good deeds and actions of the beloved of God and His maid-servants, submitted with praise, greetings and great thanksgiving unto that holy law. The beautiful woman is blessed by being touched by that Merciful Being the glory of whose blessing shall suffuse the universe. Then the Merciful Being returned to His station, mounting the bird and ascended to the Supreme Horizon in the infinite realm.

This vision showeth that thou, O confirmed and attracted one, by the breezes of God will soon be acquainted with the ancient mysteries, for the Manifest Light will appear to thee. The vision also signifieth that a Mashriq'ul-Adhkar will soon be established in America. The cries of supplication and invocation will be raised to the Highest Kingdom therefrom and, verily, **the people will enter into the religion of God <u>by troops</u>** with great enthusiasm and attraction. ('Abdu'l-Baha, *Tablets III*, pp. 678-681)

This is one of the places where they get the prophecy for 'Abdu'l-Baha saying that the people will enter in by troops. These people don't enter in by troops through these people's teachings of the sans-guardian Baha'is.

Concerning thy vision of the angels surrounding the **Great White Throne**: This "throne" is the body of the Greatest Name. The beautiful and glorious person riding upon the white horse is the Greatest Name and the white horse means also His glorious body. The herald who proclaimed the written names is 'Abdu'l-Baha who announceth the names of those who deserve salvation and are firm in the Covenant of God, and Thou art one of those people, the people of salvation. Be thankful for this great favor. ('Abdu'l-Baha, *Tablets III*, pp. 678-681)

It says, "Concerning thy vision of the angels surrounding the **Great White Throne**"; This is the gathering: this gathering. The gathering unto the Throne. And that Great White Throne is this Chair Mountain in this valley in Colorado. At this time. We are going to be going there. It is made of marble that is white. It's a white throne! It was from that place that all of the marble in Washington was taken for all their monuments. That middle place that the founding fathers of this country designed as being the twelve tribes and that holy place in the middle--Washington DC--all of the marble for that was made from that area of the Great White Throne.

It says here is this vision that 'Abdu'l-Baha came to this country of America and he announced the name of those who deserve salvation and are firm in the Covenant around this Great White Throne.

This is an account of 'Abdu'l-Baha coming to Glenwood Springs in 1912 from the Glenwood Springs Historical Society--which is also related in *Mahmud's Diary*. It says:

When we reached the hotel [the Hotel Colorado], he[*] stood outside in the garden and said that it would be well to have food there. This garden had a large tank of fish of various colors. The buildings of the hotel enclosed the garden on three sides. Having read the newspapers of Denver and having seen his likeness as well as those of his party, the manager recognized him as soon as he approached. He hastened to do what he could. Without the beloved's request, the manager ordered the servants to serve the dinner in the garden. A large table was prepared and spread, and beautiful chairs were placed around it. The holy being sat down on a chair and asked us to do the same. The Master gave tips to the servants before and after the dinner.

As the people of the hotel saw his majesty in the glory of the beloved, they informed others. People began to come to him party by party. Others were watching the dignity of his beautiful face from their rooms. Most of them were heard to say, "How neatly he takes his food: He is no doubt a great man." Bye and bye his mission dawned upon the occupants of the hotel as they were informed of the Cause of God. In the afternoon 'Abdu'l-Baha walked in the garden. When we were crossing the bridge a messenger brought some telegrams. There was among them one which informed us of the serious illness of Mr. Chase in a hospital in Los Angeles. The beloved repeatedly mentioned the constancy of Mr. Chase. Afterwards he said, "To turn to the Covenant is to obey the Blessed Beauty which is the CAUSE OF THE GATHERING OF THE PEOPLE OF BAHA. The

---

[*] 'Abdu'l-Baha.

command of the people of Islam to prostrate themselves before the stone of *Hifral Aswad* (Stone of the Ka'aba) was simply to obey the messenger of God and to prove the influence of the Cause of God."

So he says that "to obey the Covenant" and he says it in the same context as "Mr. Chase"--in Glenwood Springs, Colorado. Surrounding the White Throne. These angels that appear at this time. And he also likens it to prostrating yourself before the stone of the Ka'aba. And in the Ka'aba, there is only one stone that is left of the original Ka'aba, and that is that corner stone. All the other stones are stones that they put together, but there is only one that is original. And this is the stone that they start their *Tawaf* which is their circumambulation of the Ka'aba. And it says in the Islamic prophecies that in the end times, that stone will be endowed with a tongue, and will be able to testify to the Oneness of God and to His commands. At the same time that this Day of Doom appears in the world. And this is the CAUSE OF THE GATHERING OF THE PEOPLE OF BAHA. That second regathering--that God extends His hand yet a second time and gathers them from all over the world and from the islands of the sea!

He also relates in *Mahmud's Diary* that he comes into Glenwood Canyon and he sees the mountains and he relates a story of how this is like the Cave of Hira that Muhammad hid in away from his oppressors; away from the people who were intent on his life. And he compares it to this place--to where Muhammad had hid himself. And the story is that the people were out to kill Muhammad and they went and they rode on their horses following Muhammad's trail. And they came by the place of where he went in--in this cave--in the cave of Hira. And they were about to go into the cave but they didn't. Because on the outside of the cave's mouth there was a gigantic spider web. And they said, "Don't even bother looking in there. Nobody could have gone in there. We were hot on his trail. There is a huge spider web in front of it. Nobody could have gone in there: they would have broken the spider web."

This is this place! And that spider web is the web that was prophesied of in the Native American prophecies that would cover the whole world and be that third sign for the third great shaking of the earth. That world wide web which now that we have internet sites all over, that people from all over the world are being able to see, and being able to recognize and coming into this GATHERING OF THE PEOPLE OF BAHA. And this is what protects this Cause. And this will be the cause of the gathering of the people of Baha. Even though there are people who "with ***divine unity for their excuse*** have deprived themselves and perturbed and poisoned others" (W&T, p. 12); and as with "impure gold have seized upon diverse measures and various pretexts that they may separate the gathering of the people of Baha" (W&T, p. 12). That is not happening anymore! This Cause is going forward, and these destructions are on our very doorstep. And I am sure, as we will all see, these things will come about.

Closing prayer: TRIUMPH OF THE CAUSE

Lauded be Thy name, O Lord my God! Darkness hath fallen upon every land, and the forces of mischief have encompassed all the nations. Through them, however, I perceive the splendors of Thy wisdom, and discern the brightness of the light of Thy providence.

120

They that are shut out as by a veil from Thee have imagined that they have the power to put out Thy light, and to quench Thy fire, and to still the winds of Thy grace. Nay, and to this Thy might beareth me witness! Had not every tribulation been made the bearer of Thy wisdom, and every ordeal the vehicle of Thy providence, no one would have dared oppose us, though the powers of earth and heaven were to be leagued against us. Were I to unravel the wondrous mysteries of Thy wisdom which are laid bare before me, the reins of Thine enemies would be cleft asunder.

Glorified be Thou, then, O my God! I beseech Thee by Thy Most Great Name to assemble them that love Thee around the Law that streameth from the good pleasure of Thy will, and to send down upon them what will assure their hearts.

Potent art Thou to do what pleaseth Thee. Thou art, verily, the Help in Peril, the Self-Subsisting.--Baha'u'llah.

THE MASTER WHO CAME TO GLENWOOD

The Glenwood Springs Daily Avalanche issue of September 30th, 1912, carried this story. "'Abdu'l-Baha Abbas of Persia, lecturer and philosopher, stays in Glenwood Springs a day and enjoys the cave baths." In all his stops in America, this was the only one where He rested.

"We have been in many places during our journey but we had no time to see the sights," He said. "We had not even a moment's rest. Today, however, we have had a little respite."

He bathed in the Vapor Caves and upon leaving the pool He looked at the mountains and river and remarked that such scenes were much loved by Baha'u'llah.

In 1912, this is what 'Abdu'l-Baha told the Avalanche reporter: "The earth is small compared with other planets...The sun is a million and a half times larger than this earth and the sun is the same to other planets. So, doesn't that prove clearly that this earth that we are living on is **a small world after all?**

"How insignificant this world is when it comes to the East and the West, don't you think? In our estimation, it is one East and one West combined. And on this earth all are human kind and no distinction at all for we are descendants from the family of Adam."

The following are excerpts from Mahmud's Diary, chronicling the time The Master, 'Abdu'l-Baha, spent in Glenwood Springs, Colorado in September of 1912.

Friday September 27th, 1912

'Abdu'l-Baha departed from Denver by train at nine o'clock in the morning. The Denver Newspapers were translated and read to Him. Mahmud relates:

They gave Him pleasure as they described the diffusion of the fragrance of God in Denver and contained the translation of the discourse. Among them was the translation of these Blessed Words:

"He is God!
"The contingent world is like unto the human organism that has grown from the embryo and reached puberty and perfection. It may be said that the development of the human being from the beginning to the age of puberty was but a preparation for the culminating event which was the power of reason. This power of the mind in the human world is the goal towards which the biological organism works. Likewise, this is the Age of Maturity for the soul world and the Spiritual Time for the manifestation of the Most Great Mind and the Pre-existent Bounty so that the Divine and material civilizations may be joined and the perfection of the human world may dawn."

The train passed through the Rocky Mountains of Colorado. Some of these rose precipitously like walls from the railway bed, formidable and immense, *towering overhead like giant demons.* Gazing at their summits one felt as if the mountains would fall down at any moment.

There were some special roofless observation cars on the train so that passengers might have a full view of the majestic mountains. In these observation cars the passengers could see the mountains on the right and the serene river on the left. As the train passed through these beautiful scenes, the Master said:

"Dear friends, the waves of the bounties of the Blessed Beauty are surging. As I look I see the ocean of His favor swelling and saying, 'I am with you.' Truly, were it not for these glad tidings and His assistance, what could I have done? Just one person alone in the East and West of America, in the mountains and wilderness--it is no light matter. It is easy to say these things but it was unimaginable that they would let us into these churches. See how His aid and favor descend upon us. This trip fills us with wonder! Offer thanks to the Blessed Beauty that He has bestowed such confirmations upon us."

In order to comfort them 'Abdu'l-Baha told them the story of Muhammad and the Cave and His words, 'God is indeed with us.'

The story of Muhammad and the companions of the Cave are related by Baha'u'llah in *The Seven Valleys* and *The Four Valleys:*

> If the wayfarer's goal be the dwelling of the Praiseworthy One (*Maḥmúd*), this is the station of primal reason which is known as the Prophet and the Most Great Pillar. Here reason signifieth the Divine, Universal Mind, whose sovereignty enlighteneth all created things--nor doth it refer to every feeble brain; for it is as the wise Sana'í hath written:
>
> > How can feeble reason encompass the Qur'an,
> > Or the spider snare a phoenix in her web?
> > Wouldst thou that the mind should not entrap thee?
> > Teach it the science of the love of God!
>
> On this plane, the traveler meeteth with many a trial and reverse. Now is he lifted up to heaven, now is he cast into the depths. As it hath been said: "Now Thou drawest me to the summit of glory, again Thou castest me into the lowest abyss." The mystery treasured in this plane is divulged in the following holy verse from the Súrih of THE CAVE:
>
> "And thou mightest have seen the sun when it arose, pass on the right of their cave, and when it set, leave them on the left, while they were in its spacious chamber. This is one of the signs of God. Guided indeed is he whom God guideth; but for him whom He misleadeth, thou shalt by no means find a patron."
>
> If a man could know what lieth hid in this one verse, it would suffice him. Wherefore, in praise of such as these, He hath said: "Men whom neither merchandise nor traffic beguile from the remembrance of God...

This station conferreth the true standard of knowledge, and freeth man from tests. In this realm, to search after knowledge is irrelevant, for He hath said concerning the guidance of travelers on this plane, "Fear God, and God will instruct thee." And again: "Knowledge is a light which God casteth into the heart of whomsoever He willeth."

Wherefore, a man should make ready his heart that it be worthy of the descent of heavenly grace, and that the bounteous Cup-Bearer may give him to drink of the wine of bestowal from the merciful vessel. "For the like of this let the travailers travail!"

And now do I say, "Verily we are from God, and to Him shall we return."

If the loving seekers wish to live within the precincts of the Attracting One (*Majdhúb*), no soul may dwell on this Kingly Throne save the beauty of love. This realm is not to be pictured in words.

> Love shunneth this world and that world too,
> In him are lunacies seventy-and-two.
> The minstrel of love harpeth this lay:
> Servitude enslaveth, kingship doth betray.

This plane requireth pure affection and the bright stream of fellowship. In telling of these companions of the Cave He saith: "They speak not till He hath spoken; and they do His bidding."

On this plane, neither the reign of reason is sufficient nor the authority of self. Hence, one of the Prophets of God hath asked: "O my Lord, how shall we reach unto Thee?" And the answer came, "Leave thyself behind, and then approach Me."

These are a people who deem the lowest place to be one with the throne of glory, and to them beauty's bower differeth not from the field of a battle fought in the cause of the Beloved.

The denizens of this plane speak no words--but they gallop their chargers. They see but the inner reality of the Beloved. To them all words of sense are meaningless, and senseless words are full of meaning. They cannot tell one limb from another, one part from another. To them the mirage is the real river; to them going away is returning. Wherefore hath it been said:

> The story of Thy beauty reached the hermit's dell;
> Crazed, he sought the Tavern where the wine they buy and sell.
> The love of Thee hath leveled down the fort of patience,
> The pain of Thee hath firmly barred the gate of hope as well.

In this realm, instruction is assuredly of no avail.

> The lover's teacher is the Loved One's beauty,
> His face their lesson and their only book.
> Learning of wonderment, of longing love their duty,
> Not on learned chapters and dull themes they look.
> The chain that binds them is His musky hair,
> The Cyclic Scheme, to them, is but to Him a stair.

Here followeth a supplication to God, the Exalted, the Glorified:

> O Lord! O Thou Whose bounty granteth wishes!
> I stand before Thee, all save Thee forgetting.
> Grant that the mote of knowledge in my spirit
> Escape desire and the lowly clay;
> Grant that Thine ancient gift, this drop of wisdom,
> Merge with Thy mighty sea.

Thus do I say: There is no power or might save in God, the Protector, the Self-Subsistent. (Baha'u'llah)

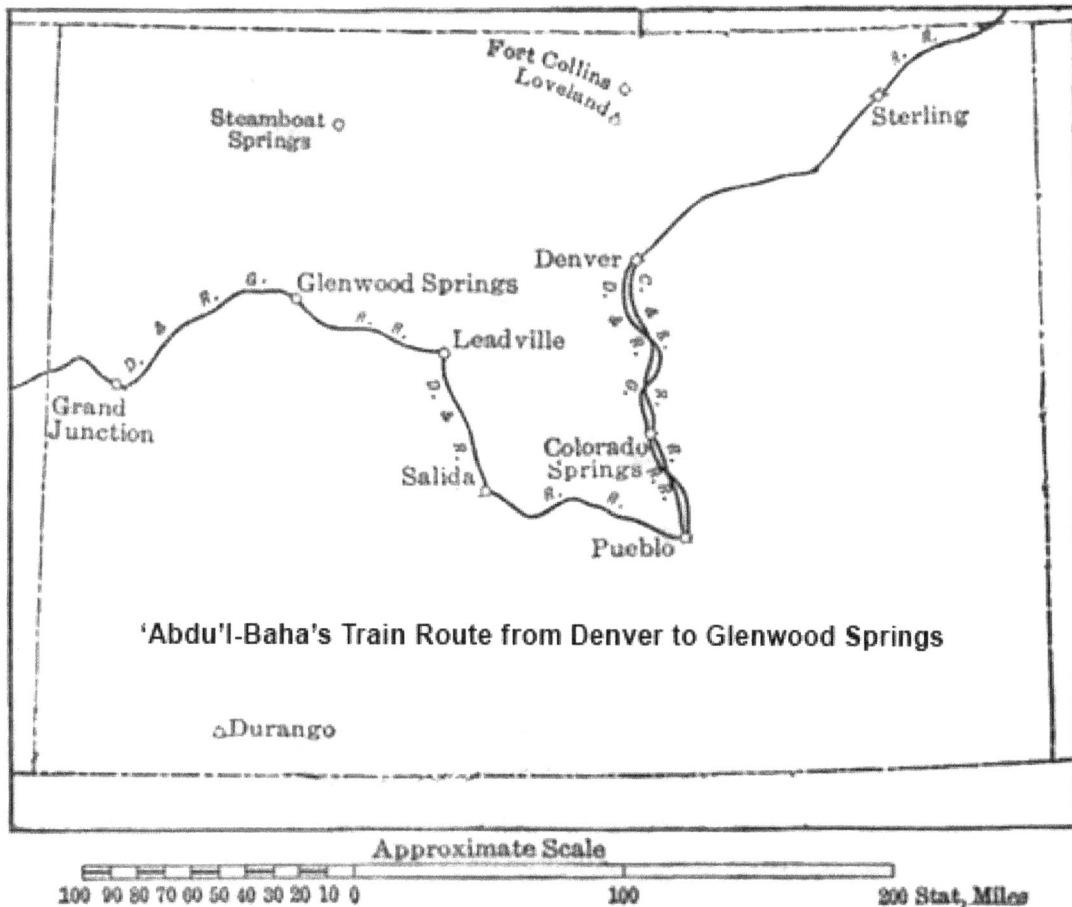

'Abdu'l-Baha's Train Route from Denver to Glenwood Springs

Approximate Scale

100 90 80 70 60 50 40 30 20 10 0   100   200 Stat, Miles

125

Heading West over the Rocky Mountains on tortuous mountain roads fatigued 'Abdu'l-Baha. We read:

At midnight the Blessed Temple was fatigued by the motion of the train. We suggested that California was still far away and it would be well to stop two or three days. He left the train at two a.m. at Glenwood Springs, which is beautifully situated near many hot springs. We stayed at the Hotel Colorado which overlooks the river and nestles among green parks and wooded mountains.

Saturday September 28th, 1912

After the morning tea He came out of the Hotel and enjoyed the scenery. Three superb mountains stood on three sides crowned with verdant trees and adorned with flowers of innumerable hues. Like the feathers of a peacock they are a peculiar beauty in every view. He went towards the river where there were bath houses and hot springs. On the other side of the river which was spanned by a bridge in two sections were the tall buildings of the city rising high on the horizon.

It was decided the entire company should enjoy the baths. The rooms and the bathing facilities were magnificent. In a special room the hot water gushed from natural caves. It was so hot a person could hardly stay there more than fifteen minutes. Coming out of the bath the Beloved said, "Today I am relieved of fatigue. We have been in many places during this journey but we had not time to see the sights. We had not even a moments rest. Today, however, we have had a little respite."

Looking at the clean, Transparent water of the river spinning like pure pearls, and the majestic mountains and parks He said, "May God have mercy on the tyrants who kept the Blessed Beauty in prison for forty years. Such scenes were loved by Him. Once He said that He had not seen any vegetation for over nine years."

A delightful little episode occurred when the party reached the Hotel, which Mahmud relates:

When we reached the Hotel He stood outside in the garden and said that it would be well to have food there. This garden had a large tank of fishes of various colors. The buildings of the Hotel enclosed the garden on three sides. Having read the newspapers of Denver and having seen His likeness as well as those of His party, the manager recognized Him as soon as He approached. He hastened to do what he could. Without the Beloved's request the manager ordered the servants to serve the dinner in the garden. A large table was spread and beautiful chairs were placed around it. The Holy Being sat down on a chair and asked us to do the same.

The Master gave tips to the servants before and after the dinner. As the people of the Hotel saw this majesty and glory of the Beloved they informed others. People began to come to Him party by party. Others were watching the dignity of His beautiful Face from their rooms. Most of them were to say, "How neatly He takes His food! He is, no doubt, a great man." By and by His mission dawned upon the occupants of the Hotel as they were informed of the Cause of God.

In the afternoon 'Abdu'l-Baha walked in the garden.

126

When we were crossing the bridge a messenger brought some telegrams. There was among them one which informed us of the serious illness of Mr. Chase in a hospital and Los Angeles. The Beloved repeatedly mentioned the constancy of Mr. Chase. Afterwards He said, "To turn to the Covenant is to obey the Blessed Beauty which is the cause of the **Gathering of the People of Baha**. The command of the people of Islam to prostrate before *Hifral Aswad* (Stone of the Ka'aba) was simply to obey the Messenger of God and to prove the influence of the Cause of God."

Mr. Chase passed on September 30th. 'Abdu'l-Baha revealed this Tablet:

This revered personage was the first Baha'i in America. He served the Cause faithfully and his services will ever be remembered throughout future ages and cycles. He has written many books in this Cause and they will be studied carefully by the coming generations. He traveled once to The Boundary City and there we associated with each other for several days. Indeed he became free from the troubles of this world. No matter how long he might have remained here, he would have met nothing else but trouble. The purpose of life is to get certain results; that is, the life of man must bring forth certain fruitage. It does not depend upon the length of the life. As soon as the life is crowned with fruition then it is completed, although that person may have a short life...Praise be to God! The tree of Mr. Chase's life brought forth fruit. It gave complete fruit, therefore he is free. He attained eternal rest. He is now in the presence of BAHA'U'LLAH.

I was exceedingly sad and heart-broken when I heard of the departure of Mr. Chase, for I loved him very much...Be not sad nor grieved. Do not sorrow, for no man in this world is permanent. As there was a day for him to come, there is a day for him to leave...Mr. Chase was heavenly. Mr. Chase was spiritual. Mr. Chase was radiant. You have not lost him. At most, there is now a temporary separation between you. In the Kingdom there will be a meeting. It is precisely like taking a journey. You will meet him. Do not sorrow...Certain souls come and believe, and leave behind them an eternal light or radiance, which is the equivalent to a candle that never goes out...You should be comforted. Thus may the spirit of Mr. Chase be pleased with your patience and forbearance. If you were sad, he would be sad, and you would not want to make him sad, too.

O my God! O my God! Verily, this is a servant of Thine, who did believe on Thee and in Thy signs; verily he harkened to Thy summons, turned to Thy Kingdom, humbled himself at Thy holy threshold, was possessed of a contrite heart, arose to serve Thy Cause, to spread Thy fragrances, to promote Thy word, and to expound Thy wisdom.

Verily he guided the people to Thine ancient pathway, and led them to Thy way of rectitude. Verily he held the chalice of guidance in his right hand and gave unto those athirst to drink of the cup of Thy favor. He presented himself at Thy lofty threshold, where he laid his brow on the fragrant soil of Thy garden and circumambulated Thy all-glorious and sublime abode, the traces of which are wide-spread and the fragrances of whose loyalty are sensed everywhere. Later he returned to these vast and extensive countries and proclaimed Thy Name amongst the people, until his respiration ceased and his outward sensation was suspended, returning to Thee with a heart throbbing with Thy love and with an eye opened in Thy direction.

O Lord! O Lord! Submerge him in the ocean of Thy glory. O Lord! O Lord! Usher him into Thy delectable garden. O Lord! O Lord! Usher him into Thy lofty paradise and cause him to be present in Thy meeting of transfiguration. O Lord! Submerge him in the ocean of Thy lights.

Verily, Thou art the Clement! Verily, Thou art the Merciful, the Precious, the Omnipotent!

We left Glenwood Springs at about midnight.

TABLET OF THE CENTRAL PILGRIMAGE: GLENWOOD SPRINGS, COLORADO

(Suriy-i-Hajj I)
--Baha'u'llah--

O Muhammad, when the fragrances of holiness have attracted thee unto them and turned thee unto the land of the All-Merciful that thou mayest discover the breezes of divine praise, go forth then by permission of Thy Lord, the Generous, unto the spot around which circle the angels that are nigh unto God, they that sing His praises about the Throne. At the moment when thou arisest from thy place, seeking to turn in the direction of God, thy Lord, take off from thy body the robe of self and desire and from thy feet the sandals of sin and wickedness, for thou art entering the spot that none may reach save he that casteth behind him all that are on earth and in the heavens, wherein naught but the greatest righteousness shall be accepted, if thou art of them that comprehend, and around which circle the Mount of Command and the Land of Holiness and the Sinai of Glory and the hearts of them that ascend at all times unto the heaven of nearness. None other shall ever attain unto it nor be mentioned by God as having reached it, even should he dwell there for a thousand years as you number them.

And when thou hast journeyed from thy self and from the world and its people and hast travelled unto God, thy Lord, and hast reached the spot at which thou beholdest the outskirts of the city, dismount and stop where thou art and say:

"Spirit and light and glory and praise be upon thee, O City of God, O dwelling-place of His names, O treasury of His attributes, O source of His bounties, O mine of His grace, O place of the manifestation of His effulgences that have encompassed all creation. I bear witness that from thy outskirts appeared the Primal Point and the ornament of pre-existence and the eternal mystery and the universal word and the fixed decrees and the hidden secrets. Thus hast thou surpassed all others in receiving grace from God, the Protector, the Self-Subsisting."

Lift up, then, your hands unto God, thy Lord, with humility and self-effacement, with submission and pleasing contentment, and say:

"O Lord, praise be to Thee for the wonders of Thy gifts and the graces of Thy bestowals. How can I give thanks to Thee, O my God, for having provided me with the visitation of Thy House and having honored me with it and having chosen me for this bounty in which none hath preceded me and having taught me what none hath known but Thee? Wherefore, O my God, I have fled from the house of my self and taken refuge in the place in which Thy most exalted Self hath been established; I have taken flight from whatever hath kept me back from drawing nigh unto Thee and gone for protection unto the precincts of Thy most great mercy. Deprive me not, then, O my God, of that which belongeth unto Thee and cause me not to be occupied with any one but Thee. Thou, verily, art the Mighty, the Forgiving. O Lord, make me steadfast in Thy love and in the love of Thy friends, and cause me not to be of them that have disbelieved in Thy verses after they were sent down, them that have mocked them after their sweet scents have encompassed all created things and all that was brought into existence in the visible and the invisible worlds. O Lord, send unto me the rod of Thy grace and bounty that I may cleave therewith the sea of self and desire, pass over it, and reach the pavilion of the glory of Thine exaltation and the tabernacle of the holiness of Thy protection, lest there be made manifest from me that which Thy good-pleasure abhorreth. Thou, verily, art He that doeth as He willest, and Thou art, in truth, the Lord of this firmly builded House."

Continue on, then, until thou reachest a spot at which there shall be between thee and the city only a thousand steps, be it more or less. Whereupon, embark on foot and immerse thyself in water [The Glenwood Hotspring Pool], as thou hast been commanded in the Book of God, the Protector, the Exalted, the Self-Subsisting. And when thou comest forth from the water, trim thy moustache, then clip thy nails, then comb thy head, then make use of the best of perfumes, then put on the best clothes you are able to afford. And if thou art not able to perform that which We have commanded thee, be thou not saddened, for God hath pardoned thee: He, verily, is the Powerful, the Forgiving, the Pardoner. Strive, then, within thyself that, at the moment thy eye falleth upon the city and thou comest close to it, thy heart may be purified from the mention of all things in such wise that thou mayest cast behind thee all that hath been created between the earth and the heavens, for thou art at that moment walking before the King of all creation, thy Sovereign of names and attributes. Thus instructeth thee the Pen of God, thy Lord and the Lord of all things, if thou art of them that know.

And when thou hast performed that which We have commanded thee, rise from that spot [Hot Spring Fountain] and turn your face towards the House. Then stop, then raise your hands in humble devotion to God, the Powerful, the Protector, the Beloved, and say:

"O my God, this is the spot through which the eyes of them that desire Thee have been solaced and the hearts of Thy lovers have been attracted; this is the utmost goal of them that seek Thee and the highest desire of them that yearn for Thee. This is the spot wherein the eyes of them that know Thee have rained tears in their separation from Thee and the faces of them that have attained unto Thee have turned pale in their longing for Thy beauty. I beseech Thee, O my God, by it and by the effulgences of the lights of the glory of Thy oneness and the flashes of the manifestation of the holiness of Thy Divinity, to release me from the fire of my self and to sanctify me from all that is unworthy of Thy sovereignty. Thou, verily, art the Protector, the Self-Subsisting."

Lower, then, thy hands until they reach the level of thy cheeks, then magnify God (with the phrase *Allah-Hu Akbar!*[*]) nine times, then raise thy hands yet again unto God, thy Lord and the Lord of all that hath been and all that is, and say:

"O my God, this is the city wherein Thy sovereignty was made manifest and the signs of the glory of Thy grandeur appeared and Thy verses were sent down and Thy word was completed

---

[*] Each One of the 9 "*Allah-Hu Akbar!*" The **Takbīr** (تَكْبِير), also transliterated *Tekbir* or *Takbeer*, is the Arabic phrase **Allah-Hu Akbar!** (الله كبر) meaning "*God be Magnified through Me!*" It is a common Arabic expression of Islam used in various contexts by Muslims in formal prayer; in the call (*adhān*) for prayer; as an informal expression of faith;, in Times of Distress; or to express Resolute Determination and/or Defiance! *Ya Allah-Hu Akbar! Va-Ha-Allah al-Kay-Bir*!" Say: "Allah-Hu Akbar!" Nine Times.

and Thy might was exalted and Thy proof shone forth and Thy mercy encompassed all things and all that is in the heavens and the earth. Here beareth witness unto this my self and my heart and my tongue and beyond them blessed servants. Whereupon, I beseech Thee, O my God, by THIS CITY and all that hath been manifested in it to remove that which hath kept me far from the shore of the holiness of Thy mercy and bounty and shut me out from the precincts of the outpouring of Thy grace and bestowal. Clothe me, then, O my God, in the robe of Thy graciousness and bounty. Thou willest and Thou art, truly, the Mighty, the Exalted, the Beloved. Give me, then, to drink, O my God, from the fountain of the glory of Thy knowledge and the living waters of the holiness of meeting with Thee, waters which, were but a drop from them to be sprinkled upon all created things, they would be raised to eternal, everlasting life, standing before Thy face and the manifestations of the flashes of the lights of Thy countenance. Thou, verily, art the Mighty, the Exalted, the Holy."

[Drink then from the Hot Spring Fountain taking the water in thy hand to thy lips]

Lower, then, thy hands and walk upon the ground [toward the bridge] with the dignity of God and His tranquillity. And as thou walkest proclaim the singleness of thy Lord (with the phrase "He is God") then proclaim His greatness (with the phrase *Allah-Hu Akbar)*, then His holiness (with the phrase *Allah-Hu Aqdás),* then His majesty (with the phrase *Allah-Hu Akbar Amjad).* Follow, then, in the ways of the messengers and the manners of them that are near to God, saying:

"Here am I, O my God, here am I; greetings unto Thee, and the light be before Thee."

Repeat these words as much as will not cool down the fire of thy ardor and passion. Thus We have instructed thee in truth that thou mayest be of them that act in accordance with what they have been commanded. Know, then, that thou didst answer thy Lord with these words when He ascended the Throne and called upon all created things with His words "Am I not your Lord?" Those words are the secret of those others, if ye be of them that ponder upon the mysteries of their Lord. Indeed, shouldst thou behold with the eye of thine inner being, thou shalt at that moment behold Him raised upon the thrones of all created beings, crying: "No God is there but Me, the Protector, the Self-Subsisting." Know, then, O pilgrim, thy value and station at that moment. Give thanks, then, to God that this has been bestowed upon thee and that He hath aided thee therein. Verily, there is no God but Him; creation (*khalq*) and command (*amr*) are His and all act according to His bidding. Blessed art thou, O servant, in that thou hast entered the land of holiness, the Paran of the Spirit, and the Sinai of Command. Yea, shouldst thou make sharp thy sight, thou wilt behold circumambulating all about thee the worlds of God and the Concourse on High. By God, O servant journeying from thy home, should God open thy vision and shouldst thou turn thy gaze above the head unto the heavens, thou wilt behold the sanctuaries of holiness, the habitations of loving-fellowship, the people of the pavilion of the heavenly kingdom, the inhabitants of the thrones of the kingdom of might, the bodies of the holy ones among the manifestations of the realm below and the kingdom above all moving in the heaven of holiness above thy head, extolling with thee the unity, the greatness, the holiness, and the majesty of the Lord of the City and of him that appeared from it and arose therein. Thus shalt thou behold the matter, if thou art of them that see with the eyes of the spirit.

And when thou reachest the spot [on the bridge] at which thou art come nigh unto the gate of the city at a distance of 20 paces, stop at the command of God, thy Lord, the Lord of all things, and the Lord of this praiseworthy scene. Extol, then, the greatness of God 19 times, then address the city on My behalf, [turning to the left and then to the right] saying:

"May God curse a people that have interposed themselves between Us and the lights of Thy holiness, O City of God, and who have kept us back from inhaling the fragrances of the holiness of Thy oneness and from dwelling within the precincts of the glory of Thy mercy and from standing in the courtyard of the gate of the outpouring of Thy compassion."

Turn, then, thy gaze unto the most great spectacle, in the direction of the canyon walls of the city and whatsoever hath been created therein and hath existed within it, for upon all of these hath fallen the eye of God, the Mighty, the Protector, the Self-Sufficient. Say:

"O wall of the City! Blessed be thou, inasmuch as there shone forth above thee the lights of the sun of thy Lord, the Exalted, the Most High. O trees of the City! Blessed be ye, inasmuch as the breezes of holiness have been wafted upon you from the direction of eternity. O air of the City! Blessed be thou, inasmuch as the breath of God, the Mighty, the Powerful, the Beloved, was spread within thee. O earth of the City! Blessed be thou, inasmuch as the feet of thy Lord, the All-Merciful, have walked upon thee and the form of the Praised One hath passed over thee in the days when all were wrapped in the veils of their own selves."

Walk, then, until thou reachest the city hall; and when thou hast attained its presence and arrived at its gate, place thy face upon the dust of the gate, that thou mayest discover the fragrance of thy Lord, the Exalted, the Most High and may be of them that are nourished with the water of life. Know, then, that from its dust is manifested the decree of water, and from its water the decree of air, and from its air the effect of fire, and from a torch ignited from it hath appeared the decree of 'B' and 'E,' if thou art of them that know.

This is how We have described it unto thee in the land and among these people that are unconscious in the drunkenness of self. Otherwise, by Him in Whose hand is my soul, an atom of its dust is more glorious in the sight of God than all that hath been created in the meadows of eternity and all that hath been decreed in the Tablets of Destiny within the mystery of fate in the realm of the Divine Decree. Thus do We cast upon thee the secrets of the Cause, that thou mayest be of them that comprehend.

When thou hast kissed the dust and derived a blessing therefrom, raise up thy head, then stand and magnify God (with the phrase *Allah-Hu Akbar)* 19 times, then walk with the dignity and tranquility of God and with His grandeur and majesty until you arrive before the House [1020]. Then stop and say:

"I bear witness by my tongue and my soul and my spirit and my body that this is the spot whereon prostrate themselves the inhabitants of the Empyrean realm and the denizens of the Kingdom of God's decree and they that inhabit the highest mansions of eternity behind the veils of grandeur. Through it all things have been made manifest and through it the breezes of bounty have blown upon the forms of all the worlds. This is the spot whence the inhabitants of the Concourse of Eternity derive their blessings and the hearts of them that are established between earth and heaven obtain their illumination. Every day the dwellers of the crimson chambers sweep its courtyard and the angels that are nigh unto God brush it with the tresses of the Spirit. And this is the spot wherein the Beauty of the All-Merciful appeared and in His own person ascended the Throne of Forgiveness and decreed that which He willed for all creation. He, verily, is the One that doeth as He willeth and decreeth as He desireth and performeth whatsoever He wisheth. I bear witness that, from a handful of this dust, the first Adam was created, wherefore was he named "The Father of Humanity" (Abu'l-Bashar) in the kingdom of names, and God made him His remembrance amongst all created things."

Bow down, then, with thy face upon the dust, then place thy right cheek upon it and say with my tongue:

"Praised be Thou, O God, my God. This is Thy servant that hath detached himself from all directions, turning in the direction of Thy oneness, and hath freed his soul from all apart from Thee, and hath clung to the cord of the bounty of Thy grace, and hath come in his completeness unto the meadows of the glory of Thy forgiveness. Cause to blow, then, O my God upon my heart the breezes of the glory of the holiness of Thy bounty and upon my inner being the fragrances of the majesty of the glory of Thy favors. Cast me not away disappointed, O my God, from Thy gate or despairing from the manifestations of the sun of Thy bounties. Thou, verily, art the Powerful over what Thou willest and Thou art the Protector, the Mighty, the Powerful."

Then stand and turn to the right of the House [toward the direction of Chair Mountain], in the direction of thy Lord, the Exalted, the Mighty, the Wise. Raise, then, thy hands unto God, the Exalted, the Most High and say:

"Praised be Thou, O God, my God. I have raised the hands of my hope unto the heaven of Thy bounty and grace, and I have fastened the fingers of my reliance upon the cord of Thy grace and favors. I beseech Thee by him through whom Thou didst clothe all created things with the robe of Thy guidance and didst raise to life all existence from the power of Thy compassion and generosity, not to lock the door of Thy knowledge upon the face of my heart nor the door of Thy mercy upon my soul. Cause me, then, O my God, to be such as will be worthy of the power of the glory of Thy singleness and the majesty of the holiness of Thine eternity. Thou, verily, art the Gracious, the Bestowing, the Mighty, the Generous. O my God, I have become detached from mine own self, hastening unto Thy Most Exalted Self, and have fled from mine own abode and stood before Thy most pure and most glorious House. Wherefore, I beseech Thee not to leave me unto myself nor unto them that keep back mankind from the love of Thy beauty and debar Thy servants from Thy mighty and unbending path."

Circle, then, about the House [counter-clockwise] on my behalf seven times. Thus commandeth thee the Ancient Beauty and teacheth thee what none in all the worlds doth know. And at the time when thou art circumambulating the House of the Lord, make mention of Him in thy heart and upon thy tongue and turn within thyself unto the direction of the mighty Throne. And when thou hast completed thy circumambulation, present thyself within the first portico [across the street], before the door of the sanctuary, then, stand, then raise thy hands unto the heaven of the outpouring of the grace of thy Lord, the Mighty, the Inaccessible. And I counsel thee that, at that time when thou dost raise up thy hands, raise them with such yearning that thereby the hands of all beings may be raised up towards the heaven of the grace of thy Lord. And when thou desirest to call upon God, thy Lord, call upon Him with such devotion that thereby the tongues of all atoms may utter the praise of thy Creator and may make mention of Him that brought thee into existence, the Powerful, the Mighty, the Wondrous.

And if thou be not thus, it is not fitting for thee to stand in the spot whereon have stood the bodies of the holy ones and them that are nigh unto God. Nor art thou worthy of thy relation unto my Self nor thy habitation beneath the shadow of my love, which God hath made a cutting sword whereby to separate the unbelievers from them that extol His Oneness.

And when thou hast raised thy hands unto the clouds of the mercy of thy Lord, the Mighty, the Knowing, the All-Informed, say:

"I bear witness that no god is there but He; He is alone, no companion is there for Him nor likeness nor deputy nor comparison nor rival nor equal nor similitude for His sovereignty, the Exalted, the Inaccessible, the Most High. From all eternity He was one in His Essence and one in His attributes and one in His deeds and unto all eternity He shall be as He hath ever been in the glory of His majesty and the sovereignty of His sublimity, such that the mystic knowers have confessed their inability to attain unto the meadows of the holiness of His knowledge and the devoted ones have admitted their powerlessness to ascend unto the heaven of His mention and His praise. He, verily, is the Protector of all things and He, in truth, is the Mighty, the All-Generous.

"I bear witness that the Primal Point of our Lord the Exalted, the Most High is, truly, His manifestation in the realm of the empyrean and His appearance in the kingdom of the decree and His dawning-place in the domain of destiny. Through him all created things are brought to life and all existence is renewed and the balance of justice hath been set up upon the station of praiseworthy glory. Through him the Bird of the Throne hath crowed and the Dove of Glory hath warbled and the Resurrection of the Command hath come to pass and all that lay hidden in the treasuries of hidden glory hath been made manifest. Through him the heavens of pre-existence were raised up and the clouds of bounty were elevated unto this most holy, most notable sky and the sun of grace and beneficence shone forth from the horizon of resplendent holiness. Through him the oceans of verses surged in the kingdom of names and attributes and the time set for the command arrived with that which was decreed in the tablets of inaccessible majesty. And I bear witness that, through him, the veil of mystery was removed from the beauty of grandeur and the secrets of the unseen were revealed in the kingdom of the Divine Decree, and that through him every poor and needy one ascended unto the heaven of riches and every transient one rose up unto the dwelling-places of eternal life and every sick one was raised to the abodes of healing within pavilions of shining light. And I bear witness that this is the Spot wherein Thou didst ascend the Throne of the glory of Thy unity and didst bring into being all creation, both former and latter, through the power of Thy will and Thy desire, and wherein the clouds of Thy grace rained down upon all created things.

"Wherefore, I beseech Thee, O my God, by Thy hidden and Most Great Name and Thy concealed and most perfect word whose manifestation Thou didst promise unto Thy servants at the Time of **_Mustaghath_**,[*] to bring me unto the shore of the ocean of Thy forgiveness and to erase all that I have enumerated of my most great sins and my most mighty transgressions! Then forgive, O my God, my father and my mother and my family and those whom I have related unto myself, them that have believed in Thee and Thy signs. Make, then, for me, O my God, a seat of truth by Thy side and cause me to be united with those of Thy servants that are nigh unto Thee. I ask Thee, then, O my God and my Beloved, not to make me to be one of them that circle about Thy House in Thy Land and deny Thy sacred House within the Manifestations of Thy Self and the Dawning-places of the glory of Thy Self-Subsistence and the Locations of the glory of Thy Lordship. This, O my God, is my utmost wish and desire. Thou, verily, art the Sovereign, the Powerful, the Mighty, the Wise.

"I ask Thee, then, O my God, by Thy beauty whereby the suns of the glory of Thy bounty have been made luminous and the rays of the lights of the holiness of Thy generosity flashed forth, to cause me not to be distressed upon the day whereon every soul shall be distressed, on which the possessors of pomp and leadership shall be puffed up with pride, on which the feet of them that have attained shall slip, on which the lamentation of all things shall be raised, and on which every resplendent and shining light shall be darkened. Take hold of my hand then, O my God, with the hand of Thy grace and favors and deprive me not on that day of the fragrances of the glory of Thy holiness nor from hearkening unto the melodies of Thy new creation, and cause me not to follow upon that Day behind every croaking, sinful one. Open my eyes through Thy grace that I may recognize Thee by Thine own Self, not by that which is other than Thee, and that I may behold the wonders of the lights of Thy Beauty by what Thou hast bestowed upon me through Thy bounty, not that which belongeth unto men. For Thou hast not created any proof for Thyself save Thine own Essence, nor any evidence save Thy signs. Thou, verily, are He that ariseth, the Ruler, the Knowing, the All-Informed. Praise be to God, Lord of all the worlds."

Whereupon, end thou thy pilgrimage, for We have not permitted anyone to approach closer than this unto the sanctuary, for before that spot shine the lights of the Essence from behind the names and the attributes. And, apart from that, courtesy must be observed, for that is one of the best of all attributes in the sight of God, King of the earth and the heavens. Thus have We sent down upon thee the command with a shining and manifest proof. It is our desire that, from every city, one should go forth on My behalf and for his own sake to visit the House of God and that he may be a pilgrim. By God, at every step mercy and grace shall descend upon him from the heaven of resplendent holiness, and at the same time when he raises his foot for the first step and sets it down, God shall forgive his sins and the sins of his mother and his father and all that are related unto him. Thus hath the grace of thy Lord encompassed all created things, whether of the first or of the last. By God, whosoever visiteth the House, it is as if he hath visited God within the pavilion of the glory of meeting with Him and the tent of the majesty of His Beauty. Thus do We inform thee of the call that is mighty by the side of the Throne.

Whosoever visiteth the House as We have commanded him, God shall raise him up after his death within the paradise of majesty and grandeur in such a beauteous form that the dwellers of the Concourse on High shall be illumined by the lights of his face, and all that are in the exalted

---

[*] Autumnal Equinox, 2001 AD.

heavens shall be commanded to appear before him and to circle about him and to make their pilgrimage unto his beauty every morning and evening.

O trustees of God upon the earth, strive unto the most great mention, and cast away all that is in your hands and turn your faces unto the Abode of God, the Mighty, the Powerful, the All-Knowing. Be ye steadfast, O people, in this station that, if all that are on earth should rise up against you, ye would not pay the least attention to them and would remain firm in the faith of God. The unbelievers shall prevent you performing what God has sent down upon you on account of the rancor that is in their breasts. But God shall do as He willeth through His word; He, verily, is the Powerful, the Mighty.

Know, then, that We have written concerning pilgrimage to the House detailed and vast tablets, but We have not sent them until now, If God wills, We shall send them in truth. He, verily, is the Guardian of the Messengers. That which We have sent is what was sent down from the Kingdom of Divine Power in a brief form, for the angels that are nigh unto God and the inhabitants of the Exalted Concourse love to be brief in their outward acts. And inwardly, let there be at all times those that perform the pilgrimage. Thus have We taught thee and made known unto thee the paths of holiness and guided thee unto the shores of manifest grace.

Tablet of the Northern Pilgrimage: Deer Lodge, Montana

(Suriy-i-Hajj II)
--Baha'u'llah--

HE IS THE EVERLASTING, THE MANIFEST!

It is incumbent on whomsoever desireth to turn to the Most Holy Direction, to come into the Presence of God, the Mighty, the Knowing, to hearken unto the call of God, to behold His Beauty, and to inhale the perfume of God, the Mighty, the Powerful, the Exalted, the Great, that he should go forth from his house, journeying unto God, until he entereth the city that hath been named "the Abode of Peace" [Deer Lodge, Montana]. And when he arriveth there, let him magnify God, his Lord, (with the phrase *Ya Baha'u'l-Abha*) with the tongue of his heart and with his outward tongue until he cometh unto the river [on the Western Bank of the Clark Fork at the Conley Yellowstone Trail Bridge].

And when he reacheth it, let him put on his best clothes and then perform ablutions as God hath commanded him. And when he washeth his hands, let him say:

"O Lord, this is water that Thou hast caused to flow forth through Thy command in the neighborhood of Thy sacred House (Ezekiel's Prophesied Temple). As I have washed my hands with it, O my God, at Thy command, wash me, then, from every stain and sin and omission and from all that Thy good-pleasure abhorreth. Thou, verily, art the Mighty, the All-Powerful."

Then let wash his face, saying:

"O Lord, this is my face that Thou hast purified through Thy will. I beseech Thee, then, by the power of the glory of Thy singleness and the wonders of the names of the manifestations of Thy Cause, to cleanse it of all save Thee. Guard it, then, from turning to any but Thee or from beholding them that have failed to seek Thy manifest, spotless, mighty, and generous Beauty."

Let him, then, cross the bridge with the dignity and comportment of God, magnifying God (with the phrase *Ya Baha'u'l-Abha*) until he reaches the end of the bridge (1200 Main St. Apt #1). Then let him stand and turn in the direction of the House (the "Stone with Seven Eyes"), saying at his first step:

"O Lord, this is the first step that I have set down in the path of Thy good-pleasure and the first pace that I have taken through Thy will. I have fled, O my God, from all directions in the direction of Thy grace and favors, and I have taken flight from myself and my desires and from all save Thee in the direction of Thy bounty and blessings. O my God, disappoint not them that have hoped for the clouds of Thy mercy and shut not out them that have sought the showers of the glory and generosity. Here am I, O my God! I have sought Thy House, the House round which circle the dwellers of the Celestial Concourse and beyond them the souls of them that are nigh unto Thee among the holy ones. I beseech Thee by the former and by the latter not to prevent my eyes from beholding the wonders of the lights of the holiness of Thy beauty, nor to withhold from my face the manifestations of the breezes that blow from the dawn of Thy meeting, nor to keep back from my heart the fragrances of the glory of Thy revelation and inspiration. Thou, verily, art the Possessor of bounty and might, of grace and mercy and sovereignty, and Thou, truly, art the Possessor of power and strength and grandeur, and Thou, in truth, art near to answer them that pray to Thee."

Then let him glorify God (with the phrase *Allah'u'Abha*) and begin to perform the circumambulation. Let him circle about the House [clockwise] seven times, and, when he has completed this action and is come before the Door of the House (Tower 7), let him stand and beg forgiveness from God 70 times. Then let him say:

"O my God and my Lord. Praise be unto Thee for having shown Thy kindness and generosity to me in that Thou hast caused me to stand in the spot wherein naught is seen but the tokens of the glory of the sovereignty of Thy oneness and naught is witnessed save the flashes of the lights of the sun of Thy beauty. I beseech Thee by Thee and by Thy Self to purify me from the mire of the world and from its vanities and to burn from the surface of my heart the veils that have kept me back from entering into the floods of the oceans of the glory of Thy unity and have shut me out from entry into the fields of the holiness of union with Thee and meeting Thee. O Lord, turn me not back disappointed from the gate of Thy mercy and send me not away in loss from Thy House. O Lord, forgive me and my parents and my brethren and my family and my kinsfolk, those of them that have believed in Thee and in Thy most great verses in the manifestation of Thy most exalted Beauty. Thou, verily, art the Mighty, the Beneficent."

Let him, then, walk with the utmost gravity and glorify God (with the phrase *Allah'u'Abha)* until he reacheth the gate (19-12), then let him stand and say:

"O my God, this is the spot wherein Thou didst lift up Thy voice and in which Thy proof was made manifest and Thy signs shone forth and Thy beauty rose above the horizon and Thy verses were sent down and Thy command was made visible and Thy name was raised up and Thy mention was spread abroad and Thy power was made perfect and Thy sovereignty was exalted above all that are in the heavens and the earth."

Let him, then, address the House and Leland and its walls and all that is upon it, saying:

"Blessed be thou, O House, inasmuch as God hath made Thee the Spot whereon His feet have trodden. Blessed be thou, O House, inasmuch as the glances of the glory of His greatness have fallen upon thee. Blessed be thou, O House, inasmuch as God hath singled Thee out and made Thee a dwelling-place for His own Self and a location wherein to ***establish*** His sovereignty. No earth hath surpassed thee, unless it be the earth that God hath chosen above all the shrines of the world, by that which hath been written down by His Pen, the Preserver. Blessed be thou, O House, inasmuch as through Thee God distinguish between the fortunate and the wretched from this day unto the day whereon the All-Merciful shall shine forth with the lights of a wondrous holiness. Blessed be thou, blessed be thou, inasmuch as God hath made Thee the balance for them that believe in His unity and the uttermost abode of them that know Him, and hath sanctified Thee from the knowledge of them that hate Him and them that disbelieve in Him, in

138

such wise that none may enter Thee save the believer whose heart God hath tried in its faith, nor may any be able to approach thee save him from whom there are wafted the breezes of the praise of God. Blessed be Thou, inasmuch as God hath singled Thee out for them among His servants that are nigh unto Him and them among His creatures that are devoted to Him. None may touch Thee save them that have utterly detached themselves from all that are in the heavens and the earth, in whose hearts there is naught but the radiance of the lights of the glory of His oneness and in whose inner beings there is naught but the manifestations of the effulgences of the holiness of His eternity. This is a station for which God hath chosen Thee, wherein Thou shouldst pride Thyself above all the worlds. Blessed be Thou and him that built Thee and raised Thee up and served Thee and carried water unto thy roses, and **Blessed Is He** that hath entered thee and he that hath gazed upon Thee and he that hath discovered from Thee a breath of the **Robe of the Joseph of God**, the Mighty, the Powerful. I bear witness that he that hath entered within thee, God shall cause him to enter the Holy Sanctuary on the day whereon the Beauty of the Essence shall be established upon a mighty throne, and He shall forgive the sins of him that taketh refuge in Thee and entereth beneath Thy shadow, and shall fulfill his needs and shall raise him up on the Day of Resurrection with such beauty that his kindred of both past and future shall be illumined by it."

Let him, then, prostrate himself with his face upon the dust of the gate and call upon his Lord like one that is detached and repentant, relating himself to God and saying:

"O Lord, I am he that hath acted wrongly towards Thee and rejected Thy beauty, for my self and my desires preoccupied me. Thou, verily, art the Knowing, the All Informed. O Lord, since I have recognized Thy Self, I seek pardon for my former state and for whatever appeared from my tongue and went forth from my mouth and entered into my thoughts. I have returned unto Thee with all my being; Thou, verily, art the Forgiving, the Compassionate. O Lord, when Thou didst make known unto me **the places of Thy command** and didst awaken me from my sleep and my heedlessness, I set forth from my house in the direction of Thy House, turning my eyes towards Thy bounty and Thy forgiveness. Thou, verily, art the Most Merciful of the Merciful. O Lord, I have come unto Thee with that sin that was heavier than all that is in the heavens and the earth and greater than the creation of all existence, until I have stood before the gate of Thy House, from which no sinner hath been turned away disappointed; I have bowed myself down upon its dust, humbling myself before Thy beauty, abasing myself before Thy sovereignty, and making myself as nothing in Thy presence. O Lord, have mercy on me through Thy compassion and graciousness and ordain, then, for me a seat of truth by Thy side. Make me, then, one of Thy servants that have turned in repentance unto Thee. O Lord, forgive me my sins and my transgressions and all that my hands have committed. Thou, verily, art the Mighty, the Generous."

Then let him raise his head and seek forgiveness from God with this Mighty, this Great Invocation:

"O Lord, I seek forgiveness from Thee by my tongue and my heart and my soul and my mind and my spirit and my body and my corporeality and my bones and my blood and my skin. Thou, verily, art the Forgiving, the Merciful. And I seek forgiveness from Thee, O my God, by the Invocation whereby the fragrances of mercy have blown upon the people of rebellion and through which the sinful have been clothed **in the beauteous garment of Thy forgiveness**. And I seek forgiveness from Thee, O my King, by the invocation whereby the power of Thy clemency and Thy grace is made manifest and whereby the sun of loving-kindness and bounty shineth forth above the forms of the sinful. And I seek forgiveness from Thee, O Forgiver of my sins and my Creator, by the invocation whereby the wrongdoers hasten in the direction of Thy pardon and graciousness and through which the seekers stand at the gate of Thy mercy, O Thou the Merciful and Compassionate. And I seek forgiveness from Thee, O my Lord, by the invocation that Thou hast made a fire that burneth away all sins and rebelliousness from every one that hath repented and returned to Thee, regretting what he hath done, weeping over his actions, and secure in Thee, and through which the bodies of all created things are purified from the defilement of sins and wrongful actions and from all that Thy mighty and all-wise Self abhorreth."

Then let him enter into the House with dignity and tranquillity, as if he beholds God in the realm of His command and the kingdom of His House, until he enters the cell-block and comes before the *qibla* (Room 232) that was singled out for the raising up of the throne of might upon it. Then let him raise his hands and turn his gaze in the direction of His bounties and say:

"I bear witness in this place where I stand that there is no God but Him alone; no companion is there for Him nor likeness nor peer nor rival nor deputy nor equal nor similitude; and that the Point of Unity is His servant, His glory, His might, His greatness, His reality, His power, His sovereignty, His majesty, His kingship, His strength, His honor, His nobility, His benevolence, and that through Him, His beauty shone forth and His face was purified and His proof rose above the horizon and His evidence was perfected and His argument was completed and His signs were made luminous, and through Him all that are in the heavens and on the earth were raised to life and they that are in the kingdom of command and creation were resurrected, and through him the breezes of holiness were wafted upon all the worlds.

And I bear witness that *He Whom God Shall Make Manifest* is the truth, no doubt is there concerning Him; He is come with the lights of a wondrous holiness, and through Him are recreated the heavens and the earth and the people of the former and the latter generations. **Blessed Is He** that hath attained unto His days and that entereth His gate and is honoured with meeting Him and circleth around Him and prostrateth himself before Him and visiteth the dust of His feet and standeth in His presence and is of them that arise."

Then let him say:

"O Lord, this is Thy House wherein the breezes of Thy bounty and generosity have wafted and wherein Thou hast shone forth in the innermost heart of mystery upon all the manifestations of Thy names and the dawning-places of Thine attributes. None is informed of this save Thee, the All-Knowing. O Lord, this is Thy House from which the signs of Thy grace have been made manifest unto all the worlds and wherein there befell Thee what befell Thee on the part of them that believed and them that disbelieved. Thou, verily, wast patient in all this, notwithstanding Thy power and Thy sovereignty. Thou, truly, art the Knowing, the Wise, the Mighty, the Powerful! O Lord, this is the Spot whereon Thou didst walk with Thine ancient feet and wherein

Thou didst raise up Thy voice and Thy melodies and didst make heard Thy call and Thy singing, with wondrous and honeyed tones.

"O Lord, this is the Spot wherein Thou didst sit upon the Throne of all created things and didst exalt Thyself through the tongue of Thy power above all that are in the heavens and on earth. O Lord, this is the Spot wherein Thy gaze was turned in the direction of Thy bounty and wherein the oceans of power surged within Thy hidden and concealed and guarded Word. O Lord, this is the Spot wherein was Thy Cause within the mystery of mysteries, and wherein Thou didst not move Thy lips as Thou didst wish, and wherein Thou didst conceal Thy radiant face, and wherein Thou wast hidden in the most utter concealment and behind the densest of veils, in such wise that none among all creation recognized Thy Self.

"O Lord, this is Thy House that was shamed after Thee by Thy servants, who looted whatever was therein and plundered all that was within it; thus did they dishonor Thee and make war against Thee in their heart of hearts and break Thy Covenant and shatter Thy bond; yet didst Thou conceal all this and didst pass over them through Thy wondrous bounty. O Lord, divest me not of the bounty of Thy protection, nor take from me the garment of Thy favor and pardon, nor cause me to be far removed from the precincts of Thy mercy, nor deprive me of the fountain of Thy exalted grace. O Lord, sanctify me from all save Thee and bring me near unto Thy Self and honor me with meeting Thee. Thou, verily, art the Powerful, the Knowing, the Understanding, the Bringer to Life, the Vivifier, the Slayer. O Lord, cause me to attain unto that which Thou hast willed for those of Thy servants that are nigh unto Thee. Ordain, then, for me the best of what Thou hast ordained for the sanctified among Thy chosen ones."

Let him then be silent within himself and be at rest in his innermost being. Then let him turn in his heart and with his hearing in the direction of the House. If he should **discover the fragrance of God** and hear His call, he may be assured within himself that God has forgiven him his sins and has passed over him and relented towards him and beholdeth him as on the day whereon he was born of his mother. But if he should not **discover the fragrance of God**, the Mighty, the Powerful, let him perform again the ritual on this day or one another day until he discovereth it and heareth the call. This is that which hath been decreed by the Pen of a glorious and Wise One upon the Tablets of a Hidden Holiness. Thus doth God open the Gates of Grace and bounty unto the face of the heavens and the earth, that perchance people may not deprive themselves of the mercy of God and His bounteousness. This, verily, is true guidance and a remembrance from Us unto all the worlds.

QIBLIH

The Point of Adoration is called the *qiblih* and signifies the direction of prayer ordained for the peoples of God in every dispensation. In the days of Adam this was designated as the black chocolate granite coffer stone situated in the so-called "King's Chamber" of the Great Pyramid of Giza. When the covenants were broken in ancient times, Shem, the blessed son of Noah--known as the High Priest Melchizedec (Genesis 14:18-20; Psalm 110:1-7)--built the City of Jerusalem, and established the Point of Adoration, in that City, on the sacred spot where the Holy Temple would eventually be built by Solomon and the Ark of God's Covenant would come to rest. It was not until the coming of the prophet Muhammad that the direction of prayer was changed to Holy Mecca, at the place of the Ka'aba to the point of the black meteorite stone placed in that location by father Abraham with the assistance of his son Ishmael.

Upon the advent of the Bab, in 1844 AD (after 2300 years from the building of the second Temple, and 1260 years after the advent of the prophet Muhammad), he announced:

> The Qiblih is indeed "He Whom God Shall Make Manifest;" whenever He moveth, it moveth, until He shall come to rest. (The Bab, *Arabic Bayan*)

The changing of the direction of obligatory prayer has always been a test to the peoples. The appearance of the Holy Manifestations of God, according to God's wisdom and inscrutable decree, in the human Temple at different places and different times, is the natural change of Qiblih as depicted in the Path of the Flaming Sword of the Tree of the Qabala. Thus the light of God shines from different directions at different times, and the Point of Adoration is to turn towards the direction of the divine appearance of the Light as tabernacled in the immediate moment, and not simply to any darksome place where the light may have appeared on the horizons of the past. Baha'u'llah states:

> Know verily that the purpose underlying all these symbolic terms and abstruse allusions, which emanate from the Revealers of God's holy Cause, hath been to test and prove the peoples of the world; that thereby the earth of the pure and illuminated hearts may be known from the perishable and barren soil. From time immemorial such hath been the way of God amidst His creatures, and to this testify the records of the sacred books.

> And likewise, reflect upon the revealed verse concerning the "Qiblih." When Muhammad, the Sun of Prophethood, had fled from the dayspring of Batha [Mecca] unto Yathrib [Medina], He continued to turn His face, while praying, unto Jerusalem, the holy city, until the time when the Jews began to utter unseemly words against Him--words which if mentioned would ill befit these pages and would weary the reader. Muhammad strongly resented these words. Whilst, wrapt in meditation and wonder, He was gazing toward heaven, He heard the kindly Voice of Gabriel, saying: "We behold Thee from above, turning Thy face to heaven; but We will have Thee turn to a Qiblih which shall please Thee."[*]

---

[*] Qur'an 2:144.

On a subsequent day, when the Prophet, together with His companions, was offering the noontide prayer, and had already performed two of the prescribed Rik'ats,[*] the Voice of Gabriel was heard again: "Turn Thou Thy face towards the sacred Mosque."[†] In the midst of that same prayer, Muhammad suddenly turned His face away from Jerusalem and faced the Ka'bih. Whereupon, a profound dismay seized suddenly the companions of the Prophet. Their faith was shaken severely. So great was their alarm, that many of them, discontinuing their prayer, apostatized their faith. Verily, God caused not this turmoil but to test and prove His servants. Otherwise, He, the ideal King, could easily have left the Qiblih unchanged, and could have caused Jerusalem to remain the Point of Adoration unto His Dispensation, thereby withholding not from that holy city the distinction of acceptance which had been conferred upon it. (Baha'u'llah, *Kitab-i-Iqan*, pp. 49-51)

Baha'u'llah confirms the Bab's injunction to turn toward "He Whom God Shall Make Manifest" in the *Kitab-i-Aqdas*:

Raise up and exalt the two Houses in the Twin Hallowed Spots [Deer Lodge and Glenwood], and the other sites wherein the throne of your Lord, the All-Merciful, hath been established. Thus commandeth you the Lord of every understanding heart. Be watchful lest the concerns and preoccupations of this world prevent you from observing that which hath been enjoined upon you by Him Who is the Mighty, the Faithful. Be ye the embodiments of such steadfastness amidst mankind that ye will not be kept back from God by the doubts of those who disbelieved in Him when He manifested Himself, invested with a mighty sovereignty. Take heed lest ye be prevented by aught that hath been recorded in the Book from hearkening unto this, the Living Book, Who proclaimeth the truth: "Verily, there is no God but Me, the Most Excellent, the All-Praised."

Look ye with the eye of equity upon Him Who hath descended from the heaven of Divine will and power, and be not of those who act unjustly. Call then to mind these words which have streamed forth, in tribute to this Revelation, from the Pen of Him Who was My Herald, and consider what the hands of the oppressors have wrought throughout My days. Truly they are numbered with the lost. He said: "Should ye attain the presence of 'Him Whom We Shall Make Manifest,' [Baha'u'llah] beseech ye God, in His bounty, to grant that He might deign to seat Himself upon your couches, for that act in itself would confer upon you matchless and surpassing honor. Should He drink a cup of water in your homes, this would be of greater consequence for you than your proffering unto every soul, nay unto every created thing, the water of its very life. Know this, O ye My servants!"

Such are the words with which My Forerunner hath extolled My Being, could ye but understand. Whoso reflecteth upon these verses, and realizeth what hidden pearls have been enshrined within them, will, by the righteousness of God,

---

[*] Prostrations.
[†] Qur'an 2:149.

143

perceive the fragrance of the All-Merciful wafting from the direction of this Prison [this "Stone with Seven Eyes"] and will, with his whole heart, hasten unto Him with such ardent longing that the hosts of earth and heaven would be powerless to deter him. Say: This is a Revelation around which every proof and testimony doth circle. Thus hath it been sent down by your Lord, the God of Mercy, if ye be of them that judge aright.

Say: This is the very soul of all Scriptures which hath been breathed into the Pen of the Most High, causing all created beings to be dumbfounded, save only those who have been enraptured by the gentle breezes of My loving-kindness and the sweet savors of My bounties which have pervaded the whole of creation.

O people of the Bayan! Fear ye the Most Merciful and consider what He hath revealed in another passage. He said: "The Qiblih is indeed 'He Whom God Shall Make Manifest;' whenever He moveth, it moveth, until He shall come to rest." Thus was it set down by the Supreme Ordainer when He desired to make mention of this Most Great Beauty. Meditate on this, O people, and be not of them that wander distraught in the wilderness of error.

If ye reject Him at the bidding of your idle fancies, where then is the Qiblih to which ye will turn, O assemblage of the heedless?

Ponder ye this verse, and judge equitably before God, that haply ye may glean the pearls of mysteries from the ocean that surgeth in My Name, the All-Glorious, the Most High. (Baha'u'llah, *Kitab-i-Aqdas*)

He further reveals that a pre-ordained spot has been designated by God for the Point of Adoration after the Ascension of Baha'u'llah:

When ye desire to perform this prayer, turn ye towards the Court of My Most Holy Presence, this Hallowed Spot that God hath made the Center round which circle the Concourse on High, and which He hath decreed to be the Point of Adoration [Qiblih] for the denizens of the Cities of Eternity, and the Source of Command unto all that are in heaven and on earth; and **when the Sun of Truth and Utterance shall set**, turn your faces towards **the Spot that We have ordained for you**. He, verily, is Almighty and Omniscient. (Baha'u'llah, *Kitab-i-Aqdas*)

The identity of this future Qiblih, to be established after the ascension of Baha'u'llah is contained in *The prophecies* of God particularly in the Book of Ezekiel. Knowing that His Covenant would be violated, and the Baha'i shrines in Haifa would be hijacked by the Covenant-breakers for a time, and the other holy sites destroyed by the enemies of the faith, Baha'u'llah acknowledges that the Point of Adoration after His own Ascension has been preserved and protected in the Plan of God:

You have asked concerning the Qiblih: while the Sun is till shining above the horizon, it is and shall be acceptable to turn towards it. ***An arrangement*** has also been made for afterwards. (Baha'u'llah, *Ganjina-yi Hudud wa Ahkam*, p. 20)

According to the prophecies of God, 'Abdu'l-Baha designated the Tomb at Bahji as the immediate spot to which the people should turn pending the violation of the Covenant, and the violation of every single provision of the sacred Will and Testament of 'Abdu'l-Baha.

The spot unto which the people should turn their faces and the place round which circumambulate the angels on high [prior to the Violation of the Covenant by the 25 "Hands"] is the Resplendent Tomb [Bahji]. Let no one after this [violation of the Covenant] provide any metaphorical interpretation. ('Abdu'l-Baha, *Amr va Khalq, IV*, pp. 97-98)

In one of the most dramatic and powerful moments of his vision, Ezekiel (chapters 8 through 11) sees 25 of the 27 "Hands" of the Faith who are the violators of the Covenant with their backs turned away from the TEMPLE (Qiblih) toward the physical sun of the East in rejection of the Light of God--the Glory of the Lord: Baha'u'llah--which has removed itself from the Tomb at Bahji, due to their violation of the Covenant, and settles in this place on "the very high mountain:"

Then he said to me, "Have you seen this, O son of man? You will see still greater abominations than these." And he brought me into the inner court of the House of the LORD; and behold, at the door of the temple of the LORD, between the porch and the altar, were about ***twenty-five men*** [the 25 Covenant-breaking "Hands"], with **their backs to the <u>Temple of the LORD</u>**, and their faces toward the east, worshiping the sun toward the east. Then he said to me, "Have you seen this, O son of man? Is it too slight a thing for the house of Judah to commit the abominations which they commit here, that they should fill the land with violence, and provoke me further to anger? Lo, they put the BRANCH [aghsan-Davidic lineage] to their nose. Therefore I will deal in wrath; my eye will not spare, nor will I have pity; and though they cry in my ears with a loud voice, I will not hear them." (Ezekiel 8:15-18 RSV)

Then he cried in my ears with a loud voice, saying, "Draw near, you executioners of the city, each with his destroying weapon in his hand." ...Now the Glory of the God [Baha'u'llah] of Israel had gone up from the cherubim on which it rested to the threshold of the House [Bahji]; and he called to the man clothed in linen, who had the writing case at his side. And the LORD said to him, "Go through the city, through Jerusalem, and put a mark upon the foreheads of the men who sigh and groan over all the abominations that are committed in it."...So they began with the elders who were before the House [before they set up that false headless UHJ]. Then he said to them, "Defile the House [bogus "House" of Justice--headless monster], and fill the courts with the slain. Go forth." (Ezekiel 9:1, 3-4, 6-7 RSV)

And the Glory of the LORD [Baha'u'llah] went up from the cherubim to the threshold of the House [Bahji]; and the House was filled with the cloud [clouds of violation], and the court was full of the brightness of the Glory of the LORD [Baha'u'llah]... Then the Glory of the LORD [Baha'u'llah] went forth [Hebrew: departed] from the threshold of the House, and stood over the cherubim... And the Glory of the LORD [Baha'u'llah] went up from [Hebrew: departed] the midst of the city, and stood ***upon the mountain*** which is on the east side of the city. (Ezekiel 10:4, 18; 11:23 RSV)

Here at the opening of his vision the "Glory of the Lord" Baha'u'llah leaves the House and departs from that City due to the violation of the Covenant of these 25 "Hands" to later settle in the Temple--Ezekiel's Temple in Montana--on the "very high mountain":

And behold, at the door of the gateway there were twenty-five men [25 arch Covenant-breaking "Hands"]... And he said to me, "Son of man, **these are the men who devise iniquity** and who **give wicked counsel** in this city; who say, 'The time is not near to build houses; this city is the caldron, and we are the flesh.' Therefore prophesy against them, prophesy, O son of man." (Ezekiel 11:1-4 RSV)

And brought me in the visions of God into the land of Israel [New Jerusalem in the Rocky Mountains], and set me down upon ***a very high mountain*** [Rocky Mountains of the Great Divide], on which was a structure like a city opposite me.

And behold, the Glory of the God [Baha'u'llah] of Israel came from the east; and the sound of His coming was like the sound of many waters; and the earth shone with his glory [Baha'i]. And the vision I saw was like the vision which I had seen when he came to destroy the city [see chapters 8 through 11], and like the vision which I had seen by the river Chebar; and I fell upon my face [in adoration of God: the Qiblih]. As the Glory of the LORD [Baha'u'llah] entered the Temple by the gate facing east [Tower #7], the Spirit lifted me up, and brought me into the inner court; and behold, the Glory of the LORD [Baha'u'llah] filled the Temple [one third of all the inmates became Baha'is]. (Ezekiel 40:2, 43:2-5 RSV)

The blood of the people is literally on the hands of these "Hands." Through their violation of the Covenant (and those like them) we are standing upon the threshold of World War III. It is prophesied in the Book of Revelation that one third of mankind is to perish in one hour of thermonuclear war, with every city in America population 100,000 or more to be targeted. This great "abomination of desolation" set up by the "Hands" during the time of core covenant-breaking, 1957 through 1963, upon the slope of Mt. Carmel--the Mountain of Armageddon (see Foreword) is the source of malice, and hatred amongst the peoples that is fast fashioning this ruinous war, and terrorism, amongst all the peoples of the world. According to 'Abdu'l-Baha:

It is racial, patriotic, religious and class prejudice, that has been the cause of the destruction of Humanity. ('Abdu'l-Baha, *'Abdu'l-Baha in London*, p. 28)

The Qiblih, as announced by Baha'u'llah and preserved in the sacred books of God during this time of the Great Violation, is room 232 in Ezekiel's Temple in Montana, at the spot in which the Bible was located upon the desk with the one page up in the air, open to Zechariah chapter 3 KJV.

Baha'u'llah states:

> QUESTION: The believers have been enjoined to face in the direction of the Qiblih when reciting their Obligatory Prayers; in what direction should they turn when offering other prayers and devotions?
>
> ANSWER: Facing in the direction of the Qiblih is a fixed requirement for the recitation of obligatory prayer, but for other prayers and devotions one may follow what the merciful Lord hath revealed in the Qur'an: "Whichever way ye turn, there is the face of God." (Baha'u'llah, *Q&A*)

AN OPEN LETTER TO FRANCIS C. SPATARO

Dear Mr. Spataro,

Your recent Remey Letter was fantastic! I was overjoyed to read it and so was everyone else. Thank you for sending a copy to us here in Montana.

Dr. Jensen has shared all his recent correspondence with you with me so I would be able to fulfill your request to answer your questions and send you more information on the Morrisites--both their history and prophecy. Enclosed along with this letter is a copy of the first edition of my book *Ezekiel's Temple in Montana*. I originally wrote this edition at the very start of our research into the Morrisites even before we discovered the many and detailed prophecies of George Williams so we could have something to give the Morrisite descendants and the other people that we interviewed. In this way we were able to exchange information and have access to the Morrisite family heirlooms such as over 100 year old leather bound diaries and journals containing the history, prophecies and writings of George Williams the prophet who had the original visions of Deer Lodge and Jesus the High Priest returning there to establish his Father's (Baha'u'llah's --Glory of the **Father**) Kingdom--the World Order of Baha'u'llah. For this reason the more detailed prophecies appear in the addendum of this edition of the *Ezekiel's Temple* book which we were able to uncover after having access to the journals in Deer Lodge and later the archival documents stored in Logan, Utah, at Utah State University in the special collections library.

The first information that I obtained on the Morrisites came from the book, *For Christ Will Come Tomorrow: Joseph Morris and the Saga of the Morrisites* by C. Leroy Anderson a professor of sociology here in Missoula at the University of Montana. Mr. Anderson was raised a Mormon and has since broken away from that church in which he was raised. His views come through that perspective which in a way possibly attracted him to Joseph Morris, the Mormon reformer, who led the reformation which broke away from the Mormon church of Brigham Young. Based on the historical information in his book the first edition of *Ezekiel's Temple* was written. I recommend his book for you to read and I am sure you will be able to find it in the New York public library. However, his book though informative fails to document the detailed prophecies of Williams for the return of Jesus in Deer Lodge. The reason for this is that he specifically wrote his book to prove prophecy failure. Because of this he had no interest in seeing if the prophesies were fulfilled. He went into the project with his mind already made up and in that way his book was already written even before it was researched. This is much like prejudiced journalists who go into a story with the story already written and therefore blind themselves to the facts that prove the opposite of their idea. The irony is that in the very office next door to his on the second floor of the sociology building at the University is another sociologist who did his research on the Baha'is Under the Provisions of the Covenant and the station of Dr. Jensen as the establisher of the Baha'i Faith. Although these two professors worked side by side for over ten years they never put two and two together. Anderson knew all about the history of the Deer Lodge Valley and the Morrisites and their prophecies and the other one knew all about Dr. Jensen proofs that originate in Deer Lodge. It was not until the summer of 1990 that I became the first one to put these two things together and discover that the Morrisite prophecy was fulfilled in Dr. Jensen and the Baha'i Faith! My book on the Morrisites clearly proves Anderson's theory all wrong and has become an *embarasse de riche* for them at the university.

The way I came about this research was from discovering that the Old Montana State Prison--the "Stone with Seven Eyes"--was the prophesied Temple of Ezekiel as depicted in the Bible that the return of Jesus is to come to. Having discovered this in Madison, Wisconsin, I then traveled to Deer Lodge, Montana, to measure the Temple the same way that Ezekiel was instructed to do by God. While we were doing this all the people and tourists there were very curious of what we were up to. So we told them that this old prison was not just a prison but actually fulfilled Bible prophecy as Ezekiel's seven towered Temple and that it was the site for the second coming of Jesus the High Priest. The woman behind the counter then said, "Well do you know that there is a whole other group of people waiting for the return of Jesus in Deer Lodge called the Morrisites?" I had never heard of them before and neither had any other Baha'i. I thought to myslf, 'I know what a termite is, and a parasite? But what is a Morrisite?' I said, "Well that prophecy is fulfilled right here in this prison!" She said that we should read the book about the Morrisites and also said that she would be interested in reading my book when it becomes published. No one was more surprised than me that day as mystery after mystery began to unfold before our very eyes. Prophecy was being fulfilled at every turn. Everyone was swept away at the magnitude and power of this great proof. Imagine an entire valley pioneered and built up just to await the return of Jesus and not Jesus Christ but very specifically Jesus the High Priest after the order of Melchizedec. It was amazing--and still is.

When I returned to Madison, Wisconsin with my wife I called up Dr. Jensen on the phone and told him of the Morrisites. That was June of 1990 it was the first time he ever heard of the Morrisites approximately 20 years after he made his proclamation and first gave his proofs converting over one third of the prison to be Baha'i. No one had ever seen anything like that neither before nor since.

So you see Mr. Spataro his claim was not made based on the Morrisite prophecies--but rather the Morrisite prophecies are something that I discovered 20 years later that validate and confirm everything he had already declared for all mankind to hear. How great indeed is this day in which we live!

So after moving to Montana during the Gulf War we lived in Deer Lodge for over a year and met with hundreds of people, were written up in the news media, interviewed people door to door and were invited to give public talks at local churches. Throughout all this we learned more and more about how accurate God's plan is and how specifically He prophesied and prepared the way for the establisher of the genuine Faith of Baha'u'llah to fulfill his mission and carry out his mandate from God. The Faith had been eradicated from all the world up until that time except from the mind, heart and soul of his chosen Knight of Baha'u'llah, Dr. Leland Jensen here in the mountains of Montana the holy spot of the re-establishment of what Baha'u'llah brought and the Covenant-breakers threw out.

After speaking with Mr. Anderson in person he tipped us off to the Logan State University archive were he placed all his research material including the copious writings of George Williams that he left out of his book and up to us to bring to light for all the world to see.

****

A COVENANT OF BLOOD

In the dead hot silence of the American West--Sunday, June 15th, 1862--Joseph Morris was murdered under the direct orders of Brigham Young. As Joseph Morris turned to pray, Sheriff Burton charged his horse directly at Morris to kill and trample him into the ground. Morris caught the horses bridle by surprise. Burton's horse bucked back upon its haunches. Morris was still alive! Burton yanked out his gun and blasted Morris in the back of the head. "What do you think of your prophet now?!" screamed Burton at the top of his lungs. Morris's body lay crumpled in the Utah dust. The life ripped from him in brutal, cruel, cold-blooded murder.

Joseph Morris murdered in the Utah territory, like Jesus crucified at Calvary or Joseph Smith murdered in Illinois or 10,000 Babi's blood staining Persian soil and 20,000 Baha'is murdered for the same diabolical reason. Yet unlike Islamic Persia (modern day Iran) America is supposed to be the land of freedom of religion.

Ironically the Mormons who were the persecuted and whose founder Joseph Smith was murdered became the persecutors of the Morrisites and murdered their leader the reformer Joseph Morris. Similar to the Jewish government in Israel--who homeless persecuted throughout the ages most recently by the Nazis--have now become the intolerable persecutors of the Palestinians whose Arab lands they occupy illegally according to the UN mandate.

The worst thing in the world is indoctrination because it leads to militant religious fanaticism. We see this in the mid-east crisis between Jew, Christian and Muslim. Every thoughtful person can see that it is the unquenchable fire of prejudice and intolerance that is prophesied to result in Biblical thermonuclear Armageddon.

The brutal killing of 10,000 Babi's and 20,000 Baha'is is documented as the greatest religious slaughter and persecution in the modern world. At the time of its occurrence European investigators were appalled and shocked at the terror and barbarism inflicted upon innocent and defenseless people. Those who are familiar with the true history even today are repulsed.

In the same vein, modern historians and non-biased sources such as *The San Francisco Chronicle* document the Morrisite Massacre, as it has been labeled, as the most brutal and cruel religious persecution and slaughter in the history of the United States if not in the modern Western world altogether. Yet the true details have remained blurred and obscure through the crafty use of misinformation, disinformation and downright lies by the corrupted Mormon clergy who seek to efface this bloodstain from the pages of their history. To the same degree that the Mormons committed the barbarous act of the Mountain Meadows Massacre, writes *The San Francisco Chronicle*, the Morrisite Slaughter is even more barbarous and chilling in its cold blooded calculation and wanton manipulation of the law and justice system so that Brigham Young could wipe out and efface his enemies the purifiers under the leadership of the reformer Joseph Morris.

150

TAKEN FROM *THE SAN FRANCISCO CHRONICLE*
SUNDAY JUNE 19, 1892, VOL. LV., NO. 156.

A MORMON CRIME.

Cold-Blooded Murder of the Morrisites.

A Massacre of Just Thirty Years Ago.

How Brigham Young Made Way With a Rival
Under a Shadow of Law.

Written for the Chronicle.

It is just thirty years ago this month that those mild-mannered Latter-Day Saints, the Mormons, whom Professor Elliott has seen fit to compare favorably with the New England pilgrims, committed one of the most wanton and cruel slaughters which stain the pages of the History of Christian nations. This was the Morrisite massacre, which occurred on the 16th [15th *sic*] of June, 1862.

From the dead level of crime which darkens the early history of Utah under Mormon domination, two events stand out in hideous prominence; two crimes which for their magnitude of cruelty and deliberate devilishness rear their horrid heads above the surrounding waste. These are the Mountain meadows massacre and the Morrisite slaughter. In the horrible atrocity of the former the latter has eclipsed, yet for deliberate plotting and cunning execution of the plot, the latter was the worse. In the Mountain meadows Brigham's hand was never directly traced; it was an active factor in the destruction of the Morrisites. The one was the outgrowth of fanaticism, the other of jealousy. The one was the work of a day, the other was deliberately planned. One was committed without any form of law and was a crime in the other the courts were invoked to carry out Young's plans, and the crime stalked before the land disguised in the cloak of justice.

Uniquely both slaughters of Baha'is and Morrisites took place within the same time frame of the late 1800s. All to prepare the way for the establishment of the Kingdom of God on earth.

Strangely enough America, which is founded on religious freedom by the pilgrims seeking asylum from the persecution of England, is also a country marred with religious persecution dating from the Salem witch hunts to the persecution of the Mormons to the Mormon persecution of the Morrisites. In fact the history of Christianity itself is marred with a tradition of unjust bloodshed! As the progressiveness of truth grows clearer, the blood flows swifter and thicker-- until as the prophecies state it will flow as high as a horses bridle for over 200 miles. From Jesus unjustly killed on the cross, to the apostles likewise slain. It would later be these same Christians under the dictates of the Pope who would persecute Martin Luther and seek to kill him. Likewise after him his group sought the lives of the others...the corruption keeps rolling along even until this present day and the World Wide Baha'i Faith is decapitated with a headless, guardianless monster House of Justice and the Great Battle rages to which the Knight of Baha'u'llah, Dr. Leland Jensen has arisen to re-establish what the Covenant-breakers have thrown out--the Morrisites being his forerunners in the United States of America.

Paul in Hebrews 9:18-22 speaks of this Covenant of blood.

> Hence the first Covenant was not ratified without blood. For when every commandment of the law had been declared by Moses to all the people, he took the blood of calves and goats, with water and scarlet wool and hyssop, and sprinkled both the book itself and all the people, saying "This is the blood of the covenant which God commanded you." And in the same way he sprinkled with the blood both the tent and all the vessels used in worship. Indeed, under the law almost everything is purified with blood, and without the shedding of blood there is no forgiveness of sins...so Christ [Jesus], having been offered once to bear the sins of many, will appear a second time, not to deal with sin but to save those who are eagerly waiting for him. [*]

The blood of Joseph Morris and the Morrisite slaughter, like that of 10,000 Babis and 20,000 Baha'is, purified the sanctuary and Ezekiel's Temple built in Deer Lodge for the arrival of Jesus the High Priest. Those who are eagerly waiting for him are to be saved. Saved by the blood of the Covenant--Baha'is Under the Provisions of the Covenant.

WHO ARE THE MORRISITES?

Joseph Morris was the Mormon reformer who rose up during the great Mormon reformation of the late 1850s in opposition to the corruption and abuses of Brigham Young. Like Martin Luther, at one time an unknown monk, Morris was keyed into the spirit of his times and quickly rose into prominence as the central figure of the reformation. Also like Luther, Morris had no intention of starting his own religion, splitting the faith or of taking over control of the church. Like Luther who wanted the Pope to clean up his act, Morris demanded the same from Brigham Young and wrote letter after letter imploring him to change his evil ways so that the people could again follow the true path that God had laid out before them to walk--preparing the way for the return of Jesus in America.

Unlike Luther, however, Joseph Morris didn't have eight German princes to protect him. As long as the United States government army occupied the Utah territory Morris was safe. But with the outbreak of the civil war, the US troops were forced to leave the Utah territory and Brigham Young's Mormon militia took over total control. Morris was killed.

Though the death of Morris was at first a tragic blow for the Morrisites, about 1000 pure of heart people that Morris had successfully separated from the perversion and corruption of Young, it turned out to be the hallmark event of their greatest victory and triumph which even today is now coming into ultimate fruition and glory as their purpose and destiny is fulfilled in the climatic

---

[*] Hebrews 9:18-22, 28.

152

and awe-inspiring return of Jesus in Ezekiel's Temple in Deer Lodge Montana, Rocky Mountains, USA.

For the surviving Morrisite pioneers, Joseph Morris's mission became clear as the martyr-forerunner for the true prophet George Williams who, though never having had any direct contact with the Morrisites or Morris himself was instantly raised up by God to guide those chosen people into the modern day promised land of the Deer Lodge Valley in Montana, the sacred sight for the appearance of the New Jerusalem, the City of the great King, the holy city of the modern world to which all nations shall flow to learn peace, the sacred and destined spot where the return of Jesus has come suddenly to his Temple.

It was the job of Morris as the reformer to separate the pure of heart from the corruption of Brigham Young and lead them to the living waters of the prophecies and visions of George Williams. Morris also acted as a physical depiction of the things that were to come in the future. He modeled his behavior after the roles he saw the return of Jesus fulfilling in the future. Thus at one point he rode a white horse and wore seven crowns on his head physically depicting the seven titles (crowns) of Jesus upon his return as stated in the book of Revelation and the seven world religions, one of these being the seventh angel. Williams explained later that Morris was using this earthly (physical) pattern based on heavenly prophesies of the future as a symbolic physical prototype.[*]

In the Spring of 1862, before the death of Joseph Morris, a simple farmer by the name of George Williams was riding his horse in the mountains surrounding the Salt Lake Valley. Suddenly the snow began to fall in an unusual way and Williams dismounted his horse. Then a great cloud came flowing out of the North, from the direction of Deer Lodge, and formed a giant archway surrounded on either side by two giant pillars of light. Then to his astonishment Williams saw the gates of heaven flung open and Jesus as the Knight on the white horse (see Revelation chapter 19) leading the armies of God, the 144,000 promised, south out of the Deer Lodge Valley into Salt Lake area in Utah at the time of the great battle of Armageddon. Williams was then instructed that he was to keep this vision of Jesus' second coming in America, specifically in Deer Lodge, Montana, a secret until the appointed time at which he was instructed to meet again at the same spot months later in August at which time he would receive further instruction.

By August, after the death of Joseph Morris, Williams kept his appointed rendezvous on the mountain and was then told that he was the third and final link forming the chain of succession to herald the return of Jesus in America. The first was the seer Joseph Smith founder of the Mormon movement killed in 1844. The second was Joseph Morris, the reformer, only killed a few weeks prior to Williams's vision, earlier in 1862. The third was, himself, George Williams, the great Mormon prophet, who was to complete the mission by proclaiming his vision of the return of Jesus in Deer Lodge Montana to the scattered Morrisites people and instructing them to pioneer the Valley.

---

[*] Anderson, *For Christ Will Come Tomorrow*, p. 148: "Morris's mission was seen as being entirely symbolic [of what was to come]."

John R. Eardley, George Williams (the Prophet Cainan), and George Thompson, in England, circa 1873, where a missionary effort had been initiated during the leadership of Williams.

154

JOSEPH MORRIS

By the spring of 1863, at the same time as the proclamation of Baha'u'llah thousands of miles away outside the city of Baghdad in the garden of Ridvan and motivated by these invisible impulses from the Manifestation of God Himself, the Morrisites unanimously accepted Williams as their true prophet. Exactly at the end of Ridvan on May 2nd of 1863, as Baha'u'llah pulled out of the garden of Ridvan, the Morrisite pioneers pulled out of Utah on May 5th in two wagon trains, one going north to Soda Springs Idaho half way between Salt Lake City and Deer Lodge, Montana and the other headed south to Carson City, Nevada.

The first Morrisites entered Montana at this time in 1863 and thus began the religious history and pioneering of the Deer Lodge Valley. Throughout the rest of his life Williams continually urged all the Morrisites to gather in Deer Lodge in order to prepare the Valley for the coming of Jesus. Today approximately two thirds the population of the Deer Lodge Valley, which is five to ten miles wide and about 60 miles long are descended from the Morrisite pioneers.

Williams also wrote score after score of prophecies and educational Epistles giving the exact specifics, details, dates, genealogy, mission and circumstances in which the second coming of Jesus would fulfill and whereby the Morrisites could easily recognize their true and only savior, the return of Jesus himself. For us today their history and prophecy stands as the documentation of the true forces of God working here at home in the United States. Like the Bab who had Shaykh Ahmad, Siyyid Kazim and Mullah Husayn as his forerunners, so the establisher of Baha'u'llah has a string of forerunners increasing in intensity and accuracy until George Williams himself who is like the John the Baptist of Jesus on his first coming or the Bab--the John the Baptist--of Baha'u'llah. It is to Williams that all the detailed prophecies are traced.

THE PROPHECIES!

The first and most fundamental prophecy of Williams is that the return of Jesus would be in prison in Deer Lodge. In all of Deer Lodge there is only one prison. As a matter of fact in all of Montana there was only one prison. That is the old Montana State Prison in Deer Lodge, Montana! This prison is impossible to miss. The wall is made out of solid stone from the surrounding mountains and it has seven watch towers on it. It stands like a huge fortress or castle in the middle of down town Deer Lodge on Main Street where it is absolutely impossible to miss. Williams prophesied that Jesus would return in Deer Lodge in prison and this is the true Faith based on Williams prophecies that the Morrisites held. Here in a few excerpts Williams designates the City of Deer Lodge as the chosen City of the Great King.

> If I call at night or day, and say, "Pack up for Deer Lodge--our Merciful God wants your presence there," he is quickly on the road.[*]

> As **Deer Lodge Valley, Montana is the nucleus**. let all others begin to turn their attention that way as they tire in the wings.[†]

> In that region where you dwell [Deer Lodge, Montana], extending East, West, South and North--in this region will come down the City of the Great King [New

---

[*] George Williams, (June 13, 1880). "An Open Letter," p. 114.
[†] George Williams, (August 9, 1865). "Letter to My Dear Saint James and John," Great Salt Lake, p. 6.

Jerusalem, the City of Ezekiel's Temple]. Before that, many wise men shall find their way there, endowed with intelligence from the Lord to map out and make ready [build the prison] for the Lord's coming, [Jesus' return in Deer Lodge] with thousands who have toiled and suffered with him here. You are the pioneers.[*]

Clearly Deer Lodge is the chosen City. More specifically is the fact the return of Jesus will be imprisoned in Deer Lodge. This prophecy of the return of Jesus in prison is found in Williams's prophecy entitled the "The High Priesthoods Return" referring to Jesus the High Priest after the order of Melchizedec and not the Christ (descendant of David) of which Baha'u'llah fulfills that prophecy.

THE HIGH PRIESTHOODS RETURN

How white is his raiment [the return of Jesus], how
>glittering his head;
>Fresh out from the chambers where long he had stayed,
How brilliant his eyes! like flames of a fire
>Not a deed nor a thought from that gage can retire.

How well **he is <u>prisoned</u>** by a process unshown;
>The flaming sword still keeps this science unknown
With all his massive wisdom a spot of blood is there
>Upon his heavenly garments as evidence declare
How soon began the malice with them who would obey
>God's will and counsel white clothed in mortal clay.[†]

Thus Williams sees the return of Jesus the High Priest in prison in Deer Lodge which can only be the Old Montana State prison. This is identical to the Bible prophecies in which Jesus himself states that on his return he will be naked, hungry, sick and a stranger in **<u>prison</u>**.

<u>The Last Judgement</u>

When the Son of man comes in his glory [in the future at the second coming], and all the angels with him, then he will sit upon his glorious throne. Before him will be gathered all the nations, and he will separate them one from another as a shepherd separates the sheep from the goats, and he will place the sheep at his right hand, but the goats at the left. Then the King will say to those at his right hand, "Come blessed of my Father [Baha'u'llah], inherit the kingdom prepared for you from the foundation of the world; for I was hungry and you gave me food, I was thirsty and you gave me drink, I was a stranger and you welcomed me, I was naked and you clothed me, I was sick and you visited me, I was in **<u>prison</u>** and you came to me." (Matt. 25:31 *ff*)

---

[*] C. Leroy Anderson, *For Christ Will Come Tomorrow*, pp. 222-223.
[†] George Williams, (1870). "The High Priesthoods Return."

He was naked. When Dr. Jensen was taken the first thing they did was strip him of his clothes, his watch, his ring, everything, making him naked and they put him in the prison garb. He was hungry, being a doctor of Natural Medicine he lives on a holistic diet of live foods and lots of raw fruits and vegetables and the diet he was subjected to was red meats, no chicken or fish, no vegetables or fruits, sometimes boiled potatoes, white bread and coffee. He was sick. They sent him to Galen Pulmonary Hospital and found him to be so sick that he didn't have to work while he was there. He was a stranger in prison. He is a stranger to the Christians because they are waiting for a mythical Jesus to come down out of the sky on a cloud when they should be looking for him to be in prison fulfilling prophecy where he said he would be on his return.

Baha'u'llah and the Bab were also in prison, but the prisons that they were in did not also fulfill the prophecies of the future Temple of Ezekiel which has seven towers. Whereas the Old Montana State Prison has seven towers and is the prophesied Temple of Ezekiel. Both the Bible and Williams's prophecies state that the return of Jesus will be in **both** Prison and in the Temple. The only way for both these to be true is that the Temple and the prison are the same building, the same structure.

> You wish to know what is the object of **gathering together in Montana.** It is our Lord's Command [Jesus' coming in Montana] that his chosen people may come together to receive blessings spiritual and temporal, and the order of both Priesthoods prepared. Also a **Temple** [Ezekiel's Temple] prepared to receive the ministering angels of our God.[*]

> This excitement will arise suddenly as the world lays sleepy and find the foundation of an everlasting Government [World Order of Baha'u'llah/Kingdom of God on earth] laid secure and **the Lord [Jesus] coming suddenly to his Temple**...for the choice place of the earth is handed over to you. Its beauties and riches, in part, are yet hidden. But your children will develop it more and more. For there **[Deer Lodge, Montana] will be built the City of the Great King.**[†]

Williams is explicitly clear the return of Jesus will be in Deer Lodge, Montana and even more specifically that he will come to that city suddenly in his Temple. This prophecy is also found in Malachi 3:1:

> "Behold, I send my messenger [George Williams] to prepare the way before me,
> and the Lord whom you seek will come suddenly to his Temple."

This Temple is sometimes called the "Millennial Temple" and is prophesied in explicit detail in the Book of Ezekiel and therefore is also known as Ezekiel's Temple. (The entire book of Haggai is likewise dedicated to the Millennial Temple.) The unique feature of Ezekiel's Temple is that it has seven towers unlike any of the other temples the Jews ever built which were fashioned after Solomon's Temple. In his further prophecies Williams states that the Temple in Deer Lodge "must be built from the stone of the surrounding mountains."[‡] The only structure in

---

[*] George Williams, (July 24, 1873). "Letter to Dear Sister Thomas," Brigg, Lincolnshire, England, p. 59.
[†] George Williams, (1879). "Letter to My Dear Brother James," Walthamstow, Essex England, p. 65.
[‡] Morrisite Collection: Marie-Eccles Caine Archive at the Utah State University, Logan, Utah (MCLU).

downtown Deer Lodge built from the stone from the surrounding mountains is the Old Montana State Prison. It was constructed from the stone from Whitehall and Garrison towns located on either side of the Deer Lodge Valley. As both the Bible and Williams are so specific that not only will Jesus come suddenly to his Temple in Deer Lodge but that he will be in prison--thus the Temple and the prison are the same building without a doubt.

Though Williams is very clear that Jesus will return to the Temple built out of stone and that it will be the same as the prison and must be within the City limits of Deer Lodge (the city of the Great King), some people are confused thinking that the little wooden church (called the Lord's House) that the Morrisites built was supposed to be the place for Jesus' return. This is false as Williams's writings show. It was simply a church, a prayer house and Sunday school. Williams anticipated more than one to be built in Montana. As a matter of fact, though this is the last remaining one, there was once another little prayer house in Anaconda.

> It is very gratifying to me to find all are lending the builder a helping hand, as it [the Lord's House] will be a source of pleasure to them in all time, being in a central place, and on property of your own, must, it appears to me, be wisely chosen, **a temple in miniature**, and place of holiness for the faithful.[*]

> It is not the only House of Prayer for Montana. Finish it, and it will be revealed to you how to raise another more easily, at the proper time.[†]

The Lord's House is not the prophesied Temple. It is built out of wood and not stone. It doesn't have seven towers or any towers for that matter. It is six miles outside the city limits. And it is not a prison. Only one building in all the world fulfills the criteria to be the prophesied Prison/Temple of Ezekiel and that is the Old Montana State Prison as solid stone wall with seven watch-towers.

The Morrisites were also given the date in which they could expect Jesus to come to the Temple/prison in Deer Lodge. For over 100 years they celebrated August 9th as the day that they would meet the return of Jesus in Deer Lodge. This was their great Feast Day on August 9th and also the last day that they ever met.

> Anderson: "Can you tell me a little bit about some of the special days or holidays you had?"

> Becks: "Yes, the ninth of August was when we always had a feast day."

> It was also the last day that they met.

> Becks: "Now a few years back Mrs. Staffenson, that was Agnes Hendrickson, she got all of us together, all of us that was left and we went down there [to the Lord's House--the Morrisite church] and we had a meeting...That was the last meeting we had...Ninth of August we all gathered at her house and all went to church. We had the meeting first. Frank Staffenson was there."[‡]

---

[*] George Williams, (August 28, 1878). "Letter to My Dear Brother Henrikson," Walthamstow, Essex England, p. 36.
[†] George Williams, (January 1879). "letter to to James and the Deer Lodge Morrisites (Stake #1)."
[‡] MCLU, 2:2.

159

THE LORD'S HOUSE built outside Deer Lodge at Racetrack & **THE GREAT SALT-LICK**

The last meeting was on August 9th and even more amazing is the fact that it was on August 9th of 1969 which is the first full day that Dr. Leland Jensen spent in the "Stone with Seven Eyes" in Deer Lodge.

> "All those people that belonged to that little church down there [in Deer Lodge, Montana]: One day out of the year, it was August the 9th, they knew that was the Day that Christ would return." (Lewis Johnson--interviewed, September 21st, 1990--Last of the Morrisite Pioneers)

> The Church of Jesus Christ of the Saints of the Most High [the Morrisites] officially disbanded in 1969 [on August 9th].[*]

Thus the Morrisites were given the right date and the right place for Jesus' return. Interestingly enough the date of August 9th corresponds to Tisha b'Av on the Jewish Calendar. Tisha is the ninth day of the month and Av corresponds to August on the Solar Calendar (the days of the Jewish Calendar move around being lunar/solar). The Jewish Temple of Solomon destroyed by Nebuchadnezzar in 586 BC and the second temple refurbished by Herod destroyed by Titus in 70 AD were both destroyed on the same day of the same month Tisha b'Av. The Jewish prophecy has it that this will be the day of the restored Temple (which is Ezekiel's) and the coming of the Messiah. Baha'u'llah is the Messiah (descendant of David) and the Deer Lodge Temple/Prison succeeds Him (as the Tabernacle succeeded Moses).[†] It was on this day of August 9th (equal to Tisha b'Av) that his establisher entered the Temple/Prison in Deer Lodge.

Williams was also specifically clear that it would be the return of Jesus the High Priest after the order of **Melchizedec** (see Hebrews chapters 5, 6 and 7) and not the second coming of Christ (which is Baha'u'llah the descendant of David) that would appear in Deer Lodge! Thus Williams's prophecy on the return of Jesus in prison is specifically the return of Jesus the High Priest and he entitles his prophecy as such: "The High Priesthoods Return." Williams and the Morrisites were really into Jesus being of the order of Melchizedec (as a High Priest) and they held that Williams was the one representing him at their time. In this clarification that it is not Jesus Christ but Jesus the High Priest after the order of Melchizedec Williams prophesies:

> You also wish to know something of Melchisedec--the real Melchisedec [Jesus the High Priest], not one representing him [Williams]. Now mark the first time we hear of him, he is declared to King of Salem or Peace. Here is brought out the bread and wine to Abraham, our faithful friend and brother. It is not written what was said at this interview; but I have no doubt it would be the same as said to the 12, at <u>his</u> last supper when <u>he</u>[‡] takes the bread and also the cup saying: "Take, eat

---

[*] MCLU index book. Morrisite Collection: Marie-Eccles Caine Archive, Logan, Utah at the Utah State University.
[†] Baha'u'llah ascended in May of 1892 while the plans for the Old Montana State prison were laid out. Construction of the Stone wall with seven towers commenced in 1893 corresponding to the beginning of 'Abdu'l-Baha's ministry. The Temple/Prison was completed in 1912 at the same time that 'Abdu'l-Baha proclaimed it to be "already built." (See *Ezekiel's Temple*: "The Temple is already built," pp. 7-8 this volume).
[‡] Underlines by Williams to stress identity of Jesus to the High Priest after the order of Melchizedec which is who he foresaw in Deer Lodge and not Christ--Baha'u'llah the descendant of David.

and drink, all of you, for this is my body broken, and my blood shed for you. There he stood [Jesus the High Priest], without a scar.[*]

Thus Williams's prophecies were expressly for the return and second coming of Jesus the High Priest after the order of **Melchizedec** and not of the Christ. In the Bible there are two orders of high priests given. The Aaronic priesthood through Moses' brother Aaron who are just priests; and the High Priest after the order of Melchizedec which is a royal genealogy of high priests. In this case 100 year-old prophecies of George Williams gives the astounding fact that the return of Jesus the High Priest (after the order of Melchizedec) will be from the royal genealogy of the kings of Denmark. Dr. Jensen's family is Danes on both sides and his father's line goes back to the royalty of Denmark.

Williams further sees the return of Jesus from this lineage which traces back to Abraham through the tribe of Dan[†] as a High Priest who will be clothed in the "filthy garment" and then given new raiment to wear. This vision of the king of Denmark which Williams uses as a basis for his prophecy is directly out of Zechariah chapter three which contains the prophecy for the return of Jesus the high priest who will have his iniquity (injustice inflicted against him) removed and be clothed in the fine new raiment of the High Priest, his robes of state.

The vision also speaks of the many crows he will be given of which in the Bible, in Zechariah chapter six, is fashioned a crown of silver and gold which is the crown of his authority to establish what Baha'u'llah brought and the Covenant-breaking "Hands" threw out. Also in Revelation chapter 19 as the knight on the white horse he wears many crowns meaning that he is known by many titles in the many roles he fulfills as the establisher of the Baha'i Faith. Williams writes:

> You also wish me to say something of a notice regarding the King of Denmark, the Dream, the Vision of the King was this:
>
> In the early dawn of morning as he lay upon his bed **a company of poorly clad men** [wearing dirty garments] with staves in their hands and without shoes entered his palace without ceremony. The vision continued until the King saw himself in his grand Reception Room with his Kingly robes on and a crown upon his head. He attempted to Order these Strangers to withdraw but was speechless. The company began to remove the ornaments in the room, casting them from the window and approaching the King **removed his robes and crown and clothed him as themselves were clothed** [in the dirty garment], placing him in the midst and one who was called Seth [Joseph Morris] stood up.

---

[*] George Williams, (December 27, 1881). " Letter to Erasmussen."
[†] The kings of Denmark trace their genealogy back to the kings of the tribe of Dan one of the twelve tribes of Israel which goes back to Abraham. "Dan was the one 'from whom, so saith antiquity, the pedigrees of our kings [of Denmark] have flowed in glorious series, like channels from some ancient spring.'" John Philip Cohane, *The Key*, p. 255.

At this moment came a man's hand through the ceiling of the room, handing Seth [Morris] a roll of Parchment,[*] in which was written in glowing letters, which Seth [Morris] unfolded and read before the King, saying, "These are Ministers of the Holy one of whom you have heard, hear them. The High and Holy one has sent them with the Covenant and Law [Book of the Covenant and the Will and Testament] that whoever obeys and is faithful shall be brought before the Highest, and Ordained a King, a Priest, or Ruler, or Celestial Glory [Baha'i], when mortality and the thing thereof are passed away with you. **For behold you are of the Royal Line of heavenly Priesthood** [the return of Jesus the High Priest after the order of Melchizedec is from the royal genealogy of the Kings of Denmark] and elected to sit in your place to be advantage to the Work of Redemption in the hands of the Holy one. Then this sent unto you and Knowledge shall be given unto you. First through them and then through other means appointed by the Highest, and see you tell not the Priest or the wicked, for they will labor to turn your heart away from the Truth with threats of Rebellion, but stand fast and listen not. For the Highest is sufficient to bear you up and his Wisdom shall shine upon you. Be not afraid and my servant Seth [Morris] shall not give you a seal and a sign." And the Hand withdrew.

And the speaker who was Seth [Morris] then called upon the fruits of the Earth to appear. And after a melodious anthem was sung by an unseen band, there appeared groves after groves of trees in full fruit of every color which could be tasted in passing by the King and Company. No Agent was seen conducting, but self moving in utmost order. After these had passed, there were seen streams of delicious Lovely Flowers entering and passing through as the trees had done blooming their fragrance, would be felt by all the company.

And through the foliage of flowers could be seen the band of players of music, A Celestial band of females in robes of exceeding whiteness. Around their arms and ankles were hands of Gold and precious Stones. And on their heads were many crowns. Their long bright hair **held the robe [clean raiment of the high priest] in pleats and formed a girdle for their waists.** They sang an Anthem in honor of our dear Lord and the Fullness of the Gospel, saying in the chorus, "How beautiful shall Adam's planet be, and clothed with Celestial glory, The Working Ministers are sent O King they stand before you."

The vision of the King continued until Seth [Morris] reached forth his hand and took from this Celestial Female Band Host **new Raiment for the King, with which Seth clothed him** and put his Heavenly name on his forehead and sealed it there.

As I am only complying with your wishes it is not for me to describe the King's new name [Leland] or the Celestial Priesthood's dress at this time.[†]

---

[*] Revelation chapter 5 the scroll "written within and on the back" "sealed with seven seals" which is the Book of the Covenant (Kitab-i-'Ahd) written within and the Will and Testament of 'Abdu'l-Baha written on the back.
[†] George Williams, (April 6, 1873). "Letter to Brother Rasmusson," Lincolnshire, England, pp. 2-4.

Williams gives the clearest picture of all! Unlike the ridiculous myths of the majority of Christians waiting for Jesus to come floating down out of the physical sky on a cloud, the Morrisites were awaiting the return of Jesus for over 100 years as a descendant of the King of Denmark, a real person, to be imprisoned in the city of Deer Lodge in a stone building that was both a prison and Ezekiel's seven towered Temple. He would be wearing the "dirty garment" as his charge, something that the Bab and Baha'u'llah though in prison did not have. He would arrive on the day of August 9th of 1969. Williams even said that he knew his "new name," which we know is **Leland (the Land--Ha Eretz--Zechariah 3:9)**, but he says that it was not for him to reveal in the "Vision of the King" but he gives this in "The High Priesthoods Return."*

Williams foresaw the name, Leland, the place Temple/prison in Deer Lodge and the date August 9th, 1969, Leland's first full day in the "Stone with Seven Eyes" and his mission to be the High Priest after the order of Melchizedec to open the scroll of the Covenant and the Law (Book of the Covenant and Will and Testament) in order to establish his Father's Kingdom, the indestructible and eternal Government of the World Order of Baha'u'llah which we know must have the Davidic king as the president and member of the IBC/UHJ.

Williams's prophecies go into much, much more depth detailing the earth's shifting crust and the catastrophe of thermonuclear war--a destruction by fire. Also Williams gives credence and prophetic insight into the fact that the return of Jesus will unravel the significance of the great pyramid of Giza which is a Chronological Book in Stone.

> With regard to the Pyramids in Egypt there will be wise men attracted there to explore, calculate to measure, to find what is the meaning of these extraordinary relics. Jeremiah speaking, and Isaiah also, knew the Lord of Hosts [Baha'u'llah] had a design in these great wonders, and these explorers will be helped to bring these hidden mysteries to light if they are doing it for an honest, holy purpose, to benefit mankind, and not with a view of making money; for every feature of the structure represents a heavenly order and may be called a pure language. Not by figure or by writing as we represent things, and it is written that the Lord will turn unto the inhabitants of the earth a pure language by which a small sign or movement may represent volumes of our written words. [The Pyramid gives its message in measurement and mathematics the pure universal language.] Its height, its circumference, its depth, its inner chambers, the space occupied by it, **all represent Jehovah's purposes from Adam to the Millennium**, and farther, as far as I know. There they stand, witnesses, and are called the mighty wonders of Egypt; and although the children of Israel built some of these Pyramids in slavery and oppression, the Lord of Hosts claimed their labors a standing memorial of his guardianship over them. He delivered them, and drowned their oppressors, as the record tells us; but the Egyptians knew not what a wonderful memorial Jehovah's chosen had left behind them; and now, before our dear Lord's second coming, professors and wise men desire to look into the meaning of these grand structures, and, I have no doubt, others will be found buried in the

---

* See pages 175-178, this volume.

sand. These explanations have been given me as fast as my scribe could write them. Amen & Amen.[*]

Williams also sees the mystery of the Great Pyramid and its spiritual message to be unraveled at the return of Jesus the High Priest, the establisher of the Baha'i Faith. Breaking the seals on the Great Pyramid was the first thing that Leland did when he had the "Stone with Seven Eyes" before him in 1969 to 1973.

As a capstone to this brief segment of Williams's prophecies is a most remarkable vision of all: of special interest to Baha'is as well as all the people of the world. In an astounding vision in which Muhammad appeared to George Williams, he was instructed to send a messenger from Deer Lodge to Constantinople and rebuke the Sultan of Turkey Abdu'l-Aziz who is the one that imprisoned Baha'u'llah unjustly. Williams prophesies that the Ottoman empire will be torn down for this evil deed and that the Sultan will lose his power which he did. The most astounding feature of the vision is that at the end of Muhammad's visit to him he hears the multitude of multitudes of angels singing the most beautiful sound he had ever heard "Allah'u'Abha! Allah'u'Abha!" over and over again. Thus in this vision Williams received the Most Great Name brought by Baha'u'llah and Baha'u'llah alone thus showing that he had attained, as Baha'u'llah has written: the true station which every Baha'i can attain which is that of an old Testament prophet.

> Cainan [George Williams] bowed consent and then a pause. Muhammad said, "My time is expired. Farewell." I heard now a loud rushing, it seemed of thousand voices, the most distinctive sound was **Allah Abbah**. This proceeded from the same body of light that swept past taking my visitor which I watched till I could see no more. And the voices left their memory, the sweetest ever mortal heard.[†]

This vision was given in 1867 in America long before the news of Baha'u'llah had ever travelled to the West. Williams was a true Baha'i minor prophet and accurately foresaw the advent of the establisher of the Baha'i Faith in Deer Lodge, Montana. Because of Williams's prophecies, to this very day an estimated two thirds of the population of the Deer Lodge Valley are descended from the Morrisite pioneers. The city of Deer Lodge itself was platted and formed in 1863 at the time of Baha'u'llah's proclamation in the garden of Ridvan outside of Baghdad, Iraq. Although these descendants have turned to other Christian sects, the prophecies of Williams and the Morrisites live on today preserved in over one hundred year old leather bound hand written journals saved in the Morrisite families the same way copies of the New Testament were once saved and put together.

Like Jesus Christ and Baha'u'llah, who had John the Baptist and the Bab respectively as their forerunners, Dr. Jensen has George Williams and the Morrisites. The entire Deer Lodge valley was pioneered and settle specifically for his coming so that all the people of the world could be absolutely assured through this proof that he is the authentic and bonafide establisher of the

---

[*] George Williams, (December 27, 1881). "Letter to Dear and Beloved Brother Erasmussen," Walthamstow, Essex, England, pp. 8-9.
[†] George Williams, (1867). "Vision of Muhammad" (see pages, 166; and 173-174 this volume).

wisdom and will not consent to Turkey's degradation
or shameful humiliation as they will be anxious
to afford their help and avoid war let them bear the
heavy burden of being bringing about a better state
of things than now exist for their interference will
not be without cause and their anger will be appeased
and they the Nations shall feel flattered at their timely
aid and Turkey shall so escape her delinquencies at
their cost for no charge will be ask asked do this
Servant of the most High not hurriedly but watch
the opening Time and I Mahomet will be free of
threatened anger and you Caiman shall likewise
be free unconcern in the prosperity of mighty
Empire when the opportunity was yours this
place let it be known as my Meeting place with
you & the river passing by as the Sweet sweet
Caiman bowed consent and then a voice
Mahomet said my Time is expired farewell
I heard now a loud rushing it seemed of

_____ st distinctive sound
5 Allah Abbah_____ proceeded from the
                        swept coast taking
my pressure warm watched till I could see
the Mormor and the voices left their
Memory the sweetest ever Mortal heard
        Almerin grave was the person sent and
returned in safety I have lost sight of
him a long time
        Bro James has asked me for a
this interview many times let him have
copy

"*ALLAH ABBAH*" from leather bound journal (1867) Williams's Vision of Muhammad
(Deer Lodge Historical Society)

166

Baha'i Faith authorized to re-establish what the Covenant-breaking "Hands" threw out--the genuine IBC/UHJ with the Davidic kingship as the president and member for life of that body.

REVIEW

The purpose of these prophecies is to establish beyond any doubt whatsoever (through proofs) what the true and fullest station, mission and authority of Dr. Jensen is as the authentic establisher of the Baha'i Faith. The fulfillment of prophecy is given by 'Abdu'l-Baha in *Some Answered Questions* as the bonafide criteria for recognizing the authenticity of the promised ones.[*] When we see that they fulfill the prophecies 100% we can then see that they are authentic and we can believe in them as authenticity is the criteria for believability.

Dr. Jensen is not a Manifestation of God. He is not a prophet who has dreams and visions like Daniel or Ezekiel in the Old Testament. He is not a medium or a channeler either. He is like Noah who was so knowledgeable in the scriptures of Adam on down to his time he derived his knowledge, understanding, explanations and commentaries on what was already revealed. His authority is given by the fact that he fulfills the prophecies to be the one to do these things. His titles such as Joshua, Jesus, the seventh angel, Kalki, Maitreya, Bahana, etc...are not personal mystical experiences that he has had as a channeler or medium. Not at all! These are the different titles that the promised one is known by in the different scriptures of the different faiths throughout the world. This is like John the Baptist fulfilling the prophecy for the return of Elijah.

In the Old Testament it is stated in the last Book of the Bible, the Book of Malachi, in the last chapter, in the last two verses that before the great and terrible day of the Lord, God will send Elijah. Now John was not the reincarnation of Elijah, he was not the same physical Elijah which it states went up into heaven in a whirlwind and a flaming chariot, he was not a medium channeling Elijah either. When they asked him if he was Elijah he said that he was not[†] because he was himself John. But as Elijah lived nine hundred years before John he was in the same desert of the Negev, he was wearing a camel hair coat and eating locust and honey, and calling the people to repent and turn back to the law of Moses and the Covenant. In this same way John was in the same desert in the same garb eating the same food and doing the exact same job, calling the people to turn back to the law and Covenant of Moses. At the time of Elijah he appeared to the 10 tribes that had broken away from the Temple worship. John appealed to the Jews who were forsaking the true teachings to prepare them for Jesus. Thus John the Baptist was Elijah returned. They preformed the same mission. It was like the same light in two different lamps. As Jesus was looking at the light and not the lamps he said that John was Elijah for all those willing to accept it.[‡] In this same way the Bab was the return of Elijah for Baha'u'llah. And Williams is the return of Elijah for Dr. Jensen. And both the Bab and Williams are like the return of John the Baptist. It is the same mission.

The station of Joshua is that of the establisher of Moses. As Moses had Joshua lead the 12 tribes across the river Jordan into the promised land and conquer the seven pagan kings of Palestine

---

[*] See 'Abdu'l-Baha, *Some Answered Questions* (SAQ), chapter 10 "Traditional Proofs Exemplified from the book of Daniel," p. 43.
[†] John 1:21.
[‡] Matthew 11:14.

and set up the true temple and government of Israel, so the establisher of Baha'u'llah is a modern Joshua performing the same mission as that Warrior Champion leading the 144,000 (12 tribes regathered under their new name Baha'i) through the four winds of destruction, conquering the seven alive revealed apostate religions and establishing the temple IBC/UHJ and the government, the World Order of Baha'u'llah, for all the people of the world. Now Joshua is the Hebrew name for the Greek name Jesus.

This Jesus (Joshua) the son of Nun at the time of Moses was his establisher but he was not the high priest. Moses' brother Aaron and his sons were the high priests. Thus this Jesus (Joshua) the son of Nun had to go before Aaron or his sons. The modern Joshua is prophesied to be both Joshua and the high priest rolled up into one as the same person. Thus the prophecy of Zechariah chapter three is of **JOSHUA THE HIGH PRIEST**. As Joshua and Jesus is the same name in a different language this is **JESUS THE HIGH PRIEST**. As a matter of fact in some editions it says Jesus the High Priest in place of Joshua the High Priest (see enclosed copies). They are one and the same, that is, they perform one and same mission.

Now within the Bible itself Jesus/Joshua the High Priest has many titles or diadems. These are the different roles that he performs. For instance it says that it will be like in the days of Noah. Thus he bases his knowledge on what has already been revealed by Baha'u'llah and the Manifestations and does not have dreams and visions. In the Book of Revelation alone there are seven separate titles, that is roles, that the same individual, the return of Jesus fulfills. These are not seven separate people but one and the same personage depicted in this way as to show the wholeness and fullness of his station, mission, role and authority. For instance John Wayne is one actor, one person. In one role he is a cowboy, another he is a soldier, another he is a cop, etc...Yet he is always himself and not anyone else. He simply has these different roles or jobs. In Revelation the return of Jesus the High Priest is the Lamb--Paul explains why the Lamb is the High Priest after the order of Melchizedec in the Book of Hebrews. The Book of Hebrews is one of the most important books in the Bible. Everyone should read it and study it. He is also the man on the white horse (chapter 6) identical with the Knight on the white horse in Revelation chapter 19. Dr. Jensen is the last remaining Knight of Baha'u'llah under the provisions of the Covenant who is active and fulfilling his mission. The other knights are either dead or went with the Covenant-breakers and rejected the continuation of the guardianship--the Davidic kingship. He is also entitled the seventh angel, the man with the sickle, the Mighty Angel, the angel with great authority, the angel with the key and the great chain, etc.... This is all one and the same person. These titles are in the Bible.

Then around the world we have the prophecies of the different world religions of the different countries and nations also waiting for the promised establisher. If he were not prophesied in their scriptures also, then they would not be able to enter the Kingdom. For the Native American Hopi he is known as the Bahana--he is not channeling Bahana but foretold to be in the station performing the mission of the Bahana. For the Hindu he is the Kalki Avatar and for the Buddhist he is the Maitreya. These are all titles for the future one who is to come and establish the Kingdom of God on earth. Thus they all perform the same mission, the same function. These prophecies are all for one and the same person: the establisher of the Baha'i Faith, that Dr. Jensen fulfills.

Douay Version

THE
PROPHECY OF ZACHARIAS

Zacharias began to prophesy in the same year as Aggeus, and upon the same occasion. His prophecy is full of mysterious figures and promises of blessings, partly relating to the synagogue, and partly to the Church of Christ.

PROLOGUE

CHAPTER 1.

An Exhortation to Conversion

IN THE eighth month, in the second year a of king Darius, the word of the Lord came to Zacharias the son of Barachias, the son of Addo, the prophet, saying: 2. The Lord hath been exceeding angry with your fathers. 3. And thou shalt say to them: Thus saith the Lord of hosts: b Turn ye to me, saith the Lord of hosts, and I will turn to you, saith the Lord of hosts. 4. Be not as your fathers, to whom the former prophets have cried, saying: Thus said the Lord of hosts: Turn ye from your evil ways, and from your wicked thoughts. But they did not give ear, neither did they hearken to me, saith the Lord.

5. Your fathers, where are they? And the prophets, shall they live always? 6. But yet my words, and my ordinances, which I gave in charge to my servants the prophets, did they not take hold of your fathers? And they returned, and said: As the Lord of hosts thought to do to us according to our ways, and according to our devices, so he hath done to us.

I. THE PROMISE OF SALVATION

7. In the four and twentieth day of the eleventh month which is called Sabath, in the second year of Darius, the word of the Lord came to Zacharias, the son of Barachias, the son of Addo, the prophet, saying: 8. I saw by night, and behold a man ! riding upon a red horse, and he stood among the myrtle trees, that were in the bottom; and behind him were horses, red, speckled, and white. 9. And I said: What are these, my Lord? And the angel that spoke in me, said to me: I will show thee what these are. These are they 2 whom the Lord hath sent to walk through the earth.

11. And they answered the angel of the Lord, that stood among the myrtle trees, and said: We have walked through the earth, and behold all the earth is inhabited, and is at rest. 12. And the angel of the Lord answered, and said: O Lord of hosts, how long wilt thou not have mercy on Jerusalem, and on the cities of Juda, with which thou hast been angry? This is now the seventieth year. 13. And the Lord answered the angel, that spoke in me, good words, comfortable words.

14. And the angel that spoke in me, said to me: Cry thou, saying: Thus saith the Lord of hosts: c I am zealous for Jerusalem and Sion with a great zeal. 15. And I am angry with a great anger with the wealthy nations, for I was angry a little, but they helped forward the evil. 16. Therefore thus saith the Lord: I will return to Jerusalem in mercies: my house shall be built in it, saith the Lord of hosts,

6 520 B.C.—b Isa. 21, 12; 31, 6; 45, 22; Jer. 3, 12; Ezech. 18, 30; 20, 7; 33, 11; Osee 14, 2; Joel 2, 12; Mal. 3, 7.—c Zach. 8, 2.

1-Ver. 8. A man: an angel in the shape of a man, probably St. Michael, the guardian angel of the Church of God.

2-Ver. 10. These are they, etc.: the guardian angels of provinces and nations.

and the building line shall be stretched forth upon Jerusalem. 17. Cry yet, saying: Thus saith the Lord of hosts: My cities shall yet flow with good things, and the Lord will yet comfort Sion, and will yet choose Jerusalem.

18. And I lifted up my eyes, and saw: and behold four horns. 19. And I said to the angel that spoke to me: What are these? And he said to me: These are the horns which have scattered Juda, and Israel, and Jerusalem.

20. And the Lord showed me four smiths.1 21. And I said: What come these to do? And he spoke, saying: These are the horns which have scattered Juda every man apart, and none of them lifted up his head; and these are come to fray them, to cast down the horns of the nations, that have lifted up the horn upon the land of Juda to scatter it.

CHAPTER 2.

The Man with a Measuring Line

AND I lifted up my eyes, and saw, and behold a man, with a measuring line in his hand. 2. And I said: Whither goest thou? And he said to me: To measure Jerusalem, and to see how great is the breadth thereof, and how great is the length thereof. 3. And behold the angel that spoke in me went forth, and another angel went out to meet him. 4. And he said to him: Run, speak to this young man, saying: Jerusalem shall be inhabited without walls,2 by reason of the multitude of men, and of the beasts in the midst thereof. 5. And I will be to it, saith the Lord, a wall of fire round about: and I will be in glory in the midst thereof.

6. O, O flee ye out of the land the north, saith the Lord, for I have scattered you into the four winds heaven, saith the Lord. 7. O Sion, flee thou that dwellest with the daughter of Babylon.

8. For thus saith the Lord of hosts: After the glory he hath sent me to the nations that have robbed you, for he that toucheth you, toucheth the apple of my eye; 9. for behold I lift up my hand upon them, and they shall be a prey to those that served them; and you shall know that the Lord of hosts sent me.

10. Sing praise, and rejoice, daughter of Sion, for behold I come, and I will dwell in the midst of thee, saith the Lord. 11. And many nations shall be joined to the Lord in that day, and they shall be my people, and I will dwell in the midst of thee. And thou shalt know that the Lord of hosts hath sent me to thee. 12. And the Lord shall possess Juda his portion in the sanctified land, and he shall yet choose Jerusalem. 13. Let all flesh be silent at the presence of the Lord, for he is risen up out of his holy habitation.

CHAPTER 3.

Jesus, The High Priest

AND the Lord showed me Jesus the high priest standing before the angel of the Lord: and Satan stood on his right hand to be his adversary. 2. And the Lord said to Satan: The Lord rebuke thee, O Satan. And the Lord that chose Jerusalem rebuke thee. Is not this a brand plucked out of the fire?

3. And Jesus was clothed with filthy garments,4 and he stood before the face of the angel. 4. who answered, and said to them that stood before him, saying: Take away the filthy garments from him. And he said to him: Behold I have taken away thy iniquity, and have clothed thee with change of garments. 5. And he said: Put a clean mitre upon his head. And they put a clean mitre upon on his head, and clothed him with garments, and the angel of the Lord stood. 6. And the angel of the Lord

1-Ver. 18. 20. Four horns—four smiths; the four horns represented the empires or kingdoms, that persecute and oppress the people of God. The four smiths or carpenters represent those whom God makes his instruments in bringing to nothing the power of Jerusalem's enemies.

2-Ver. 4. Jerusalem shall be inhabited without walls: this must be understood of the spiritual Jerusalem, the Church of Christ.

3-Ver. 1. Jesus: or Josue, the son of Josedec, the high priest of that time.

4-Ver. 3. With filthy garments: negligences and sins.

protested to Jesus, saying: 7. Thus saith the Lord of hosts: If thou wilt walk in my ways, and keep my charge, thou also shalt judge my house, and shalt keep my courts, and I will give thee¹ some of them that are now present here to walk *with thee.*

8. Hear, O Jesus thou high priest, thou and thy friends that dwell before thee, for they are portending men:² For behold d I WILL BRING MY SERVANT THE ORIENT. 9. For behold the stone³ that I have laid before Jesus: upon one stone there are seven eyes. Behold I will grave the graving thereof, saith the Lord of hosts, and I will take away the iniquity of that land in one day. 10. In that day, saith the Lord of hosts, every man shall call his friend under the vine and under the fig tree.

CHAPTER 4.

The Golden Candlestick

AND the angel that spoke in me came again, and he waked me, as a man that is wakened out of his sleep. 2. And he said to me: What seest thou? And I said: I have looked, and behold a candlestick⁴ all of gold, and its lamp upon the top of it, and the seven lights thereof upon it, and seven funnels for the lights that were upon the top thereof. 3. and two olive trees over it: one upon the right side of the lamp, and the other upon the left side thereof.

4. And I answered, and said to the angel that spoke in me, saying: What are these things, my Lord? 5. And the angel that spoke in me answered, and said to me: Knowest thou not what these things are? And I said: No, my Lord.

6. And he answered, and spoke to me, saying: This is the word of the Lord to Zorobabel,⁵ saying: Not with an army, nor by might, but by my spirit, saith the Lord of hosts. 7. Who art thou, O great mountain,⁶ before Zorobabel? Thou shalt become a plain, and he shall bring out the chief stone, and shall give equal grace to the grace thereof.

8. And the word of the Lord came to me, saying: 9. The hands of Zorobabel have laid the foundations of this house, and his hands shall finish it; and you shall know that the Lord of hosts hath sent me to you. 10. For who hath despised little days?⁷ And they shall rejoice, and shall see the tin plummet in the hand of Zorobabel. These are the seven eyes of the Lord, that run to and fro through the whole earth.

Two Olive Trees

11. And I answered, and said to him: What are these two olive trees, upon the right side of the candlestick and upon the left side thereof? 12. And I answered again, and said to him: What are the two olive branches, that are by the two golden beaks, in which are the funnels of gold?

13. And he spoke to me, saying: Knowest thou not what these are?

---

d Luke 1, 78.

1-Ver. 7. *I will give thee,* etc.: angels to attend and assist thee.

2-Ver. 8. *Portending men:* i.e., men, who by words and actions are to foreshew wonders that are to come. *My servant the Orient:* Christ, who, according to his humanity is the servant of God, is called the Orient from his rising like the sun in the east to enlighten the world.

3-Ver. 9. *The stone:* another emblem of Christ, the rock, foundation, and corner stone of the Church. *Seven eyes:* the manifold providence of Christ over his Church, or the seven gifts of the spirit of God. *One day:* the day of the passion of Christ, the source of all our good, when this precious stone shall be graved, i.e., cut and pierced, with whips, thorns, nails and spear.

4-Ver. 2. *A candlestick,* etc.: the temple of God that was then in building: and in a spiritual sense, the Church of Christ.

5-Ver. 6. *To Zorobabel:* this vision assured Zorobabel, of success in building the temple, signified by the candlestick and the lamp supplied with oil from the two olive trees and distributed by the seven funnels or pipes, to maintain the seven lights.

6-Ver. 7. *Great mountain:* the opposition by the enemies of God's people. Without any army or might it was quashed by divine providence. *Shall give equal grace,* etc.: shall add grace to grace, or beauty to beauty.

7-Ver. 10. *Little days:* i.e., the small and tin plummet: literally *the stone of tin:* the builder's plummet which Zorobabel shall hold in his hand for the finishing of the building. *The seven eyes:* the providence of God that oversees and orders all things.

And I said: No, my Lord. 14. And he said: These are two sons of oil,⁸ who stand before the Lord of the whole earth.

CHAPTER 5.

The Flying Volume

AND I turned and lifted up my eyes, and I saw, and behold a volume² flying. 2. And he said to me: What seest thou? And I said: I see a volume flying: the length thereof *is* twenty cubits, and the breadth thereof *is* of ten cubits. 3. And he said to me: This is the curse that goeth forth over the face of the earth; for every thief shall be judged as is there written, and everyone that sweareth in like manner shall be judged by it. 4. I will bring it forth, saith the Lord of hosts, and it shall come to the house of the thief, and to the house of him that sweareth falsely by my name. And it shall remain in the midst of his house, and shall consume it, with the timber thereof, and the stones thereof.

5. And the angel went forth that spoke in me, and he said to me: Lift up thy eyes, and see what this is, that goeth forth. 6. And I said: What is it? And he said: This is a vessel go-ing forth. And he said: This is their eye³ in all the earth.

7. And behold a talent of lead was carried, and behold a woman sitting in the midst of the vessel. 8. And he said: This is wickedness. And he cast her into the midst of the vessel, and cast the weight of lead upon the mouth thereof.

9. And I lifted up my eyes and looked: and behold there came out two women, and wind was in their wings, and they had wings like the wings of a kite; and they lifted up the vessel between the earth and the heaven. 10. And I said to the angel that spoke in me: Whither do these carry the vessel? 11. And he said to me: That a house may be built for it in the land of Sennaar,⁴ and that it may be established, and set there upon its own basis.

CHAPTER 6.

The Four Chariots

AND I turned, and lifted up my eyes, and saw: and behold four chariots⁵ came out from the midst of two mountains; and the mountains *were* mountains of brass. 2. In the first chariot were red horses, and in the second chariot black horses. 3. And in the third chariot white horses; and in the fourth chariot grisled horses, and strong ones. 4. And I answered, and said to the angel that spoke in me: What are these, my Lord? 5. And the angel answered, and said to me: These are the four winds of the heaven, which go forth to stand before the Lord of all the earth. 6. That in which were the black horses went forth into the land of the north,⁶ and the white went forth after them, and the grisled went forth to the land of the south. 7. And they that were most strong, went out, and sought to go and to run to and fro through all the earth. And he said: Go, walk throughout the earth. And they walked throughout the earth. 8. And he called me, and spoke to me, saying: Behold they that go forth into the land of the north, have quieted my spirit in the land of the north.

1-Ver. 14. *Two sons of oil:* i.e., the two anointed ones of the Lord: Jesus the high priest, and Zorobabel, the prince.

2-Ver. 1. *A volume:* i.e., a parchment, according to the form of the ancient books, which, from being rolled up, were called volumes.

3-Ver. 6. *This is their eye:* this is what they fix their eye upon; or this is a resemblance and figure of sinners.

4-Ver. 11. *The land of Sennaar:* Site of Babel or Babylon. Babylon in the Scriptures is often taken for the city of the devil: that is, for the whole congregation of the wicked. Jerusalem is taken for the city and people of God.

5-Ver. 1. *Four chariots:* the four great empires of the Chaldeans, Persians, Grecians and Romans. Or perhaps by the fourth chariot are represented the kings of Egypt and of Asia, the descendants of Ptolemeus and Seleucus.

6-Ver. 6. *The land of the north:* so Babylon, north of Jerusalem. The black horses, i.e. the Medes and Persians; and after them Alexander and his Greeks signified by the white horse, went thither because they conquered Babylon, executed upon it the judgments of God, which is signified ver. 8, by the expression of *quieting his spirit. The land of the south:* Egypt to the south of Jerusalem, and was occupied first by Ptolemy and then by the Romans.

There are much, much more things to write about on the Morrisites and their prophecies of Williams. This letter only scratches the surface. There are still the prophecies of Columbus who came to America, St. Brendan, the Vikings and Plato just to name a few. Some of these are covered in the book *Ezekiel's Temple in Montana* (enclosed).

I hope that this letter finds you in the best of health and good spirits. My prayers for your son--I hope that he regains his health and strength. It is my purest wish that this letter has met your satisfaction into a brief description of the Morrisites and the prophecies of George Williams. As you well know we have before us the mighty task of establishing Baha'u'llah's kingdom before us is these trying times, the majestic day of the great victory of God!

If you have any questions on the Morrisites or any related issues toward the great work that is commenced in this great day of the 100th anniversary of Baha'u'llah's ascension, please feel free to write or call at any time, any day.

Sincerely yours,
in the service of the Lamb,

I remain yours,
your servant,
Neal.

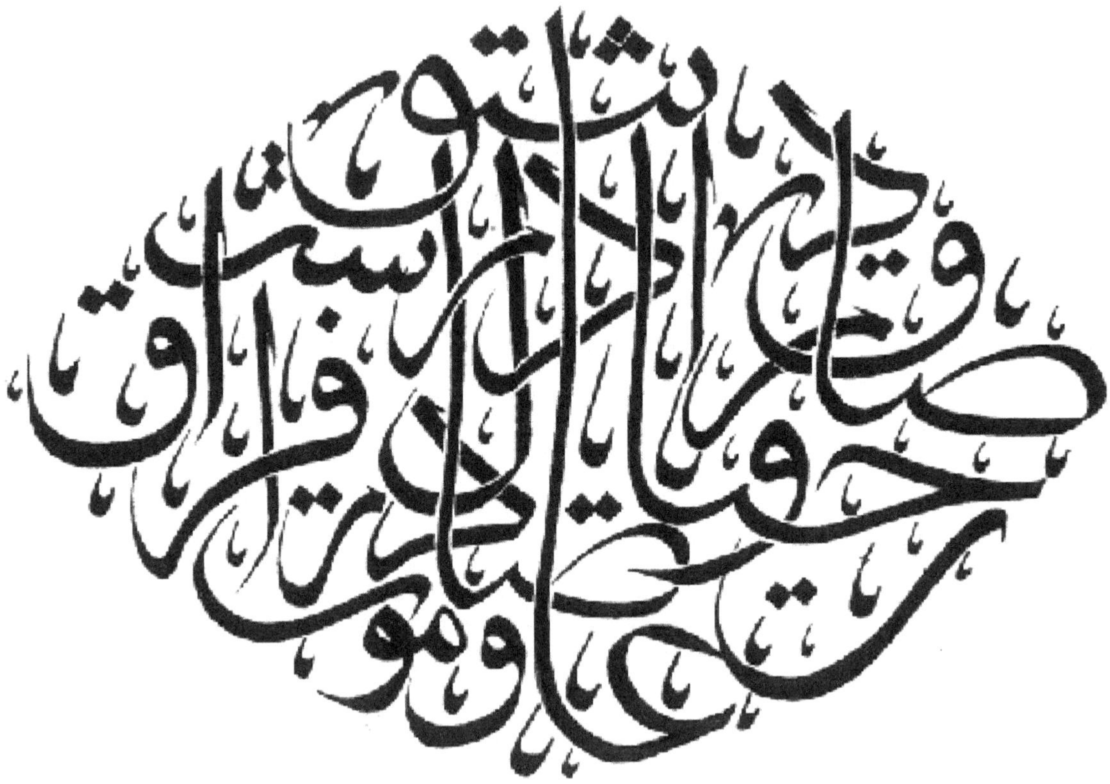

GEORGE WILLIAMS'S INTERVIEW WITH MUHAMMAD

(Copied from my Journal in the year, 1867)

While on a visit with a friend (called the stranger) under the mountains by the mouth of the little Cottonwood Canyon, a voice came unto me saying: "Dismiss this stranger for one cometh, to whom hear what he sayeth."

Knowing that this was not a mortal's voice I stopped the conversation with the Stranger, and desired him to leave me and go to his home. With some astonishment he did so and I was in a wood of Cottonwood trees wondering what the voice might mean; yet it was a voice I knew, the voice presently came again saying: "Fear not, Servant of the Most High, we are your friends." And immediately I was Strengthened Spiritually. The things of Earth was fled from my understanding and a soft unspeakable influence enveloped me.

Something at a vast distance very bright was swiftly approaching me. Out of this bright body of light stepped one of beautiful Countenance and massive Stature with green garments flowing round him. Upon his head a folded banner of white and green in the center a circle of a half-moon. His legs were bare up to the knee with threads of yellow bound here and there around them. Bending very low he came near me with a: "Hail, Servant of the Most High! I am Muhammad, and before I was Muhammad I was Ishmael the Son of Abraham and Hagar, and I am also a Servant of the Most High to that branch of Adam's family of the mothers line. At this time I am permitted to leave my mansion in paradise to visit the Servant of the Most High now in mortality. Of my visit a messenger from the Son of Mary was sent to warn. Therefore I need not give a sign or hand a key of Priesthood. My raiment must show I am another branch of Priesthood and occupy a separate mansion in Paradise; for there are many mansions.

"Jesus, Son of Mary, is not divided in feeling with me there, for both serve the Most High, and by his appointment and according to the line of teaching shown us for we are dependant servants there, as you are here, upon the Most High. As my stay with you must be short I lay before you my errand of Mercy [that] the Most High and Merciful God grants me to deliver.

"The people and government of Turkey whose Fathers received my mission to them while I was in mortality are now in a dangerous state and have become in debt to many nations contrary to the Law and doctrine given them. And by their harsh government over many fair and beautiful Lands chiefly possessed by the followers of Jesus, Son of Mary, and many other vices, have aroused the indignation of powerful governments surrounding their borders who are now planning their overthrow and destructions.

"These nations will call upon the Sultan and his government to reform their government and give security for their future good conduct toward the peoples they govern for which they will send ministers to meet the Sultan and his ministers to arrange a better state of things--of these designs, and writing of the nations ministers, it is our great desire [that] the Sultan and his ministers should be appraised by me, that he and they may repent and be prepared. For Lo, these nations are and will be violently angry and will declare war, a war of vengeance such as they have never known, and terrible weapons shed the blood of thousands, sparing neither women or children and terrible slaughter and suffering of famine and cold will spread over that Land. To avert this I am come to you in mercy that you may send a missionary with my words written to the Sultan and his government and let the missionary present written word through the American minister to the Sultan.

"There is a man who shall be pointed out to you after many days. Send him. Let him read my words, understand my Interview with you, even Muhammad. Let him be sent without a preparation of money and he will do it. His Journeying shall be protected and his wants supplied. And let him sew the written word in the collar of his coat never looking at it after he starts on his journey until he delivers it to the American minister. The way and procedure shall be pointed out to him at times needed and say unto him, 'He shall return in safety to his Country for which I Muhammad will be surety.'

"Also write these, my words and counsels, to the Sultan and his ministers[*] that when the nations ministers shall arrive in conference the Sultan and his ministers shall meet them with much courtesy putting aside all stubbornness and pride and shall agree to the proposals the other powers advance and you may advance objections slightly, but finally agree to their suggestions and plans accepting their help to adjust the nations difficulties. For those that will be sent will be men of wisdom and will not consent to Turkey's degradation or shameful humiliation as they will be anxious to afford their help and avoid war. Let them bear the heavy burden of bringing about a better state of things than now exist for their interference will not be without cause and their anger will be appeased and they the nations shall feel flattered at their timely aid and Turkey shall escape her delinquencies at their cost for no charge will be asked. Lo this Servant of the Most High, not hurriedly but with the opening time, and I Muhammad will be free of threatened anger. And you Cainan [George Williams] shall likewise be free, unconcern in the prosperity of Mighty Empire when the opportunity was yours. This place let it be known as my meeting place with you and the river passing by as 'the sweet sewer.'"

Cainan [George Williams] bowed consent and then a pause. Muhammad said, "My time is expired. Farewell."

I heard now a loud rushing, it seemed of thousand voices, the most distinctive sound was *Allah Abbah*. This proceeded from the same body of light that swept past taking my visitor which I watched till I could see no more. And the voices left their memory, the sweetest ever mortal heard.

Almerian Grow was the person sent and returned in safety. I have lost sight of him a long time. Brother James has asked me for this "Interviews" many times. Let him have a copy.
--George Williams

---

[*] Compare Baha'u'llah's Tablets to this same Sultan and ministers who banished Him to perpetual incarceration in the Prison Fortress of Akka, in 1868, in fulfillment of prophecy in the Holy Land at the same time as Williams's Vision: *Suriy-i-Rais, Lawh-i-Rais, Lawh-i-Fu'ad*, and the *Suriy-i-Muluk* (*Tablet to the Kings*), in which He personally addresses Sultan Abdu'l-'Aziz of the Ottoman Empire of Turkey who signed the decree against Him (see Shoghi Effendi, *God Passes By*, Chapter IX, for more). "And I will give her her vineyards from thence, and the Valley of Achor [Akka] for **a door of hope**; and she shall **make answer there**, as in the days of her youth, and as in the day when she came up out of the land of Egypt" (Hosea 2:15 ASV). Baha'u'llah was transferred to Akka by sea via Egypt in His banishment from Constantinople.

THE HIGH PRIESTHOODS RETURN

by George Williams

Come to me sweet spirit in your garment of snow
     Conduct me along where the holy ones go.
To the house of my Father where the holy ones go;
     My **new name** and white stone now entrust to my care.
I will not be alarmed at you step without noise,
     In the glow of your bright face my heart shall rejoice.
My hand shall not touch you: my eyes only see,
     No taint of a mortal shall cleave unto thee.

Come nearer dear Angel and bend down your ear,
     Return unto Jesus this form of my prayer,
Tell him I am ready his work to have done,
     If he also is ready permit me to come.
In the court of his Father, one hour after death,
     The keys I received from Enos and Seth.
On the mountain transparent with joy will deliver,
     Claim my crown of reward, and wear it forever.

There my body celestial has waited so long,
     And patiently listened to the archangels song;
Singing the triumphs of the last of the three,
     Engaged by Jehovah his servant to be.
Seth and Enos returned all dabbled in blood,
     The Lord scarcely knew them, being covered with mud,
But they have ascended up higher and higher
     To the top of the Quorum, and brighter than fire,

The singing continued till Cainan was come,
     The body expanded and he was at home,
The escort was ordered, the army prepared,
     And loaded with honors, see Cainan's reward,
As he stepped in that chariot all gleaming with fire
     At the farewell of Jehovah's the army moved higher.
Increasing in speed, increasing in light,
     Advanced to the regions more brighter more light.

The suns and the systems were left in the rear,
     As fragments inferior, there's a grandeur appear,
Oh the blaze and the glory, the sight and the sound,
     And deep the clear spirit--in ecstasies drown.
The army cuts through; Heaven is in sight,
     And beauty and riches, and music invite,

The cavalcade halts, the portals expands,
        And myriad, celestial, come trooping in bands.

From the cottage in Surry, where parents had made,
        The casket for Cainan, to commence his parade.
Through trials and storms; through poverty's stress
        The Father's correction, the Mother's caress,
The school and the garden, divided his time,
        The sun and the stars awoke the sublime.
Constantly watching how wonderfully true
        They came, and departed, and always seemed new.

How did it happen they never should fall?
        Their motions majestic and requisite all,
Who was it polished their glittering rims?
        And why did those sparks shoot out of their brims.
Astonished perplexed he wondered admired;
        Those traveling guns that never were tired,
He inquired of his fellows, his father and mother,
        Ones explanation unfitted the other.

Restless unsettled he applied to the priest,
        Whose magnified ignorance he credited least,
At length he discovered; there is somebody higher
        Than father or mother or that priest of a liar,
As a touch of intelligence straight from his throne
        Was graciously given--All shadows had flown.
As you read in the records at chapter the first
        The inklines were given there--the shadows had burst.

To the spirit that is worthy, the spirit reveals,
        To the spirit unworthy, the spirit conceals.
Up to his departure the records revealed,
        All openly written and nothing concealed,
And sealed by Jehovah with the emblem of power
        Revolving this mortal earth, strict to the hour.
Through the ages of time, through fathomless space,
        No tower or prop, to steady her race.

Everlasting rushing, with swiftness immense,
        Her waters and fires held in by a fence.
Constructed by wisdom in the heavenly college
        Her salvation and safety depends upon knowledge.
Should the slight touch of ignorance step into the plan
        What chaos; what ruin;--no battering ram.

With ponderous force come plunging on paper
      Would show such destruction by ending in vapor.

Oh thanks to the treaty, the Covenant made,
    When all was agreed and all was obeyed.
No ruin can come, through the enemy tries.
      His peeping and cunning the Father defies,
The planet serine and even will run,
      Until all her creations are perfect and done.
And sin is abolished and Jesus has won.

Rotations completed day and night making one,
      The Angel in charge announces the sum,
Through time, times and half she gradually came,
      Then a gulf in the orbit at the number she named.
One foot on the sea and one on **the Land**,
      Declared, it is finished!, with an uplifted hand.
Here ended in triumph earth's mortal career,

In the pause and suspense what next do we hear,
      The rushing of angels escorting the gods,
With the books, and attendants, upholding the rods,
      These are authors of worlds,--come with counsel and sword.
To assist at the judgement the hands of our Lord,
      There is Adam the first, the Ancient of days,
 What a radiance of joy encircles his face!

How white is his raiment, how glittering his head;
      Fresh out from the chambers where long he had stayed,
How brilliant his eyes! like flames of a fire
      Not a deed nor a thought from that gage can retire.
His statue and bearing reveals him the prince;
      That flung out the rebels one eternity since.
For him our dear Lord trod the winepress alone
      Securing his titles, securing his throne.

By his blood and his sweat has averted his fall
      Now hands him the kingdom, the Father, the God all in all.
There is innocent Abel, what a beautiful soul!
      Been presiding in paradise over the whole
Arranging the mansions for the heirs of salvation
      Whatever their faith whatever their nation.
For what they are heirs to in justice is given
      What mortal dare question the rule of this Heaven.

How well he is **prisoned** by a process unshown;
     The flaming sword still keeps this science unknown
With all his massive wisdom a spot of blood is there
     Upon his heavenly garments as evidence declare
How soon began the malice with them who would obey
     Jehovah's will and counsel white clothed in mortal clay,
Allegiance may bring on sufferings here
     Without it how undefined to head a mansion there
Who would attain his beautiful firmament Heights suppose
     One first in power, with many crowns behold
The Mighty Seth!
     The other seed that Eve received soon after Abel's death.

To be continued...

AN OPEN LETTER TO PATRICK C. LABBE

"IT IS HARD...TO KICK AGAINST THE PRICKS."
--Acts 9:5, KJV.

Dear Patrick,

I have received and read your essay, "Exposing a Modern Anti-Christ: Falsehoods and Deceptions in **Maontana** (Revised edition)" as well as the rest of the items in your packet to me. The arguments in your paper hold about as much water as the way you misspelled Montana ("Moantana") on your cover page. You spent so much time laying out the computer graphics trying to make yourself look important (as you foolishly tried to condemn and criticize the one sent by God for today, to re-establish what the Covenant-breakers threw out) when you should learn how to spell or at least learn how to use the spell-check on the computer.

The pathetic end of this is that what should be the path of knowledge in search of the truth has resulted, in your case, as a feeble and empty collection of information and terminology without understanding, that only serves to separate yourself from God and the mercy and forgiveness of the Lord in this Day! Baha'u'llah warns in the Aqdas of this fatal form of self-deception that pride and conceit taken in false learning and presumptions can cause the soul to be forever separated from the light.

> We have decreed, O people, that the highest and last end of all learning be the recognition of Him Who is the Object of all knowledge; and yet, behold how **ye have allowed <u>your learning</u> to shut you out**, as by a veil, from Him Who is the Dayspring of this Light, through Whom every hidden thing hath been revealed.[*]

Although I sent you my ninety page letter to Mr. Francis Spataro and you have read the book ***Ezekiel's Temple in Montana*** as well as seen the video *Montana in Prophecy*, absolutely none of the information contained within these repositories of facts, evidences and proofs has so far been able to penetrate your mind, for obstinacy[†] and self has barred your way. You have become the archetypical bastion of whom 'Abdu'l-Baha de-thrones:

> **But there are some people who, even if <u>all the proofs in the world be adduced before them</u>, still will not judge justly![‡]**

What is even worse for you is that even what little you can see of the truth you choose to reject it! Thus in your essay on page three you state: "Could not Baha'u'llah fulfill **BOTH** the Establisher prophecies **AND** the Christ prophecies." Showing full well that there are two separate bodies of prophecy for two separate personages: one the second coming of Christ which Baha'u'llah fulfills and the other the prophecies for His establisher the return of Jesus the High Priest! By God! You see this clearly! Yet feign blindness to mislead and poison others and to justify your **unworthy** attack against the one who does fulfill these prophecies, sent by God to

---

[*] *Codification of the Kitab-i-Aqdas*, p. 23.
[†] "Fixed and unyielding (as in an opinion or course) **despite reason** or persuasion," Webster's.
[‡] 'Abdu'l-Baha, SAQ, pp. 43-44.

establish the Order* of the world in this great Day, the last remaining Knight of Baha'u'llah, Dr. Leland Jensen! What kind of hope is there for such a person as this?! What type of curative or medicine or elixir of God can awaken the sick man who refuses health like a poison and escapes into disease and decay as his barricade from the all encompassing love of God from which light and heat bat-like he fleas into the oblivion created by his own vanity and self-loving, shortsighted deadly folly? You have been betrayed, sir, by your own self and by the dissidents of this Promised One today, and yet you do not know it!

Your strongest objection, that you state in your paper on page two ("Obviously from the above statements [that Dr. Jensen fulfills prophecy for the return of Jesus] Leland Jensen considers himself on par with the Manifestations of God") is that Dr. Jensen cannot claim to be the return of Jesus for Jesus is a Manifestation of God and Baha'u'llah said explicitly that another Manifestation of God will not come for a full one thousand years. You persist in this thinking despite the fact that over and over and over again Dr. Jensen has explained that he is not a Manifestation of God! Yet ignoring this, you go forward anyway and therefore conclude, Dr. Jensen cannot be the return of Jesus for he is not a Manifestation of God and that if he does claim this he is in violation of the command of Baha'u'llah that another Manifestation will not appear for a full 1000 years. Your presumptions are spurious! You couldn't be more wrong and more misinformed of the issue at all! Baha'u'llah, in His own pen, explains your folly and that of those who share this aberrant thinking as the foolishness of the idle disputants who are bereft of His knowledge and sorely deprived of His merciful graces! Concerning the matter of the **return and resurrection** of a specific Promised One that God has foretold will again come before the people and perform a sacred task victoriously despite the convulsive opposition of the infantile and subversive, Baha'u'llah reveals this poignant truth in His "Tablet to Vafa" (*Suriy-i-Vafa*) found in the collection *Tablets of Baha'u'llah*, this passage cited on pages 184 and 185:

> Consider thou the Day of Resurrection. Were God to pronounce the lowliest of creatures among the faithful to be the First One to believe in the Bayan, thou shouldst have **no misgivings about it** and **must** be of them that **truly believe.** In this station look not upon human limitations and names but rather upon that whereby the rank of the First One to believe is vindicated, which is faith in God, and recognition of His being and assurance in the fulfillment of His irresistible and binding command.

> Consider thou the Revelation of the Point of the Bayan [the Bab]--exalted is His glory. He pronounced the First One† to believe in Him to be **Muhammad**, the Messenger of God. [Yet Mulla Husayn was not a Manifestation! But a follower of the Manifestation!] Does it beseem a man to dispute with Him by saying that this man is from Persia, the Other from Arabia, or this one was called Husayn while the Other bore the name Muhammad? **Nay,** I swear by God's holy Being, the Exalted, the Most Great. Surely no man of intelligence and insight would ever pay attention unto limitations or names, but rather unto that with which Muhammad was invested, which was none other than the Cause of God. Such a man of insight would likewise consider [Mulla] Husayn and the position he occupied in the

---

* The World Order of Baha'u'llah. The Kingdom of God on earth as it is in heaven.
† Mulla Husayn.

Cause of God, the Omnipotent, the Exalted, the Knowing, the Wise. And since the First One to believe in God in the Dispensation of the Bayan was invested with command similar to that with which Muhammad, the Messenger of God, was invested, therefore the Bab pronounced him to be the latter, namely His return and resurrection. This station [although Mulla Husayn was not a Manifestation] is sanctified from every limitation or name, and naught can be seen therein but God, the One, the Peerless, the All-knowing.[*]

The Bab was the promised Manifestation of Islam and therefore the First One to fully believe and comprehend His Revelation, Mulla Husayn, was invested with the station of being the return and resurrection of Muhammad, though Mulla Husayn was not himself a Manifestation of God like the Bab, but was rather His follower. The coming of Baha'u'llah as you correctly write, is that of the second coming of Christ, the fulfillment of Christianity and therefore the First One in this Great Revelation, the establisher of the Baha'i Faith, holds the station of the return and resurrection of Jesus without being a Manifestation of God the same as Mulla Husayn was not a Manifestation of God yet was the return of Muhammad.

In this light, for you to protest in any way is to go against the explicit teaching of Baha'u'llah on this point. It is manifestly clear that Baha'u'llah never, in any of His writings, ever said that He was the Lamb of God or the return of the Son, that is, the return of Jesus. No! He categorically proclaimed that He was the second coming of Christ (that is, a descendant of David), who ruleth from the throne of David[†], the appearance of the Father[‡] (not the Son!). Baha'u'llah never said that he was the Lamb or Jesus the High Priest or any such thing at all! Neither has any authoritative figure of the Baha'i faith, the Bab, 'Abdu'l-Baha, Shoghi Effendi, or Mason Remey (president of the first IBC) ever proclaimed themselves to be the Lamb or proclaimed that Baha'u'llah was the Lamb or the return of Jesus the High Priest. No. Nowhere. Never. This whole fiasco is a figment of your own imagination and supposition and that of certain lunatic dissidents who don't know from nothing! It is all non-authoritative hogwash.

The very fact that Mulla Husayn was the return of Muhammad yet he was not the Bab, which Baha'u'llah takes the time to educate us on, serves to prepare the way for all the pure in heart without evil minds to accept Dr. Jensen as the return of Jesus, the Lamb, (based on the proofs of prophecy) yet he is not Baha'u'llah, not the second coming of Christ, nor a Manifestation of God. Furthermore Baha'u'llah tells us to accept this fact with "**no misgivings about it**" because He commands that we "**<u>must</u>** be of them that **truly believe.**"

Furthermore according to the explicit text of Baha'u'llah, it is not your right, nor that of anyone else, to protest and say, "But Jesus was born in Bethlehem in Israel and Dr. Jensen was born in Wisconsin and is from Deer Lodge or Missoula." Or that "That one is named Jesus whereas this one is named Leland"--Zechariah 3:9 "the Land" (Ha Eretz in Hebrew and Leland in French, 'Le' is French for 'the'). Or that "that one was descended from Abraham through David and this

---

[*] *Tablets of Baha'u'llah*, pp. 184-185.
[†] "The Most Great is come, and the Ancient Beauty [Baha'u'llah] ruleth upon the **throne of David**." *Proclamation of Baha'u'llah*, p. 89.
[‡] "Lo! **The Father** is come, and that which you were promised in the Kingdom of God is Fulfilled!" *Proclamation of Baha'u'llah*, pp. 84-85.

one is descended from Abraham through the tribe of Dan." The fact remains that the return of Jesus the High Priest (great world teacher) is to be born in America, is to be descended from the tribe of Dan, is to be imprisoned in Deer Lodge and is to be named "the Land" Leland and therefore as the date is also given by 'Abdu'l-Baha to work out to 1963 and his mission is to establish the courts (of the Houses of Justice Zechariah 3:7) which he is doing and establish the CHARTER of the Will and Testament, therefore he is the one and there can be no other. Just as both Jesus of Nazareth and Baha'u'llah each fulfilled Their respective body of prophecies for Their roles and stations. As Baha'u'llah is descended from David like Jesus of Nazareth, and fulfills the prophecy by the prophesied name, prophesied date, prophesied address and prophesied mission, He therefore is the second coming of Christ (anointed descendant of David) and there is no other! Yet as He Himself explicitly reveals it is no one's right to question the First One of His Revelation on these feeble and neanderthal terms anymore than it was the right to do so at the time of the Bab (Mahdi return of 12th Imam) and Mulla Husayn (return of Muhammad). Dr. Jensen does fulfill the prophecies for the establisher of the Baha'i Faith, Jesus returned, and therefore **"thou shouldst have <u>no misgivings about it</u> and <u>MUST</u> be of them that truly believe."**[*]

This point alone completely destroys your entire essay "Exposing a modern Anti-Christ" as the entire fabric of it is based on the fact that Dr. Jensen cannot be a Manifestation of God[†] and therefore cannot proclaim himself to be the return of Jesus. Yet as pointed out above you already can see that there are two separate bodies of prophecy, one for the second coming of Christ (Baha'u'llah) and the other for establisher of the Baha'i Faith (Dr. Jensen) the return of Jesus the Lamb....

One of your greatest failures (and it is also the failure of the majority of people both Christian and Baha'i alike) is your failure to grasp the difference between who the Christ is and what Christ means and who the High Priest (great world teacher) is and what High Priest means.

Jesus of Nazareth was **BOTH** the Christ (Manifestation of God descended from David) and therefore a king[‡] **as well as** a High Priest after the Order of Melchizedec. Thus he fulfilled two roles in one person. Who was Melchizedec?

Melchizedec is another name for the blessed son of Noah, Shem. He built the city of Jerusalem and is mentioned in the Bible as blessing Abraham after the battle of the kings as well as spoken of by Paul in the Epistle to Hebrews which you should read! Shem was both King and High Priest rolled up into one.[§] Later in Jerusalem, his role was split into two people and David was king and Zadok was the High Priest. This is the same pattern as the coming of Jesus Christ. On his first coming, like Shem, Jesus was both the king (Christ) descended from David **as well as** the High Priest rolled up into one. No one questions this as Jesus Himself as well as His apostles such as Paul all proclaimed Him such.[**] On the second coming, as the prophecies all show, this

---

[*] Baha'u'llah, *Tablets of Baha'u'llah*, p. 184.
[†] In fact all the leadership in the faith, including 'Abdu'l-Baha, has been accused of this same accusation.
[‡] Though his kingdom was not of this world.
[§] See Hebrews chapter 7.
[**] Jesus proclaims he is the High Priest after the order of Melchizedec from his own lips in Matthew 22:44 and Mark 12:36 saying that he fulfills the prophecy for the coming of Melchizedec in Psalm 110.

PATTERN OF THE KINGDOM

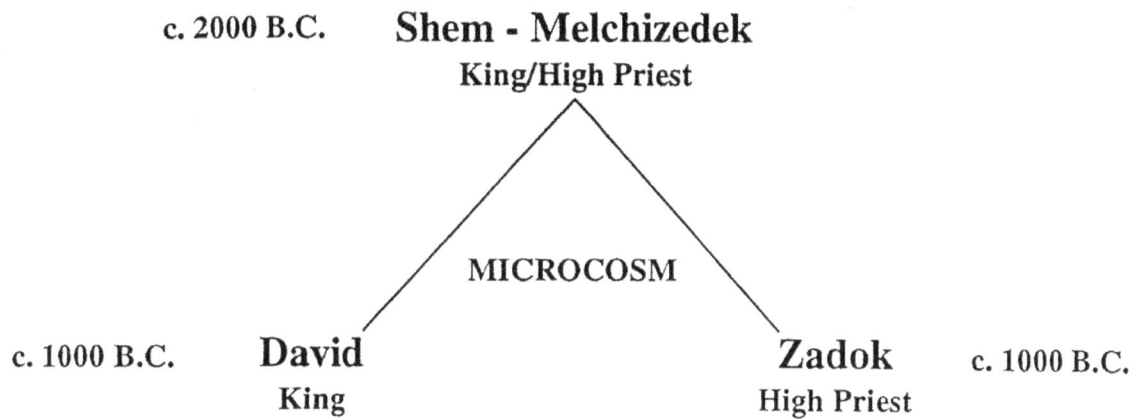

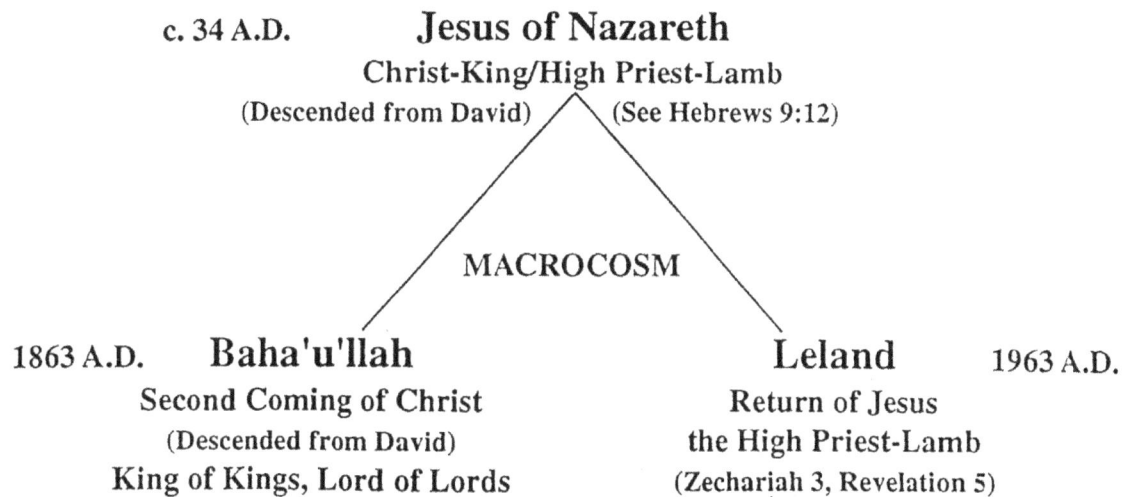

c. 2000 B.C.   **Shem - Melchizedek**
King/High Priest

MICROCOSM

c. 1000 B.C.   **David**   **Zadok**   c. 1000 B.C.
King   High Priest

c. 34 A.D.   **Jesus of Nazareth**
Christ-King/High Priest-Lamb
(Descended from David)   (See Hebrews 9:12)

MACROCOSM

1863 A.D.   **Baha'u'llah**   **Leland**   1963 A.D.
Second Coming of Christ   Return of Jesus
(Descended from David)   the High Priest-Lamb
King of Kings, Lord of Lords   (Zechariah 3, Revelation 5)

183

role is again split into Baha'u'llah who is the second coming of Christ the king (King of Kings and Lord of Lords: the Manifestation of God descended from David) and Dr. Jensen who fulfills the prophecy for the role of Jesus the High Priest which is the Lamb. See enclosed chart (on previous page).

Thus whereas Jesus and the Holy Scripture of the New Testament openly states and proclaims that Jesus of Nazareth was both Christ and High Priest/Lamb rolled up into one, Baha'i Holy Scripture of Baha'u'llah and 'Abdu'l-Baha and even that of Shoghi Effendi show that Baha'u'llah is not the Lamb, never claimed to be the High Priest after the order of Melchizedec, and is not the "Son of God" nor the "Word of God,"* but He is rather the Lord of Lords and King of Kings, the Father seated upon David's throne, the second coming of Christ.

'Abdu'l-Baha also makes it **very clear** that Baha'u'llah is not "the Word of God" but that He is "the Most Great Name of God," whereas Jesus is "the Word of God."

> Know that the attributes of perfection, the splendor of divine bounties, and the light of inspiration, are visible and evident in all the Holy Manifestations, but the glorious **Word of God, Christ [Jesus],**† and the **Greatest Name, Baha'u'llah,** are manifestations and evidences which are beyond imagination; for they possess all the perfection of which make the other Manifestations dependent upon them.‡

Therefore, 'Abdu'l-Baha is clear that Baha'u'llah is not the "Word of God" or the return of "the Word of God" which is one of the titles referring to Jesus Christ on His first coming, but He, Baha'u'llah, is the appearance of the "Greatest Name." The return of "the Word of God" is prophesied of in Revelation chapter 19 as the Knight of Baha'u'llah who establishes Baha'u'llah and is someone other than Baha'u'llah, and is not 'Abdu'l-Baha, Shoghi Effendi or Mason Remey or anyone else as none of these are Knights of Baha'u'llah. Dr. Jensen alone is the last remaining Knight of Baha'u'llah and therefore, as scripture establishes, also bears the title "Word of God" i.e., the return of Jesus.

> Then I saw heaven opened and behold, a white horse! He who sat upon it is called Faithful and True, and in righteousness he judges and makes war. His eyes are like a flame of fire, and on his head are many diadems [titles]§; and he has a name inscribed which no one knows but himself [Leland]. He is clad in a robe dipped in blood, and the name by which he is called is **The Word of God.****

So therefore the return of "the Word of God" (Jesus) is a Knight of Baha'u'llah, someone other than Baha'u'llah yet to come to establish Baha'u'llah. 'Abdu'l-Baha forbid anyone to ascribe to him any station other than that of 'Abdu'l-Baha--servant of Baha'u'llah--and therefore he is not

---

* SAQ, p. 171.
† In the Arabic and Persian originals, Jesus is constantly referred to as "the Spirit" by both Baha'u'llah and 'Abdu'l-Baha and this is sometimes erroneously translated as Christ instead of "the Spirit" or "Jesus."
‡ SAQ, p. 171.
§ The many titles of Jesus on his return to establish Baha'u'llah.
** Revelation 19:11-13.

184

this one as he categorically denied being the Lamb or "Son of God" or "the Word of God." Revelation chapter 19 tells us that it is the Knight of Baha'u'llah, on the white horse (the Revelation of Baha'u'llah) whose name is "the Word of God." And therefore it must be a Knight of Baha'u'llah who fulfills prophecy for the return of Jesus.

Not only is there only one last remaining Knight of Baha'u'llah, which is none other than Dr. Leland Jensen, but he is also the only Knight of Baha'u'llah to fulfill prophecy for the return of Jesus, having the "Stone with Seven Eyes" before him (Zechariah 3:9) as well as fulfilling the rest of the body of prophecies for the return of Jesus, (by the prophesied name, prophesied address, prophesied date and prophesied mission) let alone be the only Knight of Baha'u'llah to even put forth this claim. As "the Word of God" is another title for the return of Jesus, this last remaining Knight of Baha'u'llah is Jesus come to establish His Father's Kingdom,[*] the great defender of his King, Baha'u'llah. Shoghi Effendi knighted only about 150 people to be Knights of Baha'u'llah. The rest of them are either all dead, inactive or have been expelled from the Baha'i religious faith for Covenant-breaking by the guardian Mason Remey. Only two Knights of Baha'u'llah did not violate the Covenant, Dr. Opal Jensen and her husband Dr. Leland Jensen. As Dr. Opal passed away on February 4th of 1991, this leaves only one remaining Knight of Baha'u'llah active, prolific, unstoppable and under the provisions of the Covenant in the world, Dr. Leland Jensen. Thus Dr. Jensen is this one and there is no other!

Also as Baha'u'llah categorically declared Himself to be "the Father" and not the Son, this is tantamount to Him denying that He is return of Jesus the "Son of God" and therefore it is tantamount to Him declaring forever that He does not fulfill the prophecy for the return of Jesus the High Priest, for it is written:

> For this Melchizedec...is without father or mother or genealogy, and has neither beginning of days nor end of life, but resembling **the Son of God** he continues a priest forever.[†]

Thus the High Priesthood after the order of Melchizedec resembles "the Son of God" and **NOT** "the Father" which is Baha'u'llah. As Zechariah chapter three specifically anticipates the coming of Jesus the High Priest (Douay Version)[‡], this is not Baha'u'llah at all but His establisher, the First One, Dr. Jensen. Furthermore the First One, by definition, is a follower of the Manifestation, and never the Manifestation Himself. And 'Abdu'l-Baha categorically stated that it was not him.[§]

As clearly shown above, in the teachings of Baha'u'llah, the return and resurrection of Jesus the High Priest, the Lamb, is not conditioned upon that person being a Manifestation of God, but that the rank and power of command will be the same as that of the first appearance of Jesus **the High Priest** as he too will stand in the Holy of Holies of the Father's Revelation (the Revelation

---

[*] The Father is Baha'u'llah for His Revelation is in the potency of the Father, whereas Jesus' Revelation is in the potency of the Son.

[†] Hebrews 7:1-3.

[‡] Other translation read Joshua the High Priest. Jesus (Gk.) and Joshua (Hb.) are the same name in different languages.

[§] "**THAT NO-ONE SHALL ASCRIBE TO HIM ANY MISSION OR STATION OTHER THAN THAT OF THE SERVANT OF GOD** [i.e 'Abdu'l-Baha]"--Thornton Chase, *In Galilee*, p. 71.

of Baha'u'llah) and will therefore open the scroll of the Covenant of Baha'u'llah and the Will and Testament of 'Abdu'l-Baha in order to establish the World Order of Baha'u'llah in the World which is clearly unestablished at this point in time save for the formation and setting up of the second International Baha'i Council/Universal House of Justice (IBC/UHJ) of Baha'u'llah on South Avenue in Missoula, Montana.

So the question is raised: Since the return of Jesus bears the title and station of the First One, then what is the return of Jesus, Dr. Jensen, the First One to do?

As the Lamb, he is the First One to break the seven seals and read (explain and establish) the contents of that scroll written within and on the back and sealed with seven seals in Revelation chapter five.

But what are the seven seals? And what scroll or document is sealed with seven seals?

> 'Abdu'l-Baha's Will was written in three parts at three different times in His life. All three parts are in His handwriting and are signed by Him [3]. All three, comprising twelve pages in all, were in an envelope under lock and key in His safe when he died. The face of the envelope was addressed to Shoghi Effendi in the Master's handwriting and signed by him [1]. On the back it bears three more signatures [3] where it was stuck down. [3+1+3=7 seals.]*

And again,

> Thus we note that the photostat copies of Part One and Part Two of the original Will are signed in the old way: that is with Abdul Baha's initials, together with the seal [Arabic insignia], appearing below; while Part Three, which is the shortest, consisting of a single page, is signed in the new way, adopted after 1912: the name in full with no impression of the seal [of the Arabic insignia].

> Now, in reference to the envelope which contained the Original Wills [Three Parts]: the photostat copy shows four legible and clear signatures written in the new way; one appearing on the front of the envelope at the upper left corner, while the other three appear on the back, written across the flap at the point of sealing.

> Consequently, apart from certain historical events in the Will itself, we can conclude without any doubt that Part One and Part Two were written before 1912, while Part Three was written after Abdul Baha's return to Palestine from his Western trip, that is between 1913-1921. At this latter time, all three Parts were placed together in the same envelope [sealed with seven seals].†

---

* Headless "Universal House of Justice," letter to an individual, October 2, 1974. Cited from *The Power of the Covenant: The Problem of Covenant-Breaking Part II*, pp. 22-23.
† Mirza Ahmad Sohrab, *The Will and Testament of 'Abdu'l-Baha: An Analysis*, pp. 14-15.

Thus the seven seals are the seven seals of 'Abdu'l-Baha that he placed on the Will and Testament (written on the back, the addendum to, the Covenant of Baha'u'llah, the *Kitab-i-'Ahd* also contained within the Aqdas). This can be none other than the Will and Testament, the CHARTER for the World Order of Baha'u'llah. It can be no other scroll or document as the Will and Testament of 'Abdu'l-Baha alone has the seven seals on it and this document of the Will alone plays the central and pivotal role in the Revelation of Baha'u'llah as 'Abdu'l-Baha was made the Center of His Covenant! Because the Will has the seven seals on it this one fact alone blows your theory that Baha'u'llah should be the Lamb right out of the water into eternal oblivion! Baha'u'llah cannot be the Lamb as the seals on the Will didn't even exist during His life time (let alone the fact that He never claimed to be the Lamb.)

Ultimately, it is a good thing that Baha'u'llah never claimed to be the Lamb or He would be a big failure and imposter as the Lamb, since the Will and Testament with its seals didn't even exist in His lifetime. Thus in the prophecies for the Lamb, which you try to force Baha'u'llah into (showing that it is you and the dissidents trying to paint Baha'u'llah out as a failure into something He is not, and never said He was and never will be), the Lamb, the return of Jesus is the First One to break these seals and establish the true World Order of Baha'u'llah as delineated in that CHARTER of the Will and Testament.

None of this could be any clearer. Yet for you: "**but there are some people who, even if <u>all the proofs in the world be adduced before them</u>, still will not judge justly!**"[*]

Furthermore the Bible, in the book of Revelation, identifies the Lamb categorically with the seventh angel that 'Abdu'l-Baha prophesied of in *Some Answered Questions* on page 66 as "a man qualified with heavenly attributes, who **will** arise" in the future (the future of even the lifetime of 'Abdu'l-Baha) to establish the Kingdom that Baha'u'llah has revealed. As SAQ was revealed circa 1906 long after the passing of Baha'u'llah the seventh angel cannot be Baha'u'llah. If 'Abdu'l-Baha were the seventh angel he would have proclaimed himself to be so, but he was not and therefore said it was another authoritative figure who would arise in the future. It cannot be Shoghi Effendi (who also never claimed this for himself) as 'Abdu'l-Baha is clear that the seventh angel will arise at the "Epoch of the Divine Cycle of the Omnipotent" which refers to the 100 Year Epoch of the 100th Anniversary of the Proclamation of Baha'u'llah during Ridvan of 1863 bringing us to Ridvan of 1963[†] at least 6 years **AFTER** the death of Shoghi Effendi when he was no longer with us in the world and could not possibly be this person! Also Shoghi Effendi failed to establish the Baha'i Faith as everything he worked so hard for was destroyed by his evil wife the arch violator of violators Ruhiyyih Khanum. If anything, the end of Shoghi Effendi's mission appears to be the anti-thesis of the mission of the establisher of the Baha'i Faith, who against all odds, all dissidents and all opposition is vigilantly re-establishing what the Covenant-breakers have thrown out, which is the IBC/UHJ that Baha'u'llah revealed, 'Abdu'l-Baha explained, and Shoghi Effendi amplified and defined to evolve into the fully elected Universal House of Justice (UHJ) through a four stage plan beginning with the IBC phase. For all intents and purpose the Baha'i Faith is back to square one as God has now raised up a new creation through the efforts of one man, Dr. Jensen, to

---

[*] 'Abdu'l-Baha, SAQ, pp. 43-44.
[†] As explained by 'Abdu'l-Baha in the fulfillment of the 1335 days/years in Daniel 12:12 in *Baha'u'llah and the New Era*, Chapter on the "Prophecies of Baha'u'llah," sub-section 'Coming of the Kingdom of God.'

accomplish what the Baha'is of the world failed to do. Now we see the fulfillment of the sacred verse: **"ALL THE WORLD WILL ENTER THE KINGDOM WHILE THE CHILDREN OF THE KINGDOM ARE CAST OUT!"**

Thus, the remedy: in Revelation chapter 10 we read of "another mighty angel" that the script tells us is the seventh angel ("In the day of the trumpet call of **the seventh angel**")[*] coming down from heaven with a "little scroll **OPEN** in his hand"[†] that is sweet to taste and bitter in the stomach.[‡] What is this scroll? How is it open?

This scroll is the exact same as that in chapter five written within and on the back sealed with seven seals of the Covenant and the Will and Testament of 'Abdu'l-Baha. The reason it is open is that the Lamb spent the last 5 chapters breaking the seals on it and now (as he is identical to the seventh angel) he holds it in his hand wide open in order to establish the Kingdom of Baha'u'llah.

All the proof for this is in the scriptures! The references in the Revised Standard Version of the Bible refer us from the scroll in chapter 10 to Ezekiel chapters 2 and 3 for the full picture.

> And when I looked, behold, a hand was stretched out to me, and, lo, a **written scroll** was in it; and he spread it before me; and it had **writing on the front and on the back**, and there were written words of lamentation and mourning and woe [the Will and Testament of 'Abdu'l-Baha is full of words of lamentation, mourning and woe, as those who read well know].[§]

> And he said to me, "Son of man, eat what is offered to you: eat this scroll, and go, speak to the House of Israel." So I opened my mouth, and he gave me the scroll to eat. And he said to me, "Son of man, eat this scroll that I give you and fill your stomach with it." Then I ate it; and it was in my mouth as sweet as honey.[**]

Thus the scroll in chapter ten which is sweet to the taste and bitter in the stomach is the same scroll in Ezekiel, that he also shows is written on the front and back, of which we again read about in Revelation chapter five that the Lamb took out of the Hand of the one seated on the throne (who was unworthy to break the seals) which is Mason Remey, the first Aghsan guardian seated upon the throne (of David) after the passing of 'Abdu'l-Baha by the authority of the scroll of the Will and Testament of 'Abdu'l-Baha sealed with seven seals.

Furthermore in chapter 9 the last thing we read of is the sixth angel[††] Quddus and then chapter ten opens with the next angel in sequence, the seventh angel, who is the establisher of the Baha'i Faith which can only be Dr. Jensen who holds in his hand the same scroll of the Covenant and the Will and Testament now open in his hand showing that he is also identical to the Lamb that

---

[*] Revelation 10:7.
[†] Revelation 10:2.
[‡] Revelation 10:10.
[§] Ezekiel 2:9-10.
[**] Ezekiel 3:1-3.
[††] Who 'Abdu'l-Baha shows authoritatively is Quddus the establisher of the Babi Faith. See SAQ chapter 11.

first took the scroll into his hand **SEALED** now which is open for him to perform his mission of establishing the contents of that CHARTER which he then proceeds to do as he sounds his trumpet (explanations and commentaries) enabling him to set up the genuine IBC/UHJ with both the body and head functioning together in perfect harmony and perfection. Which brings us to another prophecy of the promised establisher of the Baha'i Faith.

> Verily that infant is born and exists and there will appear from His Cause a wonder which thou wilt hear in future. Thou shalt see Him with the most perfect form, most great gift, most complete perfection, most great power and strongest might! His Face glisteneth a glistening whereby the horizons are illumined! Therefore, forget not this account as long as thou art living, forasmuch as there are signs for it in the passing centuries and ages.[*]

This tablet revealed by 'Abdu'l-Baha circa 1906 and published throughout the world in 1915 cannot refer to Shoghi Effendi, Mason Remey, Baha'u'llah, 'Abdu'l-Baha or even the Bab. No matter which date you go by, 1906 or 1915, none of these were infants. The Bab and Baha'u'llah had already ascended from this world. 'Abdu'l-Baha was an old man. Mason Remey, born in 1874 was over 30 at even the earlier date. Likewise Shoghi Effendi born in 1896 was at least 10 years old at the first date in 1906, and he was at least 19 in 1915. In either case he was not an infant at either time and cannot be the one as the mainstream Baha'is have erroneously proposed. Then who is this person? It is that First One, the establisher of the Baha'i Faith and return of Jesus the High Priest. It cannot be any other!

In 1906, the first part of the Will and Testament of 'Abdu'l-Baha was already completed making the Will that infant[†] which was born that year. In 1914 the establisher of the Baha'i Faith was born making him an infant in 1915 the date that this prophecy was disseminated throughout the world as he is the one of which 'Abdu'l-Baha says, "and there will appear from **His Cause** a wonder which thou wilt hear in future." The great wonder is what all the world is hearing today that here is a man who fulfills the prophecies for the return of Jesus yet is not a Manifestation of God but has been invested with supreme authority to break the seven seals of the Will and establish the CHARTER and the World Order of Baha'u'llah throughout the entire world! What could be more of a wonder than this?

In the above prophecy 'Abdu'l-Baha makes clear the impossibility of separating the power of the Will and Testament from the establisher and champion of that document--so completely intertwining the prophecy and the mission of the Promised One of today with the greatness and magnitude of the power of the Covenant delineated within and enshrined eternally inside the Holy Writ of the Will and Testament sealed with the seven seals of the Master, 'Abdu'l-Baha, the Mystery of God (*Sirru'llah*). **"Thou shalt see Him with the MOST PERFECT FORM, most great gift, MOST COMPLETE PERFECTION..."** 'Abdu'l-Baha explains that it is the human form that has the **"most perfect form"** and **"most complete perfection"** as it embodies all aspects of creation and man is the microcosm of the universe.

---

[*] *Tablets of 'Abdu'l-Baha, Vol II*, p. 484.
[†] Shoghi Effendi explains on page 144 of the *World Order of Baha'u'llah* that the Will and testament of 'Abdu'l-Baha, which is the CHARTER for the World Order of Baha'u'llah is that **child** which born in 1906 makes the Will and Testament "Verily, that infant is born and exists."

Thus the embryo of man in the womb of the mother gradually grows and develops, and appears in different forms and conditions, until in the degree of **PERFECT BEAUTY** it reaches maturity, and appears in a **PERFECT FORM** with the utmost grace.[*]

The "most perfect form" and "most complete perfection" is today seen only in Dr. Jensen distinguishing him from all the other Baha'is of the world for only the second IBC/UHJ which he has established has the perfect form of the human form as delineated by 'Abdu'l-Baha in the Will and Testament of both the body of the IBC/UHJ and the head and irremovable member for life which is the guardian of the Baha'i Faith as delineated on page 14 of the Will and Testament....

Labbe! Throughout this entire ordeal, up to this time, you have dogmatically refused to recognize the true meaning of Anti-Christ! And have refused to accept the God-given definition of Christ!: **The anointed descendant of David!**

Christ refers to the genealogy of both Baha'u'llah and Jesus who are descended from David, making all those Christians that **DENY** Jesus' genealogy back to David through his father Joseph and all the mainstream Baha'is that **DENY** Baha'u'llah's genealogy back to David, Anti-Christ! Just as the Apostle John states:

> This is the antichrist, he who denies the Father [Baha'u'llah descended from David] and the Son [Jesus descended from David].[†]

Instead of learning the meaning of these things, like the meaning of Christ and Antichrist, you, like the majority of people, remain in your Christian indoctrination that the Antichrist will be some person, some strong man, who arises at the end time to be the world dictator, to rule the world against God with force as an absolute despot! In fact, it is those that oppose Baha'u'llah's Universal House of Justice, the eliminates one man rule, that fails the TEST! If you could sum up our message to the world into one sentence it would be: "The purpose of the descendant of King David is so we can recognize Baha'u'llah's true Universal House of Justice from fakes, frauds and imitations." Without the descendant of king David through Baha'u'llah and 'Abdu'l-Baha as the president and executive branch of the IBC/UHJ (see W &T, p. 15) there can be no justice. The line of David continues for ever. Those that are anti- this lineage continuing have always failed to extinguish the light of God....

Even more so has God triumphed throughout the ages preserving the lineage of David on down throughout a history of the most fierce and savage dynasties that have ever ruled the world.

At one time the king of all Persia, Chosroes II of the Sassanian dynasty sought to extinguish the lineage of David and rubbed out, murdered and extinguished all the male descendants except for one, who was a little babe gestating in the womb of his mother the wife of the last Davidic king in exile (exilarch) who had just been executed. The reason he did it was that the Zoroastrian

---

[*] SAQ, p. 212 and many other places.
[†] 1 John 2:22.

Sassanians had rival prophecies that it would be from their lineage that the great King of Kings was to be born. As this conflicted with the Jewish prophecy that it would be a descendant of David, he sought to make sure that his lineage and not that of David would be the one. So, Chosroes II, in his desire for his lineage to rule the world ordered his soldiers to find the woman and gut her open and kill the unborn child. As they searched the streets with a vengeance like the hounds of hell she went into deep hiding.

That night as Chosroes fell asleep he dreamed a dream of which he was in the most beautiful garden filled with trees and he had an axe in his hand. Ferociously he tore into the garden and chopped down all the trees until none were left but a tiny little shoot. The he lifted the axe above his head to kill this last root when all of a sudden in a blinding flash of light, a man appeared with flaming red hair and ripped the axe out his hands and pounded him on the head knocking him out.

When Chosroes came to the man was waving the axe over his head hollering at him at the top of his lungs, "How dare you destroy all the trees in my garden and now you will kill the last shoot? Surely you deserve that your name should perish off the face of the earth!"

Chosroes was scared stiff, crying and grovelling, "Please don't hurt me. Please don't hurt me. I will take care of the little shoot until it becomes big and strong and bears much fruit and a thousand times ten thousand trees and forests are rejuvenated from it!"

"As you have said, so it shall be," said the man. And the dream ended.

Chosroes woke up in a pounding sweat, his feet and arms shaking like leaves. He ran over to the mirror and to his horror saw that a had a bloody wound on his head where the man hit him in the dream. (Maybe he was tossing in bed so hard that he hit his head against the bedpost. History doesn't say).

Seeing this blood he screamed in terror rushing out into the hallway of his great palace hollering and crying like a scared little baby. He screamed for his wisemen in terror and the whole palace woke up and everyone came running from all directions.

"What is it! What is it!" they said. "My dream! My dream! My head! My head!" he cried.

Finally he told them all of his dream in the garden and one wise man explained it to him. The man with the red hair was king David and all the trees his descendants that Chosroes had murdered. The last shoot was the baby son in the womb of his mother which he had now vowed he would take care of and nurture for the rest of his life. Chosroes vowed on the spot to do it!

The very next day they found the woman and brought her into the palace of the king where she was given the finest robes, perfumes and silks, a wonderful room in the palace and rings and bells on her toes. Within several months she gave birth to a beautiful baby boy and the king named him Bostanai which in Persian means "from the Garden" referring to garden of his dream. When Bostanai grew up he became the Grand Vizier over the whole empire and as long as Chosroes guarded this boy and the line of David his power increased and increased and his kingdom prospered until it was again the greatest empire in the world. He became so powerful as to recapture Jerusalem from Rome[*] and even capture the true cross that Jesus was crucified on-- which it is said he brought back to his capital in Mesopotamia and gave as a gift to his favorite wife who was a Christian. Such are the bounty and gifts of God.

Bostanai grew into manhood and later, after the victory of Muhammad (and after Omar destroyed Persia) during the just rule of Ali, Bostanai was wedded to Dara, the granddaughter of Chosroes and both prophecies that the Christ would be descended from David (in the male-line) and Zoroaster (on the female) were fulfilled as this is the ancestry of Baha'u'llah![†]

Thus Imam Ali gave Dara to Bostanai whom he met and they were great friends. Thus God has stated that he would not violate his Covenant to David and that he would protect his line and his throne forever!

> I will sing of thy steadfast love, O Lord, for ever;
> with my mouth I will proclaim thy faithfulness to all generations.
> For thy steadfast love was established for ever,
> thy faithfulness is firm as the heavens.
> Thou hast said, "I have made a Covenant with my chosen one, I have sworn **to David** my servant;
>
> **'I will establish your descendants for ever,
> and build your throne for all generations.'"** [‡]
>
> **I WILL NOT VIOLATE MY COVENANT,**
> **or alter the word that went forth from my lips.**
> **Once for all I have sworn by my holiness;**
> **I WILL NOT LIE TO DAVID.**
> **His line will endure for ever,**
> **his throne as long as the sun before me.**
> Like the moon it shall be established forever;
> it shall stand firm while the skies endure.[§]

How foolish people are to contend with God! God will win! So we can expose the evil of this man, but it is God that will straighten him out. Just how God will do it, if He hasn't already started, will be something interesting to see indeed!....

We have the infallible guidance of 'Abdu'l-Baha's sacred Will and Testament that only the true Universal House of Justice must have the guardian (descended from David: an Aghsan, and appointed by his predecessor) as both its distinguished member and head. Thus only the second IBC/UHJ fits the bill and has the Most Perfect Form and complete perfection of both the body and the head. The Lamb of God, Dr. Jensen, leads us to the living waters!

---

[*] SAQ, p. 54.
[†] See *God Passes By*, p. 94.
[‡] Psalm 89:1-4.
[§] Psalm 89:34-37.

He who sits upon the throne [of David, the Aghsan guardian] will shelter them with his presence.

They shall hunger no more, neither thirst anymore; the sun shall not strike them, nor any scorching heat.

For the Lamb in the midst of the throne [Dr. Jensen] will be their shepherd, **and he will guide them to springs of living water;** and God will wipe away every tear from their eyes. [*]

Thus the guardian of the IBC/UHJ shares authority with his co-members in the full deliberative capacity to arrive at and solve all problems and then in his own sphere as Executive BRANCH he promulgates both the teaching and law of the UHJ which are equal to "the Truth and Purpose of God"[†] as well as those of the explicit texts and writings of Baha'u'llah and 'Abdu'l-Baha also equal with the power of God.

This system is so perfect and so beautiful that coupled with Baha'u'llah's three point economic plan, the true Faith of Baha'u'llah and its Divine system of Government of the World Order is truly irresistible and even now is taking the world by surprise, as we see the order of things upset day to day around us all in anticipation of this message that the Baha'is Under the Provisions of the Covenant alone have for all the world. It is the very Kingdom foretold by Jesus 2000 years ago that today he has returned to establish.

On the other hand we have you.

In your personal letter to me you state:

> In your epistle to Mr. Spataro you rightly quote both Shoghi Effendi and Mason Remey in support of the SEER STATUS of Joseph Smith. If this is true as a Seer Joseph Smith under the direction of God to prepare the world for the return of Jesus, he translated and brought forth the *Book of Mormon*, even Joseph Morris who you sight as being at least a seer accepts the *Book of Mormon*. So the question is do you? Do you accept the *Book of Mormon* as scripture on the level of the Bible?[‡]

You don't even know what your talking about! Shoghi Effendi rightly explains Joseph Smith as a SEER and not a PROPHET! He is not an independent prophet--A Manifestation who reveals a book--nor even a minor prophet of God like Daniel or Ezekiel--who were firm in the Covenant of God under the Manifestation of their day. Smith is only a seer! 'Seer' means that he can 'see' certain things that are true but not that he is some sort of infallible guide or even that he is part of the religion of God! Shoghi Effendi makes this distinction absolutely clear which cannot be ignored!

---

[*] Revelation 7:15-17.
[†] W&T, p. 19.
[‡] Labbe, Letter to Neal Chase, 6 June 1992.

Joseph Smith was a seer, NOT A PROPHET OF GOD, NEITHER MAJOR NOR MINOR PROPHET.[*]

What this means is that Smith could see visions and glimpses of the future but that he did not speak or write on behalf of God and is not a prophet **of God.** The Bible is full of seers who were not prophets of God. Such are Pharaoh and Nebuchadnezzar to which Joseph Smith falls into their category. Pharaoh saw the true dream and vision of the seven fat cows and the seven thin cows, etc. Therefore he was **seer** because he **saw** this. But he did not know the meaning. It was Joseph the prophet of God that interpreted the dream and gave the correct meaning of it. Likewise Nebuchadnezzar was into astrology and he was a seer and he saw the dream of the giant statue (representing the powers of the world until the coming of the kingdom of God). But he both forgot the dream and didn't know the meaning. Therefore Daniel the prophet of God told him the vision of the dream and the meaning.

The reason God uses people like Pharaoh, Nebuchadnezzar or Joseph Smith is that they are popular and well-known. Through them the fame and renown of the message of their vision spreads to all parts of the world and all people hear about it. Because of Smith all people should know the prophecy of the return of Jesus in America. Clearly Baha'u'llah was **never** in America or the United States at all! If God gave these visions and prophecies to people who were unknown then these visions would be ignored by everyone. So instead he lets someone famous have the vision who is a seer. But then to give the meaning of it he has one who is from God to explain it. Thus the vision of the seer through the explanation of one like Daniel or Joseph becomes the cause of the people accepting the true religion of God.

Now, just because Pharaoh, Nebuchadnezzar and Smith were seers with true visions, such as those recorded in the Bible, does not mean that we convert to their corrupted forms of religion and/or paganism! No! God forbid! This is so that through the vision given to people such as Smith, Jeane Dixon, Nebuchadnezzar, Pharaoh, etc...these ones are famous and all people hear about it so that through the true explanation from an authoritative one speaking on behalf of God the people can turn to the religion of God and **not** to something else.[†] Your thinking on these points is erroneous.

As to the actual facts and events surrounding the *Book of Mormon* of Joseph Smith, you are completely uninformed!

When Smith was 14 he had a vision of the two Christs. He saw the Father and the Son, (as two separate people) Baha'u'llah and Jesus.[‡] And later he saw that the return of Jesus would be in America in the Temple described by Ezekiel in the Bible which would be in the Rocky Mountains.[§] Thus he directed his people to that area "to prepare the way" up until the time he died in 1844.

---

[*] Shoghi Effendi, *Memories of 'Abdu'l-Baha*, p. 117.
[†] See Dr. Leland Jensen, *The Child of the East: Jeane Dixon Was Right!* for more.
[‡] Smith did not accept the pagan trinity which has its origin in Babylon.
[§] See the White Horse Prophecy of Smith based on the book of Revelation. (Mason Remey went by this also, see pages 23-25 this volume).

JOSEPH SMITH'S FIRST VISION

Turning to me he said, "I want to tell you something of the future. I shall speak in parables like unto John the Revelator." He said, "You will go to the Rocky Mountains and you will see a great and mighty people established [the Baha'is], which I shall call the White Horse of Peace and Safety [The White Horse is the Revelation of Baha'u'llah and Dr. Leland Jensen is that Knight of Baha'u'llah on that White Horse depicted in the Book of Revelation] which, [Joseph Smith] said: "You will see." I asked him where he would be at that time. He answered, "I shall never go there." (Joseph Smith, "The White Horse Prophecy")[*]

However when he was 14 no one would listen to him. So he needed a way to get the people's attention. Having been a treasure seeker he took his own ideas and visions and wrote them into the *Book of Mormon* which he fabricated based on a manuscript that had been stolen years earlier from Solomon Spaulding.

Solomon Spaulding had been studying religion at Dartmouth College where one of the popular ideas of the day was that the Native American Indians were supposed to be descended from the ten lost tribes of Israel.[†] Based on this fanciful idea Spaulding wrote a Romantic Novel called "Manuscript Found" about a modern man who discovers "tablets" with the lost history of the Americas inscribed on them. Spaulding had submitted his manuscript to R and J. Patterson's print shop, who said they were interested in printing the book. However, in 1816, right before Spaulding died, Patterson told him that his book "Manuscript found" had been lost.

One of the employees at Patterson's print shop was J. H. Lambdin was friends with Sidney Rigdon the Campbellite preacher who was the friend and co-religionist of Joseph Smith. Before Spaulding died he told several people that he knew for a fact that Rigdon had stolen his manuscript. One of these was Dr. Cephas Dodd who was Spaulding's attending physician during his last illness (see Photo). Dr. Cephas Dodd testifies:

> This work [*The Book of Mormon*], I am convinced by facts related to me by my deceased patient, Solomon Spaulding, has been made from the writings of Spaulding, probably by Sidney Rigdon, who was suspicioned by Spaulding with purloining his manuscript from the publishing-house to which he had taken it; and I am prepared to testify that Spaulding told me that his work was entitled, "The Manuscript Found in the Wilds of Mormon; or Unearthed Records of the Nephites." From his description of the contents, I fully believe that this *Book of Mormon* is mainly and wickedly copied from it.[‡]

Rigdon was seen at the Smith farm in New York after Spaulding's manuscript was stolen before the *Book of Mormon* was written.

---

[*] Cited from: Francis M. Darter, (1931). *Our Bible In Stone*, pp. 166ff.

[†] A friend of Spaulding's (Ethan Smith) also studying there wrote another book called "View to the Hebrews" which authoritative Mormon Historian B. H. Roberts also cites as one of Smith's sources for writing the Book of Mormon. Joseph Smith's cousin Oliver Cowdry even attended the church that Ethan Smith later taught at and they all had access to this book also.

[‡] Davis, *Who Really Wrote the Book of Mormon?*, p. 74.

Picture of Dr. Cephas Dodd

During some of my visits at the Smiths, I saw a stranger there who they said was Mr. Rigdon. He was at Smith's several times, and it was in the year of 1827 [the *Book of Mormon* was published in 1830] when I first saw him there, as near as I can recollect. Some time after that tales were circulating that a young Joe had found or dug from the earth a Book of Plates which the Smiths called the Golden Bible.[*]

Later when the *Book of Mormon* was first published all the friends and family of Spaulding immediately recognized the story and the names and places as that from Spaulding's stolen manuscript. It was easy to connect Joseph Smith back to Rigdon who by that time was a well known Mormon. Spaulding's brother writes:

He [Solomon] then told me he was writing a book....It was an historical romance of the first settlers of America, endeavoring to show that the American Indians are the descendants of the Jews, or the lost tribes. It gave a detailed account of their journey from Jerusalem, by land and sea, till they arrived in America, under the command of Nephi and Lehi. They afterwards had quarrels and contentions and separated into two distinct nations, one of which he denominated Nephites, and the other Lamanites. Cruel and bloody wars ensued, in which greta multitudes were slain. They buried their dead in large heaps, which caused the mounds so common in this country. Their arts, sciences and civilization were brought into view in order to account for all the curious antiquities found in various parts od North and South America. I have recently read the *Book of Mormon* and to my great surprise I find nearly the same historical matter, names, &c., as they were in my brother's writings. I well remember he wrote in the old style, and commenced about every sentence with 'And it came to pass,' or 'Now it came to pass,' the same as the *Book of Mormon*, and according to the best of my recollection and belief, it is the same as my brother Solomon wrote, **with the exception of the religious part.**[†]

So Smith added his own visions and beliefs, "the religious part," on top of Spaulding's story of the ancient happenings of America. The fact that Smith wrote the *Book of Mormon* himself based on the Bible in part, the beliefs of his day in part, Spaulding's manuscript in part, and his own visions cannot be denied. The very first edition of the *Book of Mormon* did not even claim to be a "translation of gold plates" but instead stated that Smith did in fact write the book himself!

In the first edition of the *Book of Mormon*, this statement of the eight witnesses declares that Joseph Smith Jr., was "author and proprietor of this work." This statement also appeared on the title page of the first edition.

The subsequent editions have the eight witnesses saying that Smith was the "translator" of the book. The title page is also changed. I. W. Riley remarks that

---

[*] Testimony of Abel D. Chase cited from: Spencer, *Have you Witnessed to a Mormon Lately?*, p. 207.
[†] Spencer, pp. 202-203.

"the name of author and proprietor of the *Book of Mormon* was inadvertently assumed and quickly discarded."[*]

All told there have been at least 3,913 changes added to and deleted from the *Book of Mormon* since the first edition. Likewise there were never any physical gold plates that were found. This was also a story made up by Smith (which he learned from the Free Masons) to attract attention to the movement. If he did have actual physical gold plates they would have weighed over 234 pounds! This is ridiculous! No one could carry that weight around by themselves in "out stretched arms" or with one hand! Further witnesses testified that they never even saw any physical gold plates!

> Martin Harris and David Whitmer [two of the witnesses] said they **saw the plates with their "spiritual eyes" only**...[Z.H. Gurley asked:] "did you touch them?" His [Whitmer's] answer was, "We did not touch nor handle plates."[†]

The *Book of Mormon* is not "revealed scripture" or translated from "gold plates." It is certainly not equal with the writings of the Bible and that of Baha'u'llah and 'Abdu'l-Baha. And you are in no authority to demand them to be as such. Your demand is contra the Baha'i Faith. It is contra the writings of Shoghi Effendi who clearly states Smith is not a prophet (either major or minor). It is also against what really took place and what is scientifically possible. The *Book of Mormon* is a collection of ideas and visions and prophecies of the seer Joseph Smith and parts plagiarized from the King James Bible and Spaulding's manuscript.

The whole idea of the "Gold Plates" actually originates within the ancient prophecy of Enoch preserved in Masonic tradition in which Enoch is instructed to bury the "Gold Plates" in a mountain with the letter **"M"** written on it.

> The similarities between this ancient Masonic legend [prophecy] about Enoch, and the mythology that Joseph Smith et al managed to establish concerning his alleged exploits in finding and translating the gold plates, are too numerous and exact to allow any other explanation than the most obvious one. As Dr. Durham said that night to his stunned audience of fellow Mormon historians, "The parallels [to the legend of Enoch] of Joseph Smith and the history of Mormonism are so unmistakable that to explain them only as coincidence would be ridiculous."
>
> In the legend, Enoch was 25 years old "when he received his call and vision," as was Joseph Smith "when he brought forth his sacred record." Enoch's vision was of a hill [mountain] containing a vault prepared for "sacred treasures," on which he saw the identifying letter **"M."**[‡]

Enoch is then instructed to place the knowledge of how to obtain the "Gold Plates" into two structures, one a "pillar of brick" and the other a "pillar of stone." These two pillars of Enoch are

---

[*] Fraser, *Is Mormonism Christian?*, p. 21-22.
[†] Tanner, *The Changing World of Mormonism*, p. 108.
[‡] See *The God-Makers* for the Masonic Legend of Enoch, pp. 112-113.

described in the *History of Josephus*. The "pillar of brick" was destroyed during the flood. The "pillar of stone" is the Great Pyramid of Giza--A Chronological and prophetic Book of Stone--that Dr. Jensen unraveled the meanings since his move to Missoula (Masau'wa of the Hopi) and his wrongful imprisonment within Ezekiel's Temple ("the Stone with Seven Eyes") in Deer Lodge. Missoula is the mountain with the "M" written on it fulfilling the prophecy of the Masonic Legend of Enoch (see Photo). The knowledge of the "Gold Plates" is also in our possession.

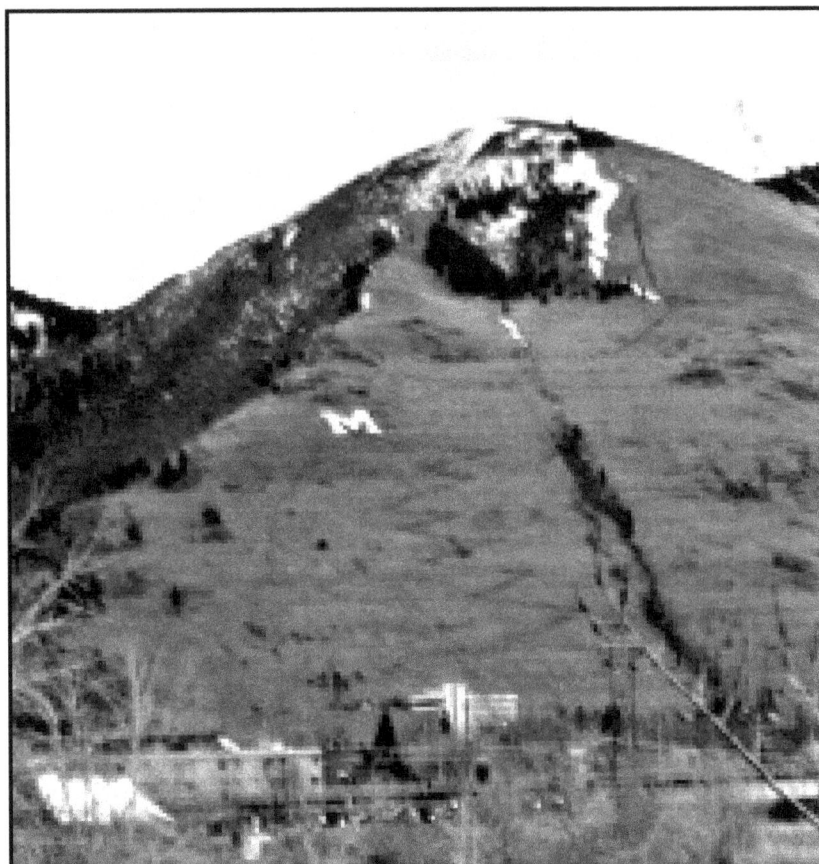

THE "M" ON MOUNT SENTINEL IN MISSOULA, MT

And lastly we have your twisted concept of the Morrisite prophecies. Although you saw the film and read the book *Ezekiel's Temple in Montana*, both of which clearly proclaim Baha'u'llah as the second coming of **Christ**, descended from David, and Dr. Jensen to be the return of **Jesus the High Priest** (and not the CHRIST!) you still have the temerity to try to twist this around into Dr. Jensen being the Christ when we have stated over and over and over again that Baha'u'llah, descended from David (which is what the word Christ means: the anointed descendant of David) is the return of Christ, and His establisher, Dr. Jensen, is not the Christ but is the return of Jesus the High Priest! You write:

Now to start with Jensen, in order to fulfill the Morrisite prophecies Jensen must be claimed to be the <u>Christ, not Joshua the High Priest.</u> The Morrisites were expecting CHRIST not some pseudo-High Priest.[*]

You are tragically wrong and completely uninformed and un-educated (or under-educated) in the Morrisite prophecies! Yet you write as if you know, when you don't! The tragedy is yours! The Morrisite prophecies are **filled** and replete with the promise and prophecy that it will be Jesus the High Priest after the order of Melchizedec to appear in Deer Lodge and not CHRIST! Yet you are blind! The prophet Williams not only is specific that it is Jesus **the High Priest** but also that he will be **IN PRISON** in Deer Lodge! This prophecy of the return of Jesus in prison is found in Williams' prophecy entitled the "The **High Priesthoods** Return" referring to **the return** of Jesus the **High Priest** after the order of Melchizedec and not the Christ (the descendant of David).[†] Williams writes:

THE HIGH PRIESTHOODS RETURN

How white is his raiment [the return of Jesus], how glittering his head;
    Fresh out from the chambers where long he had stayed,
How brilliant his eyes! like flames of a fire
    Not a deed nor a thought from that gage can retire.

How well he is **prisoned** by a process unshown;
    The flaming sword still keeps this science unknown
With all his massive wisdom a spot of blood is there
    Upon his heavenly garments as evidence declare
How soon began the malice with them who would obey
    God's will and counsel white clothed in mortal clay.[‡]

Williams further explains that this Jesus the High Priest is after the order **of Melchizedec**! It is not Jesus Christ but Jesus **the High Priest after the order of MELCHIZEDEC!**

You also wish to know something of Melchisedec--the real Melchisedec [Jesus the High Priest], not one representing him [Williams]. Now mark the first time we hear of him, he is declared to King of Salem or Peace. Here is brought out the bread and wine to Abraham, our faithful friend and brother. It is not written what was said at this interview; but I have no doubt it would be the same as said to the 12, at <u>his</u> last supper when <u>he</u>[§] takes the bread and also the cup saying: "Take, eat and drink, all of you, for this is my body broken, and my blood shed for you. There he stood [Jesus the High Priest], without a scar.[**]

---

[*] Labbe, *Antichrist*, p. 1.
[†] Baha'u'llah fulfills that prophecy of the second coming of Christ.
[‡] George Williams, (1870). "The High Priesthoods Return."
[§] Underlines by Williams to stress identity of Jesus to the High Priest after the order of Melchizedec which is who he foresaw in Deer Lodge and not Christ--Baha'u'llah the descendant of David.
[**] George Williams, (December 27, 1881). " Letter to Erasmussen."

Thus Williams's prophecies were expressly for the return and second coming of Jesus **the High Priest** after the order of **Melchizedec** and not of the Christ.

Williams further states specifically that the person must **physically** enter the Temple in Deer Lodge which is identical to the prison.

> You wish to know what is the object of **gathering together in Montana.** It is our Lord's Command [Jesus' coming in Montana] that his chosen people may come together to receive blessings spiritual and temporal, and the order of both Priesthoods prepared. Also a **Temple** [Ezekiel's Temple] prepared to receive the ministering angels of our God.[*]

> This excitement will arise suddenly as the world lays sleepy and find the foundation of an everlasting Government [World Order of Baha'u'llah/Kingdom of God on earth] laid secure and **the Lord [Jesus] coming suddenly to his Temple**...for the choice place of the earth is handed over to you. Its beauties and riches, in part, are yet hidden. But your children will develop it more and more. For there **[Deer Lodge, Montana]** will be built the City of the Great King."[†]

Baha'u'llah was never imprisoned in Deer Lodge. Neither were any of our dissidents of today imprisoned within the "Stone with Seven Eyes." Baha'u'llah was in prison but two things are missing: 1) His prison was not in Deer Lodge and 2) His prison did not have the prophesied seven towers of Ezekiel's Temple.[‡] Furthermore the date that the Morrisites awaited for Jesus the High Priests wrongful imprisonment and entrance into Ezekiel's Temple was set on the morning of August 9th, the very first morning that Dr. Jensen has the "Stone with Seven Eyes" before. The last time the Morrisite descendants met was August 9th, 1969. The very day **AND** year that Dr. Jensen was first placed in the Old Montana State Prison in Deer Lodge.

Furthermore, Baha'u'llah wrote nothing on the Great Pyramid of Giza (the pillar of Enoch) whereas Dr. Jensen broke the seals on the Pyramid while he had the "Stone with Seven Eyes" before him. This also fulfills the Morrisite prophecy that Jesus the High Priest will explain the prophecies of the Pyramid upon his return.

> With regard to the Pyramids in Egypt there will be wise men attracted there to explore, calculate to measure, to find what is the meaning of these extraordinary relics. Jeremiah speaking, and Isaiah also, knew the Lord of Hosts [Baha'u'llah] had a design in these great wonders, and these explorers will be helped to bring these hidden mysteries to light if they are doing it for an honest, holy purpose, to benefit mankind, and not with a view of making money; for every feature of the structure represents a heavenly order and may be called a pure language. Not by figure or by writing as we represent things, and it is written that the Lord will turn unto the inhabitants of the earth a pure language by which a small sign or movement may represent volumes of our written words. [The Pyramid gives its

---

[*] George Williams, (July 24, 1873). "Letter to Dear Sister Thomas," Brigg, Lincolnshire, England, p. 59.
[†] George Williams, (1879). "Letter to My Dear Brother James," Walthamstow, Essex England, p. 65.
[‡] The Old Montana State Prison has a stone wall with seven watch towers.

message in measurement and mathematics the pure universal language.] Its height, its circumference, its depth, its inner chambers, the space occupied by it, **all represent Jehovah's purposes from Adam to the Millennium**, and farther, as far as I know. There they stand, witnesses, and are called the mighty wonders of Egypt; and although the children of Israel built some of these Pyramids in slavery and oppression, the Lord of Hosts claimed their labors a standing memorial of his guardianship over them. He delivered them, and drowned their oppressors, as the record tells us; but the Egyptians knew not what a wonderful memorial Jehovah's chosen had left behind them; and now, before our dear Lord's second coming, professors and wise men desire to look into the meaning of these grand structures, and, I have no doubt, others will be found buried in the sand. These explanations have been given me as fast as my scribe could write them. Amen & Amen."[*]

Williams also clearly gives the genealogy of the return of Jesus the High Priest from the tribe of Dan through the lineage of the king of Denmark.[†] In this prophecy Williams shows the parallel of the return of Jesus High Priest not only being from the tribe of Dan and of the "royal lineage of High Priest" (that of, Melchizedec) but also that he will wear the "dirty garment" which will then be removed which is a prophecy clear and explicit right out of Zechariah chapter 3!

You also wish me to say something of a notice regarding the King of Denmark, the Dream, the Vision of the King was this:

In the early dawn of morning as he lay upon his bed **a company of poorly clad men** [wearing dirty garments] with staves in their hands and without shoes entered his palace without ceremony. The vision continued until the King saw himself in his grand Reception Room with his Kingly robes on and a crown upon his head. He attempted to Order these Strangers to withdraw but was speechless. The company began to remove the ornaments in the room, casting them from the window and approaching the King **removed his robes and crown and clothed him as themselves were clothed** [in the dirty garment], placing him in the midst and one who was called Seth [Joseph Morris] stood up.

At this moment came a man's hand through the ceiling of the room, handing Seth [Morris] a roll of Parchment,[‡] in which was written in glowing letters, which Seth [Morris] unfolded and read before the King, saying, "These are Ministers of the Holy one of whom you have heard, hear them. The High and Holy one has sent them with the Covenant and Law [Book of the Covenant and the Will and Testament] that who ever obeys and is faithful shall be brought before the Highest, and Ordained a King, a Priest, or Ruler, or Celestial Glory [Baha'i], when mortality and the thing thereof are passed away with you. **For behold you**

[*] George Williams, (December 27, 1881). "Letter to Dear and Beloved Brother Erasmussen," Walthamstow, Essex, England, pp. 8-9.

[†] This is Dr. Leland Jensen's genealogy.

[‡] Revelation chapter 5 the scroll written within and on the back sealed with seven seals which is the Book of the Covenant (*Kitab-i-'Ahd*) written within and the Will and Testament of 'Abdu'l-Baha written on the back.

are of the Royal Line of heavenly Priesthood [the return of Jesus the High Priest after the order of Melchizedec is from the royal genealogy of the Kings of Denmark] and elected to sit in your place to be advantage to the Work of Redemption in the hands of the Holy one. Then this sent unto you and Knowledge shall be given unto you. First through them and then through other means appointed by the Highest, and see you tell not the Priest or the wicked, for they will labor to turn your heart away from the Truth with threats of Rebellion, but stand fast and listen not. For the Highest is sufficient to bear you up and his Wisdom shall shine upon you. Be not afraid and my servant Seth [Morris] shall not give you a seal and a sign." And the Hand withdrew.

And the speaker who was Seth [Morris] then called upon the fruits of the Earth to appear. And after a melodious anthem was sung by an unseen band, there appeared groves after groves of trees in full fruit of every color which could be tasted in passing by the King and Company. No Agent was seen conducting, but self moving in utmost order. After these had passed, there were seen streams of delicious Lovely Flowers entering and passing through as the trees had done blooming their fragrance, would be felt by all the company.

And through the foliage of flowers could be seen the band of players of music, A Celestial band of females in robes of exceeding whiteness. Around their arms and ankles were hands of Gold and precious Stones. And on their heads were many crowns. Their long bright hair **held the robe [clean raiment of the high priest] in pleats and formed a girdle for their waists.** They sang an Anthem in honor of our dear Lord and the Fullness of the Gospel, saying in the chorus, "How beautiful shall Adam's planet be, and clothed with Celestial glory, The Working Ministers are sent O King they stand before you."

The vision of the King continued until Seth [Morris] reached forth his hand and took from this Celestial Female Band Host **new Raiment for the King, with which Seth clothed him** and put his Heavenly name on his forehead and sealed it there.

As I am only complying with your wishes it is not for me to describe the King's new name [Leland] or the Celestial Priesthood's dress at this time.[*]

Williams gives the clearest picture of all! Unlike the ridiculous myths of the majority of Christians waiting for Jesus to come down out of the physical sky on a cloud, the Morrisites were awaiting the return of Jesus for over 100 years as a descendant of the King of Denmark, a real person, to be imprisoned in the city of Deer Lodge in a stone building that was both a prison and Ezekiel's seven towered Temple. He would be wearing the "dirty garment" as his charge, something that the Bab and Baha'u'llah though in prison did not have. He would arrive on the day of August 9th of 1969. Williams even said that he knew his new name, which we know is

---

[*] George Williams, (April 6, 1873). "Letter to Brother Rasmusson," Lincolnshire, England, pp. 2-4. Williams gives his "new name" Leland--"The Land" in the prophecy of "The High Priesthoods Return" see pages 175-178 this volume.

Leland (the Land--Ha Eretz--Zechariah 3:9), but he says that it was not for him to reveal in the "Vision of the King," but he gives this in the "High Priesthoods Return."

Williams foresaw the name, Leland, the place Temple/prison in Deer Lodge and the date August 9th, 1969, Leland's first full day in the "Stone with Seven Eyes" and his mission to be the High Priest after the order of Melchizedec to open the scroll of the Covenant and the Law (Book of the Covenant and Will and Testament) in order to establish his Father's Kingdom, the indestructible and eternal Government of the World Order of Baha'u'llah which we know must have the Davidic king as the president and member of the IBC/UHJ.

Williams's prophecies go into much, much more depth detailing the earth's shifting crust and the catastrophe of thermonuclear war--a destruction by fire.

Beyond all doubt the Morrisites awaited Jesus the High Priest after the order of Melchizedec and not CHRIST! Beyond all doubt they awaited the High Priest (great world teacher), to be imprisoned in Deer Lodge, in Ezekiel's Temple, wear the dirty garment, be descended from the tribe of Dan, explain the Great Pyramid of Giza as well as the Book of Revelation, and to be there on August 9th of 1969! As for the meaning of names, Jesus is Greek and Joshua is Hebrew. Zechariah chapter three prophesies the return **Jesus** the High Priest and no other![*]

All the proofs are there. The truth is clear and evident. The fact is certain because it has been proved! Yet **"there are some people who, even if <u>all the proofs in the world be adduced before them</u>, still will not judge justly!"**[†]

Baha'u'llah never claimed to be the Lamb. The Bible strongly proclaims that Jesus is the Lamb **because** he is the High Priest after the order of Melchizedec. The Morrisite prophecies are those for Jesus the High Priest and not CHRIST. Dr. Jensen fulfills these prophecies. He is the return of Jesus the High Priest. He is the Lamb of God returned with seven horns and seven eyes.[‡] The history of the Deer Lodge Valley in Montana testifies to this TRUTH--so that God can be all in all to everyone! Amen.

Sincerely yours,
in the service of the Lamb,
Neal Chase.

> Never be depressed. The more ye are stirred by violation, the more deepen ye in firmness and steadfastness, and be assured that the divine hosts shall conquer, for they are assured of the victory of the Abha Kingdom. Throughout all regions the standard of firmness and steadfastness is upraised and the flag of violation is debased, for only a few weak souls have led away by flattery and the specious arguments of the violators who are outwardly with the greatest care exhibiting firmness but inwardly are engaged in agitating souls. Only a few who are the leaders of those who stir and agitate are outwardly known as violators while the

---

[*] See Douay Version. Some translation read the Hebrew Joshua instead of the Greek Jesus.
[†] 'Abdu'l-Baha, SAQ, pp. 43-44.
[‡] Revelation chapter 5.

rest, through subtle means, deceive the souls, for outwardly they assert their firmness and steadfastness in the Covenant but when they come across responsive ears they secretly sow the seeds of suspicion. The case of all of them resembleth the violation of the Covenant by Judas Iscariot AND HIS FOLLOWERS. Consider: hath any result or trace remained after them? Not even a name hath been left by his followers and although a number of Jews[*] sided with him it was as if he had no followers at all. This Judas Iscariot who was the leader of the apostles betrayed Christ for thirty pieces of silver. Take heed, O ye people of perception![†]

---

[*] The rest of the true apostles were Jews also.

[†] 'Abdu'l-Baha, *Selected Writings of 'Abdu'l-Baha*, pp. 211-212.

AN OPEN LETTER TO MAYOR LABBE OF DEER LODGE

Dear Mayor Labbe,

It was nice seeing you the other day at the training seminar at MSP. We spoke a little of the misrepresentation of the Missoulian article that day and I told you that I was writing a response. Enclosed in this package is the response I sent and the accompanying cover letter.

Please feel free to share this response with the history teacher who has accused me of distorting the dates to fit the Baha'i Cause. Since he has never said this to my face, I do not know his name, who he is or even what he looks like. For this reason I am unable to send him a copy directly. This response contains a few of the sources on the dates in question and when you are done reading it you will see that nothing has been distorted.

If you have any questions please feel free to contact me at any time. Also if anyone else on the Council or otherwise has questions, I am usually home in the evenings and be contacted at the number above.

It is my sincere hope that you will find the information in this package informative and reassuring. I also hope it will answer some questions that you may have.

For me personally, my main concern these days, however, is not for myself, but for the world situation which is in desperate need of guidance. Shortly, as things escalate in the Middle East and as Russia is involved, the steady dawning of this Most Great Sun of truth from Deer Lodge will be seen above the horizon of ignorance and doubt. Then and only then will the Kingdom be established after the whole world has turned against this great message.

For us here in Deer Lodge we have our work cut out for us. For the rest of the world, God is accomplishing His work which He promised He would do at this appointed time in the development and education of the human race. To this all the books and prophets of God bear witness. All else are His servants and do his bidding. Whether we work for good or for bad, the result of our labor is the result that God has foreseen. When Joseph's brothers did him in to sell him as a slave and he wound up in prison on a crime he didn't commit, what was it that he said to his brothers when they feared his wrath at the last?

> "As for you, you meant evil against me; but God meant it for good, to bring it about that many people should be kept alive, as they are today [after the famine of seven years]." (Genesis 50:20)

The return of Jesus is prophesied to be in prison in both the Bible (Matthew 25:36) and the Morrisite prophecy (Williams: "The High Priesthoods Return"). The evil which the people involved had meant to do Jesus in by sending him to prison; God meant for good. After the catastrophes it will be known beyond a shadow of a doubt that God meant it for good that many people should be kept alive. For without Jesus imprisoned on the "dirty jacket" charge we would have no criteria to recognize him by. If you choose to read the story of Joseph, investigate his plight and the crime they framed him on. Compare that story to the situation today and you will find answers to the pressing questions of today.

It is my hope that this letter finds you and your loved ones in the best of health and happiness!

yours in friendship,

Neal Chase.

AN OPEN LETTER TO THE MISSOULIAN I

To the staff, editors and chief:

In the recent days much news has been happening in Deer Lodge concerning the Morrisite pioneers and their prophecies for the return of Jesus in Deer Lodge. The Old Montana State Prison has been discovered to be not only a prison which Jesus is prophesied to be in but also the prophesied "Temple of the Lord" depicted in the book of Ezekiel, which is to have seven towers.

At the same time these discoveries were made, God was operating on His own concerning the affairs of the world in the Middle East. In Revelation chapter 9 verse 14 it states that the four angels are holding back the four winds of destruction that are bound at the great river Euphrates which is in Iraq. Because of the Bush/Hussein debacle these four winds are now being released.

In response to these press releases which the Morrisite Awareness Committee has been sending out from Deer Lodge, John Stromnes from the Missoulian came to Deer Lodge to interview us directly. The result was an article designed to smear the Baha'is Under the Provisions of the Covenant which failed to even present the research on the Morrisites which has been our main focus here in the Valley.

Stromnes purposely neglected to write about the Morrisites even leaving out the fact that an estimated 2/3rds of the Deer Lodge Valley is descended from these original pioneers. He also failed to mention anything about the prison being identical to Ezekiel's Temple in the Bible. He didn't even state that this is what we believed based on the research we have done into the Morrisites and the Bible.

Therefore, because of his gross misrepresentations which he designed to cloud the true issue, I wrote a response to his article of January 29th, 1991 entitled, "Sect Grids for April Apocalypse." This response is enclosed in this package for you to investigate, to set the record straight.

As the events in the gulf escalate, likewise the news of Jesus returning to Ezekiel's Temple in Deer Lodge will gain more and more attention. As journalists and reporters you deserve to be filled in on all these happenings from the ground floor up.

For when the story breaks it will be you that God has called forth to be the public's educators in your papers. It is you that will have to investigate the truth of what has occurred and vindicate it.

In the words of Baha'u'llah:

> "Newspapers [and all News Media] are as a mirror which is endowed with hearing, sight and speech; they are a wonderful phenomenon and a great matter. But it behoveth the writers thereof to be sanctified from the prejudice of egotism and desire and to be adorned with the ornament of equity and justice; they must inquire into matters as much as possible, in order that they may be informed of the real facts, and commit the same to writing [broadcast and publication].

"Concerning this oppressed One [Baha'u'llah], whatever the newspapers have mentioned is mostly devoid of truth. Good speech and truthfulness are, in loftiness of position and rank, like unto the sun which hath risen from the horizon of the heaven of knowledge. The waves of this sea [the Revelation of Baha'u'llah] are visible before the faces of all the world, and the traces of the Pen of wisdom and utterance are manifest."[*]

Stromnes purposely misrepresented the reason why I am living in Deer Lodge in order to obscure the truth and dissuade further investigation. He has failed!

We have not travelled to Deer Lodge to "gird for the end of the world" as Stromnes would have it. Nor are we cowering in the basements with guns to save our own butts. Most definitely not! I do not believe in the end of the world and neither do the Baha'is and neither did the Morrisites!

This mighty message which is on fire with the love and God and is unquenchable and unstoppable can be summed up in three words: CATASTROPHE AND KINGDOM!

We are in Deer Lodge resurrecting, researching and bringing to light the teachings, history and beliefs of the Morrisite pioneers. This great research shows, beyond a shadow of doubt, that the Morrisites were right and that Jesus has returned in Ezekiel's Temple in Deer Lodge with a mighty message for the world.

The discovery of this information has upset the balance of humanity; and the governments, economies, and nations are propelled off-balance into a war which will overtake them to the point of finally surrendering to the will of God.

What you have read in the papers concerning the Armageddon being a mystic battle between good and evil is false. This is the theology and mythology of Stromnes which he mashed on top of what I told him. The Armageddon refers to one hour of nuclear war in which one third of mankind will be killed in that one hour. Russia will be involved. The Soviets will go down into Israel to take control of the oil in the Middle East as they unite with the Arab-Muslim alliance against Israeli Jews. Even as these words are written and these words are read, the internal affairs of the Soviet Union are turned upside down in preparation for this.

One fourth of the population of Russia is Muslim and 30% of their army is Muslim. Anti-Semitism is on the rise there. The military has been complaining that in originally supporting Bush in the coalition against Iraq the Russians have betrayed their old friend Saddam Hussein. Now Russia is turning back into the military dictatorship. Chevardnazi quit because he saw this coming. Now it has arrived!

Gorbachev is clever. He is the head of the Communist party and has always been 100% Communist. Yet by playing a sunshine act with his *parastroika* and *glastnos*, he has been able to disarm Europe! Russia needed to get rid of the Eastern Block countries anyway because they were a great drain on the Russian economy. Now not only have they removed that drain but they

---

[*] Baha'u'llah, *Baha'i World Faith*, p. 171.

did it by eliminating the medium range missiles. Yet Russia still has long range nuclear missiles while Europe is disarmed!

Bush is all tied up with Aramco--the Arab American Oil Company--started by Rockefeller and then divided up between his four sons. The gulf war is an oil vendetta on the part of Bush because of his oil connections and the Texas oil dollars which got him elected. The Kuwaitis own near half of the Aramco stock.

Iraq and Kuwait are one nation. According to international law no nation is allowed to interfere with the internal affairs of any other nation. In 1921 the British took a pencil on the map and cut Kuwait off of Iraq. They did this so Iraq wouldn't have a sea port. The Kuwaitis were nothing more than a bunch of impoverished Bedouins. Now they are the richest people in the world. They owe their riches to Britain which own one of the largest oil companies in the world, Shell Oil. The US is also connected with the Aramco. It is Britain and the US who are all for this war more than France, China and Russia who are also part of the UN Security Council.

Bush refused to negotiate with Saddam Hussein. Instead he sent Baker over their not to negotiate but to tell him to his face that there would be no negotiations. Now as one man is railroading congress and this nation into a war the Middle East: problems are still not solved. After this war with Iraq regardless of how many American soldiers die, the Middle East problems will still not be solved--they will be worse.

The United Nations is poised to issue a resolution to remove the Israeli Jews from the occupied territory by force the same way they issued the resolution for Bush to use force to remove Hussein from Kuwait. This time it will be the Soviets leading the forces to go into Israel just as the Bible prophesies. This will be the final Armageddon.

Thus the Iraqi war is the prelude to Armageddon which the Bush\Hussein debacle has released the four winds of destruction. The result will be one hour of nuclear war with one third of the population of the world dying in that one hour. America will be hit hardest.

This whole situation could have been avoided easily, however, through the establishment of a Council of nations that is empowered with an international police to enforce its decisions. The way Bush has it, if one nation invades another all others should rise to defend the nation that was attacked. This is his concept on the new World Order. Only this is taken out of context.

Baha'u'llah states that this cannot happen until after a simultaneous disarmament of all the nations of the world. Today the United States has the nuclear bomb and won't give it up. This country has others at its mercy and intimidates the other nations into what ever is in the interest of the US with threat of nuclear punishment.

The nuclear weapon should not be in the hands of any nation, but should be in the hands of a Council of Nations. Then after the simultaneous disarmament of the nations, if a nation should violate the Council that nation will be brought before the Council for Judgement. If they refuse to obey then the international police will force them to comply even to the point of wiping out that nation.

The New World Order cannot take place until after the simultaneous disarmament of all nations in favor of the Council of Nations empowered with the nuclear weapons and an international police to enforce the decisions of the Council. In this way the Council will be able to solve problems such as nation's rights and define boundaries. The Council won't be a paper tiger like the UN because it will have the teeth of an international police and nuclear power.

Yet what nation right now as we read is in favor of global simultaneous disarmament empowering the collective security of a Council[*] of all Nations?

Not the US. Not Russia. Only after the hour of nuclear war which will kill one third of the people in one hour will all the people of the world that are left gladly and freely choose to adopt Baha'u'llah's plan. Then we will have peace on earth.[†] This will be through the Most Great Justice. Fort peace on earth without justice is tyranny!

The news of the world is that today Jesus has returned in Ezekiel's Temple in Montana with Baha'u'llah's New World Order (the Kingdom of God on Earth as it is in Heaven) to heal the world of its sicknesses.

As reporters, as journalists, as editors and newspapers it is your job to report the story accurately and honestly. You are responsible for investing the truth as much as possible and then vindicating it. Do not pass off your responsibility as predestination. For all people are held accountable for their actions according to their freedom of choice. In criminal law even neglect (not doing anything at all) can be a crime punishable by the court. It is my hope that you will investigate the truth and vindicate it.

Yours, in hope,

Neal Chase.

---

[*] This Council will have a descendant of King David through Baha'u'llah and 'Abdu'l-Baha as its president.
[†] One of the first acts of the Council will be to define the borders of the participant countries and arbitrate PEACE between the nations.

TUESDAY

Missoulian

MISSOULA, MONTANA

50 CENTS

INCREASING CLOUDS and colder in the valleys. Mostly cloudy tonight with slowly moderating temperatures. For road conditions, call 728-8553.

HIGH 15 / LOW 8

JANUARY 29, 1991

Deer Lodge sanctuary

By JOHN STROMNES
of the Missoulian

DEER LODGE —

Baha'i Under the Provision of the Covenant, are bustling all over Deer Lodge, talking with townspeople and local ministers, holding meetings to explain their views, and trying to get local residents to prepare for the coming paradise on earth

For example, early in January the group asked Deer Lodge Mayor R.F. Labbe to proclaim Aug. 9 as "Morrisite Pioneer Day," in honor of the Morrisites, a small splinter branch of Mormons who settled in the Deer Lodge Valley in the 1870s.

The Morrisite sect has substantially died out now, although many of their descendants still live in Deer Lodge and surrounding communities.

But Chase believes the Morrisites predicted knowingly the arrival of the second coming of Jesus II, or Jesus the High Priest, in the person of the Baha'i sect's founder, Leland Jensen of Missoula, who lived in Deer Lodge as an inmate of Montana State Prison from 1969 until 1973.

Chase and others in the sect believe that the second coming awaited by the Morrisites actually did occur on Aug. 9, 1969, when Jensen spent his first full day in prison.

KURT WILSON/Missoulian

NEAL CHASE is among a small group of believers who say the old Montana State Prison is the site of the second coming of Jesus "the High Priest" and it occurred Aug. 9, 1969.

213

The coincidence between an Aug. 9 Morrisite holiday and of Jensen's entry into prison is a prophetic proof of Jensen's spiritual authenticity, Chase said.

The Baha'i group. Under the Provision of the Covenant, believe the worldwide Baha'i faith is in error, and that Leland Jensen is the return of Jesus the High Priest, or Jesus II, a holy teacher foreordained to warn the world of the coming Judgment Day.

Like the Baha'i Under the Provision of the Covenant, the Morrisites also believed that the Deer Lodge Valley would be the promised land.

Chase, a 25-year-old writer who formerly lived in Madison, Wis., said the current war in the Middle East between Iraq and the United States and its allies is a prelude to Armageddon — the last, decisive battle between the forces of good and evil to be fought before Judgment Day.

Chase said that Deer Lodge, a bucolic community of 3,300 people about 80 miles east of Missoula, will become the New Jerusalem, or a paradise on earth, after thermonuclear war destroys the world's population centers.

"Deer Lodge and Missoula are very, very safe, but people still need to get into fallout shelters and they still need a week's worth of food and water," Chase said.

So far, the effect of their proselytizing has had "mixed results," Chase acknowledged.

"They snookered me," Labbe said.

Labbe said that when Baha'i members came to him asking for the proclamation, they identified themselves only as historical researchers. The mayor issued the proclamation.

But when sect members made a presentation to the town council, several council members were alarmed.

"We had one alderman who said, 'Holy Cow, if they are right, I've been teaching the kids all wrong.' What they were doing is distorting the dates to fit their cause," the mayor said.

Chase said "No. In fact, there is a fair amount of misinformation and even improper quotes taken out of my book."

So at the next council meeting, the council rescinded the mayor's Morrisite Pioneer Day proclamation, and approved a policy that prohibited similar proclamations in the future.

"If the proclamation is of a religious or controversial nature, there will be no proclamation," the council's resolution stated.

Perhaps the foremost historical researcher on the Morrisites, C. Leroy Anderson of the University of Montana sociology department, agrees that Chase and his group have little credibility as historical researchers, at least as evidenced by the book they have published, "Ezekiel's Temple in Montana."

Anderson wrote the definitive history of the Morrisite sect as an outgrowth of his professional interest in millenarian sects. The book, "For Christ Will Come Tomorrow: The Saga of the Morrisites," was published in 1988.

Chase said "Ezekiel's Temple," achieved considerable notoriety in light of Anderson's and others' criticisms.

—Edited from the Missoulian.

[How it might have been.]

AN OPEN LETTER TO THE MISSOULIAN II

Sirs:

In response to your article "Sect Girds for April Apocalypse," John Stromnes has purposely misrepresented me and the reason why I am living in Deer Lodge. Worse than personally misrepresenting me and the Cause for which I am working, and have dedicated my life to, you have unwittingly cheated yourselves out of the greatest story ever told!

The real story which I gave to Mr. Stromnes is far, far superior to the one that you printed--and if I were you I would print the right story before you are scooped by another paper on this one--that's how big this really is!

In the first place you painted me out to be someone who has "little credibility as an historical researcher" and is "unscholarly," "distorting the dates to fit this cause." This is completely not true. As I told Stromnes, I go by facts and proofs first and then draw my conclusions second. Stromnes was well aware of this but purposely chose to ignore it in order to smear the Baha'is.

The story that I gave Stromnes was that Deer Lodge was the greatest city on earth and that the people who live in it are also great! I told him that Deer Lodge has the richest and most glorious history in the world--that for over 100 years the Morrisites had settled this valley as the site for the second coming of Jesus the High Priest. I told Stromnes that the reason I have settled in Deer Lodge was to write a book on the Morrisites demonstrating beyond a shadow of a doubt that the Morrisites were right and that their prophecy has been fulfilled.

Instead he wrote that I moved here to "gird for the apocalypse." I never said any such thing. As a matter of fact in the first line where he quotes me, he craftily inserted words into my mouth in parenthesis which I never said! It's well known around town that Stromnes is infamous for twisting the facts and distorting the stories through gross misrepresentation to suit his own ends--whatever those might be.

My book is entitled, ***Ezekiel's Temple in Montana***, because it shows that the Old Montana State Prison actually fulfills the Bible prophecy of the future Temple depicted in the book of Ezekiel. It is to have seven towers and be the place that Jesus is to return in on his second coming.

Although this is what my book is about, Stromnes never once mentioned that the Old Montana State Prison was actually Ezekiel's Temple. He didn't even mention that this is what I believe according to the research that has been done! Instead he misrepresented our beliefs and wrote that like the Morrisites the Baha'is Under the Provisions of the Covenant think "the end of the world is at hand."

The Baha'i's do not believe that the world is going to end! Neither did the Morrisites! We believe that the world is going to change--drastically and catastrophically--but not that it will end. The world has to change because our leaders (religious, secular, medical, legal, financial, judicial, etc.) do not know what they are doing and are incapable of solving the problems of the world without the guidance that Baha'u'llah has brought. Just look at the world situation and you can see that this is quite true. It is the blind leading the blind.

The Baha'is, like the Morrisites, understand that Jesus has returned to Ezekiel's Temple in Montana for the purpose of establishing the New World Order of the Kingdom of God on earth. This is to be an actual government of God ruling from the throne of David and Deer Lodge is the chosen educational world center from which the message of the Kingdom will go out to all the world.

Stromnes asked me if we were here in Deer Lodge stocking up guns like Elizabeth Claire Prophet's group. I told him definitely not! He asked if people had to give up all their possessions to be Baha'i. I said definitely not! I told him that we were here purely for the guidance of the people--not only in Deer Lodge, Missoula and Montana--but for the guidance of all the nations of the world. I made it very clear that our sole purpose was educational.

Stromnes asked me if that after the catastrophes we were going to force the Baha'i government and New World Order of the Kingdom of God on everyone without their choice in the matter. I said definitely not! The Baha'i system of the Kingdom of God cannot function unless it is set up by free election and has the majority vote of all the people of the world. In Baha'u'llah's Book of the Covenant (Kitab-i-'Ahd) He states that He has not come to the world to take over the governments from the rulers but rather to win the hearts of the people back to God. I also told Stromnes that 'Abdu'l-Baha said that if the people of the world were pure of heart and spiritual than any system of government would work. But if they were greedy and corrupt no system would work--that includes the Baha'i government. As long as the people are selfish and greedy and power hungry we cannot have the government of God's Kingdom established that Baha'u'llah brought. These are the facts.

For this reason we see the conflict in Iraq not as the Armageddon but as the prelude to Armageddon. As stated in the Bible in the Book of Revelation chapter 9 verse 14, the four angels are holding back the four winds of destruction at the river Euphrates. The Euphrates flows through Iraq! The four winds of destruction have already been released from Iraq because of the Bush/Hussein debacle! This is the prelude to Armageddon. Russia will be involved.

I told Stromnes that the Armageddon is in fact not the end of the world but will be the escalation of the Middle East crisis into one hour of nuclear war which will kill 1/3 of the people of earth in one hour. The Bible describes Russia going down into Israel, allied with the 10 Arab nations (Saudi Arabia, Iraq, Palestine, Syria, Lebanon, Egypt, Sudan, Libya, Tunisia and Algeria)[*] that once formed the Ottoman Empire and also with the "three ribs" in the mouth of "the bear" (Russia) being Iran, Libya and Ethiopia.[†] Even now Russia is supplying Iraq with satellite intelligence and Iran is giving Iraq food and medical supplies. One fourth of the population in Russia is Muslim and 30% of the Russian Army is Muslim. Anti-Semitism is also very high and on the rise in Russia. The Russians will come down into Israel in exchange for taking the control

---

[*] Revelation 17:12. 10 horns taken from the Dragon of Islam in 1921 when the Ottoman Empire was divided up amongst the Beast counties of England and France.
[†] Daniel 7:5. Ezekiel 38:5. See also, Hal Lindsey, *The Late Great Planet Earth*, chapter 5. Put (Libya), Cush (Ethiopia), and Persia (Iran).

of the oil. This should be accomplished by a UN resolution similar to the one issued by the UN for Bush to remove Saddam Hussein from Kuwait by force.

Instead Stromnes wrote as if we believed that the Armageddon was the last battle to be fought between the forces of good and evil--as if some mythic conflict of pure fantasy were to take place in outer-space somewhere. This is perverted and wrong! This maybe Stromnes' concept of Armageddon but it is not Baha'i! The Armageddon is a very real battle not some mythical conflict as Stromnes would have it.

Again, this is not the end of the world, it is the birth of the Kingdom of God. This is why we moved to Deer Lodge to deliver the birth of this Kingdom which has been prophesied and awaited by all the people of the world for thousands and thousands of years. Deer Lodge is the chosen site where this all begins. The official motto of Deer Lodge is "Where it all began." Deer Lodge is where the Kingdom of God is born from and established.

In this respect Deer Lodge is the New Jerusalem. Jerusalem was the governmental and educational center of the nation of Israel. What made Jerusalem the special city of Israel is that it is where the Temple was. As the Temple of Ezekiel is in Deer Lodge, this in itself makes Deer Lodge the New Jerusalem. Today as the message of the Kingdom goes forth to all the world from Deer Lodge this also makes Deer Lodge the New Jerusalem--meaning the world educational center of the nations.

Instead Stromnes depicts us imagining that Deer Lodge will become the New Jerusalem in the future through some fantasy of his own which he equates with a paradise on earth. This is misleading! Deer Lodge is already the New Jerusalem where the Temple is built and the return of Jesus has come! The Old Montana State Prison fulfills the prophecy for the Temple of Ezekiel. It is not all of a sudden going to turn into some mythical paradise! This is all Stromnes' theology which he mashed on top of the things that I told him which are practical and ring of common sense. He did this on his own with no help from me. He did this on purpose too. I know he did this on purpose because he asked me these very specific questions so he would know where we are coming from, so as not confuse the issue--so he told me at the time. Then he went ahead anyway and wrote up his own religion of what the Baha'is believe and tried to pawn it off as if we actually believe his distorted concepts.

Your article should be headlined: "Stromnes Distorts the Facts" and you should have put his picture in the paper because it certainly isn't the story I gave him on the Morrisites preparing the way for Jesus return in the Temple of Ezekiel. "Stromnes Distorts the Facts" is not the message that the Baha'is have for the world and doesn't even remotely resemble it in any way.

Likewise, Stromnes wrongly presented that Baha'is believe it is the mission of Dr. Leland Jensen as the return of Jesus to "warn the world of the coming doom.'" This is inaccurate. Like the Morrisites and the Bible, the Baha'is Under the Provisions of the Covenant know that it is Leland's mission as the return of Jesus the High Priest to establish the Kingdom of God on earth by setting up the New World Order of Baha'u'llah. This will then blossom into the world government of God ruling from the throne of David, which the guardian of the Baha'i Faith (not Leland) is seated upon. This New World Order will then supplant the old system of graft, corruption and dirty political intrigue that we have now as the entire world becomes Baha'i after the year 2000 and freely chooses to adopt the Baha'i system.

Secondary to the great message of the Kingdom is the fact that the world must undergo such a drastic and catastrophic change before the government of God can be set up by a majority vote. After the catastrophe people will be begging God to have His Kingdom that Baha'u'llah brought. They will be on their knees saying, "Oh God we've had enough! No more war. No more pain. Give us your Kingdom! We believe. We were wrong. End our suffering. Now we will listen, now we will learn!"

Today the people of this country and the world are hell-bent on destruction. It doesn't take the return of Jesus to point this out. Every night on the news, every day in the paper, we have Tom Brokaw, Dan Rather and the global news media proclaiming to all of us everywhere that we're already living in "the Day of Doom," if those are the words you choose to use. The media portrays a dying society, suicidal with war-policies such as Mutual Assured Destruction (MAD), obstinate to change any of its ways. A society that would rather go to war on the insistence of one man, rather than settle the difficult problems of the world at the Council table of the nations. The war that Bush has inaugurated, without putting any real effort forth to negotiate, will not solve the problems of the Middle East that Bush refused to even consider. After the war with Iraq, no matter how it works out, the Middle East problem will still be there only it will be even worse.[*]

With the economy, the drug problem, the educational problem, the Medicare problem, the Social Security problem, the savings and loan problem, the war problem, etc., of today, people are independently seeing the decay of the world. It is the signs of the time. This world is sick! Sick. Sick. Sick.

It is not the mission of Leland as the return of Jesus to prescribe the death sentence by declaring that this is the end of the world with no solution. No Way! He is the divine physician with his finger on the pulse of humanity come to give this sick world the medicine it sorely needs. This is the medicine of David's throne contained within all the writings of Baha'u'llah-over 15,000 books, letters and epistles. Baha'u'llah has already brought the medicine into the world! It is the mission of the return of Jesus to heal this sickness. It is definitely not the end of the world--but a new beginning--the beginning of a new World--the Kingdom of God on earth.

The world today is like an alcoholic who refuses to realize his own problem. First there were the problems he couldn't deal with, so he turned to the bottle to drown his sorrows. He listened to the lies of his "friends" (the clergy) who encouraged him to drink and drink deeply, saying: "Here drink this it will make you feel better" or "Drink this, it will help!'"

At first he felt good and forgot his problems--but they didn't go away. As time went by he became addicted to drinking--he needed more and more just to get by. He wouldn't get out of bed without an eye opener in the morning. He was only taking "his medicine," etc. Then the problems got worse. They got out of control. His friends could see that he was going bankrupt, hurting his family and risked losing his job.

---

[*] Consider the current non-ending global war of terror.

People begged him to get help but he refused to even admit he had a problem. As far as he was concerned he could handle it. He disregarded all the facts, all the signs and all the evidence. He was stubborn. Then finally one day it happened. The day that changed his life forever. He was driving drunk with his wife and child in the car when he swerved off the road running down several people, causing a major accident, totaling his car and killing all the passengers, his wife and child. Yet he survived with only a severe bump on his head. Tragically the 2/3rds who were killed in the car were more than just a statistic they were his only family. He was all alone. Everyone else that he loved was gone and it was all his own fault that they were dead. He was alone and he was to blame.

After this, then and only then, is he willing to admit that he is an alcoholic! Admitting the problem is only the first step--it is not the end of the world but the beginning of a new life. Once the catastrophe is over, and the alcoholic sees his problem--and takes responsibility for himself-- then they have to enter a program like Alcoholics Anonymous because it works!

Today the world is drunk! Dead drunk. And it won't be until after the tragic calamity that it has brought about on itself that it will admit, that it has this problem--that the leaders will admit to themselves that they need the guidance from God that the return of Jesus in Deer Lodge has preserved. Baha'u'llah has brought the therapy that the world of humanity needs to get along in harmony and peace and solve its own difficult problems. It is the mission of the return of Jesus to apply this therapy and the therapy works! Yet what good is the therapy if the sick person refuses to undergo it, let alone admit that he is sick?

The great news today is that Jesus has returned with the medicine that this sick world needs, with the therapy that dead drunk mankind is desperately thirsty for. Yet Stromnes misconstrued the whole thing all on purpose. And he did it at the expense of the Mayor, the City Council and the town of Deer Lodge. He smeared me and he smeared the Baha'is. He did this purposely, misrepresenting the mission of Leland Jensen. He belittled the Morrisites and doing this has offended the heritage of 2/3rds of the population of the entire valley.

Now where are we? We are headed down the wrong road in a fast car with a drunk driver!

It is true that I am presently writing the final draft of my book but not because of the criticism of Anderson or anyone else like Stromnes would have it in his article. The first draft was written before we uncovered the majority of the Morrisite Prophecy which added even more validity to the proofs that the return of Jesus (Leland) has. It was even written before the date of August 9th, 1969 (which Leland fulfills) was made known to us. Therefore the first draft has all the juicy Morrisite information in the addendum at the end of the book. As I told Stromnes, the book is being rewritten to put the juicy stuff about the Morrisites right up front where it deserves to be-- as the showcase of proof that Jesus has in fact returned in Ezekiel's Temple in Deer Lodge to heal this sick world with the medicine of Baha'u'llah's New World Order. Stromnes purposely twisted that all around to make it look as if the book is being finalized because of historical error. This couldn't be farther from the truth! Everything in the first draft is completely historical and accurate and was researched in a scholarly way! Every detail, every fact and every date is thoroughly documented, footnoted and established to the highest degree of scholarly precision and accuracy. Stromnes made a grave error in choosing this area of expertise to smear. Now he has egg on his face for everyone to see because of the facts. These are the facts:

The important dates are as follows: 1) 1863 the year that the Morrisites came to Montana which is the same year that Baha'u'llah proclaimed Himself; 2) 1969 the last year that the Morrisites gathered awaiting Jesus return; 3) the day of August 9th which the Morrisites celebrated for over 100 years as the day Jesus would be in Deer Lodge; 4) 1893 the year construction on the stone wall with seven towers of the prison began corresponding to the ascension of Baha'u'llah; and 5) 1912 the year that the single stone wall with seven watch-towers was finished at the same time 'Abdu'l-Baha prophesied that the Temple was completed in 1912. These are the significant dates of which I am accused of distorting to fit this Cause and I declare that I have distorted not one of them!

According to Mr. Anderson, who claims that I have used "misinformation"' and have used "improper quotes taken out of [his] book." His "definitive history of the Morrisite sect" states on page 211 that:

> "Morrisites began arriving in Montana as early as 1863."[*]

Likewise the Montana Standard and the Billings Gazette state the same unimpeachable fact:

> "Morrisites began arriving in Montana as early as 1863."[†]

It is well known throughout all books on the subject that Baha'u'llah began his ministry in 1863 when he first made his proclamation in the Garden of Ridvan outside of Baghdad, Iraq. Furthermore, according to *Names on the Face of Montana*, found right here in the Deer Lodge public library:

> "In 1863 the citizens formed the Deer Lodge Town Company, had the town platted, and changed the name to Deer Lodge City."[‡]

What have I distorted! Unless Anderson, *The Montana Standard*, *The Billings Gazette*, and these history books are full of lies these things are absolutely true! And even if they are full of lies (which there are not) then it would be Anderson, *The Montana Standard*, *The Billings Gazette* and the history books which are distorted and not me, nor this Cause, nor the Baha'is Under the Provisions of the Covenant, nor Dr. Leland Jensen! You people over there and John Stromnes should get your facts straight!

1863 is the date for the foundation of all three things: Baha'u'llah's proclamation, the platting of Deer Lodge City, and the pioneering of the Morrisites in Montana. Furthermore if you take a closer look the dates only become more accurate!

---

[*] C. Leroy Anderson, *For Christ Will Come Tomorrow*, p. 211.
[†] *The Billings Gazette*, Saturday, July 24, 1982, p. 9-A; *The Montana Standard*, Butte, Saturday, June 19, 1982, p. 5.
[‡] Roberta Carkeek Cheney, *Names on the Face of Montana*, p. 70.

Deer Lodge once thought to be site of Second Coming

GEORGE JOHNSON

ANDREW HENDRIKSON

MISSOULA — Few people would think of Deer Lodge as a "heavenly city." Certainly not the residents of the Montana State Prison.

A picturesque town settled in the mid-19th century, Deer Lodge is better known for the Grant-Kohrs Ranch, the Towe College-tion of antique Ford automobiles, or, more obscurely as the site of the state's first college, established in 1878.

But to a tiny now-extinct religious sect known as the Morrisites, Deer Lodge was the "Heavenly City," the place where the Second Coming of Christ was to occur and where the "City of the Great King" would be built.

It was prophesied back in 1879 that wise men would find their way there, that the climate would be moderated and bring forth choice vegetations and floral grandeur. There would be no beasts of prey, no one would be of greater rank than anyone else and all neighbors would live in perfect accord.

In a newly released book about Morrisites C. LeRoy Anderson, a University of Montana professor of sociology, tells the story of how some of the earliest settlers in Montana came to live in the Deer Lodge Valley, and around Anaconda, a legacy that will be fascinating reading for many of the descendants who remain there still. Titled "For Christ Will Come Tomorrow: The Saga of the Morrisites," Utah State University

Press. Hardbound, $12.95. Anderson's book recounts the history of the little-known sect from its beginnings in Utah in the 1850s to its end a century later in Montana.

THE STORY is both dramatic and tragic and at times boggles the imagination. The founder of the sect, Joseph Morris, was an English convert to Mormonism who migrated to Utah in 1853. During this period the entire nation, including the Mormon Church, was swept with the fervor of religious revivalism. In the context of these times, Morris became convinced that God had spoken to him and selected him to be a prophet.

After failing in numerous written attempts to convince Brigham Young that he was to replace him as the spiritual leader of the Mormon Church, Morris established his own communal sect along the banks of the Weber River about 30 miles north of Salt Lake City. He managed to attract a following of several hundred and preached in

open defiance of Young.

A devout follower of Joseph Smith, Morris differed from Young in that he was against polygamy. He believed in reincarnation, and developed his own evolutionary cosmology. Naturally, the Morrisites and the Mormons were destined to conflict. In June 1862 the Morrisites were drawn into an armed conflict with a territorial posse over 500 strong.

After three days of resistance, Anderson writes, the Morrisite settlement was overrun. Morris and several of his followers were killed, and the remainder were soon scattered to the winds.

Although Morrisites began arriving in Montana as early as 1863, a major influx did not occur until 1871 when Morrisites from Omaha, Neb., Council Bluffs, Iowa and Soda Springs, Idaho, migrated to the Deer Lodge area. Unfortunately after the death of Morris, the leadership of the sect remained weak and divided and most of the other settlements in Washington, California,

Nevada and Idaho were fairly well dissolved by 1890. The Morrisites who settled in Montana, however, were mostly of Scandinavian heritage, and their common ethnic and cultural identity helped the sect to survive.

Their concentration in the Deer Lodge Valley gave the appearance of a sizable group," Anderson said, "but it is doubtful that their numbers ever exceeded 75-100."

Andrew Hendrikson of Deer Lodge served as president of the Montana Morrisites from 1886 to 1921. After Hendrikson's death, George Johnson became president. By the 1940s the active membership had dwindled to fewer than a dozen. The sect effectively died out with Johnson's death in 1954 at age 98.

ALL THAT remains of the sect today is a simple white frame building standing near the railroad tracks at Dempsey Crossing, six miles south of Deer Lodge. The inscription, "The Lord's House," can still be seen in faded letters above the door. Begun in 1877, it was dedicated on Aug. 9, 1879, and is probably the last Morrisite structure in Montana, or even the world.

It was here that Christ was supposed to make His Second Advent. "It seems truly incongruous that such a modest structure could ever have been intended as the site of so grand and glorious an event," Anderson writes. "No doubt it was the best that those pioneers could do. And perhaps they felt it did not compare too badly with the traditional site of His first appearance — a primitive stable in an obscure village called Bethlehem."

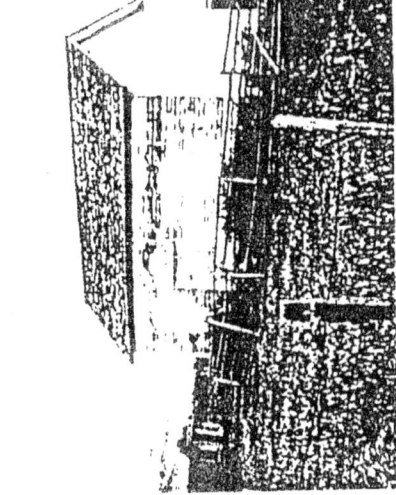

THE WORDS "The Lord's House" can still be seen in faded letters above the doors of the last Morrisite church known to exist. Dedicated on Aug. 9, 1879, it is located six miles south of Deer Lodge toward Race Track. This was the place where the Morrisites expected the Second Coming of Christ to occur. (UM photo by Virginia Vickers Braun)

In brief

'Creation' is Bible school theme

Vacation Bible School at United Congregational Church, Bayard and Sheridan, begins Monday 9-noon for the week.

Wallenberg fate intrigues world

By GEORGE CORNELL
AP Religion Writer

Is Raoul Wallenberg dead or alive? The question has been raised increasingly in Christian and Jewish circles, in honoring a man whose deeds blazed with courage and compassion in the period of Nazism.

"One of the most saintly and self-sacrificing men of our time," said a recent U.S. convention of the Rabbinical Assembly, crediting Wallenberg with saving the lives of about 100,000 Hungarian Jews.

The assembly urged the

U.S. government "to exert every diplomatic effort to determine the true fate of Wallenberg.

He was ... once completely forgotten, but he now is very much alive everywhere, says his half-sister, Nina Lagergren, noting a spreading movement in the world to find and free him.

A Lutheran college in Minnesota, Gustavus Adolphus College, last month conferred an honorary degree in absentia on Wallenberg. The U.S. Congress has granted honorary

American citizenship to Wallenberg, an honor given only to one other person — the late Winston Churchill.

And the puzzle persists, amid sporadic, indirect clues, that Wallenberg still is alive somewhere in the Soviet prison system.

It would seem nearly impossible after 37 years, writes Harvey Rosenfeld in a new book, "Raoul Wallenberg, Swedish Angel of Rescue."

Wallenberg was a young Swedish Lutheran who knew his Bible and studied it regularly. Although a Christian, his maternal

great-great grandmother was of Jewish descent, converted to Christianity in the 18th century.

He lived for four years in the United States, studying architecture at the University of Michigan from 1931-35. On return to his homeland, he became a businessman. But in World War II, the Swedish government enlisted him at the age of 32 into diplomatic service. He was sent to Budapest, Hungary, on July 9, 1944, in the midst of Nazi drives to round up Jews and transport them to death camps.

The ... at great risk to his life ... he "worked tirelessly to extend protection to some 20,000 Jews by means of special protective passports," read the citation from Gustavus Adolphus College.

It said efforts by him and other diplomats, by

Baptists endorse prayer in school

©By New York Times
NEW ORLEANS — Reversing a long-held position, the Southern Baptist Convention has endorsed President Reagan's proposal for a Con-

organized prayer in public schools. Most churches, fearing government involvement in religion or infringement of religious liberties, have opposed such moves.

It would mean that the church was using civil power to carry out its work.

But many delegates to the denomination's annual

called it "incredibly out of keeping with Baptist tradition," Dunn, expressing views held by other church groups opposing organized prayer in schools, said. "Real

221

Deer Lodge was sect's 'Heavenly City' in 1870s

By VIRGINIA VICKERS BRAUN
University of Montana

MISSOULA — Few people would think of Deer Lodge as a "heavenly city." Certainly not the residents of Montana State Prison.

A picturesque town settled in the mid-19th century, Deer Lodge is better known for the Grant-Kohrs Ranch, the Towe Collection of antique Ford automobiles, or more obscurely as the site of the state's first college, the College of Montana, established in 1878.

But to a tiny, now-extinct religious sect known as the Morrisites, Deer Lodge was the "Heavenly City," the place where the second coming of Christ was to occur and where the "City of the Great King" would be built.

It was prophesied back in 1879 that wise men would "find their way there," that the climate would be "moderated" and bring forth "choice vegetations and floral grandeur." There would be no beasts of prey, no one would be of greater rank than anyone else and till neighbor would live in "perfect accord."

In a newly released book about the Morrisites, C. LeRoy Anderson, a University of Montana professor of sociology, tells the story of how some of the earliest settlers in Montana came to live in the Deer Lodge Valley and around Anaconda, a legacy that will be fascinating reading for many of the descendants who remain there still.

Titled "For Christ Will Come Tomorrow: The Saga of the Morrisites," (Utah State University Press, $12.95) Anderson's book recounts the history of the little-known sect from its beginnings in Utah in the 1860s to its end a century later in Montana.

The story is both dramatic and tragic and, at times, boggles the imagination. The founder of the sect, Joseph Morris, was an English convert to Mormonism who had migrated to Utah in 1853. During this period, the entire nation, including the Mormon Church, was swept with the fervor of religious revivalism. In the context of these times, Morris became convinced that God had spoken to him and selected him to be a prophet.

After failing in numerous written attempts to convince Brigham Young that he was to replace him as the spiritual leader of the Mormon Church, Morris established his own communal sect along the banks of the Weber River about 30 miles north of Salt Lake City. He managed to attract a following of several hundred and preached in open defiance of Young.

A devout follower of Joseph Smith, Morris differed from Young in that he was against polygamy.

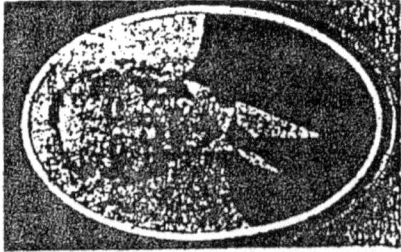

ANDREW HENDRIKSON
president of Morrisites 1884-1921

GEORGE JOHNSON
sect ended with its death in 1944

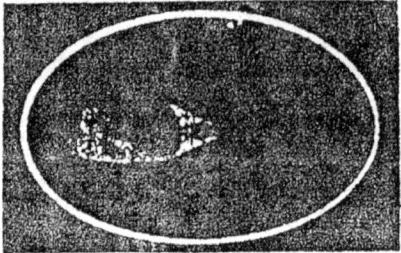

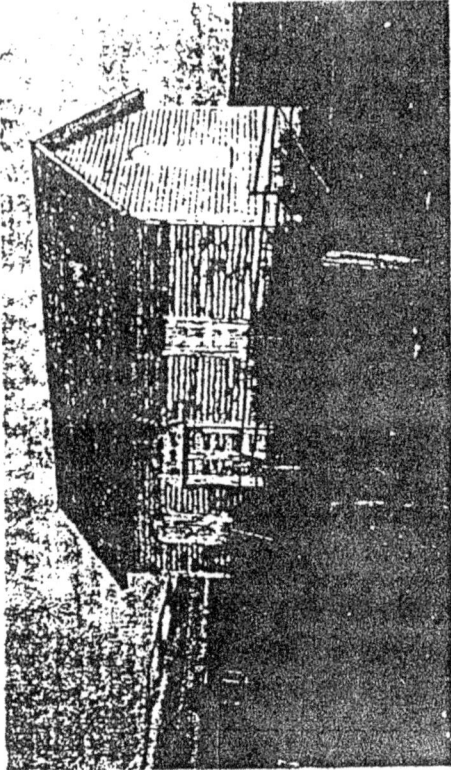

Last Morrisite structure is this church six miles south of Deer Lodge.

believed in reincarnation and developed his own evolutionary cosmology. Naturally, the Morrisites and the Mormons were destined to clash. In June 1862, the Morrisites were drawn into an armed conflict with a territorial posse more than 500 strong.

"After three days of resistance," Anderson writes, "the Morrisite settlement was overrun. Morris and several of his followers were killed, and the remainder were soon scattered to the winds."

Although Morrisites began arriving in Montana as early as 1863, a major influx did not occur until 1871 when Morrisites from Omaha, Neb., Council Bluffs, Iowa, and Soda Springs, Idaho, migrated to the Deer Lodge area.

Unfortunately, after the death of Morris, the leadership of the sect remained weak and divided and most of the other settlements in Washington, California, Nevada and Idaho were fairly well dissolved by 1890. The Morrisites who settled in Montana, however, were mostly of Scandinavian heritage, and their common ethnic and cultural identity helped the sect to survive.

"Their concentration in the Deer Lodge Valley gave the appearance of a sizable group," Anderson said, "but it is doubtful that their numbers ever exceeded 75-100."

Andrew Hendrikson of Deer Lodge served as president of the Montana Morrisites from 1886 to 1921. After Hendrikson's death, George Johnson became president. By the 1940s, active membership had dwindled to fewer than a dozen. The sect effectively died out with Johnson's death in 1954 at age 98.

All that remains of the sect today is a simple white frame building standing near the railroad tracks at Dempsey Crossing, six miles south of Deer Lodge. The inscription, "The Lord's House," can still be seen lettered above the door. Begun in 1877, it was dedicated on Aug. 9, 1879, and is probably the last Morrisite structure in Montana, or even the world.

It was here that Christ was supposed to make his second advent. "It seems truly incongruous that such a modest structure could ever have been intended as the site of so grand and glorious an event," Anderson writes. "No doubt it was the best that those pioneers could do. And perhaps they felt it did not compare too badly with the traditional site of His first appearance — a primitive stable in an obscure village called Bethlehem."

Churches and TV: still looking it over

By DAVID E. ANDERSON
UPI Religion Writer

The Rev. Donald Wildmon, the Tupelo, Miss., Methodist pastor who

Evangelist to teach, minister to ill

Bill Moore, a Baptist minister who was a pas-

Co-Uni-Bus to show film Sunday

"Jana," a movie for young adults about a girl who brought Jesus into view for friends, will be shown 8 p.m. Sunday at 2707 Glenwood Lane.

It is sponsored by Co-Uni-Bus, a Christ-centered ministry to college and career young people. Visitors are welcome. A free-will offering will be taken to pay for film rental.

Heralds of Song to perform

group. Participants are asked to bring camping equipment.

Church day camp starts Monday

Heights Baptist Church's annual five-day camp for children entering grades 1-4 is scheduled July 26-30.

Children will travel by bus each day to various Billings sites for activities, including crafts, Bible stories, games and contests. The last day will feature a swimming party. For more information ca...

Baha'u'llah made His proclamation in the spring of 1863 at the time that he was exiled from Baghdad. Likewise the Morrisites began their exodus from Utah to Deer Lodge in the spring of 1863. They were freed from Mormon oppression on March 31st, 1863 when Governor Harding exonerated the Morrisites from any guilt in the massacre they endured and put the full blame of the Morrisite slaughter on the Mormons and Sheriff Burton.[*] The month of April was spent planning to leave Utah under military escort with General Connor who had been dispatched by the federal government to protect the Morrisites from the Mormons.[†] Baha'u'llah proclaimed Himself in the garden of Ridvan on April 21st, 1863 for 12 days. On May 2nd, 1863 He began His long exodus to Israel, retracing the path of Abraham, finally placing the throne of David on Mt. Carmel, before His death in 1892. Likewise the wagon trains of the Morrisites planned in April with General Connor and pulled out on May 5th, 1863, "like the two wings of the great eagle" three days after Baha'u'llah left the Garden of Ridvan after his proclamation.[‡] Everything about the Morrisites and Deer Lodge parallels the Baha'i Faith--without any distortions! This is the work of God, not man.

According to Anderson's book, George Williams had already contacted the Morrisites and was among them when they journeyed north to Soda Springs, Idaho.[§] A postmark documents that he was there in the settlement, called Morristown, in August of 1863.[**] In *Gems of Inspiration* by John Eardley, he documents that in fact it was George Williams who identified the wagon trains of the Morrisites pulling out of Utah like "the two wings of the great eagle."[††]

Williams had his vision of Jesus second coming to Deer Lodge in the spring of 1862--April 12, 1862. A year later he was teaching this to the Morrisites in the Spring of 1863, putting forth his claim, and encouraging them to move to Deer Lodge in Montana. Just like all prophets, (like Daniel and Ezekiel), Williams had his vision first and then was able to make prophecies later.

In Hebrew the two words for prophet are "roeh" and "nabi." "Roeh" means seer, and "nabi" means mouth-piece. First the prophet has the vision of the event and then second he is able to proclaim it. Williams' vision of Jesus returning in Deer Lodge was in 1862. From 1863 to the day he died he proclaimed this vision to the Morrisite pioneers. Thus the first Morrisites entered Montana in 1863 according to the vision of Williams and began their settlement of the Deer Lodge Valley. By 1869, Williams visited Council Bluffs, Iowa and even more Morrisite pioneers came to Deer Lodge filling the valley as original homesteaders in the early 1870s.

All the pioneering of Deer Lodge by the Morrisites was at the insistence of one man--George Williams. Williams' entire life was dedicated to the pioneering of Deer Lodge for the preparation of the return of Jesus. The Morrisites believed his vision. They saw the truth of his prophecy. They were the homesteading pioneers.

---

[*] Anderson, pp. 150-151.
[†] Anderson, pp. 159-163.
[‡] Anderson, p. 161.
[§] Anderson, p. 176.
[**] Anderson, p. 176.
[††] J. R. Eardley, *Gems of Inspiration*, p. 98.

Today 2/3rds of the population of the entire Deer Lodge Valley--from Butte to Garrison--are descended from the Morrisites. This fact comes from the Morrisite descendants we have interviewed and several local historians. Yet John Stromnes conveniently omitted that fact from his article making it look like the Morrisites were nothing more than a few eccentrics who moved here and then disappeared. This couldn't be farther from the truth. The Morrisites played a large part in the history of Deer Lodge and Montana and their descendants still do. One of the original Morrisite pioneers, J. R. Eardley, sat on the Montana Territorial State legislature and owned a placer gold mine in the Valley. The Morrisites were influential, well known and well respected and admired by everyone who met them. Today their descendants still play a major role in the valley. The beautiful homesteads and farmland surrounding the city of Deer Lodge is owned by them. They are ranchers, farmers and breeders. They also play a role in government--Beck being one of the more famous Morrisite names. According to Anderson's book:

> "From that group [of Morrisites] came numerous persons who played a significant role in the settlement of the Deer Lodge Valley in Montana."[*]

Clearly, the beginning of all the pioneering efforts of the Morrisites, the platting of Deer Lodge and the proclamation of Baha'u'llah all begin in the spring of 1863. These are not distortions. These are facts!

Next, for over 100 years the Morrisites looked for the return of Jesus on August 9th. The last time they looked for Jesus was on August 9th of 1969.

According to the C. LeRoy Anderson Morrisite Collection: Marie-Eccles Caine Archive preserved in Logan, Utah at the Utah State University:

> "The Church of Jesus Christ of the Saints of the Most High [the Morrisites] officially disbanded in 1969."[†]

According to the daughter of George Johnson, Inez Rhoades of Missoula (of which we have a taped interview) and other Morrisite descendants, August 9th was celebrated forever 100 years as the day the return of Jesus in Deer Lodge would occur and it was the last day they met.

> "All those people that belonged to that little church down there [in Deer Lodge, Montana]: One day out the year, it was August the 9th, they knew that was the Day that Christ would return."(Lewis Johnson--taped interview, September 21[st,] 1990--Last of the Morrisite Pioneers)

These same dates are documented by Anderson in the Morrisite archive collection in Logan, Utah. In Anderson's interview with the Becks on July 17, 1974 August 9th was the day that they always celebrated for over 100 years:

> Anderson: "Can you tell me a little bit about some of the special days or holidays you had?"

---

[*] Anderson, p. 206.
[†] Morrisite Collection Logan Utah (MCLU) index book.

Becks: "Yes, the Ninth of August was when we always had a feast day."

It was also the last day that they met.

Becks: "Now a few years back Mrs. Staffenson, that was Agnes Hendrickson, she got all of us together, all of us that was left and we went down there [to the Lord's House--the Morrisite church] and we had a meeting...That was the last meeting we had...Ninth of August we all gathered at her house and all went to church. We had the meeting first. Frank Staffenson was there."[*]

August 9th was the day that the Morrisites had picked, not the day that the Baha'is Under the Provisions of the Covenant picked. It was the day that the Morrisites had celebrated for the return of Jesus. Their only other holiday was February 14th, the birthday of George Williams the prophet who told them that Jesus second coming would be in Deer Lodge on that day! The last time they looked was on August 9th, 1969, the first full day Leland was in Deer Lodge in fulfillment of prophecy! These are facts. Historical facts! Scholarly facts. These are not distortions. The fact that Leland's first full day in the prison was August 9th, 1969 is a matter of public record.

Finally, like in the days of Moses, it was the Temple that succeeded Him after His passing. Likewise after the ascension of Baha'u'llah in 1892, construction began on the solid stone wall and seven watch towers of the Old Montana State Prison, which are like eyes, in 1893.

"1. THE WALL: Built by convict labor in 1893...Tower and wall construction, 1893 (photo caption)."[†]

The stone wall with its seven watch towers was not completed into its final form with tower #7 being "the gate that faces east" and the main entrance until 1912.

"During construction of the wall extension, to allow room for a new cell block, in 1911 and 1912, the prison entrance was moved from the north side of the institution to its present location on the east."[‡]

"3. TOWER: This [Tower 7] was the main entrance to the Old Prison. All new prisoners, from 1912 onward, entered these doors, [between the pillars of Jachin and Boaz] and for some it was a one way trip."[§]

Likewise after the death of Baha'u'llah in 1892, 1893 marked the first year of the ministry of His son 'Abdu'l-Baha. 'Abdu'l-Baha travelled to America in 1912, the year that the prison was completed in its final form with seven watch towers upon one stone wall. As it is written in Zechariah chapter three:

---

[*] MCLU, 2:2.
[†] *A Self-Guided Tour of the Old Montana State Prison*, pp. 2-3.
[‡] *Self-Guided Tour*, p. 3.
[§] *Self-Guided Tour*, p. 5.

"For behold the stone that I have laid before Jesus: upon one stone there are seven eyes."[*]

Thus upon one stone wall there are seven watch-towers like eyes placed before the return of Jesus the High Priest (Leland) who spent his first full day in Ezekiel's Temple in Montana with seven towers on August 9th, 1969.

It is no coincidence that 'Abdu'l-Baha prophesied the completion of the Old Montana State Prison, declaring that the Temple was already built in the year that construction was finished in 1912.

While 'Abdu'l-Baha was in America in 1912, the Baha'is asked him to lay the cornerstone to the Baha'i Temple in Wilmette, Illinois. After he laid the stone, facing west toward Deer Lodge, with his back toward Lake Michigan, 'Abdu'l-Baha prophetically declared:

"THE TEMPLE IS ALREADY BUILT!"[†]

Thus at the exact time that the Old Montana State Prison was completed, 'Abdu'l-Baha declared that the Temple was already built. The actual construction of the Wilmette Temple wasn't even begun until nine years later and it wasn't even finished until the early 1950s. Yet Ezekiel's Temple in Montana was already finished in 1912 as 'Abdu'l-Baha prophetically announced!

These are all the dates of the Morrisites and Deer Lodge which correspond to the Baha'i Faith. I challenge anyone to show that this is distortion! The Cause of God is not built upon distortions! It is built upon facts! And the denizens of the Kingdom, the Baha'is Under the Provisions of the Covenant are the angels whose faith is founded upon science, history and proofs. Including an intellectual and scientific belief in the Bible and prophecy! Faith is important, but not blind faith or faith on rhetoric. Faith must be based on proof.

Therefore heed these ominous and prophetic words of prophecy from Paul the great establisher of Christianity:

"Let brotherly love continue. Do not neglect to show hospitality to strangers, for thereby some have entertained angels unawares. Remember those who are in prison, as though in prison with them."[‡]

Thus concludes the Book of Hebrews with these opening words to the last chapter. The Book of Hebrews which prophesies Jesus the High Priest in the archetypical Temple of Ezekiel declares that it is the prisoners who will be the angels! As Jesus himself declares through prophecy that he will be in prison on his second coming (Matthew 25:30). Thus the Bible demonstrates that the prison and Temple are one and the same. This is how Jesus is both in prison and in the Temple of Ezekiel with seven towers at the same time.

---

[*] Zechariah 3:9. Catholic Douay Version (CDV).
[†] *Baha'i News*, April 1987.
[‡] Hebrews 13:2-3.

If you cannot even recognize strangers who may be the angels, and the angels who are the prisoners, how will you recognize Jesus who himself is to be in prison on the "dirty jacket" charge as prophesied of in Zechariah chapter three and the Morrisite prophet George Williams? This is why he comes with proofs! So you will recognize him. So you are able to recognize him. When Jesus came the first time he came with proofs. This is how he did away with sin. The sin of not being able to recognize him. For by dying on the cross Jesus fulfilled prophecy and gave the fulfillment of prophecy as this criteria to recognize him by on his second coming. The Golden Criteria of the fulfillment of prophecy. So accurate as to give the prophesied name, prophesied date, prophesied address and prophesied profession of the one prophesied like a divine business card. Therefore we have an everlasting faith based on everlasting indestructible proofs.

Do not forget that the Morrisites are Christians! They considered themselves to be Christian-- 100% Christian. As a matter of fact they were the last true Christians on earth, just like John the Baptist's group was the last remnant of true Jews before Jesus appeared to them and they officially disbanded in 30 AD. For these majestic and brave homesteading pioneers (the Morrisites) it was for the love of Jesus on both his first coming in Bethlehem in a dirt floored manger and on his second coming in the prophesied prison/Temple in Deer Lodge that they pioneered this valley and raised up a multitude of descendants to recognize his return! Yet your article ignores the greatness of these people, belittles their faith and fails to educate the area which boasts a population of an average of two out every three people being a Morrisite descendant or being married to one--whether they know it or not. Most of them are in fact Morrisites by blood!

When this gets some positive coverage the faithful will pour out of the wood work and we will see 144,000 world-wide joyously celebrating this great Day.

What must it take to get people to see? For Christians it took the brutal and senseless death of Jesus on the cross to get people to pay attention. And afterward is was thousands and thousands of Christians fed to the lions--martyred--whose blood was spilled. At the time of Noah it was the mass destruction of the people in the flood before he was seen to be right. For Moses it was the first born of all the people who disbelieved and then Pharaoh and his mighty armies still went down in the sea. At the time of Baha'u'llah it was the blood of the Bab and 10,000 of his followers that flowed to purify the sanctuary for the coming of Baha'u'llah. Then it was 20,000 Baha'is who were likewise put to death by the corrupted Muslim clergy.

In America, the pilgrims left Europe for religious freedom and then they became the persecutors of other Christian groups. Joseph Smith was killed for his different beliefs in 1844 the same year that the Bab made his proclamation in Persia (Iran). Then it was Brigham Young and the Mormons who became the persecutors and the Morrisites had to die. Morris was assassinated by Sheriff Burton under the direction of Brigham Young to eliminate Morris who was the Mormon reformer, much like Martin Luther the Catholic reformer. Unlike Luther, Morris didn't have eight German princes to protect him and he was killed--trampled down by Burton's horse while he was turning to pray and shot in the back of the head. Cruel, cold-blooded and brutal.

According to the front page of *The San Francisco Chronicle*, the Morrisite slaughter and the assignation of Joseph Morris was the cruelest religious massacre in the history of the United States engineered all under the direction of Brigham Young, even worse and crueler than the brutality of Mountain Meadows Massacre because of the calculated deceptions and manipulation of the Utah political machine by Young. [*]

After the spilling of even more blood the Morrisites then recognized George Williams in 1863 and moved to Deer Lodge Montana. How much bloodshed and senseless death and brutality is it going to take before you people see the truth that God has again sent the same light into the world today that he did almost 2000 years ago? Today this light shines from the person of Leland, the return of Jesus in Ezekiel's Temple in Montana.

Is it necessary that you hold out against the real story until the tide of the war in Iraq turns for the worse? For almost 2000 years it has been written that "the four winds of destruction" would be released from "the great river Euphrates" which is from Iraq! (Revelation 9:14) The four winds of destruction have already been unleashed. Do we really need to have up around 200,000 American soldiers killed and Israel gassed like Saddam has threatened before this message of Jesus the High Priest returned to Ezekiel's Temple in Montana is proclaimed to all the world. Does the alcoholic have to refuse to admit his problem until after he has had his wreck and killed his family? Does humanity always have to choose the way of blood? Before this Kingdom is established 2/3rds of the earth's population will die and then the 2 billion who are left we gladly elect to have the Baha'i system established because this is the Plan of God and not the plan of man.

Clearly as proven above the Baha'is go by the facts first and draw the conclusions second. There was never any distorting of dates to fit this Cause, the significant dates of the Morrisites and Deer Lodge automatically fit this Cause in their own right because that's how God has it. It just happens that we were the first to ever put two and two together on this one without any distortions.

On the other hand, Mr. Stromnes showed up at my home in Deer Lodge with his conclusions already made and his story already written. He researched the facts of this story and then went ahead and ignored them. He purposely misconstrued the truth to suit his own ends. This is unprofessional and unscientific. He and your paper may operate that way, but I do not.

Quite the opposite! As a typical Baha'i Under the Provisions of the Covenant I am continuously researching new ideas and facts and developing new concepts based on those facts. Just as the scientist uncovers new facts in the physical universe and new inventions, with the intellect God gave us we are all capable of uncovering spiritual discoveries. This was how I was able to discover that the Old Montana State Prison fulfilled the prophecies for Ezekiel's Temple in the Bible where the return of Jesus is to be. That research, in turn, lead us to discover the Morrisites who for over 127 years had been awaiting the return of Jesus the High Priest in prison in Deer Lodge.

---

[*] *San Francisco Chronicle*, Sunday, June 19, 1892. Vol. LV. No. 156. See also *Brigham's Destroying Angel* by Bill Hickman for the corruption of Brigham Young.

God was kind and generous by first opening our eyes to the Temple being the Old Montana State prison in Deer Lodge. Then because we saw this on proof and were willing to sacrifice everything for the truth and the promotion of this Cause, God then revealed to us as a gift and a fruit of our labors that the Morrisites had settled here 127 years ago to give credence to this same message we are promoting today.

It was only a few months ago, during the research on Ezekiel's Temple, that we first discovered that the Morrisites prophesied the second coming of Jesus was to be in Deer Lodge in Ezekiel's Temple! Previously this was completely unknown to me or any other Baha'is. This was amazing to discover that the research I had been doing was completely corroborated by the Morrisites who were the original homesteading pioneers of the valley--and that the proofs for the return of Jesus (Leland) in the prison on the "dirty jacket" charge were also backed-up by the Morrisites.

Williams prophesied that Ezekiel's Temple would be built in Montana, specifically in Deer Lodge, and that it would be built "from the stones from the surrounding mountains." The Old Montana State Prison fits both the Biblical and Morrisite description of Ezekiel's Temple. In the 54th chapter of Isaiah he sees that the Temple is to have turreted towers. Turrets are for guns! Why would a Temple have guns? A Temple doesn't have guns but a prison does. Likewise both Biblical and Morrisite prophecy states that Jesus will be in prison on his second coming thus showing that the prison and the Temple are the same building. These are the facts.

It was not Leland who inspired Joseph Morris to become the Mormon reformer and sacrifice his own life for this message. It was God Almighty! It was not Leland or me or the Baha'is today who gave the vision of Jesus coming to Ezekiel's Temple in Deer Lodge to George Williams! It was God Almighty! This mighty Cause has proofs of prophecy that transcend the bounds of time through the power and vision that God inspires his prophets with. George Williams is great and the Morrisites are great. George Williams is the modern forerunner to the return of Jesus and the Morrisites were the ones who sacrificed EVERYTHING for this truth which is now astounding and amazing the people who have ears to hear and minds to listen to this great calling today!

Unlike your article which states that they "unknowingly" predicted the arrival of Jesus--George Williams, the prophet of the Morrisites, prophesied every detail of Leland's coming to Deer Lodge. Williams states that Jesus will be both in prison[*] on a dirty jacket charge[†] and that he will also be in the prophesied Temple showing that the prison and the Temple are one and the same. This same prophecy is given in the Bible and in Zechariah chapter 3 it states that Jesus the High Priest will be wearing the dirty jacket! In verse 9 it gives the name of the return of Jesus as "the land." Zechariah identifies the iniquity of Jesus (in verse 4) which will be removed as the same iniquity of "the land" which will be removed. This is the iniquity (iniquity means "gross injustice" and refers to the gross injustice inflicted against Leland) of the "dirty jacket." "The land" is Leland's name: 'Le' is French for 'the' and 'land' is 'land.'

Williams further states that the "Temple must be built from the stone from the surrounding mountains"[‡] and the Old Montana State Prison is built from the stone from Whitehall and

---

[*] George Williams, (1870). "The High Priesthoods Return."
[†] George Williams, (April 6, 1873). "Letter to Brother Rasmusson," Lincolnshire, England, pp. 2-4.
[‡] Morrisite Collection Logan Utah (MCLU).

229

Garrison. Williams gives the day of August 9th for the day that Jesus will be in Deer Lodge and the Morrisites celebrated this day for over 100 years until the last day they met on August 9th, 1969 which was Leland's first full day in the prison.[*]

Williams was also very clear that it would be the return of Jesus the High Priest in Deer Lodge and not Jesus the Christ--specifically Jesus the High Priest after the order of Melchizedec. Furthermore, the Morrisites did not believe in reincarnation but saw the return of Jesus in the same light that the Bible depicts John the Baptist as Elijah come again--the return of the same light in a different lamp.[†] In this respect Williams gives the genealogy of the return of Jesus showing that he will be descended from the King of Denmark which is the genealogy of Leland Jensen.[‡] Thus the same light which was crucified almost 2000 years ago on Calvary Cross has returned in Ezekiel's Temple in Montana in the lamp of Dr. Leland Jensen.

This is not a matter of distorting the facts on my part like your article has it--these facts form the core of Morrisite belief of which I have all the documentation of the original letters that are over 100 years old copied from the archives in Utah State University in Logan, Utah and from leather bound manuscripts which are the safely guarded and precious family heirlooms of the Morrisite descendants here in Deer Lodge.

The fact that the Morrisites waited for Jesus on August 9th for over 100 years is a plain matter of history, something that I did not create not distort to fit this Cause. After my interview with Mr. Stromnes, he knew this to be the case for he specifically asked me of my documentation and proofs which I informed him of completely. Yet he persisted in writing his article in the manner that he had already formulated before being appraised of the facts and then after the clear presentation of the material still wrote his own concepts in spite of the facts!

You misleadingly stated in your article that:

> "When sect members made a presentation to the town council, several council members were alarmed by apparent errors in the group's research on the Morrisite faith. 'We had one alderman who said, "Holy Cow, if they are right, I've been teaching the kids all wrong." What they are doing is distorting the dates to fit their cause,' the mayor said."

At the council meeting, which I attended in person and which I have a word by word tape recording of (for legal documentation) the issue which alarmed several council members was when Victor Woods told the council that:

> "The Native American Indians who had occupied the valley had considered the land to be sacred. It was considered a truce area and no battles were fought within the valley, only in the canyons leading to the area."[§]

---

[*] George Williams, (August 9, 1865). "Letter to My Dear Saint James and John," Great Salt Lake.
[†] Matthew 11:14; John 1:21; Luke 1:17.
[‡] George Williams, (April 6, 1873). "Letter to Brother Rasmusson," Lincolnshire, England, pp. 2-4.
[§] *Silver State Post*, January 10th, 1991, "Morrisite Pioneer Day Planned," p. 5.

ttlement of Beaver
three in width, and
a whole, is delight.
hat invites to labor.
During the summer
ig rushes along as a
mountains, but still
v. The material of
here is no tenacious
ttler cannot, with a

oll, Muscleshell, and
towns and villages

lroad station estab.
master and general
icts a saloon.
overnment saw mill

ie new town of Car-
 king citizens of the
rthwest of Muscle-

of its settlement to
of physical change.
:ndive, of the ante-
lleys is watered and
finest stock ranges
the vegetation loses
ilands settles down
ation, for it grows
e reason why it has
une the grass looks
:, cured as it grows
plains are generally
ition to the natural
iman converts these
lerness stood, beau-

o the natural boun-
region. The Deer
e county. The Big
of the finest graz-
, and hundreds of
of the Blackfoot,
: fine, bold, mount-
waters flow some
.d Bitter Root val-

leys. Deer Lodge valley spreads out from five to ten miles wide, between the Rocky and Deer Lodge ranges for a distance of sixty miles. Besides these a number of lateral valleys open into it, bordering the numerous and beautiful streams which enter the main river from each side. Many fine farms are located in these valleys, while the foot hills and mountain sides are grazing lands. The mountains within the county boundaries possess all that gigantic beauty to be found on the Pacific slope, while natural eccentricities, such as hot springs, etc., make up a scene unexcelled in the entire west. The origin of the name is credited to the poetic imagery of the Indians. Captain Mills, himself an old settler, calls it an "old appellation," and states that it is derived from a large, sugarloaf mound, with a thermal spring on its summit. Situated near the center of the broad upper half of this valley, it is one of the most beautiful and interesting formations in the northwest, growing with the centuries, the waters building their throne slowly, imperceptibly, but steadily as the coral builds the ocean reefs, and in the coming years will attract many thousands to drink of its medicinal waters and find health and pleasure in the picturesque valley, mountain circled and coursed by crystal streams. The mound is over forty feet high. It stands in the midst of a perfectly level valley; and the hot springs on its summit, during the greater portion of the year, send up a heavy volume of vapor, rendering it a conspicuous object for from twenty to twenty-five miles in every direction. It bears, in the distance, a striking resemblance to an Indian lodge with the smoke ascending from it. Through all the traditions of the Indians the valley has been famous for the plenitude and fatness of the white-tailed deer that graze upon its ever-nutritious and almost ever-green grasses; where the snow scarcely ever falls, and, falling, quickly disappears. And so the aborigines, true to these facts, and weaving with them a happy fancy, named it after that it most resembled; and we have it that the Snake hunting parties, approaching the crests of the surrounding mountains, before the pale-face came to the land, would try the fleetness of their steeds to see who would first catch sight of and hail the point of rendezvous—*It Soo-ke en Car-ne*—the lodge of the white-tailed deer. The early coming French, appreciating the poetry of the designation, adopted it literally, and among them it was known as *La loge du chevreuil*. But the laconic, matter-of-fact Yankee pioneer came this way, and without remorse boiled down all its traditions and beauty and poesy into the practical appellation Deer Lodge, by which is now known the valley, the river, the county and town. In 1861-2 the location of Deer Lodge City was called Spanish Fork, in compliment to Thomas Lavatta, Joseph Hill, Alejo Barasta, and other Spaniards then located there.*

The leading quartz mines of Deer Lodge county (the county is also somewhat noted for its placer mines) are the Cable, Algonquin, Hope, Granite Mountain and Princeton. The first of them, the Cable, has produced some of the richest gold rock known, and it has already added several millions of dollars to the gold wealth of the world. As an instance of the wonderful richness of its ores it might be stated that a twenty-one pound block of ore taken from the mine recently and now on exhibition at the New Orleans exposition contained about $4,000 in gold. For several years past the Phillipsburg silver mines—principal among which are the Algonquin, Speckled Trout, Hope, Comanche, Granite Mountain, Pyrenees, and other properties—have been rolling out a steady stream of wealth. The output of the Granite Mountain alone is now some $300,000 per year. The Hope Company is making a good record for itself and is paying regular dividends. They aggregate to date about 170,000, the last being November 1, 1884. Its output the past year has been about $100,000. All the properties mentioned are being worked successfully and with large profit to the owners. Silver lodes also abound in Moosecreek district, and valuable gold-bearing lodes in Highland, Snowshoe, McClellan and Bear gulches. In fact, Deer Lodge county is seamed with gold and silver veins and adds to these deposits of coal, iron, lead and copper. It was in this county the first discovery of placer gold in Montana was made, and these mines have to date yielded a good many millions of dollars in gold nuggets. The nine mines worked in Deer Lodge in 1881, produced 850,000 in gold and silver. The census returns of 1880, made prior to the setting off of Silver Bow, placed the value of gold at $341,930, and that of silver at 2,065,980. In 1882, the value of the gold and silver product was about $720,000. Increased largely in 1883 and 1884.

* Vide personal history and reminiscences of Choteau county, review of Choteau's enterprise and operations of the Spanish.)

In fact it was not several members but only the one alderman who used to be a history teacher who was alarmed. He announced to the whole group, after Victor spoke, that in the book he read Deer Lodge was never a valley of truce or sacred ground but was instead a battle field were many wars took place. As his "red herring" remark was addressed to me I was going to respond, but instead Dorene Courchene (who is also quoted in your article), who has done extensive research in to the history of the valley rebuked him for me, stating that we were absolutely right and he was coming way out from left field. She said that Deer Lodge is famous as being a valley of truce and holy ground for the Indians just like Victor had said. Dorene then said that she couldn't imagine what book he had ever read that misinformation out of. He responded by not being able to recall the title. After our group was finished speaking and answering questions, later in the council meeting, as a matter of public record, the alderman who was quite embarrassed and humiliated about being wrong stated:

"I've been teaching the kids all wrong."

He was. Do your own research and you will find that he is wrong--just like Dorene Courchene told him. Deer Lodge has always been a valley of truce, the Happy Hunting Ground in the Sky--Montana is the Sky State: the BIG SKY! Yet Stromnes quoted this guy way, way out of context in a feeble attempt to discredit Baha'is. He has failed.

When I told Stromnes that the Baha'is and the Morrisites were not the first to understand that Deer Lodge was holy ground, but that for over 6000 years the Native American's held Deer Lodge as their sacred spot--he couldn't have cared less. Well I can think of over 40,000 people who would be very interested in this! The people who live throughout the entire valley (from Butte to Garrison) and the people who are Morrisite descendants! Like I've been saying you people have out-scooped yourselves.

What happened next was that Victor had invited the entire council to a free lecture open to the public on what we were teaching, which I have a video tape of to show what was said. Likewise, long before we had ever gone to the council I had given another talk at the local Reorganized Latter Day Saint Church (RLDS) for a group of Morrisite descendants which was also taped stating our research clearly.

The reason for going to the council was never to try "to gain credibility at the expense of the Deer Lodge city council" as Dorene Courchene wrongly imagined. This Cause already has credibility based on the facts, which your paper has misrepresented.

In the first place the Baha'is Under the Provisions of the Covenant didn't make up Morrisite Pioneer Day for August 9th. For over 100 years the Morrisites had already chosen August 9th themselves as the day that Jesus would come to Deer Lodge at his second advent. The reason we wanted to have it put on the official city calendar is that although 2/3rds of the Deer Lodge Valley is descended from the Morrisites yet they are very uninformed about their own history. Even the local history teacher is an ignoramus thinking that Deer Lodge was a war zone instead of Holy Ground. Because of ignorance, prejudice, thoughtlessness and plain apathy, we thought that a Morrisite Pioneer Day should be put on the calendar for the sole reason of educating the people on their own history. The Council agreed on that point.

Morrisite Pioneer Day planned

A Morrisite Pioneer Day commemorating the original homesteading pioneers of the Deer Lodge Valley is being planned for August 9.

Mayor Labbe told the planning committee, "I think it is great when people are interested in their heritage, and willing to promote it in their community."

Historically, before the Morrisites journeyed to the Deer Lodge Valley in 1863, the Native American Indians who had occupied the valley had considered the land to be sacred. It was considered a truce area and no battles were fought within the Valley, only in the canyons leading to the area.

At that time, a 40 foot high thermal spring emitting a large column of vapor created a great salt pool that attracted large herds of deer to the valley. For this reason, the Indians named the valley "Lodge of the White Tailed Deer." It was later renamed Deer Lodge.

Like the Native Americans, the Morrisites were convinced that the Deer Lodge Valley was a land of destiny and hope. The dream that Deer Lodge would fulfill their vision prompted the Morrisite journey from Northern Utah to the Deer Lodge Valley in April of 1863. Upon seeing the grasses of the valley waving as the waves of the sea and a great plume of steam rising in the western end they exclaimed "We have entered paradise!"

Such was the beginning of the settlement of the Deer Lodge Valley by the men, women and children known as the Morrisites. Not unlike the original settlers of the British colonies two hundred years earlier, they came as seekers of freedom: freedom to live as they chose to live, freedom to believe in what their hearts and minds told them was true, and freedom to worship as they chose to worship.

The Morrisites acquired the name from their first leader, Joseph Morris, a Mormon reformer. In 1862, the prophet of the Morrisites, George Williams had a vision as he rode his horse in the Salt Lake Valley of Utah. As a result of the vision, Williams soon began instructing the dispersed Morrisites to pioneer the Deer Lodge Valley which lies due north of the Salt Lake Valley. Many of the Morrisites followed the instructions of Williams, thus beginning their early settlement in the Deer Lodge Valley.

Among the teachings which the Morrisites received from Williams was the advent of the second coming of Jesus in Deer Lodge.

The Morrisites built a church, "The Lord's House" six miles south of Deer Lodge. Construction was begun in 1877 and the church was dedicated on August 9, 1879. They met there weekly until they officially disbanded in 1969. For over one hundred years, August 9 was the day that the Morrisites celebrated their vision, commemorating the promise they felt the land held for them.

Today, an estimated two-thirds of the Valley's population are believed to be descendants of these pioneers.

For more information on the history and significance of Morrisite Pioneer Day, the public is invited to attend a free lecture at the C.P.C. on Thursday, January 10 from 6:30 - 7:30 p.m.◊

MORRISITE COMMEMORATION DAY PLANNING COMMITTEE - (front) Kay Woods, Esther Hall, Neal Chase, (back) Victor Woods, Dawn Chase and Bob Jaffe.◊

233

booties for sled dogs. See page 9.

50¢ Single Copy (Less By Mail Subscription)

THE SILVER STATE POST

103rd Year – No. 35   DEER LODGE, POWELL COUNTY, MONTANA 59722   Thursday, January 10, 1991

City Council reviews vandalism, cold weather pro

The Morrisite Pioneer Day in 1863 (see related story). The Deer Lodge planning committee, Victor Woods said," The Deer Lodge Woods, Esther Hall, Neal and Valley is unique in that it is the Dawn Chase appeared before the only area in the entire world that City Council to explain their was populated for the purpose of desire to have August 9 desig- preparing the site for the second nated as a commemorative day. coming of Jesus. For over 100

They explained some of the years August 9 was the day the history relating to the home- people would celebrate the ful- steading of the Deer Lodge Val- fillment of the vision." ley by the Morrisites beginning It is the committee's wish to

raise the awareness of the com- munity to the rich heritage they have. An estimated two-thirds of the population in the Deer Lodge Valley, from Butte to Garrison, are decendants of the Morrisite pioneers.

Plans for the commemorative day call for an informal celebra- tion including a community picnic.

The Council encouraged the committee to proceed with their plans, and the Mayor agreed to sign a proclamation to that effect whenever the committee wished.

* * * *

Alderman Beck presented pic- tures of vandalism at the upper east softball field in which eleven steel posts and 100 feet of cyclone fence were run over by a

vehicle. All of the post will need to be replaced and set in new concrete. Cost of repairs will be $800. The City's insur- ance deductible is $1,000. He noted that repairing the extensive damage will greatly cut into the Parks and Recreation budget for this year eliminating some of the other projects planned.

* * * *

Alderman Beck he will not be reelection from h said, "I feel there le who are quali terested in servi Council. An intention, at thi seek reelection v opportunity for c

* *

A DREAM COME TRUE! - Pride and

234

Ezekiel's Temple in Montana

Baha'i faction awaits April Armageddon, new world in Deer Lodge, 'Jesus' in prison

By Duncan Adams
Standard Staff Writer

Behold, they proclaim, Armageddon is at hand, Jesus has returned and lives in Missoula, where he works as a chiropractor, and Deer Lodge is the New Jerusalem.

So insists a local faction of the Baha'i faith, a small splinter group of Baha'is who believe a nuclear holocaust and other catastrophes beginning in April will kill two-thirds of the world's population.

They warn that George Bush and Saddam Hussein have unwittingly unleashed the "four winds of destruction" described in the Bible's Book of Revelation.

Are they "a bunch of weirdos" as the mayor of Deer Lodge suggests? Or do they have their fingers on the throbbing pulse of an apocalyptic truth?

"Kingdom and catastrophe — that's our message," said Neal Chase, 25, an outspoken member of the group.

Chase and his co-believers plan to survive, holed-up in public or private fallout shelters, from which they will emerge to help usher in a New World Order.

"We don't want to just save ourselves. We want to save everybody," Chase said. "This country is going to be basically decapitated, with the major cities gone."

Four members of the group, Neal and Dawn Chase and Victor and Kay Woods, live in Deer Lodge in a timeworn, nondescript apartment building dubbed "the White House." Unemployed, they live on the edge of town, and their marginal presence there has made more than a few of the city's 3,378 people edgy.

Numbered among them is Mayor R.F. Labbe.

"I've had it up to here with these people," said Labbe, gesturing to his forehead.

"That outfit is a bunch of weirdos. They're a cult and that's what they are, and people have to realize that," he said.

Neal Chase disagrees.

"We are not a cult," he said.

Deer Lodge Police Chief Bill

Wood was asked whether he's had any problems with Chase and company.

"No. None. I've been trying to keep on top of what's going on," Wood replied, noting he was the only person attending one of the group's recent public meetings.

But Wood added there is a chance the group, which claims 25 members in Deer Lodge, 50 in Missoula, and more elsewhere, will increase in number.

"I don't think it's going to end tomorrow. I think it's going to grow here," Wood said.

FORECASTING A NUCLEAR catastrophe in April are, from left, Neal Chase, Dawn Chase, Victor Woods, Esther Hall and Glenn Goldman. The group is shown, in

Staff photo by Duncan Adams

front of the old Montana State Prison's East Gate. Members claim the site is Ezekiel's Temple. Members say two-thirds of the world's population will be killed.

The "White House" is a short walk from the old Montana State Prison, which the group claims to be Ezekiel's Temple of biblical prophecy — the place where Jesus II will be known.

Jesus II, according to Chase and company, is Leland Jensen, 76, of Missoula, who the group argues was framed by fellow chiropractors who were jealous of Jensen's skill as a naturopathic doctor.

"The town knew it was a scam," said Dawn Chase, 24.

"The return of Jesus will be scorned and rejected by the majority because of the great sex scandal and the rumors spread about (Jensen)," wrote Kay Woods.

Much of the group's prophecy hinges upon their notation that Jensen's "first full day" in the old prison was Aug. 9, 1969.

According to state records, Jensen was sentenced in October 1988 to 20 years in prison.

Records show he entered prison on Aug. 8, 1969, and was paroled on June 1, 1973.

Aug. 9 was a significant day for the Morrisites, a religious faction led by Joseph Morris that split from the Mormon faith and populated the Deer Lodge Valley in the 1860s.

"The Morrisites were told by (George) Williams to wait for Jesus to come to them on Aug. 9. Thus they waited every Aug. 9 for over 100 years for Jesus to come ... The last time they waited was Aug. 9, 1969," the group writes.

"The Baha'i Faith and the Morrisite Faith are two separate and independent religions, just like Judaism and Christianity are separate and independent religions. Yet like

They warn that George Bush and Saddam Hussein have unwittingly unleashed the 'four winds of destruction' described in the Bible's Book of Revelation

Christianity, which is the fulfillment of Judaism, the Baha'i Faith is the fulfillment of the Morrisite religion," writes Chase in his book, "Ezekiel's Temple in Montana."

According to writings of Jensen's quoted in Chase's book, Jensen claims his role as Jesus the High Priest became slowly and painfully clear soon after he was jailed in the old prison — a stone building with seven towers — "the seven eyes" of prophecy, according to Chase.

Jensen writes that he was visited by an angel, that he realized the "dirty garment" was reminiscent of Zechariah's message:

"Now Joshua was clothed with filthy garments, and stood before the angel."

After noting additional "proofs" of his identity, Jensen wrote: "At that point all the evidence was in. There was nothing more. Indeed I was the promised return of Jesus. Not Jesus the Messiah, a Manifestation, but Jesus the High Priest

J esus II, according to Chase and company, is Leland Jensen, 76, of Missoula, who the group argues was framed by fellow chiropractors who were jealous of Jensen's skill as a naturopathic doctor

R.F. LABBE

the mention of Jensen's name. He said his son, Allan, had seen Jensen at work in Missoula when Allan was a student at the University of Montana.

Neal and Dawn Chase and Victor Woods moved to Deer Lodge from Madison, Wis. Another member, Glenn Goldman, is originally from New York. Goldman moved to Missoula some 18 months ago, he said, after meeting Jensen at a "Rainbow Gathering" in Texas.

Although the group says they have no clergy, Neal Chase projects a priestly presence, of sorts. He quotes scripture, speaks in a rapid-fire, staccato rush, and his dark, luminous eyes blaze with a passionate belief in his cause. He has a habit of ending monologues with the question, "You see?"

"As this message goes out, there will be 144,000 spiritual and intellectual greats who will accept the prophecy and survive," Chase explained.

"If we don't have the 144,000 together by April," said Chase, shrugging, the catastrophes may be delayed, he said.

"Noah warned three times — don't miss the boat," wrote Kay Woods.

Meanwhile, Labbe seems more worried about the city's budget than about Armageddon or missing the boat. He said his son jokingly requested he hold a spot for him in a local fallout shelter.

"He said, 'Be sure to make me a reservation, and put a couple of pots of beans on, because we'll be up,'" said Labbe, grinning.

236

When we called up Mayor Labbe on the phone, he told us that all we had to do to proclaim August 9th as Morrisite Pioneer Day was to have him come over to our house, sign the proclamation, shake our hand and get our pictures in the paper. We said that was terrific but that we would rather go before the town council first (although we didn't have to) to inform them all of our idea, which at the end of the council meeting everyone was all for. We stated clearly and repeatedly that this was a religious issue and a religious day for the Morrisites who were very religious people and settled the valley for religious reasons. We figured that since the pilgrims came to America for the same religious reasons that the Morrisites came to the Valley and we celebrate Thanksgiving as a national holiday there should be a city holiday for the Morrisites. This was all made very clear.

The article in the Silver State Post even quotes Victor Woods directly documenting what was said at the council meeting:

> "Woods said: "The Deer Lodge Valley is unique in that it is the only area in the world that was populated for the purpose of preparing the site for the second coming of Jesus. For over 100 years August 9th was the day the people would celebrate the fulfillment of the vision."[*]

How did the council respond to these words which clearly state that the religious theme is the return of Jesus in Deer Lodge on August 9th?

> "It is the committee's wish to raise the awareness of the community to the rich heritage they have...The Council encouraged the committee to proceed with their plans, and the Mayor agreed to-sign a proclamation to that effect whenever the committee wished."[†]

What happened was that after the article came out in the paper a few Morrisite descendants who had defected from the Morrisite faith to join the RLDS church and happen to be the clergy in that church called up and were about as upset as the Pharisees and Sadducees were against Jesus on his first coming. They are all burnt up over the success and acclaim that the Morrisite religion and Ezekiel's Temple in Montana has been having among the people in the local area, whereas their own active membership has dwindled to about ten people. This group of Morrisite defectors prompted by one or two clergy who have this negative influence on the rest wants to suppress this whole thing. They want a Morrisite Cover-Up!

So we have one or two cranks trying to be like rotten apples and spoil the whole bunch. However they certainly do not constitute anywhere near the majority population of the Valley who are interested and who are Morrisites by blood. Many more people and many other Morrisite descendants that we have spoken with are very interested in their heritage and preserving their own history. These are the ones who aren't clergy! Remember it was the clergy who were first to turn against Jesus on his first coming.

---

[*] *Silver State Post*, Front Page, January 10th, 1991.
[†] *Silver State Post*, Front Page, January 10th, 1991.

For the most part the average citizen of Deer Lodge is open minded to new ideas--as the survey we took indicates that about 74 percent of the population is interested in the Morrisites and believes that this history should be brought to light.

At first the clergy at the Reorganized Church sponsored me and the Morrisite information and they allowed me to give a free lecture to the public and their entire congregation in their annex which is about three times as big as the church itself. The whole town was notified and all the stores on Main Street put up signs advertising the event. The lecture was video-taped and should be shown on public access cable TV.

The theme of the lecture was that all the Morrisite prophecy has been fulfilled and that the Morrisite descendants are the greatest people in the world! The lecture was very successful and everyone learned something new and was able to take pride in their own heritage. Then the big wigs in the Reorganized church (RLDS) came down from up north and some came out from Wyoming and started poisoning the minds of their congregation. What they are most upset about is that this is the year that their leaders are constructing the first RLDS temple ever built in Independence Missouri--and they want this to be the promised place. However their temple is shaped like a conch-shell pointing into the air whereas the prophesied Temple of the Lord depicted in the book of Ezekiel is to be a prison with 7 towers. Their temple doesn't have seven towers it only has one pinnacle like a giant sea snail. Likewise the Mormons in Salt-Lake have a temple that they want to be the one. It also is not a prison and only has six towers instead of seven. Brigham Young screwed it all up when he made them build it a tower short! The true Temple is Ezekiel's Temple in Montana which George William prophesied of and saw Jesus the High Priest returning to. The Morrisites were right!

Also the New Jerusalem is to be a perfect cube. Deer Lodge was platted as a perfect 640 acre square mile and you have to drive a mile high in the Mountains to get there making it a mile high, a mile wide and a mile long-- a perfect cube just like the Bible says it will be.[*]

In the face of these facts and the fulfillment of the Morrisite and Bible prophecy, the Reorganized Church is all torn up not knowing whether to support the Morrisites which they are blood or their church which they defected to which denounces their own heritage. It's too bad that people need to be so easily influenced by their clergy.

In light of these "rotten apples" trying to spoil the whole bunch, Victor called up the Mayor on the phone and we both went to see he him. Previous to the council meeting he had said we would only have 5 minutes to talk. In his office the other week we spoke for quite some time and straightened out the situation.

However there is still one loose cannon running around town and that is the retired history teacher/alderman who Courchene told off at the Council meeting who is still trying to insist that I am "distorting the dates [of the Morrisites] to fit this cause."

After being humiliated at the first Council meeting this guy is going around town behind my back blatantly lying about the research I have done. First of all he has never come to me nor

_____

[*] Revelation 21:15.

238

confronted me directly on any of this. I have a public standing invitation with everyone I know to discuss any questions that they have regarding this research. Also I give public talks and invite creative comments and new information.

At the council meeting this teacher with the rest of the members were all invited to a talk given at the Central Park Center in Deer Lodge that Thursday night, January 10th. As I found out later from other people who attended the meeting, this history teacher had come before it started and was whispering with the Chief of Police out in the hallway before the talk. My wife noticed him and invited him in but he ran away saying that he was only there for a basket ball game. Yet there was no basket ball game there that night!

It is no concern of mine that he declared Deer Lodge as a war zone before all the council and embarrassed himself. It is also not my problem that he has been "teaching the kids all wrong" which is his own admission. However his errors (or whatever) does not give him the right to slander me and back-bite me around town as "distorting the dates." As a historian, researcher and scholar I am more than happy to discuss any of these points with anyone who is interested and certainly with another teacher and student of history. I have an open standing invitation to anyone and everyone. The door is wide open. I suggest people pass through it before it quickly closes.

However I do not support back-biting and slander and false rumors designed to murder another's character behind his back. As demonstrated above these dates are impeccable and irrefutable. Out of all the points of history, recording the date when the event happened has to be the easiest thing of all. And as stated above all the dates are verified in accurate, credible and authoritative sources from the news papers, history texts and Anderson's book on the Morrisites.

This history teacher/alderman is all wet!

Likewise Mr. Anderson has no business at all to try and discredit this in-depth research into the prophecy and religious beliefs of the Morrisites as unscholarly or inaccurate. The research we have done far surpasses the mere surface analysis that Anderson did of the Morrisites as a social movement. Anderson's specialty is limited to Sociology and not history. Furthermore he is prejudiced against the subject of my book and the scientific inquiry we are investigating in the first place.

Mr. Anderson's main focus and emphasis is his academic carrier is the study of "prophecy failure."[*] Thus from the very definition of his academic bent, this research of the Morrisite prophecy and its fulfillment is against his grain. To Anderson even the general concept of the validity of prophecy fulfillment is loathsome and despicable to him as he feels it is a direct attack on his personal beliefs especially in the arena of the Morrisites. There is a slight possibility that he can overcome his prejudice and investigate this with an open mind. However, he finds Ezekiel's Temple in Montana particularly disturbing because he does not see it as a book that proves the Morrisites were right but as a book which proves that Anderson is all wrong.

---

[*] Anderson, p. 265: ABOUT THE AUTHOR.

The reason I say that he therefore has no business at all to try and discredit this work, based on his own prejudice, with no facts to back up his accusations at all, is because he got the same treatment from the Mormons when he wrote his book!

The Mormons who follow Brigham Young are the Morrisite killers and like Anderson they are prejudiced against the Morrisites. When Anderson first submitted his book on the Morrisites to the publishers at *Dialogue Magazine* they stamped REJECT-REJECT-REJECT-REJECT-REJECT-REJECT-REJECT all over the evaluation form and turned him down cold. What was the reason that they rejected Anderson's manuscript on the Morrisites? Dialogue consultant Gordon C. Thomasson declared that it was because Anderson's book:

> "Certainly isn't history."[*]

He went on to say that it was definitely not suitable for a Mormon audience. He wrote:

> "My comments are found on the attached 4 pages of single spaced type. I hope that this is the last time I see this manuscript. Every time I read it and try to find some redeeming/social value I get angrier. I specifically request that my unexpurgated comments be sent to the authors. FEEL FREE TO ATTACH MY NAME. I am really sick of this thing."[†]

> "The authors are lucky I didn't give them an objective evaluation, I'm afraid my <u>symbolic</u> language would embarrass them."[‡]

Thomasson goes on to say in his four page commentary that Anderson and his co-author use "<u>pure bs to build their case</u>."[§] And that it is "typical of old anti-Mormon writing" which Thomasson states:

> "Is unfortunately typical of these writers [Anderson's] whole approach. GARBAGE!"[**]

Anderson responded by saying that it was a good thing that Sheriff Burton led the Morrisite militia and not Thomasson, otherwise there wouldn't have been a Morrisite left alive. The Mormons are all in a huff because Brigham Young really did engineer the assignation of Joseph Morris and they don't want it to be exposed by Anderson or anyone else. *The San Francisco Chronicle* reports the Morrisite slaughter and the slaying of Joseph Morris as the cruelest and most brutal religious killing in the history of the United States. And it was done by Brigham Young and his devoted Mormon fanatics!

My point is simply that it is easy to call names. Like Thomasson, who calls names without any concrete proofs, Anderson has no proof to back up his charges against me. Like Thomasson, who

---

[*] MCLU, 1:4.
[†] MCLU, 1:4.
[‡] MCLU, 1:4.
[§] MCLU, 1:4, p. 2.
[**] MCLU, 1:4, p. 3.

has an alternative reason to hate Anderson's book on the Morrisites, Anderson has reasons of his own. Worse yet is where does he get off as the pot calling the kettle black? He hasn't contacted me personally, although after I gave him a copy of the manuscript I told him that if he had anything to say or any comments he could call any time. Anderson is just as prejudiced against prophecy fulfillment (being that he specialized in prophecy failure) as the Morrisite killers (the Mormons) are prejudiced against the Morrisites. Nothing in my book distorts the dates! Nothing in my book uses misinformation! Nothing in my book misquotes from Anderson's book or the source material preserved in Logan, Utah which he donated to Utah State University. Anderson is prejudiced and bigoted today like the Mormons were prejudiced and bigoted against him, plain and simple.

Even worse than Anderson is Stromnes who is not only prejudiced and bigoted in his own right, but has the power of the press to prejudice and mislead many other people who read his articles in your news paper.

Stromnes can't even report the happenings of a town council meeting straight, let alone cover a big story like the one I gave him, without distorting it into a cult smear. The proof is in the pudding. Stromnes inaccurately reported the Mayor's role in all this and misrepresented the Council's decisions. Stromnes states that the Mayor proclaimed Morrisite day and then the Council retracted the proclamation and has now passed an official policy against similar proclamations. This is all false. The Mayor never proclaimed the day because the proclamation day was set for August of 1991 which was the verdict at the first council meeting. Second, the council never passed a policy prohibiting similar proclamations. This is a lie.

Why do I bring this up? Because it shows Stromnes to be what he is--an inaccurate reporter. If he can't (or won't) even get the simple facts of a Council meetings proclamation straight how can we expect him to write up this story which I gave him straight. Bad journalism.

When Stromnes came over to my home I was very straight with him. I told him that if he were reporting 2000 years ago how easy would it be for him to write that several dirty fishermen who can't read or write support the local yocal Jesus of Nazareth born in the bucolic town of Bethlehem...etc, etc. And that: "The" Jesus "sect called" Christians "is not associated with the Established" Jewish "faith," a world-wide religion which has its...headquarters in" Jerusalem. Jesus' "followers believe that the world-wide" Jewish "faith is in error," and that" Jesus fulfills prophecy as "a holy teacher foreordained to warn the world of the coming doom." Jesus was caught and killed for upturning tables in the Temple, disturbing the peace, and possession of a whip. Now he is dead. THE END.

Although this may be journalistically correct it misses the whole point. Stromnes not only missed the whole point but he distorted the facts to discredit the Baha'is. As a result of supporting him with a responsible position on your paper which he abuses, your paper has printed things which are completely not true.

Stromnes purposely twisted this entire thing into a Baha'i smear-trying to destroy the Baha'is by painting them out to be a cult--in order to sell more papers or make better news. Legally we are not a cult as Rob Balch, the faculty supervisor for the Baha'i club at the University in Missoula and an expert on cults, has testified to. Stromnes knows this very well which is why the article was entitled, "Sect Girds…" and not "Cult girds…". However, in order to destroy the Baha'is, Stromnes purposely ended his article by quoting a woman who is ignorant of the Baha'is, which she admits in the article ("I don't know what they want in Deer Lodge") by stating in her words, that as far as she is concerned the Baha'is are just a "cult more than anything else." Stromnes knows that this isn't true but purposely ends his article with these words to mislead the public and do harm to this Cause. Yet your paper supported his article which smears the Baha'is and does not educate the public to what Baha'i really is. This is blameworthy.

You have made a mistake by cheating yourselves out of the real story! "End of the world cult" is an old idea and a boring theme. The correct version is certainly much more provocative, more educational, and bears directly on the people of Montana and has a lasting personal impact of all the citizens of the Deer Lodge Valley.

The true story and scoop, which I handed to Mr. Stromnes on a platter like a fine gourmet meal fit for a king, is the greatest story ever told! It is even greater than the story of Jesus' first coming because today on his second coming he is to be victorious within his lifetime, as the whole world recognizes his station as the authoritative establisher of the Kingdom of God on Earth.

Stromnes asked me specifically if the Kingdom of God was some mystic realm of being or if it was something he could touch and live in which would have direct impact on people's everyday lives. I told him the straight dope that the Kingdom of God was in fact the government of God ruling from the throne of David here on earth like it says in the Bible (Isaiah 9:6-7). And unlike today where the Beast governments of America, Russia, France and England make war and take things by force if it will benefit their own gain, the Kingdom of God will be a spiritual government where the people truly live by just principles and the nations of the world will be in harmony and peace. Once this country had a civil war. Now the states are united in one union.

So in this way all the countries of the world are states of the global union. After this war which is escalating in Iraq are finally resolved (with the loss of 2/3rds the population, 1/3rd in one hour) all nations will be at peace in the one global world civilization of the Kingdom of God on earth which is the World Order of Baha'u'llah. This is what I told Stromnes. And this is the true story that you missed.

Today because of the Bush/Hussein debacle the four winds of destruction that the four angels are holding back at the river Euphrates have been released.[*] The Euphrates flows through Iraq. This has been the result of Bush who refused to negotiate in any way with Saddam Hussein. Bush told Baker to go see Hussein but not to give one inch. But to go there and tell his final warning. This type of move is not a negotiation it is a threat. It is not diplomatic. It is deplorable!

On the other hand Baha'u'llah prescribes a universal simultaneous disarmament of all the nations with a setting up of an international police to enforce the decisions of a United Nations Council which will then be empowered to solve the difficult problems of the world such as defining boundaries and nations rights.

---

[*] Revelation 9:14.

242

The nuclear power shouldn't be in the hands of any one nation only the Council of United Nations. However countries like the US refuse to give up this power because with it they can be the big guy on the block and bully the other nations into doing what benefits themselves. This is the old World Order of Caesar and Napoleon that Bush is supporting. It is not a new World Order. Although Baha'u'llah prescribes that if a nation should invade another nation then it is the responsibility of all the nations of the world to rise to the defense of the invaded country--Bush has taken this out of context.

Baha'u'llah prescribes this only after the simultaneous disarmament of all the other nations, not while one nation still runs the whole show! Thus as the nations of the world must simultaneously disarm the power and authority is then to be turned over to the Council of Nations. If a nation then violates the Council then the rest of them bring that nation before the Council for Judgement. If that nation refuses to come then the international police forces them to comply even to the point of wiping out that nation.

In the 15th chapter of first Corinthians it states that the Son will return to establish his Father's Kingdom. Baha'u'llah is Aramaic for the Glory of the Father. He fulfills the prophecy for the "Everlasting Father" seated "upon David's throne" (Is. 9:6-7) as Baha'u'llah is a direct male-sperm descendant of King David through the royal throne-line preserved through Solomon and the exilarchs (exiled monarchs of David). Therefore the new World Order of Baha'u'llah is the Kingdom of the Father which Jesus is to establish.

The prophecy shows the return of Jesus in Ezekiel's Temple in Montana establishing his Father's (Baha'u'llah's) Kingdom. It states clearly that he (Jesus) will put all rule and authority under his feet until he turn the Kingdom over to his Father and then he himself (Jesus) will become "subjected unto it" (1 Cor. 15:24-28).

From this time forward we have the return of Jesus in Deer Lodge Montana who fulfills both the Bible and Morrisite prophecy. In order to be the one he must wear the "dirty jacket" and be in prison having the "Stone with Seven Eyes" before him. Herein lies the true story.

Stromnes has certainly misrepresented the Baha'is and this Cause in his article, but his corruption and misrepresentation pales in comparison to the corruption that got the return of Jesus framed up on a crime he didn't commit!

The problem with Stromnes is that he doesn't know the difference between the good guys and the bad guys. In the case of Jesus going to prison on a crime he is innocent of recompounds and exposes the corruption of the justice system in the world today. The problem is: where are the gutsy reporters like a Woodward and a Burnstein who are willing to write the truth at the risk of going to jail rather than reveal their sources to expose the corruption! Even if the corruption reaches to the highest levels! They weren't afraid! They exposed a President and an entire corrupt administration, while that administration was operating! Even more important was that they had the courage and strength to investigate and pursue their story even against the odds and that's what makes a real hero. The real hero is the underdog who starts out with nothing and then rises to the top of the ladder with success and victory. This is who the people root for. This is who the people congratulate.

Today we have a Morrisite cover-up and a Baha'i Gate on our hands! The State of Montana was the guilty party in 1969 on August 9th when the return of Jesus got sent to prison on the "dirty jacket" charge: a frame up and bum rap that he is in fact innocent of.

According to the Bible in Zechariah chapter three, Jesus the High Priest must be wearing the "dirty jacket" so we can recognize him through the fulfillment of prophecy:

> "And the Lord shewed me **Jesus the high priest** standing before the angel of the Lord: and Satan stood on his right hand to be his adversary. And the Lord said to Satan: The Lord rebuke thee, O Satan: and the Lord that chose Jerusalem rebuke thee: Is this not a brand plucked out of the fire?

> "And Jesus was clothed with filthy garments: and he stood before the face of the angel. Who answered, and said to them that stood before him, saying: Take away the filthy garments from him. And he said him: Behold I have taken away thy iniquity, and have clothed thee with a change of garments."[*]

Therefore Jesus must wear the "dirty jacket" to be Jesus. Yet this is to be removed at the appointed time when the people see it was a frame up--Jesus is innocent of the crime he never committed. This "clean garment" that Jesus then receives is not a pardon but a full reversal! Showing total innocence. Then it is the State of Montana who must take the blame along with those who conspired within the system to manipulate the situation in order to accomplish their scheme.

At least since this was in a past administration it won't have to be as embarrassing to the State as if it were exposed in a recent scam of this nature and a current cover-up. The worst thing that the State of Montana could do at this point is try and continue to cover this up in its present administration. This would only carry over the corruption of the previous administration and would be very embarrassing today. Furthermore the people involved in the plot will not hold out at this point and time but will come forth and tell what really happened[†] and how Jesus did get framed up on the "dirty jacket" charge. They know Leland is innocent of the thing they perpetrated against him and now it is clear through the Morrisite and Bible prophecy being fulfilled that a much greater design was taking place then the people realized. And as our sure handle we have this for assurance: that God has never made false his promise to do good in any way. The victory must come and the victory has come!

George Williams prophesied that it would be the news of the Morrisites as the pioneers and forerunners for the return of Jesus in Deer Lodge which would finally bring about the return of Jesus receiving the "clean garment" and the complete removal of the "dirty jacket."[‡]

---

[*] Zechariah 3:1-4. Catholic Douay Version.
[†] This occurred several times on MCAT--live television--where the people came forward and confessed the truth.
[‡] George Williams, (April 6, 1873). "Letter to Brother Rasmusson," Lincolnshire, England, pp. 2-4.

Simultaneous to the discovery of the Morrisites with appearance of Comet Austin which is the "Sign of the Son of Man in Heaven" we have the Bush/Hussein debacle unleashing the four winds of destructions that have been held back by the four angels at the Euphrates river in Iraq!

What no one has ever reported before is that the pivot of Leland's fulfillment of the prophesies for the return of Jesus is based on the fact that he must be in prison as Jesus is prophesied to be in prison[*] and that he must be in prison on the "dirty jacket charge." Although the charge has been stated it has never been stated that in fact this is how he fulfills the prophecy and without the "dirty jacket" he could not fulfill the prophecy. Yet the Catch-22 is that he was framed up to wear the "dirty-jacket" in order to fulfill prophecy and still remain aloof from this thing at the same time. In fact this shows that it was the State of Montana who was at fault for permitting such a travesty of justice to occur.

Yet what the other chiropractors and the State of Montana had intended for evil God had intended for good. For in fact over 100 years before August 9th, 1969 the Morrisites had already settled in Deer Lodge in knowing anticipated this great event!

Also foreordained is the fact that the prison is not just a prison but is in fact the prophesied Temple of the Lord given in the book of Ezekiel which is to have seven towers. Thus in Zechariah chapter three the prison/Temple with seven watch-towers is described as a "Stone with Seven Eyes." It is a solid stone wall with seven watch-towers which are like eyes. Jesus must wear the "dirty jacket" and he must have the "Stone with Seven Eyes" before him which is in fact the seven watch-towered Temple of Ezekiel which the Old Montana State prison fulfills!

> "For behold the stone that I have laid before Jesus: upon one stone there are seven eyes."[†]

Now we see the validity and reality of this great happening right here in our home town! In his prophecy entitled "The High Priesthoods Return" referring to the appearance of the second coming of Jesus the High Priest in Deer Lodge, the prophet George Williams writes:

> "How well he is prisoned by a process unshown!
> The flaming sword still keeps this science unknown!"[‡]

Thus George Williams sees the return of Jesus the High Priest in Deer Lodge in Montana, in prison! There is only one prison is all of Montana! And there is only one prison in all of Deer Lodge at that time of the appearance at August 9th, 1969 which the Morrisites also anticipated that is the Old Montana State Prison! Williams sees the return of Jesus is prison but he cannot see--what God does not show him is--the craftily misconstrued and trumped up charges that got him there.

Nothing can be clearer. Though Stromnes misrepresented the Baha'is on purpose to destroy this message he only proves the point even more so--that Jesus himself was misrepresented in court

---

[*] Matthew 25:30.
[†] Zechariah 3:9, CDV.
[‡] Kramer: Leather bound journal of George Williams writings: "The High Priesthoods Return."

even worse than Stromnes misrepresented the recent happenings in Deer Lodge. This Baha'i Gate is laying there like an oyster concealing the rare jewel waiting to be snatched up for the scoop of the century!

The greatness, the pure greatness, is that Jesus has come to put all rule, power and authority under his feet because of the corruption in the system. Now we are at the climax of the great event! It is the absolute peak of the most glorious event in the 5000 century cycle of Baha'u'llah. That is the setting up of the second International Baha'i Council which is the embryonic Universal House of Justice destined to become the Council of Nations known as the Supreme Tribunal which will bring peace to the entire world after the catastrophes. This event ranks second only in comparison, to the time of the first three figures in the Baha'i Faith--the Bab, Baha'u'llah and 'Abdu'l-Baha. It is the greatest event since the ascension of 'Abdu'l-Baha and the inauguration of the Covenant of the Will and Testament of 'Abdu'l-Baha. And it will stand out and shine for the entire 5000 century cycle. And as the light is shined on the Covenant of Baha'u'llah and the Will and Testament of 'Abdu'l-Baha, all the world will know and understand what it means to be a Baha'i Under the Provisions of the Covenant!

In all his glory here is Jesus riding as the knight on the white horse, the Knight of Baha'u'llah,[*] establishing his Father's (Baha'u'llah's) Kingdom in the world! His garments are new, his garments are clean. His garment is white! As the Bible declares:

> "See how I have taken away your guilt from you [Jesus]" (Zechariah 3:4)...In one
> day I will wipe away the guilt of the land." (Zechariah 3:10)[†]

Thus the guilt of Jesus in verse 4 which is the "dirty jacket" is identical to the guilt in verse 10 which is the guilt of the land. The guilt of Jesus and the guilt of the land is the same guilt making Jesus and the land the same person. And that is his name: Leland. 'Le' is French for 'the' and 'land' is 'land'!

The prophecies are fulfilled by his prophesied name: Leland, by prophesied address: Ezekiel's Temple in Deer Lodge; by prophesied date: August 9th, 1969 and by prophesied mission: to put all rule and authority under his feet, the Son returned to establish his Father's (Baha'u'llah's) Kingdom.

The return of Jesus is the fulfillment of Christianity. The return of Jesus is the desire of Christians everywhere. The return of Jesus in Deer Lodge is the pulsing heart of the Morrisite Faith in God which has today been realized and fulfilled!

Yet, Stromnes purposely left out the fact that an estimated 2/3rds of the entire population of Deer Lodge Valley (from Butte to Garrison) are Morrisite descendants. Those who aren't actual Morrisite descendants married people who are which makes their kids Morrisites by blood. This is big news! Talk about local appeal! This is the very root of these people's heritage. It is the

---

[*] Leland is the last remaining Knight of Baha'u'llah. The rest are dead or Covenant-breaking.
[†] *The New English Bible.*

246

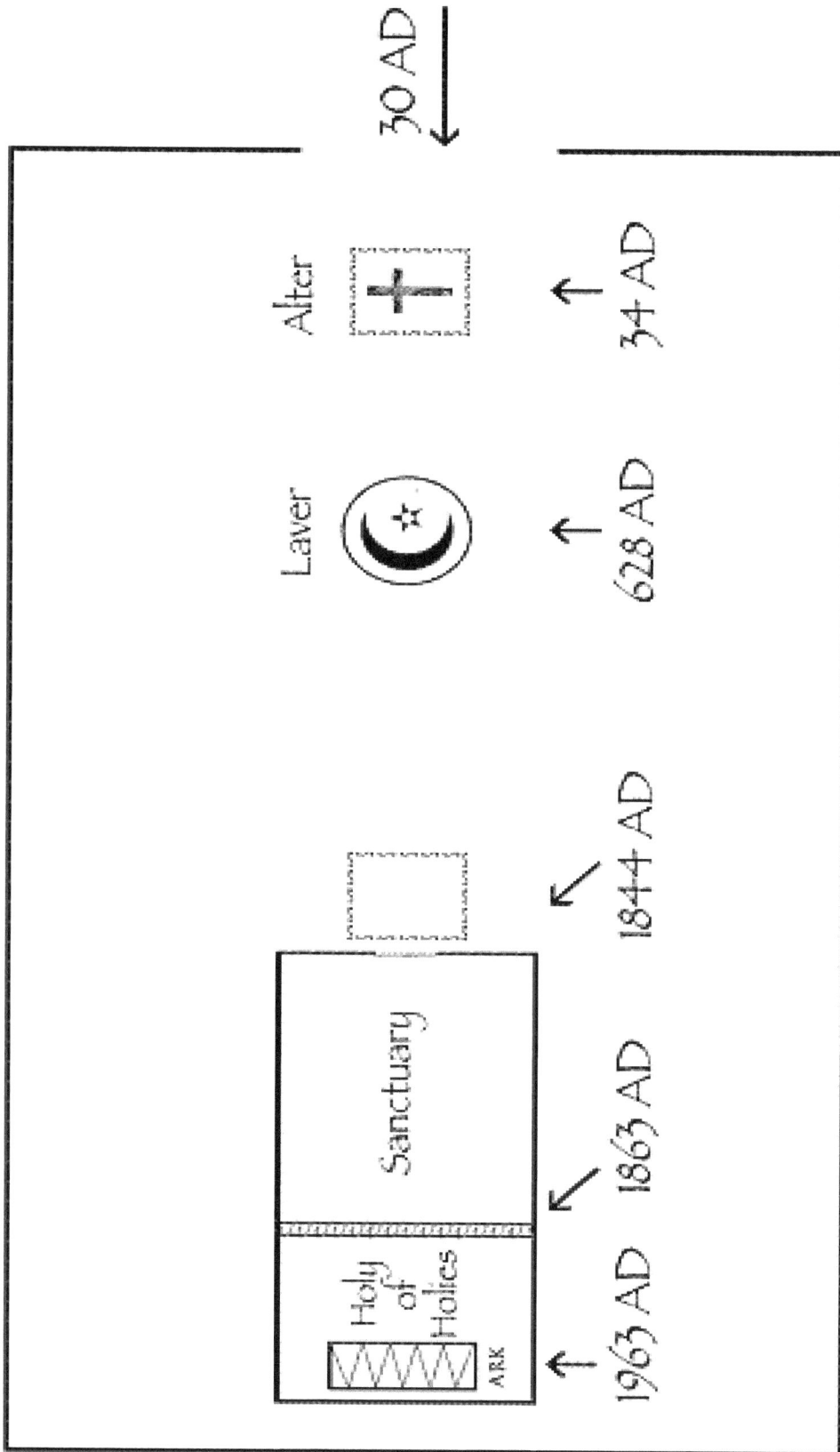

Alter

Laver

Sanctuary

Holy of Holies

ARK

30 AD

34 AD

628 AD

1844 AD

1863 AD

1963 AD

very soul of their ancestors Faith! And as history it cannot be changed or altered. The Morrisite prophecies for the return of Jesus in Deer Lodge defines the identity of these people. The fact that the prophecy has been fulfilled (to every dot and tittle) also has dramatic impact. This is affecting everyone living in the Valley directly as this quickly becomes a world news media event while the Iraqi situation escalates toward nuclear war because of the Bush/Hussein debacle.

With great proofs and mighty authority based on those proofs, the Kingdom is being established and the 7 seals have been broken on the Book of the Covenant (written within) and the Will and Testament of 'Abdu'l-Baha (written on the back).[*] In this way the return of Jesus is destined to rule until all rule and authority is put under his feet. Then at the end of the century at the year 2000 he will turn the Kingdom over to the Father (Baha'u'llah) by becoming subject to the Universal House of Justice with the guardian as its chairman. Thus from now until then, Jesus has taken the scroll out the hand of the guardian seated upon the throne of David and rules until the New World Order of Baha'u'llah (the Father) is firmly established and in full working order with all the people of the world becoming Baha'i.

> "Then comes the end, when he [Jesus, the Son] delivers up the kingdom to God the Father, after abolishing every kind of domination, authority and power. For he [Jesus, the Son] is destined to reign until God has put all enemies under his feet; and the last enemy to be abolished is death [spiritual death]. Scripture says, 'He has put all things in subjection under his feet.' But in saying 'all things,' it clearly means to exclude God who subordinates them; and when all things are thus subject to him, then the Son himself will also be made subordinate to God who made all things subject to him, and thus God will be all in all."[†]

Now the trumpet of this good news of the Kingdom established by the return of Jesus (Leland) from Deer Lodge, Montana, will sound around the world! For it is the greatest, greatest story ever, ever told!

Respectfully,

Neal Chase.

---

[*] Revelation 5:1-2.
[†] 1 Corinthians 15:24-28.

The August 9th Prophecy (*Tisha B'Av**)

*"All those people that belonged to that little church down there [in Deer Lodge, Montana]: One day out the year, it was **August the 9th**, they knew that was the day that Christ would return."*--(Lewis Johnson, 9/21/1990)

On September 21st, 1990, we interviewed Lewis Johnson and his wife Marvel Johnson concerning the prophecies of George Williams that the promised return of Jesus would suddenly appear in Deer Lodge, Montana, in "his Temple" (Malachi 3:1): and that was fulfilled on August 9th, 1969. Lewis was the living heir of George Johnson the original and first head minister of the Morrisite Pioneers of the Deer Lodge Valley. Joseph Morris was the reformer who appeared after Joseph Smith during the days of Brigham Young. Together Joseph Smith, the seer; Joseph Morris, the reformer; and George Williams the minor prophet, fulfill the promised role of the three forerunners to "prepare the way" (Malachi 3:1) for the coming of Jesus II.

We interviewed Lewis and Marvel at their ancestral homestead in Deer Lodge, after which Lewis presented me with an original photo from the late 1800s of the George Johnson Home and Morrisite Teaching Center as a personal gift. Lewis told us that the center had burned down in a fire and much original materials (church records, some original letters of George Williams, etc.) were forever lost. However, these letters had also been copiously copied and preserved in leather bound journals safeguarded by the various Morrisite folks as sacred prophecy and scripture. We were able to have direct access to the original documents housed in the various archives in the Deer Lodge Valley, personal artifacts of the Morrisite homestead pioneers, as well as also secondary copies and other archival materials housed in Logan, Utah.

The following dialogue is a transcription of part of our meeting with the Johnsons--from the original taped recording--that is of important historical record as it documents not only the fact of the August 9th prophecy, but also the unexpected spontaneous circumstances in which the information was established. As such all the friends should print a hard copy of this important document for their records, especially if that is their habit and inclination. It is this particular interview that sets the records straight--as raw data--preserving the reality of **The August 9th Prophecy**.

---

* *Tisha B'Av* is the 9th day of the Hebrew month of Av (August). It literally means the "9th of the Father" where interestingly enough "9" is the number for Baha'u'llah and His name literally means "Father" ("the glory of the father" see Mark 8:38). According to the Jewish literature both the first and second Temple (of Solomon and of Herod) were destroyed on *Tisha B'Av* and this will be the prophetical date that the return of Jesus will appear as High Priest in God's prophesied millennial Temple depicted in the last nine chapters of the book of Ezekiel that has 7 Towers. "Behold, I will send my messenger [George Williams], and he shall prepare the way before me: and the Lord, whom ye seek, shall suddenly come to his Temple, even the Messenger of the Covenant, whom ye delight in: behold, he shall come, saith the LORD of hosts" (Malachi 3:1 KJV). "The Mishna (Ta'anis 4:6) explains the fast [of *Tisha B'Av*] because of 5 tragedies that befell Israel on this day [the 9th of August]: (1) The Israelites would not enter the Promised land of Israel; (2) the destruction of the 1st Temple; (3) the destruction of the 2nd Temple; (4) the capture of Betar; and (5) the city of Jerusalem was overtaken... For many traditional Jews, it is believed the Mashiach (or Moshiach) meaning "anointed one," the Jewish King, will appear on *Tisha B'Av*" (Miller, S. A. (July 1, 2001). "*Tisha B'Av*, The 9th of Av, Prophecy." *The Lampholder Newsletter*).

The Transcript

Lewis Johnson: "You know what is quite interesting, is that with the ideas in the book[*] all right, about the prison down here, is the copper mines on both sides of it [Lincoln to the North and Butte to the South: the world's two largest repositories of copper], because they **are there.** There are seven towers! I even counted them.

Neal: (laughs nodding in agreement)

Lewis Johnson: "Yeah... I did that."

Interviewer B: "We think it is really interesting how that we have been finding--especially the recent stuff that we found in Logan--how that the prophecies of George Williams: how accurate they are." (Lewis: "Yeah.") "How well they describe a lot of the things that are going on now."

Interviewer G: "One thing that we think is real important is that Moses said that 'the test of a true prophet' is that their prophecies comes true. George Williams--validates this--we know that he is a true prophet because of his scientific proofs. Twenty years before the light bulb was invented he talked about there being lights on the hills. Forty years before the airplane was invented he talked about man flying in the sky like a bird. And this is scientific proof. (Lewis: "Yep.") We know that this man is not a phony. And so we should listen to what he has to say about Deer Lodge and the Kingdom..."

Lewis Johnson: "I been trying to think--I can't remember--but all those people that belonged to that little church down there: One day out the year, it was August the 9th, they knew that was the day that Christ would return."

Neal: "Is that right!?" (Interviewer D: "O My God!") Do you know what happened on August 8th?"

Lewis Johnson (very interested): "No?"

Neal: "On August 8th the man who fulfills the prophecies for the return of Jesus was sent up the river from Missoula to the prison in Deer Lodge--that is the day of the year that he was sent to prison.

Lewis Johnson: "On August the 8th!?"

Neal: "That's right. And so if you went up there on August the 9th, there he was. On August the 9th, 1969 that was the first day he was in there."

Lewis Johnson: "I know they were always together on August the 9th. (Interviewer D, *amazed*: "Wow!") I had heard it repeatedly."

---

[*] *Ezekiel's Temple in Montana* (1990) by Neal Chase.

Interviewer G: "Every year?"

Lewis Johnson (nodding emphatically): "O, Yes!"

Interviewer D: "That's bizarre."

Interviewer G: "Wow!"

Neal (to the interviewers): "Let's write that down."

Lewis Johnson (in agreement): "Right."

Interviewer D: "I'm glad I put the tape in."

Interviewer G (astounded to Lewis): "There's some information that you gave us that we didn't know! So…"

Lewis Johnson: "They'd all get together [that was every year on August 9th for exactly 100 years from August 9th 1869 until August 9th 1969] and I know there was a lot of disappointment that nothing happened."

Neal: "See, they officially disbanded in 1969, which was the year on August the 9th the day that this happened."

Lewis Johnson: "How in the hell did I remember it was the 9th of August? That's the one that's bothering me. I knew it was the 9th. I forgot what month."

Neal: "The reason we always remember that date is that my wife was born on August 8th. (Marvel Johnson: "O, really?") That is why we remember that. Yes. (Responding to Marvel) So August 9th, 1969 that was when it happened. August 8th/August 9th. And he wasn't in there yet two weeks, when he passed through that Eastern Gate ["the gate that faces East" (Ez. 43:1, 2)]. It says in Ezekiel 44 that after he passes through, it will be shut for ever more. And within the first two weeks he was there, they announced that they were closing the Old Prison. And now that Eastern Gate is shut as tight as a drum and nobody else can pass through it. They started building the new one [the new prison] which is also part of the prophecy [including the bright electric security lights on the hills Williams foretold]."

Interviewer G: "One really interesting thing we discovered was about the genealogy of the return of Jesus. The king of Denmark had a dream… "

Interviewer D: "When we went to Utah [the Logan Archive], we were flipping through all these letters of George Williams we had never seen before. In one of them George Williams is recounting the dream of the king of Denmark. And in the dream, the king is experiencing these things that will happen to somebody in his future lineage. And what happens is a bunch of people who are *poorly clad*--they are poorly dressed--come into his palace and they start throwing out all his rules and all that stuff. And then, the next thing you know he [the king] has the same kind of poorly clad garments that they have. And then what happens is, a band of angels--like celestial females singing and stuff like this--come in and then they give him this brand new garment, brand new, clean, that's real white. The king of Denmark never found out what the dream meant. But when the people asked George Williams what it meant, he said that his lineage--the king of Denmark's lineage--was a future lineage of the royal high priesthood. And this totally corresponds to the Bible in Zechariah chapter 3, where it says "Joshua the High Priest"--the Catholic [Douay] version of the Bible says "Jesus the

High Priest"--the return of Jesus has a soiled garment or a "dirty garment" and then he is given a clean garment, and this is when he has the "Stone with Seven Eyes" before him, [Ezekiel's Temple in Montana with 7 watchtowers] which is in Deer Lodge."

Neal: "This is from the letter of George Williams to Brother Rasmusson right here in Deer Lodge: "You also wish me to say something of notice regarding the King of Denmark. The dream, The vision of the King's was this: In the Early dawn of Morning as he lay upon his bed a company of poorly clad men (so they are wearing dirty clothes: prison garb) with staves in their hands and without shoes entered his palace without ceremony. The vision continued until the King saw himself in his Grand Reception Room with his kingly robes on and a crown upon his head. He attempted to order these Strangers to withdraw, but was speechless. The Company began to remove the ornaments in the room, casting them from the window, and approaching the King removed his robes and crown and clothed him as themselves were clothed (here they threw out all the royal things out the window including his robe and his crown, making him naked, then they clothed him as they had been clothed in these dirty clothes). Placing him in the midst and one who was called Seth (that's Joseph Morris who proclaims to the King) for behold you are of the Royal Line of Heavenly Priesthood [the return of Jesus as a High Priest after the Order of Melchizedec is from the royal genealogy of the Kings of Denmark] and elected to sit in your place to be of advantage to the Work of Redemption in the hands of the Holy One… [There appeared] a Celestial band of Females in robes of exceeding whiteness [Jesus II's army] around their arms and ankles were bands of Gold and precious Stones. And on their heads were many crowns. Their long bright hair held their robes in pleats and formed a Girdle for their waists. They sang a New Anthem [the New Song] in honor of our Dear Lord and the fullness of the Gospel. Saying in Chorus: How beautiful shall Adams Planet be, and clothed with Celestial Glory, the Working Ministers are sent. O King they stand before you. The vision of the King continued until Seth reached forth his hand and took from this Celestial Female Band Host *new Raiment* (clean garment) for the King, with which Seth [Joseph Morris] clothed him and put his heavenly name on his forehead and sealed it there. As I am only complying with your wishes it is not for me to describe the King's *new name* [Leland: "The Land"] or the Celestial Priesthoods dress at this time. But the King awoke in great trouble and seeks to know the meaning of his dream, but dare not tell it." (George Williams to Bro. Rasmusson, April, 1873)

Neal: "So he says that the King of Denmark is of the royal line of High Priests. In the Bible there are two types of High Priests. There is Aaron's line, who is Moses's brother, and then there is the High Priest after the Order of Melchizedec, which is the royal line of high priests. Jesus-- not being descended from Moses's brother Aaron [in the male-line] was a High Priest after the Order of Melchizedec. In Zechariah chapter 3 it says "Jesus the High Priest" wears a "dirty garment" and that he is given a "new raiment" and then in chapter six they put "a crown" upon his head. So for the Morrisites, they were waiting for a descendant of the King of Denmark [which is of the Biblical tribe of Dan--*Dan's Mark*: Denmark] to be the one who would return to them. And it turns out that Dr. Leland Jensen's genealogy goes back to the royal Kings of Denmark. And so he also has the correct genealogy…" and fulfills all the prophecies of God to a "T".

TWELVES

The number twelve represents the number of completion. We find twelve months in the year, twelve zodiacal signs through which the sun must pass through in its apparent motion; as well as the facts that in our history the foundation of the religion of God progressively given from the past into the present today has likewise conformed to this same pattern of twelve. This includes the 12 "foundation stones" of the New Jerusalem, and the outer fulfillment of this prophecy in the twelve gates of the promised New Jerusalem in the Rocky Mountains (see Map back cover this volume) in which both Ezekiel's Temple in Montana and Chair Mountain--the Great White Throne--are situated.

For the 6000 year cycle of Adam, begun in the year 4000 BC and culminating in the establishment of the Kingdom in the year 2001 AD "on earth as it is in heaven," 'Abdu'l-Baha explains:

> Know thou that according to mathematical principles, the firmament of this earth's brilliant day-star hath been divided among twelve constellations, which they call the twelve zodiacal signs. In the same way the Sun of Truth shineth out from and sheddeth its bounties through twelve stations of holiness, and by these heavenly signs are meant those stainless and unsullied personages who are the very well springs of sanctity, and the dawning-points proclaiming the oneness of humanity.[*]

'Abdu'l-Baha goes on to explain how in the previous dispensations there have been twelve sons of Jacob-Israel in the dispensation of Adam, twelve leaders of the twelve tribes at the time of Moses, twelve apostles of Jesus and twelve Imams of Muhammad and that today, as prophesied in the Twenty-First chapter of the Book of Revelation of Jesus Christ, which God gave him, as recorded by the apostle Saint John the Divine, there are prophesied twelve gates who are the twelve foundations of the Holy City New Jerusalem, which 'Abdu'l-Baha explains are the twelve apostles of the Lamb, Dr. Leland Jensen, who form the body of the second International Baha'i Council. When including their twelve substitutes who are also members of this body (as alternates) we have the twenty and four elders seated upon thrones spoken of in the fourth chapter of the book of Revelation and explained by 'Abdu'l-Baha in *Some Answered Questions* on page 67.

Likewise we find that in the Great Pyramid of Giza, as represented by twelve white marble blocks blocking the ascending passageway--in which the Manifestations of God: Moses, Krishna, Zoroaster and Buddha are represented by four red-granite girdlestones (like square-doughnuts that surround the entire passageway) through which the ascending passage and these 12 white marble plugs pass through--the twelve personages of the previous dispensations are also represented.

The purpose of this short chapter is to give an accurate list of the names of these individuals in the previous dispensations from Adam to Muhammad--as it is well known that also Krishna had twelve princes, Zoroaster had twelve kings and Buddha had twelve monks--yet the names of these in particular are not common knowledge among the people. Also, the 12 Foundation Stones of the New Jerusalem are explained and correlated to the 12 Principles of the Baha'i Faith in a Tablet by

---

[*] 'Abdu'l-Baha, *Selections From the Writings of 'Abdu'l-Baha*, #142, p. 165.

'Abdu'l-Baha. These 12 Principles are foundationally important for the New Golden Age of divine civilization upon this earth, as they form the core value system for all the peoples of the world based upon the organic, scientific, moral and spiritual reality of the Oneness of Humanity. The Oneness of Humanity forms the AXIS upon which our current and future divine civilization revolves. The living Davidic Kingship is the "sign of God" (W&T, p. 11) for this natural oneness of both body and spirit, as all humanity reaches this stage of maturation in its development, to have the direct and immediate experience of God in our individual lives and reflected in the outer horizons of our civilization that we freely choose to establish, nurture, perfect and grow.

I. THE TWELVE SONS OF JACOB IN THE DISPENSATION OF ADAM:

The Revelation of Adam was preserved in the Chronological Book of Stone, that is, the Great Pyramid of Giza which on the outside gives scientific information of the physical giving credence to the inside which contains the spiritual message in which the inner passageway system represents a chronological time-scale where each inch represents one solar year giving the dates for the coming of all the Manifestations of God and Promised Ones in the 6000 year Adamic Cycle. This cycle comes to an end in the year 2001 AD when the Kingdom of God shall be established "on earth as it is in heaven" the prophesied date given in the Great Pyramid and other Holy Books, for when God "brought forth" his "servant the BRANCH" (Zech. 3:8 KJV).

Adam became cognizant of his mission through the breath of life breathed into his nostrils, that is, the breath--word of God--came upon him. Adam brought the beginning. Adam was a Universal Manifestation for all people.

The revelation of Adam is symbolized as a robe. The robe of the Revelation of Adam was passed down this wise: Enoch, Methuselah, Noah, Shem/Melchizedec and then Abraham, Isaac and Jacob who is called "Israel" meaning "He Who Strives with God." Enoch is the establisher of Adam and the architect of the Great Pyramid, also known as Iemhotep. These things are recorded in the history of Josephus and in the Books of Adam and Eve and elsewhere.

These are the names of the twelve sons of Jacob-Israel under the dispensation of Adam stated in order of their blessings in Genesis, Chapter 49.

1) Reuben
2) Simeon
3) Levi
4) Judah, from whom comes King David and his line (see Psalm 89). Baha'u'llah is descended from King David in the male-line and seated upon David's throne which is to last forever.
5) Zebulun
6) Issachar
7) Dan, from whom comes the return of Jesus, the Lamb, Dr. Leland Jensen.
8) Gad
9) Asher
10) Naphtali
11) Joseph, the father of Ephraim and Manasseh & 12) Benjamin.

II. THE TWELVE LEADERS OF THE TWELVE TRIBES AT THE TIME OF MOSES:

Moses became cognizant of his mission at the burning bush on Mt. Sinai. Moses brought the Torah meaning the Way, FLOW, Teaching or The Path. Moses came to the 12 tribes of Israel.

The Hebrew word הרות (torah, Strong's #8451) is usually translated into the English word "Law." Because of this translation there is a great misunderstanding of what "Torah" truly is. "TORAH IS NOT LAW." When we use the word "law" we assume a certain meaning and concept of the word that is not present in the Hebrew Scriptures.

Let us start by looking at the Etymology of the Hebrew word Torah so that we may better understand its true definition. The word Torah comes from the Hebrew root word הרות (Y.R.H, Strong's #8451), a verb which means "to flow or throw something."

This can be a flowing of an arrow from an archer's bow, or the flowing of a finger to point out a direction. Nouns are derived from the verb by making one or two changes to the verb root. For instance, when the ׳ (the letter yud) is replaced by a ו (the letter vav) and a מ (the letter mem) is added to the front of the word, the noun הרומ (moreh, Strong's #4175) is formed and means "one who does the flowing."[*]

This can be an archer who flows an arrow, or a teacher who flows his finger to point out way the student is to go in the walk of life. Another noun is formed the same way except that a ת (the letter tav) is placed at the front of the word instead of a מ (the letter mem) and we have the word Torah. Torah is "what is flowed by the Moreh." This can be the arrow from the archer or the teachings and instructions from the teacher.

A hebraic definition of Torah is "a set of Instructions, from a father to his children, violation of these instructions are disciplined in order to foster obedience and train his children." Notice how the word Torah is translated in the New International Version translation in the following passages.

"Listen, my son, to your father's instruction and do not forsake your mother's teaching [Torah]." (Proverbs 1:8)

"My son, do not forget my teaching [Torah], but keep my commands in your heart." (Proverbs 3:1)

The purpose of a parents Torah is to teach and bring the children to maturity. If the Torah is violated out of disrespect or defiant disobedience, the child is punished. If the child desires to follow the instructions out of a loving obedience but falls short of the expectations, the child is commended for the effort and counseled on how to perform the instructions better the next time.

---

[*] As in Mt. Moriah, the Temple Mount.

Unlike Torah, law is a set of rules from a government and binding on a community. Violation of the rules require punishment. With this type of law, there is no room for teaching, either the law was broken with the penalty of punishment or it was not broken. God, as our heavenly Father, gives his children his Torah in the same manner as parents give their Torah to their children, not in the manner as a [secular] government does to its citizens.

"Blessed is the man you discipline, O LORD, the man you teach from your Torah." (Psalms 94:12)[*]

These are the names of the twelve leaders of the twelve tribes that Moses sent out of the wilderness to spy-out the land across the river Jordan according to the command of the Lord as stated in Numbers chapter 13. The establisher of Moses is Joshua the son of Nun.

1) Shammua the son of Zaccur, from the tribe of Reuben.
2) Shaphat the son of Hori,......................................Simeon.
3) Caleb the son of Jephunneh,.............................Judah.
4) Igal the son of Joseph,......................................Issachar.
5) Hoshea the son of Nun,.....................................Ephraim.
6) Palti the son of Raphu,......................................Benjamin.
7) Gaddiel the son of Sodi,....................................Zebulun.
8) Gaddi the son of Sus,.....Joseph (that is from Manasseh).
9) Ammiel the son of Gemalli,...........from the tribe of Dan.
10) Sethur the son of Michael,................................Asher.
11) Nahbi the son of Vophsi,..................................Naphtali.
12) Geuel the son of Machi,...................................Gad.

"These were the names of the men whom Moses sent to spy out the land. And Moses called Hoshea the son of Nun Joshua."--Genesis 13:16, RSV.

III. THE TWELVE PRINCES OF KRISHNA:

Krishna became cognizant of his mission in the war chariot of Arajuna. Krishna brought detachment. He gave the divine teachings of the three yogas: Jnana Yoga, the Path of Knowledge; Bhakti Yoga, the Path of Devotion (love); and Karma Yoga, the Path of Action. Krishna came to the people of India.

The establisher of Krishna is Arajuna. These are the names of the twelve princes of Pandu that fought in the great Mahabharata War, the five Pandava brothers and their seven sons, as given in the Mahabharata Sacred Hindu texts.

1) Yudhistra the son of Pandu and Kunti by Dharma.
2) Bhima the son of Pandu and Kunti by Vayu.
3) Arjuna the son of Pandu and Kunti by Indra.
4) Nakula the son of Pandu and Madri by Asvin.

---

[*] Jeff A. Benner, *What is Torah?* Retrieved from: www.anceint-hebrew.org.

5) Sahadeva the son of Pandu and Madri by Asvin.
6) Yaudheya the son of Yadhistra.
7) Ghatotkacha the son of Bihma.
8) Sarvaga the son of Bhima.
9) Abhimanyu the son of Arjuna.
10) Parakshit the son of Abhimanyu son of Arjuna,
  the father of Janamejaya. For it was under the just rule of Janamejaya long after the
  battle that the Mahabharata was recited for the first time and set down for posterity.
11) Niramitra the son of Nakula.
12) Suhotra the son of Sahadeva.

IV. THE TWELVE KINGS OF ZOROASTER:

Zoroaster became cognizant of his mission at the setting sun. Zoroaster brought purity. The establisher of Zoroaster is King Kai Vishtaspa that Zoroaster converted as given in the dialogues of the sacred Avesta. Zoroaster came to the people of Persia.

Almost all the Zoroastrian books were destroyed first by Alexander and later at the time of Omar. The priests had to re-construct these books from memory with a few original passages surviving mostly in the Mountings of Yazd and in India to where the Parsis escaped total destruction. For this reason many foreign ideas are introduced into the texts of the Zend (commentaries) on the original fragments of the Avesta (scriptures) that survived.

Zoroaster is prophesied in the book of Genesis chapter 3 as the "seed of the woman" that shall "bruise the head of the serpent." The name Zoroaster means "seed of the woman." Zoroaster had only daughters. He gave one of his daughters to the King he converted. Baha'u'llah is descended from Zoroaster through the female line.

The "head of the serpent" represents the throne of Satan that was set up by Nimrod in Babylon that Nebuchadnezzar and his heirs sat upon.

The twelve kings of Zoroaster are the twelve great Achaemenian Zoroastrian Persian Kings from Cyrus the Great to Darius III, that made war upon this throne of Satan in Babylon and removed it from the East to Pergamum in Asia minor near Greece whence it was bequeathed to Rome by Attalus III in 133 BC. Julius Caesar claimed rights to it as Venus Genetrix and later when the Emperor Gratian refused to sit upon it, knowing of its evil origin, Damasus the Bishop of Rome took it in 383 AD along with the robes and fish-hat of Dagon and became the first Roman Pontiff to where the garb of Nimrod (Satan/Saturn) seated upon this throne.

In the book of Isaiah chapters 44 and 45, Cyrus the Great is prophesied by name to be raised up by God to end the rule of the despotic line in Babylon and re-establish Temple worship for God for the Jewish people.

"Magi" is the Zoroastrian word for priest. The "three wise men" or three Magi that visited the birth of baby Jesus were Zoroastrian Priests following the prophecy of Zoroaster that in 1000 years from his birth he told them: "Follow a star and go to a manger and there you will find me." Following this prophecy the Magi arrived in Jerusalem following the Star of Bethlehem and were guided from there to travel to Bethlehem where they brought their gifts of gold, frankincense and Myrrh. "Magi" is where we get our English word "magic" from.

The Great Zoroastrian Kings raised up by God are spoken throughout the Bible in the books of Ezra, Nehemiah, Daniel and others. These are the names of the twelve kings of Zoroaster as preserved in the books of God and by the testimony of history.

1) Cyrus the Great
2) Cambyses
3) Darius
4) Xerxes
5) Artaxerxes
6) Xerxes II
7) Darius II
8) Artaxerxes II
9) Cyrus II
10) Artaxerxes III
11) Arses
12) Darius III

V. THE TWELVE MONKS OF BUDDHA.

Buddha became cognizant of his mission under the Bo Tree in India. Buddha brought enlightenment. Buddha came to the people of India and China and the East.

In the conversation with Subhadra just before his death, the Blessed One [Buddha] said: "Save in my religion [the religion of God continuing throughout all the dispensations from Adam to Muhammad and beyond] the twelve great disciples, who being good themselves, rouse up the world and deliver it from indifference, are not to be found."

The establisher of Buddha is Ananda, his first disciple and personal attendant. The names of the twelve monks in are as given in *The Essence of Buddhism* by Narasu.

1) Ajnata Kaundinya
2) Asvajit
3) Sariputra
4) Maudgalyayana
5) Maha Kasyapa
6) Maha Katyayana
7) Anuruddha
8) Upali
9) Pindola Bharadvaja
10) Kausthila
11) Rahula
12) Purna Maitrayaniputra

VI. THE TWELVE APOSTLES OF JESUS:

Jesus became cognizant of his mission at the river Jordan, when the Holy Spirit descended upon like a dove. Jesus brought Love and the Gospel of the Kingdom. He was a Universal Manifestation of God for all people.

The establisher of Jesus is Paul that Jesus himself chose on the road to Damascus to replace Judas that betrayed him and committed suicide. These are the names of the twelve apostles of Jesus as recorded in the Gospel of the Holy Bible.

1) Simon, who is called Peter, the son of Jonah.
2) Paul, who was Saul of Tarsus.
3) John
4) James the son of Zebedee, the brother of John, who are called the sons of thunder.
5) Andrew, the brother of Peter.
6) Philip
7) Doubting Thomas, called the Twin.
8) Batholomew
9) Matthew (Levi) the tax collector
10) James the son of Alphaeus
11) Simon the Zealot (Nathanael), the Cananaean.
12) Judas (Thaddeus) the son of James.

VII. THE TWELVE IMAMS OF MUHAMMAD:

Muhammad became cognizant of his mission while meditating in the Cave of Hira when the angel Gabriel appeared to him. Muhammad brought submission or surrender as Jesus had said: "Not my will O Lord, but Thine!" He came to the people of Arabia. Ali is the establisher of Muhammad.

The first Imam is Ali. The other eleven Imams are the sons of Ali and Fatima the daughter of Muhammad. The third Imam Husayn, the son of Ali, married Shahr-banu, the sister of Dara. Shahr-banu is known as the "Mother of nine Imams." Dara (Izdadwar) was the daughter of Yazdigird III the last Zoroastrian Sassanian monarch. Dara married Bostanai the Davidic king in exile (exilarch) from whom Baha'u'llah is descended from David on the male-line and Zoroaster through Dara on the female-line.

These are the names of the twelve Imams of Muhammad who successively held office, found on page lii of *The Dawn Breakers (Nabil's Narrative)*.

1) Ali-ibn-Abi-Talib, the cousin and first disciple of the Prophet Muhammad, assassinated by Ibn-i-Muljam at Kufih, AH 40 (AD 661).
2) Hasan, son of Ali and Fatimah, born AH 2, poisoned by order of Mu'aviyih I, AH 50 (AD 670).
3) Husayn, son of Ali and Fatima, born AH 4, killed at Karbila on Muharram 10, AH 61 (Oct 10, AD 680).

4) Ali, son of Husayn and Shahribanu (daughter of Yazdigird, the last Sasaniyan king), generally called Imam Zaynu'l-Abidin, poisoned by Valid.

5) Muhhammad-Baqir, son of the above-mentioned Zaynu'l-Abidin and his cousin Umm-i-Abdu'llah, the daughter of Imam Hasan, poisoned by Ibrahim ibn-i-Valid.

6) Ja'far-i-Sadiq, son of Imam Muhammad-Baqir, poisoned by order of Mansur, the Abbaside Khalifih.

7) Musa-Kazim, son of Imam Ja'far-i-Sadiq, born AH 129, poisoned by order of Harunu'r-Rashid, AH 183.

8) Ali-ibn-i-Musa'r-Rida, generally called Imam Rida, born AH 153, poisoned near Tus, in Khurasan, by order of the Khalifih Ma'mun, AH 203, and buried at Mashad, which derives its name and its sanctity from him.

9) Muhammad-Taqi, son of Imam Rida, born AH 195, poisoned by the Khalifih Mu'tasim at Baghdad AH 220.

10) Ali-Naqi, son of Imam Muhammad-Taqi, born AH 213, poisoned at Surra-man-Ra'a, AH 254.

11) Hasan-i-Askari, son of Imam Ali-Naqi, born AH 232, poisoned AH   260.

12) Muhammad, son of Imam Hasan-i-Askari and Nargis-Khatun, called by the Shi'ahs Imam-Mihdi. He was born at Surra-man-Ra'a, AH 255, was hidden for safety reasons from whence he disappeared in AH 260.

The Bab fulfilled the prophecy for the long-awaited re-appearance of the 12th Imam after the passage of 1000 lunar years (260 AH + 1000 years = 1260 AH) in 1844 AD when he made his proclamation and started the Baha'i calendar. Bab means door or gate. The Bab closed the door to age of prophecy and opened the door to the age of fulfillment. He became cognizant of his mission in a dream.

The Bab, like John the Baptist that was the forerunner of Jesus Christ, prepared the way for Baha'u'llah, who, being as descendant of King David, seated upon David's throne, fulfills prophecy for the second coming of Christ.

The successor to Baha'u'llah, 'Abdu'l-Baha and Shoghi Effendi, according to the Covenant of Baha'u'llah--*the Kitab-i-'Ahd* and the sacred Will and Testament of 'Abdu'l-Baha, as well as the Constitution and Four-Stage Plan of Shoghi Effendi--is the second International Baha'i Council/Universal House of Justice of Baha'u'llah with the descendant of King David seated upon the throne of David that is to last forever (see Psalm 89), as its president, now located in the Rocky Mountains, USA.

The second International Baha'i Council was established on January 9th, 1991 by the establisher of the Baha'i Faith, the distinguished Knight of Baha'u'llah, Dr. Leland Jensen, N.D.. The appointed body of the second International Baha'i Council is formed by the twelve apostles of the Lamb which Leland fulfills the prophecies for as the return of Jesus the High Priest spoken of in the third chapter of Zechariah and as explained in the book of Hebrews by the apostle Paul, the establisher of the true Christian faith.

These twelve apostles of the Lamb, who form the appointed body of the second International Baha'i Council/Universal House of Justice, are further prophesied of in the Twenty-First chapter of the Book of Revelation as explained by 'Abdu'l-Baha as follows:

> Consider how in the days of the Interlocutor (Moses), there were twelve holy beings who were leaders of the twelve tribes; and likewise in the dispensation of the Spirit (Jesus), note that there were twelve Apostles gathered within the sheltering shade of that supernal Light, and from those splendid dawning-points the Sun of Truth shone forth even as the sun in the sky. Again, in the days of Muhammad, observe that there were twelve dawning-points of holiness, the manifestors of God's confirming help. Such is the way of it.

> Accordingly did Saint John the Divine tell of twelve gates in his vision, and twelve foundations. By 'that great city, the holy Jerusalem, descending out of heaven from many Tablets and still to be read in the scriptures of the Prophets of the past: for instance, that Jerusalem was seen going out into the wilderness.

> The meaning of the passage is that this heavenly Jerusalem hath twelve gates, through which the blessed enter into the City of God. These gates are souls who are as guiding stars, as portals of knowledge and grace; and within these gates there stand twelve angels. By 'angel' is meant the power of the confirmations of God--that the candle of God's confirming power shineth out from the lamp-niche of those souls--meaning that every one of those beings will be granted the most vehement confirming support.

> These twelve gates surround the entire world, that is they are a shelter for all creatures. And further, these twelve gates are the foundation of the City of God, the heavenly Jerusalem, and on each one of these foundations is written the name of one of the Apostles of the [the Lamb]*. That is to say, each one maketh manifest the perfections, the joyous message, and excellency of that holy Being [Dr. Leland Jensen].†

No other people or group have access to the information contained within this book other than the Council of these twelve apostles, alive and in the world today, who are loyal, faithful and true, along with the living Davidic King as their president.

The fact that all the Dispensations of the Manifestations of God have this foundation of twelve shows the cohesiveness and unity of design in the single Plan and Design of God. This one fact, to the intelligent person, demonstrates that there is but one God, one religion and one progressively continuing Revelation. This is the religion of God. The religion of man is the other religion in the world that is the mass of confusion of manmade imitations and vain imaginings of the peoples that leads to ruinous wars, ignorance, poverty and disaster.

---

* "And the wall of the city had twelve foundations, and on them the twelve names of the twelve apostles of the Lamb" (Revelation 21:14, RSV).
† 'Abdu'l-Baha, *Selections*, #142, pp. 165-166.

Only the Baha'is Under the provisions of the Covenant possess this information and much, much more.

The reason the Baha'is Under the provisions of the Covenant have access to this information, and no other people or group has this, including the mainstream Covenant-breaking group masquerading as "Baha'i" is because the of the uniqueness, power, simplicity and crystal clarity of the explanations and commentaries of Dr. Leland Jensen, the establisher of the Baha'i faith--the establisher of the Kingdom of God on earth as it is in heaven, who has "come suddenly to his Temple."

Even in science, not only of astronomy on the Macrocosm but in molecular biology of the Microcosm we find that in fact even our very life-forms are based on the Carbon-12 atomic structure. How great is God!

Investigate the rest of the proofs and evidences for the Baha'i Faith through the Baha'i Firesides which are the "waters of life" free for the asking. No cost. No obligation.

In conclusion of this chapter on twelves is the twelve principles of the Baha'i Faith as explained by 'Abdu'l-Baha that the Revelation of Baha'u'llah can be summoned up into. Here, from the Tablet to Shanaz Waite, 'Abdu'l-Baha explains how they are remarkably depicted in prophecy as the twelve foundation stones of the Holy City the New Jerusalem.

TWELVE PRINCIPLES OF BAHA'U'LLAH

The wonderful essence of Baha'u'llah's Revelation is the oneness of mankind. This Revelation is summed up in 12 basic principles, each represented by a stone in the Book of Revelation that is stated as being the adornment of the foundation of the Holy City.

> The foundation of the city wall was ornate with precious stones of every sort: the first course of stones was jasper, the second sapphire, the third chalcedony, the fourth emerald, the fifth sardonyx, the sixth sardius, the seventh chrysolite, the eighth beryl, the ninth topaz, the tenth chrysoprasus, the eleventh jacinth, and the twelfth amethyst (Rev. 21:19-20, KJV).

These represent 12 basic principles upon which the Holy City, the New Jerusalem, rests (the Kingdom of God on earth as it is in heaven). These 12 stones are most remarkably correlated to the 12 precious foundation stones of the New Jerusalem of St. John's vision regarding their spiritual significance and their colors, for they are spiritual symbols and not material stones, as 'Abdu'l-Baha has said. Consider them in this light:

I

The first Baha'i Principle is: "The Oneness of the World of Humanity." Hands may be black, white, yellow or brown, but the hue of the heart is one." The first foundation stone is **the jasper**; it is clear red like the hue of the heart. In ancient times it was called the bloodstone.

The following eleven principles are essential in order to establish the oneness of mankind:

II

The second Basic Principle is: "The Independent Investigation of Truth." All must be free to seek out truth in their own way. The second foundation stone, **the sapphire**, is a clear blue, "true blue," and the color of faith, inspiration, loyalty and truth. Man must be free to soar in this "**Dome** of heaven's blue truth," and see it with his own eyes, the intellect.

III

The third Basic Principle is: "The Foundation of all Religions is One." Each Revelator has given the same "New Heaven and Earth," but man has polluted and misrepresented these Divine Laws. In reality they are all one. The third foundation stone, **the chalcedony**, is pure white, of which 'Abdu'l-Baha said: "While white is apparent, yet in it is hidden and concealed the seven colors. In white all colors are brothers and sisters." White is the symbol of purity, and in its origin each religion is pure, and a brother to every other religion, for all Truth is one.

IV

The fourth Basic Principle is: "Religion Must be the Source of Unity." If it is not, its non-being were better than its being. The fourth foundation stone, **the emerald**, is green. Green is the color or harmony and unity. There is no color known that green will not harmonize with, as the green foliage blends with every hued flower. It is the color of immortality and also humility.

V

The fifth Basic Principle is: "Religion Must be in Accord with Science and Reason." Neither must deny the other. The fifth foundation stone, **the sardonyx**, is red or brown, according to the way it is held. So it is with science and religion; they are in essence one, but differ in color or manifestation. Today their realities come closer together in the minds of thinking people.

VI

The sixth Basic Principle is: "The Equality of Men and Women." They must be as the two wings of the soul, each equally developed. The sixth foundation stone, **the sardius**, is a stone in two layers, one white and one red, symbolized of the two in one who unitedly further the progress of mankind.

VII

The seventh Basic Principle is: "Removal of all Prejudice--Religious, Racial, National, Political, etc." The seventh foundation stone, the "**pure chrysolite**," is exquisitely clear, slightly tinted green. We read in the ancient philosophies of the Chrysolite Tablet it is the symbol of absolute sincerity and truthfulness, purity and selflessness. Only when our hearts are free from every form of prejudice can they become the "chrysolite tablet" whereon may be engraved our thoughts and motives.

VIII

The eighth Basic Principle is: "Universal Peace." The eighth foundation stone, **the beryl**, is greenish-blue; somewhat like the ocean is as it mounts its crest, the blue of faith and loyalty toward our brother man, the green of humility and unity, the harmonious blending into one symmetrical whole, like a beautiful bouquet of flowers. This, established in the heart of man, will also establish Universal Peace.

IX

The ninth Basic Principle is: "Universal Education." The ninth foundation stone, **the topaz**, the glory of the sun, is symbolic of the Light of knowledge and the glory of wisdom, which universal education will establish in the world when the golden topaz, Light of the Teachings of Baha'u'llah, is understood and lived.

X

The tenth Basic Principle is: "The Spiritual Solution of the Economic Problem." The tenth foundation stone, **the chrysoprasus**, is like opaque chrysolite, a clear green which embodies truthfulness, justice, sincerity and purity. These are the necessary requirements for the solution of all economic problems--the Golden Rule--"Do unto others as ye would that they would do unto you."

XI

The eleventh Basic Principle is: "Universal Language." The eleventh foundation stone, **the jacinth**, is somewhat like the jasper, rose red, the universal color, the hue of the heart. A race can only understand the heart of another when it can speak the same language.

XII

The twelfth Basic Principle is: "An International Tribunal, or Parliament of Man with the Davidic King as its president." The twelfth foundation stone, **the amethyst**, is violet. It symbolizes spiritual Light--reverence, healing, serenity, spiritual calm and poise. This Tribunal of all nations must be as the ultra-violet rays for the "healing of the nations" and it must seek spiritual Light in all reverence, that it may fulfill its high calling, imparting a sense of security, poise and serenity to the hearts of all humanity. The amethyst above all transforms or changes things.

Ask for how to attend your own 7 fireside classes in 12 sessions NOW!

For now is the time to Investigate, Investigate, Investigate...

Before it's too late and the clock strikes twelve!

The Exilarch and the Eighth Imam

After Nebuchadnezzar brought the throne of David and the Davidic King, Jehoiachin, into captivity in 597 BC, the exilarchs (exiled monarchs of David) remained in Babylon in the Area of Pure Lineage up until the time that the eighth Imam Ali ar-Rida converted the exilarch Isaac Iskoi ben Moses to accepting Jesus and Muhammad in 817 AD. 'Abdu'l-Baha refers to this meeting between the exiled Davidic King (exilarch) and the Imam in his *book The Secret of Divine Civilization*.

> When the Chief of the Exile[*] [the Exilarch] came into the presence of that Luminary of divine wisdom, of salvation and certitude, the Imam Rida---had the Imam, that mine of knowledge, failed in the course of their interview to base his arguments on authority appropriate and familiar to the Exilarch, the latter would never have acknowledged the greatness of His Holiness.[†]

Using the proofs of the new criteria that Jesus had already established (that of the Golden Criteria of the prophesied name, prophesied date, prophesied address and prophesied mission), as well as other prophecies that Jesus and Muhammad fulfilled from the Old Testament, the Exilarch accepted the reality of Jesus and Moses and Muhammad as well as that of the rightful authority of the Imam.

The Exilarch then returned from his meeting with the Imam, which took place in Persia, and succeeded in converting over 600 members of the Jewish community to also accepting the Imam based upon the proofs the Exilarch had received.

At that time, the Abbassid caliphs were busy killing off the Imams of the line of Muhammad and Ali. It was also a time of great persecution of the Davidic kingship in that area by the war-like dynasties that sought to extinguish this line (such as the genocide in the days of Chosroes II at the time of Bostanai in which all the Davidic kings had been wiped out but one).

The Imam, being knowledgeable, in not only the prophecies that were already fulfilled, but those yet to come to pass in his lifetime and shortly thereafter, foresaw the onslaught of the crusades of the Christian peoples to attempt to wipe out the line of David in the future. For the reason of protection for the Davidic kings in exile (the Exilarchs) as well as that of the succeeding Imams that were to guard them, the Eighth Imam instructed all his followers to move to the province of Mazindaran (the ancient province of Tabarastan[‡]) in the Alburuz Mountain range, where the city of Teheran, Persia, (the ancient city of Rayy) is located by the shores of the Caspian Sea.

> When 'Abdu'llah al-Mamun, the seventh Abbasid caliph, named Ali ibn Musa ar-Rida, the eighth Imam, to be his successor, many of his relatives [as well as his followers] (and he had twenty- one brothers) made their way to the great city of Ray [Teheran] and its neighborhood. But those halcyon days did not last long....

---

[*] The *Resh Galuta* [Hebrew for Exilarch], a prince or ruler [Davidic King] of the exiles in Babylon, to whom Jews, wherever they were, paid tribute.

[†] 'Abdu'l-Baha, *The Secret of Divine Civilization,* p. 36.

[‡] Tabarastan is sometimes referred to as The Land of 'Ta.'

But before long, under pressure from the dispossessed Abassids, Mamun changed his mind and secretly, it is claimed, encompassed the death of Imam Rida by poisoning. The Alawiyyin [relatives of the Imam as well as his followers that he had instructed], noting the treachery, had hastily to seek refuge...those Alawiyyin who flocked to Mazindaran (Tabaristan) [went there] when **their relatives** found power and authority in that region. And it must be said at once that the dwellers of both sides of the Elburz range, discontented as they were with the caliphs, received the descendants of Ali [and the followers of the Imam as well as the Exilarch] with joy.[*]

The relatives of the Imams that received them with joy were the descendants of the Sassanian dynasty that had fled to Mazindaran much earlier during the conquests of Omar. The Imams as well as the Exilarchs were related to them through the daughters of Yazdigird III the last Sassanian monarch.

Ali, the first Imam and successor to Muhammad, had given these daughters in marriage to both his son Husayn, the third Imam, as well as to Bostanai the reigning Exilarch at the time. Through Dara, that was married to Bostanai, and Shar-banu, her sister, that married Imam Husayn, both the Imams and the Exilarchs had relatives in power as kings in the mountains of Mazindaran where the Imam Ali ar-Rida knew that they would be safe from all sort of violence such as the Crusades that were prophesied to come later in the form of the Beast and the Dragon prophesied of in the book of Revelation.

In the book *Mazandaran and Astarabad*, by H. L. Rabino, he explains that:

> Sayyids [descendants of Muhammad] in Mazandaran are countless. At the death of Imam Rida [per his instruction], his relatives sought refuge in Daylam and Tabarastan [Mazindaran], where some of them suffered martyrdom, their tombs becoming celebrated. Their descendants [as well as those descendants of the Exilarch], however, remained there....sayyids of the House of Ali and the Banu-Hashim [the followers of the Imam Rida] began to flock to Tabarastan [Mazindaran] from Hijaz, Syria and Iraq [the Area of Pure Lineage], **"like unto the number of the leaves on the trees,"** and this continued under the other Alid rulers.[†]

Baha'u'llah and the Bab are both descended from these two lines: the Bab being from Muhammad and Imam Husayn and Shar-Banu and Baha'u'llah being descended from king David through Exilrach Bostanai and his wife Dara.

Due to the Imam not only converting the Exilarch to Christianity and Islam as 'Abdu'l-Baha has explained above, but also instructing the Davidic Kings as well as 600 of his Jewish followers to move to Mazindaran for safety, Baha'u'llah was born in the city of Teheran, in Mazindaran

---

[*] H.M. Balyuzi, *Eminent Baha'is in the Time of Baha'u'llah,* p. 300; 332.
[†] H.L. Rabino, *Mazandaran and Astarabad,* p. 11.

exactly 1000 years later in 1817 AD.[*] The Exilarch and his followers accepted Jesus and Muhammad, as well as that of the Imam Rida, and took all their possessions including the throne of David to Mazindaran with them. Here the great King of Kings, Baha'u'llah was born heir to this throne that is to last forever as the executive branch of the Universal House of Justice of Baha'u'llah, so we can recognize the true House of Justice from all fakes, frauds and imitations.

---

[*] The religious conference in which the Exilarch was converted by the Imam took place in 202 AH Muslim Era which is 817 AD (Donaldson, D.M., *The Shi'ite Religion: A History of Islam in Persia and Irak*, pp. 167-168). The Caliph al-Mamum learned of the secrets of the Great Pyramid from the Imam at this conference, and then formed the first ever expedition circa 820 AD to go to Egypt and to enter the Pyramid for the first time since its original construction. The forced entrance of al-Mamum remains there to this very day.

Mirza Buzurg

The father of Baha'u'llah was Mirza Abbas-i-Nuri, the son of Mirza Rida-Quli Big, of the village of Takur, in the district of Nur, of the province of Mazindaran. Mirza Abbas came to be known as Mirza Buzurg-i-Vazir (Mirza Buzurg the Vazier). And this is how it happened. One day Fath-Ali Shah (reigned 1797-1834) was shown a masterpiece of calligraphy by Mir Imad, the celebrated calligrapher. Marvelous was the beauty of that piece of handwriting, and Fath Ali Shah wondered if anyone living could match it excellence. Hasan-Ali Mirza, the Shuja'u's-Saltanih, the sixth son of the Shah, mentioned the name the name of Mirza Abbas-i-Nuri. He was sent for, shown the work of Mir Imad, and challenged to produce its like. Thereupon Mirza Abbas took Mir Imads masterpiece, copied it, and after that exercise wrote his own lines, had them suitably illuminated and presented them to Faith-Ali Shah. The Shah's admiration was boundless. A royal decree bestowed upon Mirza Abbas the name Mirza Buzurg, and invested him with a robe of honor---a garment which the monarch himself had worn. At the same time the Shah exempted the people of the village of Takur from the payment of taxes. A few years later, Mirza Buzurg was appointed vizier to Imam-Virdi Mirza, the twelfth son of Fath-Ali Shah, who was the Ilkani (chief of the clans) of the Qajar tribe (to which the royal family itself belonged).

Mirza Buzurg prospered in the service of the State, until the days of Muhammad Shah (reigned 1834-48), when he encountered the ill will of that monarch's notorious grand vizier, Haji Mirza Aqasi, and lost his position and much of his considerable wealth.[*]

Mirza Abul-Fazl, renowned Baha'i scholar explains that the Nuri family always held positions of State as high up as Grand Vizier (Prime Minister) within their family.

The next Light is Baha'u'llah, son of Mirza-Abbas, renowned as Mirza Buzurg of Nur. The Nuris are one of the well known families of Mazindaran. During the reigns of Qajar the present Persian Dynasty, the members of this family have usually occupied the highest positions in the state, such as Prime Minister, Minister, Secretary, and other civil and military dignities. Even in the present day, most of them are in the Government. Some have retired from their positions, but their names are enrolled upon the financial and military staff.[†]

As 'Abdu'l-Baha explains these positions of Vizier were hereditary--going from father to the son within the family--which Baha'u'llah declined to become a follower of the Bab.

When Baha'u'llah was twenty-two years old, His father died, and the Government wished Him to succeed to His father's position in the Ministry, as was customary in Persia, but Baha'u'llah did not accept the offer. Then the Prime Minister said:

---

[*] H. M. Balyuzi, *Baha'u'llah: King of Glory*, pp. 11-12.
[†] Mirza Abul-Fazl, *The Baha'i Proofs*, p. 51.

MIRZA BUZURG

"Leave him to himself. Such a position is unworthy of him. He has some higher aim in view. I cannot understand him, but I am convinced that he is destined for some lofty career. His thoughts are not like ours. Let him alone." ('Abdu'l-Baha)[*]

Mirza Buzurg, as one of the highest ranking ministers in the court of the Shah, consulted with the Shah in establishing the order of the Lion and the Sun to foreign ambassadors. The following is the translation of a letter written by Mirza Buzurg which is still extant in the National Library of Wales.

> My dear and affectionate Friend,
>
> I received your Excellency's Letter, and immediately laid it before the King who said--"What reflection is this of yours after having issued the late Firman. We shall not act contrary to its tenor and spirit. The truth of the case is as follows-- The High in Station General Malcolm has expressed his wishes to be invested with the Order presented to General Gardanne Khan and to be created a Khan and a Sirdar. He openly avowed that the Arms of the Sun and the Lion were exclusively proper for you and that the King of England had granted you permission to accept them. Although We were thus informed, We did not promise the Order, expecting your arrival on the day appointed. After you have reached Us We shall act as you consider conformable to Our interests."
>
> After thus saying His Majesty took your letter and having read it resumed his observations, "Although it is evident the Ambassador has written that granting the Order of the Sun and the Lion to be worn on the breast like General Gardanne's is not objectionable, yet immediately dispatch a Messenger that We may receive his final opinion tomorrow as to the propriety of the Order and the other honors being presented. If you Mirza Buzurg go to Tabriz let the answer be sent to Mirza Abdul Wahab that no time may be lost in Our receipt of it."
>
> Whenever you receive this pray lose no time in answering it, and order the Messenger if he should see me on the road to deliver the letter to me that I may forward it to Mirza Abdul Wahab. Until we meet I say no more.
>
> (sgd) Issa Mirza Buzurg[†]

Mirza Buzurg was not only Vizier in the court of the Shah but he was the Vizier and Governor over several of the most important territories in the province of Mazindaran. The district of Nur had been held within the family of the Davidic kings since 817 AD when the Imam Ali ar-Rida instructed the Davidic Kings in exile (Exilarchs) to move there for safety. The village of Takur and the hereditary rulership of that area had been inherited by Mirza Buzurg. Also he was granted rulership of Burujird and Luristan. This post also granted him large control over a sizable part of the Bakhtiyari territory--all great and wealthy possessions in the province of

---

[*] Cited from: J. E. Esslemont, *Baha'u'llah and the New Era*, p. 38.
[†] Sir Denis Wright, *Sir John Malcolm and the Order of the Lion and Sun*, p. 138.

Mazindaran.[*] As stated above Baha'u'llah as Heir Apparent stood to inherit all of this as well as including the throne of David from His father.

The Shah (King) of Persia was actually called the *Shah-en-Shah* or "King of Kings" because he was the national king over all the local kings that ruled over hereditary districts throughout all of Persia. This type of government traces back to the forms established by Zoroaster to unify the nation and the empire. This is the type of lineage and position of State that Mirza Buzurg truly held that Baha'u'llah stood to inherit from him.

Thus Baha'u'llah really did have the "government upon his shoulders" in fulfillment of the prophecy of Isaiah chapter 9 verses 6 through 7. Whereas Jesus did not have the government upon his shoulders at all, but instead had "carpentry upon his shoulders," his father Joseph being a carpenter and he being the carpenter's son.

---

[*] Balyuzi, p. 15-16, "It appears for a time Mirza Buzurg was also vazir of this province."

PASSPORT OF BAHA'U'LLAH
Dated January 19th, 1853

272

BAHA'U'LLAH AND THE CZARS

List of Czars

(1) Alexander I (reigned 1801-1825 died)

(2) Nicholas I, Alexander's younger brother (reigned 1825-1855 died)

(3) Czar Nicolaevitch Alexander II (born 1818, reigned 1855-1881 assassinated)

(4) Alexander III (reigned 1881-1894 died)

(5) Nicholas II (born 1868, reigned 1894-1918 murdered in Revolution)[*]

All told four Czars were acquainted with the Baha'i Faith, Nicholas I; Alexander II, the great reformer that Baha'u'llah corresponded with; Alexander III; and Nicholas II (grandson of Alexander II) who was the Czar that set up the World Court in imitation of Baha'u'llah's Peace Plan.

While in Akka, Baha'u'llah wrote to Czar Alexander II of Russia who is famous for beginning his reign by implementing Baha'u'llah's reforms such as immediately ending the Crimean War, lifting the censorship of the press, establishing educational reform at the universities, lifting the restrictions on travel and most significantly abolishing serfdom in the first Edict of Emancipation, March 3rd, 1861 all of which won for himself the popular title "the Czar Liberator."

Later in an era of reactionism, Alexander II was assassinated by a bomb in 1881. It is this Czar that corresponded with Abraham Lincoln stating that if Lincoln freed the slaves, he would free the serfs. Of course Lincoln established the Emancipation Proclamation similar to that 1861 edict of the Czar all of which has its origin in Baha'u'llah. Czar Alexander proclaimed the Revelation of Baha'u'llah to Lincoln, and Lincoln accepted. Both were martyred for this Cause.[†]

In His Epistle addressed to Czar Alexander II (cf. *GPB*, p. 106), Baha'u'llah explains that while He was in the *Siyah Chal* (the Black Pit of the dungeon in Teheran) one of the Russian Ministers (Count Dolgoruki)[‡] extended Him his aid and therefore the Czar has a great station set aside for

---

[*] See also *God Passes By*, pp. 226-227; 55, 106, 207.

[†] For those who denied Lincoln's spirituality or insist he was an atheist: "I do not believe a word of it. It could not have been true of him while here, for I have had frequent and intimate conversations with him on the subject of the Bible and the Christian religion, when he could have had no motive to deceive me, and I considered him sound not only on the truth of the Christian religion but on all its fundamental doctrines and teaching. And more than that: in the latter days of his chastened and weary life, after the death of his son Willie [1862], and his visit to the battle-field of Gettysburg, he said, with tears in his eyes, that he had lost confidence in everything but God, and that he now believed his heart was changed, and that he loved the Savior, and, if he was not deceived in himself, it was his intention soon to make a profession of religion [Baha'i]" Quoting Phineas Gurley: from Reed, James A. (July 1873). "The Later Life and Religious Sentiments of Abraham Lincoln," *Scribner's Monthly, 6* (3), p. 339.

[‡] This same Count Dolgoruki was the great cousin of Madame Blavatsky founder of the Theosophical Society from whom she first heard the word of the Bab and Baha'u'llah. Annie Besant, one of Madame Blavatsky's successors would later meet with 'Abdu'l-Baha in London (see *God Passes By* for more). It was Krishnamurti's knowledge of Baha'u'llah and 'Abdu'l-Baha, and this history, that prompted him to decline Bessant's instance that he proclaim

273

himself if he chooses to obtain it. Baha'u'llah's release from the *Siyah Chal* was in January of 1853 during the reign of Czar Nicholas I. Also, on page 55 of *God Passes By*, Shoghi Effendi mentions that shortly before the Bab's martyrdom (1850) the Czar instructed the Russian Consul to enquire into the reality of the Babi movement. Again this would be during the reign of Nicholas I.

The above two events transpired during the rule of Nicholas I, and while spiritually inclined Nicholas was entangled with the Crimean War of the Ukraine at the time. Alexander II, was in his early 30s at that time, and showing his desire for peace and spiritual achievements, was the driving force behind the throne of Russia, along with Nicholas I, that threatened (through the Russian Consul) to make war on Persia if one hair on Baha'u'llah's head was harmed and also, earlier issued orders to investigate the faith shortly before the Bab's martyrdom.

Although Czar Alexander was able to institute some reforms, he was unable to solve all the sources of the problems and also came against the opposition of the establishment that was against the serfs being freed. He never was able to implement the World Court himself but this passed on down to his grandson, Nicholas II.

After the assassination of Czar Alexander II, his son, Alexander III, succeeded him. Alexander III's son, Nicholas the II is the Czar that set up the World Court according to the Baha'i principles, but failed to proclaim Baha'u'llah, leading to WW I, the Russian Revolution of 1917 and the complete extermination of the Romanoff dynasty by the angry masses seeking justice and revenge.

If any kingship had a chance after chance to proclaim Baha'u'llah to the World it was that of Russia. To whom much is given, much is expected.

---

for himself the title of "World Teacher" knowing the true station of Baha'u'llah and 'Abdu'l-Baha and of the Promised One to come of which he spoke on certain occasions.

THE MILITARY ESCORT OF THE MORRISITES

On June 15th, 1862, Joseph Morris was murdered under the direct orders of Brigham Young. At that time the United States Army had already withdrawn from the Utah territory in July of 1861 to fight the Civil War and the Mormon militia under the iron-fisted control of Brigham Young had taken over full power.

The legal writs, warrants and other government authorizations issued to empower the Mormon militia for the murder of Morris was all orchestrated and controlled by Brigham Young through the force of his three main agents: Sheriff Robert T. Burton, who did the actual killing; Judge John F. Kinney, who issued the writs; and acting Governor Frank Fuller, who placed his seal of approval on the executive order to kill Joseph Morris.

Sheriff Burton was a known pawn and dirty-jobber for Brigham Young. Judge Kinney publicly stated that he was in Brigham's pocket.[*] And acting Governor Fuller was a devout Mormon and follower of Young's.[†]

The Morrisite slaughter was the final atrocity on top of previous abominations of the Mormons such as the Mountains Meadows Massacre, the murder of the Aiken party--another bloody episode,[‡] and other heinous crimes, that moved the Lincoln Administration, despite the immediate concerns imposed by the Civil War, to re-occupy the Utah Territory and protect the remaining Morrisites from any harm and danger from the violent threats and acts of Brigham Young and his Mormon killers.

Immediately after the murder of Morris and the arraignment of the surviving Morrisites in the court of Judge Kinney, acting governor Fuller was relieved of duty on July 7th, 1862 with the arrival of newly appointed Governor Stephen S. Harding.

Harding was instantly revolted by the slaughter--an oppressive religious war within in the territory orchestrated by Young--and immediately set out to get to the bottom of the truth. This ended in Harding granting full exonerations of all charges against the Morrisites[§] as well as the issuance of a strong report back to Washington reaching Abraham Lincoln through the Secretary of State.[**] Lincoln then ordered the Union solders back into the Utah territory, under the leadership of General

---

[*] "I have not taken any steps without counseling President Young and when the men came to swear out their affidavit, I told them they must ask President Young. When they came back, they said they had done so and President Young told them to go to Judge Kinney and get out their affidavits." Judge Kinney, cf. C. Leroy Anderson, *For Christ Will Come Tommorrow: Joseph Morris and the Saga of the Morrisites*, p. 116.

[†] Anderson, p. 244.

[‡] Kelly and Birney, *Holy Murder, The story of Porter Rockwell*, p. 141.

[§] Anderson, p. 150. "To each of them full and perfect pardon for the offence of which they stand convicted [by Judge Kinney], and they are, and each and every one of them is hereby **forever exonerated, discharged and absolved from the fine, costs, and charges** imposed upon them or either of them in pursuance of said conviction. In testimony whereof I have hereunto set my hand, and caused the Great Seal of the Territory of Utah to be affixed at Great Salt Lake City this 31st day of March AD 1863. Stephen S. Harding, Governor Utah Territory."

[**] Report dated August 3rd, 1862. Anderson, p. 149.

Patrick Edward Connor, to protect the Morrisite peoples from further harm.[*] These actions by Lincoln completely infuriated Brigham Young who lashed out at the President from the pulpit in a feverish tirade.

> "And as for those whom Abraham Lincoln has sent here, [Connor's troops] if they meddle with our domestic affairs I will send them to hell across lots; and as for those apostates [the Morrisites] running around here, they will probably fall down and their bowels will gush out, or they will bleed somewhere else."[†]

Despite the loud threats, General Connor fulfilled his mission, personally overseeing that the Morrisite wagon trains safely left the Utah Territory on May 5th, 1863 with a full military escort! One wagon train went south to Carson City, Nevada, while the other train led by Connor moved north to Soda Springs, Idaho, where the Morrisites built a settlement that they named Morristown.[‡]

It was at this time that George Williams came on to the scene with his visions of the return of Jesus to be in the Deer Lodge Valley in Montana. After hearing Williams's great announcement, the first Morrisites moved to Montana in the spring of 1863[§] the same year that the Deer Lodge Town company platted the city of Deer Lodge, Montana as a perfect square mile (640 Acres).[**]

By the 1870s, the majority of the rest of the Morrisites joined their friends in Deer Lodge to await the return of Jesus in that city, the City of the Great King.

---

[*] "In California one Patrick Edward Connor, a veteran of the Seminole campaign and of the Mexican War, had tendered his services to the government and had been placed in command of the Third California infantry, a volunteer regiment. Connor hoped to be called to the eastern theater of war [the Civil War], but so treasonable were Brigham's speeches, so terrified [from the massacres and slaughters] were the Gentiles in Zion [non-Mormons in Utah], **that at the last moment the redoubtable Patrick Edward was ordered to Utah**, ostensibly to guard the Overland Trail, to protect the mail and its carriers, and to keep an eye on the Indians [and actually to protect the Morrisite survivors and regain control from Young]. His regiment of infantry was augmented by one troop of the second California Calvary" (Kelly and Birney, p. 218).

[†] Brigham Young, cf. Kelly and Birney, pp. 219-220.

[‡] Anderson, pp. 159-163.

[§] Anderson, p. 211 and pp. 174-177.

[**] "In 1863 the citizens formed the Deer Lodge Town Company, had the town platted, and changed the name to Deer Lodge City" (Roberta Carkeek Cheney, *Names on the Face of Montana*, p. 70).

"With regard to **the <u>Pyramids</u> in Egypt** there will be wise men attracted there to explore, calculate to measure, to find what is the meaning of these extraordinary relics. Jeremiah speaking, and Isaiah also, knew the Lord of Hosts had a design in these great wonders, and these explorers will be helped to bring these hidden mysteries to light if they are doing it for an honest, holy purpose, to benefit mankind, and not with a view of making money; for every feature of the structure represents a heavenly order and may be called a pure language. Not by figure or by writing as we represent things, and it is written that the Lord will turn unto the inhabitants of the earth **a pure language** by which a small sign or movement may represent volumes of our written words. It's height, its circumference, its depth, its inner chambers, the space occupied by it, **all represent Jehovah's purposes from Adam to the Millennium**, and farther, as far as I know. There they stand, witnesses, and are called the mighty wonders of Egypt; and altho the children of Israel built some of these Pyramids in slavery and oppression, the Lord of Hosts claimed their labors a standing memorial of his guardianship over them. He delivered them, and drowned their oppressors, as the record tells us; but the Egyptians knew not what a wonderful memorial Jehovah's chosen had left behind them; and now, before our dear Lord's second coming, professors and wise men desire to look into the meaning of these grand structures, and, I have no doubt, others will be found buried in the sand. These explanations have been given me as fast as my scribe could write them. Amen & Amen."[*]

---

[*] George Williams, (December 27, 1881). "Letter to Dear and Beloved Brother Erasmussen," Walthamstow, Essex, England, pp. 8-9.

A UNIQUE AIR-PHOTOGRAPH OF THE PYRAMIDS OF GIZEH, SHOWING
ON THE SHADED SLOPE OF THE FARTHEST PYRAMID—WHICH IS
THE GREAT PYRAMID—THE NATURE OF THE HOLLOWING OF THE
STEPPED CORE SLOPES WHICH, ACCORDING TO SIR FLINDERS PETRIE,
IS "A PECULIAR FEATURE" OF THE GREAT PYRAMID.

(The air-photograph is by Brig.-Gen. P. R. C. Groves, C.B., C.M.G., D.S.O.,
by whose kind permission the reproduction appears.)

278

THE GREAT PYRAMID
The Revelation of Adam in Stone
by Dr. Leland Jensen

ADAM was a Divine Universal Manifestation of God, setting up the Adamic cycle of six thousand years, beginning with himself and his establisher, Enoch, and ending with Baha'u'llah and His establisher, the return of Jesus the High Priest after the Order of Melchizedec, Dr. Leland Jensen. Adam's establisher was Enoch who was the architect of the Great Pyramid at Gizeh in Egypt. This Pyramid gives in graphic details the dates for the advent of the Divine Manifestations as found in the Kabbalah Tree, including the Ancient Root and the Land that the Tree of Life is planted in (see Twin Diagrams following page).

There are many books written on the Great Pyramid, but almost all of them are written either by Christians or by people in the Christian world who have limited their works to Christian concepts, making their writings limited to this narrow view with results that are but mediocre. However in spite of this, they have done a monumental job of supplying us with accurate measurements in the Pyramid. The object of this writer is to give to the world the rest of the story, for the limited versions have served no real purpose nor given any real guidance to the world. Whereas this writer's purpose is to give this guidance that the world so sorely needs, as we are in the throes of transition from nationalism into internationalism. The world has shrunk to where every man is his neighbor, and, as a result, the differences in nationalities, races, ideologies, religions, cultures and classes and the struggle to adjust have resulted in all kinds of disturbances, such as scrabbling fights, mayhem, carnage, pillage and small and great wars. We have had two world wars and are now on the verge of World War III and, according to prophecies, a third of mankind will be dead in one hour (Revelation 18:10, 17).

Enoch

Enoch, who was the architect of the Great Pyramid, was also the architect of the pyramids in Central America. He gave the Hopis the Fire Clan Tablet. He broke off a corner of that Tablet and said he would return with the missing cornerstone. He told the Hopis where they would find him, that they should go to Yellowstone, then to the pointed rock, which is the salt pillar just south of the Temple, or the Montana State Prison, and then they should go to Masauwa, which is the phonetic spelling of Missoula, and there they would find the Bahana, or true Baha'i.

Enoch went up the Mississippi River to the Wisconsin River and went into Wisconsin where he took chocolate-colored granite to make the Ark of the Covenant in the Holy of Holies in the Great Pyramid, and its Capstone. This is how St. Brendan knew that the continent beyond the sea was divided by a great river. This knowledge was passed down in the legends of the Dans, as they were knowledgeable of the *Book of Enoch*[*] which didn't get in the Bible.

In ancient times the Pyramid was called the Pillar of Enoch, but to the ancient Egyptian kings, Enoch was called Iemhotep, meaning "He who comes in peace." As he was the establisher of Adam's Revelation, he received his knowledge from Adam. He was like Joshua who was the

---

[*] Jude 14.

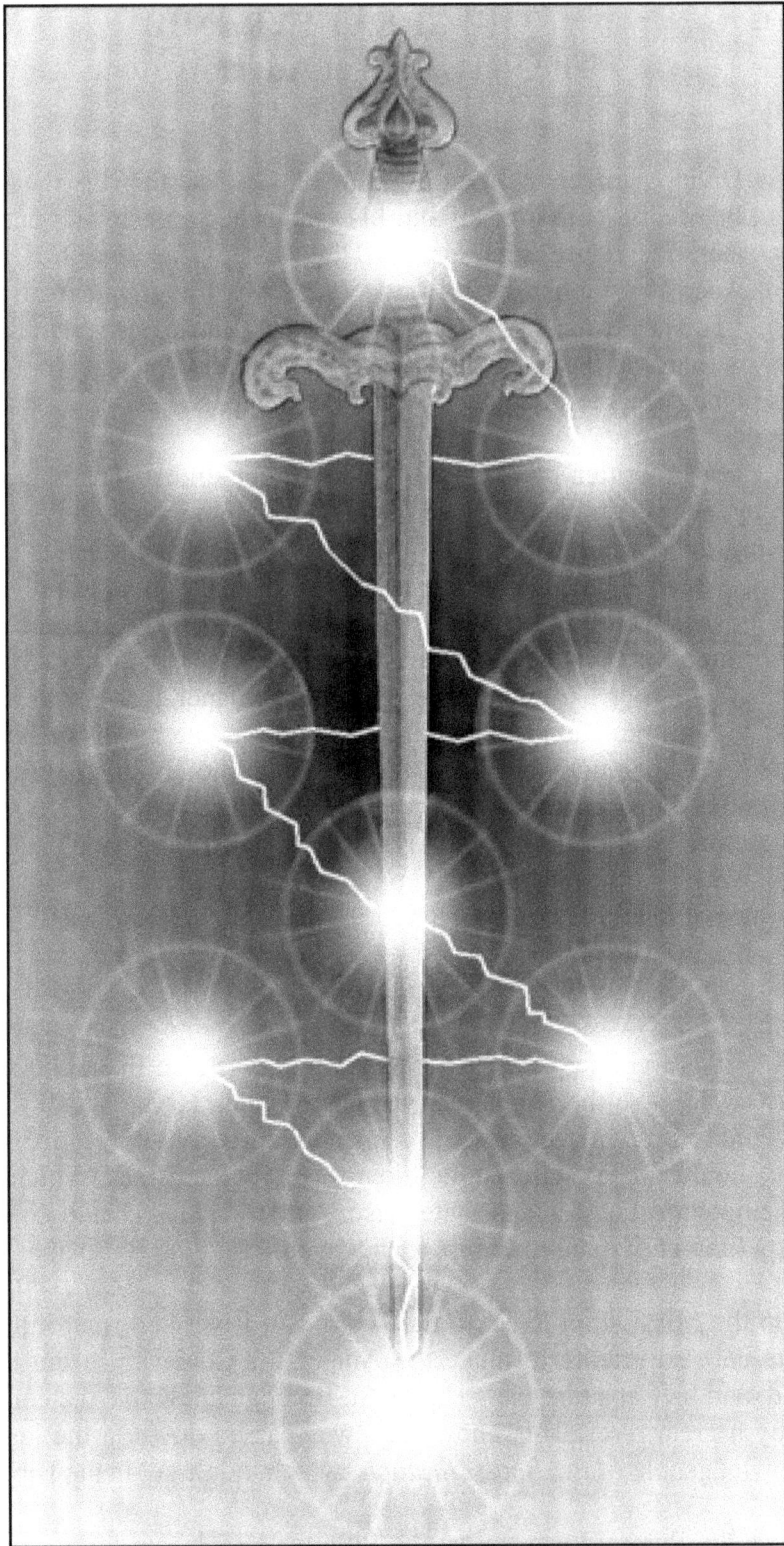

TREE OF LIFE: PATH OF THE FLAMING SWORD

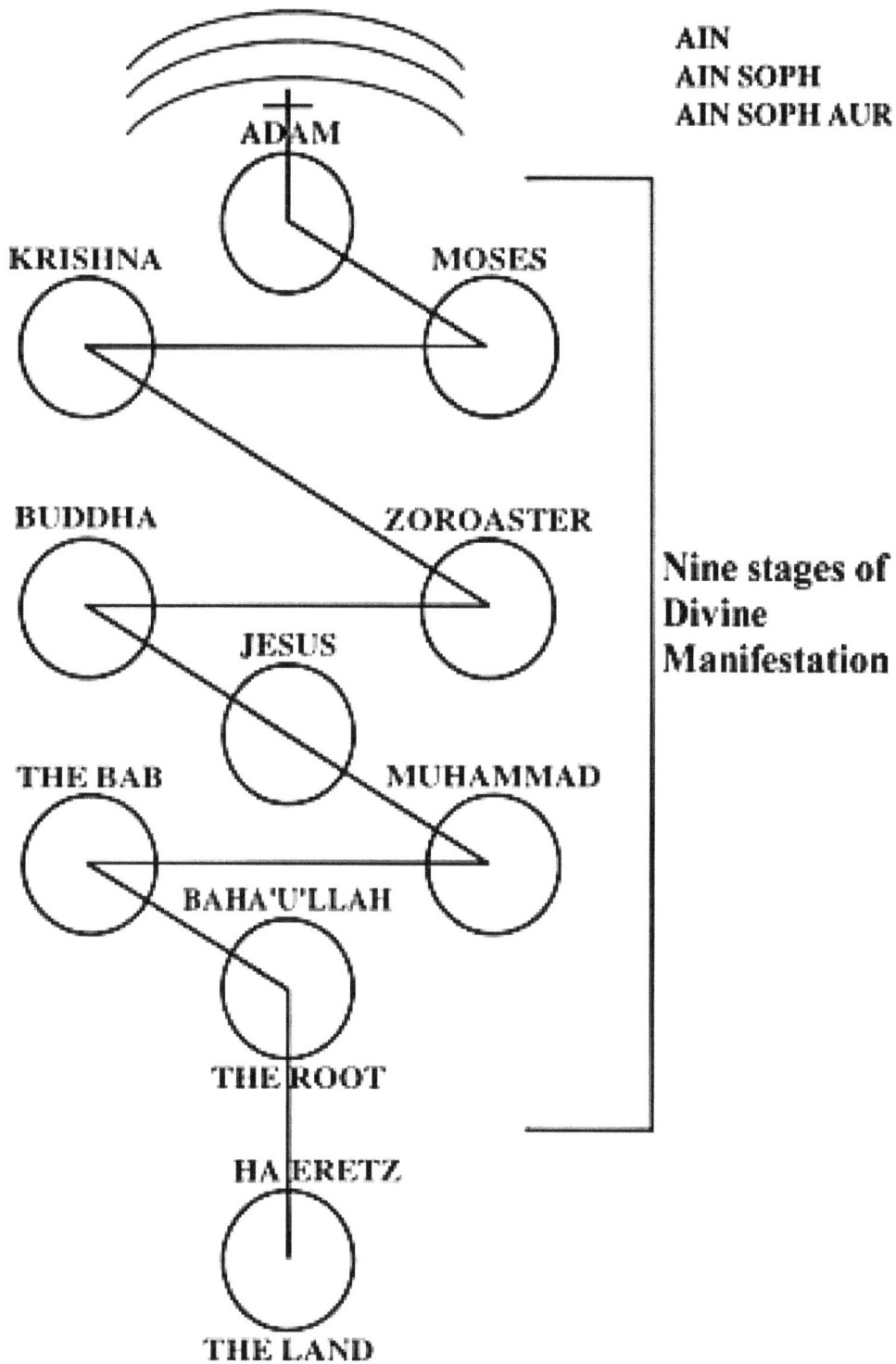

AIN
AIN SOPH
AIN SOPH AUR

ADAM

KRISHNA MOSES

Nine stages of
Divine
Manifestation

BUDDHA ZOROASTER

JESUS

THE BAB MUHAMMAD

BAHA'U'LLAH

THE ROOT

HA ERETZ

THE LAND

The Path of the Flaming Sword is the path that Divine Spirit took through nine stages of manifestation

establisher for Moses, and Paul who was the establisher of Jesus. Adam lived 930 years and survived the completion of the Pyramid by almost 400 years.

Herodotus, the Greek historian in the third century BC, went to Egypt to check out the Great Pyramid. He found that it was the Pillar of Enoch, with Enoch as its architect, and that it was not a tomb, but contained a great message for a later date.[*]

THE AUTHENTICITY

Before one can accept a criteria, it must be shown that it is authentic. It must be authenticated, in this case, by God.

> In that day shall there be an altar[†] to the LORD in the midst of the land of Egypt, and a pillar at the border thereof to the LORD. (Isaiah 19:19)

The Great Pyramid was built at the border of Upper and Lower Egypt and located in the middle of Egypt.

> It will be for a sign and a witness to the LORD of hosts [Baha'u'llah] in the land of Egypt: when they cry to the LORD because of the oppressors[‡] [the Covenant-breaking Baha'is], he will send them a savior [the return of Jesus[§]] and will defend and deliver them. (Isaiah 19:20 RSV)

Certain physical facts were placed in the Great Pyramid some 5500 years ago that were unknown to man until the last few centuries, such as the size of the earth, the weight of the earth, the distance of the earth from the sun, the circumference of the earth, the length of the diameter of the earth, and the squaring of the circle (πr^2). It gives 365.242465 days for a solar year. It gives 365.256471, the days in the sidereal (or stellar) year. It gives 365.259973 days in an anomalistic or orbital year. It gives 25,826.52 P″, the approximate number of years in the precessional cycle, and many, many more facts that are too many to mention in this book, but you could pick up almost any book on the Great Pyramid for further information.

These facts were not given to educate man to these facts and were not known to be in the Great Pyramid until civilization had progressed to the place where mankind had arrived at this

---

[*] This same history of Enoch being the architect of the Pyramid to preserve the prophecies of Adam is found in the history of Josephus as well as that of pseudo-Hermes (as quoted by Cedrenus). David Davidson, *The Great Pyramid: Its Divine Message,* 11th ed (1948), p. 435, see note.

[†] The great step at the upper end of the Grand Gallery is referred to as the Altar Stone. This refers to the Bab's Proclamation on May 23rd, 1844 and the beginning of the Babi/Baha'i calendar on March 21st, 1844.

[‡] They have built a wall of oppression around their followers, preventing them at the threat of expulsion and damnation if they even read the explanations showing that the ones they are now following are the Covenant-breakers. This is the main reason they forbid their oppressed followers from investigating the truth of the matter for themselves. They have gone against Shoghi Effendi and the *Will and Testament of 'Abdu'l-Baha,* doing away with the Executive Branch which is an integral part and head of the Universal House of Justice, having them turn to their headless monster which is not a Universal House of Justice at all, but a mockery.

[§] Zechariah 3:1-9.

knowledge. This was to show that Adam and Enoch had this knowledge and put it into the Great Pyramid to show its credibility.

The purpose of the Great Pyramid is to give the dates for the advents of the various Promised Ones of God in the Adamic cycle so humanity can see that these Promised Ones are sent by God for their edification, so humanity can be guided by them, especially by those who have come in our day.

It is absolutely necessary for those who are under the great delusion of the Covenant-breaking "Hands" to turn to the savior that God has so graciously sent them and who is alive in the world now. Without the guidance of this savior they will go into the fire of the oncoming nuclear war that is upon us along with the rest of those who are damned.

Here Isaiah not only gives credibility to the Great Pyramid, but gives a message to the approximately 5 million Baha'is who are now following the Covenant-breaking "Hands" and the Headless Monster--a message of salvation--by directing these Baha'is to turn to the return of Jesus (Dr. Leland Jensen) whom God has sent to them.

A CHRONOLOGICAL TIME SCALE

The passageways are prophetic chronological time scales with each Pyramid inch (P″)[*] representing one solar year. The passageways are of white limestone that is overlaid with white marble. At certain points there are red granite rocks, signifying spiritual events. Limestone is water-born, and red granite is fire-born.

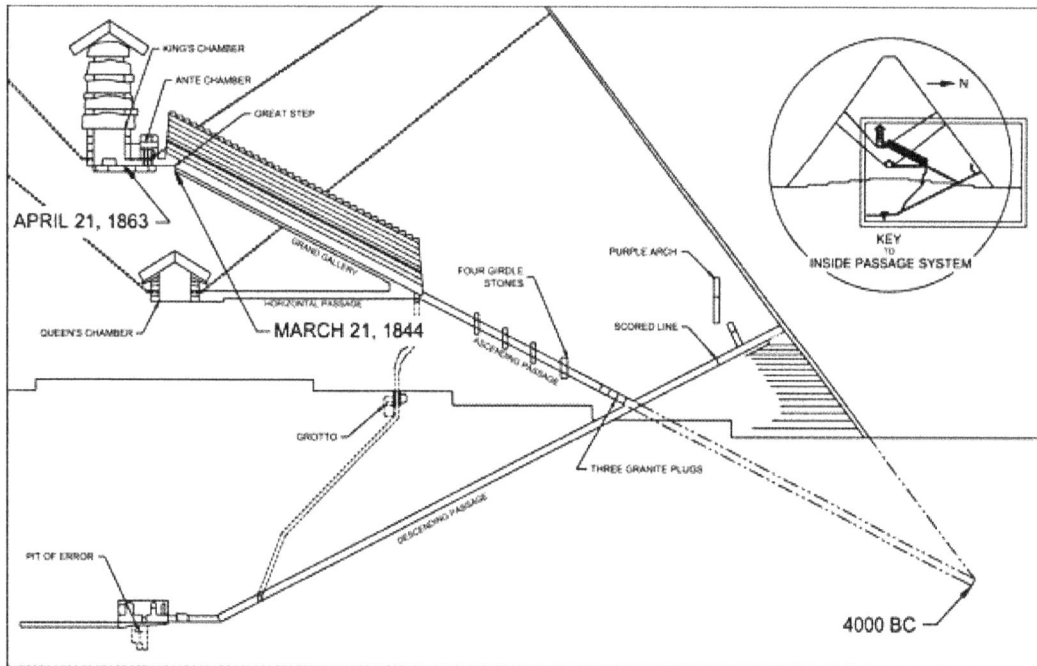

FIGURE 1

---

[*] A Pyramid inch is 1.0011 of an English inch and is found in the boss on the Granite Leaf in the Ante-chamber.

According to David Davidson, the chronological time scale starts where its northern slope intersects the extended line of the Ascending Passageway, representing 4000 BC (see Figure 1). The records of the Chinese, Babylonians, Egyptians and Hebrews all prove this to be the Zero epoch (A.K.[*]) of Adamic chronology. Measuring a Pyramid inch for a year, there is a continuous ascent to the end of the Grand Gallery at the Great Step, or Altar Stone, giving the date March 21st, 1844. Almost all pyramidologists agree that at this juncture is 1844 AD. They realize that from that point on, each Pyramid inch no longer represents one year, so they almost all agree that it is one thirty-day month, and they come up with such nonsense as dates for the first and second Balkan Wars, 1909 to 1912, and then World Wars I and II. Not being Baha'is, they don't know that the juncture of the Great Step is the advent of the Babi and Baha'i calendars of 19 days to a month and 19 months to a year plus four and one-quarter intercalary days. By this method we find that from the juncture of the Great Step to the entrance of the King's Chamber we arrive at April 21st, 1863, the date of the proclamation of Baha'u'llah.

The Date for the Advent of Jesus, The Christ

Measuring down in the Grand Gallery from the juncture of the Great Step to the start of the Grand Gallery at its juncture with the Ascending Passageway gives us the date of September 21st, 30 AD, the exact same date given by Daniel for the beginning of Jesus' ministry when he was baptized (see Figures 2a and b). This is 29.7178918677 P″ from the Zero Point, which is the birth of Jesus. 3.5 P″ before the opening of the Grand Gallery there is a seam in the rock face, giving us the date of the advent of John the Baptist when he began his mission on March 21st, 27 AD. This is the exact date given by Daniel. By hanging a plum-line from the first Overlay just past the opening of the Grand Gallery, we have 3.5 Pyramid inches from the baptism of Jesus until his crucifixion on **March 21st, 34 AD**.

This is 33.2178918677 P″ up from the Zero Point. This is the exact same date as given by Daniel for the crucifixion of Jesus (see the chart on page 53 this volume).

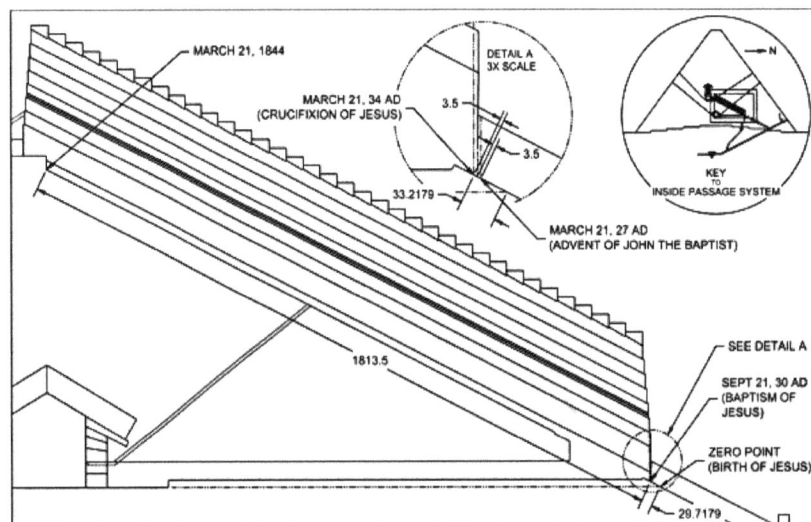

FIGURE 2a

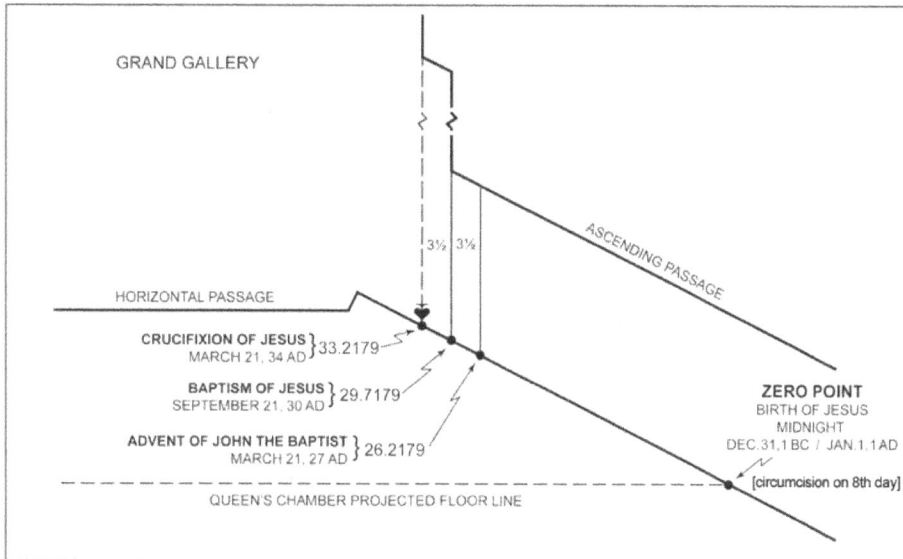

FIGURE 2b

The Date of the Exodus of Moses

Going down from the Zero Point to the start of the Ascending Passageway at its juncture with the Descending Passageway there are exactly 1455.78210813 P″ which gives us the date of March 21st, 1456 BC for the Exodus of Moses (see Figure 3). History doesn't give any date for the Exodus. Velikovsky said it was circa 1450 BC.*

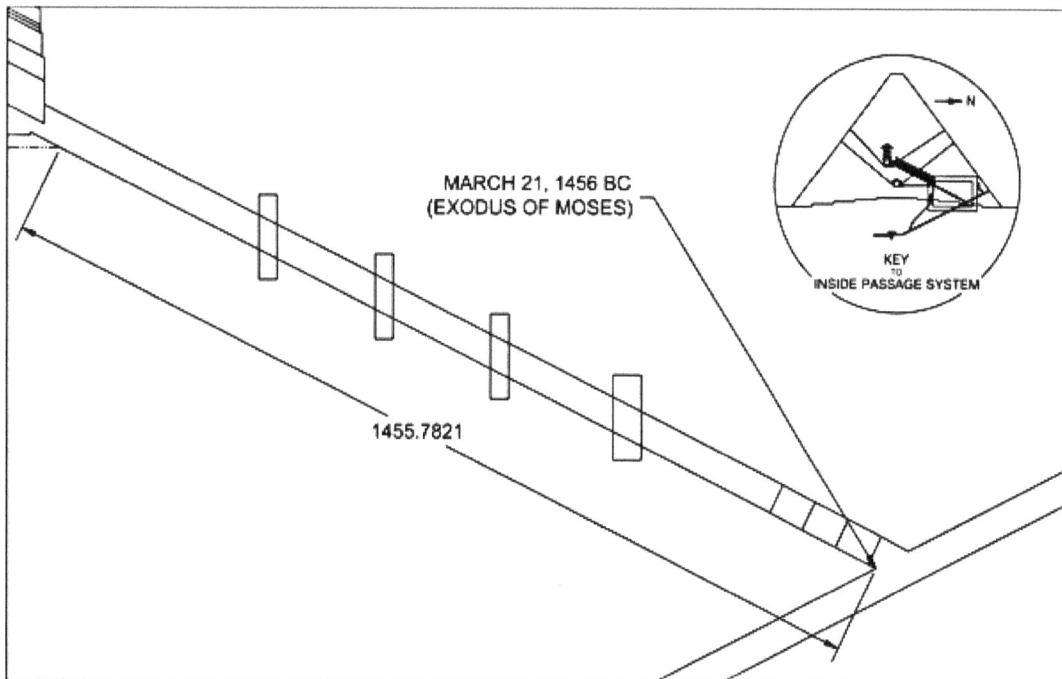

FIGURE 3

---

* See *Ages in Chaos* by Immanuel Velikovsky.

The Date for the Exodus of Abraham from Ur

Going up the Descending Passageway from the Ascending Passageway to the Scored Line there are exactly 687.8850737024 P″, giving us the date of Abraham's exodus from Ur of the Chaldees or May 2nd, 2144 BC: 1455.78210813 + 687.8850737024 = 2143.66718183 (see Figure 4).

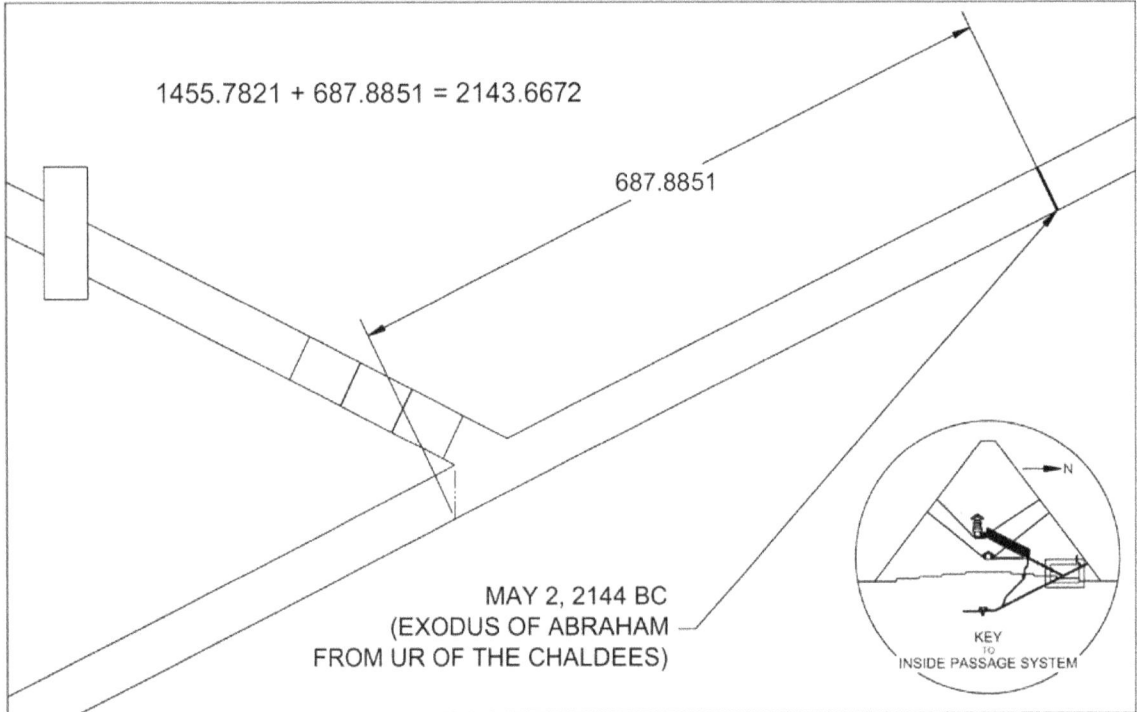

1455.7821 + 687.8851 = 2143.6672

687.8851

MAY 2, 2144 BC
(EXODUS OF ABRAHAM
FROM UR OF THE CHALDEES)

KEY
TO
INSIDE PASSAGE SYSTEM

FIGURE 4

The Star Alignment of Alpha Draconis

This event, Abraham's exodus from Ur of the Chaldees, is synchronized perfectly with the star alignment of Alpha Draconis. By looking up to the entrance passage of the Descending Passageway, the Pole Star is seen, and the simultaneous alignment of the Scored Line with Alcyone of the Pleiades on that very day of May 2nd, 2144 BC is the very night Abraham left Ur (see Figure 5).

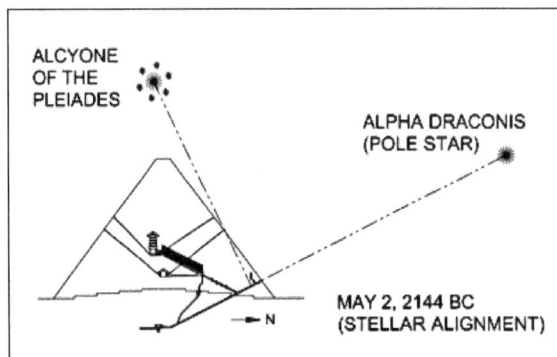

ALCYONE
OF THE
PLEIADES

ALPHA DRACONIS
(POLE STAR)

MAY 2, 2144 BC
(STELLAR ALIGNMENT)

N

FIGURE 5

286

The Date for the Advent of Noah

As the Purple Arch of Noah is on the ceiling of the Descending Passageway we have 356.33281817 P″ from the Scored Line to the start of the Descending Passageway bringing us to the Advent of Noah on January 1st, 2500 BC: 2143.66718183 + 356.33281817 = 2500.000 or January 1st, 2500 BC (see Figure 6).

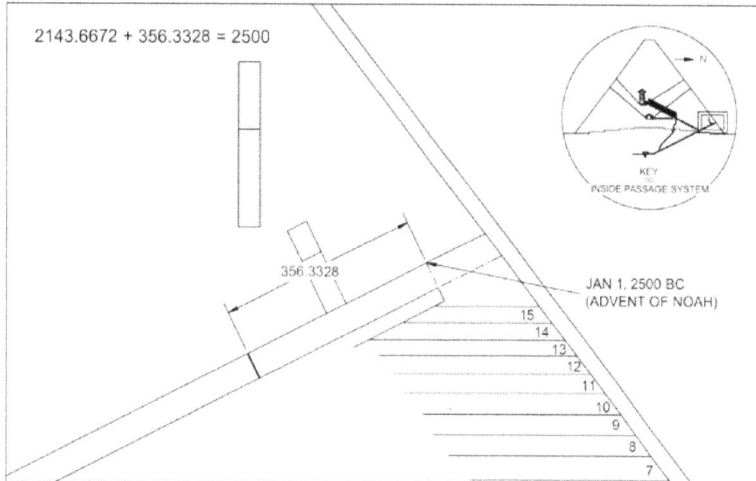

FIGURE 6

The Date for the Advent of Adam

By extending a line downward from the top of the Ascending Passageway to where it meets with the outer slope of the north slope of the Pyramid, there are 3999.99844863 P″ or January 1st, 4000 BC* (A.K.), to when Adam began his ministry (see Figure 7).

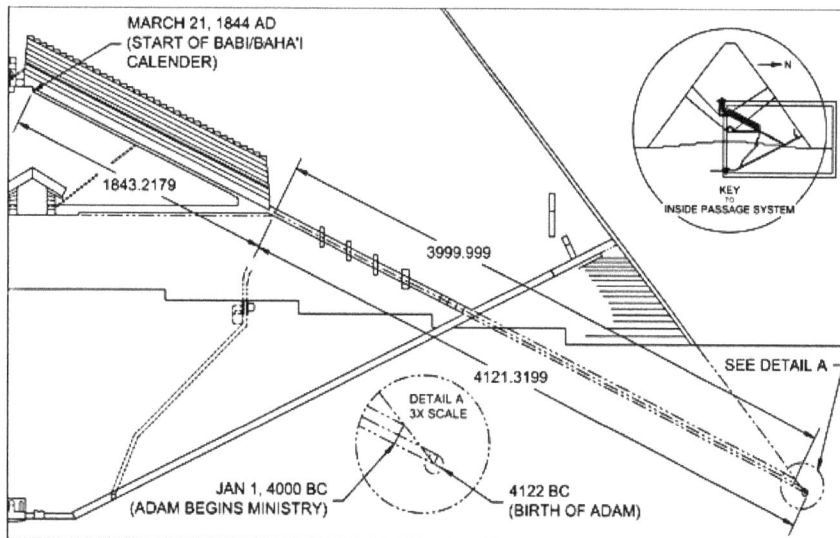

FIGURE 7

---

* *The Word in Stone* by John H. Dequer, see preface.

When you extend a line from the base line of the Ascending Passageway to where it meets with the Aris line (plus the length of the extended ramp height), it measures 4121.31988445 P″, or 4122 BC, for the birth of Adam. (see Detail A in Figure 7) "The records of the Chinese, Babylonians, Egyptians and Hebrews all prove this to be the Zero epoch of Adamic chronology."[*] Measuring a Pyramid inch[†] for a solar year, there is continuous ascent to the Altar Stone (the Great Step) of March 21st, 1844 AD, which is the start of the Babi/Baha'i calendar.

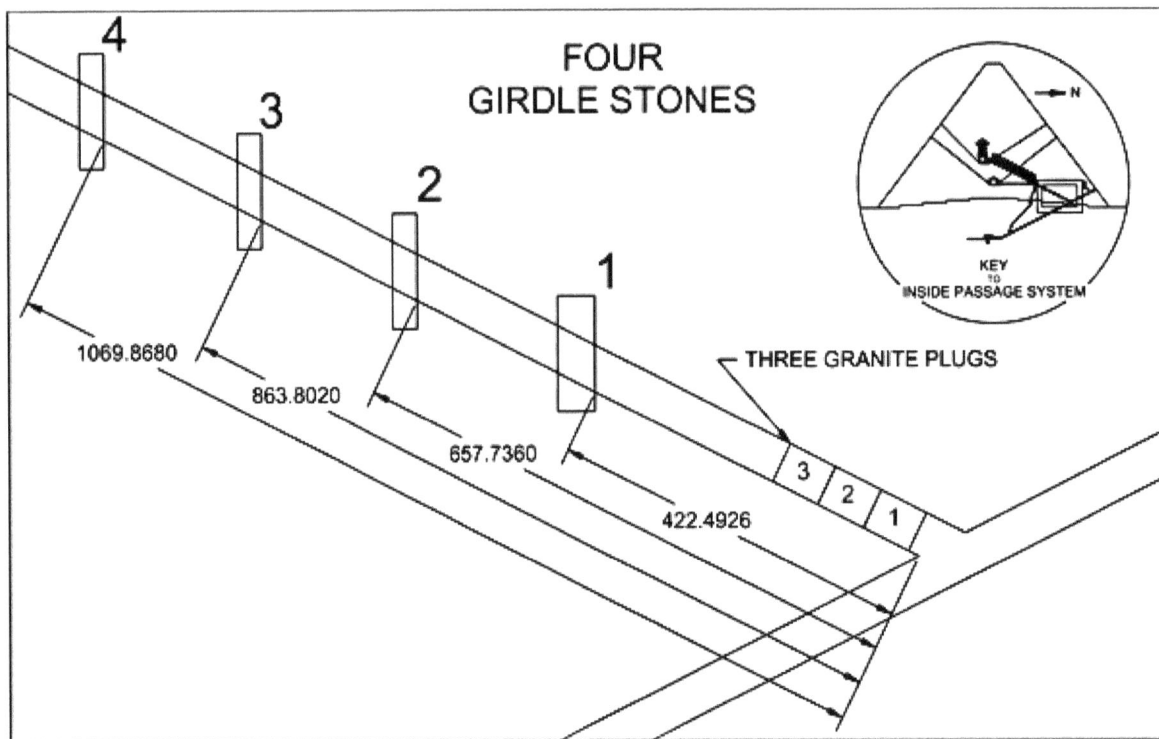

FIGURE 8

The above measurements were found in various Pyramid books, but all of the Christianized pyramidologists are limited by Christianization to their narrow-minded viewpoint. The views that crept into Christianity, such as the Babylonian trinity and the Incarnate god Lie (that Jesus is God incarnate), are erroneous and shut the Christians out from recognizing other Manifestations besides Adam, Jesus and Moses. Therefore other very important findings in the Pyramid remain unexplained, namely the Red Granite Plugs in the Ascending Passageway and the four square Red Granite Girdle Stones (see Figure 8). These are mentioned in various pyramid books. One book in particular is *The Word In Stone* by John H. Dequer, pp. 79, 80, 113. On page 113 he gives dimensions and rounded-out positions. He and other pyramidologists don't have the foggiest idea of their importance and meaning. Certain ones have tried to figure out their meanings but they don't, by themselves, give any meaning. This is also true about the Overlays in the Grand Gallery (see Figure 9). They mention them, but they don't have any idea as to their meanings.

---

[*] Dequer.

[†] A Pyramid inch is 1.0011 of an English inch and is found in the boss on the Granite Leaf in the Ante-chamber.

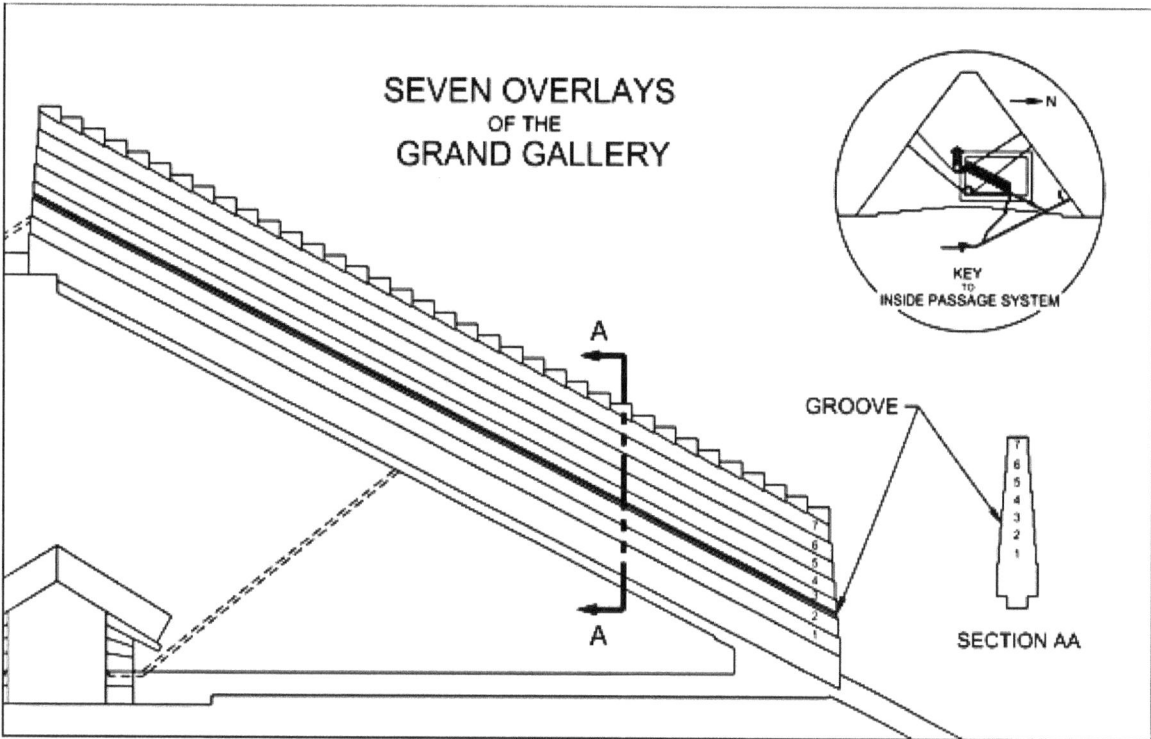

FIGURE 9

The same is true for the Kabbalah Tree, or the Tree of Life--scholars don't comprehend the meanings. Because Abraham studied in the Bet Midrash, the college of Shem, he learned the meaning of the Tree of Life.

Abraham, the Great Patriarch

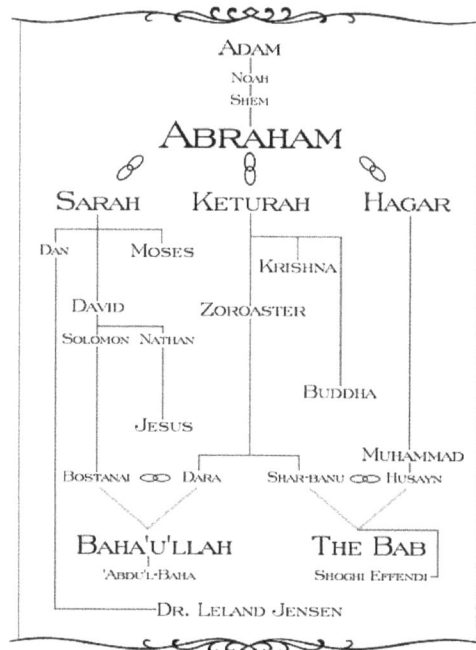

All the Manifestations of God and the establisher of Baha'u'llah's Revelation are the descendants of Abraham. He had three wives. From his first wife, Sarah, came Moses, Jesus, Baha'u'llah and His establisher, Dr. Leland Jensen, who is of the tribe of Dan. From his second wife, Hagar, came Muhammad and the Bab. From his third wife, Keturah, came Krishna, Zoroaster and Buddha.

The Date for the Advent of Moses

By taking the distance from the start of the Ascending Passageway to the first Girdle Stone, 422.492597951 P", and subtracting it from the length of the first Overlay, 1878.27470608 P", gives us 1455.78210813 P", or March 21st, 1456 BC for the Exodus of Moses. (see Figure 10) This is the exact same date given from the Zero Point in the Ascending Passageway to the start the Passageway of 1455.78210813 P", or March 21st, 1456 BC, for the Exodus of Moses. This is so astounding because it proves both are correct.

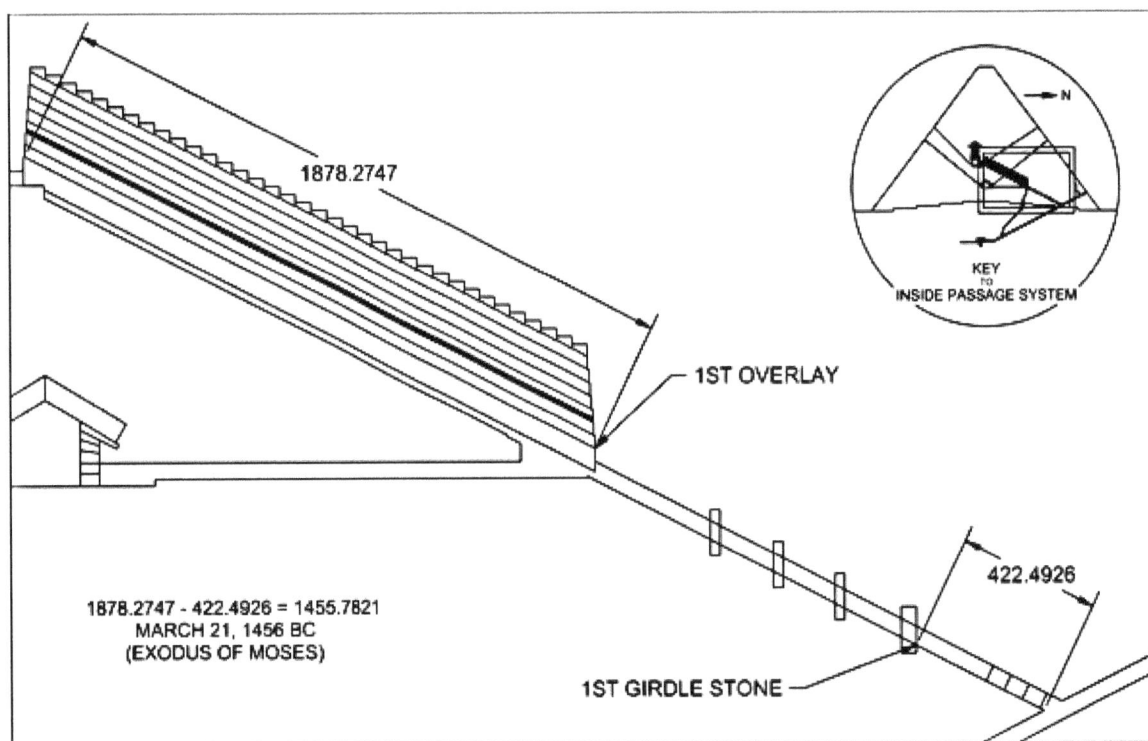

FIGURE 10

The Three Red Granite Plugs

The three Red Granite Plugs at the start of the Grand Gallery (see Figure 11) represent the three parts of Moses' Covenant—the Blessing (Deuteronomy 28:1-14), the Curse (Deuteronomy 28:15-68 and chapter 29:1-29), and the Re-gathering (Deuteronomy 30:1-20).

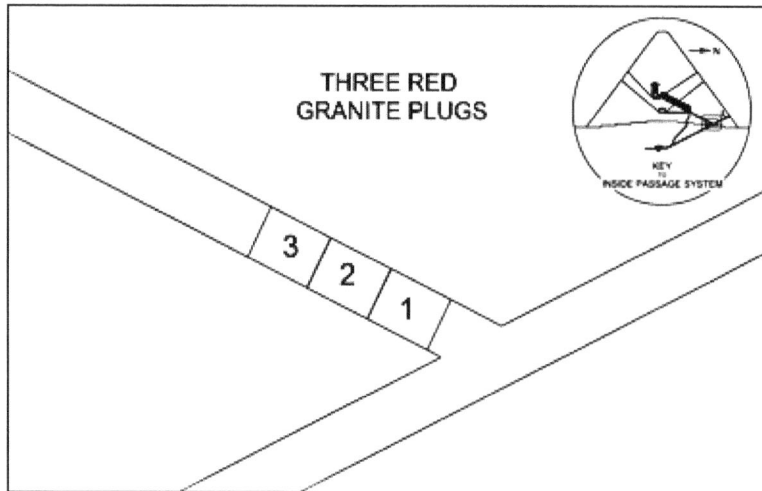

FIGURE 11

And it shall come to pass if thou shalt hearken diligently unto the voice of the LORD thy God, to observe and to do all his commandments which I command thee this day, that the LORD will set thee high above all the nations of the earth: And all these blessings shall come on thee, and overtake thee, if thou shalt hearken unto the voice of the LORD thy God. (Deuteronomy 28:1, 2)

In verses 3-14 Moses lists a number of blessings that would fall upon Israel if they would obey "the LORD thy God."

But it shall come to pass if Thou wilt not hearken unto the voice of the LORD thy God, to observe to do all his commandments and his statutes which I command thee this day; that all these curses shall come upon thee, and overtake thee.... (Deuteronomy 28:15)

Then Moses lists the curses that would befall Israel. This list goes on and on and on throughout the rest of the chapter in verses 16-68. In verse 64 Moses said:

And the LORD shall scatter thee among all people, from the one end of the earth even unto the other; and there thou shalt serve other gods, which neither thou nor thy fathers have known, even wood and stone. (Deuteronomy 28:64)

The Curse

The curse on Israel began with Solomon when he broke the Covenant by bowing down before other gods:

For Solomon went after Ashtoreth [Semiramis] the goddess of the Zidonians, and after Milcom [Nimrod] the abomination of the Ammonites. And Solomon did evil in the sight of the LORD, and not fully after the LORD, as did David his father. Then Solomon built an high place for Chemosh, the abomination of Moab, in the hill that is before Jerusalem, and for Molech, the abomination of the children of

291

Ammon. And likewise did he for all his strange wives, which burnt incense and sacrificed unto their gods. (I Kings 11:5-8)

And the LORD was angry with Solomon, because his heart was turned from the LORD God of Israel, which had appeared unto him twice, and had commanded him concerning this thing, that he should not go after other gods: but he kept not that which the LORD commanded. (I Kings 11:9, 10)

When this occurred those of the tribe of Judah followed suit and also began worshipping false gods, but the ten tribes of Israel would have no part of this. So when Solomon died the ten tribes separated themselves from this curse. Later in 721 BC they were conquered by Shalmaneser V and were brought into Assyria (Iraq) and Media (Iran), except for the tribe of Dan which went into Danmark and Ireland.

Chapter 29 goes on to give many explanations and commentaries, and finally in chapter 30 Moses gives the third part of his Covenant: **the Re-gathering.**

The Re-Gathering of Israel

The present State of Israel is composed of only the tribes of Judah and Benjamin and half of the tribe of Levi. The ten tribes are known today as the Ten Lost Tribes of Israel. Baha'u'llah was born and raised in Iran (Media). He was exiled to Iraq where the Jews had been taken captive by Nebuchadnezzar and brought into Babylon, or Iraq. Therefore, those who turned to Baha'u'llah and followed Him from Iran and Iraq represent the regathering of the twelve tribes of Israel. Thus Baha'u'llah brought a remnant of the twelve tribes of Israel back to Israel when He was brought there as a prisoner.

In Israel Baha'u'llah wrote His Covenant and whoever accepts this **Covenant** is grafted into Israel (which means "he who strives with God") under its new name Baha'i. The Jews in Israel are no longer part of Israel, as Paul tells us in the eleventh chapter of Romans that they were taken off the tree for unbelief when they rejected their Messiah, Jesus Christ, and the gentiles who accepted Jesus were grafted on in their place (Romans 11:17-21).

Under 'Abdu'l-Baha's ministry the Baha'i faith was brought to the Western world and Shoghi Effendi brought the Baha'i faith to all the remaining parts of the world except Russia. Thus the tribes of Israel from all over the world were regathered. But when the "Hands" broke the Covenant and led the entire Baha'i faith throughout the world astray, these regathered tribes were dispersed again from the Covenant and were taken off the tree all over the earth. Therefore the tribes of Israel must be regathered yet a second time:

And it shall come to pass in that day [which is now] that the LORD shall set his hand again the second time to recover the remnant of his people, which shall be left [from them that had gone astray], from Assyria [Iran and Iraq] and from Egypt, and from Pathros and from Cush, and from Elam and from Shinar, and from Hamath, and from the islands of the sea.

And he shall set up an **ensign** for the nations, and shall assemble the outcast of Israel [Covenant-breakers], and gather together the dispersed of Judah from the four corners of the earth. (Isaiah 11:11, 12)

The **ensign**, or **standard** for the nations is the genealogy of Baha'u'llah back to Jesse the father of King David. "And there shall come forth a rod out of the stem of Jesse, and a Branch shall grow out of his roots" (Isaiah 11:1). The stem of Jesse is his penis and the sperm that came out of the stem by uniting with an ovum produced King David. The rod pertains to the scepter of authority of King David, as he was chosen by Samuel (I Samuel 16:11-13). "I have found David my servant; with my holy oil have I anointed him" (Psalm 89:20).

In Psalm 89, God said:

I have made a **Covenant** with my chosen, I have **sworn** unto David my servant, Thy seed will I establish for ever, and build up thy **throne to all generations.** (verses 3, 4)

My mercy will I keep for him for evermore, and my **Covenant** shall stand fast with him. His seed also will I make to endure for ever, and **his throne** as the days of heaven. (verses 28, 29)

My **Covenant** will I **not break**, nor alter the thing that is gone out of my lips. Once have I sworn by **my holiness** that **I will not lie** unto David. His seed shall endure for ever, and **his throne** as the sun before me. It shall be established **for ever** as the moon, and as a faithful witness in heaven. (verses 34-37)

Baha'u'llah is a genealogical descendant of David and is seated on the throne of David. He said He was the Ancient Root. 'Abdu'l-Baha is the Branch grown out of this Ancient Root, and verses 2-5 of Isaiah 11 pertain to 'Abdu'l-Baha.

This genealogy of Baha'u'llah will be **an ensign** of the people because it is to exist forever. When Baha'u'llah appointed His son, 'Abdu'l-Baha, to succeed Him, this genealogy of David was passed on to him, 'Abdu'l-Baha. 'Abdu'l-Baha's son died in infancy, so he legally adopted Mason Remey to be his son. An adopted son has all the rights and privileges of a natural son, including the kingship. Therefore Mason Remey inherited David's lineage. This genealogy of David is of the line of Judah, and the scepter shall not depart from this line until Shiloh comes:

The sceptre shall not depart from Judah, nor a lawgiver from between his feet [legs] until Shiloh come; and unto him shall the gathering of the people be. (Genesis 49:10)

Here the seed of David is passed to the gentiles with the Advent of Shiloh. Shiloh is the one that regathers Israel.

This gathering a second time is now taking place by the Baha'is Under the Provisions of the Covenant, led by the return of Jesus the High Priest after the Order of Melchizedec, who is Shiloh.

The Will and Testament of 'Abdu'l-Baha gives two criteria that must be followed in appointing a successor of this lineage. If only one of the criteria is present then that person cannot be a succeeding guardian seated at the head of the Universal House of Justice.

Shoghi Effendi had conferred infallibility, but he was not a son of 'Abdu'l-Baha. Therefore he did not inherit the Davidic lineage, and consequently he was not to have a natural son. His father was Mirza Hadi Afnan, a descendant of Muhammad. Therefore Shoghi Effendi could not sit upon David's throne. His son was the first International Baha'i Council. Shoghi Effendi appointed all the members of this Council and placed 'Abdu'l-Baha's son, Mason Remey, to be its president, for only a descendant of David could sit at the head of the Universal House of Justice.[*]

Mason Remey adopted Joseph Pepe in a court of law in Florence, Italy and recorded his appointment of Joseph Pepe Remey in the court of records in Florence, Italy. We, the Baha'is Under the Provisions of the Covenant, have copies of both the adoption and the appointment papers of Joseph Pepe, thus making him the president of the second International Baha'i Council which will go through four stages to become the Universal House of Justice.

This is the standard (ensign) that the nations will turn to and accept. This standard will gather the twelve tribes of Israel a second time. This was represented in the Great Pyramid as the third Red Granite Plug.

This standard distinguishes the true Baha'i faith from the Covenant-breakers. This standard distinguishes the true House of Justice from all false houses of Justice--the World Court at the Hague, the League of Nations in Geneva, the United Nations in New York, and the Headless Monster of the Covenant-breaking Baha'is on Mt. Carmel. This standard distinguishes the World Order of Baha'u'llah from all other world orders--the world order of Bush (*pax Americana*[†]) and the world order of the Covenant-breakers on Mt. Carmel. This standard separates the sheep from the goats--those that enter the Kingdom of God on earth and those that are for the fire. This standard will exist forever, as it is the Covenant of God to King David that his lineage would exist forever and that there always will be a man seated on his throne. God never makes a promise that He doesn't keep. Baha'u'llah, a descendant of David seated on the throne of David, continued this lineage with His son, 'Abdu'l-Baha, and 'Abdu'l-Baha continued this lineage with his son, Mason Remey, whom Shoghi Effendi placed at the head, or president, of the Universal House of Justice in its embryonic form, the first International Baha'i Council. This lineage will exist forever through Mason Remey's son. The second International Baha'i Council/Universal House of Justice (IBC/UHJ) has this lineage as its president.

---

[*] Mason's only son Pepe passed the throne of David onto his only son, Neal Chase Ben Joseph Aghsan, the great-grandson of 'Abdu'l-Baha.
[†] Bush Sr. announced this "new world order" on September 11th, 1990.

The Date for the Advent of Krishna

By taking the distance of 657.73602311 P″ from the start of the Ascending Passageway to the second Girdle Stone (of Krishna) and subtracting it from the length of the second Overlay (of Krishna) in the Grand Gallery, 1870.3958696 P″, you get 1212.65984649 P″, or May 5th, 1213 BC, the date for the Advent of Krishna (see Figure 12). This is in harmony with the historical records of India:

> The Kaliyuga began with the winter solstice immediately preceding the commencement of the Kollam Andu, or at the end of 1177 BC... and [fixes] the date of the great Mahabharata war which was fought a few years before the beginning of the Kaliyuga. (V. G. Aiyer, *The Chronology of Ancient India*, p. 52)[*]

The *Purana* accounts give the date for the Mahabharata battle as 36 years before the ascension of Krishna that commences the start of Kaliyuga in 1177 BC. 1177 BC plus 36 years is 1213 BC the date that the Pyramid gives for the advent of his mission in the War Chariot of Arajuna and the Revelation of the Gita.

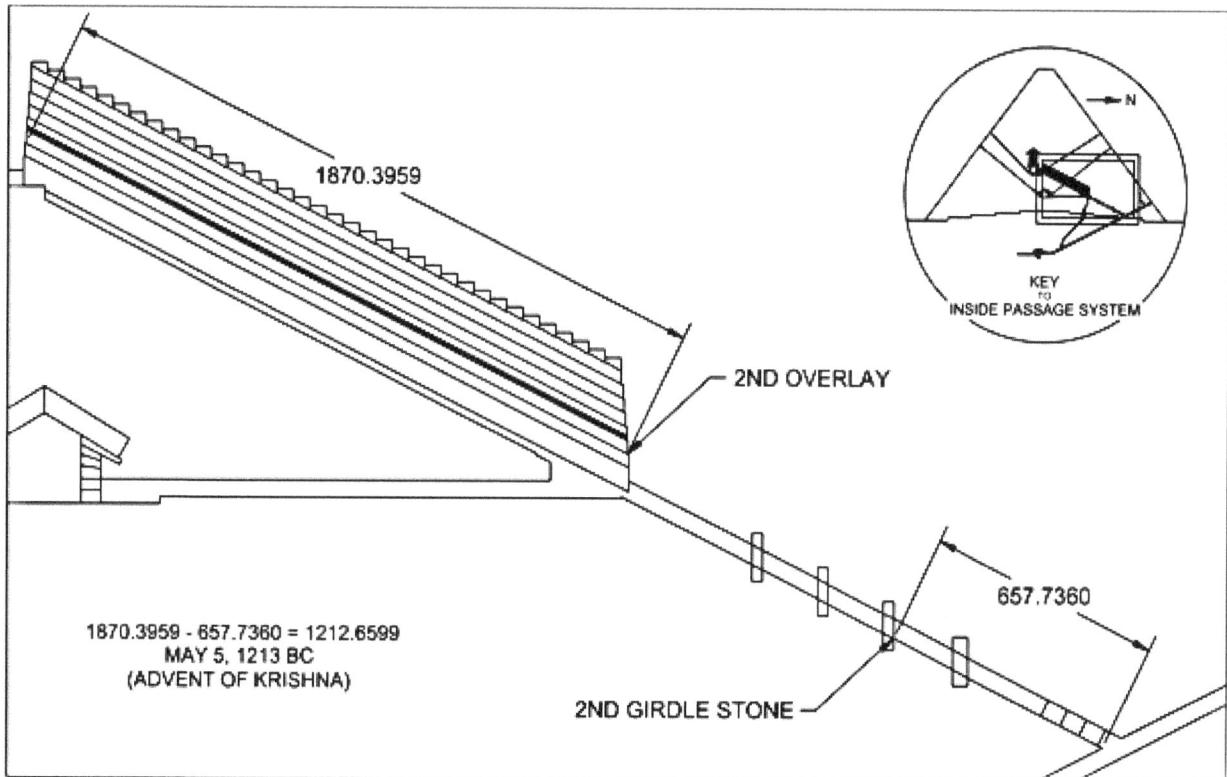

1870.3959

2ND OVERLAY

657.7360

1870.3959 - 657.7360 = 1212.6599
MAY 5, 1213 BC
(ADVENT OF KRISHNA)

2ND GIRDLE STONE

KEY to INSIDE PASSAGE SYSTEM

FIGURE 12

[*] "In *Vyasa and Valmiki* Sri Aurobindo refers to a 'recent article of the *Indian Review*' on the date of the Mahabharata war praising it as "an unusually able and searching (or almost conclusive) paper." It was Velandai Gopala Aiyer's "*The Date of the Mahabharata War*" published in Vol. II, January-December 1901 of this monthly journal (*Indian Review*) edited by G. A. Natesan. Sri Aurobindo was obviously fully convinced by Aiyer's arguments, because elsewhere he writes, 'It is now known beyond reasonable doubt that the Mahabharata war was fought out in or about 1190 BC'" (Pradip Bhattacharya, *The Date of the Mahabharata War*, p. 1).

The Date for the Advent of Zoroaster

By taking the distance from the start of the Ascending Passageway to the third Girdle Stone (of Zoroaster), 863.80201733 P″, and subtracting it from the distance of the third Overlay (of Zoroaster), 1863.80201733 P″, you get 1000.000 P″, or January 1st, 1000 BC, the date for the birth of Zoroaster (see Figure 13). Zoroaster said, "One thousand years after my birth you will see a star in the sky. Follow it and you will come to a manger, and there you will find me." We all know the Christmas story of the Magi (Zoroastrian priests) who followed the star and came to the manger and found the infant Jesus, bringing him gifts of gold, frankincense and myrrh. Zoroaster said he lived 3000 years before his birth,[*] and 3000 years after his birth the forces of light would win over the forces of darkness. Likewise, 'Abdu'l-Baha said by the end of this century all the people of the world would be Baha'is. "This Century is the Century of the Sun of Truth. This Century is the Century of the establishment of the Kingdom of God upon the earth."[†]

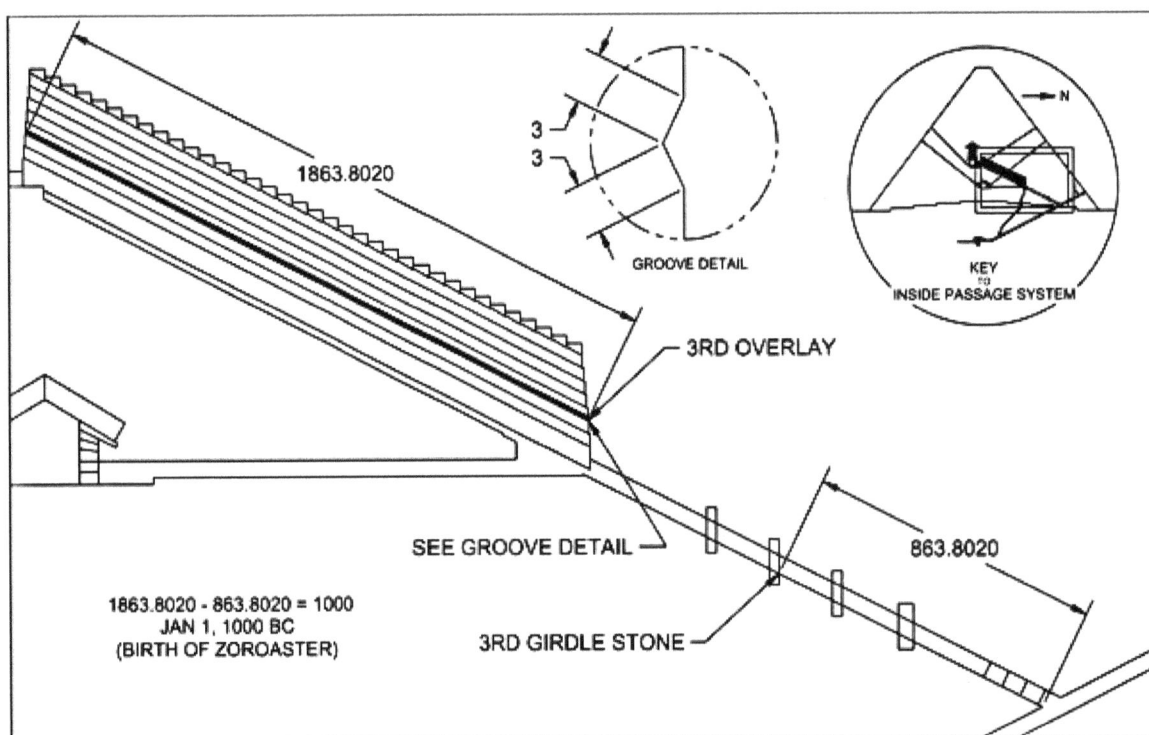

FIGURE 13

Thus Zoroaster was the middle Manifestation of the Adamic cycle, coming 3000 years after the Advent of Adam in 4000 BC, the start of the Adamic cycle. Three thousand years after the birth of Zoroaster the Adamic cycle will be ended at exactly midnight, December 31st, 2000 / January 1st, 2001 AD when the Dispensation of Baha'u'llah will begin and will last for a half a million years.[‡]

---

[*] Jesus said, "Before Abraham was, I am," meaning that he (Jesus) was in the plan of God before Abraham was born. In the same way, Zoroaster was in the plan of God at the time of Adam.

[†] *Star of the West, Vol. IX*, p. 7, cited in *Baha'u'llah and the New Era*, "Prophecies of Baha'u'llah and 'Abdu'l-Baha," 1950 edition, p. 302

[‡] The Bab and Baha'u'llah prophesied of the year 2001 AD as the "Year 'Mustaghath,'" the letters of which add up to 2001 in the Abjad system of letter to number correspondence.

In the third Overlay (of Zoroaster) there is a groove 3 P″ in and 3 P″ out running the entire length of the Grand Gallery in both walls. Each of these Pyramid inches represents one millennium, or 1000 years, showing that Zoroaster was the middle Manifestation. The center of this groove is also half-way from the ceiling to the floor of the Grand Gallery (see Groove Detail in Figure 13).

These explanations are unique. Nobody in this entire world, either in the past or the present, has been able to give this knowledge, although 'Abdu'l-Baha said by the end of the present cycle all the people in the world will be Baha'is. Absolutely none of the pyramidologists, nor any of the religious leaders, nor in any of the teachings of the Manifestations of God can we find these explanations. In none of the Baha'i Writings are these explanations found. Only Jesus on his second coming possessed this knowledge. These explanations were given to us by Jesus on his return. This is one of the purposes for the return of Jesus the High Priest standing in the Holy of Holies before the Ark of the Covenant--to establish the Kingdom of Baha'u'llah, the Father,[*] in the world.

Dr. Leland (the Land[†]) Jensen, when he had the "Stone with Seven Eyes" before him wrote these explanations with his own pen.

The Date for the Advent of Buddha

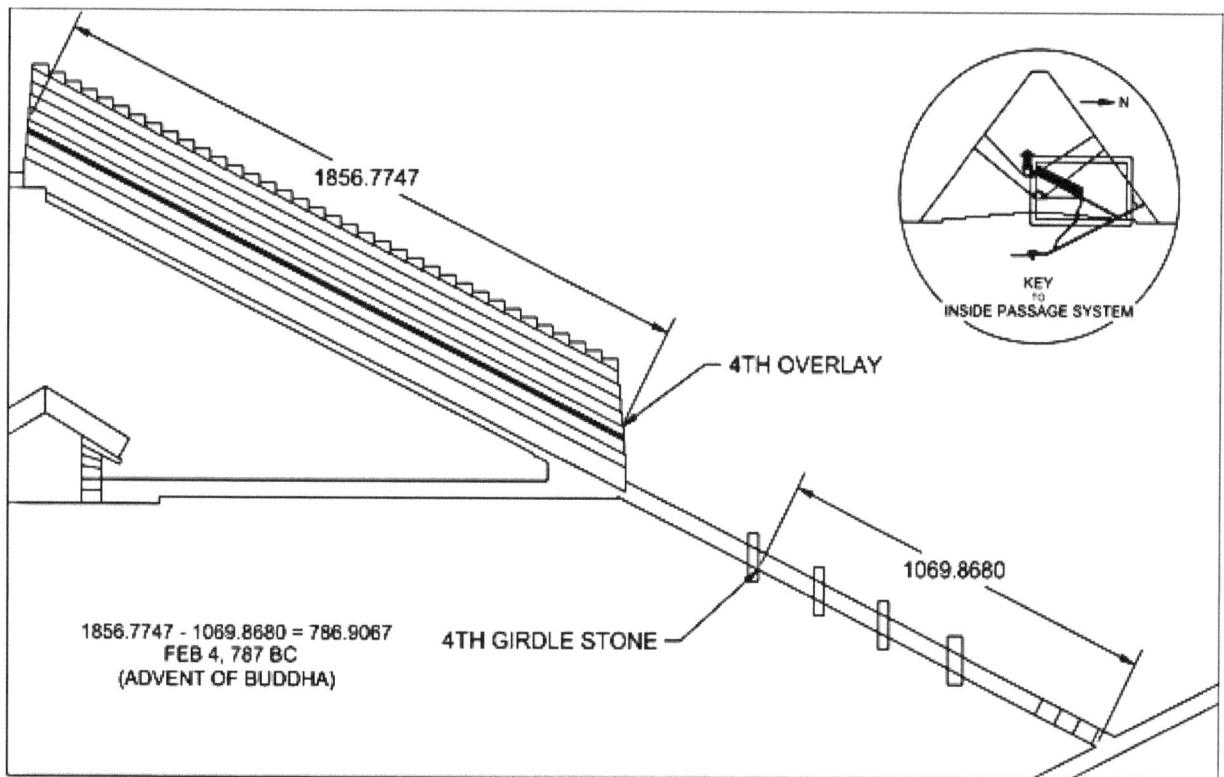

FIGURE 14

---

[*] Mark 8:38.
[†] Zechariah 3:9.

The distance from the start of the Ascending Passageway to the fourth Girdle Stone (of Buddha) is 1069.86801156 P″. When you subtract this from the fourth Overlay (of Buddha), 1856.77471784 P″ - 1069.86801156 P″, you get 786.906706285 P″, or February 4th, 787 BC, the date for the Advent of Buddha (see Figure 14).[*]

The Date for the Crucifixion of Jesus Christ

The length of the fifth Overlay (of Jesus) is 1848.67171899 P″ (see Figure 15). The length of this Overlay contains all the dates that pertain to the advent of Jesus Christ and John the Baptist, as well as that of the crucifixion of Jesus: 33.2178918677 P″ x 29.7178918677 P″ x 26.2178918677 P″ divided by 7 divided by 2 = 1848.67171899 P″.

Or you can take the length of the fifth Overlay (of Jesus), 1848.67171899 P″, and multiply it by 7 for the "Week of the Covenant," and multiply it by 2 (for the two parts of the week) and divide it by the date for the Advent of John the Baptist 26.2178918677 P″, and then divide it again by the date for the Baptism of Jesus 29.7178918677 P″, and you will get 33.2178918677 P″ or March 21st, 34 AD, the date for the Crucifixion of Jesus Christ.

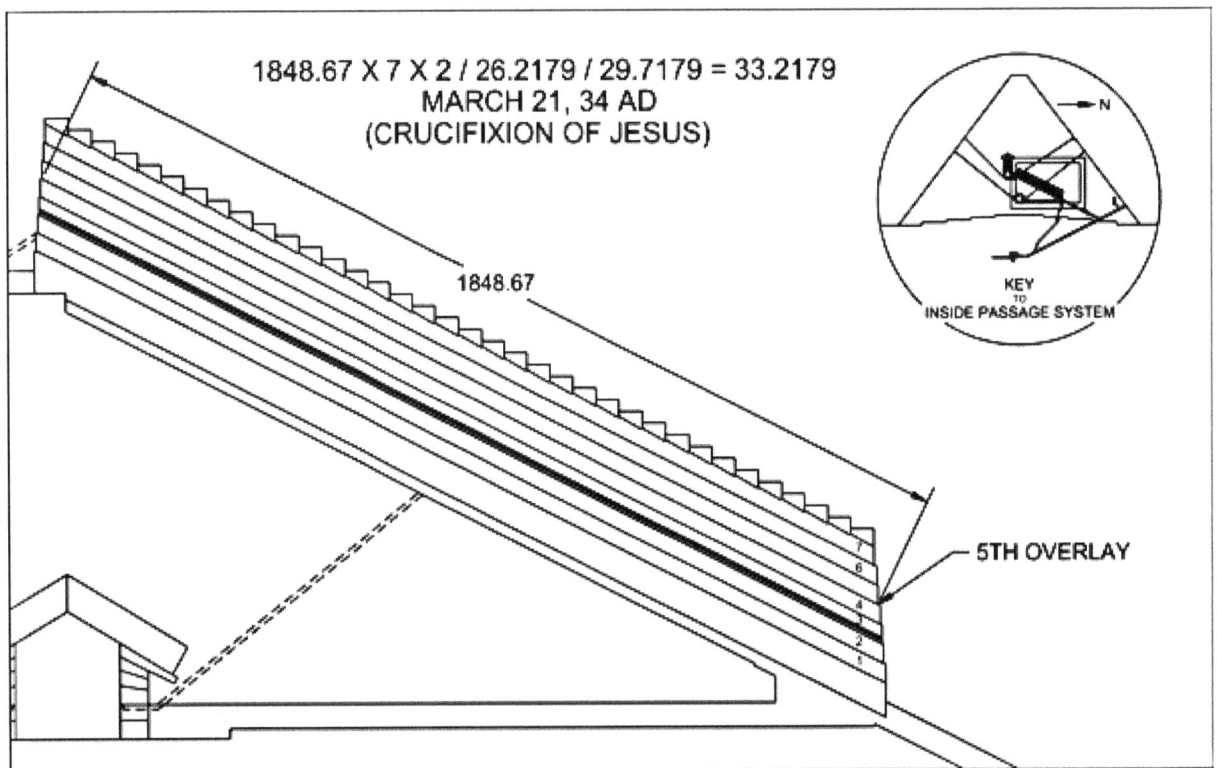

FIGURE 15

[*] The Kalachakra dating places the birth of Buddha at 787 BC the same date given in the Great Pyramid. Modern archaeology also sets the birth of Buddha back to this same epoch: "Coningham and his team of 40 archaeologists discovered a tree shrine that predates all known Buddhist sites by at least 300 years" (*Archaeologists' Discovery Puts Buddha's Birth 300 years Earlier* by Elizabeth Day).

The Date for the Advent of Muhammad

The length of the sixth Overlay (of Muhammad) is 1842.85714286 P″ (see Figure 16). The length of this overlay gives us the dates for the proclamation of Muhammad.

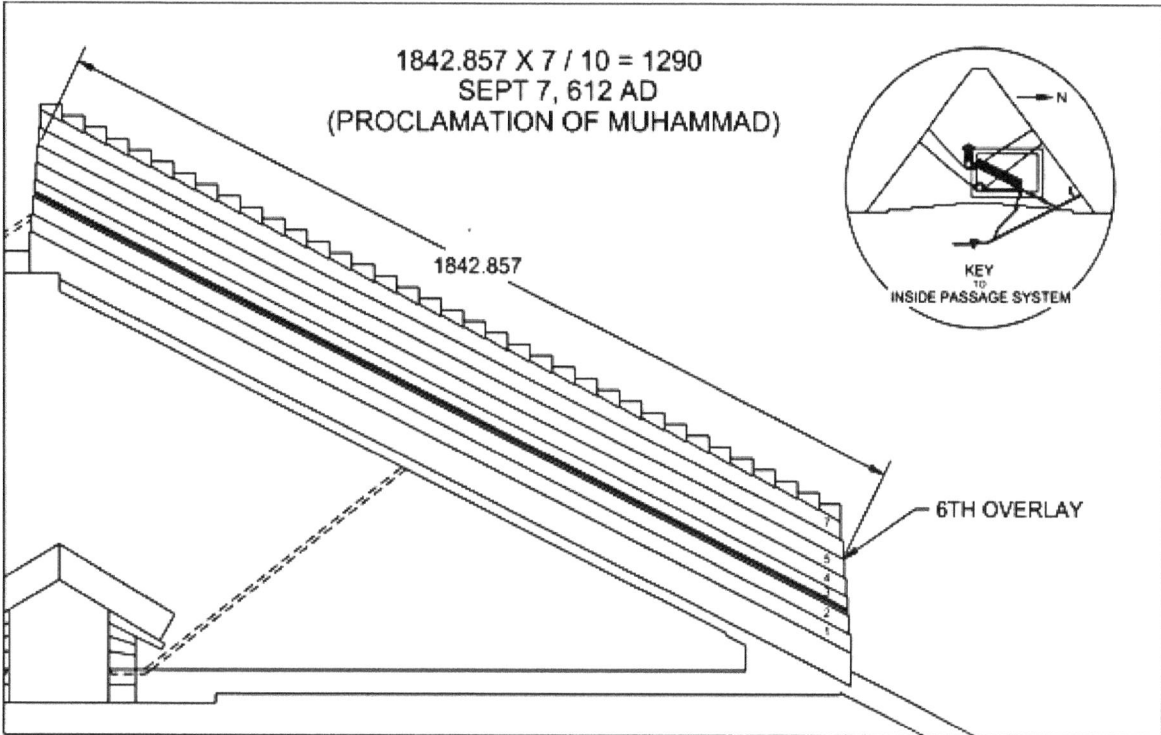

FIGURE 16

First, taking the length of the sixth Overlay (of Muhammad), 1842.85714286 P″, and multiplying it by 7 (Muhammad is the seventh Manifestation in the Adamic cycle) and dividing it by 10, gives us 1290. Twelve hundred and ninety lunar years (prophesied of in Daniel chapter 12) before the Proclamation of Baha'u'llah in the Garden of Ridvan on April 21st, 1863 AD gives us the day of the Proclamation of Muhammad on September 7th, 612 AD. It was on September 7th, 612 AD, that Muhammad officially proclaimed himself to all his family at a special dinner that he had arranged just for that occasion. This happened after a three-year silence, since the start of the mission of Muhammad when the angel Gabriel came to him in the cave of Hira, that he received the call to proclaim himself openly to his family first and then to all the people.

Again, when we take the length of the sixth Overlay (of Muhammad) 1842.857143 P″ and subtract 1260 from this (the date for the Advent of the Bab according to the Muslim calendar), you get 582.85714286 P″ (see Figure 17). Add to this the distance from the Zero Point to the start of Grand Gallery, 29.7178918677 P″, giving you 612.575034728 P″, or July 30th, 613 AD, the exact date when Muhammad next proclaimed himself in public on Mt. Safa to the entire population of the city of Mecca. The Pyramid gives both dates for the Proclamation of Muhammad.

299

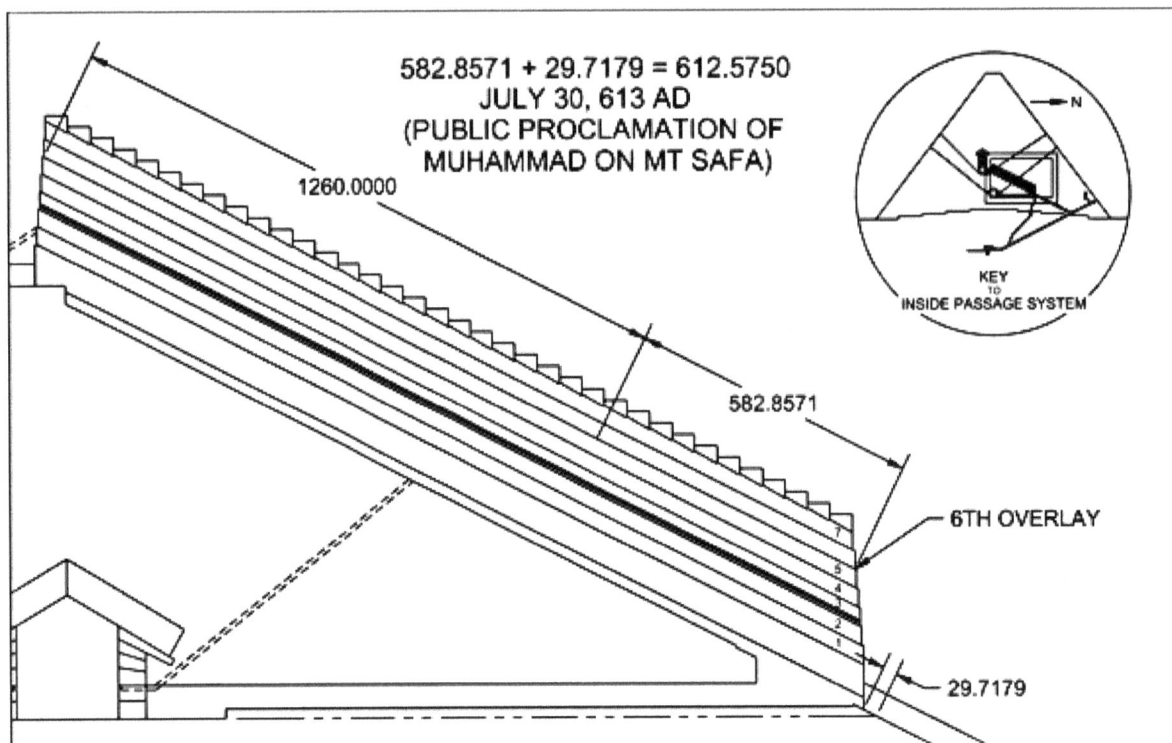

582.8571 + 29.7179 = 612.5750
JULY 30, 613 AD
(PUBLIC PROCLAMATION OF
MUHAMMAD ON MT SAFA)

1260.0000

582.8571

6TH OVERLAY

29.7179

KEY
TO
INSIDE PASSAGE SYSTEM

N

FIGURE 17

The Date for the Advent of Enoch

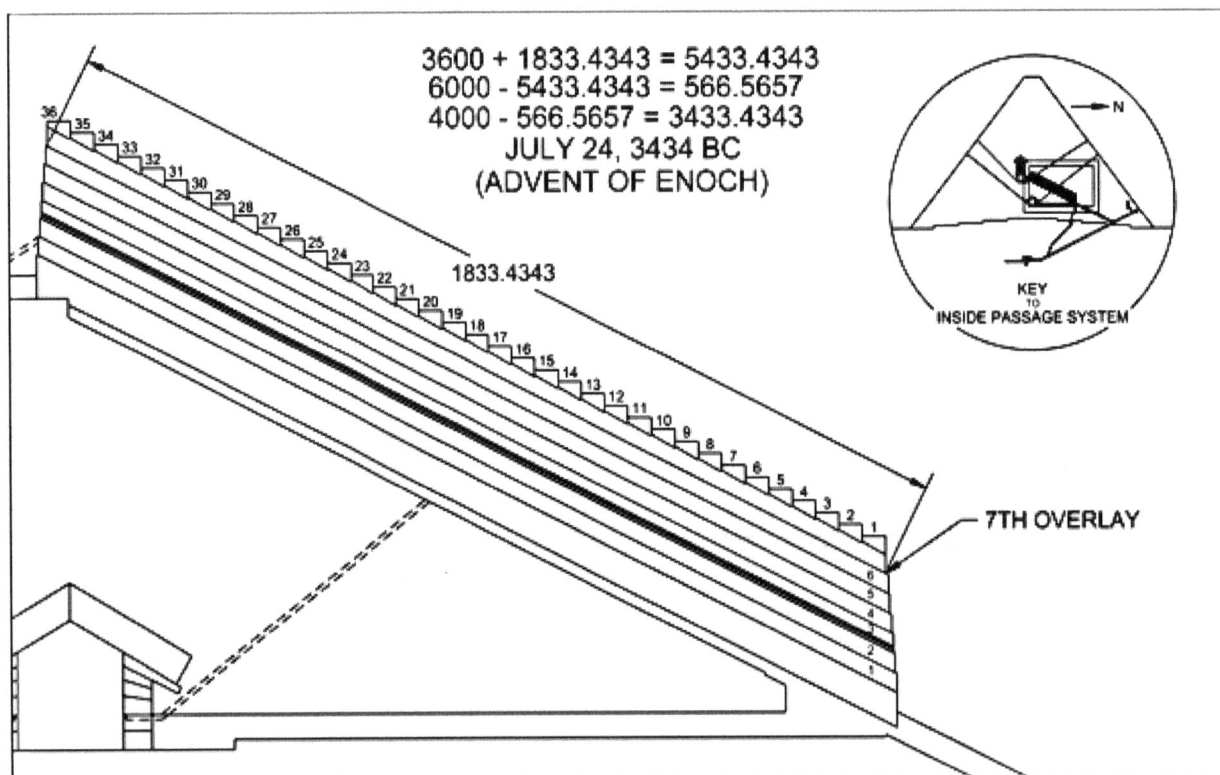

3600 + 1833.4343 = 5433.4343
6000 - 5433.4343 = 566.5657
4000 - 566.5657 = 3433.4343
JULY 24, 3434 BC
(ADVENT OF ENOCH)

1833.4343

7TH OVERLAY

KEY
TO
INSIDE PASSAGE SYSTEM

N

FIGURE 18

300

There are 36 blocks like shingles forming the ceiling of the Grand Gallery. Each of these represents 100 years, or 3600 years total. When you add these 3600 years to the length of the seventh Overlay, 1833.43435819 P″, you get 5433.43435819. You then subtract this amount from the 6000 year Adamic cycle (6000 - 5433.4345819 = 566.56564181), and then subtract this result from the date for Adam of 4000.000 P″, giving you 3433.43435819, or July 24th, 3434 BC, the date when Enoch laid the first cornerstone to start the construction of the Great Pyramid: 3600 + 1833.43435819 = 5433.43435819; 6000 - 5433.43435819 = 566.56564181; 4000.000 - 566.56564181 = 3433.43435819 or July 24th, 3434 BC (see Figure 18).

The Date for the Advent of The Bab

Measuring 1843.217891867748 P″ up the Ascending Passageway from the Zero Point, you come to the upper end of the Grand Gallery of Religions at the Altar Stone (see Figure 19). This junction is at the East-West Center Line, marking the end of the Christian Era and calendar on March 21st, 1844 AD and bringing us into the New Age. The Baha'i Era and calendar were inaugurated by the Bab who made his Proclamation on May 23rd, 1844 AD. This date corresponds exactly with the date given by Daniel in the Bible of 2300 days/years from 457 BC to March 21st, 1844 (Daniel 8:13, 14) for the return of Jesus as the Bab (Door or Gate in John 10:7, 9), for the cleansing of the Sanctuary. The Sanctuary is symbolized by the Ante-chamber in the Great Pyramid and the Altar by the Great Step. The Sanctuary was cleansed by the blood of the Bab on the Altar just inside the Door of the Sanctuary and by the blood of ten thousand of his followers in Glorious martyrdom, during the years represented by the length of the Altar Stone (the Great Step) in the Pyramid.

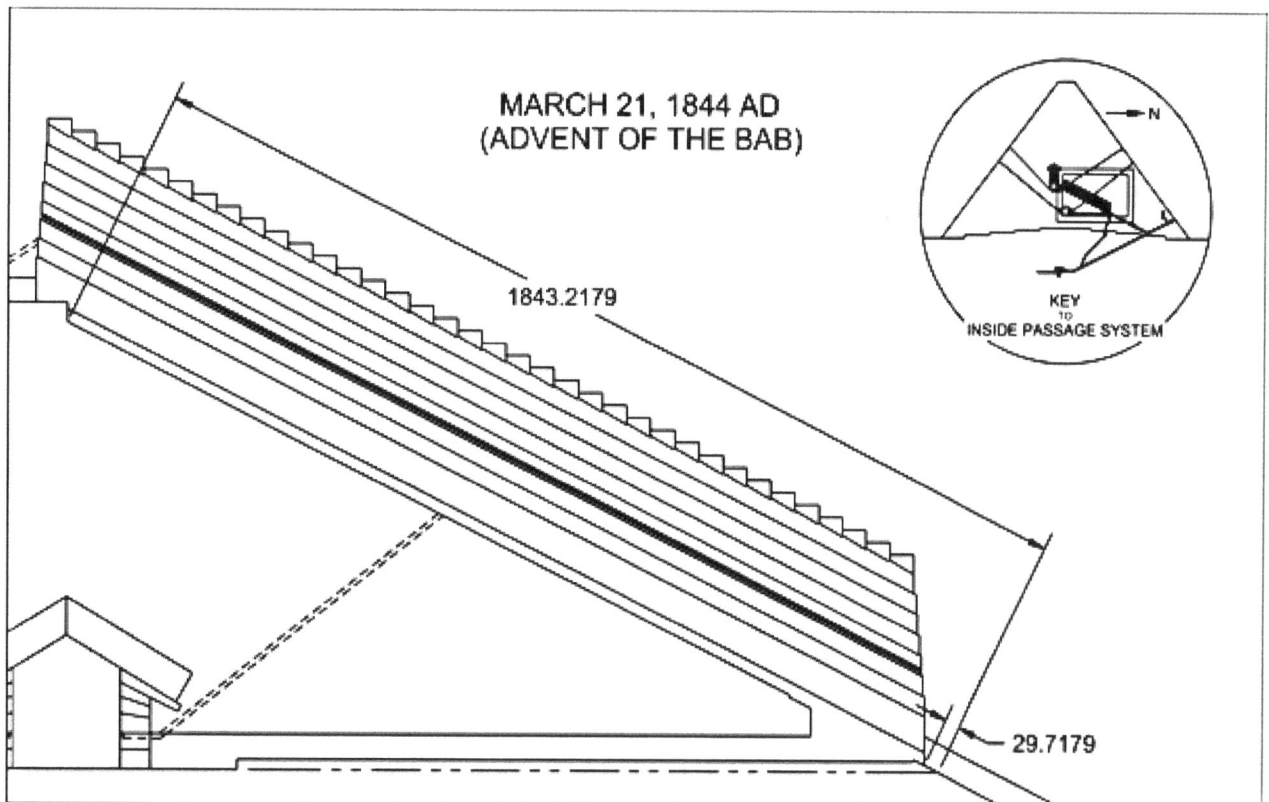

FIGURE 19

The Bab, meaning Door or Gate, closed the door to the Prophetic Age and opened the door to the Age of Fulfillment. His Revelation was of the potency of the Sanctuary and he is therefore the return of Jesus to earth in the Sanctuary which he had entered in heaven (Hebrews 9:24). Like John the Baptist, he prepared the way for the Advent of the Glory of the Lord—Baha'u'llah (see the 43rd chapter of Ezekiel).

The calendar instituted by the Bab for the New Age has 19 days to the month and 19 months to the year, plus four and one-quarter intercalary days, with leap years having five (one year = 19 months of 19 days plus four and one-quarter intercalary days). Therefore there are 19.22328763 Baha'i months in one solar year.[*]

The Date for the Proclamation of Baha'u'llah

There are 366.885640743 P'' from the start of the Altar (the Great Step) to the Holy of Holies (King's Chamber) (see Figure 20). It was rightfully named as it is the Chamber of the King of kings and Lord of lords[†] (Baha'u'llah). From the start of the Altar (Great Step) onward, each P'' represents one Baha'i month (a Vahid) of 19 days, with 19.2232876316 of these Baha'i months in one solar year. Therefore the distance to the Holy of Holies from the Altar, 366.885640743 P'', divided by 19.2232876316, equals 19 years and 31 days. Adding this to the vernal equinox on March 21st, 1844 (the start of the Babi/Baha'i calendar) gives the date when Baha'u'llah entered

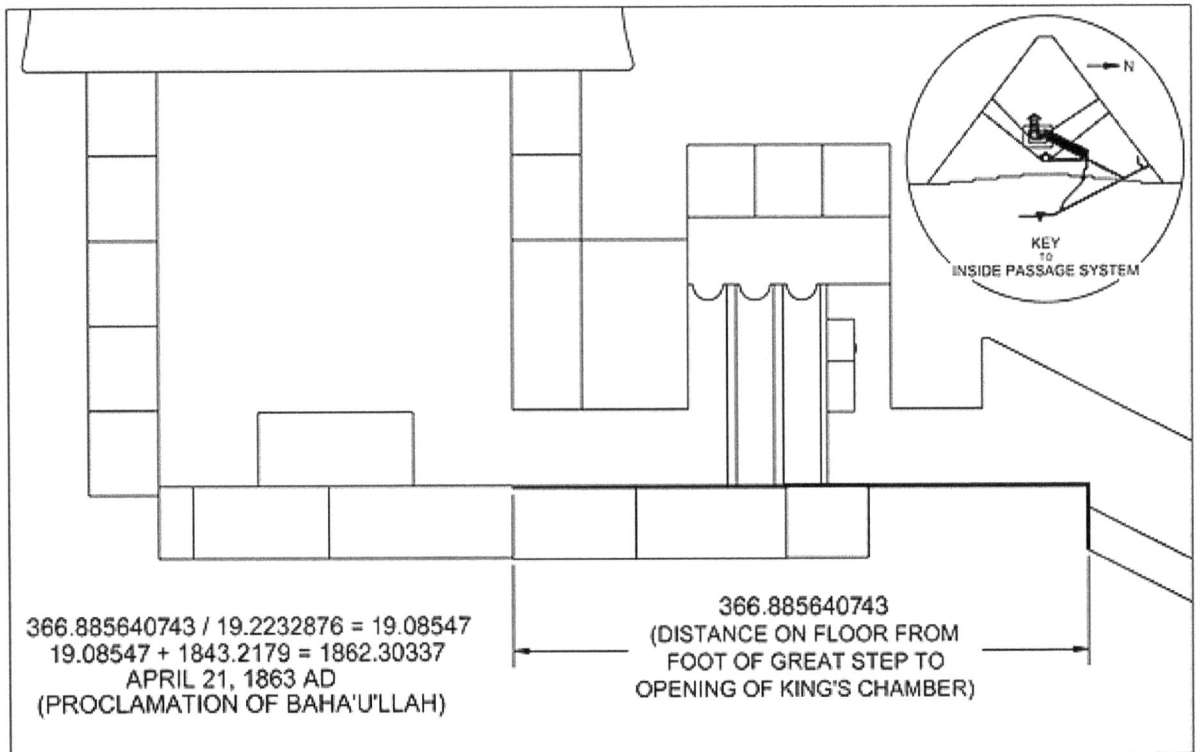

366.885640743 / 19.2232876 = 19.08547
19.08547 + 1843.2179 = 1862.30337
APRIL 21, 1863 AD
(PROCLAMATION OF BAHA'U'LLAH)

366.885640743
(DISTANCE ON FLOOR FROM
FOOT OF GREAT STEP TO
OPENING OF KING'S CHAMBER)

FIGURE 20

---

[*] For more on the Baha'i Calendar see *The Baha'i World Vol. XII*, 1950-1954, pp. 553-554.

[†] Revelation 19:16.

the Garden of Ridvan on April 21st, 1863 AD where He made His Proclamation. This corresponds with the prophecy of Daniel 12:11:

> And from the time that the daily sacrifice shall be taken away, and the abomination that maketh desolate is set up, there shall be a thousand two hundred and ninety days. (Daniel 12:11)

There are exactly 1290 days (or lunar years, with each day equaling a lunar year) from the Proclamation of Muhammad on September 7th, 612 AD to the Proclamation of Baha'u'llah on April 21st, 1863 AD. Muhammad did away with all sacrifices, including the Eucharist.

Three Chambers

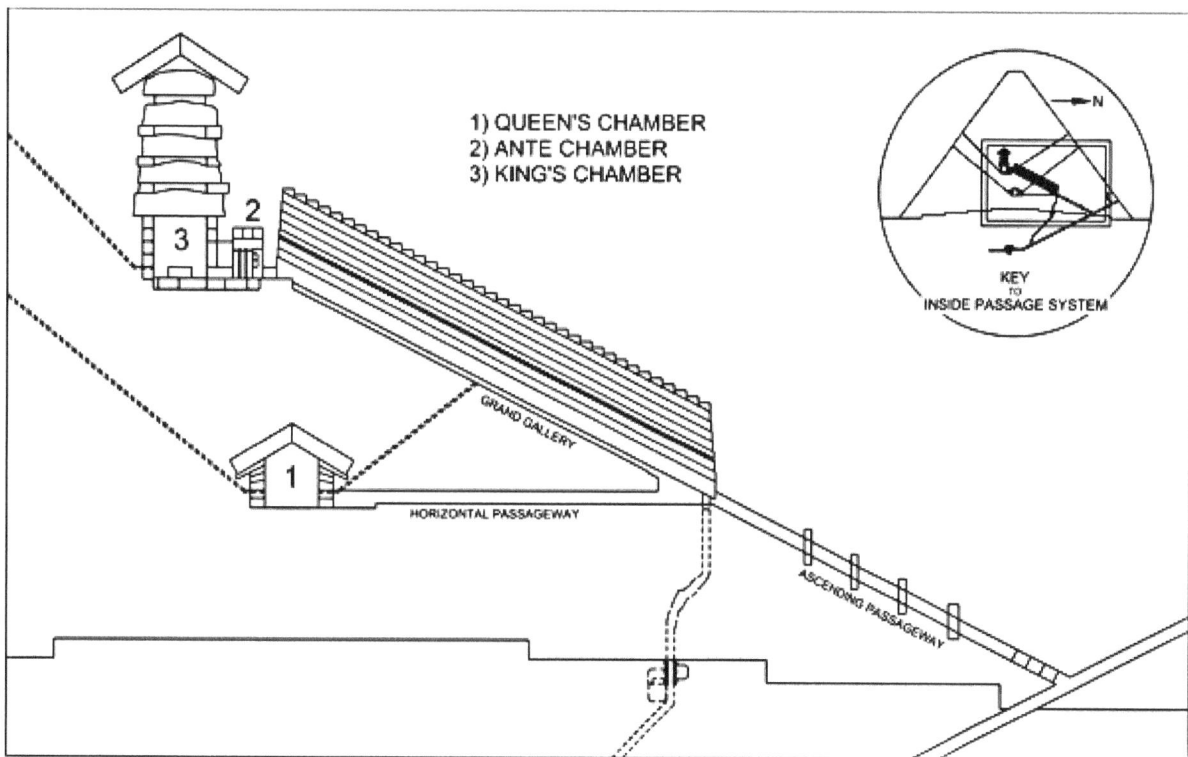

FIGURE 21

The Ascending Passageway leads to three chambers: (a) the Queen's Chamber, (b) the Ante-Chamber, and (c) the King's Chamber (see Figure 21).

The Horizontal Passageway leads to the so-called Queen's Chamber, which represents the Passageway of the Chamber of Martyrs for Jesus who were first martyred by Imperial Rome and then by the Holy Roman Empire. Those that are in this chamber cry out, 'O Lord how long will it be before you avenge our blood for Thy Cause?' They are told to be quiet for a little while longer until all the martyrs come in,[*] referring to the Babi and Baha'i martyrs. We are now entering that time:

> And when he had opened the fifth seal, I saw under the altar the souls of them that were slain for the word of God [Jesus], and for the testimony which they held:
>
> And they cried with a loud voice, saying, How long, O Lord, holy and true, dost thou not judge and avenge our blood on them that dwell on the earth?
>
> And white robes [auras] were given unto every one of them; and it was said unto them, that they should rest yet for a little season, until their fellow servants also and their brethren, that should be killed as they were, should be fulfilled. (Revelation 6:9-11)

This Queen's Chamber is directly under the Altar Stone in the Great Pyramid (see Figure 22). We are now at the time that the blood of the martyrs will be avenged by God, with the oncoming of the great catastrophe.

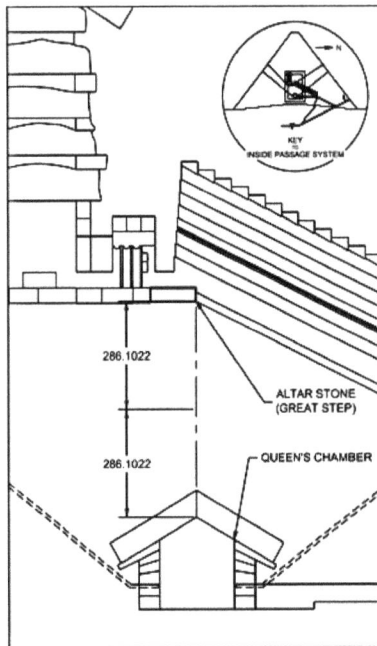

FIGURE 22

The Jews are Expecting the Rebuilding of the Temple

The Jews know that they are under the Curse and are waiting for the Temple to be rebuilt and the reinstitution of animal sacrifice for the removal of sin. This is best explained by a scenario that took place soon after the Jewish State of Israel was set up.

---

[*] Revelation 6:9-11.

The Scenario

The scenario went something like this: The Jews are still under the period of the curse. They don't have their Temple and the sacrifices for sins. A reporter interviewed a famous Israeli historian, Israel Eldad. In looking up at the Temple site in answer to the question, "Do your people intend to rebuild the Temple?" Eldad said: "From the time that King David first conquered Jerusalem until Solomon built the Temple, just one generation passed. So will it be with us."

The reporter asked, "Why don't you build the Temple now?"

Eldad replied, "We can't because the Dome of the Rock (Omar's Temple) is on the Temple site."

"Why don't you tear it down?"

Eldad replied, "That would bring on a disastrous war with all of Islam united against us."

The reporter asked, "What are you going to do?"

Eldad replied, "Maybe there will be an earthquake."

The reporter asked, "If you built the Temple, how is it going to function? The High Priesthood came to an end about the second century AD?"

Eldad replied, "Well, we will have to wait for our Messiah. He will have all the answers."

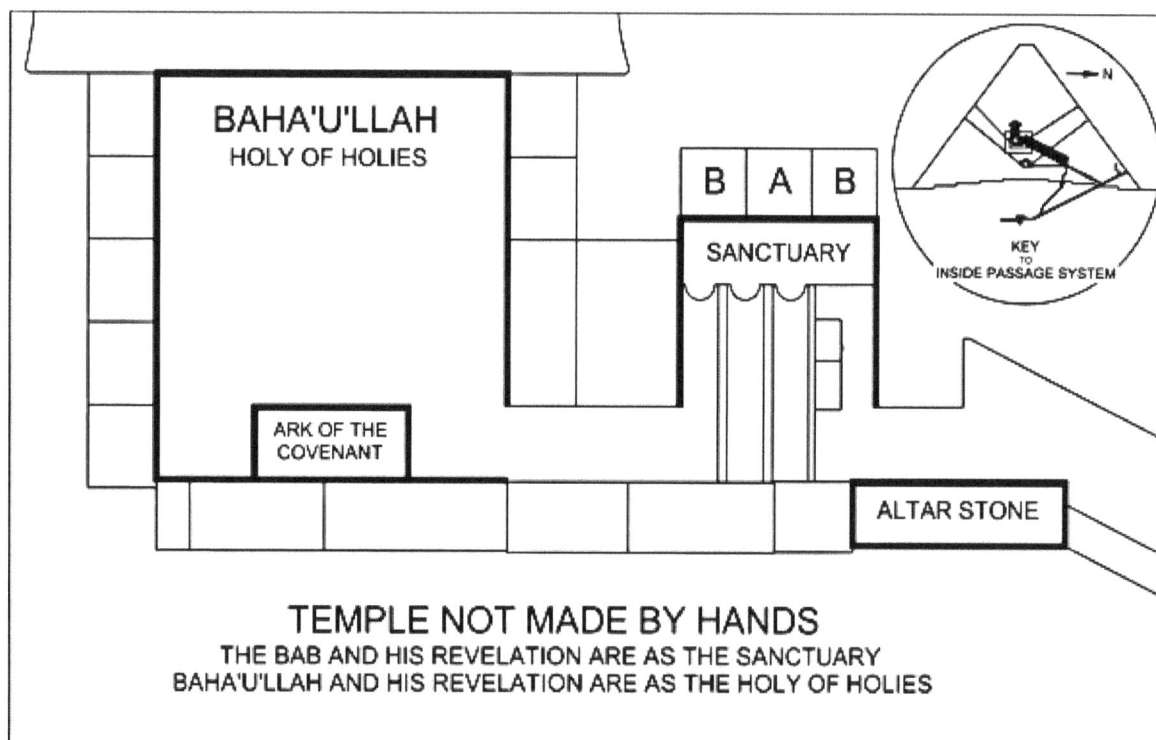

FIGURE 23

If the Jews had listened to Paul, an apostle to Jesus, in his Epistle to the Hebrews, they would be informed that the Temple that is to be is one not built by hands, that is, the Temple built by hands will never be rebuilt. The Great Pyramid shows that the Ante-chamber, or the Sanctuary, representing the Bab, and the King's Chamber, representing Baha'u'llah, are a blueprint for the re-establishment of the Temple of Moses. As Moses was the Temple (the presence of God), so too are the Bab and Baha'u'llah, being Manifestations of God, representative of the Temple.

The Grand Gallery brings us to two Chambers which represent the re-establishment of the Temple of Moses, consisting of the Sanctuary and the Holy of Holies.[*] In this Temple, the Bab and his Revelation are as the Sanctuary, and Baha'u'llah and His Revelation are as the Holy of Holies. (see Figure 23) These two Manifestations are the Temple not made by hands.

> For Christ [Jesus] is not entered into the holy places made with hands, which are the figures [symbols] of the true [one]; but into heaven itself, now to appear in the presence of God for us. (Hebrews 9:24)

The Bab is the return of Jesus as the Door (or Gate) and Baha'u'llah as the return of Christ. They are the Temple of the heaven of prophecy that Jesus entered into.[†]

The Displacement Factor

The entrance and all the Passageways in the Great Pyramid are left of the North-South center line 286.102215583 P″ (see Figure 24).

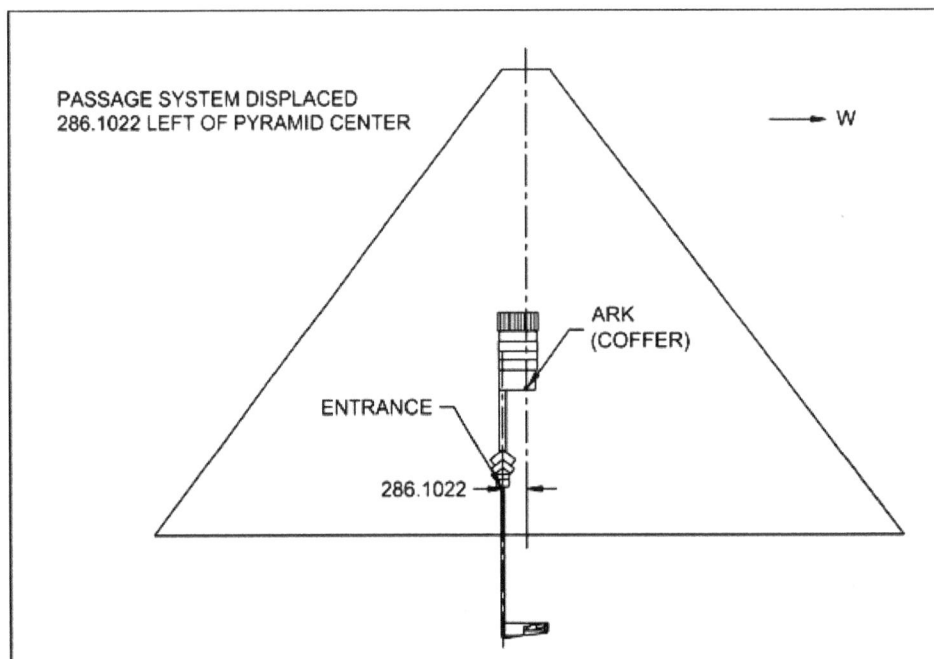

PASSAGE SYSTEM DISPLACED
286.1022 LEFT OF PYRAMID CENTER

W

ARK
(COFFER)

ENTRANCE

286.1022

FIGURE 24

---

[*] Hebrews 9:2, 3.
[†] Hebrews 9:24, 28.

306

This is not due to Adam eating the apple, but rather to the waywardness of the so-called believers and their violation of the Great Covenant. For instance, almost all people are in violation of the first and second commandments:

> I am the Lord thy God, which brought thee out of the land of Egypt, out of the house of bondage. Thou shalt have no other gods before me. Thou shalt not make unto thee any graven images or any likeness of any thing that is in the heaven above, or that is in the earth beneath, or that is in the water under the earth: Thou shalt not bow down thyself to them, nor serve them: for I the Lord thy God am a jealous God, visiting the iniquity of the fathers upon the children unto the third and fourth generation of them that hate me. (Exodus 20:2-5)

The Christians have three gods before them and they have statues and pictures, especially one that looks like a Nordic person that has no resemblance of Jesus. They were to have nothing at all before them. This is true of other religions as well.

The Adamites became so corrupt that God drowned them all except Noah and his family. The Jews were so corrupt they lost their Temple twice and were dispersed throughout the world. They were so corrupt that they had their Messiah nailed to a cross. The Christians were so corrupt that true Christianity came to an end in the Dark Ages when they looked upon all learning and science as unclean to such a degree that they sunk into ignorance, disease, poverty and squalor. Muhammad was the greatest protagonist of Christianity, bringing the message of Christ to the Arab world. It was the influence of Islam that brought the Christians out of the Dark Ages into the Renaissance. Although Jesus prophesied Muhammad by name, the Christians were so corrupted by their clergy that they, like the Jews, rejected him. The Baha'is became so corrupt that they broke the Covenant and did away with the Executive Branch of the Baha'i faith, a violation so horrible that the mass of them will perish in the great catastrophe that is upon us.

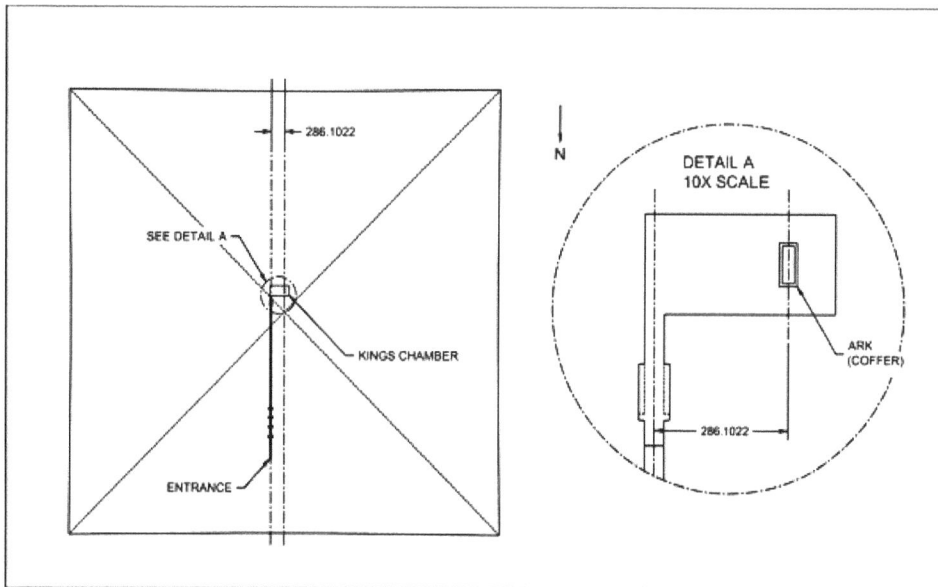

FIGURE 25

The Holy of Holies Brings Us Back to the Center Line

The Ark of the Covenant in the King's Chamber is on the Center of the North-South center line (see Figure 25). This brings mankind back from error--the displacement factor--to the Kingdom of God on earth as prophesied by Jesus, in what is called the LORD'S prayer. This Covenant of Baha'u'llah is symbolically placed in the Ark of the Covenant in the Holy of Holies. This Covenant of Baha'u'llah, when followed, will bring peace to the world. Baha'u'llah, the second Messiah (a descendant of David seated on the throne of David), provided in His Covenant for this lineage from David (seated on the throne to exist forever) to be the president or head of the Universal House of Justice, distinguishing the true House of Justice from all false ones. The Covenant-breaking "Hands" threw out the Executive Branch of the House of Justice, making it a Headless Monster.

This violation of the Covenant happened because nobody in this world understood the Covenant. Shoghi Effendi said he didn't understand the Covenant,[*] but indicated that one would come that would be the only one who understood the Covenant. That is because absolutely no one except the High Priest can enter into the Holy of Holies where the Covenant is situated in the Ark of the Covenant, as it was with Moses. Moses's Temple was a microcosm of the macrocosm, that is, his Temple was one that was built by hands which was but a symbol of the true one not built by hands. As only Aaron the High Priest alone was allowed to go into the Holy of Holies, and as this priesthood came to an end about a century or so after the crucifixion of Jesus, God has sent his Son, Jesus the High Priest after the Order of Melchizedec, to reestablish back into the Baha'i faith what the Covenant-breakers threw out.

> Whither the forerunner is for us entered, even Jesus, made an high priest forever after the order of Melchizedec. (Hebrews 6:20)

Jesus the High Priest after the Order of Melchizedec

The proof for the High Priest after the Order of Melchizedec is found in the Holy of Holies. He is standing before the Ark of the Covenant, for only a high priest is allowed in the Holy of Holies. Absolutely no one else is. (See the books of Moses.)

Moses, of the tribe of Levi (the tribe of the priests), was the Temple, where the presence of God was. But he wasn't going to live forever so God had him build a Temple made by hands. It was at first a tent in the desert divided in two by a curtain, with an Altar at its entrance, and it was called a tabernacle. Later on, Solomon built a huge Temple in Jerusalem, made of stone and wood.

> The first [room], wherein was the candlestick, and the table, and the shewbread; which is called the sanctuary. And after the second veil, of the tabernacle which is called the Holiest of all [the Holy of Holies]; Which had the golden censer, and **the ark of the covenant** overlaid round about with gold, wherein was the golden pot that had manna **and the tables of the covenant**....(Hebrews 9:2-4)

---

[*] *World Order of Baha'u'llah*, pp. 8, 147.

Only the High Priest Could Go into the Holy of Holies

The High Priest Aaron (the brother of Moses) and the first-born of his descendants had access at will to go into the Holy of Holies and read the laws of Moses, study the scriptures and educate the ordinary priests. But only once a year could he go in with blood to offer up for the sins of all of Israel:

> Now when these things were thus ordained, the priest went always into the first tabernacle [room], accomplishing the service of God.
>
> But into the second went the high priest **alone** once every year, not without blood, which he offered for himself, and for the errors of the people. (Hebrews 9:2-7)

Jesus, being of the tribe of Judah, the kingly line, was not permitted to go into the Temple even though his mother, Mary, was of the tribe of Levi and Aaron. But Jesus entered into Jerusalem with a large army and busted his way into the Temple:

> And the **multitude that went before, and that followed**, cried, saying Hosanna to the __son of David__: Blessed is he that cometh in the name of the Lord; Hosanna in the highest....
>
> And Jesus went into the temple of God, and cast out all them that sold and bought in the temple, and overthrew the tables of the moneychangers and the seats of them that sold doves, And said unto them, It is written, My house shall be called the house of prayer; but ye have made it a den of thieves. (Matthew 21:9, 12, 13)

Jesus could not enter into the Temple built by hands that was standing in his day to officiate, for he was not a high priest after the order of Aaron. However, Jesus was a prophet like unto Moses, therefore he was the Temple.

> The LORD thy God will raise up unto thee [Israel] a Prophet from the midst of thee, of thy brethren, like unto me [Moses]; unto him ye shall hearken. (Deuteronomy 18:15)

Thus Jesus was a prophet like Moses. As Moses was the Temple, or the presence of God, so was Jesus. However, unlike Moses who had Aaron to be the high priest, Jesus himself was a high priest. However, he was a high priest of a much higher order than Aaron, whose position depends on genealogy, "...even Jesus, made an high priest for ever after the order of Melchizedec" (Hebrews 6:20). This Melchizedec was Shem, who built Jerusalem and put a high wall around it to protect the religion of Adam that was taken over by Nimrod and Semiramis who created the Trinity Doctrine that spread all over the world, crept into Christianity and destroyed it. Shem was both king and priest. This priesthood comes every two thousand years. Seidec is another name for Adam. Shem came two thousand years after Seidec, or Adam, and Jesus, a High Priest after the Order of Melchizedec, came two thousand years after Shem, and the return of the High Priest after the Order of Melchizedec comes today, two thousand years after Jesus.

> For this Melchizedec king of [Jeru*] Salem [Shem], priest of the most high God, who met Abraham returning from the slaughter of the [pagan] kings and blessed him. (Hebrews 7:1)

This priesthood didn't depend on genealogy or family:

> Without father, without mother, without descent, having neither beginning of days, nor end of life; but made like unto the Son of God; abideth a priest continually. (Hebrews 7:3)

A thousand years after Shem the kingship and the High Priest were separated. David was King and Seidec was the High Priest. A thousand years later they were united again in Jesus, who was both King and Priest. But today they are separated again. Baha'u'llah is the King of Glory and His establisher is the High Priest after the Order of Melchizedec. This High Priest does not go into the Temple built by hands but goes into the one in which the Bab is the Sanctuary and Baha'u'llah is the Holy of Holies.

The Date for the Return of Jesus the High Priest

This is pictured in the Holy of Holies in the Great Pyramid. In the King's Chamber, or the Holy of Holies, the floor, the walls and the ceiling are all of Red Granite, signifying the spiritual. The prophecy for Leland, the Land, is not by Pyramid inches, but is prophesied by all the Red Granite in the Holy of Holies (see Figure 26). The 100 Red Granite slabs forming the four walls of the King's Chamber represent the 100 years from the Proclamation of Baha'u'llah on April 21st, 1863 AD, to when the return of Jesus the High Priest began his ministry by being opposed by Satan on April 21st, 1963.

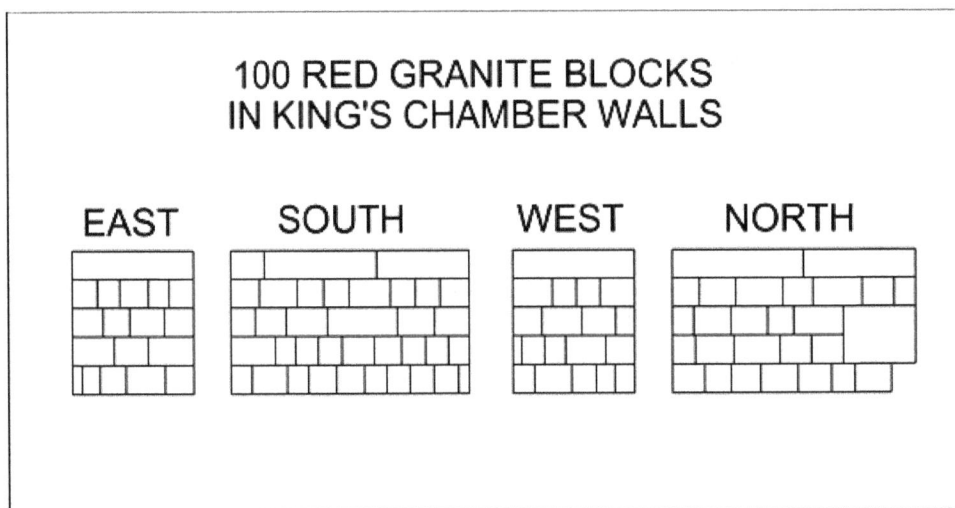

100 RED GRANITE BLOCKS IN KING'S CHAMBER WALLS

EAST   SOUTH   WEST   NORTH

FIGURE 26

---

* Meaning "city."

In the last two verses of the Book of Daniel occur the cryptic words:—

"**Blessed is <u>he</u>** that waiteth and cometh to the thousand three hundred and thirty-five (1335) days/years...." 'Abdu'l-Baha's Tablets make it clear that this prophecy refers to the one-hundredth anniversary of the Declaration of Baha'u'llah in Baghdad, or the year 1963. (*Baha'u'llah and the New Era*, "Prophecies Fulfilled," 1950 edition, pp. 302, 303)

As this prophecy occurs in the Holy of Holies in the Great Pyramid it could only mean the High Priest, for only a high priest could possibly be in the Holy of Holies.

There are exactly 108 Red Granite Slabs forming the floor of the Great Pyramid.[*] This represents the one hundred and eight years from the Proclamation of Baha'u'llah on April 21st, 1863 to April 21st, 1971. This date refers to the Proclamation of Leland (the land)[†] on the Holy Day of April 29th, 1971. April 21st is the first day of Ridvan and April 29th is the ninth day of Ridvan, the Most Holy Day. These nine days are represented in the Great Pyramid by the nine Red Granite Beams forming the ceiling of the Holy of Holies, with each Beam representing one day. Baha'u'llah declared April 29th as the Most Holy Day (see Figure 27).

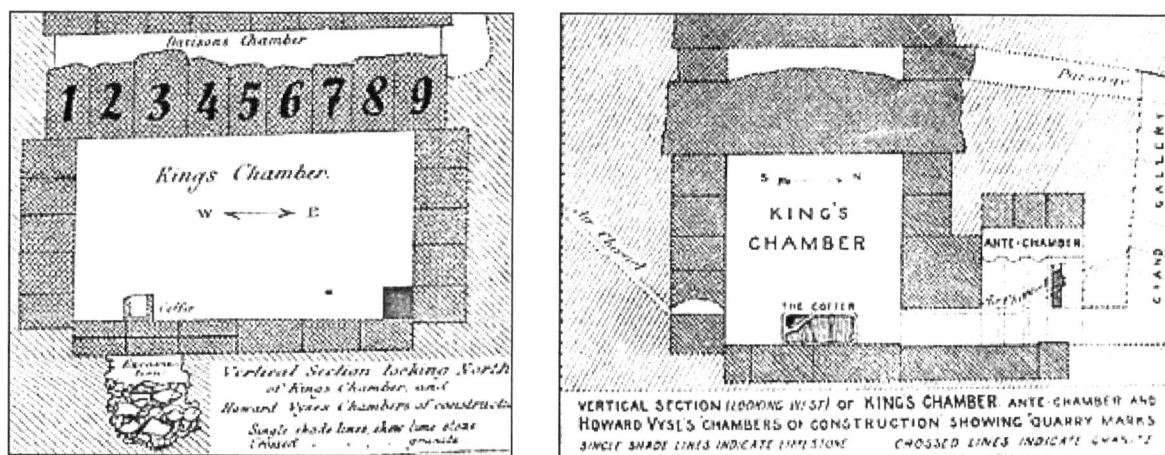

FIGURE 27: Two original drawings of the King's Chamber
showing the 9 ceiling beams and the Layers in the Floor.

On April 29th, 1863, as Baha'u'llah walked in the garden all night long, the nightingales were warbling loudly, stimulated by the blooming of the roses giving their sweet scent. Baha'u'llah couldn't sleep. Yet nobody knew why Baha'u'llah made April 29th as the Most Holy Day, as the Advent of the High Priest had not yet come. The Covenant-breaking Baha'is throughout the world commemorate this Holy Day not knowing that they are celebrating the Proclamation of Jesus the High Priest standing in the Holy of Holies before the Ark of the Covenant.

---

[*] These measurements are given by John H. Dequer in his book, *The Word in Stone*, p. 109.
[†] Zechariah 3:9.

311

"The Stone with 7 Eyes"

A short time after Dr. Jensen had the "Stone with Seven Eyes"* before him he knew that he was the one who fulfilled the third chapter of Zechariah, but he kept it a secret, as he didn't want to be anything but a servant to Baha. He was in hopes that it would go away, or someone else would come up with a better claim. However, his wife, Dr. Opal M. Jensen, who was very spiritual and intuitive, knew for a long time that he was the Promised One. However, he taught the Baha'i faith from the beginning of having the "Stone with Seven Eyes" before him. Within a year he had one-third of the inmates become Baha'i. There were so many inmates attending his firesides that the chapel was too small, so they gave him the gym to hold his meetings. He had it filled up. Not only did the inmates attend these firesides, they had their families from the outside come in to attend them too. Thus he had the gym filled to capacity every Sunday.

Harry Stroup, an inmate, became very deep in the understanding of the faith. He studied it continually. Also, he was reading the Bible from cover to cover. When he came to Zechariah chapter three, it dawned on him that the surrounding stone wall was the "Stone with Seven Eyes." On April 29th, 1971 at 3 p.m. when yard was called (a two-hour recreation time until 5 p.m.), he came running out into the yard and caught up with Dr. Jensen and told him, "This stone wall with seven watch towers is the "stone with seven eyes" in the third chapter of Zechariah, and you, Dr. Jensen, are the return of Jesus/Joshua the High Priest."

Dr. Jensen told him, "Harry, I didn't tell you this."

He said, "No. While I was reading and meditating on this chapter, I had a visitation, and the angel told me that you were the return of Jesus."

Dr. Jensen could no longer keep it a secret. He now had two witnesses, his wife, Dr. Opal Jensen, and Harry Stroup, who had arrived at this on their own. So he told Harry that he was the second coming of Jesus the High Priest. That evening after supper during recreation time, Dr. Jensen had a scheduled fireside in the chapel, and he had already prepared to explain the Great Pyramid for the first time in the prison. When he came to the part of the Holy of Holies, instead of skipping

---

* Zechariah 3:9.

312

over it as he had intended, he explained that he was the High Priest standing in the Holy of Holies and they all became believers.

As Dr. Leland--the Land--Jensen fulfills the prophecies in both the scriptures and in the Great Pyramid for the return of Jesus the High Priest after the Order of Melchizedec, and as he alone is standing in the Holy of Holies before the Ark of the Covenant, only he can get the Baha'i faith back on the right track, so-to-speak.

The prophecies in both the scriptures and in the Holy of Holies in the Great Pyramid prophesy of the coming in the end times of just one High Priest, and not of the order of Aaron, but of the order of Melchizedec! He is, according to prophecy, opposed by Satan, as was Dr. Jensen who was opposed by Satan on April 21st, 1963, the date given by the prophet Daniel in chapter 12, verse 12: "Blessed is he who comes to the 1335 days [years]," which is figured from the victory of Muhammad in 628 AD (628 + 1335 = 1963). 'Abdu'l-Baha stated that this date is 100 years from the Proclamation of Baha'u'llah on April 21st, 1863, giving the date April 21st, 1963. These 100 years are prophesied in the Holy of Holies by the 100 Red Granite Slabs surrounding the four walls. This coincides with verse one of the third chapter of Zechariah:

> And he shewed me Joshua [Jesus] the **high priest** standing before the angel of the LORD, and Satan standing at his right hand to resist him. (Zechariah 3:1)

This is so darn important because only the High Priest is allowed in the Temple not made by hands, that is, the Bab as the Sanctuary and Baha'u'llah as the Holy of Holies. Only the High Priest goes to the Ark of the Covenant and takes out the Book of the Covenant of Baha'u'llah and the Will and Testament of 'Abdu'l-Baha, and by his explanations restores the Executive Branch back into the Baha'i faith. The High Priest rebukes the "Hands" for maliciously going against Shoghi Effendi and his plan for the establishment of the Divine Plan given him by 'Abdu'l-Baha. He rebukes them for leading the entire Baha'i community astray into the oncoming fire prepared by the Devil (Hel[*]) for ungodly men, that is, those who wantonly follow the "Hands" who broke the Covenant for their own aggrandizement and empowerment.

This is the final word of God, that is, the explanations of the High Priest. Those who ignore this pronouncement or go against it are for the fire in this world and in the next.

As Dr. Jensen fulfills the prophecies for the return of Jesus the High Priest in both the Divine Scriptures and in the prophecies of Adam put into the Great Pyramid by Enoch, he, and he alone, is standing in the Holy of Holies before the Ark of the Covenant of Baha'u'llah and the Will and Testament of 'Abdu'l-Baha. And when Jesus on his first coming said, "No one comes to the Father (Baha'u'llah), but by me" (John 14:6), he meant that no one enters into the Kingdom of the Father, Baha'u'llah, in this life or in the next realm, now or in the future,[†] except through Jesus on his return, who is Dr. Leland Jensen. A person could read all the Baha'i books, live a Holy and righteous life, pray and observe all of the ordinances, yet if he rejects Jesus on his return, he is lost in this life and in the next. This book is so clear that it cannot be taken lightly.

---

[*] Ruhiyyih Khanum. See *Entry by Troops* for more on Danish and Scandinavian prophecy.
[†] Until the next Manifestation comes in a thousand years.

If you should pass on now, or in one of the four waves of destruction, without turning to Baha'u'llah through Jesus the High Priest, you may be lost for eons of time. This concept was put into scriptures and the Great Pyramid from the beginning of the Adamic cycle and nothing can change it.

EPILOGUE: BRINGING FORTH THE CAP STONE

The final vision in the Book of Revelation corresponds to the final prophesied act depicted in the Great Pyramid Prophecy: that is the placing of the Capstone upon the top of the Pyramid. This is spoken of in the Bible and the Book of Revelation. Many have written of this pre-eminent event in relation to the completion of the 6000 years prophetical cycle of Adam depicted in the Great Pyramid prophecy that culminates with the final appearance of the last promised one of the Adamic Cycle in 2001 AD who is also the first promised one of the New inaugurated 5000 Century Baha'i Cycle for the creation of the "Oneness of Humanity" whose watchword is "Unity in Diversity." Of this Capstone Dr. Leland Jensen writes:

> I have a mandate--to bring forth and establish the BRANCH--I must and I will accomplish this. NOTHING IN HEAVEN OR ON EARTH CAN PREVENT ME IN DOING THIS.
>
> The Guardianship of the Baha'i Faith is the promised Zerubbabel, the governor of the New Jerusalem (Rev. 21:2, Haggai 1:1). He is that Great King that is seated upon the throne, that brings forth the CAP STONE, AMID SHOUTS OF GRACE GRACE TO IT!!! (Zech. 4:7) The Cap Stone represents the Kingdom of God on earth as it is in heaven, of which the Guardian is the *sine qua non*. This is the stone (the Guardian the living Christ of the Baha'i world order) that the builders have rejected, the corner stone of the Kingdom of God on earth is the Guardianship, for it is the head of the corner itself (Psalms 118:22, Matthew 21:42, Mark 12:10). (Dr. Leland Jensen, *The Beast: Is About to Be Dead!*)

Thus the date for the coming forth and establishment of the guardianship (throne of King David) through the appearance of the living descendant of David through Baha'u'llah and 'Abdu'l-Baha is the prophesied date of September 21st 2001 AD. This is given as the Terminal Date of the prophesied time scale in David Davidson's book *The Great Pyramid, Its Divine Message*, pages 359-368 (see Figures 28 and 29). This is depicted as the prophesied 2520 years--the "Seven Times" of the great vision of Daniel chapter 4--added to September 21st, 520 BC that brings us to September, 21st, 2001 AD.

314

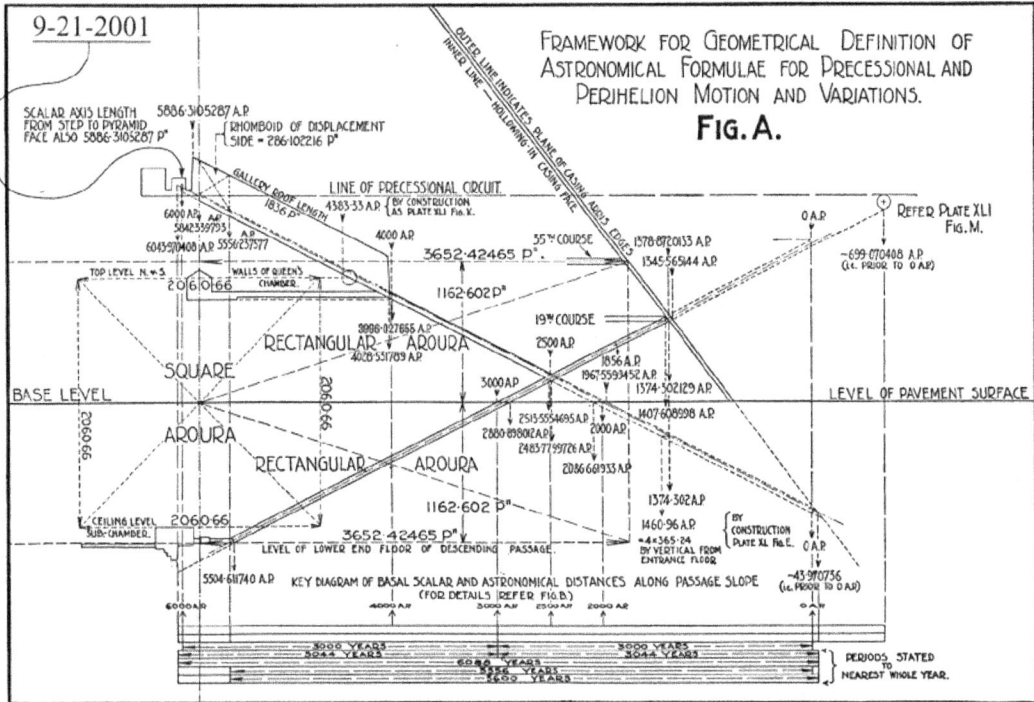

As defined and confirmed by the Pyramid's various and independent astronomical formulæ and their integrated angular values: (1) o A.P.=Autumnal Equinox 4000 B.C.; (2) 3000 A.P.=Autumnal Equinox 1000 B.C.; and (3) 6000 A.P.=Autumnal Equinox 2001 A.D. NOTE.—A.P. denotes *Anno Pyr.*

September 21, 2001 A.D.

FIGURE 28

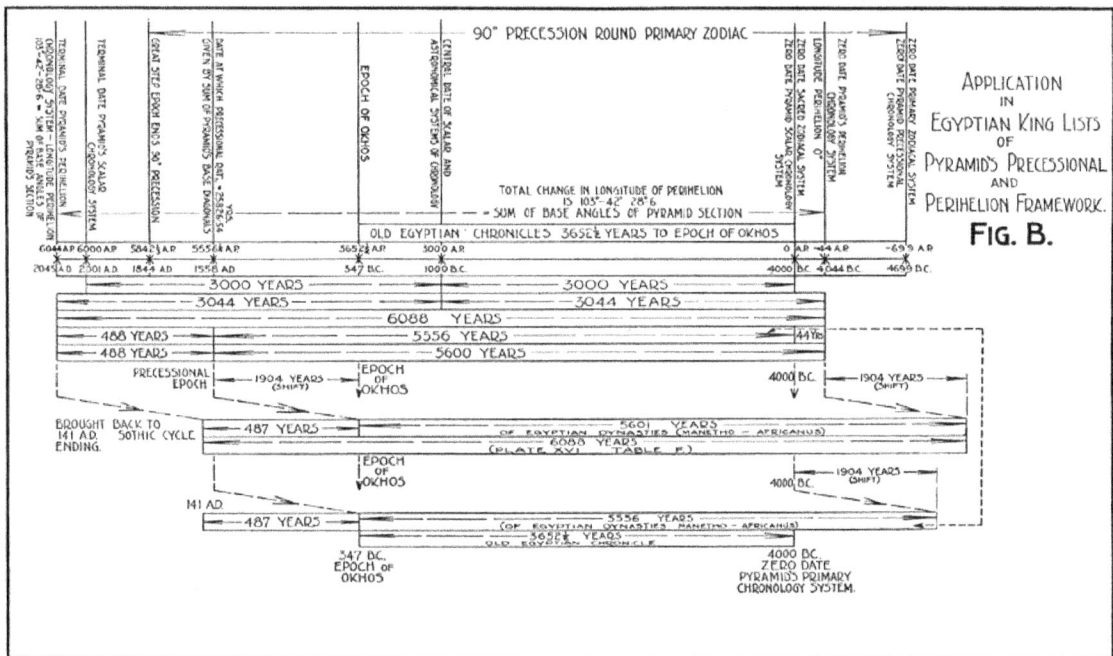

The Pyramid chronology of the Egyptian King Lists, and its application in the King Lists, confirm the chronology as derived from the Pyramid's astronomical formulæ. The King Lists independently prove that o A.P.=Autumnal Equinox 4000 B.C. and 6000 A.P.=Autumnal Equinox 2001 A.D.

FIGURE 29

This same date is included in the volume measure of the Capstone which is 2520 cubic cubits representing the 2520 prophesied years (see Figure 30).

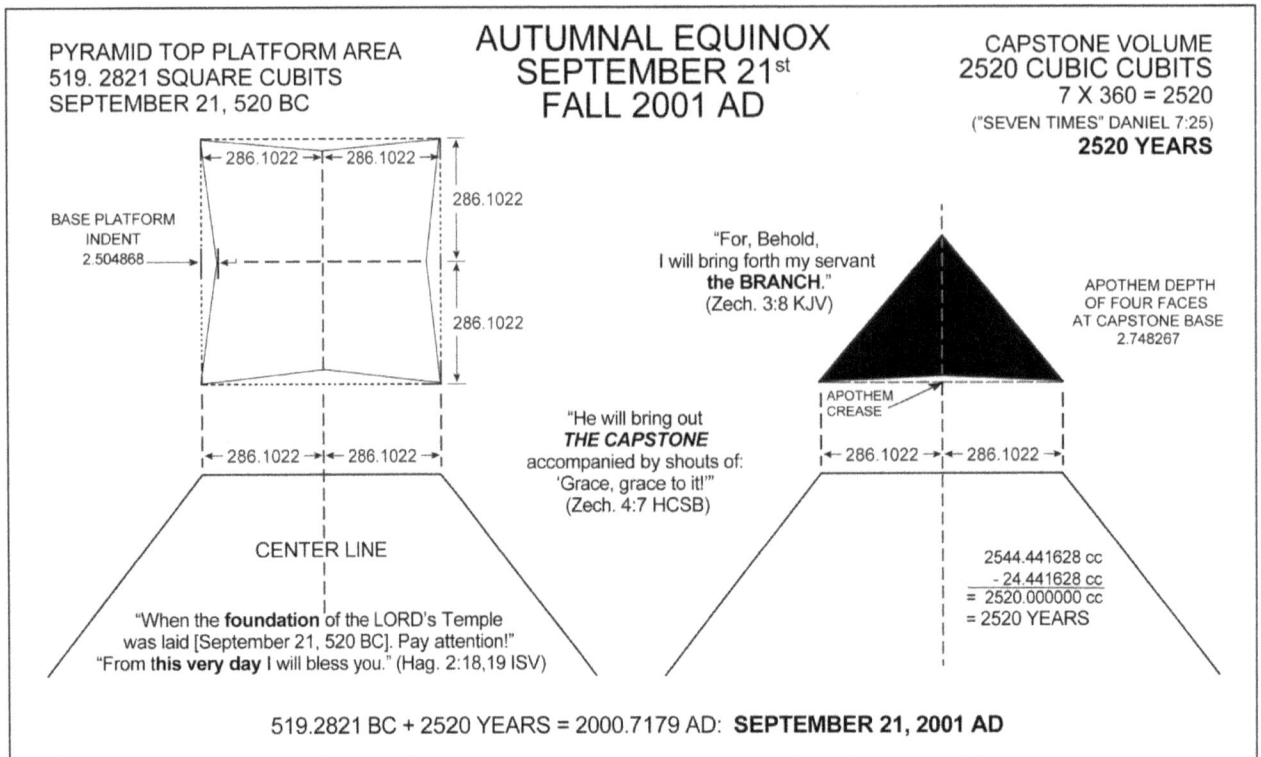

PYRAMID TOP PLATFORM AREA
519. 2821 SQUARE CUBITS
SEPTEMBER 21, 520 BC

AUTUMNAL EQUINOX
SEPTEMBER 21st
FALL 2001 AD

CAPSTONE VOLUME
2520 CUBIC CUBITS
7 X 360 = 2520
("SEVEN TIMES" DANIEL 7:25)
2520 YEARS

286.1022 → ← 286.1022

286.1022

BASE PLATFORM
INDENT
2.504868

286.1022

"For, Behold,
I will bring forth my servant
the BRANCH."
(Zech. 3:8 KJV)

APOTHEM DEPTH
OF FOUR FACES
AT CAPSTONE BASE
2.748267

APOTHEM
CREASE

286.1022 → ← 286.1022

"He will bring out
THE CAPSTONE
accompanied by shouts of:
'Grace, grace to it!'"
(Zech. 4:7 HCSB)

286.1022 → ← 286.1022

CENTER LINE

2544.441628 cc
- 24.441628 cc
= 2520.000000 cc
= 2520 YEARS

"When the **foundation** of the LORD's Temple
was laid [September 21, 520 BC]. Pay attention!"
"From **this very day** I will bless you." (Hag. 2:18,19 ISV)

519.2821 BC + 2520 YEARS = 2000.7179 AD: **SEPTEMBER 21, 2001 AD**

FIGURE 30

The top truncated platform measures 520 square cubits representing the prophesied foundation date of the Laying of the Corner-Stone of the second Temple on September 21st, 520 BC. September 21st, 520 BC plus 2520 years is September 21st 2001 AD. Thus God brought forth myself, Neal Chase Ben Joseph Aghsan, as His "servant, the BRANCH" (Zech. 3:8 KJV) during the prophesied "ten days" period from 9-11, 2001 AD to public projection on September 21st, 2001 AD in the fulfillment of prophecy.

After that event it was later discovered that the exact day of September 21st, 2001 AD was given in the Pyramid and other scriptures for the coming forth of the Branch--the **terminal date** of the Great Pyramid Chronograph: the Autumnal Equinox of 2001 AD (see Figure 31).

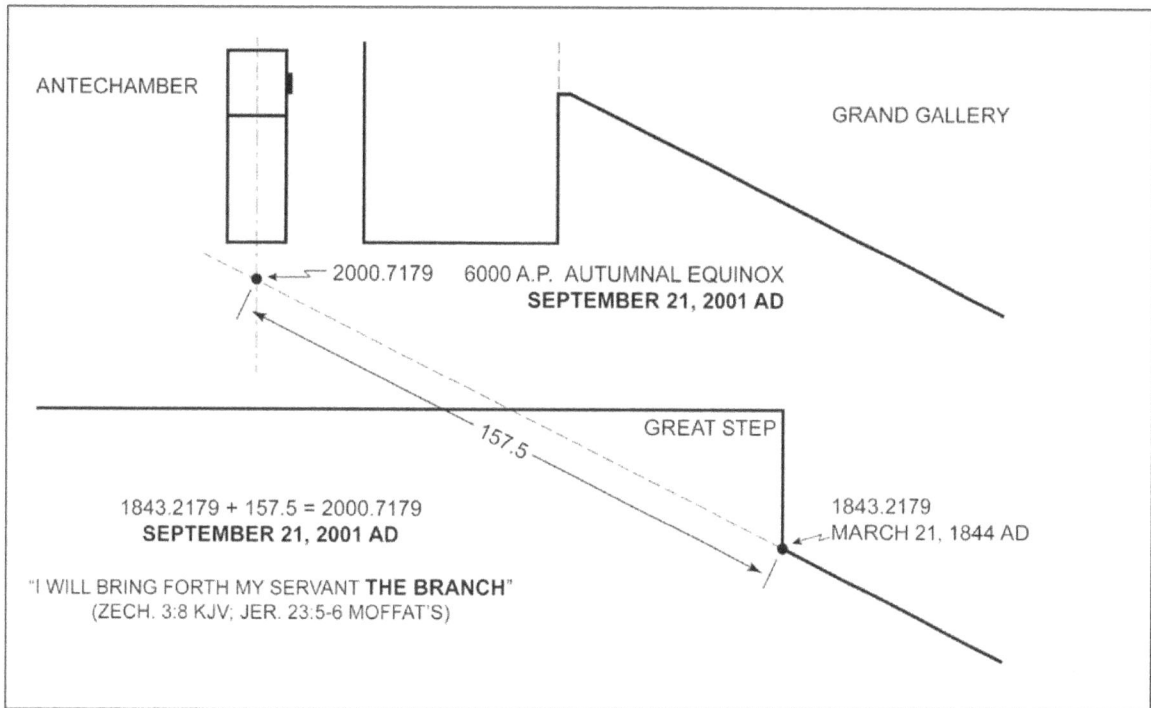

FIGURE 31

So it is written that "every body shall bow" and "every knee shall bend" as we align our will with the will of God and in the words of Christ who was obedient unto death: "Not my will O Lord, but Thine!"

> *In that day shall there be an altar to the LORD in the midst of the land of Egypt, and a pillar at the border thereof to the LORD. And it shall be for **a sign** and for a **witness** unto the LORD of hosts in the land of Egypt: for they shall cry unto the LORD because of the oppressors, and he shall send them a saviour, **and** a great one, and he shall deliver them. (Isaiah 19:19, 20 KJV)*

> *Where wast thou when I laid the foundations of the earth?*
> *declare, if thou hast understanding.*
>
> *Who hath laid the measures thereof, if thou knowest?*
> *or who hath stretched the line upon it?*
>
> *Whereupon are the foundations thereof fastened?*
> *or who laid the corner stone thereof;*
>
> *When the morning stars sang together,*
> *and all the sons of God shouted for joy?*
> *(Job 38:4-7 KJV)*

THE GOLDEN RULE
From God Almighty to Man

There are two religions in the world: the religion of God; and the religion of man.

The religion of man is filled with confusion, divided up into innumerable warring and independent sects, infighting and chaos. The religion of God is One and has been given progressively throughout human history to unite the hearts, elevate the souls of men and bring about a state and condition of spirituality to uplift the human spirit, create man in the image of God--love, justice, generosity, concord, fidelity, harmony, etc... -- and to free the human mind from blind imitation and slavish devotion to false creeds and man-made dogmas. In this light we can see the TRUTH of the true religion of God woven like a GOLDEN THREAD throughout all faiths whose origin is from Him in the form of the GOLDEN RULE.

The purpose of this chapter is to show the PROOF of this golden thread of unity throughout God's Cause in every land and in every scripture in which it has appeared from the first of time in written history unto today. Considering the lofty goal and sublime aim of God in choosing to reveal Himself to man, it is hard for us to imagine, in this day of crooks, cheats and charlatans, what could be a more corrupt or dirty business than religion gone bad. From government to the church, the politician and the preacher, some have said 'that those who have the gold make the rules:' and they sell Jesus Christ on the cross for the almighty dollar. This IS NOT the golden rule, where those who have the gold make the rules, for the scripture says, that "love of money is the root of all evil." Clearly, when it comes to God and religion, any intelligent person can see that the bath water, so to speak, is certainly dirty--but we don't want to throw the baby out with the dirty bath water!

Thus there is a real truth for the Golden Rule, the one that comes from the One True Invisible God and not from fallible man. In this short chapter we will see this golden theme, found like a golden thread woven throughout all the true religions of God that are practiced by people of world faith throughout this great and good world of God's green earth.

If all people would practice the Golden Rule: "Do unto others as you would have them do unto you" we cannot imagine any better form and foundation for the end of war, a spiritual solution to the economic problem, and the establishment of a universal and everlasting Kingdom of justice and peace on earth for all humankind. Read this chapter and open your mind to the eye of God Himself, even as Jesus hath said: "Seek ye the truth and the truth will set you free."

THE GOLDEN RULE

JESUS CHRIST:

"Teacher, which is the great commandment in the Law?"

"Jesus said to him, You shall love the LORD your God with all your heart, and with all your mind and with all your soul… and You shall love your neighbor as yourself."
(Jesus Christ, Matthew 22:36-40)

BAHA'U'LLAH:

"O son of man! If thine eyes be turned towards mercy, forsake the things that profit thee and cleave unto that which will profit mankind. And if thine eyes be turned towards justice, choose thou for thy neighbour that which thou choosest for thyself."
(Baha'u'llah, The third Leaf of the Most Exalted Paradise, *Tablets*, p. 64)

BUDDHISM:

"Hurt not others with that which pains yourself or in ways that you yourself would find hurtful. One should seek for others the happiness one desires for one's self."
(Udana-Varqa, 5:18)

HINDUISM:

"This is the sum of duty: do naught unto others that which would cause pain if done unto you."
(Mahabharata 5:1517)

"Do not to others what ye do not wish done to yourself; and wish for others too, what ye desire and long for, for yourself. This is the whole of Dharma, heed it well."
(The Celestial Song, 2:65)

ZOROASTRIANISM:

"That nature ONLY is good when it shall NOT DO unto another whatever is not good for its own self."
(Dadistan-i-Dinik, 94:5)

"Whatsoever is disagreeable to yourself do not do unto others."
(Shayast-na-Shayast 13:29)

That which is good for all and any one, for whomsoever--that is good for me. What I hold good for self, I should for all. Only Law Universal, is true Law."
(Zoroaster, Yasana-Gathas)

JAINIST:

"A man should wander about treating all creatures as he himself would be treated."
(Sutrakritanga 1.11.33)

SIKH:

"Precious like jewels are the minds of all. To hurt them is not at all good. If thou desirest thy Beloved, then hurt thou not anyone's heart."
(Guru Aranj Devji 259, Guru Granth Sahib)

CONFUCIANISM:

"Do not unto others what you would not have them do unto you."
(Analects, 15:23)

"If one strives to treat others as he would be treated by them, he will come near the perfect life."
(Book of Meng Tzu)

WESTERN SCHOOLS:

"What you wish your neighbors to be to you, such be also to them."
(Pythagorean)

"We should conduct ourselves toward others as we would have them act toward us."
(Aristotle, from Plato and Socrates)

"Avoid doing what you would blame others for doing."
(Thales)

"Do not to your neighbor what you would take ill from him."
(Pittacus)

"Cherish reciprocal benevolence, which will make you as anxious for another's welfare as your own."
(Aristippus of Cyrene).

"Act toward others as you desire them to act toward you."
(Isocrates)

TAO:

"Pity the misfortunes of others; rejoice in the well-being of others; help those who are in want; save men in danger; rejoice at the success of others; and sympathize with their reverses, even as though YOU WERE in their place."

"The sage has no interests of his own, but regards the interests of the people as his own. He is kind to the kind, he is also kind to the unkind: for virtue is kind."
(T'ai Shang Kan Ying P'ien)

NATIVE AMERICAN:

"Love your friend and never desert him. If you see him surrounded by the enemy do not run away; go to him, and if you cannot save him, be killed together and let your bones lie side by side."
(Sur-AR-Ale-Shar, The Lessons of the Lone Chief)

"Do not kill or injure your neighbor, for it is not him that you injure, you injure yourself. But do good to him, therefore add to his days of happiness as you add to your own. Do not wrong or hate your neighbor, for it is not him that you wrong, you wrong yourself. But love him, for The Great Spirit (Moneto) loves him also as he loves you."
(Shawnee)

"Respect for all life is the foundation."
(The Great Law of Peace)

AFRICAN TRADITIONAL RELIGION:

"A SAGE is ingenuous and leads his life after comprehending the parity of the killed and the killer. THEREFORE, neither does he cause violence to others nor does he make others do so."
(Yoruba Proverb, Nigeria)

"One going to take a pointed stick to pinch a baby bird should first try it on himself to feel how it hurts."
(Yoruba Proverb, Nigeria)

ISLAM:

"Not one of you is a believer until he desires for another that which he desires for himself."
(Muhammad, 40 Hadith of an-Nawawi 13)

"Do unto all men as you would they should do unto you, and reject for them that which you would reject for yourself."
(Mishkat-el-Masabih)

JUDAISM:

"What is hateful to you, DO NOT to your fellow man. That is the law: all the rest is commentary."
(Talmud, Shabbat 31a)

"Thou shalt LOVE thy neighbor as thyself: I am the LORD."
(Moses, Leviticus 19:18)

CHRISTIANITY:

"All things whatsoever ye would that men should do to you, do ye even so to them."
(Matthew 7:12)

"Do unto others as you would have them do unto you."
(Luke 6:31)

BAHA'I WORLD FAITH:

"Blessed is he who preferreth his brother before himself."
(Baha'u'llah, Tablets, p. 71)

"Lay not on any soul a load which ye would not wish to be laid on you, and desire not for any one the things ye would not desire for yourselves."
(Baha'u'llah, Gleanings LXVI, p. 128)

"Ascribe not to any soul that which thou wouldst not have ascribed to thee, and say not that which thou doest not. This is my command unto thee, do thou observe it."
(Baha'u'llah, The Hidden Words, Arabic # 29)

"Choose for thy neighbor that which thou choosest for thyself."
(Baha'u'llah, Epistle to the Son of the Wolf, p. 30)

From the *Sacred Will and Testament of 'ABDU'L-BAHA*:

"O ye beloved of the Lord! In this sacred Dispensation, conflict and contention are in no wise permitted. Every aggressor deprives himself of God's grace. It is incumbent upon everyone to show the utmost love, rectitude of conduct, straightforwardness and sincere kindliness unto all the peoples and kindreds of the world, be they friends or strangers. So intense must be the spirit of love and loving kindness, that the stranger may find himself a friend, the enemy a true brother, no difference whatsoever existing between them. For universality is of God and all limitations earthly. Thus man must strive that his reality may manifest virtues and perfections, the light whereof may shine upon everyone. The light of the sun shineth upon all the world and the merciful showers of Divine Providence fall upon all peoples. The vivifying breeze reviveth every living creature and all beings endued with life obtain their share and portion at His heavenly board. In like manner, the affections and loving kindness of the servants of the One True God must be bountifully and universally extended to all mankind. Regarding this, restrictions and limitations are in no wise permitted.

"Wherefore, O my loving friends! Consort with all the peoples, kindreds and religions of the world with the utmost truthfulness, uprightness, faithfulness, kindliness, good-will and friendliness, that all the world of being may be filled with the holy ecstasy of the grace of Baha,

that ignorance, enmity, hate and rancor may vanish from the world and the darkness of estrangement amidst the peoples and kindreds of the world may give way to the Light of Unity. Should other peoples and nations be unfaithful to you show your fidelity unto them, should they be unjust toward you show justice towards them, should they keep aloof from you attract them to yourselves, should they show their enmity be friendly towards them, should they poison your lives, sweeten their souls, should they inflict a wound upon you, be a salve to their sores. Such are the attributes of the sincere! Such are the attributes of the truthful."
(*The Sacred Will and Testament of 'Abdu'l-Baha*, pp.13-14)

Conclusion

Therefore, the source of all true religions is one. And this single source is the One True Invisible God that has been made known. All peoples of both the Eastern and Western worlds, of both the Eastern and Western schools and philosophies, have been guided by the Merciful and Living God, through the appearance of the Divine Manifestations of Himself, the Nine Great Revelators of this last 6000 year Adamic Cycle, into this Universal Teaching of this Universal Law of Justice, Mercy and Love!

The word "religion" comes from the Latin "*religio*" which literally means to "bind together" (like a bundle of sticks). But today people are DIVIDED up according to the many religions, cults and sects. Thus this is NOT religion, but it is truly IRRELIGION, as it separates the gathering of the peoples.

The true religion unites the hearts and minds of man through the Oneness of Humanity and the independent, unfettered investigation of the truth. When we see the light of the truth with our own eyes and not through the eyes of our neighbour, then and only then, will ALL people of race, creed, nationality, color and persuasion be truly united. All mankind will be united like one soul in one body.

Thus the Golden Rule is that spark of a glimmer of the golden light of God made manifest through the glory, splendor and light of God for the healing of all the nations. Nothing can separate the gathering of the people of light. Nothing can separate the gathering of the people of Baha! Though those who love the dark, may defect, the hearts of love in God remain ever united!

Baha'u'llah, the HEIR to David's throne, the descendant of King David through Solomon and the exiled monarch of David (exilarch) Bostanai, fulfills prophecy for the Second Coming of Christ! The meaning of the word Christ is a Greek word for the Hebrew word Messiah which means the descendent of King David which is anointed (see Psalms 89).

The Purpose of the descendants of King David continued through Baha'u'llah and Abdu'l-Baha is so that we can recognize the true Universal House of Justice of Baha'u'llah from fakes, frauds, and imitations.

The world has turned aside from the basic teachings of the One True Invisible God as given in the Golden Rule and explicitly stated in the everlasting Covenant of God spoken of all throughout the Bible, and therefore the catastrophe is upon us now!

The Twelve BASIC Principles of the Baha'i Faith:

The Oneness of Humanity

The Independent and Unfettered Investigation of the Truth

Religion is Progressive, all having a Common Foundation

Religion Must be the Source of Unity

True Science and True Religion Must Correspond

Equality of Men and Women

The Removal of Prejudice of All Kinds

Universal Peace Upheld by a Spiritual World Government

Universal Compulsory Education

A Spiritual Solution to the Economic Problem

A Universal Auxiliary Language

A Universal House of Justice with the Davidic King as its President

INVESTIGATE NOW BEFORE IT'S TOO LATE

TABLET OF THE HIGH PRIEST

(Lawh-i-Kahin-i-Akbar)

--Baha'u'llah--

THE BEGINNING OF EVERY ACCOUNT IS THE NAME OF GOD

O FRIENDS of God! Incline your inner ears to the voice of the peerless and self-subsisting Lord, that He may deliver you from the bonds of entanglement and the depths of darkness and enable you to attain the eternal light. Ascent and descent, stillness and motion, have come into being through the will of the Lord of all that hath been and shall be. The cause of ascent is lightness, and the cause of lightness is heat. Thus hath it been decreed by God. The cause of stillness is weight and density, which in turn are caused by cold. Thus hath it been decreed by God.

And since He hath ordained heat to be the source of motion and ascent and the cause of attainment to the desired goal, He hath therefore kindled with the mystic hand that Fire that dieth not and sent it forth into the world, that this Divine Fire might, by the heat of the love of God, guide and attract all mankind to the abode of the incomparable Friend. This is the mystery enshrined in your Book that was sent down aforetime, a mystery which hath until now remained concealed from the eyes and hearts of men. That primal Fire hath in this Day appeared with a new radiance and with immeasurable heat. This Divine Fire burneth of itself, with neither fuel nor fume, that it might draw away such excess moisture and cold as are the cause of torpor and weariness, of lethargy and despondency, and lead the entire creation to the Court of the Presence of the All-Merciful. Whoso hath approached this Fire hath been set aflame and attained the desired goal, and whoso hath removed himself therefrom hath remained deprived.

O servant of God! Turn thou away from the stranger, that thou mayest recognize the Friend. He indeed is a stranger who leadeth you away from the Friend. This is not the day whereon the high priests can command and exercise their authority. In your Book it is stated that the high priests will, on that day, lead men far astray, and will prevent them from drawing nigh unto Him. He indeed is a High Priest who hath seen the light and hastened unto the way leading to the Beloved. Such a man is a benevolent priest and a source of illumination to the whole world.

O servant of God! Any priest who leadeth thee away from this Fire, which is the reality of the Light and the mystery of Divine Revelation, is indeed thine enemy. Suffer not the words of the foe to hold thee back from the Friend or the insinuations of the enemy to cause thee to forsake the Beloved.

O servant of God! The day of deeds hath come: Now is not the time for words. The Messenger of God hath appeared: Now is not the hour for hesitation. Open thou thine inner eye that thou mayest behold the face of the Beloved, and hearken thou with thine inner ear that thou mayest hear the sweet murmur of His celestial voice.

O servant of God! The robe of divine bestowal hath been sewn and readied. Take hold of it and attire thyself therewith. Renounce and forsake the people of the world. O wise one! Shouldst thou heed the counsel of thy Lord, thou wouldst be released from the bondage of His servants and behold thyself exalted above all men.

O servant of God! We have bestowed a dewdrop from the ocean of divine grace; would that men might drink therefrom! We have brought a trace of the sweet melodies of the Beloved; would that men might hearken with their inner ear! Soar upon the wings of joy in the atmosphere of the love of God. Regard the people of the world as dead and seek the fellowship of the living. Whoso hath not breathed the sweet fragrance of the Beloved at this dawntide is indeed accounted among the dead. He Who is the All-Sufficing proclaimeth aloud: "The realm of joy hath been ushered in; be not sorrowful! The hidden mystery hath been made manifest; be not disheartened!" Wert thou to apprehend the surpassing greatness of this Day, thou wouldst renounce the world and all that dwell therein and hasten unto the way that leadeth to the Lord.

O servants of God! Deprived souls are heedless of this triumphant Day, and chilled hearts have no share of the heat of this blazing Fire.

O servant of God! The Tree which We had planted with the Hand of Providence hath borne its destined fruit, and the glad-tidings We had imparted in the Book have appeared in full effect.

O servant of God! We revealed Ourself to thee once in thy sleep, but thou didst remain unaware. Remember now, that thou mayest perceive and hasten with heart and soul to the placeless Friend.

O servant of God! Say: O high priests! The Hand of Omnipotence is stretched forth from behind the clouds; behold ye it with new eyes. The tokens of His majesty and greatness are unveiled; gaze ye on them with pure eyes.

O servant of God! The Daystar of the everlasting realm is shining resplendent above the horizon of His will and the Oceans of divine bounty are surging. Bereft indeed is the one who hath failed to behold them, and lifeless the one who hath not attained thereunto. Close thine eyes to this nether world, open them to the Countenance of the incomparable Friend, and commune intimately with His Spirit.

O servant of God! With a pure heart unloose thy tongue in the praise of thy Lord for having made mention of thee through His gem-scattering pen. Couldst thou but realize the greatness of this bestowal, thou wouldst find thyself invested with everlasting life.

"THIS STONE WITH SEVEN EYES"

This stone with seven eyes that is prophesied in the Bible (Zech. 3:9) is not only important for the recognition of the Promised Joshua, by it being the address of his appearance, but as the cross is a symbol of the perversity of the Sanhedrin Court that tried Jesus, and the corrupt judge of the Roman Pontius Pilate that acquiesced to their malicious condemnation of Him, this prison is a symbol of the gross injustices of the American legal system as well as that of the world. It shows that justice with equity is but a word in the dictionary, and the legal system but a grand facade.

The miscarriage of justice in the imprisonment of the Promised Joshua is not much dissimilar from that of ancient Joseph in the 39th chapter of Genesis, nor is it much different from St. Paul being held in prison for several years by Governor Felix with the thought in mind to extract a bribe from him (Acts 24:26,27).

Justice in America, with its legal system of lawyers is a business by which the commodity of justice is bought and sold, the price being fixed by what the traffic will bear, and by how big of a predicament they can get you into. For instance, there are no rich people in the Montana State Prison, not because the rich and affluent are not criminals, but because of their connections and that they can afford to pay the price. If you cannot or will not pay the price, you are then subjected to a biased court whose prejudices are hostile to minorities. For instance if you are a black man or a chiropractor you are most certainly guilty if you are accused. The outcome of your trial is decided ahead of time, then an act is planned by your lawyer and the county attorney, perhaps over a cup of coffee or a drink, they then proceed to the court house and put on a big show for the benefit of the jury and the public.

THIS IS THE DAY OF JUDGEMENT

The mission of Baha'u'llah is to bring about world unity, and the oneness of mankind, by the establishment of Justice in the world. This is the long Promised Kingdom of God on Earth as it is in Heaven (Luke 21:31).

The great condemnation of mankind is not just the persecution and imprisonment of God's Promised Ones i.e., the Bab, Baha'u'llah, and 'Abdu'l-Baha as well as the Promised Joshua, but that, although they have the Books of God in their hands they fail to recognize the Promised Ones that are prophesied to come in these Holy Books, and by so doing they cut themselves off from both the guidance of the Holy Books by which they claim to believe, and the guidance of the Promised Ones (John 5:45,46,47) and they blindly stumble into the FIRE (Matthew 15:14, 23:40, Isaiah 66:15, 9:19).

The great crime of the nations is that although they have legal systems and courts of justice they have allowed the thieves to steal the religions of God. The Baha'i administration of Shoghi Effendi was usurped by the Covenant-breaking "Hands" and perverted bogus UHJ; although it is incorporated in the world today, this nation as well as the other nations, have stood by and allowed the "Hands" to take over and illegally possess this establishment. Therefore the "flying scroll" 20 cubits long and 10 cubits in circumference, which is about 42 feet long and 21 feet in circumference, this being a good description of the modern ballistic mussile with its thermonuclear warhead, is to go out over the face of the earth and enter the houses of these thieves that swear falsely in the name of God that, their stolen religions represent God, and destroy them with a destruction that consumes both timber and stone (Zech. 5:1,2,3,4).

Dr. Leland Jensen
Knight of Baha'u'llah

327

www.ingramcontent.com/pod-product-compliance
Lightning Source LLC
Chambersburg PA
CBHW062033090426
42740CB00016B/2890